STUDIES IN
WORD-ASSOCIATION

STUDIES IN
WORD-ASSOCIATION

EXPERIMENTS IN THE DIAGNOSIS OF PSYCHOPATHOLOGICAL CONDITIONS CARRIED OUT AT THE PSYCHIATRIC CLINIC OF THE UNIVERSITY OF ZURICH

UNDER THE DIRECTION OF

C. G. JUNG, M.D., LL.D.

(FORMERLY OF THE UNIVERSITY OF ZURICH)

AUTHORIZED TRANSLATION BY

Dr. M. D. EDER

LONDON

ROUTLEDGE & KEGAN PAUL

First published in 1918
by William Heinemann (Medical Books) Ltd.

Reissued in 1969
by Routledge & Kegan Paul Ltd.
Broadway House, 63–74 Carter Lane
London, EC4

Printed in Great Britain by photolithography
by Unwin Brothers Limited
Woking and London

SBN 7100 6376 8

TRANSLATOR'S PREFACE

THIS book is a translation of a series of papers on the results of the association method applied to normal and abnormal persons, which appeared in the *Journal für Psychologie und Neurologie* (vols. iii–xvi) and were afterwards collected into two volumes.

The experiments were carried out at the instance and under the guidance of Dr. Jung. The work which Drs. Jung and Riklin published in 1904 gave an entirely new direction to association experiments. The principle of mental association is, of course, of reputable antiquity : "Do you not know, then, that lovers when they see a lyre, or a garment, or anything else which their favourite is accustomed to use, are thus affected ; they both recognize the lyre and receive in their minds the form of the person to whom the lyre belonged." [1]

Its experimental phase begins with Galton's work in 1879 and Wundt's in 1880.

The new departure which we owe to Dr. Jung is the application of the association method to *unconscious* mental processes ; the theory of unconscious complexes was developed by these experiments ; the results obtained by Freud's psycho-analytic technique were confirmed by the use of a very different method.

This confirmation by experimental methods compelled many who had hitherto looked askance at the psycho-analytic theory of the unconscious to investigate the phenomena for themselves. These studies in word-association have now acquired a permanent place in the historical development of this theory. Every serious student of psychology, every educationist, every one who wishes to engage in the study or treatment of morbid mental processes, will find in these "Studies" a storehouse of facts which will serve not only as a solid basis for his own studies but also as a starting-point for further research.

It was a most arduous and delicate task to establish objective criteria by which unconscious complexes could be recognized. Much thought and great ingenuity went to the discovery of these

---

[1] The *Phædo*.

" complex indicators " as they are called, and the resulting theses as elaborated in this work by Dr. Jung and his collaborators have all been found to be reliable.

Since the beginning of this work in 1904 it has been extremely productive in many different directions and is still reaping a rich harvest. Its application to education has been made quite recently ; here we may hope to establish some standard tests for normal and abnormal children, which will be complementary to the intellectual tests standardized by Binet.

In the investigation of nervous and mental disorders the association method is still opening up new paths, as seen, for instance, in the remarkable investigations by Dr. Josef Lang on familial associations in cases of schizophrenia.

I cannot refrain from pointing out that the germ of some of the views recently developed by Dr. Jung can be found in these early studies.

The work on association among normals had led to the establishment of psychological types. There are certain obvious relationships between the " objective " type here described in chapter ii and his later " introversion " type, and again there are certain resemblances between the " egocentric " type of the experiments and the " extraversion " type of the later view.

Indeed, in Dr. Jung's most recently published work (" Psychology of the Unconscious Processes," in *Analytical Psychology*, 1917), a foot-note (p. 405) indicates that psychology is not limited to two types : " other possibilities are known to us " ; this is perhaps a return to the position of these experiments where six principal types are described.

The extraverted and introverted types are, of course, not strictly comparable with the earlier types described in this work, but there are certain fundamental common qualities.

Again, Dr. Jung's introduction of an energic view-point into the psychology of the unconscious (paper given before the Thirteenth International Medical Congress in London, 1913) is foreshadowed in chapter vii, " On Psycho-Analysis and Association Experiments," written in 1906, in which Jung ascribes a patient's obsessional ideas to the locking up of energy, whilst the strengthening of the will, transferring this energy to new channels, is regarded as the chief therapeutic aim.

The results of the experiments on familial associations must, one imagines, have contributed to the formulation of Jung's conception of the composition of the *persona* and the composition of the collective psyche.

I have endeavoured in the translation to give the ideas of the different contributors as clearly and literally as possible. In a number of illustrative examples of word-associations, when clang-associations, assonances, alliterations, or rhymes occur impossible of literal translation, I have substituted reactions from my own experiments or constructed reactions on the lines of the original model. This nowhere impairs the interpretation or understanding of the text, and it has not been considered necessary to note these substitutions. In a few cases the German has been retained, a translation of the word being also given.

As the series of words used in Zurich does not altogether suit English requirements, I subjoin a list of words modified from Dr. Jung's list, of which I have made considerable use.

1. head	26. blue	51. frog	76. wait
2. green	27. lamp	52. try	77. cow
3. water	28. carry	53. hunger	78. name
4. sing	29. bread	54. white	79. luck
5. dead	30. rich	55. child	80. say
6. long	31. tree	56. speak	81. table
7. ship	32. jump	57. pencil	82. naughty
8. make	33. pity	58. sad	83. brother
9. woman	34. yellow	59. plum	84. afraid
10. friendly	35. street	60. marry	85. love
11. bake	36. bury	61. home	86. chair
12. ask	37. salt	62. nasty	87. worry
13. cold	38. new	63. glass	88. kiss
14. stalk	39. habit	64. fight	89. bride
15. dance	40. pray	65. wool	90. clean
16. village	41. money	66. big	91. bag
17. pond	42. silly	67. carrot	92. choice
18. sick	43. book	68. give	93. bed
19. pride	44. despise	69. doctor	94. pleased
20. bring	45. finger	70. frosty	95. happy
21. ink	46. jolly	71. flower	96. shut
22. angry	47. bird	72. beat	97. wound
23. needle	48. walk	73. box	98. evil
24. swim	49. paper	74. old	99. door
25. go	50. wicked	75. family	100. insult.

Finally, the grateful thanks of all students of psychology are due to Mrs. Harold F. McCormick, whose generosity has enabled this translation to be produced.

M. D. EDER

CONTENTS

CHAPTER I

UPON THE SIGNIFICANCE OF ASSOCIATION EXPERIMENTS

By PROFESSOR BLEULER

EVERY psychical activity rests upon the interchange of the material derived from sensation and from memory traces, upon *associations* ; apart from the somewhat questionable capacity to perceive pain and pleasure which is perhaps inherent in the smallest organism, even in the atom, any psychical activity without association is unthinkable. The investigation of association activity is, therefore, of fundamental importance for psychology in general, and peculiarly so for psychopathology in particular.

The sensations chiefly studied up till now [1] vary but little from individual to individual ; even in psychopathology, apart from gross analgesic disturbances, hallucinations, and illusions, they are of slight importance.

Variations in emotions are, on the contrary, so great that there can be no agreement about what is normal. Is it not still debated whether the absence of moral feeling is to be regarded as a disease or not ?

Memory, so far as concerns the building up and the maintenance of its dynamic traces, is still entirely unapproachable, and the accessible part of the function, the capacity for recollection, rests chiefly upon the activity of association ; thus an understanding of the anomalies of recollection can only be arrived at when the function of association is accurately known.

The will, despite all attempts, seems almost to elude psychological investigation. A man's psyche can be fully described without making use of this vague concept. Psychopathology frequently ignores the will altogether. The facts, which lie behind the abstraction termed the will, can be traced back to the centrifugal tendencies which dwell within the elemental and complex psychical structures ; according to this very plausible conception the resultant of all these tendencies is the will.

[1] I omit naturally the many mere speculations about will, emotion, etc., which prove nothing.

It has indeed been maintained that the will cannot possibly be the resultant of strivings supporting and opposing one another ; for the resultant of the desire to skate and the desire to write an article is a something inconceivable, at any rate a something which could never lead to a choice. If I have one wish to go east and another to go south, I do not go south-east but walk east or south.

This conception of a psychical resultant is quite absurd. It is not a question of the resultant of diverse directions of the desires, but of the resultant of the desires themselves. As an illustration : a railway train comes to a station where many lines intercross, and thus its further course will be determined by the points. Suppose there are various persons whose interests would send it in different directions ; it is to the interest of any one person to have his points open and all the others closed ; the strongest achieves his aim. When the points are fixed the train moves in the desired direction ; the wishes of the other persons have become ineffective unless they make them good at a subsequent station. There can be no question of a resultant of these different directions. The resultant can only express itself positively, not negatively, in the choice of points ; the opening of the points is analogous to the decision of the will.

A compromise between the different strivings is only thinkable as resulting from some reciprocal influence, acting directly, or in such a way that both act upon a third (e.g. upon the ego-complex), i.e. they associate with it. The " will " can be likewise explained by the activity of association ; at any rate, at the moment of our investigation association offers the most adequate explanation.

In our observations on the psyche we come upon the process of association again and again. Everything else in these investigations is found to be subordinate to association.

It is self-evident that a number of other mechanisms condition the play of our psyche. *Dynamic* differences in the individual presentations must play a great part. If the train in our illustration is very heavy or very rapid it will be more difficult to turn it aside from its direction. The strength of the desires themselves can be conceived as dynamic qualities, but we are not compelled to make such an assumption. The *number* of factors which control the points (i.e. the number of associated individual presentations which form the presentation complex) can be just as well the determining condition as the dynamic relationship of the presentations. Thus the entire psychic mechanism could be conceivably explained solely in terms of association. On the other hand, we have at present no fixed point from which to determine the relative strength of a presentation. What we usually regard as such is decomposed into the number of the associative elements, and the " strength " of the accompanying feelings ; the strength of the feelings themselves can only be recognized by their effects, inhibitory and stimulating, upon the associations.

The function of attention has usually received a dynamic explanation, but this is never convincing ; what we really observe in alterations of attention are alterations in the number and direction of the associations.

Association is a fundamental phenomenon of psychical activity. Perception, thinking, doing, cease as soon as association is impeded. This process may be conceived physiologically quite as well as psychologically, and, in both, closely unites the psychical with the (other) neurophysiological functions.

The passage of a sensory stimulus to the motor part of the reflex arc is, in principle, the same process as we must assume occurs in the physiological processes that run parallel with the psychical events. The analogy becomes much stronger if the effects of several (simultaneous) stimuli upon the reflex process are considered. Simultaneous stimuli can, it is known, evoke reflexes which take their course quite independently of one another ; these stimuli do not associate with one another. Others, even when they arrive at remote parts of the spinal cord, can produce a (simultaneous) reflex process inhibiting or affecting the path. Here the stimuli must in some way flow together or act upon one another by a process comparable with induction ; they form inter-associations.

In psychical associations current processes generally link up with memory-traces, which are revivified by the association process. But there is no difference in principle from the reflex associations, for even here the after-effects of previous experiences are demonstrable and may be compared with the function of memory.

It is self-evident that associations lie at the foundation of sensation (so far as it is conscious), i.e. the connexion of the inflowing nerve stimulus with processes which represent the psyche. If this connexion is inhibited, whether reflexly in the lower centres or in the higher regions by distraction of the attention or by any kind of psychical anæsthesia, no sensation occurs.

Perception is always understood as association of the new sensation with memory-traces of earlier experiences. At the sight of a man, of a house, we have colour sensations in definite relationships and forms ; we have had similar sensations in connexion with a great number of other houses and men which make up the concept man or house. These other elements are aroused by the new sensation, and so we interpret the sensation as the image—of a man—of a house ; we " perceive " the men, the house.

That our laws of thought are but rules of association processes is strangely enough still contested. And yet law of thought and law of association must seem almost identical once it is realized that the law of association is not so simple as to be exhausted by a few shibboleths (association by similarity, contrast, simultaneity, relationship). *Every association in real thinking is accompanied by an almost endless number of more or less distinct presentations ;* at first those of the whole personality with its inner and outer past so far as this can come into consideration ; next a hierarchy of purposeful presentations insufficiently worked up for thought. First of all comes the general aim of our endeavour, then the aim of our thought in the particular case, then all the aims which give the special direction of our thinking and doing, right down to the aim of the thought expressed or the movement undertaken at the moment. Earlier experiences also have their effect in the measure in which they were recently real for our psyche and, *ceteris paribus*, can be more easily associated than others. This factor is termed a constellation. Of great importance also are the moods which supply adequate, or inhibit contrary associations, and much else which it would be too lengthy and tedious to enumerate. When, e.g., I am writing about associations there is at work in the background first of all that portion of my personality interested in scientific research, then my whole scientific and especially my psychiatric past ; in addition, the special call to this piece of work must always be present in condensed form. I must have before me not only the general aim of writing about associations, but at every moment some survey of all that preceded and all that is yet to come. It is self-evident that a mass of detail can be determined by the accidental experience of the immediate past ; in the same way it is equally clear that I am most inclined to think (and to say) those things which are coloured in any way by some affect (some special interest, some polemic, etc.). Physical feelings, fatigue, feeling fit, etc., also enter into this, since these induce me now to shorten, now to expand, and so on.

The affects and physical feelings exert much greater influence upon the associations in all that concerns decision and action.

Thus in the activity of association there is mirrored the whole psychical essence of the past and of the present, with all their expe-

riences and desires. It thus becomes an index of all the psychical processes which we have but to decipher in order to understand the complete man.[1]

The evaluation of the associations becomes, however, extremely difficult amid the ordinary complicated relationships. Although we are often able to make the diagnosis of a specific mental disease from a letter, from the repetition of a story, and even place certain types among normals by such tests—yet for a methodological experimental study such complicated series of associations are for the present but ill adapted.

The simplest associations readily accessible for our study are to be found in *perceptions,* i.e. the union of a sensation with those memory-images which render possible the interpretation of a sense-impression.

But, like the sensations, the perceptions can have no marked degree of variation if the relationship to the outer world is not to be seriously damaged. They only occur in a few combinations—does the same sensation ever condition the same perception ?—and by constant practice become so fixed that more marked deviations seldom occur within the normal (e.g. when the stimulus is too faint or too brief, or the affect too pronounced) ; even in a series of severe mental disorders the process of perception is but little disturbed as judged by our present methods of observation. In the present state of our knowledge we must not expect the ripest harvest, even although Kräpelin's experiments on perception have shown that much valuable knowledge is to be gained about the intoxications.

Most is gained, as previous experiments have shown us, when the association is quite free, and directed thought is, as far as possible, excluded. A definite sensation of shades of red with a distinct form is always changed by association into the perception of a rose. The paths are here given. But if the completed percept (rose), all purpose being excluded, is given, the associations are pretty free and the choice of the path of the association is, in the main, dependent upon relatively few factors ; these can be determined by their effects.

When a series of associations is demanded and the subject is requested to produce all his associations without stopping, the intrusion of more or less conscious purposes cannot, as a

---

[1] In a certain sense every psychical event, every movement, is only possible to that particular man with his particular past, in one definite way. Each single action represents the whole man : the endeavour to deduce the whole man from his handwriting, physiognomy, shape of the hand, his style, even the way he wears his shoes, is not altogether folly. More especially there should be a future for graphology.

rule, be prevented. A mass of valueless co-ordinations and coexistences occur. It is, therefore, well to demand only *one* association to the given percept, and at the same time to exclude the introduction of any directed thought by requesting as quick a reaction as possible.

The most convenient way to bring up an idea to the subject is to call out a word to him, and so far this method has proved so fruitful that we have limited our experiments to it.

We employ therefore a method which has already been introduced by Wundt and his pupils in psychology, and which has been successfully transferred by the Kräpelin school (especially by Aschaffenburg) to psychopathology.

The uttering of the first word which " occurs " to the subject after hearing the stimulus-word forms the reaction. It is self-evident that this word represents only a very small part of the complicated association complex that is set free; this will be further discussed by Dr. Jung.

This method has proved most valuable. Under the direction of Dr. Jung material was brought together, which could be compared when large numbers were dealt with. This material serves not only for the presentation of psychological types among normal people, but also for the diagnosis and symptomatological understanding of a whole range of psychoses.

From the associations we are now in a position in many cases to diagnose dementia præcox, epilepsy, various forms of imbecility, certain forms of hysteria, not to speak of manic-depression with its well-known flight of ideas. By the help of associations we have also well-grounded hopes of classifying and grouping in a natural way diseases hitherto insusceptible of classification, like some paranoid forms, or those "diseases" vaguely grouped or differentiated under the names of hysteria, neurasthenia, psychasthenia.

But this does not exhaust the results. By ingenious interpretations, which can be readily proved correct, Jung and Riklin have shown that the unconscious mechanisms are accessible to this method far more extensively than we dared hope.

The word-associations not only give us information about the course of psychic processes in the exposed layer of our conscious thinking; they also furnish us with selections of the unconscious working of the mind which throw an astonishing light upon normal and pathological phenomena.

Perhaps the most important result of all is that by the help of association experiments the mechanism of the stereotypes and vagaries of dementia præcox are laid bare in a way that we could formerly have scarcely dared expect.

We hope that the work, to which these words are introductory, will open up to us new regions in psychology and psychopathology. The results reached in the course of the last two years deserve the greatest attention, and we have good grounds for the definite hope that intelligent and cautious investigations along the same paths will give us much further insight into the depth of the human pysche.

CHAPTER II

THE ASSOCIATIONS OF NORMAL SUBJECTS

By Dr. C. G. JUNG and Dr. F. RIKLIN

FOR some time past great attention has been paid in this clinic to the study of association. To obtain material scientifically comparable my honoured chief, Professor Bleuler, arranged a schedule of 156 stimulus-words and made use of them in experiments upon psychoses of all kinds. A serious difficulty, however, soon arose. There was no means of differentiating with statistical precision the associations of the abnormal from the normal. There was no material from which to ascertain the variations in normal persons, or to express as definite laws the purely haphazard nature, as it seemed, of the associations. To remedy this want to some extent, thus paving the way for the investigation of pathological associations, I arranged to collect a considerable number of normal associations, studying at the same time their main determinants. I have carried out this work conjointly with my esteemed colleague Dr. Riklin.

The general outline of our experiment is as follows : In the first place we collected the associations of a large number of normal persons in order to ascertain, first, whether any kind of law was to be deduced, and, secondly, if any individual laws were present, i.e. if certain types of reactions could be discovered. With this investigation we united another of a general psychological nature.

The association process is an extremely transient and variable psychological process ; it is influenced by innumerable psychical events which evade objective control. Among the psychical facts having a supreme influence upon the association process, *attention* is cardinal. It is attention which primarily directs and modifies the association process, and at the same time it is the psychical factor which most readily submits to experiment. Attention is also a delicate affective apparatus which immediately reacts to abnormal physical and mental conditions and thus modifies the work of association.

8

Attention is that endlessly complicated mechanism which the association process by innumerable threads binds to all the other phenomena of psychical and physical origin represented in consciousness. If we knew the effects of attention upon the process of association then we should know, at least in broad outline, the corresponding effects of every psychical event which is able to influence attention.

These considerations induced us to investigate experimentally the influence of attention upon the association process, hoping thus to clear up the following questions in particular with some measure of certainty :

(1) What are the laws of the variations of attention within the limit of the normal ?

(2) What are the direct effects of attention upon the association process ? More especially, does the specific nature of the association decrease as the field of consciousness grows more distant ?

Our experiments have disclosed a series of facts which not only encourage us to pursue the quest into the pathological domain, but, we believe, also enable us to do so.

C. G. Jung

PART I

I. General Plan of the Experiments

The experiments were carried out alternately by the two authors ; each one carried out alone the whole series of experiments upon the subject.   Altogether 38 persons took part in the experiments : 9 of the men and 14 of the women were highly educated persons ; 7 of the men and 8 of the women were ill-educated—their ages ranged from twenty to fifty years.   Care was taken to select, as far as possible, quite normal individuals for the experiments ; this, however, especially among the well-educated, gave rise to unexpected difficulties, for it is just at this level that the discrimination of what is an average normal becomes an extremely nice question.   All we can hope is that in the selection of the individuals we have not departed very far from the normal.   We give the figures in detail, occasionally adding a very brief character-sketch of the person which will facilitate the understanding of a few anomalies.   Naturally the two authors have carried out the experiments on one another.   The associations in every case were obtained by calling out the stimulus-word. Altogether we made use of 400 different stimulus-words. Grammatically they were composed of the following :

Nouns	231
Adjectives	69
Verbs	82
Adverbs and numerals	18

No attention was paid to the number of syllables (the stimulus-words were one to three syllables), nor were the stimulus-words arranged in definite categories as in Sommer's experiments. On the other hand, so far as possible, care was taken that stimulus-words similar in form or sense did not follow one another, so as to prevent the subject settling down after two or three reactions to one circumscribed domain. By an unfortunate accident it happened that among the first hundred stimulus-words there were about thirty to which there were ready associations in temporal and spatial coexistence, whilst in the second hundred there were only about twenty, thus making a notable difference in the coexistence associations between the first and second hundred. The want of stimulus-words of that particular kind is made good by verbs. Stress was placed on excluding difficult and rare words in order to prevent mistakes or prolonged reactions through want of knowledge on the part of the subjects. The stimulus-words were as far as possible taken from words in daily use.

This consideration was the more essential for us because in most of our experiments we laboured under abnormal conditions as to language. In German Switzerland the German-Swiss dialect, or rather dialects, not only differ considerably from literary German, but contain also no slight differences among themselves, especially differences in sound. The child learns literary German at school almost as a foreign language. Later on the educated acquire a fairly complete knowledge of, and practice in, the German tongue. The uneducated, however, unless he has lived for some time in Germany, retains at the most those German phrases which he has learnt at school, later adding little or nothing thereto. Literary German is not the less familiar to him in its written and printed form, and he understands it when spoken without being able himself to speak a fluent and faultless literary German. We, therefore, repeatedly tried to call out the stimulus-words in their dialect form, but we soon noticed that the ill-educated did not understand the dialect words as well as the literary German, and that they generally took pains to react in literary German. This somewhat paradoxical occurrence is due to the fact that Swiss-German is purely an acoustic-motor speech which is very rarely read or written. The Swiss is, therefore, not accustomed to sense his words as single items, but knows them only in acoustic-motor association along with other words. If he has to say one word by itself without the article he generally chooses the literary German form. We therefore gave up dialect stimulus-words entirely in our experiments. In the great majority of cases the reaction was the correct literary German ; likely reactions in Swiss dialect were accepted as valid. The reactions were written down as they were given. Persons who had never taken part in such an experiment were first of all informed as to its meaning and given practical demonstrations by examples as to how they had to react. Not a few amongst the uneducated believed it was a kind of Question and Answer game in which the object was to find an appropriate completion of the stimulus-word, e.g. *house— house-fly*, *wild—wild cat*. The experiments were only begun when it was quite clear that the nature of the experiment was understood. A case of non-understanding, we would emphasize, never occurred ; lack of intelligence is far less disturbing than affect, namely, an emotional stupidity which was not infrequent. A certain significance attaches to the kind of schoolroom attitude in which many of the uneducated approached the work, putting on a somewhat formal and stiff air.

We arranged our experiments in the following way : *First*, 200 *reactions were made without further conditions*. The reactions were timed by a one-fifth-second stop-watch, the stop-hand being released when the test-word was uttered and stopped when the reaction-word was spoken.[1]

Naturally we do not imagine that we have measured any intricate psychological times by this simple procedure. We only wanted to obtain a general idea of the average and approximate reaction-times, important in many cases, and more especially valuable in the classification of the associations. After 200 reactions the reactions were as far as possible forthwith classified with the help of subject. In the educated persons this was always done ; in the uneducated, who most rarely had any kind of capacity for introspection, this was, of course, not possible. It was there necessary to limit oneself to obtaining an explanation of the threads in the most striking associations. The result of the experiment was divided into a first and a second hundred and written down separately. During the experiment the psychical state was controlled objectively and subjectively as

---

[1] A report will be made later on about the time measurements. The time was not measured in all the persons experimented upon.

far as possible. If for any reason there was any physiological fatigue the experiment with the second hundred was deferred till the next day. Among the educated, one may say such fatigue never occurred, so that in most cases the second series could be concluded forthwith.

The second series consisted of 100 reactions which were carried out during a condition of inner distraction. The subjects were requested to concentrate their attention so far as possible upon what is called the " A-Phenomenon " (Cordes),[1] and at the same time to react as quickly as possible, that is to say, as promptly as in the first experiment. By the A-Phenomenon we understand with Cordes the sum of those psychological phenomena which are directly evoked by the perception of the acoustic stimulus. To control the compliance of the A-Phenomenon by the subjects, they had to describe directly after each reaction what they noted during the reaction. A further classification was made at the end of the experiment. Naturally only educated persons could be used in these experiments, and these unfortunately required selecting, for a certain amount of psychological aptitude is required for the attentive consideration of one's own psychical phenomena.

The third experimental series was only carried out on the second day. It consisted of 100 reactions carried out during a condition of outer distraction. The distraction in these experiments was arranged as follows : To the beat of a metronome the subject had to make pencil strokes about 1 cm. in length. The beats for the first 50 reactions were 60 per minute, for the second 50 reactions 100 per minute. The results of the first 50 reactions and of the second 50 were written down separately, and for easier comparison were calculated to 100. In some few of the subjects the metronome was accelerated after each 25 reactions in order to exclude habit being too rapidly formed. The beats, in these cases, were increased from 60 to 72, and from 100 to 108 per minute.

Even so, the factor of habit unfortunately plays a great part in these experiments, as might be a priori expected. Many persons become very quickly accustomed to the purely mechanical activity which in the second phase of the experiment only alters the beat. It is not easy to devise other distraction stimuli of similar continuity and regularity and without the additional factor of a verbal image. This is especially so in the case of the uneducated upon whose intelligence and will-power too great demands must not be made.

In seeking for some appropriate distraction stimulus we were

[1] Wundt's *Phil. Studien*, Bd. XVII, p. 30.

above all careful to exclude everything which could in any way arouse verbal presentations. In the arrangement of our experiments we believe that we have excluded this kind of influence.

With these experiments 300 to 400 associations were, on the average, carried out with each person. We also tried to complete our material in some other directions so as to obtain a kind of addendum to Aschaffenburg's results ; with this object we also carried out experiments with some of our subjects when in a state of obvious fatigue. We were able to do reactions of this kind with six persons. In one individual, associations were also carried out in a state of morning drowsiness after a good night's sleep, thus excluding the factor of fatigue. In one person associations were carried out in a state of severe depression (irritation) without fatigue.

In this way we obtained in round figures 12,400 associations.

II. Classification

1. GENERAL

Every one who does practical work in association has found the classification of the results the hardest and most tedious part. We are in general agreement with Cordes [1] when he says that in the earlier experiments the erroneous assumption was made that the psychical phenomenon of departure corresponded to the stimulus-word, and that the connexion of stimulus-words and reaction was an " association."

This conception, somewhat too simple, is at the same time somewhat too pretentious, for it maintains that the psychical connexion (the association) is given in the connexion of the two verbal signs. We need not say that we do not accept this view, for we regard the stimulus-word merely as the stimulus, and the reaction merely as a symptom of psychical processes concerning whose nature we abstain from any immediate judgment. We do not, therefore, claim that the reactions which we describe are associations in the strict sense ; we would indeed ask if it were not better to drop the word " association " altogether and to speak rather of *verbal reaction*. For the external connexion between stimulus-word and reaction is much too coarse to give any absolutely exact picture of the extraordinary intricate psychical processes, i.e. of the real associations. Stimulus-word and reaction only convey the psychical relationship in the most

[1] " Experimentelle Untersuchungen über Assoziationen," Wundt's *Phil. Studien*, Bd. XVII, p. 33.

remote and incomplete manner. When we describe and classify
the relationship expressed in speech we do not classify all the
real associations but only their objective symptoms from which
the psychical relationships must be reconstructed with due
caution. It is only in psychologically trained persons that the
reaction is what it really should be—the reproduction of the
first idea that occurs. In all others it is clearly only an attempt
to construct something out of the reaction ; in many cases it
ends by being the product of deliberation, hence of a whole
series of associations. In our association experiment we tend
to produce an exclusive excitation of the speech organism. The
more exclusive this excitation is the more strongly will verbal
relations occur in the reaction. As we shall see, this is chiefly
the case among the well-educated, among whom one may a priori
expect the psychical mechanisms to be more finely differentiated,
therefore with greater capacity for their isolated use. This must
not lead to the sophism that the educated are generally prone
to more outer combinations of ideas than the uneducated.[1]
The difference is a more psychological one, for among the
uneducated there is greater participation by the other psychical
regions than among the educated. In the second part of this
work we shall return to this difference.

Whilst we know so little about the connexions between
mental experiences we must give up all claim to evolve, from
the inner psychical data, the principles for a classification of
their external appearances. For these reasons we have contented
ourselves with a simple classification, based upon logical principles ; it was in our view safer thus to limit ourselves until we
are in a position to deduce empirical laws from the mental
associations.[2]

The logical principles of classification must also be adapted
to the special conditions of the experiment—that is, to verbal
reaction. In the classification of the associations regard must,
therefore, be paid not merely to the logical quality, but when
possible also to those outer factors which obtain by reason of
the particular arrangement of the experiment.

The employment of the speech-hearing cerebral mechanism
is naturally not without influence upon the associations. The
purely intrapsychical association cannot become the object of

---

[1] Ranschburg states that among the uneducated inner associations predominate. *Allegmeine Zeitschrift für Psychiatrie*, Bd. LVII, p. 689.

[2] Aschaffenburg also expresses himself cautiously in this respect and limits
himself entirely to the relation between stimulus and reaction as reflected in
speech. He considers it important to adhere to this, since the verbal association
by no means always accords with the simultaneous inner associations. Kräpelin,
Psychologische Arbeiten, Bd. I, p. 220.

another's consciousness without translation into the current symbolism of speech. Thus there intervenes quite a new factor in the pure association, which exercises an indefinably great influence upon it. The main determination that occurs in the direction of verbal facility, that is to say, James Mill's generally valid " Law of Frequency," affects the reaction with a more marked power of selection in the direction of the accustomed. One of the fundamental principles of our classification will, therefore, be that of verbal facility.[1]

We have given the preference on the whole to the classification of the associations by the Kräpelin-Aschaffenburg scheme. We have preferred this system to others because, from our subjective view, it is heuristically the most valuable. Ziehen describes this classification as " a failure," an expression much too strong. Nobody will pretend that Aschaffenburg's classification is exhaustive ; Ziehen would not say that of his own classification.

Ziehen's classification has certainly opened up extremely valuable points of view, but completely satisfactory it is not. The differentiation between " leaping associations " and " judgment associations " is most unsafe if this refers entirely to the absence or the presence of the copula ; Claparède also criticizes this adversely.[2] The complete failure of the Aschaffenburg scheme should, surely, be first proved ; as a matter of fact that has not been done, on the contrary, the results obtained by this classification are most encouraging. We may for some time to come work profitably on these lines, not oblivious, however, of a certain one-sidedness, common in some form or other to this and all other classifications. There is no justification for the reproach that Aschaffenburg's scheme is purely logical, for it sufficiently considers not only the logical but also the visual or other sensual interconnexion and contiguity of things as well as the verbal factor. In dealing with reactions in the form of sentences the scheme is certainly inefficient ; in regard to this it is to be remembered that sentences seldom occur with normal persons. It is of great practical importance to remember that Aschaffenburg's scheme has been tried on a great mass of material, partly pathological, and has proved itself workable. Its *conditio sine qua non* is that the subject is not subsequently questioned

---

[1] Trautscholdt says : " In that relation use or custom holds the chief and dominant place, makes certain reactions so easy that finally they are completed mechanically, and causes others by comparison not to come into question at all." " Experimentelle Untersuchungen über die Assoziation der Vorstellungen," Wundt's *Phil. Studien*, Bd. I, p. 221.

[2] Claparède, *L'Association des Idées* (Paris, 1903), p. 218.

about the reaction phenomenon as in the schemes of Ziehen, Mayer and Orth, and Claparède; it therefore permits an approximately correct classification without the co-operation of the subject, and this is of especial value in psychopathological investigations.

As we regarded our work as preparatory solely to psychopathological investigations we did not hesitate to give the preference to Aschaffenburg's scheme. The schemes of Münsterberg and Bourdon seem to us too exclusively logical; Ziehen's objection does hold true of these that they are unpsychological in that they pay no heed to the content. Claparède's [1] very subtle and ingenious proposition certainly demands careful consideration, but its practical utility must be first tested on a greater mass of material.

It should never be forgotten that in classification experiments or acoustic-verbal associations, *presentations* are not investigated, only their verbal symbols. The investigation of associations is, therefore, peculiarly liable to indirect and fertile errors conditioned by the very complexity of the process itself.

In our experiment we investigate the resultants of a whole series of psychical processes—Perception, Apperception, Intrapsychic Association. Verbal Apprehension, and Motor Expression. Each of these processes leaves traces in the reaction. By virtue of the great psychical importance of motility, especially in the speech function, a chief part in the formation of a reaction must be granted to speech and practice in speaking. This is, therefore, a factor which will receive due consideration in the classification. It may be objected that this principle of classification introduces an extremely variable and indefinite quantum into the reckoning. We must grant that practice in speaking is a highly variable quantum, that in individual cases it makes for difficulties, and that even the logical character of the classification suffers no small loss. Something arbitrary thus enters into the classification with which we would certainly prefer to dispense. But, *faute de mieux* and on the grounds already stated, we selected this classification, taking as a guide certain empirical rules which we will discuss .

With these limitations, and with all possible consideration for the subject's individuality, we hope to have practically avoided all that seems arbitrary in the employment of this principle.

In the nomenclature subsequently employed (flight of ideas, association, etc.) it must always be borne in mind that we are dealing with speech phenomena; it is from these that we deduce

[1] Claparède, *L'Association des Idées*, p. 226.

the conclusions as to the psychical experiences. We are fully aware that we are merely investigating a narrowly circumscribed psychical region, to wit, associations, chiefly displayed in the mechanism of speech. If we speak of *flight of ideas* we understand by this the verbal phenomenon, that is, outer representatives of inner processes. As a matter of fact the psychical occurrence need not be reacted *in toto* in the form of word-associations, but is only expressed by these verbal signs when it affects the speech-mechanism. The true thoughts in a state of *flight of ideas* would naturally present a very different picture if they could be directly objectivated. For instance, the *flight of ideas* where the presentations are more predominantly visual is a quite peculiar sphere which can hardly be satisfactorily made objective through speech ; hence it is almost inadequately inaccessible to external investigation. Again, as a rule, in maniacal patients the verbal excitement that is present precludes investigation.

2. Special Classification

(A) *Inner Association* [1]

a. Co-ordination.—Under this heading we classify all associations which are in any way united by coadjunction, subordination, supraordination, or contrast. The association experiments require the following special classification of co-ordinations :

α. Coadjunction.—The two terms are united by an essential similarity, that is to say, they are formulated upon some more general concept in which both are included. Examples :

Word	Reaction	General concept
Lake	sea	mass of water
Cherry	apple	fruit
Long	small	measurement
Unjust	faithlessness	wrong or vicious

The association by coadjunction need not always be a mere shifting of an obvious, common supraconcept, but can also

[1] Ziehen (*Leitfaden der phys. Psychologie,* p. 141), in a polemic against " inner association," quotes the following examples : " Lust—Brust, Herz—Schmerz " (English equivalents would be Pain—Brain, Heart—Part. TRANSLATOR), remarking that the so-called inner association is purely outer and limited almost entirely to auditory presentations of similar sounding words. It is very easy to grant Ziehen this, for nobody would designate these as examples of inner association. For the rest, with Wundt, we conceive the associative *affinity* as the principle of inner, and *practice* as the principle of outer, associations (or similarity = inner association, contiguity = outer association)

result from a more or less vague similarity. The similarity
can be so close as to be scarcely differentiated from identity
as, e.g. :

Indulgence   forbearance   Friendly   amiable   Hair   thread

But the similarity can be very remote, so that what is common
to the two presentations is not something essential, but a more
or less accidental attribute of the stimulus presentation. In
such cases the reaction seems very loosely linked to the stimulus-
word, and is thus differentiated from the other coadjuncts. The
distance of the association is to some extent a greater one. These
coadjuncts can thus be separated to a certain degree from those
already alluded to. Two categories can be differentiated amongst
these loosely linked coadjuncts :

(1) The stimulus presentation is linked to the reaction by
means of an important, but accidental, attribute, e.g. :

Father (anxiety about)	sorrow
Play (of the child ?)	youth
War (League of Peace)	Bertha v. Suttner
Murderer (hang)	gallows
Sentence (contains something)	content
Star (romantic : night ?)	romantic poetry

(2) The stimulus presentation is linked to the reaction by an
unessential, external, quasi-coexistent attribute, e.g. :

Pencil (long)	length	Lake (deep)	depth
Heaven (blue)	colour	Table (peculiar form)	style

These two modes of coadjunction can be termed " Coadjunction by inner or outer relationship." The first category includes
far more important coadjuncts than the second, justifying to
some extent the terms " inner " and " outer." The coexistence
of the attributes in the second category points to the origin of
these coadjuncts from outer associations.

As a final group of co-ordinations we propose " coadjuncts
used as examples." This category contains reactions which
present in essence nothing but the reverse of the two modes just
described ·

Sorrow	father (viz. of the father, for example)
Contents	sentence (viz. of the sentence, for example)
Colour	heaven (viz. of heaven, for example)
Trouble	old woman (for example, an old woman has trouble)

There is a series of reactions to adjectives and verbs which
do not stand grammatically in a co-ordinate relationship to the
stimulus-word, but are perhaps best included in the group

of coadjuncts, more especially in that of "coadjuncts as example."

To surrender	peaceable	Strange	emigrant
To pay attention	wiser	To pray	piety
To despise	wickedness	To help	goodness

These associations can be regarded, if the expression be allowed, as "analytical"; they are concepts which are already quasi-implied in the stimulus-word, to which they thus stand in a kind of relationship of sub- or supra-ordination. As it is, however, difficult, if not impossible, to determine this relationship in concrete cases with absolute certainty, and as, moreover, the concept of whole and part is inadmissible in the case of adjectives and verbs, we include these reactions also under the "coadjuncts as example." Certain typical reactions will always occur among the possible substantives. The reactions are here extremely general and internally independent of the stimulus-word.

The special classification of the coadjuncts would thus be as follows :

(1) By common supraconcept.
(2) By similarity.
(3) By inner relationship.
(4) By outer relationship.
(5) As example.

Examples of	(1) Father	uncle	(4) Father	our house
	(2) Father	God	(5) To pay attention	wiser
	(3) Father	sorrow		

It is to be specially noted that this classification by no means exhausts the copious differences in the coadjuncts. In individuals who associate very largely by subjective constellations there are possibilities of a series of co-ordinations which do not easily lend themselves to classification. In such cases impotence must be frankly admitted, and one must rest content with the classification "co-ordination." Consolation must be found in the fact that individual possibilities are incalculable, that no one scheme will ever be discovered by which all associations will be able to be classified typically and without a residue. But there are a number of coadjuncts which could without any extreme pressure be classified under different headings, i.e. they have no very distinctive character; the classification can here be left in suspense or the reaction be finally placed under that type with which it has relatively most similarity. The designations set out are not to be regarded as absolutely compulsory categories, but merely as names for empirically discovered types which can on occasion merge into one another without sharp demarcation. More is not to be expected in the present stage of the theory of association.

β. *Subordination.*—The reaction is thought of as a part or subconcept of the stimulus-word, e.g. :

Tree   beech-tree

Here we include also all those reactions which specify the stimulus-word, i.e. which demonstrate special cases of the universal stimulus presentations, e.g. :

House	the house in X Street	Station	Derby
Horse	Mr. X's horse		

In some cases doubt may exist whether the association is to be taken as subordination or as predicate, e.g. :

Food   to-day's (*sc.* food)

γ. *Supraordination.*—The reaction is thought of as the whole or as the generalized concept of the stimulus-word, e.g. :

Oven   town   Cat   animal

Here, likewise, the separation from predicate is often difficult, e.g. "thirteen—unlucky number." Is "unlucky number" in this case a general concept, and is " thirteen " as such included in other unlucky numbers ? According to our view it is in this case a question of a predicate ; on the other hand, we should classify Aschaffenburg's association " Baptism—obsolete custom " among the supraordinations ; " obsolete custom " is a general concept which includes many other subconcepts.

δ. *Contrast.*—The idea of contrast is intelligible without further explanation. Disproportionately difficult, on the other hand, is the classification and valuation of contrast. As a rule contrasts are not only closely connected presentations conceptually, but they are also connected visually, and above all verbally. There are indeed languages in which there only exists one and the same word for typical contrasts. In the beginning of speech and conscious thinking it was no inconsiderable effort to separate contrasts verbally and conceptually. At the present day, however, this effort of thought is ready made for us in speech ; it is imparted to us in our earliest youth with the first ideas of speech, with the first songs and reading lessons. We possess extreme verbal facility for these closely connected concepts, often strengthened by reminiscences of quotations and rhymes, e.g. :

Sorrow	joy	Bitter	sweet
Pain	pleasure	Light	dark
Good	bad		

" Bittersweet " is even a colloquialism. For these reasons we
have classified a large number of these usual contrasts among
the outer associations. · We include among contrasts only those
associations habitually linked together verbally :

Friendly	angry	Intelligence	stupidity
Good	vicious	Revenge	forgive
Animal	plant		

Despite this detailed classification of the co-ordinations there
are associations of this kind which cannot be classified in any
subgroup. For these there remains simply the universal term
" co-ordination," e.g. the association " short — silk." The
stimulus-word " short " has been taken in the sense of a proper
name, the bearer of this name has a silk business, hence the
reaction " silk." This cannot be simple coexistence, rather the
reaction is composed from a specific and a spatial coexistence,
and hence is a somewhat complicated formation. As a last
resource it might be brought under the heading " coadjunction
by external relationship," but without much justification. The
more prudent way for the present is simply to regard such
co-ordinations as incapable of any further explanation.

The foregoing may be recapitulated in the following scheme :

α. *Coadjunction.*

   1. By a common supraconcept.
   2. By similarity.
   3. By inner relationship.
   4. By outer relationship.

β. *Subordination.*

   1. True subordination.
   2. Specific.

γ. *Supraordination.*

δ. *Contrast.*

ε. *Co-ordination of undetermined quality.*

b. *Predicate.*—With Aschaffenburg, we here include all judgments, attributes and activities which in any way refer to the
stimulus presentation as subject or object. (Summarized by
Kräpelin under the term " predicate relationships." [1])

The first judgments which pertain here, may, following Kant,
be divided into analytic and synthetic.[2]

---

[1] Cp. *Psychologische Arbeiten*, Bd. I, p. 222.
[2] " In an analytic judgment I do not go beyond the given conception, in
order to arrive at some decision respecting it. If the judgment is affirmative I

This logical principle of classification is only of value for us in so far as in the analytic judgment a part of a concept, i.e. a predicate, is produced which was already necessarily represented in the concept. It, therefore, gives only that which was implicitly already present. In the synthetic judgment something is added to the concept which was not already necessarily included in the concept. In relation to associative work, therefore, synthetic judgment, if such an expression be allowed, stands above analytic judgment. Approaching the question practically we find (in so far as this mode of classification can be used at all in practice) that in simple judgment reactions the analytic judgment consists chiefly in the pointing out of a co-existent attribute perceptually evident, whilst the synthetic judgment is generally a judgment as to value, with more or less marked reference to the ego. We see here a relationship analogous to that of " coadjunction by outer relationship " to that of " coadjunction by inner relationship." In the association *pencil—length*, " length " is necessarily included in the idea, that is, it is co-existent. Whilst in *father—sorrow* the concept " sorrow " adds something new, and thus effects a displacement of the concept. We should at once accept the classification of judgment-reactions into analytic and synthetic were it not for a difficulty of practical importance. We do not know in individual cases whether the analytic predicate is or is not something necessarily included in the idea. The solution of this question can be only attempted when we are able to distinguish in individual cases between a concrete and a universal image. Ziehen opines that he is able to do this, by direct questioning, even in children. We regard this method not only as extremely unsafe, but also, so far as the differentiation between a concrete and universal presentation is concerned, as extraordinarily difficult. What I name an inner presentation consists of condensations of many memory presentations ; whether their manner of appearance is more concrete than universal or vice versa depends upon minimal differences in perceptual vividness. In many cases, even psychologically educated persons would be at a loss if they were obliged to distinguish whether by *house—roof* they had imaged a particular or a universal roof. Naturally we are far from denying the existence of general images ; but in concrete cases of acoustic-verbal experiments we cannot

predicate of the conception only that which was already cogitated in it ; if negative I merely exclude from the conception its contrary. But in synthetical judgments I must go beyond the given conception, in order to cogitate, in relation with it, something quite different from that which was cogitated in it," etc. Kant's *Critique of Pure Reason*, Meiklejohn's translation, p. 117.

refrain from the suspicion that the so-called " universal images " are merely words. They only escape the individual content because they are as a rule much less universal concepts than verbal-motor pictures where the other senses participate with very slight intensity.

To answer the question whether a judgment is analytic or synthetic we should require exact information as to whether the idea was universal or concrete. For example, *snake — green* is objectively entirely synthetic ; for green is not a necessity of thought in regard to a snake ; but when a particular snake is thought of, green must be already implicitly present, when it would then be an analytic judgment. Apart from these considerations there are other practical difficulties which prevent this mode of classification.

In order to obtain a special classification of the predicates we must realize their different possibilities :

(1) The stimulus-word is a noun, the reaction an adjective.

(2) The stimulus-word is an adjective, the reaction a noun.

We have no grounds for separating these two cases or the other forms of predicative relationship :

(1) The stimulus-word is subject, the reaction its active or passive functioning.

(2) The stimulus-word is the active or passive functioning of the reaction ; or

(3) The stimulus-word is object, the reaction the activity relating thereto.

(4) The stimulus-word is an activity, the reaction the object thereof.

Consider the first forms—the predicative connexion of noun and adjective. Two main possibilities may be differentiated :

α. The adjective denotes an essential attribute of the stimulus-image of inner import. This kind of predicate may be termed " inner." Without any particular forcing these predicates can be divided into two groups :

(1) *Judgment of Fact*, e.g. :

Snake	green	War	bloody
Glass	brittle	Grandmother	old
Mild	spring	Winter	raw
Thirst	violent		

These predicates denote certain essential and important

elements of the stimulus-image. Their purely objective emphasis differentiates them from the second group :

(2) *Judgment of Value*, e.g. :

Father	good	Pupil	good
Smell	unpleasant	Soldier	brave
Ride	dangerous	Wood	useful
Mountain	beautiful	Murderer	common
Book	interesting	Water	refreshing

In these reactions the personal element stands out more or less strongly. But where the reference to the ego stands out clearly in the shape of a wish or a defence in an entirely subjective form we can speak directly of " egocentric predicates." We should, however, prefer not to separate these reactions, as an independent group, from judgments of value, for reasons which we shall give later. We include among judgments of value reactions like :

Iron	useful metal	Scoundrel	disgrace
Water	one of the most interesting of chemical bodies		

Judgments of value which express themselves in the form of an activity, e.g. :

Smoke	smells	Apple	tastes good

are best included among the predicates.

Reactions where a value is not expressed but is required are also included among judgments of value. Example :

Good	one should be	Threaten	one should not
Industrious	the pupil should be		

These reactions are not very frequent among normals ; we add them merely for the sake of completeness.

β. The adjective denotes an outer but slightly important attribute of the stimulus-image, one coexistent and sensually evident.

We prefer to designate this kind of predicate " outer " :

Tooth	protruding	Tree	brown
Salt	granular	Water	surging
Shirt	blue		etc.

We estimate the predicate relationship between the adjective as stimulus-word and the substantive as reaction according to the principles just illustrated. That is, we judge " green — field " and " field — green " to be practically equivalent in the classification.

The *interjections* which Aschaffenburg classifies with some reason among the predicates we have placed elsewhere (see below).

A further subgroup of predicates is composed of the " relations between noun and verb."

α. *The Subject Relation.*—The noun as stimulus-word or reaction is the subject óf a definite activity :

Resin	sticks	To cook	mother
Hunter	shoots		

β. *The Object Relation* :

Doors	open	To recruit	soldiers
Throat	to stitch up	To polish	brass

If the attribute is a stimulus-word the predicates hitherto considered are often not easily to be separated from the previously mentioned " coadjuncts as example." As decisive of the latter we regard the obvious endeavour of the subject to find a reaction word or noun as far as possible suitable to the stimulus-word and of universal validity, as in :

To pray	pious	Despise	wickedness
To indulge	peaceable		

We adjudge " polish — brass " to the object relation, but " polish — bright metals " to the " coadjuncts as example."

Associations denoting place, time, means, and purpose stand in somewhat close connexion with the group of predicates. (Ranschburg's " Association Denoting Purpose." [1])

Place : to go — into town	Means : to hit — with the stick
Time : eat — noon	Purpose : wood — for burning

Occasionally doubt arises in these reactions as to whether they are perhaps to be conceived as specific, and belonging, therefore, to the subordination group. The differentiation is easy in the great majority of cases and no gross error will arise. Definitions or explanations of the stimulus-word, which on the whole occur very seldom, have a certain connexion with the above groups ; we have, therefore, included them among the predicative relationships. Examples :

Doors	noun	Blue	adjective	Star	heavenly constellation

---

[1] Ranschburg and Balint," Ueber quantitative und qualitative Veränderungen geistiger Vorgänge im hohen Greisenalter," *Allgemeine Zeitschrift für Psychiatrie*, Bd. LVII, p. 715.

Predicate relationships may be thus grouped as follows :

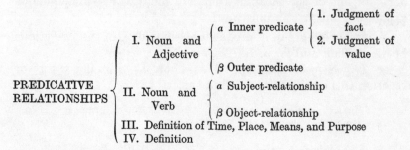

PREDICATIVE RELATIONSHIPS

I. Noun and Adjective
- α Inner predicate
  - 1. Judgment of fact
  - 2. Judgment of value
- β Outer predicate

II. Noun and Verb
- α Subject-relationship
- β Object-relationship

III. Definition of Time, Place, Means, and Purpose

IV. Definition

c. Causal Dependence (Münsterberg).

Stimulus-word and reaction are linked by a causal connexion. Examples :

Pain	tears	To cut	pain

(B) *Outer Associations*

a. COEXISTENCE.—The connexion of the coexistence is one of contiguity or simultaneity, that is to say, the union of the two images is not solely effected by similarity or relationship, but by a union in time or immediate succession. Coexistence in space is included in contiguity in time, for spatial coexistence proceeds from successive sense impressions. Examples :

Ink	penholder	Table	chair
Copy-book	knife	Mother	child
Pipe	tobacco	Handle	knife
Hospital	nurse	Lamp	family
Pupil	teacher	Sunday	church

Reactions like

Ride	horse	Ride	saddle
Eye	to see	Ear	to hear

Pencil
Paper
Copy-book } to write
Sing
Add

we likewise include here ; the associations with " write " are school memory-complexes, their connexion being essentially conditioned by simultaneity ; the remaining examples refer to reaction presentations which are linked to the stimulus-idea by essential coexistence.

b. IDENTITY.—The reaction implies no alteration or further development of the meaning, but is a more or less synonymous expression for the stimulus-word.

α. The synonymous expression arises from the same language as the stimulus-word. Examples :

Splendid	magnificent	Take care	look out
Quarrel	dispute		

β. The synonymous expression arises from a language other than the stimulus-word—it is a translation, e.g. :

Postage-stamp	timbre	Sunday	dimanche

c. VERBAL-MOTOR FORMS.—Ziehen, " Current Word-couplings and Associative Word-complements " [1] ; Kräpelin–Aschaffenburg, " Verbal Reminiscences " [2] ; Trautschold, " Word-Association." [3] In this subgroup of outer associations are included all those connected presentations which have become more or less mechanical through constant association in speech, although they perhaps have logically and historically another significance, and for that reason might be grouped under one of the above types. In the " contrasts " we have already mentioned a series of reactions which we regard as due to such verbal usage, i.e. as being mechanical.

α. *Relationship by Verbal Usage.*

(1) Simple contrast. Examples :

Light	dark	White	black
Bitter	sweet	Like	unlike

(2) Current phrases. Examples :

Hunger	suffer	Right	to be
Of age	to come	Come	go
Bat	shuttlecock	Time	space
Thanks	to give	Assault	battery
Knight	gentle	Bread	our daily
Grief	sorrow	Poor	and needy
Water	blue	Bed	board
Swim	to be able to	Walk	to go
Train	alight	Fear	never
Cat	mouse		

---

[1] Ziehen, *Die Ideenassoziation des Kindes*, p. 29. *Sammlung von Abhandlungen aus dem Gebiete der pädagogischen Psychologie*, Bd. I, p. 6.

[2] *Psychologische Arbeiten*, Bd. I, p. 223.

[3] Wundt's *Phil. Studien*, Bd. I, p. 213.

β. *Proverbs and Quotations.*—Examples :

Hammer	tongs	Eye	tooth
Liberty	equality	Solid	flesh
World	flesh, devil	Fish	fowl
House	glass	Throw	stones
Peace	and war		

γ. *Word-complements.*—(1) The reaction-word extends the stimulus-word into another complete word.

Book	-binder	Fish	-monger
Tooth	-ache	Needle	-holder
Tram	-way	Pin	-pricks
Table	-cloth	Purse	-string
Clear	-headed	Ear	-ring

The reaction can also be in the following form where the stimulus-word is repeated in the reaction :

Tear	tearfully	Glaze	glazier
Foot	football	See	seer
Horse	horse-dealer	Praise	bepraise

(2) The reaction is essentially only a syntactic alteration of the stimulus-word (Wreschner : " Association resembling an inflexion " [1]). Examples :

Die	dead	Find	found
Good	goodness	Drive	driven
Hero	heroic	Murderer	murderess
School	scholar	Fond	fondness

δ. We mention a small group of reactions which can be denoted as premature, e.g. :

Dark red	bright	Grand	small
Slow	short		

ε. We have placed the infrequently occurring *interjections* under " verbal-motor connexions," although they really denote a predicate as Aschaffenburg maintains. We justify our view by the verbal incompleteness of the reaction, which moreover contains a very strong motor element. Examples :

Grand	ah !	Love	oh !
Shame	fie !		

(C) *Clang-reactions*

The content of this group corresponds to Aschaffenburg's group of " stimulus-words that only produce effects by their sound."

---

[1] Wreschner : " Eine experimentelle Studie über die Assoziation in einem Falle von Idiotie," *Allgemeine Zeitschrift für Psychiatrie*, Bd. LVII, p. 241.

a. WORD-COMPLETIONS.—We regard these words as Aschaffenburg does, including here only those reactions which complete the
stimulus-word by a word which cannot be split up.   Examples :

Wonder	- ful	Modest	- y
Heart	- y	Friend	- ly

The completion of the stimulus-word to a name we also regard
as a word-completion.   Examples :

Liver	- pool	Dub	- lin

b. CLANG.—The reaction is determined exclusively by the
clang of the whole stimulus-word or its beginning.   Examples :

Pipe	pip	Window	winter
Fate	fat	Object	obtain
Green	greed		

c. RHYME.   Examples :

Dream	scream	Heart	part
Plate	great	Moses	noses
Make	shake		

A further classification of clang and rhymes into " meaningful
and meaningless," following Aschaffenburg, is not worth making
by reason of the great scarcity of the " meaningless " group,
We have therefore refrained from so doing.

(D) *Residual Group*

We have placed together in this not very numerous group a
few modes of reaction which do not fit into the rest of the scheme
and have but a very slight connexion with each other.

a. INDIRECT ASSOCIATION.—Aschaffenburg opposes the indirect mode of reaction to all other reactions known as the " direct."
We have rejected this as lacking in quantitative proportion, for
it can never be known, especially among uneducated persons,
how many different ideas stand between stimulus-word and
reaction.   We ourselves are often unable to state exactly how
many conscious, semi-, or un-conscious constellations interweave
in our reaction.   We do not here enter into the academic con-
troversy about the indirect association (as to whether the middle
term is conscious or unconscious), but limit ourselves to estimate
within the limits of our cases the phenomenon of " indirect
association."   *We call " indirect association " that mode of reaction
which is only understandable by the assumption of a middle term*

different from the stimulus- and the reaction-word. We distinguish five forms :

α. *Connexion by a Common Middle Term.* Examples :

White	broad	Dozen	144
Field of snow		Heap	
False	fair	Turbid	shallow
Miss X. is false and fair		Water	
Remorse	black	Red	fragrance
Mourning		Flower	
Lock	round	Bike	round
Turn		Wheel	
Sick	odourless	Walk	pears
Smell		'Mid pear-trees	
Quick	whistle	Revolve	earth
Locomotive		Turn	
Hay	green	Rich	gold
Grass		Australia	

It is to be observed that in these associations the middle term is sometimes clearly known. This kind of reaction is, on the whole, very scarce, and occurs almost exclusively in individuals of marked visual type.

β. *Centrifugal Clang-displacement* (" paraphasic indirect association " of Aschaffenburg).—At first there is inwardly a more or less clear and sensible reaction, but this is replaced during the process of reproduction into speech by a clang-like association. We therefore call this group of indirect associations the centrifugal clang-displacement. Examples :

Resolution	salve	Dress	goat
(Resolve)		(Overcoat)	
Grief	fish	Club	commit
(Selfish)		(Committee)	
Quarrel	spout	Earth	van
(Dispute)		(Heaven)	
Hair	blue	Clothes	fash
(Blonde)		(Fashion)	
Love	gate	Ear	ground
(Hate)		(Sound)	
Pair	true	Book	heaven
(Shoe)		(Heavy)	

Cordes would exclude these from the indirect reactions—with a show of right from his point of view. The direct inner association seems to be correct, i.e. no clang-association. A completely adequate and direct intention is present, which, however, at the moment of utterance is displaced, at the expense of the sense, by a clang-similarity. Such displacements can only occur when the inner picture about to be expressed does not attract to itself intensity of attention sufficient to ensure the special speech mechanism. Aberrations and divergencies only occur when what is to be expressed has too weak an emphasis. We therefore hold that the middle term, despite correct intention, has been left abnormally stranded, which agrees perfectly with the accounts given by those who have been able to observe themselves. Some simply felt that they had not said the correct thing, but were at first unable to give the middle term.

Whether the displacement to clang-similarity when the association term is but vaguely conscious occurs at the place of utterance or inception seems to us entirely unessential as regards the valuation of the reaction.

γ. *Centripetal Clang-displacement.*—The stimulus-word is inwardly replaced by a clang-word which in its turn conditions the reaction. The middle term is usually semi-conscious or unconscious. It should be noted that in all these cases the stimulus-word is correctly understood, so that there is no question of a mere misunderstanding. Examples :

Ride	wrong	Malt	vinegar
(Right)		(Salt)	
Wallow	bird	Mast	servant
(Swallow)		(Master)	
Glass	first	String	beat
(Last)		(Strict)	
Police	yearly	Misery	obstinate
(Lease)		(Surly)	
Map	sane	Paper	cut
(Mad)		(Poor)	
Green	star	Sling	tall
(E'en)		(Slight)	
Feat	mutton	Brute	hen
(Meat)		(Brood)	
Fate	pudding	Straight	stranger
(Ate)		(Strange)	

In our experience clang accounts for the large majority of indirect displacements of association. What we have said in the previous paragraph in reference to the consciousness of the middle term holds here also. The occurrence of clang-associations denotes a lack of feeling-tone or attention about the stimulus-word. The reaction to the clang middle term is likewise a result of the insufficient feeling-tone of the stimulus-word. The clang-association in this case is in our experience just as obscure as the stimulus-word, and at the first moment the individual is even uncertain as to the nature of the stimulus-word. The reaction is innervated before the act of apperception is complete.[1]

δ. *Centrifugal and Centripetal Displacement by Word-completion or Verbal-motor Association.*

Examples :

Normal	filter		Hook	shepherd
	(Solution)			(Crook)
False	fickleness		Miser	age
	(Fickle)			(Old)
Rat	poisonous		Foot	gained
	(Poison)			(-ing)
Train	ground		Milk	rosy
	(-ing)			(-maid)
Clean	fly		Dog	astronomy
	(Dirty)			(-star)
Stock	mountains		Chronic	pain
	(Alpenstock)			(Disease)
Brave	dark		Slip	motor
	(Fair)			(Side-)
Sea	spade		Stir	breakfast
	(-side)			(-about)

ε. *Displacement by Several Middle Terms.*—The middle terms may be mechanical but nevertheless highly important associations. The associations of this class are very scanty and usually of abnormal origin. Under these reactions naturally all the types above can mingle. Examples :

Ink	acid		Revenge	white
(Red	litmus)		(Sweet	sugar)
Bird	horror		Book	differ
(Cage	prison)		(Read	difficult)
Slow	weather		Severe	dead
(Sure	uncertain)		(Father	mother)

---

[1] Münsterberg is of opinion that the outer excitation does not awaken association at the moment when it is transposed into a conscious process, but that there lies between external stimulus and conscious central excitation a non-conscious intermediate stage ; here an association activity occurs which is not illuminated by consciousness (*Beiträge zur Experimentelle Psychologie*, Heft 4, p. 7). But Münsterberg imprudently denies the occurrence of indirect associations by unconscious intermediate terms (Heft 4, p. 9).

We shall not here deal more particularly with a theory of indirect associations in acoustic-verbal experiment. For the present we may say that it is closely connected with alterations in attention.

b. MEANINGLESS REACTIONS.—In moments of emotion or of confusion reactions are occasionally given which are neither words nor associations. Among those which are merely sounds we naturally separate assonances as clang-associations. Among the words not associated there are, so to say, no words whose origin would be inexplicable. They are chiefly names of objects of the environment or of accidental presentations having no connexion with the stimulus-word. Some few meaningless reactions are perseverations of type *b* (see below).

c. FAULT.—We denote the omission of a reaction as a fault. The cause of the omission is usually emotional.

d. REPETITION OF THE STIMULUS-WORD.[1]—Quantitatively a very weak group which could really just as well be included among the faults. Still, there are normal individuals who cannot refrain from quickly repeating the stimulus-word before they really react This is a phenomenon which, apart from experiment, can be observed in ordinary conversation. This latter mode of reaction would not, of course, come under this heading. The repetition of the stimulus-word is an emotional phenomenon. (This is also Wreschner's view.[2])

(E) *The Egocentric Reaction*

Certain individuals betray an obvious tendency during the experiment to form egocentric relationships, to express extremely subjective judgments which are obviously conditioned by *desire* or *fear*. Reactions of this kind have something of temperamental individuality and are characteristic for certain personalities.

a. DIRECT REFERENCE TO THE EGO.   Examples :

Grandmother	me	Praise	of me
Dancing	I don't like	Count	I can't
Wrong	I was not		

b. SUBJECTIVE CRITICAL VALUATIONS.   Examples :

Idle	pleasant	Blood	horrible
Piano	horrid	Love	stupid
Arithmetic	troublesome		

---

[1] Meaningless reactions, faults, and repetition of the stimulus-words are sometimes grouped by English writers as False Associations, e.g. C. S. Myers' *Experimental Psychology*, Part I, 2nd edition, p. 143.—TRANSLATOR.

[2] *Allgemeine Zeitschrift für Psychiatrie*, Bd. LVII.

(F) *Perseveration*

(Aschaffenburg's " association to previous words ")

Under perseveration we understand a phenomenon of persistence [1] which consists in the previous association conditioning the reaction following. In this we have chiefly considered the effect upon the reaction that immediately follows. We leave aside, therefore, the effect upon an uninfluenced reaction, for we prefer to include influence of this nature under the general concept of constellation. We wish in no way to prejudge anything regarding the nature of the phenomenon of perseveration. We therefore again direct attention to the fact that perseveration can be conditioned just as well by current unknown psychophysical causes as by peculiar constellations of feeling. There are two cases of perseveration to be distinguished in practice.

a. THE CONDITIONED REACTION IS AN ASSOCIATION to the stimulus-word to which it belongs. Examples :

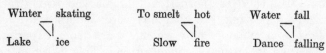

| Winter | skating | To smelt | hot | Water | fall |
| Lake | ice | Slow | fire | Dance | falling |

b. THE CONDITIONED REACTION IS NO ASSOCIATION to the stimulus-word to which it belongs. Examples :

Lid — box
Rat — basket

Softly — she comes hither
Gallant — up the steps

If a marked affect-toned complex dominates consciousness at the moment of the experiment, lengthy sequences of heterogeneous stimulus-words will be absorbed into the complex, since every reaction is conditioned by stimulus-word + complex constellation. The more powerful the complex constellation is, the more does the stimulus-image succumb to the phenomenon of assimilation (Wundt) ; that is to say, it will not be conceived in its true

---

[1] We employ the term perseveration in the sense of the investigations of Müller and Pilzecker, and denote thereby merely the continuance of the previous image so far as it is manifest in the nature of the reaction following. The term is purely formal and is not meant to explain anything. We leave aside the question of whether the " perseveration " is a cortical or cellular process (Gross), or the result of some special associative constellation. We should nevertheless like to state emphatically that our concept has no relationship to "perseveration" in organic cerebral processes, and just as little to the hypothetical " Secondary function of the cerebral cells " which is supposed to explain the psychological after-effect of the image's direction.

and usual meaning, but in some special meaning fitting in with the complex.

(G) *Repetitions*

In each experiment the same number of reactions were made ; the first and second hundred of the associations were, in normal conditions, counted off separately. We could, if necessary, distinguish between repetition of the content and of the particular form. As in normals, however, stereotyped reactions constructed with auxiliary words very seldom occur, we abandoned counting the repetition of the form.

(H) *Verbal Linking*

It is a striking fact that associations are not only connected by their meaning in accordance with the fundamental laws of association, contiguity, and similarity, but also in accordance with certain purely external motor-acoustic principles. So far as we know, Bourdon was the first to experiment on this question. In his valuable work, " Recherches sur la succession des phéno-mènes psychologiques," [1] he records investigations on phonetic linking in association. In certain selected books Bourdon took the first noun, adjective, or verb at the top of each page. In this way he compared 500 pairs of words. The total of phonetic similarities was 312 pairs, from which he argues a phonetic similarity when the words have one or several phonetic elements in common. It must certainly be admitted that Bourdon has somewhat unduly strained this similarity, e.g. *toi* and *jouer* on account of the W sound (!). Bourdon particularly investigated the *Ressemblance phonétique, graphique* (one or more letters in common), and *syllabique* (a common syllable). He found the following figures :

Ressemblance phonétique	.	.	.	0,629
,, *graphique*	.	.	.	0,888
,, *syllabique*	.	.	.	0,063

Bourdon writes : " Il reste néanmoins vrai, que les mots s'associent entre eux plutôt par leur signification que par leur ressemblance phonétique."

In accordance with these investigations we have formed a group which contains outer verbal factors.

a. SAME GRAMMATICAL FORM.—We simply counted how often the word-form of stimulus-word and reaction was the same, how often noun–noun, adjective–adjective occurred. We came to the

[1] *Rev. phil.*, T. 35, p. 225.

consideration of this problem from observing that very great individual differences exist.

b. SAME NUMBER OF SYLLABLES.—We counted how often the stimulus-word and reaction had the same number of syllables with the view of perhaps learning something about the influence of rhythm.

c. PHONETIC AGREEMENT. (1) Consonance.—We counted how often the first syllable of stimulus-word and reaction agreed as to vowels.

(2) Alliteration.—We counted how often there was alliteration in stimulus-word or reaction in initial vowels or consonants.

(3) Same ending.—-Here the phonetic influence of the stimulus-word-ending upon the reaction-ending or upon the tendency to rhyme was investigated. Only the agreement in the end syllable was counted.

Recapitulation

(A) *Inner Association*

a. Co-ordination.
    α. Coadjunction.
        1. By common supraconcept.
        2. By similarity.
        3. By inner relationship
        4. By outer relationship.
        5. As example.
    β. Subordination.
        1. True subordination.
        2. Specific.
    γ. Supraordination.
    δ. Contrast.
    ε. Co-ordination of doubtful quality.
b. Predicate relationship.
    I. Noun and adjective.
        α. Inner predicate.
            1. Judgment of fact.
            2. Judgment of value.
        β. Outer predicate.
    II. Noun and verb.
        α. Subject-relationship.
        β. Object-relationship.
    III. Definition of time, place, means, and purpose.
    IV. Definition or explanation.
c. Causal dependence.

(B) *Outer Association*

a. Coexistence.
b. Identity.

c. Verbal-motor forms.
    α. Relationship by verbal usage.
        1. Simple Contrast.
        2. Current phrases.
    β. Proverbs and quotations.
    γ. Word-complement and -change.
    δ. Premature reaction.
    ε. Interjection.

(C) *Clang-reaction*

a. Word-completion.
b. Clang.
c. Rhyme.

(D) *Residual Group*

a. Indirect association.
    α. Connexion by common middle term.
    β. Centrifugal clang-displacement.
    γ. Centripetal clang-displacement.
    δ. Displacement by word-completion or verbal-motor
       form.
    ε. Displacement by several middle terms.
b. Meaningless reactions.
c. Faults.
d. Repetition of the stimulus-word.

(E) *Egocentric Reaction*

a. Direct reference to the ego.
b. Subjective critical valuations.

(F) *Perseveration*

a. Connexion with the stimulus-word.
b. No connexion with the stimulus-word.

(G) *Repetition of the Reaction*

(H) *Verbal Linking*

a. Same grammatical form.
b. Same number of syllables.
c. Phonetic agreement.
    1. Consonance.
    2. Alliteration.
    3. Same ending.

We have classified our material according to the principles laid down in this scheme. In order not to complicate the presentation of the results unnecessarily by a heaping up of figures, the tables published in the second part give the figures of the chief groups only ; the voluminous material can be thus more distinctly grouped than by the detailed rendering of the figures for the subgroups. We have been very scrupulous in rendering an exact account of the nature of the considerations which decided us to a classification in this or that chief group. Besides, it seemed of general interest to present the various empirical possibilities of the associations so far as they are known to us.

Our figures therefore refer only to the following chief groups of the scheme :

I. *Inner Association.*
    1. Co-ordination.
    2. Predicate relationship.
    3. Causal dependence.

II. *Outer Association.*
    1. Coexistence.
    2. Identity.
    3. Verbal-motor forms.

III. *Clang-reaction.*
    1. Word-completion.
    2. Clang.
    3. Rhyme.

IV. *Residual Group.*
    1. Indirect reactions.
    2. Meaningless reactions.
    3. Faults.
    4. Repetition of stimulus-word.

(A) *Egocentric Reaction.*

(B) *Perseveration.*

(C) *Repetition.*

(D) *Verbal Linking.*
    1. Same grammatical form.
    2. Same number of syllables.
    3. Alliteration.
    4. Consonance.
    5. Same ending.

PART II

Results of the Experiments

A. On Individuals

THE subjects have reacted very diversely to disturbing stimuli. As already remarked, the experiment in inner distraction was the most difficult. It was not always successful among all the educated subjects. Outer distraction by beats of the metronome succeeded somewhat better. Nevertheless, there were also here great differences between the individuals experimented upon. Consequently we feel called upon to communicate the figures for each individual *in extenso* ; the multiplicity of tables thus occasioned cannot, unfortunately, be avoided. The figures indicate percentages.

As a whole, the character of these associations (see Table, p. 40) is a very objective one, almost entirely uninfluenced by subjective constellations. In the normal state the outer associations exceed the inner. Between the first and second hundred of the normal reactions there is a distinct difference, for there occurs an increase of 9 per cent. in the clang group. We attribute this change to the occurrence of a certain "weariness" when the second hundred words were given, which psychologically means nothing but a relaxation of attention.[1] There can be scarcely any question in this case of physiological fatigue, which, as Aschaffenburg has shown, similarly increases the clang-associations. The preceding psychical work was much too little for this. On the other hand, this relaxation of interest agrees well with "weariness" in Kräpelin's sense.[2]

The columns after the "normal state" display the change of association under the influence of an artificially disturbed attention.

In a purely dynamic conception, we could almost say the

---

[1] Aschaffenburg says : " Our attention is so extremely labile, the alterations of our psychical life—which we cannot control and cannot avoid—so great, that we are scarcely justified in deducing results from a small series of experiments. On the other hand, it must not be forgotten that during the course of longer experiments phenomena of fatigue occur ; it is not, for instance, right to compare the first twenty-five associations of a series of two hundred reactions with the last twenty-five without regard to this factor " (*Psych. Arbeiten*, Bd. I, p. 217). Aschaffenburg has therefore observed the same phenomenon but has not, in our opinion, correctly interpreted it.

[2] *Psych. Arbeiten*, Bd. I, p. 53. Kräpelin distinguishes between " weariness " (Müdigkeit) and " fatigue " (Ermüdung). " Weariness " he regards as a kind of warning sign, a subjective feeling which usually, but not invariably, develops into true fatigue.

1. EDUCATED WOMEN

Fourteen subjects with 4046 reactions

No. 1.   *Subject aged 22, very intelligent*

ASSOCIATIONS	NORMAL		DISTRACTION		
	1st hundred	2nd hundred	Inner	Outer	
				60 metro.	100 metro.
Co-ordination	26	21	16	4	12
Predicate relationship	14	14	2	4	2
Causal dependence	2	1	—	—	2
Coexistence	20	10	10	2	—
Identity	1	7	4	8	—
Verbal-motor forms	36	36	54	20	38
Word-completion	1	1	6	8	2
Clang	—	8	6	34	38
Rhyme	—	1	—	6	—
Indirect	—	—	—	4	—
Meaningless	—	—	2	4	6
Faults	—	—	—	—	—
Repetition of stimulus-word . .	—	—	—	6	—
Egocentric reaction	1	—	—	—	—
Perseveration	1	—	2	6	4
Repetition	5	8	2	0	6
Same grammatical form . . .	67	58	64	56	54
Same number of syllables . . .	43	41	56	60	42
Alliteration	10	12	12	42	48
Consonance	12	15	16	52	52
Same ending	10	6	10	14	6
Inner associations	42	36	18	8	16
Outer associations	57	53	68	30	38
Clang-reactions	1	10	12	48	40
Number of associations . . .	100	100	50	50	50

" associative energy " (Ranschburg) [1] has been conducted to a definitely new region, so that only a fraction of it is available for the formation of reaction. It follows that a proportionately easier or lighter association—that is, one for which the way is well prepared—is reacted, because to excite prepared and habitual cerebral mechanisms demands a less amount of energy than to make a track for relatively new and unusual connexions. The increase in the verbal-motor forms to 18 per cent. in inner distraction is readily understood from this point of view.[2] On the other hand, it is more difficult to understand the origin of the numerous clang-reactions in outer distraction. Aschaffenburg thinks that the motor excitation which exists in mania, exhaustion,[3] and alcoholic intoxication can be made responsible for the occurrence of clang-reactions.[4]

It has been demonstrated that flight of ideas, or modes of association similar to flights of ideas, can also occur without motor excitation, e.g. in epilepsy (Heilbronner),[5] catatonia and maniacal stupor.[6] In our experiment motor excitation is practically excluded. (The movements of writing which could be interpreted as " motor excitation " are excluded in inner distraction, and the results agree with those of outer distraction.) Therefore, the clang-reactions are not in any demonstrable connexion with motor excitation ; rather we perceive the cause of their appearance in the decline of attention. Distraction chiefly inhibits inner (" higher ") association and favours the production of outer, i.e. more mechanical, forms of association— hence predominantly of the clang-reaction. In the further course of our work we shall have ample opportunity to demonstrate the shifting of the association form towards the outer, that is, towards the mechanical association.

It is a striking fact that this obvious tendency to mechanical reactions distinctly favours clang-association. But according to

[1] Ranschburg and Hajós, *Psychologie des hysterischen Geisteszustandes*, 1897.

[2] Aschaffenburg, *Psych. Arbeit.*, Bd. I, p. 239. At the moment of origin of the outer association verbal habit predominates, whilst later, on reflection, the tendency to co-ordinatism is often added secondarily.

[3] The term " exhaustion " should be reserved for a higher degree of damage to our physical and mental elasticity (Aschaffenburg, *Psych. Arbeit.*, Bd. II, p. 47).

[4] " As the most essential factor in the origin of a number of clang-reactions exceeding the norm, the relief from the releasing of motor-impulses must be considered " (Aschaffenburg, *Psych. Arbeit.*, Bd. II, p. 69). Cp. also the works of Smith, Fürer, and Rüdin on the effects of alcohol, in Kräpelin's *Psych. Arbeiten.*

[5] Heilbronner, " Ueber epileptische Manie nebst Bemerkungen über die Ideenflucht," *Monatsschrift für Psychiatrie u. Neurologie*, Bd. XIII, 1903.

[6] There are, moreover, maniacs who still show flight of ideas, especially in the stage of subsidence, when they are no longer otherwise restless.

previous experience clang-associations are not mechanical; apparently they are not habitual associations.

In our conception clang-associations are the most primitive of similarity associations, standing very little above mere repetition. After earliest childhood they are no longer habitual but are always easily excited in the act of speech, and force themselves to the front as soon as any disturbance removes the next higher stage of association (slip in speech, mishearing). On account of their purposelessness they are constantly suppressed in normal thinking, and usually exist outside consciousness.

We call the increase in verbal-motor forms and clang-reactions the *superficial reaction type*. The attentive association, which occurs at the flash-point of consciousness, is no clang-association (unless such a one is deliberately sought); but should we succeed in directing attention to another activity—pushing the psychical reaction away from consciousness—all those associations arise which were suppressed in the fully conscious act of reaction. We shall return later to a full consideration of the importance of this hypothesis in the pathology of association.

With weak attention the stimulus-image does not rise to its full height of clearness, or, in other words, it remains in a peripheral region of the field of consciousness and is merely apprehended by means of its external, clang-like manifestation. The cause of this want of apprehension lies in the weakness of the affective tone, which is, for its part, again dependent upon the disturbance of attention. Every apperceptive process of an acoustic stimulus begins at the stage of clang-like apprehension. At each of these stages associations can be expressed through speech centres which are ready for discharge at the moment. That this does not occur normally depends upon the inhibition exercised by the direction of the attention, i.e. by the raising of the threshold of the stimulus for all inferior and non-directed forms of association.

This case is remarkable for the large number of meaningless reactions—up to 6 per cent. in outer distraction. They are partly dependent upon strong perseveration, e.g. :

Intention— out of tune (" one notices the intention," etc.)

Save — art (*sc.* art of poetry)

Strong — powerful

Hate — splendid

partly upon distraction due to the unaccustomed noise of the metronome, e.g. :

Appearance   rhythm.

These reactions show in some measure how strongly the disturbance of the stimulus affected the subject. This extreme lowering of attention explains also the unusually large number of clang-reactions. The gradual predominance of the acoustic-verbal factors is also illustrated by the distinct rise of the figures in alliteration and consonance ; agreement in number of syllables shows also a distinct increase. The increase of perseveration in distraction is not easy to explain ; perhaps it is to be referred to the failure in association caused by the distraction. It is worth mentioning that the outer distraction in this case is progressive. We make use of the clangs to demonstrate this progression. We divide each experiment in outer distraction into three parts and reckon up the clang-associations in each part.

The progression is as follows :

    I. Experiment : 5, 5, 7.
   II. Experiment : 5, 6, 8.

No. 2. The general character of the association is objective (p. 44). The outer associations predominate but very little over the inner. Inner distraction seems to have worked most intensively. After the first hundred, clang-reactions steadily increased. The group of verbal linkage shows, in comparison with the previous case, certain differences in the distraction. Agreement in grammatical form shows a distinct increase, which is also seen in agreement in the number of syllables. But consonance and alliteration somewhat decrease. The individual causes of these divergencies are naturally not within our knowledge.

The relatively numerous faults are striking, the maximum being reached in the first hundred. Of the four faults in the first hundred, three occurred in stimulus-words toned with emotion. In the second hundred there is only one fault, but numerous predicates now occur, namely, judgments as to value. This fact appears to point to the fault being essentially an emotional phenomenon, a kind of inhibition of emotion, which disappears in the second hundred with the greater ease and more assured occurrence of subjective judgments. Perseveration shows, as in the previous case, distinct increase. We draw attention to the fact that in this case the maximum of indirect associations occurs with the minimum of clang-reactions, and, inversely, the maximum of clang-reactions with the minimum of indirect reactions.

The nature of the inner distraction here, which on the whole succeeded better than in the previous case, deserves a little discussion. We purposely directed the subject's attention to visual images chiefly, for in our experience these are the sense-phenomena that most frequently accompany the association

No. 2.　*Subject about 24, intelligent, well-read*

ASSOCIATIONS	NORMAL		DISTRACTION		
			Inner	Outer	
	1st hundred	2nd hundred		60 metro.	100 metro.
Co-ordination	27	14	10	16	16
Predicate relationship	18	26	18	18	20
Causal dependence	1	3	—	2	—
Coexistence	24	16	11	22	8
Identity	2	1	4	18	12
Verbal-motor forms	21	36	50	16	36
Word-completion	—	1	2	2	6
Clang	—	1	1	—	2
Rhyme	—	—	—	2	—
Indirect	3	1	2	2	—
Meaningless	—	—	—	—	—
Faults	4	1	1	2	—
Repetition of stimulus-word	—	—	1	—	—
Egocentric reaction	1	1	—	—	—
Perseveration	1	1	2	2	4
Repetition	—	4	—	2	—
Same grammatical form	55	47	63	76	64
Same number of syllables	31	24	29	36	40
Alliteration	12	15	10	2	6
Consonance	12	17	17	8	12
Same ending	4	9	14	6	8
Inner associations	46	43	28	36	36
Outer associations	47	53	65	56	56
Clang-reactions	—	2	3	4	8
Number of associations	100	100	100	50	50

experiment, and in most of our subjects were also, relatively, the most vivid. On the other hand, the capacity to observe and to report these phenomena correctly is much rarer. Subject No. 1, for instance, gave rather unsatisfactory information in this respect ; No. 2, on the other hand, was usually a very keen observer and was able to give accurate information.

The experiment is best illustrated by some examples :

Singing   professional singing.

The subject sees directly after the apprehension of the stimulus-word a scene from *Tannhäuser* on a particular stage.

Fireplace   fire,

sees a definite memory-picture of a fireplace-scene in London.

Tile   roof,

sees red tiles.

Journey   projected journey,

sees a travelling Englishman.

Apple   -tree

sees a picture : Eve with the apple.

Honour (*Ehre*) feeling,

sees a memory-picture from a scene in Sudermann's *Honour* (*Ehre*), lately witnessed.

Sail   -cloth,

sees a sailing ship.

Deportment   rule,

sees the memory-picture of her younger brother in the dancing and deportment lesson (a recent memory).

Modest   -y,

sees the image of a certain young girl.

Vegetable   kingdom,

sees a particular picture-book with illustrations of flowers.

Sign   -post,

sees a cross-road.

Placid   placid peace,

sees a particular little kitten.

Music   enjoyment,

sees the interior of a particular concert-room (recent memory-image).

These examples show that the reactions are very simple, mostly verbal-motor forms. The inner images stand in a certain associative connexion with the reaction. According to the subject's account they all arise, if not before the reaction, then just with it. In our view the reactions are for the most part mechanical by-associations which have been aroused, as it were, at a halt on the way to a higher reaction. The stimulus-

image did not reach full clearness, for it lacked the energy necessary to ascend ; or, not to use Herbartian language, it remained
stationary in the peripheral field of consciousness on account of
the inhibition proceeding from the clear visual picture. The
following examples show still more distinctly the halt of the
reaction when the visual picture is very clear :

Praise   the singer's praise,

she sees a particular teacher who praises her.

Custom   good custom,

sees the picture of a Swiss village, of an old " custom."

Like   like unto like,[1]

sees the written sign 2 × 2 = 4.

Stretch (*Strecken*)   Cat-stretcher (*Katzenstrecher*),

sees a stretched rubber band (*Katzenstrecher* is a popular nickname
for the Lucernese).

Narrow   narrow-minded,

sees a narrow lead pipe.

Stone   chat,

sees a collection of minerals.

Change   time,

sees a bill of exchange.

Fashion   fashionable lady,

sees an elegant youth.

Hazy   eye,

sees a hazy, rainy landscape (constellation of the day of the
experiment).

Glass   smooth,

sees the display of a particular glass warehouse.

Vorwärts [2]   march,

sees a number of the newspaper *Vorwärts*.

Low   to butcher,

sees a low tabouret in a particular drawing-room.

In these reactions the connexion between reaction and inner
picture is, it may be asserted, completely detached. The reaction
proceeds as a rule quite mechanically from a lower stage of the
process of apprehension, whilst the inner picture represents quite
another conception of the stimulus-word.

[1] *Gleich und gleichgesellt sich gern.* Proverb = " Birds of a feather flock
together."—TRANSLATOR.

[2] *Vorwärts* = Forward ! march ; also the name of a well-known German
Socialist daily paper.—TRANSLATOR.

Conversely, the visual picture can be excited by a lower stage of apprehension, as the following instances show :

	Number	number, crowd,
sees a numb finger.		
	Would	you must,
sees a wooden hammer.		

No. 3.   *Subject about 21 years old, intelligent, well-read*

ASSOCIATIONS	NORMAL		DISTRACTION			FATIGUE
	1st hundred	2nd hundred	Inner	Outer 60 metro.	Outer 100 metro.	
Co-ordination	8	9	19	14	14	4
Predicate relationship. . .	16	22	13	22	4	1
Causal dependence . . .	—	—	2	—	—	—
Coexistence	22	7	4	—	2	10
Identity	3	12	6	10	6	2
Verbal-motor forms . . .	46	44	26	32	54	40
Word-completion . . .	1	2	5	10	10	—
Clang	—	—	15	6	6	1
Rhyme	3	1	9	—	—	25
Indirect	1	3	1	—	2	3
Meaningless	—	1	—	6	2	12
Faults	—	—	—	—	—	—
Repetition of stimulus-word .	—	—	—	—	—	—
Egocentric reaction . . .	—	1	—	—	—	—
Perseveration	1	2	1	2	—	—
Repetition	7	12	6	8	8	8
Same grammatical form . .	63	50	62	52	54	70
Same number of syllables . .	52	46	60	44	50	73
Alliteration	6	4	16	14	12	18
Consonance	24	7	35	18	30	47
Same ending	13	20	22	20	16	44
Inner associations . . .	24	31	34	36	18	5
Outer associations . . .	71	63	36	42	62	52
Clang-reactions	4	3	29	16	16	26
Number of associations . .	100	100	100	50	50	100

The character of the associations is objective. The outer associations, namely, the verbal-motor forms, predominate. Both distraction experiments were very successful, especially inner distraction, which gave rise to 29 per cent. clang-reactions. A few reactions in inner distraction are of interest :

> Lid   fid (meaningless rhyme),

sees a beer-jug with lid.

> Hall   hale,

sees a particular hall.

> Fall   staff,

sees a waterfall.

> Stein   fine,

sees the picture of the little town of Stein on the Rhine.

The reason why the number of inner associations remained, nevertheless, above the normal level in inner distraction and the first half of outer distraction is due to the fact that the artificial lowering of attention was not uniform and permanent, but relaxed from time to time when the reactions became normal. The reactions which were registered by the same person in a state of severe physical and mental fatigue furnish a uniform picture of associative superficiality. According to this evidence, the state of fatigue, so far as the experiment is concerned, effects nothing but a uniform lowering of attention. Its retroaction upon the association does not differ in any way from the results of distraction experiments. Moreover, in the finer shades of individual associations which could not be counted and measured there is no perceptible difference, save in some few reactions whose content was conditioned by the particular constellation of the fatigue. From further observations on this point, and from Aschaffenburg's investigations, we conclude that no specific alteration can be demonstrated in fatigue except the superficiality. This superficiality of the reaction-type in fatigue can readily be explained by the lowering of attention. We have every reason for the statement that the superficiality of the reaction-type in alcoholic intoxication and maniacal excitement as demonstrated by Kräpelin's school is nothing but a symptom of disturbance of attention. The connexion with motor excitation assumed by Aschaffenburg is in our opinion only indirect. Motor excitation lowers the intensity of attention, and thus affects the superficiality of the associations. The disturbance of attention by motor excitation is a fact long known in the conditions described as "Distraction." Since attention as an affective state is linked with certain somatic processes, the lowering or the decrease of its stability by motor excitation is readily understood. Aschaffenburg is therefore incorrect in ascribing directly to motor excitation the superficiality of reaction, for motor excitation is absent in a whole series of abnormal superficial types of reaction. All these conditions have in common a disturbance of attention which is probably always the proximate cause of all types of association that resemble flight of ideas.[1]

The origin of the disturbance of attention is naturally very diverse—if not specific for each individual process. It may depend upon motor excitation or upon a decline or lessening of kinæsthetic sensations or upon a raising of the muscular stimulus-threshold or upon psychological dissociation, as in our experiments.

The extreme variability of the intensity of attention involves great and almost incalculable error in all association experiments with alcohol and fatigue. It is quite impossible with our present knowledge to say anything positive about the range of association disturbance from alcohol, etc. To judge from the percentage relationships of the above experiment in fatigue, the subject was in a distinctly psychotic condition. According to Aschaffenburg's theory a person with only 5 per cent. inner associations and 27 per cent. clang-associations corresponds to a person in a state of severe intoxication, severe mania, or quite abnormal exhaustion. This extreme superficiality is readily explained by the fact that evident drowsiness accompanied the strong, normal fatigue. The lowering of attention with systematic increase of the outer stimulus-thresholds, peculiar to this condition, is to be regarded (by analogy with the distraction experiments) as one of the chief causes of the superficiality.[2] The intensity of the drowsiness is an immeasurable factor : how much drowsiness was there mingled with the fatigue conditions investigated by Aschaffenburg ?

Drowsiness is not merely a somatic-physiological, but to a certain extent a psychological phenomenon also, which might be almost given the name of " autohypnosis." In the first place, it is a psychological process occurring in the sphere of attention ; this process is aroused chiefly by common sensation, but it can also be produced purely by suggestion. Exactly the same holds true of the effect of alcohol. The effects of alcohol must be largely purely suggestive, especially at the beginning of the narcosis ; to this must be referred the fact that the effects of alcohol can be very different under different conditions. In alcohol experiments can the suggestive effects

---

[1] Aschaffenburg is mistaken in supposing that Nordau's descriptions refer to hypomania : they refer rather to the far more general group of individuals who are unable to concentrate, and who have a superficial association type.

[2] Cp. the experiment on drowsiness in No. 1 of Educated Men, p. 65.

of alcohol be excluded or computed ? In our opinion it is not possible. Psychological experiments on the effects of alcohol demand, therefore, great caution. The disturbance of attention in fatigue and alcohol experiments need not always have its root in motor excitation, but can be quite as well derived from suggestive causes.

To return to our experiment. The marked preponderance of outer associations can be referred to a momentary lowering of attention, But the cause of the superficial reaction type may possibly lie deeper. It is not inconceivable that there are individuals who from congenital or acquired anomalies possess a more superficial mode of reaction than others ; this anomaly may ultimately lie in the region of attention, so that weariness occurs in them much more quickly than in others. From this point of view the figures of the sister and the mother of subject No. 3 are interesting as a familial-psychological observation. (See Tables on following page.)

No. 4, aged about 20, is the sister of No. 3. The associations are on the whole objective in character ; the outer predominate largely, more especially the verbal-motor forms. The clang-reactions are also correspondingly numerous, so that the type of the normal condition looks like the result of an experiment in distraction. In the experiment on inner distraction there was found an unexpected increase of the inner associations together with a distinct increase of the clang-reactions. The superficiality of the normal experiment is, in our experience, abnormal ; we must therefore assume some disturbance of attention in this condition. She is a pronounced " type moteur." The result of further psychological experiments with this subject shows that motor presentations predominate largely over those of the other senses.[1] The motor disposition shows itself also externally in a greater vivacity of movement and a highly developed capacity for motor expression.

It should be stated emphatically that the active mobility considerably oversteps the limits of conscious innervation, expressing itself in motor automatisms which are innervated by unconscious psychological complexes. Among the reactions in the normal state there are two verbal automatisms which in all probability refer to an unconscious complex. This complex stands in close connexion with the effect of a betrothal, which was just at that time a momentous question.

---

[1] Which does not imply that some kind of motor excitation was responsible for the superficial reaction type. In individuals of a motor type the motor parts of the word-picture combination perhaps play in this respect a separate rôle, producing a somewhat more facile disposition for speech.

Nos. 4 AND 5.   *Subjects: Sister and Mother of No. 3*

ASSOCIATIONS	SUBJECT 4			SUBJECT 5	
	NORMAL		DISTRAC-TION	NORMAL	
	1st hundred	2nd hundred	Inner	1st hundred	2nd hundred
Co-ordination	3	8	16	24	17
Predicate relationship	7	8	8	10	7
Causal dependence	—	—	1	1	0
Coexistence	8	6	3	8	8
Identity	2	4	1	6	13
Verbal-motor forms	67	56	39	46	45
Word-completion	4	8	14	3	4
Clang	3	5	9	—	3
Rhyme	2	1	2	—	—
Indirect	2	3	5	1	2
Meaningless	1	—	1	1	1
Faults	1	—	—	—	—
Repetition of stimulus-word . .	—	1	1	—	—
Egocentric reaction	—	—	—	—	—
Perseveration	1	—	2	1	2
Repetition	9	7	4	9	5
Same grammatical form . . .	61	51	53	82	66
Same number of syllables . . .	48	47	35	51	38
Alliteration	13	11	13	5	12
Consonance	14	19	24	16	17
Same ending	11	14	7	18	10
Inner associations	10	16	25	35	24
Outer associations	77	66	43	60	66
Clang-reactions	9	14	25	3	7
Number of associations . . .	100	100	100	100	100

We have thus two probable grounds for the strikingly super-ficial type of reaction : the strong and abnormally independent motor disposition, and an affect partly repressed into the uncon-scious. To the latter must be ascribed the chief importance in this superficiality. (It would take us too far to enter more minutely into the individual psychology of this case.)

The increase of the inner associations in the experiment on distraction is a phenomenon which we shall again find in another person of different character, who in the normal state likewise shows a superficial type.[1] For the improvement in the type of reaction in the previous case we know no better explanation than that the attention, normally linked to the affective complex, was set free by the conditions of the experiment, and was therefore available for use. Still, there were great variations in attention, as shown by the great number of clang-reactions compared with the relatively numerous inner associations.[2]

A peculiarity of this individual was the occasional occurrence of strong synæsthesias (*audition colorée*) influencing the reactions.

Examples from the normal condition :

Küssen (Kiss)	yellow,

ü is yellow for her.

elend (miserable)	something red,

e is red.

Träge (lazy)	blue,

ä is blue.

Examples during distraction :

Orgy	orgy,

sees a yellow mass.

Pious	blessed,

sees something yellow.

Remarkably enough, the subject who has the same reaction type as No. 4 is likewise a pronounced moteur and has likewise very vivid synæsthesias, which, however, as it happens, do not appear in the reactions.

The following phenomena in the distraction experiment are worth mentioning :

Stork	-'s leg,

sees a church tower.

Ham	-let (Hamlet),

sees Hampden (village).

Fall	-chion (falchion),

sees a high wall from which one could tumble down.

Red	wine,

sees a red ball.

Carp	-et,

sees a particular pond.

---

[1] Cp. No. 2 of Educated Men, p. 68.

[2] Cp. in this respect Nos. 1 and 2 of Educated Men, pp. 65 and 68.

According to the subject's account, the visual picture fills consciousness fully and exclusively ; the verbal reaction flows off almost involuntarily, touching consciousness but quite superficially. The above examples show distinctly the purely mechanical character of the verbal reaction.

Subject No. 5 is the mother of subjects 3 and 4. In its quantitative relationships her reaction type has great similarity with those of Nos. 3 and 4. The qualitative similarity so far as concerns the objective character of the reactions is also very great. The verbal-motor forms are particularly well marked in these three persons.

Characteristic of their familial type is the occurrence of clang-reactions in the normal state, which distinguishes this type from others. For ready comparison we repeat the chief figures of these subjects in the normal state :

	Inner Asssciations	Outer Associations	Clang-reactions
Mother . . .	29·5 per cent.	62 per cent.	5·0 per cent.
Elder daughter .	27·5 per cent.	67 per cent.	3·5 per cent.
Younger daughter .	13·0 per cent.	71·5 per cent.	11·5 per cent.

The increasing degree of superficiality as we proceed towards the younger daughter should be noticed. If the figures were derived from the same individual one might believe it was an experiment in distraction. This behaviour is possibly accidental but possibly it has also its deeper psychological reasons. We refer below to a similar observation. Ranchsburg [1] found among his old men 11·8 per cent. more inner associations than among young people.

In subject No. 6 (see Table on p. 54) the outer associations predominate in the normal state. The second hundred shows a slight increase in outer associations, and a definite addition to the clang-reactions. The quality of the associations diverges significantly from the objective types hitherto considered, for in this individual some reactions of a strongly subjective character occur, some as vivid and emphatic critical valuations, e.g. :

Pupil	boring	School	beautiful
Father	good	Frog	pretty
Book	interesting	Piano	atrocious

They are partly predicates which denote more or less percep-

---

[1] Ranschburg and Balint, *Allgemeine Zeitschrift für Psych.*, Bd. LVII, p. 689.

No. 6.　*Subject about 35, intelligent, very well-read, with poetical gifts*

ASSOCIATIONS	NORMAL		DISTRACTION		
	1st hundred	2nd hundred	Inner	Outer	
				60 metro.	100 metro.
Co-ordination	9	14	8	8	6
Predicate relationship	32	14 .	30	24	36
Causal dependence	1	—	—	—	—
Coexistence	12	18	14	16	10
Identity	2	6	2	6	2
Verbal-motor forms	39	39	40	34	42
Word-completion	—	1	—	2	—
Clang	—	4	—	4	2
Rhyme	4	2	—	2	2
Indirect	1	2	2	2	—
Meaningless	—	—	—	—	—
Faults	—	—	2	—	—
Repetition of stimulus-word	—	—	2	—	—
Egocentric reaction	10	4	6	8	4
Perseveration	—	—	—	2	4
Repetition	15	5	4	4	4
Same grammatical form	43	52	48	46	40
Same number of syllables	50	33	36	42	42
Alliteration	11	13	6	8	2
Consonance	26	28	12	12	10
Same ending	8	10	6	2	8
Inner associations	42	28	38	32	42
Outer associations	53	63	56	56	54
Clang-reactions	4	7	—	8	4
Number of associations	100	100	50	50	50

tually evident qualities of the things. In the second hundred there is an increase of the co-ordinates from 9 to 14 and a decrease of the predicative references from 32 to 14. The quality of the reactions is correspondingly changed in so far as they take on a decidedly objective character with a tendency to indifferent

No. 7.   *Subject, aged over 50, highly educated, is the mother of No. 6*

ASSOCIATIONS	NORMAL 1st hundred	ASSOCIATIONS	NORMAL 1st hundred
Co-ordination . . .	9	Same grammatical form .	45
Predicate	61	Same number of syllables .	22
Causal dependence . .	8	Alliteration . . .	—
		Consonance . . .	9
Coexistence . . .	12	Same ending . . .	—
Identity	3		
Verbal-motor forms . .	4		
Word-completion . .	—	Inner associations . .	78
Clang	—		
Rhyme	—	Outer associations . .	19
Indirect	—	Clang-reactions . .	—
Meaningless . . .	1		
Faults	—	Number of associations .	76
Repetition of stimulus-word	—		
Egocentric reaction . .	40		
Perseveration . . .	3		
Repetition	25		

combinations, often clichés. The decrease of the predicate relationships is to be referred to a subsidence of the subjective valuations, so that the finer quality of the reactions also shows a marked subsidence of interest. The lax attention is very clearly marked by the increase of egocentric reactions from 10 to 4. The distraction experiments must thus be regarded as a failure. This was also shown objectively by the subject's being unable to follow the metronome beats and to react at the same time; either the writing movement stopped at the moment of the reaction or the reaction-time was prolonged to one of the succeeding intervals of the beats, when reaction occurred with concentrated attention. The disturbing influence made itself felt in the perseveration phenomena which, remarkably enough, first occurred during outer distraction. The almost unweakened personal interest at the time of outer distraction is well illustrated by the relatively great number of egocentric reactions. How far the relatively strong verbal connexion by consonance in the normal state is conditioned by the constellation of literary activity we will not judge. Many reactions of this subject betray a strongly visual disposition. According to her own account every stimulus-idea at once presents itself to her as a quite definite picture.

The completely individual character of the reactions distinguishes this subject from others, and differentiates her from those hitherto considered. It would be interesting to learn whether this type was more or less accidental or whether it was a familial condition. We are, fortunately, in a position to be able to answer this question partially.

In subject No. 7 (Table on p. 55) the number of inner associations predominates considerably over the outer. The number of predicate relations is extremely large. Most of these are due to subjective valuations, some with strong marks of feeling, as :

Cook	laborious	Ride	dangerous
Water	delightful	Prison	horrible
Star	gorgeous		

Some 40 per cent. of the reactions are egocentric in character, directly betraying a wish or a defence.

No. 8. *Subject, about 38 years old, cultured, is the elder sister of No. 6*

ASSOCIATIONS	NORMAL 1st hundred	ASSOCIATIONS	NORMAL 1st hundred
Co-ordination . . .	6	Same grammatical form .	29
Predicate	49	Same number of syllables .	33
Causal dependence . .	1	Alliteration . . .	10
		Consonance . . .	10
Coexistence . . .	18	Same ending . . .	1
Identity	1		
Verbal-motor forms . .	20		
Word-completion . .	—	Inner associations . .	56
Clang.	—		
Rhyme	1	Outer associations . .	39
Indirect	1	Clang-reactions . .	1
Meaningless . . .	1		
Faults	—	Number of associations .	78
Repetition of stimulus-word .	—		
Egocentric reaction . .	15		
Perseveration . . .	—		
Repetitions . . .	14		

In No. 8, the inner associations are more numerous than the

outer. This individual also shows a very subjective reaction type, particularly noticed in the large number of predicate relations, and especially in the numerous subjective valuations. The number of egocentric reactions is also somewhat high.

From these figures and from the individual quality of the reactions there emerges a distinct familial relationship. We can, therefore, conclude with great probability that the subjective reaction type of No. 6 rests, not upon accident, but upon a familial condition. It becomes interesting to ascertain how the relations as to quantity hold within this family : whether the superficial phenomenon, demonstrated in subjects 3, 4, and 5 of this family and progressing towards the youngest member of the family, presents anything analogous. For this purpose we reproduce the chief figures of our subjects in the normal state.

	Inner Associations	Outer Associations	Clang-reaction	Egocentric Reaction
Mother . . .	78 per cent.	19 per cent.	0 per cent.	40 per cent.
Elder daughter . .	56 per cent.	39 per cent.	1 per cent.	15 per cent.
Younger daughter .	35 per cent.	58 per cent.	5·5 per cent.	7 per cent.

These figures show complete analogy with the condition demonstrated in subjects 3, 4, and 5. The picture as a whole looks like an experiment in distraction which has extended so far as to reverse the relationships between the inner and outer associations. The increase of the clang-reactions gives a similar picture, as does the decrease in egocentric reactions, which, as subject No. 6 showed, expresses to a certain extent the measure of the personal interests. Thus this remarkable analogy between the two family types seems to be something more than mere accident. Unfortunately, our material is not sufficient to explain the observations. The complete proof and explanation of these apparent facts must await an investigation from material specially collected for this purpose.

The reaction type of the last three subjects is one very characteristic and widespread. What distinguishes it from other, less marked types is the presence of numerous predicates, including a good many subjective valuations. We call this the Predicate Type. The three subjects Nos. 9, 10, and 11 are examples of this type (see Tables on pp. 58, 59, and 60). In No. 9, the preponderance of predicate relations is distinct in all phases of the experiment. Inner distraction could not be carried

No. 9. *Subject about 20, well-read, fairly intelligent*

ASSOCIATIONS	NORMAL		DISTRACTION	
			Outer	
	1st hundred	2nd hundred	60 metro.	100 metro.
Co-ordination	4	19	18	22
Predicate	37	37	38	34
Causal dependence	5	2	2	—
Coexistence	26	14	14	14
Identity	1	3	4	12
Verbal-motor forms	25	23	20	18
Word-completion	—	—	2	—
Clang.	—	—	—	—
Rhyme	—	—	—	—
Indirect	—	—	—	—
Meaningless	—	—	—	—
Faults	2	2	2	—
Repetition of stimulus-word . .	—	—	—	—
Egocentric reaction	3	4	—	—
Perseveration	2	1	—	—
Repetitions	13	10	6	4
Same grammatical form . . .	29	33	20	46
Same number of syllables . . .	38	34	56	54
Alliteration	10	6	8	16
Consonance	15	12	10	20
Same ending	3	8	8	16
Inner associations	46	58	58	56
Outer associations	52	40	38	44
Clang-reactions	—	—	2	
Number of associations . . .	100	100	50	50

out, as the subject was not able to dissociate her attention. The experiment in outer distraction was a complete failure because the subject, like No. 6, could not carry out two activities at the same time and behaved towards the experiment exactly like No. 6. The larger figures for verbal connexion by syllable

No. 10.   *Subject about 20 years, intelligent, very well-read*

| ASSOCIATIONS | NORMAL | | DISTRACTION | | FATIGUE |
| | 1st hundred | 2nd hundred | Outer | | |
			60 metro.	100 metro.	
Co-ordination.	8	16	6	10	12
Predicate	31	17	38	34	30
Causal dependence .	1	—	—	—	—
Coexistence	14	13	10	4	12
Identity	3	11	18	14	6
Verbal-motor forms	31	35	18	20	30
Word-completion	—	—	—	—	1
Clang	1	—	—	4	—
Rhyme .	—	—	2	—	1
Indirect	1	1	—	—	2
Meaningless	—	—	—	4	2
Faults .	8	6	6	10	3
Repetition of stimulus-word	—	—	2	—	1
Egocentric reaction	9	2	—	4	3
Perseveration.	—	—	4	2	2
Repetitions	16	5	18	14	18
Same grammatical form .	48	51	44	42	48
Same number of syllables	36	33	46	40	41
Alliteration	10	3	8	10	8
Consonance	7	9	14	12	13
Same ending .	5	8	18	16	18
Inner associations .	40	33	44	44	42
Outer associations .	48	59	46	38	48
Clang-reactions	1	—	2	4	2
Number of associations .	100	100	50	50	100

numbers, alliteration, consonance, suggest perhaps a certain leaning of the reaction towards the mechanical side.

Three out of the four faults in the normal state occurred in emotionally toned stimulus-words (*wrong, rich, stupid*).

The predominance, on the average, of inner associations over

No. 11 *is the mother of the previous subject, very intelligent,
cultured, well-read, about 56 years of age*

ASSOCIATIONS	NORMAL		ASSOCIATIONS	NORMAL	
	1st hundred	2nd hundred		1st hundred	2nd hundred
Co-ordination . . .	5	4	Same grammatical form .	27	34
Predicate . . .	56	35	Same number of syllables	37	41
Causal dependence . .	2	—	Alliteration . . .	11	3
			Consonance . . .	8	14
Coexistence . . .	4	4	Same ending . .	1	10
Identity	—	1			
Verbal-motor forms . .	28	50			
Word-completion . .	3	4	Inner associations .	63	39
Clang	—	—			
Rhyme	—	—	Outer associations .	32	55
Indirect	1	—	Clang-reactions . .	3	4
Meaningless . . .	—	—			
Faults	—	1	Number of associations .	96	96
Repetition of stimulus-word	—	—			
Egocentric reaction . .	6	5			
Perseveration . . .	1	—			
Repetitions . . .	5	4			

outer is noticeable in an educated person. The reaction type is
a mixed one and does not show the same subjective character as
Nos. 6, 7, and 8.

In No. 10, predicate relations exceed on the average
the number of co-ordinates. With regard to the failure in
distraction, the same must be said as in the case of subjects
6 and 9. The reaction type, in the first hundred of the normal
state, is somewhat subjective, and this is expressed by the
9 per cent. egocentric reactions. Perseveration occurs exclusively in distraction. Like No. 9, there is an increase in the
number of syllables and consonance, which perhaps betokens
a slight dissociation. The great number of faults in all phases
of the experiment is striking. Of the fourteen faults in the
normal state ten occur in stimulus-words charged with emotion
(*must, wrong, violence, threaten, suffer,* etc.); in another two the
subjective emotional tone of the stimulus-word is only probable.
It must be stated that the subject is slightly hysterical in so far as

she has somnambulic dreams. The proof of this hypothesis we shall present in a later chapter on the association anomalies of hysteria.[1]

No. 12.   *Subject about 40, very intelligent and well-read*

ASSOCIATIONS	NORMAL		DISTRACTION		
				Outer	
	1st hundred	2nd hundred	Inner	60 metro.	100 metro.
Co-ordination.	23	12	15	12	2
Predicate	1	6	19	6	8
Causal dependence	1	1	—	—	—
Coexistence	34	18	18	22	6
Identity	7	6	9	4	10
Verbal-motor forms	34	56	34	52	70
Word-completion	—	—	—	—	—
Clang	—	—	—	—	—
Rhyme	—	1	1	2	2
Indirect	—	—	—	—	—
Meaningless	—	—	—	—	—
Faults	—	—	4	—	2
Repetition of stimulus-word . . .	—	—	—	—	—
Egocentric reaction.	—	—	—	—	—
Perseveration.	1	—	—	2	—
Repetitions	6	5	5	—	2
Same grammatical form	57	92	64	82	56
Same number of syllables . . .	50	52	57	56	38
Alliteration	5	4	10	—	4
Consonance	16	18	12	20	12
Same ending	25	16	12	18	20
Inner associations	25	19	34	18	10
Outer associations	75	80	61	78	86
Clang-reactions	—	1	1	2	2
Number of associations	100	100	100	50	50

[1] Among his experiments on normals Aschaffenburg had only one case who had a remarkable number of faults ; it was that of a dreamy, meditative, literary young man (*Psych. Arbeit.*, Bd. IV, p. 243).

No. 13.   *Subject about 22 years, intelligent, all-round culture*

The subject felt much embarrassment, hence the great number of repetitions. Only distraction with the metronome at 100 succeeded, and that but slightly. The writing movements were accordingly imperfect.

ASSOCIATIONS	NORMAL		DISTRACTION	
			Outer	
	1st hundred	2nd hundred	60 metro.	100 metro.
Co-ordination	11	21	22	10
Predicate	18	19	20	14
Causal dependence	5	1	2	—
Coexistence	10	10	16	20
Identity	3	12	16	16
Verbal-motor forms	46	31	14	34
Word-completion	—	1	—	—
Clang.	—	—	—	—
Rhyme	—	1	—	—
Indirect	—	—	—	—
Meaningless	—	—	—	—
Faults	6	—	6	—
Repetition of stimulus-word	—	4	4	6
Egocentric reaction	—	—	—	—
Perseveration	—	—	—	—
Repetitions	9	11	4	2
Same grammatical form	61	60	56	68
Same number of syllables	43	43	42	42
Alliteration	8	3	8	6
Consonance	10	14	8	14
Same ending	11	12	18	16
Inner associations	34	41	44	24
Outer associations	59	53	46	70
Clang-reactions	—	2	—	—
Number of associations	100	100	50	50

No. 14.   *Subject about 22 years, of moderate
intelligence, cultured*

We add the figures of this subject only for the sake of completeness. The reaction type is objective. Inner distraction succeeded but imperfectly. Its effect is uncertain, for owing to the absence of the second hundred of normal reactions, information is wanting as regards the deviations in the normal state. For external reasons the second hundred could not be carried out.

ASSOCIATIONS	NORMAL 1st hundred	DIS-TRACTION Inner	ASSOCIATIONS	NORMAL 1st hundred	DIS-TRACTION Inner
Co-ordination . . .	29	9	Same grammatical form.	95	69
Predicate . . .	1	10	Same number of syllables	59	40
Causal dependence . .	—	1	Alliteration . . .	10	9
			Consonance . . .	15	22
Coexistence . . .	31	12	Same ending . .	24	7
Identity	2	12			
Verbal-motor forms . .	34	51			
Word-completion . .	—	1	Inner associations .	30	20
Clang	2	—			
Rhyme	1	2	Outer associations .	67	75
Indirect	—	—	Clang-reactions . .	3	3
Meaningless . . .	—	—			
Faults	—	2	Number of associations .	100	100
Repetition of stimulus-word	—	—			
Egocentric reaction . .	—	—			
Perseveration . . .	—	—			
Repetitions . . .	14	1			

No. 11 (p. 60) is a pronounced predicate type with numerous subjective valuations. A marked relaxation is seen in the second hundred, to be attributed to distinct ennui which was also objectively demonstrated. Therefore the second hundred no longer corresponds with the normal state but is rather an experiment in distraction. If, despite this, we compare her reaction type with that of her daughter (No. 10), we notice the same phenomenon as before—namely, that the reaction type of the daughter is a more superficial one than that of the mother.

	Inner Associations	Outer Associations
Mother　.　.　.　.　.	51 per cent.	43·5 per cent.
Daughter　.　.　.　.　.	36 per cent.	53·5 per cent.

We take this opportunity of repeating that, despite this agreement, the phenomenon may be purely accidental and is one that still requires proof.

The figures for three other subjects are on pp. 61–64. No. 12, about 40, very intelligent, well-read. The lady is a North German. The great number of current phrases is peculiarly striking. Inner distraction was a failure. Outer association shows a distinct disturbance of attention. The reaction type is objective.

SUMMARY OF THE GROUP OF EDUCATED WOMEN

The material collected in this group is, unfortunately, somewhat unequal so far as concerns the quantitative relations. The speech conditions are, on the other hand, very uniform in so far as there is only one North German in the fourteen individuals; the others are all Swiss, with the dialect as their common colloquial speech. The degree of culture is, on the whole, a very high one. Two have had an academic training; six of them have command of one or two languages apart from their mother tongue; ten are relatively extremely well-read. Distraction experiments were carried out in ten subjects: in five both in inner and outer distraction, in two cases only in inner, and in three only in outer distraction. The outer distraction led to a positive result in four cases, the inner in three cases. There was a partial success in one case of inner and one of outer distraction.

Distraction failed in four cases, three of whom were pronounced predicate types. (The predicate types, as a group, who took any part in the distraction experiments showed a much slighter distraction phenomenon than the other subjects.) Of the six persons over thirty years old, three showed a preponderance, on the average, of inner associations over outer; of the eight persons under thirty, only one showed a predominance of inner associations over outer.

2. EDUCATED MEN

Nine subjects with 3793 *associations*

No. 1. *,Subject intelligent, highly cultured,* 28 *years*

ASSOCIATIONS	NORMAL		DISTRACTION			FATIGUE	DROWSINESS	
	1st hundred	2nd hundred	Inner	Outer			1st part	2nd part
				1st part	2nd part			
Co-ordination . . .	9	13	4	10	12	10·2	2	—
Predicate	6	16	19	10	4	10·2	5	2
Causal dependence . .	—	—	—	—	—	—	—	1
Coexistence . . .	18	5	6	8	4	14·1	14	6
Identity	6	8	5	10	2	2·5	5	2
Verbal-motor form . .	54	52	56	46	54	53·8	40	51
Word-completion . . .	1	—	8	4	12	2·5	2	2
Clang	—	—	2	6	2	—	4	5
Rhyme	4	4	1	2	8	2·5	20	21
Indirect	2	2	1	2	4	—	2	2
Meaningless	—	—	—	2	—	3·8	—	—
Faults	—	—	—	—	—	—	—	—
Repetition of stimulus-word .	—	—	—	—	—	—	—	—
Egocentric reaction . .	1	—	3	—	—	—	—	—
Perseveration . . .	—	—	2	2	—	2	4	—
Repetitions	5	5	2	6	2	6	9	2
Same grammatical form. .	73	47	47	54	46	63	59	60
Same number of syllables .	53	45	49	46	42	44	61	58
Alliteration	7	6	5	10	4	4	17	9
Consonance	15	23	16	24	20	5	32	36
Same ending . . .	19	15	9	18	18	14	33	36
Inner associations . .	15	29	23	20	16	20·4	7	3
Outer associations . .	78	65	67	64	60	70·4	59	59
Clang-reactions . . .	5	4	11	12	22	5	27	32
Number of associations . .	100	100	100	50	50	78	78	78

In this subject reactions were carried out in four different states of disturbed attention : in a state of inner and outer distraction, of fatigue, and of morning drowsiness after awaking.

The reaction type is very superficial, as is shown by the ratio of the inner to the outer associations, 15 : 78 and 29 : 65. The reactions are of an objective, almost a purely verbal, character. The distraction experiments do not change much as to the ratio of inner to outer associations ; as against this, the progression of the clang-reactions demonstrates the increasing disturbance of attention, which reaches its maximum in the second experiment in outer distraction. The fatigue, which was not very great in this case, shows no change of type. The drowsy state exhibits a disturbance of attention far exceeding the effect of the second outer distraction. This subject, after mental work at night, is very drowsy in the morning and it is difficult to arouse him fully. These reactions were carried out while he was in bed and had just been partially awakened. He had been previously informed that the experiment was to come off. The two experiments were carried out on two different days, at an interval of about a week. As the figures show, the type is an extremely superficial one. The clang-reactions are extremely numerous, especially the rhymes. The figures for verbal connexion are very high. The picture of this manner of reaction shows reaction almost completely reduced to the most primitive verbal mechanisms. In these experiments fatigue is quite excluded ; it is only a question of a lowering of active attention, corresponding with the associative termination of the state of sleep. It is known that during sleep attention is completely obliterated. Were we to succeed in producing reactions in a person sleeping (not somnambulic sleep), clang-reactions would certainly be the exclusive results. In our view an absolute, undistracted inner concentration of attention must have the same results. We are, fortunately, in a position to report on a case in point.

It is the case of an individual, N——, who was terribly upset by unusual emotions. Outwardly, the chief symptom was almost complete want of ability to concentrate. The cause of her emotions she kept secret. In the experiment, to which she submitted from scientific interest, she produced mainly clangs and rhymes, together with a few inexplicable (meaningless ?) reactions. We should like to compare this case with an inner distraction experiment which extended over several days. Attention was completely chained to the inner, affect-toned complex,[1] from which she could not set herself free for more or less indifferent events. For everything that does not touch the complex there is thus abnormally slight attention. To what extent this

[1] By " affect-toned complex " we understand the total number of presentations relating to a definite experience that is charged with emotion. In what follows we shall always use the term " complex " with this meaning.

barrier is more or less conscious is naturally not within our purview. According to her own account, certain vivid presentations belonging to the complex hovered before her at the beginning of the experiment ; these she constantly tried to repress, fearing lest they might be betrayed in the reaction. From the second third of the 'experiment onwards there remained only the emotional tone of the complex in consciousness without the clear presentations belonging thereto. What occurred to her were only clangs. The stimulus-words only reached her at all through clangs and never through their meaning.

These investigations prove most distinctly the dependence of clang-reactions, of the superficial reaction type in general, on disturbance of attention. But how is this abnormally superficial type to be explained ? We are dealing with a psychologically trained person who brought the greatest interest to the experiment. The superficial reaction type must be connected with the fact that many educated persons conceive the experiment entirely as a verbal one ; they endeavour, by maintaining a ready speech-excitation, to affix the first word that comes up, without entering more closely into the meaning of the stimulus-word, for they see at once that no special significance can rest within a stimulus-word standing apart by itself. This is how we explain the marked preponderance of verbal and clang combinations. All persons who allow themselves to be influenced rather by the sense than by the mere word tend to make inner associations. The conception as to the meaning of the stimulus-word is different in different persons. In our experience there are two chief types :

(1) The subject endeavours to do justice to the word as objectively as possible ; in the reaction he accordingly constructs any universal or particular connexion of objective significance ; the reaction is mostly a co-ordinate relation.

(2) The subject endeavours to characterize pertinently the object called up by the stimulus-word, which he images as distinctly as possible. He expresses something about the stimulus-word, using for this the predicate form. The reaction is hence mostly a predicate relation.

On this hypothesis the superficial reaction type of certain educated persons is not to be regarded as the result of a disturbance of attention but as a " phenomenon of adjustment " (Bleuler). By the concept " phenomenon of adjustment " we understand, with Bleuler, the occurrence of an apparently abnormal reaction type through the spontaneous preference of a definite mode of reaction. But it must be emphasized that this mode is not one accidentally selected, but one motivated by the psychological individuality of the subject. The more intense the adjustment to the clang-appearance of the stimulus-word, the more superficial must be the reaction type ; for the attention, having been specially directed thereto, will accentuate and make prominent the primitive associations suppressed in the normal act of speech. A quite paradoxical picture may thus arise in the statistical presentation of the results, one which, on the above hypothesis, we are now able to understand. The following case serves to illustrate this possibility.

No. 2. *Subject intelligent, highly educated, aged 47*

ASSOCIATIONS	NORMAL		DISTRACTION			FATIGUE
	1st hundred	2nd hundred	Inner	Outer 1st part	Outer 2nd part	
Co-ordination	16	15	12	20	20	10·2
Predicate	6	5	6	12	2	8
Causal dependence	—	—	—	4	2	—
Coexistence	4	6	8	14	8	5
Identity	6	8	2	10	10	6
Verbal-motor forms	51	45	38	28	58	38
Word-completion	2	1	—	—	—	2
Clang	8	10	24	6	—	24
Rhyme	1	3	—	—	—	2
Indirect	6	6	10	4	—	1
Meaningless	—	1	—	—	—	—
Faults	—	—	—	—	—	—
Repetition of stimulus-word	—	—	—	2	—	—
Egocentric reaction	—	—	—	—	—	5
Perseveration	1	1	—	—	—	—
Repetitions	3	13	8	4	6	10
Same grammatical form	75	63	62	70	74	58
Same number of syllables	48	37	42	48	56	41
Alliteration	25	22	38	16	6	28
Consonance	25	23	38	24	16	23
Same ending	14	12	10	10	12	10
Inner associations	22	20	18	36	24	18
Outer associations	61	59	48	52	76	49
Clang reactions	11	14	24	6	—	28
No. of associations	100	100	50	50	50	78

In this subject we again find a strikingly superficial reaction type in the normal state which is illustrated particularly by the high number of clang-reactions. The superficiality increases considerably in the experiment on inner distraction, whilst in the experiment on outer association there is a striking " improvement" in the reaction for the number of inner associations rises far above those of the normal experiment. The " improvement " is demonstrated in the clearest way by the recession and final disappearance of the clang-reactions.

This remarkable result, unique in our experiments, demands critical inquiry. We have referred to this experiment in reviewing No. 4 of Educated Women (p. 52). She presented a similar picture. We there accepted a suppressed affect as the cause of the superficial reaction type. We refer also to the interesting condition which we expounded in the critical remarks on subject No. 1 of Educated Men. The recent very strong affect which completely controlled N—— at the time was the direct cause of the occurrence of preponderant clang-associations. In that case the affect was suppressed, for it did not manifest itself directly in the reaction but only indirectly through the dissociation of attention. A similar psychological situation must be accepted for subject No. 4 of the Educated Women as explaining the superficial type. That subject No. 4 of the Educated Women and subject No. 2 of the Educated Men present the same type is probably an accidental coincidence.

Affect is perhaps entirely to be excluded in subject No. 2. We must therefore seek for another cause of the superficial type ; we find it in the phenomenon of adjustment. He is thoroughly at home in psychology and has, moreover, an extraordinary capacity for concentration. He at once directed attention to the clang-manifestation of the stimulus-word, and consequently always reproduced the first association that occurred. These cannot be anything but primitive verbal connexions and clangs, if our hypothesis is at all correct as to the associations which first arise on perceiving the stimulus-word. This explains, without any straining, the abnormally superficial type in the normal experiment.

The superficiality increases in the experiment in inner distraction. The subject executed this experiment in the most classical manner. The concentration upon the A phenomenon was excellent, as was also the reporting. We have, therefore, no reason in this case to accept any disturbance of attention ; the superficial type of this experiment must be ascribed to the lowering of attention ; it arises from a root other than that of the normal experiment, and is consequently no phenomenon of adjustment.

In most subjects outer distraction has a disturbing influence upon attention and thus causes superficiality ; in the present instance the effect is apparently the reverse. The normal state in this case is characterized by the phenomenon of adjustment ; attention is directed exclusively towards the verbal factor. This adjustment becoming disturbed by outer distraction, the subject enters into another relationship to the stimulus-word, i.e. exclusive observation of the clang-manifestation is interrupted, thus preventing the rising up of those primitive associations which lie closest at hand. If under normal conditions the suppressed associations always fall back into repression, the succeeding associations must be those determined by the sense of the stimulus-word, i.e. the number of clang-reactions must decrease, and the number of inner associations increase. That is the case here.

The figures for fatigue show remarkable agreement with those of inner distraction. From the external condition the diagnosis might be made of very severe fatigue. But this was not the fact. The fatigue was by no means extreme, but a relatively slight evening tiredness which, according to the subject's account, had not noticeably influenced the reaction. We are dealing again with a phenomenon of adjustment, and not with a disturbance of attention. That the adjustment in this state was apparently more intense is perhaps to be ascribed to the fact that the subject as a " moteur " is somewhat excited physically when in a slightly fatigued condition.

Verbal motility naturally takes part in the general motor excitation, so that the speech apparatus very readily responds to a corresponding stimulus. This circumstance must have fallen in with the specific adjustment in this case, resulting naturally in a greater number of purely mechanical combinations.

As would be at once expected from such a type, the personal and subjective kinds of reaction, with a few exceptions, disappear.

In No. 3 (p. 71) the reaction type is a rather superficial one. The predicates are especially well marked in the inner associations, and have almost without exception an objective character. As the number of egocentric reactions show, comparatively few subjective factors occur in the reactions. But as predicate types are never allowed to miss emotionally charged constellations, we find here also a small emotionally charged complex observable in the reactions. The experiment was carried out on a very hot day. Among the repetitions there were twice " snow " and twice " perspire." The following perseverations also occurred :

1. Stove	warm	4. Water	bathe
2. Walk	hot	5. To dance	perspires
3. (—	—)		

No. 3. *Subject intelligent, about* 26

ASSOCIATIONS	NORMAL		ASSOCIATIONS	NORMAL	
	1st hundred	2nd hundred		1st hundred	2nd hundred
Co-ordination . . .	9	9	Same grammatical form .	44	49
Predicate . . .	23	26	Same number of syllables	44	46
Causal dependence . .	—	—	Alliteration . . .	6	4
			Consonance . . .	14	9
Coexistence . . .	21	5	Same ending . .	2	13
Identity	—	10			
Verbal-motor forms . .	41	41			
Word-completion . .	2	4	Inner associations .	32	35
Clang	—	—			
Rhyme	—	2	Outer associations .	62	56
Indirect	2	2	Clang-reactions . .	2	6
Meaningless . . .	—	—			
Faults	2	1	Number of associations .	100	100
Repetition of stimulus-word	—	—			
Egocentric reaction . .	3	3			
Perseveration . . .	5	—			
Repetitions . . .	9	5			

No. 4 (p. 72) is a physician, 36 years old, who did not feel himself favourably disposed in the normal experiment. The experiment in outer distraction could not be executed on account of illness. The 100 associations carried out in " fatigue " were carried out after a disturbed, sleepless night.

Inner distraction and *fatigue* show striking agreement : decrease of inner associations, pronounced increase of the outer, and especially of the clang-associations and word-completions, increase of " same number of syllables," whilst the figures for "same grammatical form " remain more or less uninfluenced. In the first hundred of the normal experiment the inner associations predominate over the outer (47 : 43), in the second hundred the relation is reversed (30 : 59).

The continuously rising tide in the word-completions and clangs is beautifully seen in the experiment with inner distraction, if counted separately in each third of the 100 associations :

    1st third : 2 word-completions, 6 clangs
    2nd   „   5   „   7   „
    3rd   „   9   „   9 ,.

No. 4.　*Subject 36 years old*

ASSOCIATIONS	NORMAL		INNER DISTRACTION	FATIGUE
	1st hundred	2nd hundred		
Co-ordination	24	14	7	4
Predicate	23	13	11	—
Causal dependence	—	3	—	—
Coexistence	15	12	5	9
Identity	—	8	—	—
Verbal-motor forms	28	39	31	20
Word-completion	1	—	16	16
Clang	2	4	20	27
Rhyme	—	—	2	8
Indirect	7	6	7	8
Meaningless	—	1	1	1
Faults	—	—	—	—
Repetition of stimulus-words . .	—	—	—	—
Egocentric reaction	1	1	—	—
Perseveration	3	—	1	2
Repetitions.	2	—	—	—
Same grammatical form . . .	42	57	45	47
Same number of syllables . . .	33	30	47	53
Alliteration.	15	22	32	26
Consonance	18	27	41	39
Same ending	6	11	6	21
Inner associations	47	30	18	4
Outer associations	43	59	36	29
Clang-reactions	3	4	38	58
Number of associations . . .	100	100	100	100

The predicates begin to decrease in the second hundred of the normal experiment, decrease still more during inner distraction, and completely disappear in fatigue. Rhymes first appear in the fatigue experiment; in inner distraction there are only two, in the normal experiment none.

Constellations and Complexes

In subject No. 4 we encounter a relatively large number of associations which are only explicable by personal events of recent date or of the present moment, e.g. *ring — part of garden* ; a golden ring had just been found in a garden of the asylum where the subject was working, whose owner it was necessary to discover.

Or, for example, *clothes — Stapfer* ; a patient Stapfer, of whom the physician had charge, gave him great trouble by ordering clothes to which he constantly took exception and which he refused to wear ; there were consequently many unpleasantnesses with the tailor and other tradespeople.

Lead pencil — Koh-i-noor. The subject had at the time of the experiment first learnt the delights of this kind of lead-pencil.

Murder — Kaufmann. This physician had at the time of the experiment to give an opinion on a man named Kaufmann who had committed a murder whilst drunk.

These kinds of associations are conditioned by distinct *constellations* (Ziehen), for they refer to recent subjective events charged with feeling.[1]

With many subjects (e.g. Nos. 2 and 4 of Uneducated Women, see pp. 98, 107) we find none, or but very few. Such individuals react quite objectively and betray nothing personal in their individual associations ; e.g. they associate *river — stream* ; *pupil — girl* ; *table — floor* ; *lamp — oil* ; *mountain — valley* ; *kiss — laugh* ; *plunder — catch* ; *hit — bite* ; *prison — punishment*, etc.

Other individuals certainly make objective associations, but here and there among them are found some which, despite their objective nature, do permit of some conclusion as to the individual, without betraying in the slightest degree the inner personality. From the following collected associations it was not difficult to detect the asylum attendant (No. 4 of Uneducated Men, p. 117) : *fetch — run* ; *smell — impure air* ; *inform — report* ; *prison — asylum* ; *ill — dejected* ; *gait — run* ; *freedom — recovery* ; *consciousness — drunk* or *sober*, etc.

Still the constellation plays a very indirect part in these associations.

Then there were individuals in whose associations it was not

---

[1] We know, of course, that no reaction is accidental, but that each, even the most objective, is conditioned by definite constellations. But there is a great difference if, for example, in *murder—Meyer* the murder is associated in the mind with a definite murder, from *murder—criminal*, where murder is a general concept. It is this distinction that we want to emphasize by the special term " constellation."

the momentary constellations, but the personal events, which stand out strongly (e.g. No. 5 of Educated Men) : *lake — Lake Lucerne* (he was now and then on Lake Lucerne) ; *father — grandfather* (his grandfather is still alive) ; *mountain — Glärnisch* (he was once there—not that the trip meant anything to him) ; *hair — hair-wash* (he prescribes now and then a hair-wash for patients) ; *Sweet — Sweeting* (the proper name of a person to whom the subject is quite indifferent) ; *potato — tobacco-plantations* (accidental reminiscence of the journey from Basle to Heidelberg) ; *coffee — Brazilian* (he has sometimes drunk Brazilian coffee). These are chiefly subjective reminiscences.

If we go a step further we come across *true constellations*, such as we first referred to in subject No. 4 of Educated Men. Individuals with many constellations have usually also many reminiscences (e.g. Nos. 4 and 5 of Educated Men).

A peculiar group of constellations occurs in many persons through the influence of the momentary surroundings in which the experiment is carried out. The reaction-words : *carpet, flowers, inkstand, calendar, books, penholder, landscape, telephone, curtains, tapestry, looking-glass, sofa*, etc., refer usually, even when quite appropriate associations to the stimulus-word, to these articles present in the room where the experiments are conducted. It is not necessary that the subject should always see them, he need only know generally that the particular articles are in the room (see No. 2 of Uneducated Women).

Pathologically, pronounced cases of this association type are known to us in normal, imbecile, hysterical stupidity.[1]

If the stimulus-word sets free a subjective, affect-toned image with the reaction, we have a special kind of constellation associations, the *egocentric* (see Part I). In subject No. 4 we meet only a few, e.g. *piano — atrocious* (the subject suffers a good deal from the strumming of neighbours who are not exactly first-class musicians) ; or, e.g. *to idle — delightful* ; the egocentricity of this reaction is obvious in an extremely busy man joyously awaiting the approach of his holidays.

In many cases the egocentric reaction can directly stand for a fault by the want of any reaction (see definition in Part I). A reaction certainly occurs, but through conscious or unconscious inhibition it does not attain utterance as a reaction word. Probably all faults have not this origin, but the majority certainly have.

Girls, for instance, make faults at reaction words which impinge on the sexual sphere, as to *kiss*, to *love*, to *caress, choose*,

[1] Cp. Jung, "Ueber Simulation von Geistesstörung," *Journal für Psych. u. Neur.*, Bd. II, 1903.

faithful, etc.   Often it does not reach " a fault," but the association *love — brother* requires a relatively long reaction-time, so
that the experimenter with a little practice discovers at once
what the innocent reaction *brother* conceals.

The associations *wedding — misfortune, kiss — never,* and
others in subject No. 5 of Educated Men, have an entirely analogous significance, for he was at that time in a condition of " fear
and trembling."

An emotionally charged image-complex can stand out so
prominently and act so intensively as to form a whole number of
constellations, faults, reactions with long reaction-time, all
referring to this image-complex.   Subjects Nos. 5, 6, 7, and 8 of
Educated Men will give us occasion to return to this special
kind of constellation, the *complex constellation.*   The majority
of complexes which have hitherto presented themselves in the
association experiments refer to direct or transposed sexuality.
In the work on the association of hysterics we shall return to
the complex effect.

In subject No. 4 of this group there are exhibited, together
with many reminiscences, fifteen constellations in the first hundred
of the normal experiment, four in the second hundred, one during
inner abstraction, and twelve during fatigue.   In the normal
experiment the names of definite persons frequently occur, e.g. of
patients whom the stimulus-word recalls, e.g. *clothes — Stapfer* ;
attendant — Baum (the name of one of the attendants) ; *Zahn —
Göschenen* (in Göschenen he had had a discussion about the
writer Zahn).

In subject No. 5 of this group the constellation is often expressed
through proper names.   During fatigue, where in No. 4 of this
group the constellations increase, these nearly always consist in
the reaction being a proper name linked merely by clang-similarity
with the stimulus-word.   The inner connexion of *clothes — Stapfer*
contrasts, e.g., with the purely clang *Steel — Stapfer.*

In No. 5 (p. 76) the condition at ten o'clock at night, after a
hard day's work, was taken to be one of fatigue.

The relation of inner to outer associations is not very positive
in the different experiments.   We find the maximum for outer
associations (61 per cent.) in fatigue, but it is very little greater
than the number in the first hundred in the normal experiment
(57 per cent.).   A minimum of clang-associations corresponds to
this maximum of outer associations.

Inner distraction is stronger than outer.   The first fifty
associations were carried out with the metronome at 60 beats,
the second fifty at 100 beats, and the last eighty-five associations
at 108 beats.

No. 5. *Subject, a Physician* 28 *years old*

ASSOCIATIONS	NORMAL		DISTRACTION				FATIGUE
	1st hundred	2nd hundred	Inner	Outer			
				60 | metronome	100	108 beats	
Co-ordination	19	27	11	20	20	—	20
Predicate	9	20	10	12	6	10	13
Causal dependence . . .	—	1	2	—	—	2	1
Coexistence	11	13	8	2	2	6	5
Identity	5	10	7	—	2	12	6
Verbal-motor forms . . .	41	17	30	34	32	40	50
Word-completion	3	—	—	—	2	1	1
Clang	6	6	27	20	14	5	1
Rhyme	—	—	1	—	—	1	—
Indirect	6	5	6	12	12	18	—
Meaningless	—	1	1	—	10	—	1
Faults	—	—	—	—	—	—	—
Repetition of stimulus-word . .	—	—	—	—	—	—	—
Egocentric reaction . . .	—	—	2	2	8	—	—
Perseveration	—	4	—	2	2	—	1
Repetitions	3	2	3	4	8	21	8
Same grammatical form. . .	60	59	66	52	52	50	50
Same number of syllables . .	28	27	50	46	46	36	37
Alliteration	14	14	38	36	18	15	8
Consonance	30	23	43	28	30	20	20
Same ending	11	9	11	4	4	9	6
Inner associations . . .	28	48	23	32	26	12	34
Outer associations . . .	57	40	45	36	36	58	61
Clang-reactions	9	6	28	20	16	7	2
Number of associations . . .	100	100	100	50	50	85	78

Inner associations reach the maximum in the headings clang, same number of syllables, same grammatical form, alliteration, consonance.

The clang-associations progressively decrease in outer distraction, the indirect associations progressively increase—a relationship which we do not often meet in the experiments on distraction. In the last third of the experiment in inner distraction the subject became more indifferent, almost hypnoidal. The number and intensity of the visual images which emerged at the same time decreased, whilst the clang-associations increased as follows :

1st third :	3 clang-associations	
2nd „	6	„
3rd „	18	„

The number of perseverations oscillates within normal limits. Examples :

> Faithful ⌒ perjured
> Once   ⌄ fidel

The origin of this perseveration is obvious : *fidel* is on one side a clang-association to *fidèle*, which is itself a translation of faithful.

Stimulus-word, Fruit	Thurgau
„ False	Falk

The family orders its fruit from a place called Thurgau, from a certain Mr. Falk. Falk is a clang-association to the second stimulus-word and a coexistence to the first stimulus-word.

> Love ⌐ Stern
> Son ⌐ Isaac

Stern is the name of a Jewish young lady. Isaac, the son of Abraham, if it is not quite a verbal association, is almost one from common usage. The association to Stern is an inner one.

Alt (old)	Uchtspringe
Freiheit (freedom)	in Altman

Dr. Alt is the well-known head of Uchtspringe. Freiheit is the name of a peak in the neighbourhood of Altmann; thus a perseveration of a purely external nature.

In inner abstraction we find in this subject an example of continuous perseveration of visual images appearing at the same time as the reaction. The reaction-words are only linked to the stimulus-words by clang :

Malt	malster. Visually : a brewery.
Almighty	Halma. Visually : a cask with malt.
Well	the house at the well. Visually : at the place where a strong smell of malt was always perceptible he often saw malt-carts as a lad.

After the first reaction, *malt — maltster*, the subject could not repeat his own reaction-word—he had forgotten it ; during the associations attention was directed much more to the visual associations than to the verbal ones. We find this forgetfulness of the stimulus- or reaction-word much more frequently in pathological cases of emotional stupidity and hysteria.

Complex Phenomena and the Unconscious

On going through the associations of our subjects, the practised hand comes across complex phenomena which in normal persons are very important for comparison with pathological cases where the complexes play a great part. Unfortunately, the reaction-times were not measured in the material used in No. 5.

The material used here is not only that given in the experiments in the above table (p. 76), but was also derived from some earlier work with this subject. The following experiments were made :

On 17/9/19—	78 associations without fatigue (not used in the work)
27/12/19—	78 „ „ „ „ „ „
27/12/19—	78 „ during „ (made use of)
22/2 of ensuing year	156 „ „ „ (not used)
19/8/19—	200 „ without „ (used)
19/8/19—	100 „ in inner distraction
25/8/19—	185 „ in outer „

During the period in which all these experiments took place the subject had his emotions roused by his interest in a young lady. In order to understand the experiments, it must be further mentioned that the young man had not yet entirely escaped from the period of internal conflict, and that his feelings towards a Jewish girl caused him, who had been brought up a strict Christian, great distress. We will call her Alice Stern, which satisfies the demands of truth in so far as is necessary for the experiment In the experiment on 17/9/19— we find the following complex constellations :

1. Marriage — misfortune
2. Come — O come with me (1)
3. Suffer — my God, yes !
4. Sorrow — who never nights of sorrow !
5. Kiss — never
6. Play — by many a gay sport shall thy time be beguiled (2)
7. Sofa — a certain couch (in boudoir of the lady in question)
8. Love — is useless
9. Troth — sweetheart
10. Wreath — Jungfernkranz (thought of with the appropriate tune) [1]
11. Hope — thou shouldst us whilst living (continuation : love and solace be giving)

---

[1] From *Der Freischütz*—the Bridal Wreath (*Jungfernkranz*) song.—TRANSLATOR.

Nos. 1, 5, and 8 are concealed wishes, although their form is negative.

Nos. 2, 4, 6, 10, and 11 are quotations or verses from songs ; No. 6 is the continuation of No. 2, a quotation from the *Erlkönig*. It is very remarkable that among the seventy-eight associations there is only one other quotation :

Must   no man must must

and that quotations as a rule very seldom appear in the associations of this subject. The complex thus makes use here of a form of reaction which is otherwise unusual in this subject. It is characteristic that he—to his shame, be it said—has only remembered from the *Erlkönig* the little fragment : " O come and go with me ; by many a gay sport shall thy time be beguiled." [1]

He knows the tune of the *Jungfernkranz* perfectly, but only the fragment of the libretto " For thee we twine the bridal wreath."

In the working out of hysterical associations we shall return to the emergence of songs, tunes, and quotations, often mere fragments, which is frequently quite unconscious and automatic (cp. the corresponding manifestation in No. 3 of the group of Uneducated Women, p. 101).

In the first experiment on 27/12/19— among the associations were :

1. It	it, it, it, and it. It is a hard decision	
2. Thou	yes . . . I	
3. Separate	it hurts	
4. Stern	h'm !	
5. Play	merrymaking (with a long reaction-time)	
6. Heart	(begs not to be obliged to utter the reaction-word ; it would have been " Stern ")	

The associations 1, 2, 3, 4, and 6 explain themselves from what has been already said. The sudden long reaction-time in No. 5 is suspicious after what has gone before.

From the experiment on 27/12/19— during fatigue the following associations were taken :

1. A kiss	yesterday (*gestern*)		4. Wonder	yesterday
2. Love	yesterday		5. Pray	yesterday
3. Already	yesterday [2]			

The reaction-times were generally quite brief. He had the feeling as if the reaction slipped out unobserved. In the whole

---

[1] In the original the subject misquotes even this fragment.

[2] *Schon* (already)—*gestern* (the previous stimulus-word was *Tränen*). The subject then thought he heard *schön* (beautiful) instead of *schon* (already); possibly there was a perseveration of the umlaut.

experiment there was no repetition of any reaction, except twice *vegetable* (after *potato* and *sour*). In the remaining experiments repetitions are also few.

All these stimulus-words belong to those having close relationship to the complex " Stern." The stimulus-word *schon* (already) is apprehended as *schön* (beautiful) (see foot-note, p. 79).

It will be remembered that the examples 4 and 5 were reactions which then stood in the closest connexion with the complex (Religion !). *Kiss* and *yesterday* (gestern) is not to be regarded as a reminiscence ; that was not the kind of relationship. Whether the unconscious had allowed itself to make use of the second syllable (ge — stern) symbolically, or whether the word is connected with the fact that the experiment took place directly after the Christmas holidays, when the subject was made exceedingly happy by a little attention on the lady's part, cannot be ascertained. But the fact that this word, and only this one, is so often repeated in the experiment as the reaction to the complex stimulus-words is most striking. It stands for the quotations in the previous experiments. In this experiment there is not a single quotation.

The experiment on 22/2 of the following year took place during fatigue. The following associations are worth mentioning :

Song Nora : a complex quotation (" Of all the girls," etc., " Nora most does please me." The vowel *o* comes in the two-syllabled real name of the lady in question. The two names are very similar in clang)

Sacrifice ⌒ dog (apparently meaningless)
Marriage ⌣ wether

A perseveration of the reaction. In the combination *sacrifice — wether — marriage* the complex certainly plays a part ; in connexion with this the perseveration in the experiment on 19/8 explains itself.

⎰Love ⌐ stern
⎱Son ⌐ Isaac

One association has no sense : *rich — yesterday* (gestern). Probably yesterday occurred as the stereotype in the transferred associations. It occurs again in the experiment *people — yesterday* : here again one can only guess. Perhaps the concept ‚Jews is a middle term. The association *sport — parents* is indirect ; the middle term, unconscious in this case, is the quotation

" O come and go with me, loveliest child," etc.

the meaning of which we have learnt above.

There are also :

Inn	star (he was here conscious of the complex)		
Kiss	together	To eat	is painful
Love	roses	To caress	is painful
Parting	painful	To hit	is painful
		To sing	is painful

The first four associations belong to the complex, the remainder
are but stereotyped repetitions of " parting is painful " ; the
repetitions must be here regarded also as effects of the complex.

In the distraction experiments there were no distinct complex
manifestations :

No. 6.   *Subject: Teacher of Natural History, 25 years old*

ASSOCIATIONS	NORMAL		ASSOCIATIONS	NORMAL	
	1st hundred	2nd hundred		1st hundred	2nd hundred
Co-ordination . . .	19	21	Same grammatical form .	46	26
Predicate . . .	28	32	Same number of syllables	28	15
Causal dependence . .	2	1	Alliteration . . .	5	6
			Consonance . . .	8	14
Coexistence . . .	15	2	Same ending . .	1	—
Identity	—	—			
Verbal-motor forms . .	20	19			
Word-completion . .	2	5	Inner associations .	49	54
Clang	—	1			
Rhyme	—	—	Outer associations .	35	21
Indirect	—	—	Clang-reactions . .	2	6
Meaningless . . .	1	5			
Faults	10	11	Number of associations .	78	78
Repetition of stimulus-word	—	—			
Egocentric reaction . .	14	27			
Perseveration . . .	6	8			
Repetitions . . .	6	15			

In the second half of the normal experiment the following
increased :

(1) Inner associations from 49 to 54 per cent., while the outer
decreased.

(2) Clang-associations from 2 to 6 per cent.

(3) Perseverations from 6 to 8 per cent.

(4) Egocentric reactions from 14 to 27 per cent.

.. (5) Constellations from 56 to 73 per cent.

(6) Repetitions from 6 to 15 per cent.

The following were well above the average :

Inner associations.

Perseverations.

Egocentric reactions.

Faults.

Predicates (see section on Averages, p. 142).

The verbal-motor reactions remain about the same in both halves ; there are no indirect associations. The figures indicate that the individual's reaction is very subjective and that by analogy one may suspect some complex. In favour of this view is the high number of constellations (56 and 73 per cent.). On analysis they are found to refer overwhelmingly to *school* and to *bride*. The subject is an enthusiastic teacher. The complex bride, wedding, etc., plays a predominant part in the second half, where generally the subjective phenomena increase. In the first half :

26 per cent. of the reactions refer to the school—21 per cent. to the *bride* complex.

In the second half :

21 per cent. of the reactions refer to the school—24 per cent. to the *bride* complex.

In addition, it must be noted that in the first half two to three, and in the second half the majority, of the faults relate to the *bride* complex, e.g. the faults to the stimulus-words *caress, ill, suffer, kiss*. Otherwise the complex expresses itself much more openly than in the previous case. He is less repressed and has no use for quotations from songs like No. 5. School and fiancée, moreover, are closely connected in No. 6, as shown by a dream that they would be soon married and that his wife would hold an important position in the institute.

Among the thirteen repetitions in the first half, there occur four times the name of the institute, twice an important event in the school, three times the name of his fiancée. In the second half the fiancée's name occurs seven times in the reactions, twice the word *child*, when he was thinking of his future paternity. The other repetitions refer mostly to school affairs. Three times the subject was annoyed by the stimulus-words appearing to him nonsense, reacting each time angrily with "rubbish."

With two exceptions the perseverations refer to school and family affairs.

Finally, a few of these complex associations may be grouped :

Grandmother	S. will be (S. is his fiancée's name)
Angry	myself as teacher according to S.
{ Come	wrote S.
Year	will marry (in two years)
Sunday	S. is coming
{ Kiss	(subject does not react)
Naturally	(,, ,, ,, ,,)
Love	S.
Tears	she cried (S.)
{ Faithful	S.
Once	S.
{ Hope	we have to marry
Small	child (!)
{ Pray	I never will (presentation of a child praying)
Love	child
Where ?	in bed
Old	S.
Ring	engagement
Caress	(at first no reaction) S.
Child	my future one
{ Sweet	a box of chocolates from S.
Ride	M., the home of his fiancée, who used to ride when at home
Friendly	S.'s family
Three	members of the family (there are three in S.'s family)

The stimulus-words bracketed together directly followed one another in the experiment.

As during the course of the experiment the subjective affect increased, the critical evaluation of the individual reactions also increased ; this is shown by the figures.

Subject No. 7 (p. 84). In the second hundred of the normal experiment we come across a maximum of co-ordinations, predicate relationships, inner associations in general, whilst the outer associations decrease markedly. This maximum also extends to the perseveration and egocentric associations. Compared with the averages in Educated Men, the predicates in the second hundred, the total number of inner associations in general, as well as the perseverations and egocentric reactions, were far above the average ; their ratios are :

Predicates, 42 : 19·17 ;

Inner associations on the whole, 62 : 36·7 ;

Perseverations, 40 : 2·4 ;

Egocentric reactions, 19 : 2·8 ;

whilst the remaining figures diverge but little from the average. With the fifteenth stimulus-word of the second hundred (*kiss*)

No. 7.[1]   *Subject: Doctor, 23 years old*

ASSOCIATIONS	NORMAL		DISTRACTION		
	1st hundred	2nd hundred	Inner	Outer	
				60 metro.	100 metro.
Coordination	19	20	7	12	8
Predicate	16	42	26	20	14
Causal dependence	—	—	3	2	—
Coexistence	24	5	10	30	22
Identity	5	3	5	10	4
Verbal-motor forms	29	23	22	12	38
Word-completion	—	—	—	—	—
Clang	2	3	18	4	6
Rhyme	—	1	—	—	—
Indirect	2	1	3	2	6
Meaningless	3	2	6	8	—
Faults	—	—	—	—	—
Repetition of stimulus-word	—	—	—	—	—
Egocentric reaction	4	19	2	—	2
Perseveration	4	40	5	4	10
Repetitions	8	8	8	4	4
Same grammatical form	58	26	32	62	42
Same number of syllables	34	22	35	50	52
Alliteration	12	8	31	12	10
Consonance	18	13	33	16	8
Same ending	6	5	2	—	—
Inner associations	35	62	36	34	22
Outer associations	58	31	37	52	64
Clang-reactions	2	4	18	4	6
Number of associations	100	100	100	50	50

[1] The reactions of this subject are reproduced *in extenso* in the section on Averages under " Complex Constellation Type," p. 140.

the complex reactions begin, at first interrupted by other reactions ; then the complex persists through twenty-six associations, then again there are interruptions, and finally disappears towards the end of the second hundred. On the whole, we find as a maximum fifty per cent. complex constellations in the second hundred of the normal experiment ; in the first hundred, thirteen per cent., in inner distraction five, in outer eight. In No. 6 of Educated Men we also found a rising tide of complex reactions in the second hundred of the normal experiment. The occurrence of the complex, in this case conjured up by an adequate stimulus-word—*kiss*—likewise caused a marked increase of the inner associations, in consequence of the great stirring up of attention. That an increase of inner associations corresponds with the manifestation of a complex is a proof that our classification is to some extent correct and natural. The more affect the stimulus-words have for the individual, the more the stimulus-words claim attention, the more do the inner associations increase. This phenomenon is exactly the reverse of the distraction phenomenon ; attention is better in consequence of the irruption of an affective complex influencing the whole personality, because attention is more directed towards the significance of the stimulus-word.

If the attention is diverted from the experiment by an emotionally toned complex instead of by outer distraction, as, for example, in No. 4 (experiment after sleepless night), who was under the influence of a strong affect, we see the opposite of the phenomena which we have just described in subject No. 7 : the inner associations decrease and the result is very similar to that obtained from inner or outer distraction.

We have in the second hundred the occurrence and persistence of a complex charged with emotion, so that, contrary to what usually obtains in the second hundred, there is an increase instead of a decrease of the inner associations, predicates, etc.

The fact that among the stimulus-words in the second hundred there are rather more which arouse slight emotional presentations has no special import in this case any more than in No. 6, for the complex manifests itself in response to apparently quite indifferent stimulus-words.

It is remarkable that in the complex constellations the reactions readily occur in the form of a sentence, very seldom doing so in the remaining associations.

In distraction the complex plays no rôle. We find in inner distraction a maximum of clang-reactions (eighteen), which is slightly above the average for Educated Men.

In the first part of outer distraction we find in the reactions a maximum of "same grammatical forms" (sixty-two) and "same number of syllables" (fifty) ; in inner distraction, on the other hand, a maximum of alliterations (thirty-one) and consonances (thirty-three per cent.).

No. 8.   *Subject : Chemist, about 24 years old*

ASSOCIATIONS	NORMAL		DISTRACTION	
			Outer	
	1st hundred	2nd hundred	60 metro.	100 metro.
Co-ordinations	21	18	24	16
Predicate	20	14	2	10
Causal dependence	2	2	—	2
Coexistence	18	11	16	16
Identity	5	9	24	10
Verbal-motor forms	26	32	28	44
Word-completion	—	—	2	—
Clang	2	2	4	—
Rhyme	1	—	—	—
Indirect	2	1	—	2
Meaningless	1	1	—	—
Faults	2	9	—	—
Repetition of stimulus-word	—	1	—	—
Egocentric reaction	3	5	2	2
Perseveration	2	1	—	4
Repetitions	11	12	8	2
Same grammatical form	37	54	86	70
Same number of syllables	35	34	58	42
Alliteration	7	5	8	8
Consonance	7	11	24	12
Same ending	9	8	24	12
Inner associations	43	34	26	28
Outer associations	49	52	68	70
Clang-reactions	3	2	6	—
Number of associations	100	100	50	50

Inner Associations.—In the second hundred of the normal experiment a decrease, which is much greater in distraction.

Outer Associations.—Increase in the second hundred and in distraction. Predicates increase chiefly in the second hundred, also constellations.

Verbal-motor Forms.—Increase in the second hundred and in the second half of distraction, where we find the maximum.

Repetitions and *faults* are found mostly in the second hundred of the normal experiment, besides an increase of " same grammatical forms" " same number of syllables," " alliteration," " consonances," and " same ending " in distraction.

In the second part of distraction an improvement of the association occurs (perhaps by the subject's becoming accustomed to the distraction) ; slight increase of inner associations, predicates, faults, clangs, slight decrease of same grammatical forms, number of syllables, consonances, and same ending. Against this increase of verbal-motor forms, and those of outer associations, most of the perseverations likewise occur here.

The constellations are nearly all conditioned by love or the subject's profession. There occur :

In first hundred normal experiment . 44 per cent.
,, second ,, ,, , . 20 ,,
,, first half of distraction . . . 6 ,,
,, second ,, ,, . . . 14 ,,

The following perseverations conditioned by a complex are worth noting :

1. { Lady — of my heart
Shoulder — blade
Brace — embrace (pictures to himself some erotic situation)

2. { Square — town hall
Grass — square (the perseveration is not accidental)

Connected with the town hall is a very definite erotic affair not without importance to the subject.

We find faults of two kinds in No. 8. Often the verbal reaction fails and in its place there emerges, for example, a vivid visual image or a vivid emotional image, which he subsequently describes.

In the other kind there are inhibitions because definite erotic reminiscences emerge.

In distraction no " faults " occur. The " egocentric " reactions predominate in the normal experiment and refer mainly to erotic matters.

Of reaction-words repeated, only *bright, good,* and *beautiful* occur more than once.

The Complex.—The erotic complex took a large number of reactions into its service ; thirty were demonstrable in the normal experiment and ten in the second half of distraction, i.e. fifteen per cent. in normal experiment and twenty per cent. in the second half of distraction. In the first half, where the distraction was more complete, we came across none. The complex is hardly repressed at all ; on the contrary, it is most manifest.

The progressive decrease of the clang-associations in the course of external distraction, and increase of indirect associations correspond to the rules we have suspected (see Averages).

No. 9 (p. 89). The figures show a very moderate distraction phenomenon. The relationship of inner to outer associations is very little altered in the distraction experiment, so that, e.g., the variation between the results of the two experiments in fatigue is greater than that between normal experiment and distraction. On the other hand, the clang-associations increase in distraction, as in No. 5 of this group ; in both cases there are fewer clang-associations in fatigue. The fatigue-associations were carried out with both persons under very similar conditions (normal fatigue after professional day's work, ten o'clock at night), whilst the fatigue-associations of No. 4 of this group were preceded by a sleepless night with the mind severely taxed from affect. We there found an increase of the clang-associations in fatigue.

The inconsiderable result of distraction in No. 9 is perhaps connected with the number of inner associations being pretty small even in normal experiment (24 to 26 per cent. instead of 36·7 per cent., the average for educated men) and the number of outer associations pretty large (72 to 69 per cent. instead of the average of 52·7 per cent.).

The number of inner associations in the normal experiment is about as great as the average numbers of inner associations in distraction (Educated Men).

The effect of fatigue is visible in the first experiment on fatigue, not in the second.

In distraction the figures for alliteration and consonance have distinctly increased, as with Nos. 4 and 8 of this group.

The number of *repetitions* is also above the average ; there are relatively many words which are repeated twice, but very few which are often repeated. In nearly all the experiments *pleasant, unpleasant, willingly, unwillingly, friendly,* and similar words are among the words repeated. We will not enter here into the individual repetitions and perseverations because they do not so readily suggest affect-toned thoughts as the earlier cases ; nevertheless this background is not absent.

No. 9.   *Subject : Doctor, 25 years old*

ASSOCIATIONS	NORMAL		DISTRACTION			FATIGUE	
	1st hundred	2nd hundred	Inner	Outer		1st experiment	2nd experiment
				60 metro.	100 metro.		
Co-ordination	9	9	11	12	8	13	13
Predicate	14	17	18	16	16	6	20
Causal dependence . . .	1	—	—	—	—	—	1
Coexistence	24	7	—	8	14	7	12
Identity	5	19	8	2	10	9	5
Verbal-motor forms . . .	43	43	55	56	42	61	49
Word-completion	—	—	2	—	—	—	—
Clang	—	3	4	6	2	1	—
Rhyme	1	—	—	—	—	—	—
Indirect	2	1	—	—	4	1	—
Meaningless	1	—	2	—	4	1	—
Faults	—	—	—	—	—	—	—
Repetition of stimulus-words . .	—	—	—	—	—	—	—
Egocentric reaction . . .	3	3	—	—	—	—	—
Perseveration	5	1	2	2	—	1	4
Repetitions	16	15	22	12	10	18	18
Same grammatical form . . .	57	51	47	42	50	67	59
Same number of syllables . .	42	42	45	32	28	45	48
Alliteration	8	6	20	22	28	20	11
Consonance	14	10	28	26	38	21	14
Same ending	12	10	12	10	14	12	10
Inner associations . . .	24	26	29	28	24	19	34
Outer associations . . .	72	69	63	66	66	77	66
Clang-reactions	1	3	6	6	2	1	—
Number of associations . . .	100	100	100	50	50	156	156

The constellations are but scanty. Here we also find a decrease of the clang-associations and an increase of the indirect associations in the second part of outer distraction.

GENERAL REMARKS ON THE EXPERIMENTS ON THE GROUP OF EDUCATED MEN

There were at our disposal nine persons aged from 23 to 47 with 3793 associations. On five persons experiments were made in inner and outer distraction, on one in inner only, on one with outer only, on two there were no experiments in distraction. From five persons associations were taken during fatigue, one of them in a state of drowsiness. All the individuals in this group have had a university career. Six of them are doctors, one a medical student, one a high-school teacher, and one a chemist. They are all German-Swiss.

Only one belongs to the predicate type (No. 3). Unfortunately, distraction experiments could not be made in this case.

The inner distraction experiment was successful in four cases ; most characteristic is the great increase of clang-reactions ; the lessening of inner, with the increase of outer, associations was less noticeable. In one case (2) the success was other than might have been expected ; in one (9) there was no definite result, the subject having already had a maximum of outer associations in normal experiment.

Outer distraction succeeded distinctly in two cases ; in two cases success was but moderate ; in one case (9) there was again no distinct affect. On the whole inner abstraction acted rather more intensively than outer. The subjects in question were always better able to fulfil the experimental conditions of inner abstraction.

The associations arising in fatigue gave in three of the five cases a result similar to that in distraction. In one case (4) it was peculiarly clear ; it is possible, however, that the fatigue was not responsible or not entirely so, for the patient had had a peculiarly exciting experience in the sleepless night and was probably still very much distracted by this during the experiment.

The association experiment during drowsiness likewise gave a result similar to an experiment in distraction in subject No. 1.

In four persons (5, 6, 7, 8), in the course of the experiments, especially in the normal experiment, we came across extensive complex phenomena. In the first three (5, 6, 7) we saw how the inner associations increased in the second hundred of the normal experiment, whilst the outer decreased ; thus the opposite occurred of what one might expect ; simultaneously we find a rise in the complex constellations. In the distraction experiment the complex constellations usually decreased or disappeared.

The complex phenomena need not be conscious to the individual and often are not apparent till the association material is statistically worked out and classified. In individuals without pronounced complex types slighter complex phenomena are often discovered, e.g. in No. 4 (see below for the full discussion of association types), or again in No. 2, where in making a curve of the reaction-times some emotionally toned clang-associations came to light, part of them of quite old standing.

Every prolongation of the reaction-time, even within quite normal limits, and not reaching consciousness at all, denotes, so far as we know at present, that the stimulus-word in question has encountered an emotional complex. A later chapter deals with these investigations.

3. UNEDUCATED WOMEN

Eight subjects with 2400 associations [1]

No. 1 (Table on p. 92). Some of the associations of this individual are given on pp. 94–96.

As among uneducated persons in general, we find more inner and fewer verbal-motor reactions than among educated persons. The increase of the inner associations, especially of the predicates in the second hundred of the normal experiment, may be again referred to the occurrence of greater personal participation after the subject had become accustomed to the experiment. We have met this phenomenon repeatedly.

Distraction did succeed but was not a striking success. The outer associations increased, clang and indirect associations occurred, whilst they were absent in the normal experiment. It is remarkable that the perseverations are also more numerous.

There are many grounds for the slight effect of distraction. The subject has relatively many predicate relations without quite belonging to the predicate type, a mark of which is a lessened distraction phenomenon. It was often difficult for the subject to dissociate her attention and to react simultaneously with the metronome and to the reaction-word. Secondly, the experiments with uneducated women left us the impression that the dissociation of attention causes them more difficulty than it does the educated. They are for the most part fully occupied by the experiment and work with their attention highly concentrated. The more powerful the means of distraction, the more do they strain every nerve. Thirdly, we know that in this case the experiment had a very strong mental effect upon the subject. The affect of a strong complex that had been just recently partly

[1] On grounds of technique the experiment in inner distraction could not be carried out with any of the uneducated persons.

No. 1. *Subject : Asylum Nurse, aged 18, Swiss ; secondary school education*

| ASSOCIATIONS | NORMAL | | DISTRACTION | |
| | 1st hundred | 2nd hundred | Outer | |
			60 metro.	100 metro.
Co-ordination	23	20	16	14
Predicate	23	37	20	22
Causal dependence	2	1	—	—
Coexistence	28	14	38	30
Identity	1	5	2	2
Verbal-motor forms	23	23	14	30
Word-completion	—	—	—	—
Clang	—	—	6	2
Rhyme	—	—	—	—
Indirect	—	—	2	2
Meaningless	—	—	—	—
Faults	—	—	—	—
Repetition of stimulus-word . .	—	—	—	—
Egocentric reaction	3	—	—	—
Perseveration	1	—	4	4
Repetitions.	11	9	14	2
Same grammatical form . . .	60	53	68	58
Same number of syllables . .	36	44	48	46
Alliteration.	16	7	4	12
Consonance	15	11	12	8
Same ending	5	6	10	8
Inner associations	48	58	36	36
Outer associations	52	42	54	62
Clang-reactions	—	—	6	2
Number of associations . . .	100	100	50	50

assuaged came to the surface and this markedly influenced the reaction. The experiment was a resurrection of a complex which had already become somewhat dormant. It thus happens that even in the distraction experiment we encountered a large number of distinct complex reactions, which is very unusual.

The complex phenomena demand a brief explanatory anamnesis of the subject. She is of country origin and became an asylum nurse at the age of 17, after having brooded at home for over a year over the unhappy ending of a love affair. Her father, a violent-tempered man, would not countenance, in any way, her love affair, and on one occasion there was a scene, when he cursed her because she dared to contradict him. Shortly before the associations were carried out she had burnt her face, which gave her a great shock ; her convalescence was slow. Reflection during this period reawakened her mental pain. The association experiment itself was a further cause of exacerbating her gloomy memories ; its effect lasted some time, a proof of how intensely these experiments act as a reagent among the uneducated and with what strong affinity an emotionally toned complex can absorb and render real a fairly large mass of reaction-words or reaction-images. Now, six months after the experiment, she is objective towards the complex, whose influence is still noticeable. Whilst she then laid chief stress on her unhappiness because her father had cursed her, now she no longer hides the deeper erotic threads in attempting to elucidate the reactions. It is remarkable how acutely she still remembers some of the particular reactions of that time.

The number of complex constellations distinctly provable amount to :

	1st Half	2nd Half
In normal experiment	15	21
In distraction	16	14

As already stated, we seldom, as a rule, find complex constellations in distraction, and rarely to this extent. Naturally distraction was much prejudiced through this. As in other cases, we explain the maximum of the complex constellations in the second hundred of the normal experiment by a new adjustment, by a gain of confidence during the course of the experiment.

The complex expresses itself in such ready mintage, as quotations, snatches of songs, titles of stories, and so on ; this perhaps makes the complex less noticeable, or makes the tax on the emotions less. Quotations are frequently masks. In ordinary life we use them in this way also. Certain songs are sung in certain moods, often to avoid expressing the thoughts which are the source of this mood—hence a masking. Again, the song or the quotation is used to exaggerate a rudimentary feeling, in order to awaken a spark of this feeling by the very exaggeration

itself ; think, for example, of patriotic songs, or of birthday verses
or those composed for feasts or other celebrations.   Examples :

> Come   to the fields.

The quotation is from the story of the idle schoolboy who
wants to make the good boy play truant ; the idle boy becomes
later a scamp, the persevering, industrious boy becomes a respected
teacher.   The quotation has a very different background for the
subject herself.   It is not without reason that *fields* occurs
twice in the normal experiment.   In the orchard at home there
is a beautiful tree with a grass-plot around (*at home = field*) ;
here she often dreamed, and, watching the railway-lines near
by with the trains coming and going, her imagination would
weave travel plans.   After the unhappy ending of her love
affair she had a wish-fulfilment dream : " She lay in the tree-
garden in the grass close to her lover."   To this day the thought
of this dream gives her joy.   To the stimulus-word *dream* she
at once reacted *joy*, and her eyes sparkled at the memory of the
wish dream.

Further quotations :

> At home   it's lovely

refers to a song ; the meaning is clear.
Again :

> Once   was I happy.

She had once heard a troublesome, demented catatonaic sing :

> Once was I happy
> But now nevermore ;
> Cheated me has love, the witch, cheated me sore.

In the three subsequent associations she is still fixed to the
complex :

Once	was I happy
Wonder	love
Blood	sin (thinks of her father's curse)
Wreath	death. (For months she wished she could die. For several weeks she scarcely ate anything, in order to get ill, and she became in consequence very thin. After the experiment which had revivified the complex, and after a visit home which she paid soon after, she again, on her return to us, began to eat little and to get thin, until this was noticed and the folly of her behaviour brought home to her.)

In other places she quotes the titles of stories whose contents
refer to the complex, e.g. :

> Seven   brothers.[1]

---

[1] After breaking off her relationship her brother is the only person in whom
she can confide at all.

" The Seven Brothers " is the title of a story where the self-sacrificing brother is rewarded.

The association immediately following was :

Ill   my brother

The quotations, six in all, only occur in normal experiment, just as in No. 5 of Educated Men, and all refer to the complex.

We have already quoted two instances where the complex causes fixation to one presentation. Some others occur, e.g. the perseveration.

Friendly—⌐ friendship
Three —⌐ friends

She has an intense need of friendship ; but disappointments always arose : her best friend married another girl.

Another example from the experiment in distraction :

Meadow—⌐ the tree-garden
Bring —⌐ apples

It is not a question of direct perseveration of the reaction but of the presentation of the situation lying at its root. In the course of this work we shall include these forms under the term perseveration. The connexion between *meadow* and *tree-garden* is obvious from the preceding. The *apples* naturally arise from the same tree-garden.

Of the four (= 8 per cent.) perseverations in the distraction experiment there is only one probably that refers to the complex.

Repetitions.—In the normal experiment seven reaction-words occur several times (two to five times) ; at least thirteen of these seventeen words belong by their context to the complex. In the distraction experiment (100 reactions) there were in all eight reaction-words which occur several times (two to three times). The percentage relationship is therefore about the same as in the normal experiment ($2 \times 8 = 16$). Four of these (8 per cent.) certainly refer to the complex.

The word *man* (human being) is repeated with striking frequency, eight times in 300 associations (normal experiment + distraction). Seven of these reactions certainly belonged to the complex ; at times quite definite persons are intended by *man*, often the subject herself.

Similarly, we frequently find the reaction-word *person* as universal concept with a quite concrete meaning in the sense of the complex, e.g. :

Station   the person
Bad   the person

A quite definite person is meant—a woman friend of the subject who plays an important part in the complex, and who is not irreproachable morally—has an illegitimate child and has done various things open to criticism. By the reaction *man* this same friend is again sometimes understood, who with her easy-going ways of life has more luck in love than our more serious subject.

Lazy	man
Virtue	of man

In this instance there was a perseveration of the reaction-word itself, from which it may be gathered how strong is the emotional tone of this presentation.

We frequently find the definite article used in the reaction in the same way as in the masking of the complex constellation. Thus our subject in normal experiment used the article twenty-six times in the reaction, seventeen of these reactions certainly referring to the complex. In distraction the relation is less striking.

We find this same phenomenon again in other subjects. In illustration of the complex reaction a few instances are here given :

Proper	person (see above)
To attend to	the person
Bad	the person
Pray	the devout (referring to herself ; she prayed very much in her times of difficulty)
{ Wonder	of love (referring to herself ; also atonement)
{ Blood	of the atonement (she feels herself guilty in regard to her father. There is here a perseveration of the outer form of the reaction)
Omen	of punishment (with the same sense ; this reaction is grammatically meaningless here and is only explicable as probably the after-effect of the previous reaction forms. This reaction is separated from the above reactions by a few others)
Normal	the man (a definite one)
Meadow	the tree-garden
Bring	the apples

(see above for the elucidation of these associations)

Mild	the father
Subtle	the serpents (quite definite persons)
{ Docile	the pupil (with both associations she thought of the friend of her youth)
{ Order	the industrious one
Angry	the man (means her father)

and so on.[1]

---

[1] The brackets to the left of the stimulus-word mean that these stimulus-words followed one another in the experiment.

In the distraction experiment there were many words she did not understand, viz. *hate, love, remorse, fall, pleasant* ; and, further, *rattle, glass, hammer, entrance, ears, hinder.*

It was seen at once in the analysis that under the influence of the complex, half consciously, half unconsciously, she could not or would not understand the first series of these stimulus-words because, according to her account, all these stimulus-words intimately touched the complex which she was trying to repress.

The second series of these stimulus-words were really not understood on account of the acoustic disturbance caused by the metronome. The subject has thus found a further device for concealing her complex in an apparently innocent way. It is appropriate to the situation because, as proved by the second series of stimulus-words—those that do not touch the complex— it is easy, with the constant noise of the metronome, not to understand or to understand incorrectly the stimulus-words in the distraction experiments. (The non-understood stimulus-word was always replaced by another word.)

The not-wishing-to-understand corresponds to a more or less conscious repression of the complex ; it is not different in principle from those cases (hysteria) where failure to react or incorrect reacting occurs involuntarily.

Among the complex reactions we have a large group, that of masked complex reactions. In our subject this masking extends to the following kinds, so far as we can differentiate them :

(1) By quotations (songs, titles of books, quotations from books).

(2) By the use of simple, general concepts in the particular sense of the complex.

(3) By the addition of the article. The reaction thus receives an apparently objective varnish ; it then looks like the habitual answer of the elementary-school child.

(4) By the misunderstanding of those stimulus-words which arouse the complex.

Finally, it must be stated that in the complex reactions abnormally long reaction-times frequently occurred ; unfortunately, no complete measurements were made with this subject so that we cannot work out the point any further in this case.

In No. 2 (p. 98) the abnormally high figures for co-ordination and coexistence, in normal experiment as well as in distraction, are striking. They are in part far above the mean values. On the other hand, the number of predicate and verbal-motor reactions is relatively small, below the mean, especially the predicates. The figures certainly find their explanation in the extremely objective uniform nature of the reactions, apparently little troubled by complexes.

No. 2. *Subject : a Nurse, intelligent but not highly educated ; 22 years old ; South German*

ASSOCIATIONS	NORMAL		DISTRACTION	
			Outer	
	1st hundred	2nd hundred	60 metro.	100 metro.
Co-ordination	33	34	18	22
Predicate	3	9	2	4
Causal dependence	—	1	4	2
Coexistence	36	25	28	34
Identity	6	11	24	18
Verbal-motor forms	15	16	20	18
Word-completion	—	—	—	—
Clang	—	1	2	—
Rhyme	—	3	2	2
Indirect	4	—	—	—
Meaningless	3	—	—	—
Faults	—	—	—	—
Repetition of stimulus-word . .	—	—	—	—
Egocentric reaction	—	1	—	—
Perseveration	—	—	—	—
Repetitions	5	8	—	—
Same grammatical form . . .	91	78	92	88
Same number of syllables . . .	67	56	58	48
Alliteration	8	7	2	2
Consonance	7	18	22	14
Same ending	22	19	22	16
Inner associations	36	44	24	28
Outer associations	57	52	72	70
Clang-reactions	—	4	4	2
Number of associations . . .	100	100	50	50

There were just a few reactions with a rather longer reaction-time. In our experience reactions of over 5·0 seconds arouse a strong suspicion of emotionally toned constellations.

In this subject we found in normal experiment twelve associations with a reaction-time of over five seconds, in the distraction experiment only three.

In the following examples of delayed reaction-time the delay is presumably to be regarded as the effect of an erotic complex.

Marriage	girl :	6·8 seconds
To kiss	laugh :	6 ,,
To love	willing :	5·6 ,,
Male nurse	cupboard :	8 ,,
Dream	basket :	6·4 ,,
Ripe	fruit :	6·6 ,,
To bless	to receive :	5·8 ,, [1]

The subject usually reacted strongly at any hint of an erotic nature and blushed very easily.

She herself states that she felt awkward in replying to the first three stimulus-words.

To the stimulus-word *male nurse* she felt too embarrassed to say the word *female nurse* which first occurred to her, obviously because her thoughts at once took an erotic turn. She looked around her and named the first object she saw in the room—*cupboard*.

To the stimulus-word *dream* the erotic thoughts in the background prevent her reacting. Instead of making a sensible reaction the subject again thrust herself into the external world, saw the paper-basket in the room, and said "Basket." The meaningless reaction was thus a result of the complex action.

The reactions *ripe — fruit* and *bless — receive* are obvious instances of the same sexual *gêne*.

Distraction by objects in the surroundings is, as we know from the experiences of psychopathology, a phenomenon to be regarded as the effect of emotion.[2]

In the embarrassment or confusion which arises where the stimulus-word arouses emotionally toned presentations, which the subject consciously or unconsciously tries to repress, she allows herself to be entirely distracted by the external world and reacts verbally by simply naming some object at hand. Among certain hysterics this is a very pronounced phenomenon.

Out of sixteen stimulus-words which are repeated in the normal experiment we call attention to : *industrious*, five times ; *good*, three times ; *fine*, twice ; *right*, twice ; the remaining are

[1] The medium normal reaction is somewhere between one and two seconds.

[2] Cp. "Emotionelle Stupidität." Jung, "Ueber Simulation von Geistesstörung," *Journal f. Psychol. u. Neur.*, Bd. II, 1903.

distributed among many diverse images; these show her good moral training. It is characteristic that these suggestions of subjectivity disappear in distraction.

In the classification it became difficult to draw a precise line between co-ordination and co-existence. On the whole, it can be said that she belongs to a very objective type, one slightly influenced by constellations—a type we shall meet again in No. 4 of this group.

The following reactions illustrate to some extent her general objective reaction type:

Soft	hard	Rinse	wash	Star	moon
Youth	old age	Building	wall	Faithful	obedience
Trouble	sorrow	Sleeve	dress	Plunder	catch
Window	glass	Park	garden	Freedom	isolation
False	true	Glass	iron	Repentance	anxiety
Sweet	sour	Soft	chair	Stork	pigeon
Wide	narrow	Paint	whitewash	Bicycle	cart
Honey	bees				

The unusually large number of reactions with " same grammatical form " is a parallel to the many co-ordinations and co-existences, and confirms what has just been said.

Distraction is very distinct ; decrease of the inner, increase of the outer associations. We have clang-reactions only in the second hundred of the normal experiment and in distraction, indirect associations only in the first hundred. The rule we have suspected of the reciprocity between indirect and clang-associations would again hold here.[1]

Incidentally, it must be mentioned that the subject carried out the experiments with great zeal, and by concentrating her whole attention in distraction also strained herself to the utmost to do justice to the increased demands.

No. 3. This subject has a fairly marked tendency to make rhymes which increases in the distraction experiment, chiefly in the second hundred.

The usual distraction phenomenon did not occur, although she belongs to the predicate type. The beats were also executed very irregularly. The predicates increase in distraction ; outer associations, especially the verbal-motor reactions, decrease, the clang-reactions alone continuously increase.

Constellations are found mostly in the second hundred of the normal experiment and in the first half of the distraction experiment. The latter fact proves that the distraction experiment has been, anyway in part, well chosen, for, with the exception of No. 1 of this group, where the distraction experiment was

[1] See section on Averages, p. 130.

likewise a failure, during distraction the constellations almost entirely disappear in the other subjects.

No. 3. *Subject : Nurse,* 21 *years old ; Swiss ; secondary education*

| ASSOCIATIONS | NORMAL | | DISTRACTION | |
| | | | Outer | |
	1st hundred	2nd hundred	60 metro.	100 metro.
Co-ordinations	20	16	22	8
Predicate	5	11	16	18
Causal dependence	1	1	2	—
Coexistence	24	10	18	8
Identity	4	6	10	14
Verbal-motor forms	43	47	24	36
Word-completion	1	1	—	2
Clang.	—	—	2	2
Rhyme	1	2	2	8
Indirect	—	5	2	2
Meaningless	—	—	2	2
Faults	1	1	—	—
Repetition of stimulus-word . .	—	—	—	—
Egocentric reaction	1	—	—	2
Perseveration	2	2	2	—
Repetitions	6	5	8	4
Same grammatical form . . .	75	50	76	60
Same number of syllables . . .	48	39	56	46
Alliteration	9	8	6	2
Consonance	13	9	18	16
Same ending	13	12	12	20
Inner associations	26	28	40	26
Outer associations	71	63	52	58
Clang-reactions	2	3	4	12
Number of associations . . .	100	100	50	50

Here are a few individual examples. To the stimulus-word *lamp* she did not react till after twenty seconds with *oil-*

lamp. Shortly before, she had had a pleasant dream in which, instead of the nine-o'clock supper which she seldom took, she was to have a new lamp which she had much desired in her room.

Window-glass, ten seconds (in between, thought of *plate-glass* windows). She thought of a big shop with beautiful plate-glass windows. The subject was for some time the private nurse of the wife of the owner of a business of this kind, and remained very devoted to her former patient. One sees how apparently indifferent expressions are determined in every connexion by coincident thoughts.

Strike   6 o'clock : 2 seconds

The subject had been on night duty in an observation ward and had to get up at six o'clock every evening.

The reaction

Paint   peintre : 6·8 seconds

with its long reaction-time, refers to a sojourn of one year in French Switzerland. The subject, then quite a young girl, was adored by a painter, who was most insistent in his desire to paint her. In the reaction-word *peintre,* besides the masking of the constellation by a superficial association, there is a further constellation, since she here uses a French word with the reminiscence of an erotic event in French Switzerland. In the distraction experiment she again reacts

Painter   peintre : 13 seconds

with the same constellation. The characteristic long reaction-time at both places is worth noting. The following reactions quickly followed one another :

Wedding   to-morrow : 2·2 seconds

and

Come   to-morrow : 1·4   „

This repetition is not accidental. The day after the normal experiment she was to celebrate her birthday. She was glad, for she wanted to go out and had been invited to spend the day ; she looked forward to receiving good wishes from all and was also expecting a letter from her sweetheart.

We find also the reactions :

Rich   in love :   2 seconds

and, later,

Poor   in virtue : 2·2 seconds

The first is a quotation from Ernst Zahn's *Albin Indergand* referring to a love story, and has the force of a complex-quotation for the subject, such as we have reported in No. 5 of Educated Men and No. 1 of Uneducated Women. The second is an analogous but self-made form. She was thinking of another nurse with whom she had had a discussion on " love " the previous day ; the other had taken up a far less ideal point of view on this question. The stimulus-word *poor* had become associated to the earlier stimulus-word *rich*, and the affect-toned reaction connected with it ; she thus became conscious that her own ideal of love was contrary to that of the other nurse. By *poor—in virtue* is understood the other nurse.

The same thought gave rise to the following quotation :

Despise   dost imagine : 2·2 seconds

The quotation runs :

> Dost imagine that I should
> Hate life for ever,
> [To the desert fly
> Because not all
> Budding dreams do ripen ?]—PROMETHEUS.

She only knows the two first verses of this quotation ; the part in brackets she has quite forgotten.

She here thought of the other nurse and her base views about " love." It will be seen how closely similarly related expressions and quotations associate to emotional complexes ; helping in this way in the construction of the infinitely large unconscious material of speech which subserves emotional complexes, making it possible for the poet, for instance, to compose endless variations on a single idea.

A further quotation—

At last   endures not for ever : 5·6 seconds

again refers to her love complex. The reaction-time is strikingly long. She thought " of the brother of a woman friend," who suddenly appeared in the light of a sweetheart ; she was ardently waiting news as to whether or no he had accepted a position abroad, and wished all the time that he would not go.

To the stimulus-word *kiss* she reacted in a tone of surprise : *kiss — yes—I cannot tell you that ; we were speaking about something.* It was about the discussion with the other nurse, who said that kissing was disgusting. To the stimulus-word *time* she reacted :

Time   proportionate : 2 seconds

The second reaction following was :

To rule   proportionate : 3·8 seconds

At " to rule " an elderly nurse came into her mind who is placed in charge of a whole section. A little episode of the day made her think, " She rules over us in everything." The reaction-word *to rule* liberated these thoughts, which she could not utter; instead she gave the reaction-word *proportionate*, which she had just used; this had a meaning in relation to *time* but not to *rule*, or only a very remote one. The gap in the reaction thus conditioned by the affect is filled up by a reaction-word already present. We demonstrated a similar phenomenon in No. 5 of Educated Men, who in an experiment in fatigue invariably answered to a series of stimulus-words that aroused complexes by *yesterday*.

The reaction

Love   needed : 4 seconds

was accompanied by a sudden change in the expression of her face. This phenomenon had reference to her love complex, and is important for us because in the pathology of associations we find similar reaction phenomena (altered expression, sudden lowered voice) when important affective complexes arise.

In

Choose   advice : 3·2 seconds

the subject thought that one must be very careful in choosing a husband; she thought that one should get good advice as to whom to choose.

Hope   not abandoned : 1·8 second

The reaction is a quotation from a letter recently received from the painter (*le peintre*) in West Switzerland, and from which it was evident that he had not yet renounced hope of her.

In the reaction

Love   empty : 3 seconds

the reaction-word was strongly emphasized; it refers to her own love affair, and must be placed alongside the reaction mentioned,

Love   needed : 4 seconds

with its altered expression of face.

The reaction

Weary   why : 1·8 second

is again a quotation. The verse runs as follows :

> The maiden to the spider grieving,
> Asking : " Why so late ?
> Three long hours I sit here weaving.
> Is spinning all my fate ? "

In the stimulus-word *weary* the context of the verses is summarized. Besides this the reaction is determined by the clang between the stimulus-words *late* and *fate*. There is an obvious condensation (Freud) of two factors—situation and visible resemblance in the word, *weary* ; and this condensation took place in the unconscious. This is proved by the fact of the reaction-time being very short, thus excluding any conscious attempt at a quotation. One also sees that the sub- or un-consciousness often likes to associate quotations or complexes in such a way that chance snatches of songs or verse become linked to the complex, the subject not knowing how the rest runs at all.

In the present instance, for example, the subject does not know the verses correctly by heart. We can further prove that behind this quotation there remains an adequate emotional-toned idea.

The lines, taken from some school verses, correspond to an emotional situation which existed about this time. As has been said, the subject was on night duty for some time in an observation ward. By day she slept ; in the morning she was relieved by a nurse who had day charge of the same ward, and latterly she had been annoyed on several occasions at being relieved late by this nurse. This feeling is expressed in the reaction.

Behind the apparently very general reaction

Something   important : 1·2 second

there is concealed the thought of the festivity on the following day.

To the stimulus-words *to woo* there is no reaction. The cause of this is again the conversation with the other nurse about love. The latter had said that she had amused herself by writing to some out-of-the-way matrimonial agency and had been recommended a widower as a good *parti*. This idea displeased our subject very much. To the stimulus-words *to do* she reacts *and leave* (first section). Beneath this superficial reaction there is again masked the dispute about love.

When a complex is hidden by quotations of this kind or by superficial reactions, the reaction-time is generally a short one. Here we find a division of attention, whilst in so-called " faults " the attention is entirely absorbed by the complex, which is repressed ; that is to say, it is to be concealed either from one's own consciousness or from that of the experimenter. A part of the attention is used up in the verbal reaction, and this then bears a very superficial (verbal-motor, clang-like) character ; the other part is claimed by the affect-toned image. This part is frequently repressed, and does not reach full consciousness. This view is confirmed by the perception that such quotations and superficial reactions, which the observer may know very well, refer to and are conditioned by a powerful emotional complex, are often reproduced with the most indifferent countenance in the world.

The chief part of an affect-toned complex is dissociated and repressed from consciousness. The chain of images which occurs consciously at the same time contains, perhaps, merely a quotation as the representative of the complex. This may occur after a very short reaction-time, demonstrating to the experienced that under this cover an important complex is developing its effects in the unconscious.

In another case where the affect is already expressed in the quality of the reaction (emphasis, expression), this dissociation does not take place, the reaction becomes difficult and the reaction-time is delayed (see, for an example, *love — need* 4·0 seconds, in this subject).

In the distraction experiment, we found in No. 3 of Uneducated Women among the few cases of reaction-words repeated (*bicycle ride, Zurich, clear, sad*) two where a complex is certainly responsible for the repetition.

In the reactions

Bicycle	wheel	Tram	trip

she explained that her sweetheart frequently bicycled, and this came into her mind at once on hearing the stimulus-words.

In the reactions

Fire	Zurich

and

Railway-station	Zurich

she remembered that in the course of the discussion about love she had defended the town of Zurich and its inhabitants.

The reactions

Moves	sad
Mild	sad

are connected with family affairs.

In the reactions

Sin	world :	0·8 second
Repentance	death :	1·2 ,,

a recent accident hovered before her, when a patient tried to drink some lysol taken out of the instrument cupboard. There were no serious consequences, but the event took place in this subject's ward and left a very painful impression and a great feeling of responsibility, hence the perseveration in the above reactions.

Nos. 4 and 5.   *Subjects : Two Nurses, 27 and 28 years old respectively*

ASSOCIATIONS	SUBJECT 4				SUBJECT 5			
	Normal		Distraction		Normal		Distraction	
			Outer				Outer	
	1st hundred	2nd hundred	1st half	2nd half	1st hundred	2nd hundred	1st half	2nd half
Co-ordination – . .	46	46	54	26	21	32	14	16
Predicate	4	2	—	6	9	8	4	6
Causal dependence . .	1	3	—	—	1	1	—	—
Coexistence . . .	30	15	18	32	32	15	14	12
Identity	4	13	16	18	6	8	12	8
Verbal-motor forms . .	14	18	12	18	30	32	50	48
Word-completion . .	—	—	—	—	—	—	—	—
Clang.	—	—	—	—	—	2	2	8
Rhyme	—	—	—	—	—	—	2	—
Indirect	1	2	—	—	—	—	—	2
Meaningless . . .	—	1	—	—	—	1	—	—
Faults	—	—	—	—	1	1	2	—
Repetition of stimulus-word .	—	—	—	—	—	—	—	—
Egocentric reaction . .	—	—	—	—	—	—	—	—
Perseveration . . .	—	1	—	—	—	—	—	2
Repetitions . . .	8	5	6	4	10	9	0	2
Same grammatical form .	85	86	96	90	76	69	68	70
Same number of syllables .	60	53	58	56	54	43	48	42
Alliteration . . .	11	6	8	2	16	19	28	28
Consonance . . .	15	7	10	8	14	21	30	36
Same ending . . .	25	17	12	24	17	14	12	22
Inner associations . .	51	51	54	32	31	41	18	22
Outer associations . .	48	46	46	68	68	55	76	68
Clang-reactions . . .	—	—	—	—	—	2	4	8
Number of associations .	100	100	50	50	100	100	50	50

No. 4

Nurse, Swiss, 23 years old ; elementary-school education

The results of the experiments resemble very closely No. 2 of this group. The distraction phenomenon is less well marked (in both experiments she exerted all attention), clang-reactions are absent altogether, and the number of verbal-motor forms is still lower than in No. 3. The coexistences reach a high figure. The predicates are few, egocentric reactions are absent—a fact which speaks in favour of a very objective apprehension of the words. The figures for same grammatical form are, as in No. 2 of this group, remarkably high. The subject belongs, therefore, to the same objective reaction type without demonstrable constellations. Many associations had delayed reaction-times for which we had no subsequent explanations. We are not in possession of any more searching analysis.

No. 5

Nurse, Swiss, about 28 years old ; elementary-school education

The predicates are relatively much diminished (in the normal experiment, for example, only 8·5 per cent. instead of 20·4 per cent., the average for Uneducated Women). The co-ordinations in normal and distraction experiments are below the average—the verbal-motor forms, on the other hand, above the average—for Uneducated Women (the average is 24 per cent. in normal experiment and 28·8 per cent. in outer distraction). On the whole, we have a case with relatively few inner, but many outer associations.

Nevertheless—or rather, because the general reaction type seems somewhat superficial—the distraction experiment succeeded, whereas usually, among Uneducated Women with many predicates, distraction does not succeed so well. Although the outer associations in the second part of the distraction are not more numerous than in the first hundred of the normal experiment, still the inner associations do distinctly fall off, whilst the clang-reactions increase.

In the second hundred of the normal experiment we have an increase of the inner associations, and at the same time we find, as is fairly usual, an increase of the constellations, which we consider, as is so often the case, the cause of the alteration. (The fact that in the second hundred stimulus-words there are many more which arouse emotional images than in the first hundred may also have its influence.) In the first hundred of the normal experiment six constellations were noticed, ten in the second hundred, and two in the distraction experiment. They diminish in the distraction experiment. They are almost exclusively complex constellations.

The complex is bound up with a love affair with an unhappy ending ; after a long friendship she was jilted by her sweetheart.

The long reaction-times (mostly over five seconds) are almost entirely limited to these complex constellations. Examples :

Attendant	male nurse :	11·4	seconds (her sweetheart was an attendant)
Heart	stomach :	6·4	,,
Caress	love :	5·6	,,
Separate	go :	5·6	,,
Love	wicked :	8·8	,,
Freedom	confined :	6	,,
Despise	respected :	18·4	,,
Tie	tear :	5·2	,,
False	falseness :	7·2	,,

The subject was unwilling to give any exact account about a small remaining number of constellations and long reaction-times, which could not be set down to the complex as a matter of course ; they are, on that account, the more suspect. We have here another good instance of that special kind of complex expression—prolonged reaction-times (by this is not meant that these do not occur in other cases also, e.g. with rather difficult, unusual stimulus-words).

We have already met prolonged reaction-times as complex phenomena (subjects 3 and 4 of this group) ; here they are almost exclusively complex signs. They pass into the so-called " faults " when no verbal reaction follows at all.

The repetition of the reaction word is almost entirely limited to the normal experiment and concerns sixteen different words, the majority referring to things connected with the daily life of an asylum nurse.

No. 6

Nurse, Swiss, 18 years ; elementary-school education

A glance at the proportion of predicates to co-ordinations teaches us that this subject must be accounted a predicate type. In accordance with the rule for this type, we find no distinct effect of distraction. Clang-reactions and indirect associations only occur in the first part of distraction. The egocentric reactions are pretty well represented and equally divided. The highest number of inner and the smallest number of outer associations again occur in the second hundred of the normal experiment.

Nos. 6 and 7. *Subjects : Two Swiss Nurses, 18 and 27 years respectively*

ASSOCIATIONS	SUBJECT 6				SUBJECT 7			
	Normal		Distraction		Normal		Distraction	
			Outer				Outer	
	1st hundred	2nd hundred	1st half	2nd half	1st hundred	2nd hundred	1st half	2nd half
Co-ordination . . .	22	19	14	12	19	30	4	8
Predicate	27	45	50	48	32	32	36	16
Causal dependence . .	1	1	—	—	2	1	—	—
Coexistence . . .	31	14	6	12	26	12	10	6
Identity	2	3	6	10	2	4	6	2
Verbal-motor forms . .	16	11	18	18	18	18	36	36
Word-completion . .	—	—	—	—	—	—	—	—
Clang.	—	—	2	—	—	—	—	2
Rhyme	—	—	—	—	—	—	—	—
Indirect	—	—	4	—	—	—	—	—
Meaningless . . .	—	—	—	—	—	—	4	—
Faults	1	7	—	—	1	3	—	—
Repetition of stimulus-word .	—	—	—	—	—	—	4	—
Egocentric reaction . .	3	2	2	2	—	—	—	—
Perseveration . . .	7	1	2	—	2	—	8	14
Repetitions . . .	13	11	14	6	14	9	18	4
Same grammatical form .	50	29	28	32	31	35	38	60
Same number of syllables .	37	24	48	52	53	43	20	14
Alliteration . . .	6	3	6	6	13	9	28	30
Consonance . . .	9	5	12	6	15	12	34	30
Same ending . . .	—	2	2	4	6	11	20	28
Inner associations . .	50	65	64	60	53	63	40	24
Outer associations . .	49	28	30	40	46	34	52	74
Clang-reactions . . .	—	—	2	—	—	—	—	2
Number of associations .	100	100	50	50	100	100	50	50

We see there also a maximum of "faults" (seven), which are almost all evoked by a complex.

Unfortunately, the subject vouchsafed no real explanation, and her reserved character forbade persistence on this point. She merely stated that reminiscences of certain family affairs were concealed beneath the faults and long reaction-times. Unusual stimulus-words were responsible for a few of these.

No. 7

Nurse, Swiss, 27 years ; elementary-school education

Distraction was a distinct success ; it was chiefly characterized by a diminution of co-ordinations and an increase of the verbal-motor forms, whilst the predicates, although pretty numerous, were more stable in quantity. Perseveration occurs mainly in distraction, especially in the second hundred of the distraction experiment.

There are no egocentric reactions.

From the nature of the reactions it is not evident whether constellations or complexes do or do not play a part in the associations. Some conclusions can be more readily drawn from the reaction-times, inasmuch as some of the strikingly long reaction-times occur in reaction to insidious stimulus-words ; e.g. :

Kiss	morning kiss :	8·4 seconds
Remember	letter :	11 „
Bad	—	(fault)
Vagabond	without fortune :	12·6 seconds

Any accurate mental analysis, however, is absent in this case.

In the distraction experiment repetitions of the form of the reaction occur ; they are mostly reactions in the form of a simple sentence, e.g. :

Sin	men sin
Repentance	men repent
Love	men love
Strong	men are strong
Hate	men hate, etc.

But no strikingly long reaction-times occur. Whether this repetition of the word, especially the repetition of the word "men," denotes complex phenomena similar to those we found in No. 1 of this group cannot be elicited.

Looked at externally, the associations of this person make a very objective impression, without many subjective constellations. But the rather changing reaction-times, often remarkably long, suggest that behind the apparently objective reactions true

No. 8.   *Subject: a Swiss Servant, 27 years*

ASSOCIATIONS	Normal		Distraction	
			Outer	
	1st hundred	2nd hundred	1st half	2nd half
Co-ordination	10	13	10	20
Predicate	48	32	37	32
Causal dependence	—	—	—	2
Coexistence	11	4	14	4
Identity	2	5	2	2
Verbal-motor forms	23	42	25	32
Word-completion	—	2	2	2
Clang	—	—	—	2
Rhyme	—	—	2	—
Indirect	—	—	2	—
Meaningless	—	—	—	—
Faults	6	1	6	4
Repetition of stimulus-word . .	—	—	—	—
Egocentric reaction	—	—	2	—
Perseveration	—	1	—	—
Repetitions	15	15	8	2
Same grammatical form . . .	38	38	34	40
Same number of syllables . . .	42	36	44	54
Alliteration	3	11	6	8
Consonance	11	15	10	8
Same ending	6	8	4	6
Inner associations	58	45	47	54
Outer associations	36	51	41	38
Clang-reactions	—	2	4	4
Number of associations . . .	100	100	50	50

complex constellations are probably to be found. For practical reasons it was not feasible to carry out the mental analysis in all the subjects so exhaustively as it, fortunately, proved possible with a certain number of them.

No. 8

Servant, Swiss, about 27 *years; elementary-school education, fairly intelligent*

The marked predominance of the predicates is a characteristic of the reaction ; these are mainly responsible for the high number of the inner associations. A definite tendency to critical valuations is present, but these have no pronounced subjective (egocentric) character. The reactions denote active participation in the experiment—as to the sense of the stimulus-words. Despite a certain reserve and bashfulness, the more intimate content of the images comes out pretty distinctly. The subject is a very excellent and practical servant, very religious, and was thinking of getting married. In the reactions of the normal state the following reactions are repeated :

Practical, twice	Good, thrice
House, twice	Beautiful, four times
Room, twice	Splendid, thrice
Church, twice	Man, thrice
God, twice	Child, five times

Shortly before carrying out the associations she happened to be attacked by a big dog, which frightened her very much.

The reaction *dog* was four times repeated. Once there was strong perseveration at the picture of the dog.

Growl	dog
Lumps	lumps on the dog's paws

The reaction *wolf* was twice repeated. To the stimulus-word *sly* she reacted with *wolf*, spontaneously announcing that really *fox* was the first to come to her mind. These reactions and repetitions distinctly point to emotional complexes and to an active participation of the personality in general.

The distraction experiment—which was, however, only carried out very incompletely—had no effect at all. Thus we see here the same characteristic behaviour as in the predicate types described above.

The numerous faults in this subject can be thus grouped :

Of the seven faults in the normal experiment, four occur with undoubted emotionally charged stimulus-words (such as *heart, manners, hypocrite, faithful, rich, revenge,* etc.) ; of the ten faults in distraction 8 per cent. (four) with emotionally charged stimulus-words ; a further proof that faults in the majority of cases are referable to emotional causes.

SUMMARY

In the group of Uneducated Women we have eight subjects aged from eighteen to twenty-eight years, with 2400 associations. We have 200 associations from each in normal experiment and 100 associations in outer distraction.

Most of the subjects are fairly intelligent. More than half had attended a secondary school after the elementary school. Seven habitually spoke the Swiss dialect ; only one spoke a South German dialect (which is nearer to High German). Seven were hospital nurses, one was a servant. Two reacted with a predicate type ; in neither was the distraction experiment successful. In a third with considerable predicates, but yet not exactly belonging to the predicate type, the distraction experiment likewise miscarried. This was partly because at many stimulus-words, not wishing her attention to be distracted, she failed to make the strokes to the beats of the metronome. The distraction experiment only half succeeded in one subject, with many co-ordinations and absence of constellations. In the distraction experiment she redoubled her efforts, in order to pay attention to the stimulus-words as well as to the metronome beats. In the other four subjects the distraction experiment succeeded, although these on the whole also put forth all their efforts in the distraction experiment and strained themselves considerably more than in the normal experiment, because it was more difficult for them than for educated persons to keep their attention divided. As a whole, the Uneducated Women are the least able of all the groups to divide their attention. Clang-associations play a much slighter part as distraction phenomena than in the groups of the educated. Two subjects belong to a purely objective type with few predicates, no constellations to speak of, and remarkably many reaction-words with the same number of syllables as the stimulus-words. In two others (Nos. 1 and 3) complex phenomena come to the fore in the most diverse forms. In three subjects there was, in the second hundred of the normal experiment, an increase of the inner and decrease of the outer associations. It was then generally noticed that the complex phenomena were more distinct in the second hundred of the normal experiment, whilst they diminished more and more in distraction. In the most pronounced cases, e.g. No. 1, the manifestation of the complex in the second hundred of the normal experiment is certainly not dependent upon the increase of emotionally charged stimulus-words. This manifestation occurred with stimulus-words which possess nothing of this quality for other people.

4. UNEDUCATED MEN

In this group we give the tables of the first six cases in summary, the columns omitted having no special interest. So far as the group of verbal-motor forms is especially concerned, we get the following averages, to which all six subjects adhere pretty closely : normal experiment : first hundred twenty-seven, second hundred thirty ; outer distraction : first half twenty-two, second half thirty-four. Distinct complex constellations are hardly to be demonstrated, and in nearly all cases a thorough analysis was wanting.

	Subject 1 (Male nurse, Swiss, aged 40)				Subject 2 (Male nurse, South German, aged 25)				Subject 3 (Male nurse, aged 54)			
	Normal		Distraction		Normal		Distraction		Normal		Distraction	
			Outer				Outer				Outer	
ASSOCIATIONS	1st hundred	2nd hundred	1st half	2nd half	1st hundred	2nd hundred	1st half	2nd half	1st hundred	2nd hundred	1st half	2nd half
Co-ordination. . . .	34	12	16	16	32	37	24	20	5	22	10	12
Predicate	12	28	18	10	1	4	2	8	17	16	12	30
Inner associations . . .	49	41	34	26	33	42	26	28	23	38	22	42
Outer association . . .	50	51	62	60	64	53	64	66	75	59	56	48
Clang-reactions . . .	—	—	—	—	2	1	6	—	—	1	4	2
Residual group . . .	1	8	2	14	1	4	4	6	2	2	18	8
Number of associations . .	100	100	50	50	100	100	50	50	100	86	50	50

No. 1. *Subject : Male Nurse, aged 40, Swiss; elementary-school education, rather well-read*

The outer associations predominate over the inner, but not to the same extent as in the educated. The effect of distraction is clear. In the second hundred of the normal experiment we see the number of inner associations decrease, and the outer increase.

The figures for faults and egocentric reactions (four, eight, six, four) are remarkably high ; they exceed the mean for these reaction forms. In the absence of any exact analysis it is not possible to determine the significance of the faults in each association. There are no distinct constellation associations. The reaction-times, apart from the few faults, betray no complex constellations; they remain within small limits, 0·6 to 2·6 seconds.

No. 2. Subject: Male Nurse, about 25 years; South German; elementary-school education

The outer associations predominate over the inner, as in the previous case. In the second hundred of the normal experiment there is an increase of the inner and decrease of the outer associations. When we met this phenomenon in the other groups we were able to ascribe it to the emotionally charged association complexes emerging more distinctly. Probably this is the case here also; still, the constellation associations are not very distinct and we only possess a partial analysis. The sum of the reaction-times is greater in the second than in the first hundred; longer reaction-times are more numerous. In the second hundred there is the reaction *family — alone*, 4·4 seconds, the longest reaction-time which occurred in this subject. The young man is engaged to a hospital nurse. A series of reactions with a rather long reaction-time is very probably conditioned by this complex.

We met the strongest distraction phenomena in the first part

ASSOCIATIONS	SUBJECT 4 (Male nurse, aged 37)				SUBJECT 5 (Male nurse, aged 30)				SUBJECT 6 (Male nurse, aged 34)			
	Normal		Distraction		Normal		Distraction		Normal		Distraction	
			Outer				Outer				Outer	
	1st hundred	2nd hundred	1st half	2nd half	1st hundred	2nd hundred	1st half	2nd half	1st hundred	2nd hundred	1st half	2nd half
Co-ordination. . . .	15	15	22	10	32	16	18	12	46	27	30	22
Predicate	31	28	20	16	3	5	—	2	9	11	6	10
Inner associations . . .	49	46	44	26	35	21	18	14	56	40	38	32
Outer associations . . .	48	48	46	68	63	78	68	80	40	56	56	58
Clang-reactions . . .	1	1	4	—	1	1	8	4	1	1	—	2
Residual group . . .	2	5	6	6	1	—	6	2	3	3	6	8
Number of associations . .	100	100	50	50	100	100	50	50	100	100	50	50

of the distraction experiment, where we also found six clang-associations.

There are hints of constellations in some of the reactions, which refer to military service :

Schoolboy	soldier
Faithful	soldier
Rank	file

Others in all probability refer to his engagement and fiancée :

Love	trust :	1·6 seconds
Hope	at last :	1·6 ,,
Wreath	ripe :	3·2 ,,
Faithfulness	go a journey :	2·4 ,,
Everywhere	alone :	? ,,
Family	alone :	4·4 ,,
Separate	meet :	1·6 ,,

The reaction-times, which are rather longer in proportion to the other associations, support this idea. There were no quotations or the like in this or the previous subject.

No. 3. *Subject : Male Nurse, 54 years ; secondary education, somewhat neurasthenic*

The distraction experiment did not succeed well ; it should be stated, however, that interest in associations which belong to the clang and residual group was stronger in the distraction experiments than in the normal experiments, whilst the egocentric reactions disappeared in distraction experiment—phenomena which may be regarded as more or less the effects of distraction. There were no manifest constellation or complex associations.

No. 4. *Subject : Male Nurse, 37 years ; elementary-school education*

He can also be counted among the *predicate* types. A certain distraction result can, however, be recorded. We notice that the inner associations visibly decrease ; we meet a distinct rise of the outer associations only in the second part of the distraction experiment ; on the other hand, we see in the first part of the distraction experiment a maximum of clang-reactions. Perseverations and egocentric reactions are quite absent. There are no distinct constellation associations. We have reviewed this case (one of the previous cases from this group would have done) in a discussion about constellations and complexes (see No. 4 of Educated Men) as an example of those cases where we meet the first constellations or subjective reminiscences (p. 73).

No. 5. Subject : Male Nurse, 30 years

Inner associations diminish in this case as in the first two of this group. The predicates especially are very few in number. Obvious effects of distraction : The inner associations decrease considerably in the second hundred of the normal experiment as well as in the distraction experiment, especially in the second part. Clangs, rhymes, indirect and meaningless reactions increase in the distraction experiment, especially in the first part. In the second part they again diminish slightly, the decrease of inner and increase of outer associations being there most pronounced. The figures for " same grammatical form " are extremely high (eighty-six in first hundred of normal experiment, forty-four in second hundred ; eighty-eight each in both halves of the distraction experiment). They are also high in the next case and in Nos. 2 and 4 of Uneducated Women. In accordance with this result, egocentric associations are absent, and the constellation associations diminish altogether and are not distinctly recognizable, just as in the other cases mentioned.

In the second part of the distraction experiment there are certain repetitions, probably from embarrassment, and as a phenomenon of distraction.

No. 17.[1]	Door	castle
„ 55.	Hall	castle hall
„ 57.	Bridge	castle bridge
„ 69.	Banner	castle banner.
	Cellar	cellar door
	Corridor	door

No. 6. Subject : Male Nurse, 36 years ; secondary education

With fairly numerous inner associations co-ordinations are chiefly to be found, whilst the predicates are not particularly numerous. The verbal-motor forms are relatively scarce. A glance at the relation of inner to outer association shows at once that the distraction experiment was successful. In the second hundred of the normal experiment there is already an alteration of these figures in the sense of a distraction.

Our subject resembles No. 5 of this group and Nos. 4 and 2 of Uneducated Women by the marked occurrence of co-ordination, and of the figures for " same grammatical form," diminution of the predicate relations, and an almost entire absence of egocentric reactions and constellation associations. It is a case of strikingly objective, uniform reaction type.

[1] The numbers refer to the serial number of the stimulus-word in the scheme ; they only serve to show at what intervals these repetitions occur.

The present case differs from the others by the prominence of subordinations and definitions within the co-ordinations, whilst in the others, the three subjects referred to below, true coadjuncts are rather made.

Stimulus-word	No. 2 Uneducated Women	No. 4 Uneducated Women	No. 5 Uneducated Men	No. 6 Uneducated Men
Sunday	Tuesday	Monday	Monday	Holiday
Schoolboy	girl	teacher	teacher	boy
Head	foot	arm	neck	part of the body
Ink	pen	pen	pencil	writing material
Bread	meat	cheese	meal	food-stuff
Lamp	oil	candle	light	object in a room
Tree	chair (?)	bush	bush	plant
Wood	charcoal	charcoal	charcoal	for lighting fires
Slate	pen	pen	slate-pencil	school furniture
Helmet	glove	sword	cuirassier	head-covering

No. 7 (p. 120) may, perhaps, still be counted among the predicate type, although the predicates are not very predominant in the second hundred ; remarkably many co-existences ; no reactions in the clang group. In the residual group the number of faults is noticeable ; the maximum (five) occurs in the second hundred of the normal experiment. The sudden appearance of 6 per cent. repetitions of the stimulus-word in the second part of the distraction experiment is most surprising. We found also 2 per cent. perseverations. In the second part of normal experiment the figures for inner association rise and those of outer association fall, which, in conjunction with the occurrence of complex constellations we have already found several times. Despite the predicate type the distraction experiment was successful. The number of inner associations continued to decrease and that of outer associations to increase. The predicates, especially, diminish in the distraction experiment.

The exact number of recent constellations could not be subsequently ascertained, but a series of constellations were certainly present, among these being a great number of reminiscences from the courses in the intermediate school. Some of the specific associations with very long reaction-times are striking, e.g. :

Copy-book	squarish:	7·4 seconds
Book	interesting:	10·1 ,,
Insolent	the enemy:	17·2 ,,
Caress	*caresser* : [1]	6·4 ,,
Evil	devil:	10·4 ,,
Angry	devil :	28 ,,
Come	the yellow danger:	8·4 ,,

---

[1] Reaction in French.

Kiss	Oberon :	6·8 seconds
Love	mother :	13 ,,
To indulge	indulgent :	9 ,,
Dear	mother :	9 ,,
Strange	a poem :	11 ,,
Nausea	dirty :	6·8 ,,

No. 7. *Subject : Pupil at an Intermediate School, 17 years;
fairly intelligent, nervous*

ASSOCIATIONS	Normal		Distraction	
			Outer	
	1st hundred	2nd hundred	60 metro.	100 metro.
Co-ordination	13	22	26	12
Predicate	35	26	12	14
Causal dependence	—	1	—	—
Coexistence	26	10	22	12
Identity	3	2	14	8
Verbal-motor forms	22	34	22	44
Word-completion	—	—	—	—
Clang.	—	—	—	—
Rhyme	—	—	—	—
Indirect	—	—	—	—
Meaningless	—	—	—	—
Faults	1	5	4	4
Repetition of stimulus-word . .	—	—	—	6
Egocentric reaction	2	—	—	—
Perseveration	—	—	—	2
Repetitions	12	5	—	—
Same grammatical form . . .	44	48	82	64
Same number of syllables . . .	32	30	40	40
Alliteration	12	15	12	16
Consonance	17	18	26	22
Same ending	2	13	10	14
Inner associations	48	49	38	26
Outer associations	51	46	58	64
Clang-reactions	—	—	—	—
Number of associations . . .	100	100	50	50

In the distraction test the reactions with unusually long re-action-times are scarce. Probably a more exact analysis would have found one or more complexes behind these reactions. Eros, school, fear of a slight operation, were probably the reasons conditioning the prolongation of the reaction-times.

SUMMARY

In the group of Uneducated Men we have seven subjects with 2086 associations. They are all fairly intelligent, but, with the exception of No. 6, who had had a secondary education, and of No 7, who attends a technical school, they had only at-tended the elementary schools. Four of them are German-Swiss, speaking the current dialect; one is a South German, but long settled in Switzerland and quite adept in the Swiss dialect. Only one speaks the Swabian dialect, which is rather more like High German. The pupil at the technical school speaks High German at home.

Two of the subjects can be counted as belonging to the predicate type; as in most cases of this type, distraction did not succeed well in one case though it did in the other. In another subject, who in normal experiment had relatively few inner and many outer associations, the distraction was not a great success. In all the rest of this group the effect of distra_tion—only external distraction is referred to in this group—was evident.

Clang-associations as signs of distraction never occur as they do among the educated.

Two subjects (5 and 6 of this group) belong to a type with very many co-ordinations, few predicates, and many reactions having the same grammatical form ; at the same time they are marked by the absence of egocentric rea tions and constellations. We meet this type also in Uneducated Women (Nos. 2 and 4 of Uneducated Women). For the rest, the entire group of Uneducated Men is distinguished by the great decrease of constellations and complexes in the associations, just an indication of these being occasionally found. This does not exclude the variations in reaction-times, although within narrow limits, which denotes the action of complexes. Quotations and similar reactions which make one suspect complexes were only found in one particular case in this group. This exception was the youngest member of the group—the pupil at the technical school. He reacted by a very great number of subjective reminiscences and constellations which might be regarded partly as complex constellations.

In subjects 2, 3, and 7 we found an increase of inner associa-tions in the second hundred of the normal experiment. Whether this should always be regarded as the effect of a complex cannot be stated with certainty in all cases.

In our experiments the Uneducated Men differ from the Uneducated Women in that, subjective as they are, they exhibit their emotions much less than the latter. This difference hardly exists among the educated. Among the educated men we meet almost as many very subjective types whose reactions exhibit strong emotion as we do among women. The educated men in this respect have more feminine traits than the uneducated.

In conclusion, it is perhaps not superfluous again to call attention to the fact that the overwhelming number of complexes which we have discovered among our subjects are of an erotic nature. There is nothing very remarkable in this, seeing the great part love and sexuality play in human life.

B. GROUP STATISTICS

The Normal Experiment

Having now reviewed the subjects individually it remains for us to study the group behaviour of the reactions. The ratio of the figures among individuals is a very variable one, as a glance at the tables shows. A chief cause of these variations is, apart from specific individual causes, the intensity of attention, to the effects of which we have already referred several times. The fact that some individuals react preferably by inner association, others preferably by outer, is primarily a phenomenon of attention. Every person endowed with speech has at disposal all the different kinds of association; the nature of the association produced depends chiefly upon the degree of attention bestowed upon the stimulus-word. Where our distraction experiment succeeded, i.e. where the conditions of the experiment were carried out so as to fulfil the intentions of the experimenter, the same phenomenon was manifest—the outer associations and the clang-reactions increased at the expense of the inner associations. A change took place in the direction of habit and routine, that is, of mechanically simple or verbal connexions. With increasing distraction the effect of the "law of frequency" increases, since things which are frequently together in time and space attain expression. With the decreasing stress of attention on the images the next layer (mostly verbal elements) attains a higher valency, i.e. a lower liminal value, and thus reaches reproduction.

We do not wish to discuss here the different psychological theories of attention. We conceive attention as a state leading up to association complexes, and in the last analysis characterized by muscular tensions ; a state which supplies the psycho-physical basis to the accentuated complex. The purpose of the physical echo seems to be to make stable the accentuated image in the field of consciousness. Through this somatic connexion the accentuated image is probably kept more fluid than all the others which are also at the summit of clearness, or under other conditions of the " feeling " which is its representative. It becomes " a tendency presentation " or a " tendency feeling." Two effects proceed from this :

(1) Acceleration of all associated presentations and especially of all those having the same " tendency."

(2) Inhibition of all non-associated presentations, especially to those not associated with that " tendency."

If the tone of attention is heightened for a non-associated presentation, the tendency presentation is correspondingly put out of focus, i.e. it loses in tone.   The effects proceeding from it become proportionately lower in intensity, so that the difference in the liminal value of all the remaining associations decreases. The selection as regards the tendency becomes more difficult and becomes more subordinate to the influence of the law of frequency ; that is to say, that all those associations thrust themselves to the front which by use and practice form the most frequent content of consciousness, and thus possess the lowest liminal value. The law of frequency takes over the part which had formerly been played by the tendency presentation. Transferred to the practice of our experiments, it means that the presentations which are ready-made and mechanical in the language are substituted for the endeavour to apprehend and work out the meaning of the stimulus-word.

In the act of apperception, and of the further working out of the stimulus-words, all these purely verbal connexions are repressed, so that a part of them chime softly and vaguely and a part remain completely unconscious. If the verbal connexions enter the field of consciousness, the higher associations are pushed into the shade ; some of them chime feebly, some pass away unconsciously (according to Wundt " unperceived "). (That they do not occur at all is possible, but that is difficult to prove.) But verbal mechanism is not the lowest level in the reaction process ; mere mimicry of speech or clang-reaction is repressed during mechanical verbal reaction. If by further lowering of attention we take away verbal mechanisms, which after all do possess in most cases some meaning, the clang-reactions rise ; these represent the lowest level of verbal reaction, and on that account remain in ordinary life constantly below the threshold of consciousness. In the infantile process of speech development clang-reactions, it is well known, play a pretty large part ; later they become more and more repressed, ending in a habitual unconsciousness from which in the normal state they can only be evoked by a certain degree of effort.

We have purposely only spoken about the effect of distraction on verbal functions. We must now observe that the law of frequency occurs also in the selection of the inner pictures. We were struck by the frequency with which, while the subject was in a state of inner distraction (N.B., much more frequently than in the normal state), old, childish reminiscences emerged, even with everyday objects.

In the individual descriptions we have referred to the similarity of the phenomenon of distraction to that of maniacal reaction. The reactions in the state of distraction are in no way to be differentiated from maniacal reactions, as Aschaffenburg discovered, and as we have ourselves observed in many maniacal associations.

Liepmann,[1] who explains " flight of ideas " as due to a disturbance of attention, has arrived at the same point of view as ourselves as a result of his own investigations. Considerations similar to Liepmann's have for some time past mainly inspired our experimental investigations. The results of our experiments confirm his views. As regards the psychological mechanisms of the flight of ideas, our views agree completely with Liepmann's ; we therefore refer the reader to his work.

Aschaffenburg has acquainted us with another reaction type similar to that of the maniacal—the fatigue type. Other workers, guided by Kräpelin's elaborate investigations, record analogous results from the effect of alcohol. Aschaffenburg makes motor excitation responsible for the occurrence of clang-reactions. But against this conception it is enough to point out that the conditions in question are characterized to a large extent by disturbance of attention. Our experiments have proved that clang-reactions are conditioned, it may be said exclusively, by disturbance of attention. Motor excitation is probably an unessential by-symptom, which at the most may be the cause of the disturbance of attention. This seems to be the case in fatigue and alcoholism. In maniacal flight of ideas another factor certainly enters as the cause of the disturbance of attention, the specific excitation, the psychological nature of which is at present quite obscure. The disturbance of attention due to motor excitation in fatigue and alcoholism we should conceive as

[1] Liepmann, *Ueber Ideenflucht, Begriffsbestimmung und psychologische Analyse*, Halle, 1904.

follows : The physical correlate of the phenomenon of attention, muscular tension, undergoes, under the influence of the motor excitation, a certain abbreviation in duration and a certain abnormal variability in its nature. The psychophysical basis of the accentuated images thus become labile is psychically represented as the *Decline of the tendency images*. From this decline of the tendency image there must result, following Liepmann's views, flight of ideas, which appear in the association experiment as clang-reactions, etc. In acoustic verbal experiments there is a possibility that motor excitation, which is naturally communicated to the verbal-motor system also, encounters the mechanical reactions now set free ; but it is never the sole cause of these.

From these considerations we should expect in every case *of disturbance of attention a superficial reaction type, clang-reactions, or, inversely, where clang-reactions occur we should suspect a disturbance of attention.*

This fact seems to us to be of great diagnostic value ; moreover, it is an essential foundation for any general understanding of reactions.

With the relatively great variations in the individual figures a survey of our large number of statistics is difficult ; we have therefore prepared for easier comparison tables of certain groups giving the arithmetical mean in percentages. We do not deny' that any dealing with averages in such delicate quantitative relationships is a somewhat daring undertaking. Even though the quantitative ratio of the individual groups towards one another must be somewhat variable, we are still convinced that the chief figures at least, namely, those of the inner and outer associations and of the clang-reactions, do give, nevertheless, a pertinent picture of the nature of the reaction. The quantitative relationship of certain special groups to one another, e.g. the co-existences, is partly influenced by definite sources of error conditioned by the selection of the stimulus-words. It is obvious that reactions with nouns only show different relationships from reactions with mixed stimulus-words. Nevertheless our relative figures maintain their value, since all the subjects were examined by the same scheme of stimulus-words.

We have classified our material from different points of view ; we were, above all, interested in the question of the relationship of the educated to the uneducated. Aschaffenburg found among his educated subjects a relatively strong preponderance of outer over inner associations. On the other side, Ranschburg and Balint found a strong preponderance of the inner associations among the uneducated.

Here are the tables for the first and second hundred of normal associations :

UNEDUCATED

	Women		Men	
	1st hundred	2nd hundred	1st hundred	2nd hundred
Co-ordination. . . .	24·2 ⎫	26·2 ⎫	25·2 ⎫	21·5 ⎫
Predicate	18·8 ⎬ 44·0	22·0 ⎬ 49·3	15·4 ⎬ 41·7	16·8 ⎬ 39·4
Causal dependence . . .	1·0 ⎭	1·1 ⎭	1·1 ⎭	1·1 ⎭
Coexistence	27·2 ⎫	13·6 ⎫	21·7 ⎫	13·0 ⎫
Identity	3·3 ⎬ 52·8	6·8 ⎬ 46·1	7·8 ⎬ 55·7	12·2 ⎬ 55·7
Verbal-motor forms . .	22·3 ⎭	25·7 ⎭	26·2 ⎭	30·5 ⎭
Word-completion . . .	0·2 ⎫	0·5 ⎫	— ⎫	— ⎫
Clang	— ⎬ 0·3	0·3 ⎬ 1·4	0·7 ⎬ 0·7	0·5 ⎬ 0·6
Rhyme	0·1 ⎭	0·6 ⎭	— ⎭	0·1 ⎭
Indirect	0·6 ⎫	0·8 ⎫	0·5 ⎫	1·2 ⎫
Meaningless	0·3 ⎬ 2·1	0·2 ⎬ 2·6	0·1 ⎬ 1·4	0·2 ⎬ 3·6
Faults	1·2 ⎭	1·6 ⎭	0·8 ⎭	2·2 ⎭
Repetition of stimulus-word .	— ⎭	— ⎭	— ⎭	— ⎭
Egocentric reaction . .	0·8	0·8	2·0	1·5
Perseveration. . . .	1·5	0·6	1·0	0·4
Repetitions	10·2	8·8	14·1	10·5
Same grammatical form . .	63·2	54·7	60·1	58·4
Same number of syllables .	49·9	42·2	41·1	37·0
Alliteration	10·2	8·7	9·0	9·0
Consonance	12·3	12·2	11·1	14·0
Same ending	11·7	11·0	16·4	16·2
Total number of associations .	800	800	700	700
Total number of subjects .	8		7	

Our uneducated subjects were almost all male or female nurses in the asylum. We will agree that this selection of the uneducated was not a very fortunate one, for among the nursing staff there were a number of persons who were above the average level of education. The term half-educated would be, perhaps, better than uneducated. The level of culture and intelligence of the men is, on the whole, somewhat higher than that of the women.

The women exhibit a relatively high figure for inner associations ; remarkably enough, the number of inner associations does not rise considerably in the second half of the experiment, where the predicates show an increase. Moreover, in the second hundred there is an increase in the residual group and in the clang-reactions. With the increase of predicates and of verbal-motor forms must be connected the diminution of agreement in the grammatical forms. The figures for verbal linking are very high.

The men show, on the whole, a more superficial reaction type than the women. The second hundred does not perceptibly differ from the first, only the figures for indirect associations and consonance present a fairly striking increase.

EDUCATED

	Women		Men	
	1st hundred	2nd hundred	1st hundred	2nd hundred
Co-ordination. . . .	13·4 ⎫	14 ⎫	16·1 ⎫	16·5 ⎫
Predicate	21·8 ⎬ 36·9	18·6 ⎬ 33·2	17·3 ⎬ 34	22·2 ⎬ 39·5
Causal dependence . . .	1·7 ⎭	0·6 ⎭	0·6 ⎭	0·8 ⎭
Coexistence	16·5 ⎫	11·2 ⎫	18·2 ⎫	7·5 ⎫
Identity	2·7 ⎬ 57·2	6·7 ⎬ 58·9	3·2 ⎬ 56·6	8·3 ⎬ 49
Verbal-motor forms . .	38 ⎭	41 ⎭	35·2 ⎭	33·2 ⎭
Word-completion . . .	1 ⎫	2 ⎫	1·1 ⎫	1·1 ⎫
Clang	0·3 ⎬ 2·1	1·9 ⎬ 4·5	1·5 ⎬ 3·3	2·3 ⎬ 4
Rhyme	0·8 ⎭	0·6 ⎭	0·7 ⎭	0·6 ⎭
Indirect	0·9 ⎫	1 ⎫	2·8 ⎫	2·2 ⎫
Meaningless	0·1 ⎬ 2·9	0·1 ⎬ 2·4	0·7 ⎬ 5·2	1·2 ⎬ 6·1
Faults	1·9 ⎭	0·9 ⎭	1·7 ⎭	2·6 ⎭
Repetition of stimulus-word .	—	0·4	—	0·1
Egocentric reaction . .	2·7	1·5	3·6	2·6
Perseveration. . . .	0·8	0·5	3·1	1·8
Repetition	8·0	6·5	7·5	7·6
Same grammatical form . .	53·9	54	52·1	46·1
Same number of syllables .	43·9	39·2	37	32·6
Alliteration . . .	9·0	7·8	9·2	8·8
Consonance	14·6	15·2	15·1	16·2
Same ending	9·8	11·3	8·2	8·8
Total number of associations .	1100	1100	800	800
Total number of subjects .	11		8	

The increase of faults in the second hundred of both groups is perhaps attributable to the unfortunate accident that the number of stimulus-words with an emotional tone is rather larger in the second hundred than in the first. As we have seen, faults chiefly occur with such stimulus-words.

It is noticeable that the men present a greater number of egocentric reactions than the women, although they have a distinctly lesser number of predicates. The number of perseverations is partly connected with the egocentric reactions, i.e. with the inflow of personal wishes and valuations. In the women it is, indeed, somewhat higher than in the men; it changes, however, in accordance with the retrogression of egocentric judgments—a fact that will be confirmed later. We relate this condition to the fact that reactions with accentuated feeling have a tendency to perseveration, as we have demonstrated several times in the individual statements.

In the table on p. 127 one is most of all struck by the generally superficial type of the reactions. The men are almost all highly educated persons, the women likewise, with few exceptions, being highly cultivated.

The difference between the men and women is not considerable so far as the first three groups are concerned, with the exception of a slight preponderance of the inner associations among men over those among women, in which the co-ordinations especially participate. There are considerable differences in the residual group where the high figures in men for *indirect associations* are striking, more than double that of the women. The average of the clang-reactions is also somewhat higher in men than in women. The suspected inverse ratio between indirect associations and clang-reactions is thus again suggested here :

	Women		Men	
	1st hundred	2nd hundred	1st hundred	2nd hundred
Clang-reactions . .	2·9	2·4	5·2	6·1
Indirect associations .	0·9	1·0	2·8	2·2

We shall discuss this phenomenon in our critique of the distraction averages.

The men exceed the women in the *egocentric reactions* also. The number of *perseverations* accords here, as among the uneducated, with those of the egocentric reactions, a further proof of the largely affective nature of the perseverations (*N.B.*, only in the normal experiment).

The differences which separate educated and uneducated are best illustrated by placing the average figures for the two groups in parallel tables.

	Educated	Uneducated
Co-ordination.	15 ⎫	24·2 ⎫
Predicate	19·3 ⎬ 35·8	18·2 ⎬ 43·4
Causal dependence	0·9 ⎭	1· ⎭
Coexistence	13·3 ⎫	18·8 ⎫
Identity	5·2 ⎬ 55·3	7·7 ⎬ 52·4
Verbal-motor forms . . .	36·8 ⎭	26·1 ⎭
Word-completion	1·3 ⎫	0·1 ⎫
Clang	1·5 ⎬ 3·4	0·3 ⎬ 0·5
Rhyme	0·6 ⎭	0·1 ⎭
Indirect	1·7 ⎫	0·7 ⎫
Meaningless	0·5 ⎬ 4·0	0·1 ⎬ 2·2
Faults	1·7 ⎭	1·4 ⎭
Repetition of stimulus-word . .	0·1 ⎭	— ⎭
Egocentric reaction . . .	2·4	1·1
Perseveration.	1·5	0·8
Repetitions	7·3	10·9
Same grammatical form . . .	51·5	59·2
Same number of syllables . .	38·2	42·5
Alliteration	8·7	9·3
Consonance	10·2	12·3
Same ending	9·5	13·8
Total number of associations . .	3800	3000
Total number of subjects . .	19	15

The educated show a distinctly shallower type than the uneducated. This difference can be graphically described by the statement : *The educated exhibit a distraction phenomenon as compared with the uneducated.*

Put the case thus : the figures for the uneducated being those of a subject in normal experiment, the figures of the educated behave like those obtained in a distraction experiment. The clang-reactions and the figures for the residual group are correspondingly increased just as we have found in the individual tables.

Whence comes this difference ? It cannot be assumed that the educated really think more superficially than the uneducated ; that would be nonsense. It can merely be assumed that so far as the experiments are concerned they think more superficially than the uneducated. That seems to be really the case, and this to us seems to be the explanation of the reaction type. The following points must be considered in favour of this postulate :

(1) The agreement in grammatical forms and number of syllables between stimulus-word and reaction is decidedly greater among the uneducated. This fact speaks for the uneducated adhering more closely to the stimulus-word—being more influenced by it—than the educated.

(2) The number of meaningless reactions is considerably smaller among the uneducated. The latter controls himself more, i.e. he pays more attention to the reaction.

(3) The uneducated exceeds the educated in the number of co-existences, which are chiefly constructed from spatial perceptions ; i.e. the uneducated takes the trouble to image distinctly the object named by the stimulus-word, so that he must naturally associate what is co-existent with it. The educated, on the other hand, has fewer co-existences because he contents himself with joining verbal forms to one another.

(5) The uneducated has about one-half fewer *egocentric reactions* than the educated. This suggests that he lets himself go much less and allows fewer disguised subjective wishes and valuations to break through. He strives after the utmost possible objective apprehension of the stimulus-word.

(6) One great point is that among the educated the clang-reactions are almost seven times as numerous. Here the slackness is most distinctly evident. The subject who takes most care makes no clang-reactions, as it were,[1] except for some specific adaptation.

On these grounds we regard it as proved that the difference between the educated and uneducated reaction types, so far as it is expressed in these figures, is entirely functional, and has only the significance of a phenomenon of attention.

If it be permissible to grade the degree of attention by the figures of the clang-reaction, of the residual group and of the verbal-motor forms, the uneducated women stand highest in the work of attention, educated men the lowest. This fact is evident if we examine the groups according to sex from the above points of view.

Whence arises the difference of attention between educated and uneducated ?[2]

(1) The experiment is something foreign to the uneducated. Naturally it is for him something more unknown and more difficult than for the educated, who is in a position to survey the

---

[1] Naturally with the exception of any particular adjustment.

[2] By this must be understood a difference of attention in the quantitative sense only ; it is not any kind of qualitative dissimilarity.

range of the experiment, and who must feel at once more at ease in an intellectual activity than the uneducated. The excitation of the uneducated is thus greater and more general in the experiment, and he therefore reacts with greater strain.

(2) Words are called out to the subject without any sentence connecting them. Under ordinary circumstances, if something is called out to one in this way it is commonly a command or a question. The uneducated is, contrary to the educated, not used to being concerned with individual words apart from sentences, more especially if he has never learnt a foreign language out of books. The stimulus-word has thus something uncanny for the uneducated. Influenced by habit he instinctively apprehends it as a question, with the intensity of attention necessary for a proper answer. The stimulus-word to the uneducated is something to which he must frame for himself a connecting question, which he then answers.[1]

(3) The uneducated only knows words, as it were, in a connected sentence, especially when they occur as an acoustic phenomenon. Connected in a sentence the words always have a meaning ; the uneducated person knows the word less as a mere " word " or verbal sign than as something with a meaning. Hence single words are apprehended by the uneducated according to their meaning in some imaginary sentence ; to the educated the stimulus-word remains merely a word without any special meaning.[2]

Recapitulating, we may say that the uneducated person demonstrates, appropriately to his lower education, a narrower conception of the experiment, especially of the stimulus-words called out, than the educated, who approaches the question much more coldly and in a more businesslike fashion. In other words : the uneducated person shows a certain tendency to assimilate the stimulus-word in the sense of a question because usually verbal ejaculations denote a question. This relationship to the stimulus-word appears distinctly in certain pathological states, where the association experiment is nothing but a long conversation of 2 × 200 sentences on some emotionally charged theme. From these considerations it follows that

[1] It can be said generally that the more uneducated and unintelligent the subject is the more he will conceive the stimulus-word as a question. This is seen most clearly with idiots, who, with few exceptions, always conceive the stimulus-word as a question and thus give, in the reaction, a definition or explanation thereof.

[2] The educated person, however, proceeds in the same manner as the uneducated when it is a question of the words of a language he has never seen printed or written. If the stimulus-words are called out in dialect, the educated person has occasionally trouble in understanding them just because he is accustomed to these dialect words in connected sentences only.

the uneducated bestows greater attention, chiefly because the significance of the stimulus-word influences him more than it does the educated.

The difference between educated and uneducated is the different conception of the stimulus-word. This difference in principle might allow us to separate off two rather vague groups. This separation is, however, so general that it does not take into consideration other essential differences in the reaction types. We have, therefore, endeavoured to discover other and finer bases for a classification. We asked ourselves : Are there other universal factors, apart from the phenomena of attention, which visibly influence the reaction ?

One chief factor lies in the individual temperament. The difference in apprehension which we have just discussed is an intellectual or associative disposition which would be just the same in persons of the most diverse characters. But it is different with temperament. From our experiments two well-characterized types emerge :

(1) A type who in the reaction makes use of subjective experiences, often emotionally charged.

(2) A type who shows in the reaction an objective, impersonal habit of mind.

The first type is characterized by the occurrence of pictures of personal memories, which are often markedly emotional. The latter type preferably relates words to words or concepts to concepts, the personal element playing quite a subordinate rôle in the reaction. This may be termed the objective type.

The first type is conveniently divided into three groups :

α. *The stimulus-image evoked by the stimulus-word acts through its emotional tone.* Usually the emotional tone which the stimulus-image possesses at once excites a memory-complex which is completely equal to it. The reaction then follows under the constellation of this complex. In practice individuals of this type can be separated from others, at least in extreme cases. We term this type the *complex constellation type.*

β. *The image aroused by the stimulus-word is an individual reminiscence generally taken from daily life.* The reaction contains the image, or at least is markedly constellated by it. We term this the *simple constellation type.*[1]

---

[1] We again repeat that in this classification we merely wish to mark the quite distinct and obvious differences in the manner of reaction. We know very well that fundamentally every person belongs to the complex constellation type, for no reaction is accidental but is invariably conditioned by the psychological past of the individual. What we wish to elucidate by our classification is only the more or less of the subjective conditioning so far as it is clearly expressed in the reactions.

γ. *The image aroused by the stimulus-word acts through one or other of the attributes associated with it* (partly sensual portions of the presentation, partly emotional tones). Presumably in this type the stimulus presentation is primarily very plastic, so that first one, then another trait is thrust forward, by means of which the reaction is conditioned ; it thus generally contains a predicate of the object designated by the stimulus-word. We term this the *predicate type.*

What is common to types α, β, γ, as opposed to the objective type (2), is a strong accentuation of the individual, personal part of the reaction independent of the stimulus-word. We can therefore say that the difference between types (1) and (2) is the egocentricity of the adjustment.

These points of view elucidate the universal psychological laws which govern our experiment. This is far from disclosing all the roots of the complications in the reactions.

In the egocentric adaptation we have tacitly assumed that the reaction is a more or less distinct symbol of inner processes. So long as we know that the subject is expressing himself freely we can grant this postulate *cum grano salis.* But the picture of the reaction is altered when the egocentric adaptation leads to the raising of emotionally charged complexes which the subject will not reveal.[1] This is the case in the complex constellation type ; e.g. the stimulus-word raises the complex of an unhappy love affair hidden as far as possible. Were the subject now to react according to his inner pictures he would express in the reaction a piece of his complex, which he would thus reveal. The concealment of an affect is always characterized by a quite peculiar adjustment, a peculiar condition of feeling. Perhaps without the occurrence of any conscious critique, the complex as it emerges is immediately repressed again by the conscious emotional tendency of not wishing to reveal something—a tendency giving rise to discordant inhibitions.

Naturally this process of repression can be carried out much more consciously (or even more unconsciously, as in hysteria). In the place of the repressed complex presentation another association is substituted and expressed, one corresponding to the momentary feeling of the tendency. Thus the real inner association is concealed from the world and the secret preserved. For the experimenter who perhaps does not enjoy the subject's full confidence it may be extraordinarily difficult in some cases to

[1] We have convinced ourselves by numerous experiments that this "will not reveal" is by no means always a conscious not-willing, but very frequently an unconscious inhibition which in most cases causes a prolongation of the reaction-time also.

distinguish whether there is something concealed or not. The distinction may be impossible in some people who are able to exercise complete self-control. But in most cases the subject betrays himself after a little time. In accordance with the laws set forth above, certain phenomena occur which betray the repressed complex. Here we want to set aside the prolongation of the reaction-time, which is a regular occurrence.[1]

Repression is betrayed :

(1) By an unusual and suspicious setting of the reaction which the reaction-word by itself does not explain, but whose peculiar character must be constellated by an X. Occasionally this X can be read directly from the peculiarly forced nature of the reaction. Such reactions frequently appear in sentence form.

(2) By the phenomena of attention. A subject who is taking the stimulus-word altogether in the sense of a " question," and reproducing a series of superior associations, suddenly reacts by a clang or other strikingly superficial association, in the absence of any external disturbance. The occurrence is suspicious ; some inner disturbance, some inner distraction, must have taken place. The subject perhaps gives no information. The phenomenon is repeated at a similar stimulus-word. We are now fairly certain that there is something behind this. This suspicion has seldom led us astray. A complex has suddenly emerged, has drawn a certain intensity of attention to itself ; meanwhile the reaction takes place, and in consequence of the disturbance of attention the reaction can be only a superficial one.

(3) By fault. The emerging complex absorbs all the attention, so that the reaction is either forgotten or, in the absence of every association, cannot be expressed.

(4) By perseveration. In this case the critical reaction may be quite unnoticeable, but the succeeding one bears an abnormal character, so that the preceding reaction has undertaken the part of the constellating X. The perseverating factor is the affect excited by the preceding association.[2]

(5) By assimilation of the stimulus-word. For no obvious reason the stimulus-word is taken in a peculiarly rare sense,

---

[1] Chapter v deals with the question of the reaction-times.

[2] A subject whose mental life was influenced by an unpleasant financial transaction reacted with normal time to *ill — poor* and to the next reaction, *vain — tane,* with a prolonged reaction-time. Without obvious reason the association is a senseless rhyme. Clang associations and rhymes only occur in this subject in " critical " situations." *Poor* has a very special affective significance for him; attention remains attached to the aroused complex, thus creating disturbance by inner distraction for the succeeding reaction.

or it is misunderstood in some remarkable way in accordance with the affective idea which fills up consciousness.[1]

These points are the chief criteria of a concealed complex.[2]

We have purposely devoted so much attention to the review of these finer psychological phenomena, for the affective processes whose traces we have followed with the utmost possible care in the normal reaction play the leading rôle in pathological reactions. This we shall see subsequently in detail. What may be, perhaps, put aside in the normal reaction as capriciousness is seen to be the most important factor in pathological reactions. Provisionally, we place the greatest value upon the knowledge that the reactions are an extremely refined reagent for affective processes in particular, and for the individual outlook of the subjects in general.

In illustration of our arguments we append associations of the six chief types.

1. Objective Type

The reactions of a subject whose adjustment is essentially objective. The conception of the stimulus-word in the sense of a question is in the background. There is a great tendency merely to group the words serially, partly according to the law of similarity, partly according to verbally current connexions (No. 1 of Educated Men).

Christmas	Easter	Friendly	painful
Sunday	Monday	Cut	knife
Winter	spring	Crown	rich
Lake	sea	Saw	bone
Pupil	teacher	Prison	custody
Father	mother	Divorce	avoid
Table	leg	Ill	weak
Head	kerchief	Song	carol
Ink	pen	Potato	salt
Needle	holder	Easy	chair
Bread	earn	Coffee	drink
Lamp	shade	Sacrifice	bring
Dream	froth	Wedding	feast
Book	knife	Grandmother	father

[1] The subject quoted in the previous foot-note reacts to *pity — poor* (*poor* is a special affect). The succeeding association runs : *monkey — much*. Again a perseveration of the financial complex, monkey being assimilated as money, although this individual has been well acquainted for some time with all the stimulus-words in our scheme.

[2] In some subjects *repetitions* have also a certain significance as the indirect expression of the complex (in the special sections we have drawn attention to this more than once). Certain words are frequently repeated which are more or less closely associated with the complex, or represent it indirectly.

Tree	beat	Angry	naughty
Mountain	green	Clap	hands
Paper	cutter	Year	month
Book	read	Threaten	fist
School	attend	Long	narrow
To sing	to write	Rich	poor
Ring	finger	Sorrow	joy
Tooth	tune	Eye	tooth
Window	pane	Youth	play
Frog	leg	Inn	Goat and Compasses
Sweet	sour	Family	scandal
Ride	drive	Trouble	sorrow
Pay attention	pay heed	Once	panic
Faust	Goethe	Wonder	beyond wonder
People	insurrection	Blood	revenge
Murderer	blood	Rose	campion
Everywhere	I am at home	Choose	choice
Reckon	measure	Justice	violence
Kiss	mouth	Must	no one must must
Bad	right	Hope	be not confounded
Bond	of love	Small	all
Ripe	fruit	Unjust	faithlessness
Giver	friend	Welt	Schmerz
Play	the bells	Strange	unknown
Way	to Canossa	Slate	write
Quarrel	strife	Growl	dog
Blue	red	Knob	stick
Flower	cabbage	Fruit	eat
Cherry	stone	Sly	fox
Asylum	keeper	Handle	ornament
Piano	play	Hay	straw
Oven	town	Clean	mean
Walk	go	Guess	W. (name of an acquaintance who has suggested a particular hypothesis).
Cook	eat		
Water	drink		
Dance	music		
Cat	mouse	Chieftain	full of blood and wounds
Dozen	by the dozen		
Dark	light	At home	it's good
Heart	part	Brown	thorn
Bird	nest	Idle	lazy
White	black	Vinegar	sour
Play	cards	Hot	cold
Kaiser	Wilhelm	Pit	fall
Moon	shine	Nausea	horrible
Beat	throw	Resin	rivet
Fire	house	Throat	sew up
Shooting	star	Steep	mountain
Stroke	cat	Swing	swinging
Grand	magnificent	Fetch	carry
Child	dog	Skull	formation
Sofa	lie	Use	can
Wild	animal	Stamp	timbre
Tears	flow	Faithful	German

The subject is a doctor ; a few medical terms such as " needle-holder " and " skull-formation " point to this. We do not reckon the reactions constellated by the profession among the " constellations," using this term in the narrower sense.   Reactions of that kind are not subjective, belonging not to the individual alone, but more or less to a whole class.   The only subjective constellation is *guess — W.*

(*b*) The reactions of a person whose adjustment is objective and in whom the stimulus-word works much more by its meaning than in the foregoing.   The tendency is to give the most correct reaction possible (No. 4 of Uneducated Women).

Table	chair	Friendly	angry
Head	arm	File	hammer
Ink	pen	Crown	helmet
Needle	thread	Hit	bite
Bread	cheese	Star	sun
Lamp	candle	Caress	beat
Tree	bush	Paint	oil
Mountain	valley	Thank	ask
Wood	coal	Rough	fine
Salt	meal	Smell	taste
Dream	sleep	Prison	jail
Paper	stuff	Divide	together
Book	newspaper	Potato	bread
School	church	Fall	catch
Ripe	ring	Nausea	taste
Tooth	mouth	Resin	pitch
Sing	shout	Lazy	work
Window	floor	Coffee	milk
Frog	stork	Sacrifice	saviour
Flower	grass	Wedding	funeral
Cherry	peach	Angry	contented
Asylum	school	Soldier	civilian
Piano	violin	Clap	sing
Fern	rose	Threaten	hit
Walk	jump	Behaviour	polite
Water	wine	Fall	level
Dance	sing	Suffer	healthy
Dozen	ten	Youth	age
Heart	warm	Inn	hotel
Bird	cat	Family	man
Swim	walk	Fist	hand
Play	sing	People	household (interpolate " family ")
Emperor	king		
Moon	star	To pay attention	to listen
Haughty	gentle	Murderer	robber
Kindle	extinguish	Everywhere	here
Magnificent	wonderful	Kiss	flatter
Child	woman	Bad	good
Ride	drive	Ripe	bitter (interpolate " sweet ")
Hope	joy		

Band	stuff	Pray	believe
Ground	floor	Freedom	caught
Gait	jump	World	people
Quarrel	contented	Strange	home
Sofa	chair	Growl	bite
Love	hate	Knot	cord
Wild	tame	False	faithful
Tears	laughter	Helmet	sword
Indulge	bitter	Plate	dish
Wonder	nature	Hay	grass
Blood	man	Clean	neat
Wreath	flowers	Suppose	doubt
Choose	meet	Head	arm
Justice	false	Home	away
Violence	willing	Vinegar	wine
Revenge	freedom	Swing	throw

The subject is a nurse in our asylum. Subjective factors are entirely absent in the reactions. The tone is extraordinarily objective and quiet. In contrast with the previous case, one may notice that the meaning of the stimulus-word is here the exciting factor, as is seen by the many contrasts.

2. Egocentric Attitude

(a) Simple Constellation Type

The reactions of a person in whom numerous subjective experiences were made use of in the experiment. The attitude is egocentric in so far as the stimulus-word arouses preferably subjective memories (No. 4 of Educated Men).

Father	anxious (he is the father of a child just born)	Tausend (Thousand)	Basle (a Basle student friend is called Tausig, which is the dialect form of Tausend (1000). The stimulus-word was, of course, called out in High German but assimilated in its dialect form)
Walk	L. (name of a patient who walks a great deal)		
Head	round		
Ink	acid (interpolate " red — litmus ")		
Cook	cookery course		
Water	supply		
Needle	ear	Ring	A II-garden (a ring had been found in that garden)
Dance	concert hall (hall in which the dances of the asylum are held)	Zahn	Göschenen (Zahn, the writer, lives at Göschenen)
Bread	machine bakery		
Lamp	smells		
Tree	F. (name of a friend who is connected with a definite event)	Window	opening
		Frog	tree-frog
		Like	ball
Dark	room (he is an enthusiastic amateur photographer)	Flower	rose
		Son	little one (he has just had a son)

Mountain	Ütli mountain
Heart	valvular disease
Hair	falling out
Bird	paw (interpolate " claw")
Salz	Rhine fields where there are salt-pits
Swim	L. (name of a patient who attended the swimming-bath frequently)
Dream	R. (name of a colleague who was at the time engaged in dream analysis)
Paper	fraud (papers in the sense of documents about a case of fraud)
White	malaria (a patient called White suffered from malaria)
Wood	ebony-wood
Game	Halma (much played at the time in the wards)
Book	-seller
Pencil	Koh-i-noor (he uses this kind of pencil)
Thirteen	shorthand (interpolate write; he is greatly taken up with shorthand)
School	S. (name of the place where he went to school)
Sing	Miss S. (name of a singer who was then in the asylum)
Strange	stranger
Growl	bulldog
Rude	East Swiss (memory of student days)
Coffee	Mocha
Fruit	steal
Sacrifice	L. (name of an ill painter who preferably painted sacrificial scenes)
False	trap
Helm	house (public building in Zurich)
Wedding	no alcohol (he is a total abstainer)
Misery	hunger
Hay	Hayward (name of a place)
Asylum	R. (an asylum for feeble-minded children)

Wild	dentist (" Wild " is the name of a dentist)
Warder	R. (name of a warder)
Tears	vale
Fern	tapeworm
War	rumour
Oven	nuisance
Faithful	doggy
Once	again shorthand (see above)
Wonder	Lourdes
Bloody	English (in England the word must not be used)
Must	Lessing (interpolate " well-known quotation from Lessing ")
Rights	and duties
Revenge	thirst
Hope	pregnancy (constellation intelligible from earlier statements)
Lock	and barrel
Small	warder (Small is the name of a warder)
Arm	W. (name of a patient who injured his arm)
Play	thing
Liberty	statue (he had been admiring the Statue of Liberty in New York)
Blue	grotto in Capri
Wrong	confine (constellation from daily intercourse with querulous patients)
Sorrow	sorrowful
Stern	C (Stern is the name of a patient who was in C block)
Take care	Association experiments (momentary constellation)
Stroke	kitten
Nature	R. (patient's name)
Grand	Grant (patient's name: a clang-association)
Folk	Wundt's *Folk-Psychology* (a work recently acquired by the asylum)
Sweet	banana (cp. the reaction " wood-ebony." He has recently given a lecture on journeys in Africa)

Grand- mother	dead	Family	family day
Angry	R. (name of a patient with moral deficiency)	Murderer	G. (name of a murderer who was just then under observation in
Raspberry	garden (the raspberries in the asylum garden)	Friendly	the asylum) H. (name of an acquaint-
Need	B. (name of a colleague)		ance)
Year	and day	Everywhere	every man
Home	newspaper (*Home* is the name of a newspaper)	Hover	C. (name of a well-known aeroplanist)
Threaten	threatmonger (nickname of a patient who fre-	Count Rank	counterfeit M. (name of a person who made a joke about the
Vinegar	quently utters threats) home-made		work rank)
Trap	mouse-trap	Skull	occiput
Sour	yeast	Row	A 1 (Row is the name
Throat	epiglottis		of a patient in block
Youth	Munich (newspaper *Ju-* *gend* [youth], published	Warn	A 1)
	in Munich)	Analyse	sulphuric acid
Hit	name of a doctor who was	Prison	police-station (in Zürich)
	hit by a patient)	Ill	diabetes

The characteristic of this type is the emergence of numerous
subjective experiences, mostly of recent date, and belonging for
the most part to the daily round. It is self-evident that despite
the objective character of the constellations on the whole, some
are intermingled belonging to an emotionally toned complex.
But, compared with the others, these are relatively few and
part of them certainly well concealed. The recently experienced
joy of a father is seen in *father — anxious, hope — pregnancy,
son — little one*. This emotional-toned diminutive seems to us
to resound also in the reactions *caress — kitten, faithful — doggy*.

(b) Complex Constellation Type

(1) Reactions of a patient in whom an emotional complex
occurs undisguised in the reactions. The significance of the
stimulus-word is made to relate to the complex (No. 7 of Educated
Men).

Wood	hit	To idle	delightful
Dream	studies (simple constella- tion)	Angry Come	I am not with us to theatre (defi-
Dance	F. (hotel where dancing goes on)	Year	nite theatre) 1904
Copy-book	pen	Family	V. (subject's own family)
Paper	line	Take care	I should
Pencil	big	At last	it will end
School	bench	People	very worthy
Sing	choir	Murderer	in C (a certain criminal
Walk	long way		lunatic in section C)

Dark	room
Heart	red
Bird	feathers
To set fire	S. (name of a pyro-maniac)
Tooth	teeth
Window	frame
Flower	plant
Frog	hops
Asylum	big
Piano	I can't play
Warder	B. (name of a certain warder)
Oven	wood
Swell	fie !
Magnificent	ah !
Child	children
Dark red	again ah !
Rough	table
Divorce	name of a certain mental patient who has been divorced
Potato	mashed
Son	father and son (on account of his love affair he has had unpleasant discussions with his family)
Wild	mother (wild = angry here)
Tears	she has now (i.e. the forsaken sweetheart)
Protection	I cannot offer her
War	if there were but
Faith	I have not held
Once	and never again
Miracle	must happen
Blood	she's anæmic
Wreath	on the coffin
Choose	another
Separate	I need not
Right	she is not
Must	I must not
Violence	I do none to her
Revenge	oh no !
Hope	I know none
Small	not at all !
Pray	perhaps—
Love	I did love her
Wool	a woman's dress
Old	perhaps—
Freedom	she could have
Wrong	I was not

Every-where	is K. (name of an active catatoniac)
Do accounts	I cannot
Kiss	always again \ complex of
Natural	glorious
Bad	no
Time	not know
Ripe	I am for it

(bracketed note: complex of a love affair which had recently come to an end)

Row	soldiers
Land	and houses
Game	child
Poor	as a beggar
Stern	Miss Stern (definite person)
Ride	track
Friendly	very nice
Crown	queen
Shrill	woe
Quarrel	bah !
Sofa	soft seat
Love	ah !
World	wide
Strange	she is now
Slate-pencil	she is a teacher
Growl	poodle
Knob	stick
False	fair (interpolate " a lady" who is false and fair)
Helmet	fire brigade
Clothes	a woman's dress
Softly	she comes
Gallant	up the steps
Plate	on the table
Misery	she cries
Hay	there's a peasant there
Raspberries	in the wood
Home	(in D., where the loved one lives)
Hedge	fence
Indolent	often (i.e. she is often indolent)
Woo	a woman
Hot	live
Conscious	yes, in supraconsciousness
Vinegar	sour
Trap	in
Nausea	so so
Row	not on that account
Resin	hair
Trim	beautiful and gay
Omen	bad

Characteristic of these reactions is the strong emotionally toned complex. The stimulus-word is assimilated in the form of a conversation ; the experiment thus bears the stamp of an interrogatory in which the consciousness of the situation of the moment has, so far as the subject is concerned, receded slightly into the background. That explains the somewhat abnormal character of such a conversation. Reactions of this nature are due to extreme sensitiveness. The relatively numerous interjections and the egocentric relationships, even those unrelated to the complex, point to the same thing. The subject's egocentricity is very distinctly shown in everything. He is mentally quite healthy, and at another time would probably present a much more objective type. The abnormal character of the reaction is to be attributed entirely to the temporary, but ruling, affect. We may here remark that this abnormal state evoked by affect is the usual prototype of the hysterical anomalies in reaction.

(2) A good instance of a concealed emotional complex is No. 1 of Uneducated Women. We refer the reader to the associations already recorded in the special part.

(c) Predicate Type

Reactions of a person who evaluates the object denoted by the stimulus-word from the personal standpoint (No. 7 of Educated Women).

Sea	beautiful nature	Fern	beautiful wood
Schoolboy	industrious	Stove	glorious in cold weather
Father	something majestic, good, sacred	Work	must sometimes
		To cook	irksome
Needle	work	Water	glorious
Bread	best form of food	Dance	pleasant when one's young
Lamp	work		
Tree	something beautiful	Cat	sneak
Mountain	terrible, climbing is nicer	Dozen	exact, order
		Dark	horrible
Hair	head-dress	Heart	beating
Salt	strengthening food	Bird	glorious, fly
Wood	fire	Swim	glorious
Dream	many events	White	hard, shining
Copy-book	much work for the children	Game	pleasure
		Thirteen	clumsy
Paper	blessed because we write upon it	Moon	beautiful
		Hit	needless
Book	joy	Kindle	art, till one could
School	joy	Star	magnificent
Sing	beautiful	Grand	pompous
Ring	stupid thing	Child	God's gift
Tooth	glad that one has no more	Sweet	pleasant
		Ride	dangerous

Frog	something unnecessary	Friendly	duty
Flower	joy	Crown	unnecessary
Cherry	good fruit	Raw	winter
Asylum	narrow	Smell	sometimes, slums
Piano	troublesome	Shining	hurts
Warder	great esteem	Ill	hurts

The characteristic of this kind of reacting is an unusually marked emergence of what is personal, leading to a constant valuation of the object, mostly in reference to the self.

3. Sex Difference in the Normal Experiment

We have also considered the figures from the point of view of sex difference, and calculated the corresponding averages.

	Men	Women
Co-ordination.	19·8 ⎫	19·4 ⎫
Predicate	17·9 ⎬ 38·6	20·3 ⎬ 40·7
Causal dependence .	0·9 ⎭	1 ⎭
Coexistence	15 ⎫	17·1 ⎫
Identity	7·8 ⎬ 54	4·8 ⎬ 53·6
Verbal-motor forms	31·2 ⎭	31·7 ⎭
Word-completion	0·5 ⎫	0·9 ⎫
Clang .	1·2 ⎬ 2	0·6 ⎬ 2
Rhyme .	0·3 ⎭	0·5 ⎭
Indirect	1·6 ⎫	0·8 ⎫
Meaningless .	0·5 ⎬ 3·9	0·1 ⎬ 2·4
Faults .	1·8 ⎭	1·4 ⎭
Repetition of stimulus-word		0·1
Egocentric reaction	2·2	1·3
Perseveration.	1·5	0·8
Repetitions .	9·9	8·2
Same grammatical form .	54·3	56·4
Same number of syllables	37	43·7
Alliteration .	9·1	8·9
Consonance .	14·0	13·5
Same ending .	12·4	10·9
Total number of associations .	3000 associations	3800 associations

We are surprised when we glance at the figures to see the minimal difference between the two sexes. With few exceptions the figures are in substantial agreement; at any rate, there is an absence of the distinct difference which, e.g., separates the

group of the educated from the uneducated. The type is somewhat more superficial in the men than in the women ; the men
have rather more clang-associations, also more indirect associations—phenomena which can be directly connected with the
more superficial type. The greater number of egocentric reactions
and perseverations appears, from the considerations adduced,
to be connected with the more unembarrassed behaviour of the
men. The difference in the figures for agreement in grammatical
form and number of syllables is analogous to the corresponding
difference between the educated and the uneducated. This
must be due to the fact that in our uneducated male subjects
the level of culture is somewhat higher than in the corresponding
female subjects. These figures in the normal experiment have
disclosed nothing typical of the psychology of women, which
must not, however, be regarded as evidence that no differences
exist. Our method of investigation is obviously much too coarse
a one to discover such fine differences.

4. AVERAGES OF THE DISTRACTION EXPERIMENTS

We give here a recapitulation of the average figures from the
distraction experiments. For easier comparison we retabulate
the averages in the normal state (see Tables on pp. 145, 146,
and 147).

The figures in the distraction experiment show a progressively
more superficial type of reaction than in the normal state. The
principle change is quite obvious : the inner associations recede
during distraction in favour of the increasing outer associations
or clang-reactions.

In surveying the figures for internal association we see that
the women have higher figures in this group than the men. The
lowest figures occur among the men. The objection that the
women start with a higher number of inner associations in the
normal state is only true of the uneducated women. Educated
women have a rather more superficial type of reaction in the
normal state than educated men. The fact that the number of
inner associations in women does not fall so low as in men means
that the women have responded less than the men to the aims
of the experiment. The parallel columns of the minus differences
for inner association show clearly that the experiment appealed
less to the women.

The remaining differences cannot, unfortunately, be presented
with equal evidence, for they are divided into three groups, the
contents of which are of varying psychological value. Hence
the figures for inner associations are the best test for the amount

UNEDUCATED

	Women			Men		
	Normal	Outer distraction		Normal	Outer distraction	
		60 metro.	100 metro.		60 metro.	100 metro.
ɔ-ordination . .	25·2 ⎫	19 ⎫	15·7 ⎫	23·2 ⎫	20·8 ⎫	14·8 ⎫
ʀedicate . .	20·4 ⎬ 46·6	20·6 ⎬ 40·3	19 ⎬ 35·2	16·1 ⎬ 40·5	10 ⎬ 30·8	12·8 ⎬ 27·6
ᴀusal dependence .	1 ⎭	0·7 ⎭	0·5 ⎭	1·1 ⎭	— ⎭	— ⎭
ɔexistence . .	20·4 ⎫	18·2 ⎫	18·5 ⎫	17·3 ⎫	19·1 ⎫	12·5 ⎫
ʟentity . .	5 ⎬ 49·4	9·7 ⎬ 52·2	9·2 ⎬ 61	10 ⎬ 55·6	17·4 ⎬ 58·5	15·1 ⎬ 63·3
ᴇrbal-motor forms	24 ⎭	24·3 ⎭	33·3 ⎭	28·3 ⎭	22 ⎭	35·7 ⎭
ʿord-completion .	0·3 ⎫	0·2 ⎫	0·5 ⎫	— ⎫	— ⎫	— ⎫
ᴀng . . .	0·1 ⎬ 0·7	1·7 ⎬ 2·9	2·0 ⎬ 3·7	0·6 ⎬ 0·6	1·4 ⎬ 3·1	0·8 ⎬ 1
ʜyme . . .	0·3 ⎭	1 ⎭	1·2 ⎭	— ⎭	1·7 ⎭	0·2 ⎭
ᴅdirect . . .	0·7 ⎫	1·2 ⎫	0·7 ⎫	0·8 ⎫	3·4 ⎫	1·4 ⎫
ᴇaningless . .	0·2 ⎬	0·7 ⎬	0·2 ⎬	0·1 ⎬	1·1 ⎬	2 ⎬
ᴜults . . .	1·4 ⎬ 2·3	1·0 ⎬ 3·4	0·5 ⎬ 1·4	1·5 ⎬ 2·4	1·4 ⎬ 6·4	2·2 ⎬ 7·6
ᴇpetition of stimu- lus-word . .	— ⎭	0·5 ⎭	— ⎭	— ⎭	0·5 ⎭	2 ⎭
ᴣocentric reaction .	0·5	0·5	0·5	1·7	—	—
ᴇrseveration . .	1	2	2·5	0·7	0·5	—
ᴇpetitions . .	9·5	8·5	3	12·3	5·1	4
ᴀme grammatical form . . .	58·9	62·5	62·2	59·5	67·7	64·5
ᴀme number of syl- lables . . .	46	47·5	44·7	39	45·7	48·2
ʟiteration . .	8·4	11	11·2	9·2	8	12·4
ᴀnsonance . .	12·2	18·5	15·7	12·5	23·4	18·8
ᴀme ending . .	11·3	11·7	16·0	16·3	14·3	18·2
ᴛal number of asso- ᴄiations . .	1600	400	400	1400	350	350
ᴛal number of sub- ᴇcts . . .	8	8	8	7	7	7

EDUCATED

	Women			
	Normal	Inner distraction	Outer distraction	
			60 metro.	100 metro.
Co-ordination	13·7 ⎫	14 ⎫	11·7 ⎫	11·5 ⎫
Predicate	20·2 ⎬ 35	15 ⎬ 29·5	21·2 ⎬ 33·6	19 ⎬ 30·7
Causal dependence	1·1 ⎭	0·5 ⎭	0·7 ⎭	0·2 ⎭
Coexistence	13·8 ⎫	10 ⎫	12·7 ⎫	8 ⎫
Identity	4·7 ⎬ 58	4·3 ⎬ 44·8	10·5 ⎬ 48·9	9 ⎬ 56
Verbal-motor forms	39·5 ⎭	30·5 ⎭	25·7 ⎭	39 ⎭
Word-completion	1·5 ⎫	4·5 ⎫	3 ⎫	2·2 ⎫
Clang	1·1 ⎬ 3·3	5·1 ⎬ 11·6	5·5 ⎬ 10·2	6·5 ⎬ 9·2
Rhyme	0·7 ⎭	2 ⎭	1·7 ⎭	0·5 ⎭
Indirect associations	0·9 ⎫	1·6 ⎫	1 ⎫	0·2 ⎫
Meaningless	0·1 ⎬	0·5 ⎬	1·2 ⎬	1·5 ⎬
Faults	1·4 ⎬ 2·6	1·1 ⎬ 3·8	2 ⎬ 5·7	1·5 ⎬ 3·9
Repetition of stimulus-word	0·2 ⎭	0·6 ⎭	0·5 ⎭	0·7 ⎭
Egocentric	2·1	1	1·2	1
Perseveration	0·6	1·0	2·2	1·7
Repetitions	7·2	3·5	6·5	5
Same grammatical form	53·9	59	54	53
Same number of syllables	41·5	45·5	47·7	43·5
Alliteration	8·4	11·1	11·7	12·5
Consonance	14·9	19·3	19	20·6
Same ending	10·5	11·8	11·7	13
Total number of associations	2200	500	400	400
Total number of subjects	11	6	8	8

EDUCATED

	Men			
	Normal	Inner distraction	Outer distraction	
			60 metro.	100 metro.
Co-ordination . . .	16·3 ⎫	8·6 ⎫	15·6 ⎫	10·8 ⎫
Predicate	19·7 ⎬ 36·7	15 ⎬ 24·4	12 ⎬ 28	10·4 ⎬ 21·8
Causal dependence . . .	0·7 ⎭	0·8 ⎭	0·4 ⎭	0·6 ⎭
Coexistence	12·8 ⎫	6·1 ⎫	12·8 ⎫	12 ⎫
Identity	5·7 ⎬ 52·7	4·5 ⎬ 49·2	9·2 ⎬ 57·2	6·6 ⎬ 61·4
Verbal-motor forms . .	34·2 ⎭	38·6 ⎭	35·2 ⎭	42·8 ⎭
Word-completion . . .	1·1 ⎫	4·3 ⎫	1·2 ⎫	2·6 ⎫
Clang	1·9 ⎬ 3·6	15·8 ⎬ 20·7	8 ⎬ 9·6	3·8 ⎬ 8·2
Rhyme	0·6 ⎭	0·6 ⎭	0·4 ⎭	1·8 ⎭
Indirect associations . .	2·5 ⎫	4·5 ⎫	3·2 ⎫	6·2 ⎫
Meaningless	0·9 ⎪	1·6 ⎪	2 ⎪	1·8 ⎪
Faults	2 ⎬ 5·5	— ⎬ 6·1	— ⎬ 5·2	— ⎬ 8
Repetition of stimulus-word .	— ⎭	— ⎭	— ⎭	— ⎭
Egocentric	2·8	1·1	0·8	1·6
Perseveration. . . .	2·4	1·6	2	3
Repetitions	7·5	3·8	6·8	6·2
Same grammatical form . .	49·1	50·5	59·2	51·8
Same number of syllables .	35	44·6	46·4	41
Alliteration	9	27·3	17·6	13·2
Consonance	15·6	33·3	23·6	20·6
Same ending	8·5	8·3	11·2	10
Total number of associations .	1600	550	250	435
Total number of subjects .	8	6	5	5

of distraction. The differential figures show a certain agreemen
in the men, whilst the minus difference of the uneducated womei
is greater than in educated women, which would speak in favou
of a better adjustment to the experiment on the part of th
uneducated women.

	Educated		Uneducated
	Inner distraction	Outer distraction	Outer distraction
Men	− 5·5	− 2·8	− 8·8
Women	− 12·3	− 11·8	− 11·3

Minus difference of inner associations

Certainly the plus differences in the group of clang-reaction
again show a more important increase in the educated than i
the uneducated women.

	Uneducated women	Educated women
Plus difference of clang-reactions . .	2·6	8·3
		sometimes 6·4

The reason for this contradiction must lie in the fact that th
educated women behaved much more unequally towards th
distraction experiment than the uneducated women. Bot
groups fulfilled the conditions of the experiment, writing th
strokes and reacting at the same time, with rather more difficult
than the men. Comparing, e.g., the differences between educate
men and women in the distraction experiment, one is struck a
once by the more complete effect of distraction in men. Th
only essential difference in the two female groups appears t
be that the educated women are able, at least for a time, t
divide their attention.

It seems to us as if there were here a certain difference i
the reacting of men and women—a difference which might b
estimated quantitatively. As, however, from the paucity c
the material, sources of error cannot be excluded, we shall reserv
this for further discussion.

The figures in the individual groups of the scheme sho
certain variations which demand a critical inquiry.

Whilst the co-ordinations decrease fairly regularly wit
distraction, the predicates show in distraction a somewha
different behaviour in men and women.

	Educated Outer distraction	Uneducated Outer distraction
Women . . .	− 0·2	− 0·6
Men . . .	− 8·5	− 4·7

Minus difference of the predicates.

The table shows that in distraction the decrease of the predicates is less in women than in men.   Let us here recall the hypothesis put forward in our review of the predicate type that it is the primary sensual vividness of the stimulus-images which really evokes predicates.   This psychological peculiarity is naturally maintained also in the state of experimental dissociation of attention ; it will hinder the experiment, inasmuch as the primary vivid pictures, without the addition of active attention, engross the interest.   In this way the dissociation of attention, according to the regulations of the experiment, is hindered and made more difficult.   We shall see this phenomenon very clearly in the occurrence of distraction with the predicate type, to which we refer the reader.   Among the women there are, relatively, very many predicate types, which must be the cause of the apparently steadier maintenance of the predicates.

In contrast with the decrease of inner associations, there is a corresponding increase of outer associations, in so far as this is not influenced by a stronger increase in the clang-reactions.   In the increase of the outer associations all three groups do not take an equal part.   We shall see that the number of co-existences shows rather a tendency to diminish.   We again present the differences in a table.

Uneducated		Educated	
Women	Men	Women	Men
− 2	− 1·5	− 3·4	− 0·4

Difference between normal experiment and distraction in respect to co-existences.

Contrary to expectation, they are entirely minus differences. This shows that the co-existences do not participate in the increase of the outer association.   When we recall that co-existences frequently arise from an endeavour to represent distinctly the object of the stimulus-word, the decrease in the distraction experiment is to be understood.   Co-existence is to a certain extent a first step to inner association, and thus participates in the decrease of the latter.

The groups of identities and verbal-motor forms show, on the whole, an increase, which is, however, influenced by a strong increase of the clang-reactions, conditioning, e.g., in educated women, a decrease in both groups.   We explain this variation by the repeatedly proved irregularity of distraction.   The quantitatively lessened occurrence of word-completions is striking among the uneducated.   We think that want of verbal readiness is responsible for this, especially want of practice in literary German.   Experiments with uneducated Germans, notably North Germans, would perhaps disclose other figures.   Clang-associations are much more numerous among the educated than among the uneducated.

The indirect associations exhibit a peculiarity. We have already referred to an inverse relationship of their increase with that of clang-associations. In our averages we are at once struck by their independence of the degree of distraction.

	Uneducated		Educated	
	Women	Men	Women	Men
Normal experiment . .	0·7	0·8	0·9	2·5
Distraction . . .	0·9	2·4	0·9	4·6

These figures show that the uneducated, in normal experiment, produce on the average fewer indirect associations than the educated and that the women produce fewer than the men. In distraction the disinclination of the women to indirect associations is still clearer. Whilst in the men there is a most distinct increase, the average remains the same for educated women as in normal experiment, and there is but an insignificant increase in the figures for uneducated women. In this respect there must be some distinctive difference between the sexes, the meaning of which is at present unknown to us. The nature of indirect associations previously discussed (clang-reactions preponderating as intermediaries) enables us to understand its dependence on distraction. We should therefore expect with the increase of clang-reactions an increase also of the indirect associations. We recapitulate the figures in question :

	Uneducated				Educated			
	Women		Men		Women		Men	
	Clang	In-direct	Clang	In-direct	Clang	In-direct	Clang	In-direct
Normal experiment . .	0·7	0·7	0·6	0·8	3·3	0·9	3·6	2·5
Outer distraction 1 . .	2·9	1·2	3·1	3·4	10·2	1	9·6	3·2
Outer distraction 2 . .	3·7	0·7	1	1·4	9·2	0·2	8·2	6·2
Inner distraction (among educated only) . . .	—	—	—	—	11·6	1·6	20·7	4·5

Although these figures point in general to the expected simultaneous increase of clang-reactions and indirect associations in distraction, still the movement of the two groups is not alike in certain individual places. If there were really a common movement of the two groups one would expect that the maxima of indirect association would coincide with the maxima of clang-reactions. But that is by no means the case. If we look at the maxima of the indirect associations in the figures of the

distraction experiment we see that only in two cases are the
maxima coincident. To the maxima of the clang-reactions
there occur no corresponding increase of the indirect associations.
There is therefore no simple and clear correlation in the sense of
a direct ratio, nor do the figures give any obvious evidence of an
inverse relationship. Only in the group of educated men do
we see the coincidence of a striking maximum of indirect associations with the minimum of clang-reactions, which is certainly
a remarkable occurrence. In the two female groups we notice
that the increase in the indirect associations is strikingly less
than in the clang-reactions. In the educated men the great
increase of the clang-reactions from 3·6 per cent. normal to 20·7
per cent. in distraction corresponds to a mere 2 per cent. increase
of the indirect associations, whilst the maximum, as has been
said, coincides with the minimum of clang-reactions. This
behaviour of the indirect associations seems to us to speak in
favour of a certain dependent relationship of the two groups
to one another. We think that an increase of indirect associations chiefly prejudices the group of clang-reactions. If the
group of clang-associations is considered in its relation to indirect
associations the following picture is obtained :

| | Uneducated | | | | Educated | | | |
| | Women | | Men | | Women | | Men | |
	Clang	In-direct	Clang	In-direct	Clang	In-direct	Clang	In-direct
Outer distraction 1 . .	1·7	1·2	1·4	3·4	5·5	1	8	3·2
Outer distraction 2 . .	2	0·7	0·8	1·4	6·5	0·2	3·8	6·2

The behaviour of the pure clang-associations shows, with
few exceptions, the inverse relationship of the two groups. The
choice of clang-associations for the purpose of demonstration is
not an arbitrary one, for they are the chief part of the entire
clang-group, and are at the same time those associations which
are suppressed in the normal state—a fact that does not hold
true of all rhymes. It is just the fact that pure clang-associations
are suppressed in the normal state which is of greatest importance for the explanation of the inverted relationship. The
unspoken, for the most part quite unconscious, intermediate
terms of the indirect associations are preponderantly clang-
associations. In the normal state, clang-associations are constantly meeting inhibitions, for as a rule they are extraordinarily
ill-adapted for the process of association and are thus cast out.

There will be always present a certain tendency to suppress clangs; this will always be stronger the less the disturbance of attention, it will also be weaker the greater the distraction. With increasing distraction the reaction always becomes more inclined towards clangs, and finally nothing but a clang becomes associated. Between the inclination towards clangs and the clang-reaction there comes a point, however, where the clang-association cannot break down the inhibition opposing it, but nevertheless is able to control the sense of the reaction that follows, by breaking the connexion between stimulus-word and reaction. It is then a matter of indifference whether the sub-conscious clang-association arises centripetally or centrifugally.

This mediating clang-association, which almost reaches the threshold value of the reaction, leads to the formation of the indirect associations. It is self-evident that the intermediate terms need not always be clang-associations, they only require to attract to themselves just so much inhibition as to remain below the threshold value of the reaction. We, therefore, conceive the indirect association as a symptom of the repression of inferior associations which nearly reach the threshold value of the reaction.[1]

This conception allows us to understand readily the apparent inverse relationship of clang-associations and indirect associations. If the clang-associations gain the upper hand, it may be concluded that the inhibitions to clangs have been abolished; hence the repressions also, and consequently the indirect associations, are stopped. But if the number of clang-associations decreases, it is a sign that the inhibitions increase, and this offers the conditions for the occurrence of indirect associations. The indirect associations are therefore a phenomenon of transition which reaches its optimum at a certain stage of distraction. This explains also the apparently proportional increase in the clang-reactions and the subsequent decrease in the inverted relationship when the critical point is passed.[2]

---

[1] We only claim for this view of the indirect associations at present the value of a working hypothesis. We willingly submit our figures and our conception to further discussion, in the hope that the combined work of different investigators may result in a satisfactory solution of this question.

[2] The occurrence of indirect associations under the influence of a distraction of attention has been long known. Picture-naming in alcoholic delirium (Bonhöffer), in epileptic mania (Heilbronner), in certain catatoniac and hysterical states, is nothing but indirect association. This does not arise, as in our experiment, by a change in clang similarity but by a change in picture similarity. It is in this case, therefore, a by-product to flight of ideas in the visual sphere, and corresponds in every point with the phenomena we have demonstrated in the acoustic-verbal sphere.

Claparède, who has worked at the question of indirect associations from another side, believes that they are the " résultat du concours de plusieurs associations intermédiaires chacun trop faible pour être consciente." [1]

We agree with this view entirely, in the sense of the results of our experiment. The tendency to form associations according to the sense which proceeds from the stimulus-image prevents the occurrence of the clang-reaction. They are both, however, too weak to attain a reaction. Should the clang-association, not linked by its sense to the stimulus-image, predominate, an indirect association arises ; in the contrary case a reaction arises which has sense, though strongly affected by clang.

Piéron's [2] view, that the third term of the indirect association would have a greater interest for the individual than the middle term, does not coincide with the results of our experiment. Still, Piéron's view has something to recommend it and holds good of all those cases where the outer stimulus is unconsciously assimilated in the sense of a strongly accentuated complex filling up the conscious. (We shall consider this further possibility of an indirect association in a later work.) Piéron's view does not fit the endless number of indirect associations that occur in daily life. Out of many instances we mention one very instructive observation in our own experience. One of the authors, who had a long railway journey in front of him, was smoking a cigar, when it suddenly occurred to him that he had no more matches on him, whilst he possessed another good Havana cigar to smoke en route. He concluded he would have to light the second cigar at the end of the one he was smoking. That satisfied him, and he dropped this chain of thought. He was looking out of the window for a minute, carefully considering the landscape ; he suddenly noticed that spontaneously and quite softly he was saying Bunau - Varilla. B.-V. is the name of the well-known Panama agitator in Paris. He had read the name a few days before in the Matin. As the name seemed to have no connexion at all with the content of consciousness he at once directed his attention to the name, taking note of what came up in his mind (Freud's Method of Free Association). There came to him at once " Varinas," then " Manila " ; almost at the same time " cigarillo," accompanied by a vague feeling of a South American milieu ; the next distinct term was the Havana cigar and the recollection that this cigar had formed the content of

---

[1] Cp. Claparède, L'association des idées, p. 140 ; and Claparède, " Association médiate dans l'évocation volontaire," Archives de Psychologie, Tome III, p. 201.

[2] H. Piéron, " L'association médiate," Rev. phil., Août 1903, Tome XXVIII, p. 147.

the previous cycle of thought. The middle terms "Varinas" and "Manila" denote kinds of tobacco which have for the narrator something "Spanish" about them ; "cigarillo" is the Spanish for a cigarette, and he had smoked cigarettes made from Manila tobacco in a Spanish colony, but not in South America. Nevertheless there clung to "cigarillo" a faint image of something "South-Americanish." Whilst he had been looking out of the window he had not had the slightest feeling of any such chain of thought, his attention being concentrated on the landscape. The unconscious chain of thought which led to the formation of *Bunau-Varilla* was fashioned in the following way : Havana cigar—"cigarillo" with Spanish South-American background—recollection of a journey with "Manila-cigarillo" —Spanish-American tobaccos "Varinas" — ("Varinas" and "Manila" condensed by dream-mechanism into) *Varilla* = *Bunau-Varilla*. The sufficient basis for the unconscious carrying on of the cigar idea was that the observer had resolved not to miss lighting the Havana cigar at the end of the one he was smoking.

According to Piéron, *Bunau-Varilla* must be the emotionally toned final term desired by the thinker. That clearly it is not, but merely a condensation product arising from the concurrence of several weak middle terms (in accordance with Claparède's view). The mechanism of its rise is a verbal-motor automatism not infrequent in normals (in certain hysterics incomparably more frequent). The unconscious chain of association is stirred by picture and clang similarities, as are all associations occurring in the unconscious—i.e. external to the stress of attention (with the exception of certain somnambulic processes).

Referring to Jerusalem's article,[1] Wundt calls the middle term "unperceived," in contradistinction to "unconscious," in which we can discover no essential criticism ; it is but a mere logomachy. It will not astonish any one that Scripture obtained [2] doubtful results, Smith [3] and Münsterberg [4] none at all, for their experiments were at the outset ill devised to produce indirect associations. The best examples of indirect associations are

[1] Wundt, "Sind die Mittelglieder einer mittelbaren Assoziation bewust oder unbewust ?" *Phil. Studien.*, Bd. X, p. 1326. Jerusalem, "Ein Beispiel V. Assoziation durch unbewuster Mittelglieder," *Phil. Stud.*, Bd. X, p. 323.

[2] Scripture, "Ueber den assoziativen Verlauf der Vorstellungen," *Phil. Stud.*, Bd. VII, p. 50.

[3] William Smith, *Zur Frage der mittelbaren Assoziation.* (Diss : Leipzig, 1894.)

[4] Münsterberg, *Beiträge zur experimentellen Psychologie*, Heft 4, p. 9. Münsterberg writes : "There are no indirect associations through unconscious middle terms." Certainly in his experiments there were none.

furnished by careful self-observation in daily life.[1] Indirect verbal associations arise, as our experiment shows, chiefly in distraction experiments.

Meaningless reactions show, as was to be expected, an increase in distraction.

Faults, whose general emotional nature we have insisted upon several times in the individual accounts, are, strangely enough, quite absent among educated men in distraction. Among the others they show a consistent behaviour. We shall return to this group in reviewing the averages of the predicate type.

Repetition of the stimulus-words shows a reaction similar to that of meaningless reaction ; it increases likewise with the distraction.

We joined together the last four groups in what we called the residual group. Our original idea was to collect in this group the abnormal by-occurrences of the association experiment. From the figures of this group we hoped to obtain a certain coefficient of emotion, the subject being replaced by the experiment. We included the indirect associations in this group on the supposition, not in itself improbable, that the indirect associations, by reason of their origin from clang alterations, were really faults. The meaningless reactions we likewise held to be faults, as well as the last two groups. This view was strengthened by some experiences in the pathological sphere, by the association phenomenon in emotional stupidity.[2]

As the results of our experiments show, our earlier suspicion as to the emotional nature of the indirect associations must be relinquished, but this does not apply to the other three groups. The nature of the emotion in these three groups must be more precisely determined.

According to our experience, meaningless reactions and repetition of stimulus-words arise as a rule from the confusion which is conditioned by the rules of the experiment, whilst faults rest mostly upon the emotion which is evoked by the arousal of strong emotionally toned complexes. Confusion due to the rules of the experiment can be here entirely excluded. The inclusion of faults in the residual group is thus open to question. The

---

[1] A few beautiful examples of indirect associations are found in Cordes, *Phil. Studien*, Bd. XVII, pp. 70, 71, 75. Cordes regards the supposition that the middle terms of indirect associations are unconscious phenomena as a " theoretical construction which can never be empirically proven, for unconscious psychical phenomena are outside experience." The author would surely make this sentence less absolute were he at all acquainted with the experiences of hypnotism.

[2] Cp. Jung, "Ueber Simulation von Geistesstörung," *Journal f. Psych. u. Neurologie*, Bd. II, p. 181.

earlier name, " Emotion Group," originally chosen for this group was therefore replaced by the indifferent term " Residual Group." The statistics of the figures in this group were arranged so as to have a synoptical table, which we were fully aware was merely provisional and inadequate. Everybody who has done experimental work, especially with so intricate a material, knows that an apprenticeship must be served, and that one only knows afterwards what ought to have been known beforehand.

The egocentric reactions, which to a certain extent serve as an index of emotionally toned reactions, show a behaviour in distraction best demonstrated by a summary of the figures of the differences from normal experiment.

	Uneducated		Educated	
	Women	Men	Women	Men
Number of egocentric reactions in normal experiment . .	$+ 0.5$	$+ 1.7$	$+ 2.1$	$+ 2.8$
Difference in distraction . .	—	$- 1.7$	$- 1$	$- 1.6$

These figures show that according to our material the minus differences of the men are greater than those of the women. Although the women do not betray in normal experiment a stronger egocentricity than men, yet in distraction the women do exhibit it rather more strongly than men.

With reference to the perseverations, we have repeatedly proved a certain relationship dependent on strongly marked emotions.

We regarded the absence of association in distracted attention as the cause of its more frequent increase in distraction. Obviously, various complicated conditions are here intermingled which we cannot for the moment consider separately. The following summary of the differences from the normal experiment shows the behaviour of perseveration in distraction.

Uneducated		Educated	
Women	Men	Women	Men
$+ 1.2$	$- 0.4$	$+ 1.1$	$- 0.2$

From these figures it is clear that in distraction the perseverations decrease in men but increase in women.

The number of egocentric reactions give us a fair index of how many emotional ego-relationships occur in the reactions [1];

---

[1] In women the egocentric relationships are far from revealing themselves without protest—for the simple reason that the experimenters are males.

the number of the perseverations gives us somewhat similar help but in a less direct form.

As we have seen above, the women show a slighter effect of distraction upon the reaction. It may be concluded from this that female attention has proved itself less easily dissociable towards our experiment. With that must also be connected the slighter change in the number of egocentric reactions among the women. If the number of egocentric reactions evinces only a slight tendency to decrease, it is to be expected that the perseverations will show a similar behaviour ; but as a matter of fact they actually increase. Our explanation of this is that, owing to the lack of association artificially produced by the distraction, an emotional content of consciousness can be more easily persisted in than otherwise. But we do not know why the women to a greater degree than the men should have this tendency to perseverate more in distraction. Perhaps it is connected with more intensive feeling ?

The somewhat lesser tendency to dissociation of female attention has been based upon the following causes :

(1) We have already made it clear that different individuals (predicate types) have, it is to be presumed, primarily more vivid inner pictures than others. By more " vivid pictures " is meant such as have concentrated on themselves a greater intensity of attention, or, in other words, such as occur in company with many other associations. The greater an association complex, the more the " ego-complex " is drawn into sympathy. It is, therefore, understandable that with the vividness of the inner picture not only does the number of inner predicates grow but also, and chiefly, the number of subjective evaluations—that is, of egocentric reactions.

(2) The vividness of the inner picture is by no means always a primary, arbitrary phenomenon but can be also an artificial one. The attention can be voluntarily directed to it, or, in other words, innumerable new associations can be linked on to the picture that occurs with few by-associations. This activity is only aroused by the emerging picture, it is executed by another association complex which fills consciousness. The vividness of the inner picture is thus in one case primary and involuntary, in the other case secondary and desired. The latter form, then, stands under the influence of any other intellectual phenomenon which just happens to be present.

(3) If the inner pictures are primarily very vivid and plastic— that is, if they occur from the beginning with many by-associations—they must always possess a very definite effect upon attention ; varying with the degree of vividness, this will render

difficult or totally inhibit any dissociation of the same. This is, as we shall see, the case in the predicate type.

(4) If the inner pictures are either artificially vivid or plastic under the influence of an association complex already present, it depends only upon the stability of this complex whether the dissociation of attention becomes possible or not.

(5) We have no reason to assume that among women generally the inner pictures are primarily more vivid than among men (otherwise all women would probably belong to the predicate type). We have, however, a well-grounded supposition, as we have already demonstrated, that the reactions, relatively of high value among the uneducated, especially the uneducated women, rest upon a (quasi) intentional vividness of the stimulus-image. The association complex which executes this activity is the peculiar conception which the uneducated hold about the association experiment. Since they apprehend the stimulus-word from the point of view of its meaning, they are bound to direct greater attention to the stimulus presentation ; hence they surrender less to distraction, as our figures show.

Again, the fact that it is especially the uneducated women who submit least to distraction agrees with their being more strongly under the influence of this peculiar conception of the experiment. But that the educated women also show a lesser tendency to distraction than the men cannot rest merely upon this particular conception of the experiment. This must depend upon the condition already mentioned, that there were many predicate types among our educated women, and this type in general exhibits no distraction phenomenon.

We therefore classify the average figures of those educated women who are not predicate types in the table on page 159.

From the figures of the tables it is at once obvious that the women as such have no lesser capacity for dissociation than the men ; but it was the predicate type alone which so strongly affected the average of the educated women. Our figures show a distinct phenomenon of distraction not inferior in any way to that of men.

The *repetitions* of the same reactions decrease with distraction ; the reasons for this can be readily understood.

The figures for *verbal union* rise in distraction, so that the influence of the reaction becomes expressed quantitatively through more outer and mechanical determinants. It is noticeable among the uneducated that not only in normal experiment is there a quantitatively greater agreement in the *grammatical forms* than among the educated, but that the distraction experiment works

EDUCATED WOMEN, EXCLUDING THE PREDICATE TYPES

	Normal	Outer distraction	
		60 metro.	100 metro.
Co-ordination	15·2 ⎫	13·5 ⎫	10·8 ⎫
Predicate	14 ⎬ 30·2	14 ⎬ 28·3	9·6 ⎬ 20·8
Causal dependence . . .	1 ⎭	0·8 ⎭	0·4 ⎭
Coexistence	15·3 ⎫	12·4 ⎫	7·2 ⎫
Identity	48 ⎬ 62·6	11·2 ⎬ 50·4	8·8 ⎬ 62·8
Verbal-motor forms . . .	42·5 ⎭	26·8 ⎭	46·8 ⎭
Word-completion	1·5 ⎫	4 ⎫	3·6 ⎫
Clang	1·4 ⎬ 3·7	8 ⎬ 14	9·2 ⎬ 13·2
Rhyme	0·8 ⎭	2 ⎭	0·4 ⎭
Indirect	1 ⎫	1·2 ⎫	1·6 ⎫
Meaningless	0·1 ⎬	2 ⎬	— ⎬
Faults	0·9 ⎬ 2·4	1·6 ⎬ 5	0·4 ⎬ 3·2
Repetition of stimulus-word . .	0·4 ⎭	0·2 ⎭	1·2 ⎭
Egocentric reaction . . .	0·3	0·4	1·6
Perseveration	0·7	2·4	—
Repetitions	6·9	4·8	3·6
Same grammatical form . .	41·8	63·2	42·4
Same number of syllables . .	60·1	47·6	57·2
Alliteration	8·5	13·2	15·2
Consonance	14·7	21·2	24
Same ending	12·6	15·2	13·2
Total number of associations . .	1200	250	250
Total number of subjects . .	6	5	5

more powerfully and even more intensively than among the educated, although the uneducated show a slighter distraction phenomenon. The following differences demonstrate this clearly.

Differences between the number of same grammatical forms in normal experiment and the average figures of the experiment:

	Women	Men
Uneducated	+ 3·4	+ 6·6
Educated	+ 1·4	+ 4·7

The figure for agreement in grammatical form thus begins among the uneducated not only at a higher level, but in distraction rises still higher than the corresponding figure among the educated. The reason for this probably lies in the fact that among the educated numerous smuggled-in phrases stand ready for completion at any moment.

The figures for agreement in *number of syllables, alliteration, consonance,* etc., show nothing requiring further commentary.

The almost general decrease of the figures for verbal union in the second part of distraction is correlated with the decrease in clang-reactions. This change must be referred to habit, through which the individual factors of extreme distraction gradually diminish.

5. AVERAGE OF THE PREDICATE TYPE IN NORMAL EXPERIMENT AND IN DISTRACTION

We summarize here the average figures of all those subjects whom we term "Predicate Types." We have reckoned as belonging to this type those persons in whom the inner associations prevail as against the group of verbal-motor forms, and where the number of predicates is on the average about double that of co-ordinations. Seven women and two men are dealt with in this statistical table [1] (see Table, p. 161).

For the sake of comparison we have placed by the side of the predicate type the average of all other types. The difference is striking. In distraction the predicate type shows no change worth mentioning. The predicate type does not dissociate its attention, whilst all other types prove themselves, to some extent at least, accessible to the disturbing stimulus. This fact is extremely remarkable.

As we have already suggested, the individuals who belong to the predicate type have, we assume, primary vivid inner pictures, upon which the attention is involuntarily fixed at the moment of the appearance (in contrast to a voluntary directed vividness). We have observed in our material that among the reactions of the predicate type, together with numerous evaluations, there are found remarkably many predicates which denote sensual qualities of the stimulus-object, all of which are visual. Some of the subjects stated at once that they obtained at times quite distinct plastic pictures.[2] It is upon this that we founded the theory of the predicate type.

[1] Of the three members of one predicate family only one has been included in the table.

[2] These plastic pictures correspond pretty nearly to Ziehen's individual presentations. In the experiment we purposely did not ask about this, in order to prevent attention being at once directed thereto by suggestion. In many persons only a slight effort of attention is required to produce at once plastic pictures. In this case only the word-pictures, in themselves blank and universal, become repressed ; this, under appropriate suggestion, can occur half

	Predicate type			Non-predicate type		
	Normal	Outer distraction 60 metro.	Outer distraction 100 metro.	Normal	Outer distraction 60 metro.	Outer distraction 100 metro.
ɔ-ordination . .	12·5	14·8	13·1	21·5	18·0	14·3
ɾedicate . .	32·1 {45·7}	31·2 {46·5}	30·5 {43·8}	13·5 {36·0}	11·3 {29·9}	10·8 {25·4}
ɹusal dependence .	1·1	0·5	0·2	1·0	0·6	0·3
ɔexistence . .	13·5	13·7	11·7	17·2	16·0	12·2
ɟentity . .	4·1 {48·6}	8·0 {44·9}	8·5 {49·3}	7·3 {58·2}	13·2 {57·2}	10·8 {62·8}
ərbal-motor form .	31·0	23·2	29·1	33·7	28·0	39·8
ᵒord-completion .	0·8	0·8	0·2	0·8	1·3	1·7
ang . . .	0·3 {1·5}	1·4 {3·0}	1·1 {1·5}	1·1 {2·5}	4·7 {7·5}	4·2 {7·0}
hyme . . .	0·4	0·8	0·2	0·6	1·5	1·1
ᵈirect . .	0·8	1·7	0·2	1·5	2·2	1·9
ᵉaningless . .	—	0·2	1·1	0·3	1·2	1·3
ᵘults . . .	2·4 {3·2}	2·5 {4·6}	2·5 {4·6}	1·0 {2·9}	0·8 {5·1}	0·8 {4·7}
ᵉpetition of stimulus-word . .	—	0·2	0·8	0·1	0·9	0·7
ᵍocentric reaction .	3·6	1·7	1·4	1·0	0·6	0·7
ᵉrseveration . .	0·8	1·1	1·1	0·9	1·8	1·9
ᵉpetitions . .	9·9	8·0	4·8	8·5	6·5	4·0
ᵐe grammatical form . . .	40·7	43·1	45·4	62·1	66·9	63·8
ᵐe number of syllables . . .	37·3	44·0	47·4	42·9	47·3	43·5
ᶦliteration . .	7·9	8·8	10·8	9·4	12·4	14·1
ᵑsonance . .	12·9	15·4	14·2	14·4	22·4	20·8
ᵐe ending . .	6·7	7·7	11·1	14·0	15·4	16·6
ᵗal number of associations . .	1792	350	350	4586	1000	1085
ᵗal number of subjects . . .	9	7	7	23	20	20

An inner picture is vivid when the associations directly connected with it accord with it in sound. The closest associations to the picture of something concrete are the organs of sense—the visual, acoustic, tactile, and motor senses. A vivid visual image finds itself in a state of attention.[1] The more vivid the

unconsciously, especially in inexperienced persons. We do not know whether this presumably special vividness of the pictures is a constant feature in this subject or whether it was merely present during the association experiment.

[1] I.e. it draws the attention to itself.

picture, the stronger are the inhibitions which react to everything not associated, and the slighter therefore will be the dissociation of the attention. The practical absence of the distraction phenomenon in the predicate type is a proof of the correctness of our conception. The predicate type is unable to dissociate his attention because his primary vivid inner pictures make such a demand upon his attention that inferior associations (which make up the distraction phenomenon) cannot arise.

All the peculiarities of the predicate type can be explained on this hypothesis :

(1) *The Higher Number of Predicates.*—The subjects point to some peculiarly striking quality of the inner picture, and naturally employ the predicate for that. The great number of inner associations is to be referred chiefly to the number of predicates. The relationship of the inner to the outer association recalls the relationship among the uneducated. But what is common is merely the intensity of the attention employed. The predicates are also retained in distraction, and this we regard as a distinct proof of the spontaneity of the plastic nature of the picture.

(2) *The Great Number of Egocentric Reactions.*—The greater the vividness of the picture or the greater the association complex filling consciousness at the moment, the more must the complex arouse and attract associations, thus moulding the individual's consciousness, in order to remain conscious by means of this synthesis. In this way a whole series of personal traits reach the emerging association complex and become marked out and reacted to as peculiarly striking qualities of the picture. Thence proceed the egocentric reactions.

(3) *The Relatively Great Number of Faults.*—Faults are, as a rule, defective reactions, due to the arousal of a strong emotional complex which so chains the attention that no reaction is possible. It is highly probable that, by reason of the greater vividness of the picture, more emotional pictures are aroused in the predicate type than in other types. It is a necessary sequence of our supposition that in distraction the faults show a tendency to increase. If the minimum of free attention which is still present, together with that bound to the picture, is claimed by some activity (writing to beats), no attention is left to carry out the reaction ; in any case no diminution in faults can then occur.

From the figures of the distraction experiment it can be stated that the predicate type is no merely accidental momentary attitude, but corresponds to an important psychological characteristic—one which is maintained amid altered conditions.[1]

6. The Influence of the Grammatical Form of the Stimulus-word upon the Reaction

As may be readily understood, the choice of the stimulus-word, with all its diverse qualities, is not a matter of indifference. There is a whole series of stimulus-words which have selective reactions. There is, for instance, a whole number of terms for concrete objects to which regularly co-existent images are associated, quite apart from stimulus-words which arouse stereo-typed word-connexions : e.g. *divorce—wicked*, or *divorce—averse*, *blood — red*, etc. For the quantitative relationships it is of consequence whether the stimulus-word is a noun, adjective, or verb. The frequency of the appropriate form of word will be here a chief factor. According to the statistics to be found in any reference work, it may be said that language uses nouns twice as often as adjectives and adverbs. According to the law of frequency, therefore, a noun as stimulus-word will be " answered " more easily than any other form of word. Inversely, the lessened frequency of verbs and adjectives causes greater difficulty in the reactions. This is quite apart from the fact that for most persons an adjective or verb in the infinitive, apart from the text, seems stranger than a noun. The latter probably will denote some concrete object or other, about which something can be said. We have carried out some comparative investigations on our material from this point of view and have found the following averages :

| | React to Verbs | | | | | | React to Adjectives | | | | | |
| | Nouns | Adjectives | Verbs | Associa-tions | | Clang | Nouns | Adjectives | Verbs | Associa-tions | | Clang |
				Inner	Outer					Inner	Outer	
ducated men .	63·2	15·8	20·6	48·4	41·6	7·4	53·1	43·6	2·9	43·5	45	8·0
neducated men .	32·7	21·7	45·5	49·6	47·4	1·1	32·4	64·8	2·7	44·8	51·0	3·4
ducated women	45·7	19·4	34·7	55·5	39·2	4·5	39·1	52·6	7·4	43·3	45·4	3·1
neducated women	52·8	14·4	32·6	69	29·6	0·3	49·4	47·3	3	60·8	37·3	1·1
edicate type .	54·8	26·2	18·9	62·8	33·4	2·7	64	29·7	5·2	64·2	28·3	1·9
n-predicate type	46·7	15	38·1	52·4	41·8	4·2	35·5	59·9	4·4	42·8	51·0	4·3

[1] By which we mean, of course, only our experimental conditions. Under the influence of fatigue and alcohol the predicates practically vanish ; this branch of the work, however, remains for investigation.

The figures which we invariably give for agreement in grammatical form in the tables show generally that the stimulus-word and reaction by no means always agree in grammatical form. The above table gives the averages in percentages for the most characteristic groups among our subjects. We have refrained from presenting the separate figures of each individual, to avoid heaping up immense series of figures. The average figures show clearly enough the characteristic variations, the matter of chief interest.

In the group of verbs we find that nouns are generally reacted to verbs, with the exception of one group, the uneducated men, who generally react by verbs to verbs. Educated men react with most nouns. Remarkably enough, the uneducated women most nearly approach them, whilst the educated women came nearest to the uneducated men. It is certain that the verbal law of frequency greatly influences the preference for this or that way of reaction. It is, therefore, quite easy to understand that the educated men, who have in any case a very superficial reaction, prefer the more colloquial noun to the rarer verb ; but that the uneducated women should apparently behave in a similar way is not at first sight comprehensible and demands further investigation.

Whilst, according to our observations, the educated men mostly react current nouns to verbs, the uneducated men endeavour to do justice to the sense of the stimulus-word by reacting with a similar verb. Rather less clear is a similar endeavour in the educated women. This form of reaction, the psychology of which we have reviewed in detail, is determined by the endeavour to react according to the meaning of the stimulus-word. We have already seen that in this respect the uneducated women stand at the head. We should accordingly expect that the uneducated women would react with a still greater number of verbs than the uneducated men. But it must be remembered that the educational level of the uneducated women is lower, and that therefore their verbal facility and expression are weak ; reaction to verbs will be therefore most difficult of all for this group, for to them verbs are even more difficult than they are to the other groups.[1] Consequently they are driven to nouns which can be most readily linked on to verbs. The endeavour of the uneducated women to give a reaction that makes sense determines the selection of the noun, which is not merely strung on to the verb, but wherever possible expresses something significant to the meaning of the verb.

[1] Note also that the subjects are chiefly Swiss and thus under burdensome speech conditions.

We therefore made a further investigation to confirm this view and to discover how large is the number of inner associations which are reacted to verbs. The figures obtained enable us to prove the above hypothesis. Together with the figures which give the preferred word forms, we have placed the figures which exhibit the kind of associations which are reactions to verbs. For the chief groups in question we recapitulate the figures in question, together with those of the normal experiment :

EDUCATED MEN

	Inner association	Outer association	Clang-reaction
Normal experiment . . .	36·7	52·7	3·6
React to verbs	48·4	41·6	7·4
Plus difference	11·4	—	—

This summary shows that the reaction type is considerably less superficial for verbs as stimulus-words than for our schedule of stimulus-words, which is preponderantly composed of nouns. The figures confirm the fact that, for educated men also, far fewer casual connexions exist between verb and verb than between noun and any of the three other forms of words. Comparing these figures with the corresponding figures of the uneducated women, we find our assertion confirmed that the nouns preferred by this group possess a higher quality :

UNEDUCATED WOMEN

	Inner association	Outer association	Clang-reaction
Normal experiment . . .	46·6	49·4	0·7
React to verbs . . ; .	69	29·6	0·3
Plus difference	22·4	—	—

From these figures it is clear that by far the greater number of the associations which are reactions to verbs are of high value and correspond to the meaning of the stimulus-word. The behaviour of the clang-reactions in the two groups is also worth noting. The number, surpassing that of the normal experiment in educated men, shows how slight is the influence of the stimulus-word. Inversely, the decrease in the corresponding figures among the uneducated women is characteristic of the increased influence of the verbs. From these ratios the deduction may be made that the influence of the verbs upon attention, in consequence of their lesser frequency and the consequent greater difficulty in " answering," is greater than that of nouns.

The adjectives show, as a glance at the table teaches, a behaviour similar to that of verbs, having on the whole a somewhat lesser influence upon the reaction type. It may therefore be assumed that the reaction to adjectives encounters on the whole fewer difficulties.

The predicate type reacts to verbs preferably by nouns, whilst all the non-predicate types react by double as many verbs to verbs as the predicate type.[1]

We again investigate the quality of the associations reacted to the verbs by the predicate type.

	Predicate type			Non-predicate type		
	Inner association	Outer association	Clang-reaction	Inner association	Outer association	Clang-reaction
Normal experiment . .	45·7	48·6	1·5	36·6	58·2	2·5
Reaction to verbs . .	62·8	33·4	2·7	52·4	41·8	4·2
Plus difference . . .	17·4	—	—	16·4	—	—

As the plus differences show, the influence of the verbs is about the same in both groups ; there is no plus difference of inner associations corresponding with the numerous nouns of the predicate type which surpasses that of the non-predicate type. We have, therefore, no ground to presume that in the predicate type the verb has a greater influence upon attention or greater difficulties for the reaction. The predicate type shows no difference of attention towards the verbs, but merely the difference which the educated have in general, namely, their preference for the noun because of its greater currency. This arises from the fact that among our predicate types the majority are educated.

The behaviour of the predicate type towards adjectives is in contrast to the earlier results. As the figures of the common tables show, in the reactions of the first four groups there occur more adjectives to adjectives than verbs to verbs. In the predicate type, who is characterized by his attributes in the form of adjectives, the difference only amounts to 10·8 per cent. There is strong preference for nouns (as compared with the non-predicate type), i.e. by 28·5 per cent. more. This preference for the noun arises from the endeavour of the predicate type to

[1] Note here that among the eleven predicate types there are only two uneducated persons, of whom one is a woman.

react chiefly by attributes. Our figures show, not merely that a predicate is thus reacted, but also, inversely, a noun is given to the adjective when this is the stimulus-word.[1] Let us now investigate the relationship of the figures in regard to the quality of the adjective reactions.

	Predicate type			Non-predicate type		
	Inner association	Outer association	Clang-reactions	Inner association	Outer association	Clang-reactions
Normal experiment . .	45·7	48·6	1·5	36	58·2	2·5
Reaction to adjectives .	64·2	28·2	3·9	42·8	51	4·3
Plus difference . . .	18·5	—	—	6·8	—	—

As these figures show, the high figure for the nouns is combined with a corresponding increase of the inner associations in the predicate type. This is not the case of a mere stringing together of current nouns, but of constructions adapted to the stimulus-word and executed with regard to the adjustment, although the stringing together of similar adjectives is much easier in itself, as witness the figures which agree herein for the remaining groups. This latter fact is clearly brought out by the lesser plus difference of the inner associations in the adjective reactions of the non-predicate type.

It is clear, also, from the figures of the adjective reactions that the predicate attitude is not accidental but corresponds to a definite psychological disposition, which is maintained even when other kinds of reaction would be much easier than the predicate forms.

RECAPITULATION

The associations vary, within the range of the normal, chiefly under the influence of :

(1) Attention.
(2) Education.
(3) The individual peculiarity of the subject.

a. Reduction of attention through any kind of inner or outer impulses makes the reaction type a more superficial one ; that is,

---

[1] This behaviour can be explained from the psychology of the predicate type. The subjects of this type are distinguished by peculiarly vivid pictures. Therefore they see the adjective at once as the attribute of a particular object, which they denote in their reaction.

the inner or higher associations recede in favour of outer associations and clang-reactions.

b. The distraction of attention in our experiment effected, besides the change mentioned, an increase of the indirect associations. These must therefore be regarded as distraction phenomena derived from the concurrence of two weakly accentuated (or inferior) associations as the intermediate terms.

c. The educated have, on the average, a more superficial reaction type than the uneducated. The difference is essentially due to a difference in the apprehension of the stimulus-word.

d. As to the degree of the dissociation of attention effected by distraction, there are no essential differences between the educated and the uneducated.

e. The most important variations of association are conditioned by individual differences.

(1) As regards the influence of sex upon the reactions in normal experiment, no distinct differences result from the statistics of the averages. The peculiarities of the female subjects first appear in the distraction experiment : they have, on the average, a lesser capacity for dissociation of attention than the male subjects.

(2) The individual variations may be arranged in the following types :

I. OBJECTIVE TYPE.—The stimulus-word is apprehended objectively :

α. *Chiefly according to its Objective Meaning.* The reaction is appropriate, as far as possible, to the stimulus-word and linked by its meaning to the stimulus-word.

β. *Chiefly as Verbal Stimulus.* The reaction is partly a verbal adaptation and partly denotes a linking together of some prepared association ; any relationship to meaning falls considerably into the background.

II. EGOCENTRIC ADJUSTMENT.—The stimulus-word is taken in a subjective (egocentric) fashion.

α. *Constellation Type.* The personal elements used in the reaction belong to one or more emotionally toned complexes : two possibilities present themselves :

αα. The complex-constellation is expressed without disguise.

ββ. The complex-constellations occur in a disguised form in consequence of a repression which is not always conscious.[1]

β. *Predicate Type.* This type has presumably the psychological peculiarity of experiencing its inner pictures in a peculiarly vivid (plastic) way ; no special manner of reaction is to be

---

[1] We use the term " repression " in the sense of Breuer and Freud, to whose work, *Studies in Hysteria,* we are indebted for valuable stimulus in our investigations.

explained therefrom.   This type shows also an abnormally lesser capacity for dissociation of attention, and at times none at all; this expresses itself in the distraction experiment on the whole by an almost complete absence of the phenomenon of shallowness.

We obtain this result, which for pathology is of universal import: that the superficial nature of the reaction type in fatigue, alcoholic intoxication, and mania is to be chiefly referred to a distraction of attention.   The observations on the affective side of associations (the effects of emotionally toned complexes) should be of importance in the experimental investigation of pathological changes in emotions and their consequences.

In conclusion, we would wish to express our thanks to our esteemed chief, Professor Bleuler, for much valuable stimulus. We are also much indebted to Mrs. Jung for her active co-operation in repeatedly working over the vast material.

EXPLANATION OF THE FIGURES

The accompanying figures exhibit the arithmetical mean of the inner associations, outer associations, clang-reactions, and reactions of the residual group of the different groups.

I. signifies average of the total of inner associations.

O.	,,	,,	outer	,,
C.	,,	,,	clang	,,
R.	,,	,,	reactions in the residual group.	

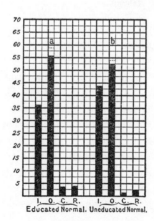

FIG. 1

a. Averages of the normal experiment among the educated of 23 subject with 3800 associations.

b. Averages of the normal experiment among the uneducated of 18 subjects with 3000 associations.

In the normal experiment the educated have fewer inner, more outer associations and more clang-reactions than the uneducated.

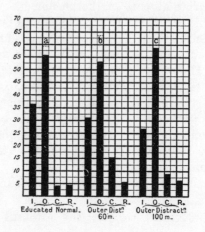

Fig. 2

AVERAGES OF THE EXPERIMENTS IN OUTER DISTRACTION
AMONG THE EDUCATED

a. Normal experiment (= Fig. 1 a, 23 subjects, 3800 associations).
b. Distraction experiment with 60 metronome beats to the minute; 13 subjects, 650 associations.
c. Distraction experiment with 100 metronome beats; 13 subjects, 835 associations.

A distinct, regular decrease of the inner associations from a to c, i.e. corresponding to the intensity of the means of distraction, is seen. Secondly, the tables show an increase of the clang-reactions in both distraction experiments. The result of the distractions consists generally of the increase of the outer associations plus increase of clang-reactions. This sum (O and C) is shown by the column O being overtopped at times by a dotted column whose height is equal to the height of C. This column (O and C) increases regularly from a to c. The decrease of I and the increase of (O and C) in the distraction experiment illustrate clearly the effect of distraction. Cb and Cc are both greater than Ca. The reactions of the residual group increase from a to c.

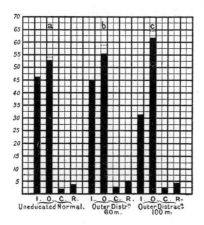

AVERAGES OF THE EXPERIMENTS IN OUTER DISTRACTION
AMONG THE UNEDUCATED

a. Normal experiment (like Fig. 1 b); 15 subjects, 3000 associations.

b. Distraction experiment; 60 metronome beats; 15 subjects, 750 associations.

c. Distraction experiment; 100 metronome beats; 15 subjects, 750 associations.

Apart from dissimilar origin, the picture is the same as in the distraction experiments among the educated.

Regular decrease of the inner associations from a to c.

Regular increase of the outer associations plus clang-reactions from a to c. R increases in the distraction, C only slightly; the clang-reactions generally play a lesser part than among the uneducated.

Fig. 4 (p. 172). Whilst among the educated the ratio of $1 : I = 2 : 3$ and among the uneducated $1 : I = 5 : 6$, here it amounts to about $1 : 1.1$. C is less than among the educated, but greater than among the uneducated in normal experiment. In the group R the ratio is reversed. In a remarkable way this ratio scarcely changes in distraction, quite contrary to the previous pictures. There is but a minimal decrease of I and a very slight decrease of (O and C). R has somewhat increased.

Fig. 5 (p. 172) offers a striking contrast to the picture in Fig. 4. In the normal experiment the ratio is $I : (O + C) = 10 : 17$, approximately $2 : 3$; in the distraction experiment $10 : 24$, approximately $2 : 5$. C increases substantially, R less so.

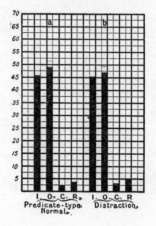

FIG. 4

AVERAGES OF THE EXPERIMENTS AMONG PERSONS OF THE PREDICATE
TYPE (EDUCATED AND UNEDUCATED)

a. Normal experiment; 9 subjects, 1792 associations.

b. Distraction experiments (outer distraction with 60 and 100
metronome beats); 7 subjects, 700 associations.

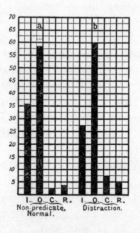

FIG. 5

AVERAGES OF ALL EXPERIMENTS IN THE REMAINING SUBJECTS
(NON-PREDICATE TYPE)

a. Normal experiment.   *b*. Distraction experiment.

CHAPTER III

THE ASSOCIATIONS OF IMBECILES AND IDIOTS

By Dr. K. WEHRLIN

At the instance of Professor Bleuler and Dr. Jung, I have for some time carried out investigations on the associations of feeble-minded children and adults. Experiments on adults have given me material which warrants certain conclusions, whilst the investigations among children are so far inconclusive. I shall limit myself in the following essay to the material obtained from the experiments on the adult feeble-minded.

The technique of the association experiments is similar to that employed by Jung and Riklin, fully described in chapter ii, to which the reader is referred for further details.

As is well known, similar investigations among idiots have already been carried out by Sommer and Wreschner.

Wreschner[1] has made experiments on an idiot in time-reactions by Sommer's schedule. He came to the following conclusions :

The quality of the stimulus-word has a great influence upon the kind of association ; the more inferior the quality of the reaction the higher the quality of the stimulus-word. The store of images in Wreschner's subject, so far as it was expressed by association, was overwhelmingly composed of adjectives.

The inner associations require generally a longer reaction-time than the verbal ones.

The worse the quality of the association, and the more unaccustomed, therefore, the subject was to the stimulus-word, the longer the reaction-time ; this holds good for inner as well as for verbal reactions.

Practice shortens the reaction-time and improves the quality of the association. The verbal associations decrease in favour of the inner ones.

[1] " Eine experimentelle Studie über die Assoziation in einem Falle von Idiotie," *Allgemeine Zeitschrift für Psychiatrie*, 1900.

Sommer [1] reviews in his *Methods of Investigations* the associations in a case of imbecility.

He found great similarity and poverty in the store of images, with in places a total absence of associations. We quote a couple of his examples which in our experience are peculiarly characteristic of the feeble-minded :

Doctor	who looks after the sick
Cleverness	who is not stupid
Memory	who remembers something
Law	who disobeys no order

Fuhrmann [2] mentions that the idiot (in contradistinction to epileptics) is unable to form sub- and super-ordinated concepts in his reactions. As will be seen below, we have not been able to confirm this view in our experiments, for universal concepts were sometimes given.

As may be gathered from the investigations of Sommer and Wreschner, these experiments on the feeble-minded meet with peculiar difficulties, due to the pathological peculiarities of the subject examined.

1. DIFFICULTIES WHICH THE EXPERIMENT ENCOUNTERS FROM THE INTELLECTUAL SIDE

It is to be expected that the apprehension of the stimulus-word among imbeciles encounters greater difficulties than among normals, for it is in general characteristic of imbeciles to apprehend slowly and with difficulty ; certain words, especially abstracts, are understood with much more difficulty by the imbecile than by a normal uneducated person.

Concrete concepts are also more difficult for him to understand, as, in consequence of the poverty of his mental life, these always find fewer related concepts. This fact must be taken into consideration in the working out of the stimulus-image which he has received. In accordance with the rules of the experiment, the subject should put into one word (the reaction-word) the first thing that occurs to him.

The intention is to arouse a succession of presentations. Among normals a presentation is generally called up in accordance with the law of contiguity or of similarity. Among imbeciles, who, unlike normals, do not possess a great mass of material derived from experience, and among whom especially

[1] Sommer, *Lehrbuch der psychopathologischen Untersuchungsmethoden*, pp. 349–355.

[2] *Analyse des Vorstellungsmaterials bei epileptischem Schwachsinn*, p. 30 (Diss : 1902).

the higher associations, constructed chiefly by similarity, are not labile—there is great difficulty in drawing on the associated presentations.

Language is a factor of great importance for the association experiment among imbeciles.

Language, as a condensation product of innumerable associated processes, is an index of feeble-mindedness.

It is here that we must expect the greatest difficulties. The imbecile's poverty in imagery is reflected in the poverty and deficiencies of his language. The imbecile lacks not only an understanding of numerous rather complicated and rare things, but also the *words* which denote them. Stimulus-words which are somewhat rare are therefore very badly understood and arouse much fewer related images because they are hardly known to the imbecile. Even if he succeeds in evoking a related image, the further difficulty arises of discovering the appropriate verbal symbol. Here again deficient verbal education is a hindrance. The result is that numerous awkward and clumsy reactions are formed which betray, on the one hand, an imperfect understanding of the stimulus-word, and, on the other, a difficulty in verbal expression. A great number of results may therefore be expected which by their peculiarity not only characteristically distinguish imbecile reactions from all others, but also afford deep insight into the essence of the imbecile activity in association.

My subjects are Swiss. As Jung and Riklin have insisted, the peculiar verbal conditions of the German-Swiss must be seriously considered in the association experiment. Jung [1] says : " The uneducated, however, retains at the most those German phrases which he has learned at school, later adding little or nothing thereto. Literary German is not the less familiar to him in its written and printed form, and he understands it when spoken without being able himself to speak a fluent and faultless literary German." As Jung shows, Swiss-German is a purely acoustic-motor language which is very seldom read and written. The Swiss, therefore, knows his words only in connexion with what is spoken and heard. He has not a sense of words as " individual things," but only as different terms, not distinctly separated, in a continuous verbal chain. " If he has to say one word by itself without the article he generally chooses the literary German form." If among the uneducated there is a certain difficulty owing to deficiency in verbal habits, it is obvious that for the imbecile the difficulty is much greater. He will not only have greater difficulty, through his imperfect knowledge in apprehending the literary German stimulus-word, but has also

[1] Chapter ii, p. 10.

more strain in constructing the verbal form of his reaction. In my experiments the reaction was frequently rendered, not in literary German, but in the dialect form. Moreover, with the idiots it was often necessary to utter the stimulus-word in this dialect form, generally adding the article also, as that considerably increases the understanding of the dialect word.

The verbal difficulties coupled with the increased difficulty of apprehension are of great importance in the peculiar formation of the imbecile reaction.

As Jung and Riklin have exemplified, the uneducated react, on the average, with greater attention than the educated. They endeavour to do greater justice to the sense of the stimulus-word, the " word " as a sound receding to the background. The inferior verbal education of the uneducated makes a word, apart from its context, seem to him something strange, unaccustomed ; hence a hypothetical context is built up for the single stimulus-word. The uneducated, therefore, betray in their reactions a distinct tendency, from the constellation of habit, to apprehend the stimulus-word in the sense of a question, something like " What does —— mean ? " " What do you know about —— ? " The contrary of the stimulus-word is also much sought for or constructed. Consequently, in the reactions of the uneducated it is much less a question of the automatic direct impressions of the educated than of something sought for and thought about.

The tendency to form these kinds of reactions increases among the uneducated, in proportion to the decrease of culture and intelligence. And, as seems to follow from some hitherto unpublished investigations made in this clinic, certain normal individuals approximate in point of culture and intelligence to a reaction type resembling that of imbecility. The similarity consists in a limitation to the meaning of the stimulus-word, with an endeavour to show by the reaction that this meaning is understood.[1]

Hence the uneducated person's way of reacting is met again in imbecility ; and, proportionate to the deficient culture of the imbecile, it plays an immeasurably greater part. If one may regard the deficient culture which most markedly influences the reaction as an index of feeble-mindedness, the associations measure in some degree the intensity of the intellectual disturbance. On the whole, one is prepared to find an uninterrupted gradation of type leading up from idiots and imbecility to the intellectual plane of the normal.

It is, therefore, a priori probable that the signs of feeble-mindedness differ merely in strength and number from the signs of a low intelligence and education in the normal.

[1] See chapter x.

2. Difficulties which the Experiment encounters from the Side of the Emotions

In any evaluation of the imbecile process of association another fact must be taken into account. The imbecile is not only intellectually undeveloped, but he is above all a degenerate, presenting as a rule, together with his weak-mindedness, other anomalies in the mental region. The most important anomalies are found, as in all psychopathic degenerates, in the *emotional functions*. The frequent anomalies of temper and the frequent moral defects are not markedly expressed in the associations, especially not the latter; but, on the other hand, various hysterical traits, so common among imbeciles, will, as one can easily imagine, markedly influence the reaction.

I have found in my experiments that a certain quickly aroused confusion can considerably disturb the experiment, and render it difficult. Jung [1] has recently called attention, with experimental proof, to this trait of the imbecile. He reports on two imbeciles, under investigation and confinement in the asylum, who fell into a state of severe dementia, characterized by marked prolongation of the reaction-time, difficulty in remembering, and the occurrence of meaningless associations. These meaningless associations had reference chiefly to objects which were accidentally in the field of vision, but had no kind of relation to the stimulus-word; they were simply liberated by the utterance of the stimulus-word. This state of obvious inhibition Jung terms " emotional stupidity."

To elucidate the nature of this disturbance I will cite a short series of associations from Jung's case :

Christmas	tree	Schoolboy	tree
Easter	book	Father	pencil
		Table	wall
Sunday	tree	Head	cloth
Winter	house	Ink	paper
Lake	school	Needle	window

We take it for granted that imbecility includes numerous and diverse groups which again present relationships to all other possible forms of psychopathic deficiency. Thus cases seem to occur which are essentially marked out by incapacity for concentration—where the intellectual weakness expresses itself chiefly by its great associative superficiality. Individuals of this kind frequently show strong social instability with a tendency to pseudological scheming. Their manner of speaking and of

---

[1] Jung, " Ueber Simulation," op. cit., p. 181.

thinking has something extraordinarily confused and vague, often recalling a slight flight of ideas. They are differentiated from manic-depressive insanity [1] by the absence of symptoms of maniacal excitement, exaltation of spirits and restlessness. These forms are frequently really difficult to separate from pure imbecility, more especially when they present structural defects similar to imbecility—which, however, can finally be ascribed to their unstable ways of life, their volatility and inattention. In cases of otherwise undoubted imbecility this condition can also occur as a by-product.

This kind of feeble-mindedness must present in its associations a picture different from that of pure imbecility.

3. ARRANGEMENT OF THE EXPERIMENT

To survey the possibilities of imbecile reaction and thus obtain a point of view of universal validity, I have collected as wide a material as possible and submitted it to a qualitative analysis. It was soon apparent that the Kräpelin-Aschaffenburg classification, which Jung and Riklin employed, was ill-adapted to the associations of imbeciles; that even where it could be used it did not bring out what was of pathognomonic importance.

I perceived that a classification adapted to the reality of the situation must proceed from other points of view. My endeavour was then to discover the points of view by which the material could be classified. From the point of view of the associations my twenty-seven patients are divisible into three groups, which are, however, not sharply divided from each other:

(1) Imbeciles of a lethargic temperament.
(2) Imbeciles of a sanguine temperament.
(3) Higher imbeciles.

As will be seen, this classification agrees also with the clinical and symptomatological one. Thirteen of the subjects certainly show a lethargic temperament, and their associations likewise show characteristic features differentiating them from the two other groups. For this reason I chose this group as the starting-point of my investigations.

This work is limited to the analysis of the associations of thirteen idiots and imbeciles, aged from seventeen to sixty-nine years, about whom clinically there is no doubt. By thus selecting

---

[1] Jung, "Ueber manische Verstimmung," *Allgemeine Zeitschrift für Psychiatrie* 1903.

my experimental material it seemed to me most possible to discover certain laws which might serve as the starting-point for later and deeper investigations. For the solution of all those problems which occur in the second and third groups I neither had time nor the requisite number of subjects. The material upon which my work is founded consists in round numbers of 2000 single reactions. The reaction-time was measured in five persons, i.e. in 764 reactions. There are eleven men and two women.

Only in the more severe cases were the stimulus-words called out in their dialect form. The reaction was always put down exactly as it was given, therefore in a large number of my patients in dialect form. The test words which I reproduce I have translated as faithfully as possible into literary German.

At the beginning of the experiment an explanation was given, with examples as to how the person had to react ; the experiment was only begun when it was quite certain that the subject had grasped the matter.[1] In most cases some two hundred reactions could be carried out, sometimes with intervals varying from a couple of days up to several weeks. In the severer cases the experiment was so laborious and tedious that after the fifty-eighth reaction one patient was hopelessly bored of the matter.

The list of stimulus-words was that used by Jung and Riklin (see chapter ii). It sometimes happened in the severer cases that the stimulus-words were not understood because they were unknown to the individual, and had then to be struck out. In cases where the subject could not react he was asked whether he knew the stimulus-word ; when it was quite certain that the word was known the missing reaction was held to be a " fault." In the severer cases the stimulus-word had occasionally to be repeated several times. In these cases the time measurement was omitted. The time was only measured in those slighter cases where the experiment went smoothly.

4. RESULTS OF THE EXPERIMENT

I have arranged my subjects clinically, according to their degree of feeble-mindedness ; first come the idiots, then the imbeciles. About thirty tests have been chosen from each

[1] I need scarcely add that those who could not understand the experiment were excluded from the investigation.

case—those which I regard as peculiarly characteristic and best adapted to demonstrate briefly the course of the experiment.

No. 1. *Total reactions* 72

1. Sunday	consists of—a day on which one does nothing	18. Flower	a pot plant
		19. Cherry	a thing in the garden, on the trees
2. Winter	consists of snow	20. Piano	where there is music, upstairs
3. Lake	consists of water		
4. Schoolboy	when he goes to school	21. Oven	good for warmth
5. Father	companion together with mother	22. Walk	that is when you stretch your legs for a pint on Sundays
6. Table	consists of wood		
7. Ink	something to write	23. Cat	four-legged animal
8. Bread	to eat	24. Bird	also of the animal kingdom
9. Tree	a part of—there are trees in the garden		
		25. Swim	in the lake, in water
10. Mountain	a high mountain	26. White	the wine
11. Hair	part of the head	27. Game	there are lots of games
12. Copy-book	consists of paper	28. Stroke	you can stroke men and animals
13. Paper	you write upon it	29. Sweet	something sugary
14. School	consists of schoolboys	30. Friendly	when you are not angry
15. Sing	consists of notes and song-books		
		31. Crown	a kind of head-covering
16. Ring	on the finger	32. Ill	when you are not well
17. Window	consists of wood and window-panes	33. Star	part of the sky

These tests give a clear view of this patient's way of reacting As is at once evident, the tendency here is to explain or to define the stimulus-word in some way. The subject seeks to explain the stimulus-words by stating of what the thing denoted by the stimulus-word consists; he denotes the material (reaction 3, 6, 12, 14, 17); the way in which this tendency runs off at a tangent in reaction 2 is characteristic of idiots:

Winter   consists of snow

The defective verbal education is here typical, as manifested in the quite inappropriate use of the phrase "consists of." This is a well-known phrase in school use, one but seldom used in later life, especially by an idiot. He is only half familiar with the limitations of its use and employs it where it does not really apply well. It is thoroughly typical of the idiot that the winter consists "of snow." He observes only the external phenomena things that occur together or that follow one another, without making any kind of deductions as to the causal connexion. have no doubt that to these patients also the cold and the snow

days are typical of the presentation "winter"; but from
their reactions it is very obvious that what is simply visual and
external has greater importance than the less striking, but
causally more important, collateral phenomena of the cold and
short days.

The most illuminating example of the idiot's purely visual
and external apprehension of things comes to light in the reaction

Sing   consists of notes and song-books

Here it is distinctly seen how the external manifestation of
the act, something really quite secondary, overcomes what is
essential. Reactions of this kind are characteristic and suffice
for the diagnosis of imbecility or idiocy, as against the so-called
secondary states of feeble-mindedness.

In order to convince himself that he understands the meaning
of the stimulus-word, our patient tries to characterize the object
it denotes by naming the place where the thing occurs or is
found (cp. reactions 9, 16, 20, 25). Or he names the purpose
of the thing (7, 8, 21) in its use or the action which it executes
(4, 13, 28); sometimes he designates the object by another
expression, synonymous as a rule, which he perhaps accentuates
by giving it some particularly typical attribute (*mountain — a
high mountain ; flower — a pot plant*), or he tries a tautological
elucidation by bringing the opposite with its negative into the
reaction (e.g. *dark — not bright* : cp. also reactions 30, 32).

Universal concepts, taken too widely, which are supraordinated
to the stimulus-word, form a characteristic group. These supraordinations are much too extensive to be able to fulfil their
object of being explanatory. Occasionally the universal concept
is so remote and indefinite that it really contains practically
nothing relating to the stimulus-word, e.g. *tree — a part*. The
disparity is here so great that the patient himself feels this gap,
and therefore adds, "The garden has trees" : cp. 23 and 24.
As this example shows, the patient tends to eliminate or limit
the extension, and therefore the inappropriateness, of his supraordinated general concept by particularizing his concept in the
actual object. This, again, he does in a way typical of feeble-
mindedness. He particularizes his general concept by affixing
some definite place to it ; this, by its naïve simplicity, often
puts it in strange contrast with the unlimited universality of
the concept (*particularized universal concept*). Almost classical
are :

Sky	part of heaven
Father	a companion together with mother
Cherry	a thing in the garden (cp. also 11, 31)

The favourite kind of explanation by means of an example is also used by our patient. Reactions of this kind are generally recognized by the form of sentence : " is, if you." The example can be *universal* (26, 28, 30, 32) or *particular*, when the subject, as a rule, takes an active part himself. In this connexion a typical reaction is *walk — that is when you stretch your legs for a pint on Sunday.*

The patient here uses the reminiscences of his Sunday excursions at the asylum. Here the great preponderance of the outer phenomenon over the meaning is very evident.

Looking at these reactions from the standpoint of Wundt's classification, we find here, as contrasted with normal persons, a marked preponderance of " inner associations " (if the use of this concept may be allowed at all in imbeciles). The number of inner associations far exceeds the average figures as given by Jung and Riklin for the uneducated, who were, however, not of the lowest grade of education.

The use here of the concept " inner association " is decidedly open to question. A calculation has shown that there are among the reactions seventy-seven per cent. of definitions, which are decidedly not the reproduction of the first impression, but rather the products of a lengthy process of reflection—that is, they are quite complicated mental structures. According to Jung's experiences with nearly twenty thousand associations in the uneducated, the intermixture of conscious reflection in the reaction begins high up in the region of the normal. The direct manner of reacting found among the educated, where practically the reaction-word is automatically linked on to the stimulus-word, is frequently neglected by the uneducated even of a relatively high grade. Conscious reflection as to the significance of the stimulus-word, with consequent tendency to explanation and to the formation of sentences, takes the place of the direct reaction ; there is almost habitually a suppression of the first words that do actually occur. As Jung and Riklin point out, the stimulus-word takes on more and more the character of a question the further we proceed from intelligence and education.

The inner associations of the uneducated are therefore not merely sudden ideas resting upon important relationships, but frequently a construction consciously sought out. This is pronouncedly the way in which imbeciles react. There is never a sharp demarcation from the normal ; they are only separated by certain differences in degree.

I have, therefore, no reason not to use the term " inner association," although there is really an essential difference between the imbecile " definition " and the " inner association " of the educated. I therefore use the word " association " rather in the sense of an intellectual reaction.

As the form of the reaction, especially the small number of outer associations, shows, the feeble-minded react with a great expenditure of attention. The association experiment means an important mental exercise to the imbecile. It seems strange that the subject should give himself such trouble instead of expressing himself, as most educated persons do, by simply giving one word for every stimulus-word. It cannot be maintained that the feeble-minded, who are able to define as our patient can, do not command a certain number of simple verbal connexions to the stimulus-word, taken from everyday language. Why do they not express themselves by these connexions, which are certainly present, in the reaction ? The stimulus-word, as Jung and Riklin show, is taken even by the uneducated normal as meaning something, by the side of which the merely verbal links fall into the background. The uneducated is not accustomed to deal with single words, but only knows them in connexions as symbols with a meaning ; under the influence of this habit constellation he is chiefly concerned with the meaning of the stimulus-word. All the reasons which hold good for this peculiar adjustment of the uneducated hold good also for the feeble-minded. His attention is fixed almost exclusively upon the meaning of the word, and, despite example and repeated admonition, can only by dint of great exertion, if at all, take up another mode of reaction. If we give any imbeciles time enough, and warn them constantly only to react with one single word appropriate to the stimulus-word, most of them will be able by training to produce a result which looks like the associations of a normal person. On the other hand, if we give the imbecile a free hand, only making clear at the beginning, by means of examples, that he has to say the first thing that occurs to him, he will force himself in the first reactions (as was frequently the case with my subject) into the mode recommended ; but he soon slips back into reacting by way of explanation, which suits him better.[1]

If the subject is constantly warned and requested to give a reaction in one single " appropriate " word, the experiment loses that freedom of its conditions by which what is specific can be brought out. A series of limited associations arise in which whatever is typical of the case cannot be recognized at all or at best with extreme difficulty. Our experiment is not designed to test the working capacity of the subject in any definite direction, but to create a method by which what

[1] There are, however, exceptions which we shall mention later.

is valuable for diagnosis may be brought out quickly and with certainty.

No. 2.   An idiot, 38 years old.   Total reactions, 66

1. Sunday	that is to-day	17. Asylum	that is one
2. Winter	that will come again	18. Attendant	sick attendant
3. Head	(points to his head) forehead	19. Oven	cylinder oven
4. Ink	ink-bottle	20. Walk	we are doing that now with Andrew
5. Bread	where we eat (i.e. what we eat)	21. Cook	the women do
6. Tree	a big and long (shows its size with his hands)	22. Dance	the others do that
		23. Cat	a kitten
7. Mountain	that is far away	24. Dark	it is now (it is rather dark in the room)
8. Salt	we want that for food	25. Heart	there (points towards his heart)
9. Copy-book	where we write	26. Bird	a vulture
10. Book	a little book	27. Moon	above in the sky
11. Lead-pencil	of lead	28. Sleep	we do that at night
12. Sing	they sing upstairs	29. Dark red	quite red
13. Ring	a large one (describes a circle in the air)	30. Sweet	quite sweet
		31. Friendly	when we shake hands
14. Frog	what hops about on the ground	32. Smell	we should stop smelling
15. Flower	bunch	33. Prison	that is a kind of little window (describes a small square in the air)
16. Cherry	where we eat		

This test exhibits essentially the same thing as the previous case—a pronounced tendency to explanation. But the manner of explanation is in some degree different from the previous case. The designations of time and purpose are common to both (5, 7, 8, 9, 16), as are also the accounts of the material (11) or the accounts of the action which the thing executes, or of the thing which executes a definite activity (2, 12, 14, 20, 21, 22, 28). The tautologies, which are partly specified by a slight external change, are relatively numerous. The particularization often takes place (as in the previous case) by the addition of an attribute characteristic of the object, or one which denotes it more concretely. Among the reactions which especially exhibit this are : tree — a big and long ; ring — a large one. These attributes serve to elucidate the object better, and to show at the same time that the subject has fully understood the stimulus-word. The same explanation holds good of those reactions where the stimulus-word is simply translated into its diminutive form (10, 23). It must be remembered that the subject only reacts in dialect. In dialect the diminutive form has a more familiar air ; hence its use by the

patient.   He wants to show that he is at home with the idea of
the stimulus-word, and that the thing is usually thus described.
If the reaction were completed to a sentence, as it probably is
at first in thought, the reaction runs :

Cat   that is a kitten
Book   that is a little book

The reaction *quite sweet* must be taken in a similar way.

The tendency to explanation is clear here ; but it is characteristic of this case that most of the associations are very brief
and arid.   The above-mentioned associations especially show
the absence of further associations.   To a certain extent the
subject contents himself with apprehending the sense of the
stimulus-word, and because he does not exactly know what to
do with it, he confirms the stimulus-word by a similar expression.   The great poverty in associations seems also to
favour a mode of reaction which could not be proved in the
previous case, i.e. the mere reference to the surroundings : *asylum
— that is one ; dark — it is now.*   These explanations again show
clearly the poverty in associations.   The subject does not go
beyond the stimulus-word at all and contents himself by showing
that he has understood it.   Reaction 33 illustrates beautifully
the imbecile manner of apprehension.   To the patient the small
square window-panes are the most important part of the presentation *prison*, because that is just the recognizable mark of it when
seen from without.

There is in these reactions, as a whole, a cleaving to the
concrete, to sensual perceptions.   There is not much beyond that.
In contrast to the previous case, we find no universal concepts
here.   The reaction is never far removed from the stimulus-word,
and the explanations are distinguished by a quite special absence
of any influx of associations.   This absence, visible in the quality
of the associations, was also shown in another way—by real
faults, that is, experiments in which no reaction at all occurred ;
although, as was proved by questioning him, the meaning of the
stimulus-word was understood.

In my opinion a good deal of the striking poverty in associations is to be ascribed to this inhibition.   As was stated in the
introductory remarks, a state of emotional stupidity occurs
relatively frequently among imbeciles, especially in the form
of an " examination paralysis " during association experiments.
As Jung has shown,[1] stupidity is chiefly characterized by an
inhibition of associative activity, the stimulus-words arousing
no associative processes.   The subject reacts with very long

---

[1] Jung, " Ueber Simulation von Geistesstörung," loc. cit., p. 181.

times naming surrounding objects, which, however, are in no way connected with the stimulus-word. The subject thus makes up for his lack of associations. If the inhibition (or rather prohibition) is stronger, perhaps he does not react at all ; faults then arise.

There is every appearance of a disturbance of this kind being present here, but a degree slighter than in Jung's case. The relatively numerous faults and the striking insufficiency of the definitions point to this. The timing of the reactions would naturally be a valuable means for the accurate recording of the momentary psychical condition ; unfortunately, my experiments were carried out at a time when our knowledge of the processes of association was very incomplete and when the great importance of the reaction-time was still unknown to us.

It is of practical importance to pay attention to anomalies of the emotions conditioned by momentary constellations. Stupidity can temporarily increase so much in a feeble-minded person as to lead one to think that it is a case of severe dementia. In forensic cases this phenomenon requires serious consideration.

No. 3. *Idiot, 65 years old*

There are no pronounced signs of dementia senilis. Patient has trouble in understanding the experiment, and throughout has very long reaction-times.

Total reactions, 58

1. Schoolboy	schoolboy repeating	16. Ring	white
2. Father	once threw me down-stairs	17. Tooth	wisdom teeth
		18. Window	of glass
3. Head	white	19. Frog	black
4. Ink	black	20. Asylum	there where people are in
5. Needle	where we sew with it		
6. Bread	white	21. Cherry	black
7. Tree	trees grow with quinces on them	22. Piano	people can play on it
		23. To cook	to cook potatoes
8. Mountain	there is a tree where quinces grow on it	24. Water	cold
		25. To dance	on the floor
9. Hair	white	26. Cat	they are white
10. Salt	white	27. Resin	black
11. Wood	black	28. Bird	white
12. Copy-book	white	29. Swim	I can also
13. Paper	white	30. Ride	on a horse
14. Book	has leaves	31. Sweet	that is white—that is sugar
15. Lead-pencil	has pictures on— pointed		

In this case we again find those traits of feeble-mindedness which we have repeatedly emphasized : statements of place, purpose, chief action or chief quality, etc. (5, 14, 15, 18, 20, 22, 25, 30). We find side by side with this the tendency to elucidation, to concrete understanding (1, 17, 23, 24). With this tendency there is connected also certain egocentric reactions in which distinct subjective reminiscences come to light, as in the characteristic reaction *father — once threw me downstairs* (cp. also 29).

A peculiarity of this case is the frequent repetition of the predicates *white* and *black*, which occur also in places where they are quite meaningless. *White* forces itself to the front, where it is only indirectly conditioned, as in 31. *White* perseverates also several times. Phenomena of this kind are occasionally found in marked stupidity, as, e.g., in the case mentioned before. In reaction 8 the subject does not hear the stimulus-word and in 15 only reacts to the stimulus-word subsequently. These phenomena require the same explanation as the abnormal perseverations of the previous case. Meaningless reactions likewise occur abundantly in emotional stupidity whenever this reaches a high degree, as Jung's case shows.

Some of the perseverations are certainly so marked that the suspicion of their being due to early cerebral atrophy cannot be put aside. As no definite observations of the effect of senile cerebral changes upon the mechanism of association have yet been made, I cannot decide how far the perseveration is conditioned entirely by emotional stupidity.

No. 4. *Idiot of a mild degree, 38 years old*
Total reactions, 145

1. Christmas	that is Christ's birth-day	17. Heart	the heart of a man
2. Sunday	for walks	18. Bird	a beast of prey
3. Winter	when it's cold	19. Swim	when we bathe in the Rhine
4. Father	when he has a son of his own	20. Hit	when we clout some one
5. Bread	for eating	21. Friendly	when we're jolly
6. Lamp	to make it light	22. Caress	flatter
7. Tree	where there are shadows	23. Grand	when they are proud
8. Mountain	when we go a journey	24. Wedding	that is when people marry
9. Hair	when we cut it	25. Sour	when it is sour
10. Sing	a song	26. Eel	a fish
11. Ring	when you are engaged	27. Eye	when we see
12. Cat	a beast of prey	28. Faithful	when nothing is taken (i.e. stolen)
13. Tooth	for eating		
14. Oven	for heating	29. Blood	that is from oxen
15. Dark	when it is night	30. Barn	at school
16. Dance	at holidays when music is heard	31. Family	when there are many children

We see again in this case a pronounced tendency to definition. It looks as if the subject had been told to say what he understood by the stimulus-word. The task is carried out in the usual way ; we have again accounts of time, place, purpose, and tautological elucidations (10, 17) in the forefront. There are, besides, a few explanations by example of a more universal character (4, 11, 15, 21, 23, 24) that are frequently but slightly separated from tautological elucidation or from a more particular character (8, 9, 19, 28, 31). Instances of the latter are the reactions : *mountain — when we go a journey* and *family — when there are many children* ; these are very characteristic of the psychology of feeble-mindedness, which adheres to concrete externality. The patient uses now and again the form of supraordination of a universal concept as a means of explanation (12, 16, 18). In 18 the general concept is not quite appropriate, but it is constellated by the previous reaction, 12 (*cat — beast of prey, bird — beast of prey*). Feeble-minded persons, especially those who are some-what inhibited by emotion, willingly lend themselves to constellations from previous stimulus- or reaction-words. In consequence of the blank association to the reaction, they make use of the same words even when they are not quite appropriate to the stimulus-word. I am inclined to regard such supraordinates as *cat — beast of prey, eel — fish*, as signs of a rather higher grade of the feeble-minded. These are universal concepts of a kind absent in a severe idiot unless they have to some extent been drilled into him in some educational asylum. General concepts, in the ordinary sense, are entirely absent ; he has only certain words which designate something general and indefinite to him, as *fact, part, thing, means, tools*, then *animal, plant, food*, etc. He brings his concrete instances under these universal concepts, which he uses quite widely and indiscriminately, even promiscuously ; if he wants to do more he particularizes, as we have seen, by simply appending the designation of a place or the like to his universal concept. All variants in concept between the concrete and universal supraconcept are either unknown to him or are unfamiliar. The occurrence of appropriate and proximate supraordinations like *dog — a mammal, tree — wood, lamp — means of lighting*, speaks, on the whole, against the presence of severe congenital feeble-mindedness. Therefore in this milder form of idiocy the occurrence of a few appropriate supraordinates cannot be entirely accidental.

No. 5. *A Peasant*, 40 *years old*. *Severe form of imbecility*
Total reactions, 200

1. Sunday	day of rest	24. Angry	when you are not
2. Winter	cold		satisfied
3. Schoolboy	they must go to	25. Proper	when he behaves
	school		quietly
4. Father	support of the house-	26. Inn	that is a restaurant
	hold	27. Family	four to five persons
5. Table	furniture	28. Fist	when you close the
6. Head	part of a man		fingers this way
7. Ink	for writing		(gesture)
8. Bread	that is a food-thing	29. People	many persons
9. Lamp	that is a lighting	30. Every-	when you are in many
10. Carriage	a pleasure-thing	where	places
11. Tree	for growing fruit	31. Gait	E. (a patient who
12. Wood	a thing for burning		limps) has a gait
13. Paper	for writing		like that
14. Book	for reading	32. Ointment	when you have some-
15. Sing	that is for enjoyment		thing on the body
16. Tooth	for biting things	33. Child	that is a person
17. Frog	an animal in water	34. Star	that is a thing in the
18. Oven	that is a thing in the		sky
	room	35. Roe	that is an animal
19. Heart	thing of a man	36. To thank	when you get some-
20. Swim	that is a favourite		thing from some-
	enjoyment		body
21. Marriage	that is for support	37. Brush	when you have dirty
22. Grand-			clothes
mother	that is a person	38. Plumb	for instance, you make
23. Hunter	he is in the wood		a fence plumb

The subject uses the definition form almost exclusively in
the reaction. The majority of the reactions are in the form of
sentences. Occasionally there is a slight tendency to abbreviation of the reaction, probably to be referred to the order given
at starting to say the first word that occurred. This is the case
in the explanatory supraordinates. Among these there are
certain universal concepts which appropriately denote the
stimulus-word (1, 5); but others are far too general and too
broad to characterize the meaning of the stimulus-word satisfactorily (10, 20, 22, 33, 35). The patient seeks to meet this
difficulty, as we have frequently seen, by adding some simple
definition to the general concept, e.g. *frog — an animal in water*,
star — that is a thing in the sky (similarly 6, 7, 12, 18, 19). These
supraordinates frequently show a certain verbal awkwardness,
as *lamp — that is a lighting* (similarly 11, 12). As usual, designations of purpose and place occur. Very characteristic of the
imbecile's external apprehension is the purpose of marriage,
which serves for *support*. Similarly the explanation of the

concept *family*, for which it is sufficient designation that it consists of *four to five persons* (similarly 25, 29).

The explanations by example show a very narrow and strongly individual view (24, 25, 28, 30, 36–38).

With the verbal awkwardness is linked a certain carelessness in the construction of new words, which are made *ad hoc.*

No. 6. *Severe form of imbecility.   Peasant, 30 years old*
Total reactions, 278

	December 9	December 15
1. Sunday	—— (fault)	Sunday has gone
2. Winter	winter is here	winter is here
3. Lake	—— (fault)	comes from a spring
4. Schoolboy	the schoolboy is active	the schoolboy must be active
5. Father	the father	—— (fault)
6. Table	the table is household furniture	the table is household furniture
7. Tree	is a vegetable	apple-tree
* 8. Mountain	the beautiful mountain	a beautiful mountain
9. Hair	the beautiful hair	beautiful hair
10. Salt	——	is a food
11. Wood	the beautiful wood	for burning
12. Sing	the beautiful song	beautiful song
13. Ring	is a beautiful	finger ring
14. Tooth	the teeth	wisdom-tooth
15. Window	the windows	house furniture
16. Frog	the frogs	frog in water
17. Piano	the beautiful piano	is house furniture
18. Dance	the beautiful dancing	on holidays
19. Bird	the beautiful bird	canary-bird
20. Swim	the birds swim	man can swim
21. Walk	—— (fault)	on Sundays
22. To cook	—— (fault)	food
23. Flowers	in the garden	
24. Cherry	is a food	
25. Oven	belongs to the house	
26. Badger	is an animal	
27. Heart	in the chest	
28. Dark	moonshine	
29. Beat	church	
30. To kindle	fire	
31. To stroke	cat	
32. Amiable	the man is amiable	
33. Ride	dragoons	
34. Cut	cutler	
35. Thirst	when you are thirsty	
36. Thumb	index finger	
37. Ill	the man is ill	

* The associations bracketed followed one another in the experiment.

December 9

38. Wedding	the wedding (dialect form)
39. Grandmother	older mother
40. Rich	when one is rich
41. Angry	when one is angry
42. Inn	the inn-house
43. Family	when father and mother are together
44. Hunger	when you are hungry
45. Murderer	with a knife
46. Pray	when you pray
47. Wrong	when you are shut up
48. Candle	a lighting up
49. Reward	when you are rewarded
50. School	day-school

We have two series of experiments from this patient. For the sake of readier comparison we have placed them in parallel tables. By comparing these two series a distinct difference can be noticed between the way of reacting on December 9 and that of December 15.

In the first experiment a series of perseverations, which I have bracketed, is noticeable. Beside these there are (as other tests show) numerous repetitions. The quality of the reaction is limited chiefly to tautological elucidations which are, in many cases, combined with a particular form of predicate (*beautiful*), used as frequently as possible, and perseverating through many terms. Another peculiarity of the tautology is the translation of the stimulus-word into the plural form (*frog —the frogs*). On the whole, these reactions show nothing which tells against the tendency to definition. Explanation and sentence-formation remain, however, stationary in the more primitive tautologies; no wider association to the stimulus succeeds. These phenomena denote a certain blankness of association like that peculiar to emotional stupidity. It is simply that nothing new occurs to the patient; he is like the nervous student at an examination. Further confirmation of this view is shown by the presence of faults. The faults mostly occur when a stimulus-word comes along to which the reaction form hitherto used can be no longer employed. The subject then finds himself bereft of all help, and makes a fault.

What is peculiar to this case is the occurrence of marked phenomena of perseveration, which were not demonstrated in the previous cases; this approximates to Jung's case, where there were a great number of perseveration phenomena. As shown by the investigations of Jung and Riklin in associations in a state of distraction, the perseveration exhibits a distinct, although not large, increase in distraction. The blankness of

association produced by this distraction seems to be the cause
of this phenomenon. In the absence of a new association the
subject takes that content of consciousness which has remained
over from the previous reaction. It seems to me that this
explanation is exactly true of this case of perseveration. The
subject when possible accepts the previous form of reaction
because nothing new occurs to him.

Now consider the second experiment of December 15. The
tendency to definition is also very pronounced here. Among the
first seven reactions, which show a stiff schoolboyish manner,
there is one fault. Only after the eighth reaction do the reactions
take on a somewhat freer appearance. The supposition that
there was at first a certain emotional inhibition is thus to some
extent justified. If we consider the other reactions we are struck
by the relatively numerous tautological elucidations—a form of
reaction which we first noticed to any considerable extent in
patient No. 2, who was shown to have emotional stupidity.
The tautologies of No. 6 show in part the quite primitive type of
repetition of the stimulus-word in its dialect form, with the
article frequently preceding the dialect word (38, 42). A further
number of tautologies show a nearer determination by combination
with a very near association, e.g. *school — day-school, tooth —
wisdom-tooth* (similarly 8, 9, 12, 16, 19). Other tautologies occur,
by way of example : " *is, if one,*" e.g. *thirsty — if one is thirsty*
(also 40, 41, 44, 46, 49). As usual, designations of time, place,
and purpose are present ; there are also found estimates of the
quality or activity in relation to the subject or, inversely, estimates
of the subject. The subject there prefers the word *man* (20, 32).
There also occur a few more or less appropriate supraordinations
(6, 10, 24, 26).

Amongst this material there are just a few reactions which
exhibit a higher value, and cannot be fitted into the form of a
definition. I mean the reactions *thumb — index finger, beat —
church* (clock), *dark — moonshine, murderer — with a knife.*
These reactions suggest an apparently creative imagination ;
the patient fashions the inner picture of a situation of which
he then names some part, without regard to the meaning of the
stimulus-word. The reactions only contain, it is true, simple
coexistent composite parts, but the fact that they occur at all
in a free form proves that the patient is not entirely chained to
the stimulus-word as a direct question. Reactions of this kind
are traces of a mental activity which has been freed to some
extent.

The personal basis of the explanations is shown in the
concept *family—when father and mother are together*; patient

was an orphan brought up in a strange family. The reaction *cut — cutler* shows a certain superficiality and verbal-clang connexion which are not very usual among imbeciles, any more than they are among the lower grade uneducated. Reactions of this kind are found chiefly among the educated. This fact also seems to suggest that association and verbal capacity are not very deep-seated.

The very primitive tautologies which we have established in this case offer a certain contrast with these signs of rather higher intellectual gifts. Clumsy and primitive reactions of this kind point, as we have seen, to emotional inhibition of associations. If we cannot prove this influence in the later reactions with all the certainty we should like, still the discovery is a warning to be cautious, for emotional stupidity can be made to represent an imbecile as much more demented than he actually is. Great care is, therefore, necessary before accepting the rapid tests of intelligence occasionally used in statistical works, with results which frequently afford such delightful bizarreries. This factor deserves consideration also *in foro*.

No. 7. *Imbecile woman, 58 years of age*
Total reactions, 59

1. Christmas	a tree like where it has presents on it	16. School	when you go to school
2. Sunday	—— (fault)	17. Sing	when you do the singing
3. Schoolboy	goes to school	18. Tooth	there in the mouth
4. Father	a father	19. Flower	it's in the garden
5. Table	for writing	20. Asylum	I am in an asylum
6. Head	headache	21. Piano	when you can play with it
7. Bread	for eating		
8. Lamp	for hanging up	22. Dark	when it is night
9. Tree	what grows apples or pears	23. Heart	—— (fault)
10. Mountain	up there on the mountain	24. Bird	when you have one in the cage there
11. Hair	up there on the head	25. Game	when you can play with it
12. Salt	when you have salt so that you can cook with it	26. Sugar	when you get sugar
		27. Ill	when you have to lie in bed
13. Wood	when you have wood for cooking		
14. Copy-book	when you have a copy-book		
15. Lead-pencil	when you have a lead-pencil		

This reaction type is obviously the same as that of the preceding cases. We again find the designations of place and

purpose, and explanations by example (1, 9, 24, 26, 27) which are
sometimes very characteristic. The tautologies are remarkably
frequent ; this, as in subjects 2 and 3, indicates a poor and
primitive temperament (4, 10–17, 25). Subsequently the tautologies are partly linked to designations of purpose. Faults
occur from time to time. (The reaction-times are extraordinarily
long.) The phenomena of perseveration are noticeable, and, as
usual, are particularly common when a series of convenient
nouns occurs. Unless such perseverations are purposely required
from the feeble-minded, care must be taken in drawing up the
lists that nouns do not directly follow one another several times.
In the list used in these experiments this, unfortunately, happens
a few times, but not to such an extent as in Sommer's schedule.

From the relatively numerous primitive tautologies, the faults
and the marked perseverations, it is justifiable to assume that
here also a slight emotional stupidity complicates the picture.

No. 8. *An idiot woman of slight grade, aged* 24

This patient exhibits a series of hysterical symptoms, chiefly
conditions of excitement, with a slight limitation of consciousness
and sexual content. Her conduct is generally shy and reserved.
It is strongly influenced by sympathies and antipathies. There
is, on the whole, inhibition towards the doctors, whilst her
behaviour towards her fellow-patients is distinctly freer.

Number of reactions, 186

1. Sunday	day after to-morrow	19. Dance	you dance
2. Lake	is big	20. Dark	when it is night
3. Father	is my father	21. Heart	the heart, which one has
4. Table	is brown		
5. Head	head with the face	22. Swim	you can swim
6. Ink	you write with it	23. White	a thing, where it's white
7. Bread	for eating		
8. Lamp	is lighted at night	24. Coffee	coffee where it's drunk
9. Carriage	for riding in		
10. Tree	is a tree	25. Wedding	when there's a wedding
11. Hair	you comb it		
12. Salt	you salt with it	26. Angry	when one's angry
13. Pencil	for writing	27. Sour	vinegar is sour
14. Sing	you sing	28. Rich	when one's rich
15. Ring	ring on the finger	29. Eyes	the two eyes, which you have
16. Window	for looking out of		
17. Frog	is a frog	30. Plant	when one plants something
18. Walk	when you go for a walk		

The tendency to definition in this case is obvious. The
patient announces what is the use of the object, what is done

with it, what she does, etc. Sometimes she explains by example (23, 27). Tautologies are most distinct, generally in the *when* form. Tautologies are particularly distinct when she adds anything to make the thing obvious (*head — head with the face ;* cp. also 21, 29). This tautology is sometimes limited to a quite primitive repetition of the stimulus-word (*tree — is a tree ;* cp. 17). In the original there was often marked perseveration in the reaction form, this could not be expressed in the tests given here.

Thus this case, too, follows the previous ones closely. Here again we find primitive tautologies and perseverations which are not to be explained by the feeble-mindedness alone, but which are complicated by slight inhibition of association based upon emotion.

The nature of the reactions agrees very well with the reserved and hampered behaviour of the patient.

No. 9. *An imbecile of severe degree, aged 32*

In jail he was taken ill with prison psychosis, was brought to the asylum and fully recovered. During convalescence a hysterical syncope occurred.

Number of reactions, 290

1.	Sunday	holiday		
2.	Lake	water		
3.	Table	for eating		
4.	Head	men		
5.	Ink	writing		
6.	Needle	sewing		
7.	Bread	eat		
8.	Lamp	light		
9.	Tree	fruit		
10.	Hair	on the head		
11.	Salt	eating		
12.	Copy-book	for writing		
13.	Book	for eating		
14.	Sing	not well		
15.	Ring	on finger		
16.	Tooth	in the mouth		
17.	Frog	legs for eating		
18.	Flowers	in the garden		
19.	Asylum	to get better		
20.	Walk	when one goes a walk		
21.	To cook	is to cook food		
22.	Cat	good for mice		
23.	Swim	when one's in the water		
24.	Beat	one hits		
25.	Star	stars		
26.	Stroke	when you stroke		
27.	Moon	the moon (in dialect form)		
28.	Ride	ride (in dialect form)		
29.	To watch	take care		
30.	Arm	an arm		

One is struck by the fact that at first the reaction is in one word ; but if we look at the quality of the reactions more closely we notice that we have only to add the usual *for* and other forms to get the same picture as in other imbeciles. This is distinctly seen in reaction 11, *salt — eating,* where the imbecile *for* is omitted. The first reactions are obviously due to the order 'to react with one word." In the later reactions the formation of sentences occurs increasingly, and thus we get the usual picture of the weak-minded (designations of purpose and place, tautologies, etc.). Tautological elucidations by translation into the dialect form occur frequently in this case (cp. Subject No. 2). The stimulus-word was given in literary German.

No. 10.   *Imbecile (see below)*
Number of reactions, 200

Sunday	beautiful	Schoolboy	young
Winter	cold	Needle	pointed
Head	clever	Father	old
Lake	big	Bread	tasty
Ink	black		

These were the first reactions in the experiment; they all had a very long reaction-time, generally over twenty seconds as measured by the watch. It was then suggested to the patient that it was not necessary for him to give an adjective to everything but just to say what occurred to him at the moment. The patient then continued:

Lamp	for burning	Salt	for eating
Tree	for bearing fruit	Wood	for burning
Hair	for protecting the head	Paper	for writing

After the patient had continued in the *for* direction during six reactions it was again pointed out to him that it was not necessary that he should constantly react by *for*. The form of the reaction then became a little freer. Nevertheless, until the end of the experiment the patient repeated this sixty-seven times in the two hundred reactions. The extremely forced style of the reaction, as seen in these experiments, gradually disappeared towards the end of the experiment and gave room to another type of reaction which, apart from the occasional repetition of *for*, gave but a slight impression of imbecility. I give some reactions from the end of the second half of the experiment:

1. Slate-pencil	for writing		13. Hot	summer
2. Growl	angry		14. Scissors	cut
3. Fruit	for cider		15. Vinegar	acid
4. False	faithless		16. Trap	catch
5. Soft	overheard		17. Sick	bad
6. Proud	haughty		18. Resin	sticky
7. Hay	dry		19. Polish	clean
8. Raspberry	sweet		20. Candle	for lighting
9. Mouth	for speaking		21. Vertical	horizontal
10. Home	for oneself		22. Pastry	food
11. Hedge	hedge (in dialect)		23. Wages	work
12. Cunning	sly		24. Lungs	for living

The *fors* which occur here are, it will be seen, in places which are less striking. The remaining reactions produce but a very slight impression of imbecility. The tendency towards explanation is, of course, not difficult to discover. The meaning of the stimulus-word is often confirmed by a synonym or the typical properties, or the actions of things are given. The meaning of the stimulus-word is reacted to with strict adhesion to its conceived meaning. This mode of reaction approximates very closely to that of many uneducated normals, and its differential diagnosis (apart from the frequent *for*) would be difficult to separate from mere want of education in a person with a rather low intellectual level. We will now compare these end reactions with a selection taken from the beginning and middle of the experiment.

Sing	for pleasure	Joke	from love
Flowers	in the garden	Right	for keeping
Piano	for music	Hope	for comfort
Oven	for warmth	Choose	for choice
Cook	for hunger	Flag	for carrying
Bird	for flying		

These reactions produce a greater impression of feeble-mindedness than the final ones. The whole course of the experiment shows that the patient was at first uncertain as to how he ought to react. When he was freed from the predicates he fell into another form which he chose spontaneously ; in this he persisted until far on in the second half of the experiment, but with decreasing intensity. Finally he arrived at a mode of reaction not far removed from the normal uneducated type.

The first reactions in the predicate form are, in my opinion, laboured constructions. Freed from this, the patient falls into another form of explanation in which he again persists for a long time. He only loses this narrow view after over one hundred reactions, the reaction then acquiring a much more normal appearance.

This behaviour appears to be only a particular expression of emotional stupidity. Here it occurs in the form of embarrassment at not knowing exactly what he is expected to do with the stimulus-word. This embarrassment is marked by an inhibition of association. The subject never sees more than one possible way of reacting, and that is always the same one ; all other possibilities seem to him remote. The inhibition thus acts chiefly upon the outer form of the reaction, and much less upon its content.

As stated above, this is not a case of severe imbecility.

The patient first came to the asylum late in life, and not on account of any intellectual weakness but chiefly because of his temperamental eccentricities. He is perverse and "obstinate," mistrustful, will only give a proper answer after much persuasion, usually much confused when first addressed, silent and very reserved even with the other patients, troubled by numerous tics. A behaviour frequently presented by hysterical imbeciles is recognizable from these traits. It is in these individuals that we most frequently find emotional stupidity.

No. 11. *An imbecile of slight grade, 40 years old, who could support himself independently*
Total reactions, 100

1. Green	hope	16. Lamp	the lamp is a room light
2. Prick	smash		
3. Angel	little angel	17. Yellow	gold is yellow
4. Ship	sailing	18. Manners	politeness is manners
5. Friendly	practise friendship	19. Despise	a criminal is despised
6. Table	keep table ready	20. Tooth	the tooth aches
7. Bear	bear sorrows	21. Frog	the frog swims in water
8. Rod	Aaron's rod		
9. Dance	dance joyously	22. Ring	a ring on the finger is a remembrance
10. Lake	sailing in the lake		
11. Ill	have often been ill	23. Lead-pencil	the pencil is used for writing
12. Swim	swim in the lake		
13. Blue	the sky is blue	24. Take care	the schoolboy must take care
14. Bread	bread is a food		
15. Threaten	somebody is threatened	25. Flower	is a garden-ornament

It is easy to see in this case how the order given at the start to react with one word only is obeyed, how its effect gradually diminishes and soon gives place to explanation and formation of sentences. By the addition of the necessary parts of the sentence the reactions, at first given curtly, are easily turned into the customary type of sentence. The later reactions are correctly phrased school expressions. The subject is back in his schoolboy attitude and tries to find the most appropriate and best-worded sentence. He is obviously more at home in this position than in the one prescribed for him by the experimenter; when he apprehends the stimulus-word it is more difficult for him to answer in telegraphic style than by forming a sentence. The sentences of this subject are differentiated from most of the previous cases by their correctness and proper grammatical form. This by itself entitles one to assume a certain education and intelligence. All the same, formations occasionally occur of a markedly imbecile nature (e.g. *room-light; garden-ornament* is also somewhat suspicious).

The stimulus-word is explained in the usual way by designations of purpose and place, by a statement of the object and subject of the activity or a statement of the action of the thing, by example or by supraordination, etc.

Contrasted with the previous subject, it is to be noted that every reaction here is more adequate, somewhat more intelligent and correct. This impression may perhaps be confirmed by the absence of tautologies. No emotional inhibition can be observed here.

I will now give the reactions of two similar patients :

No. 12.   *An imbecile, 49 years of age*
Number of reactions, 156

1. Sunday	holiday	18. Cat	is a domestic animal
2. Lake	water	19. Heart	blood flows from the heart
3. Father	man		
4. Table	room-furniture	20. Moon	shines at night
5. Head	part of body	21. Hit	the teacher hits the inattentive boy
6. Bread	food		
7. Lamp	for lighting	22. Caress	the girl caresses the cat
8. Mountain	high	23. Child	is cold in winter
9. Wood	grows in forest	24. Amiable	the man is amiable
10. Book	for reading	25. Cut	the reaper cuts the corn
11. School	good for learning	26. Ill	many people are ill in winter
12. Tooth	white		
13. Frog	is an insect	27. Star	is in the sky
14. Flower	is a plant	28. White	is a colour
15. Cherry	is sweet	29. Kindle	the baker kindles the wood
16. Walking	it is nice to walk out in fine weather		
17. Dance	people dance at a ball	30. Emperor	is a person

No. 13.   *An imbecile,* 17 *years old*
Total reactions, 200

1. Sunday	church	18. Cat	flesh, hair
2. Lake	water	19. Heart	flesh
3. Father	man	20. Moon	the moon is in the sky
4. Table	wood	21. Hit	the teacher hits the boy
5. Head	flesh	22. Caress	the mother caresses the cat
6. Bread	flour and salt		
7. Mountain	stone and gravel	23. Child	the father has children
8. Lamp	petroleum	24. Friendly	the father is friendly with the boy
9. Wood	tree		
10. Book	paper	25. Cut	I cut the bread
11. School	schoolboy	26. Ill	I have been ill
12. Tooth	the teeth are in the jaw	27. Stars	there are innumerable stars in the sky
13. Frog	flesh		
14. Flower	blossom	28. White	the sheet is white
15. Cherry	stalk, flesh, and stone	29. Kindle	the mother kindles the fire
16. Walk	the people go for a walk		
17. Dance	the people dance	30. Emperor	Germany has an emperor

In these milder cases of imbecility there is a greater wealth of ideas and a greater verbal dexterity. We find here, on the whole, an entire limitation to the meaning of the stimulus-word, but the reactions do not imply merely that the patient has understood the stimulus-word (the absence of primitive tautologies shows this) but they can also form a sentence with the stimulus-word, such sentences being no longer exclusively explanations or definitions. The examples show that a sentence is formed much as in school, when the master says, "Make a sentence with the word . . ." The sentence as such thus becomes the purpose and the tendency towards explanation recedes into the background. The tendencies are so mixed in our examples that it is difficult to decide whether we have to do with a school-sentence or an explanation.

Dr. Jung informs me that such school-sentences occur in lower-grade normal uneducated and in educated hysterical persons. For a differential diagnosis a very large material is necessary—at least one hundred reactions, better two hundred, in which signs of imbecility must be looked for that differentiate it from simple want of education.

In our experiments the most striking feature is the course of the reactions. At first, obeying the injunctions, both patients answer in a single word, but they soon relinquish this inconvenient form and make sentences, which form they retain to the end. It becomes interesting to see how the two patients conceive their tasks. No. 12 constructs mainly supraordinated concepts, together with a few designations of purpose and predicates ; No. 13 endeavours to give whenever possible the substantial nature of the thing referred to by the stimulus-word (e.g. *bread — flour and salt*). This divergence in apprehension apparently conditions a deep difference between the two. But directly they discover their own appropriate sentence-formation the difference at once disappears and the reactions assume the same, often most surprisingly similar, character.

The one-sided apprehension at the beginning has something of the imbecile about it ; this comes to light distinctly when the chosen form of reaction encounters a stimulus-word where anything rather than that kind of reaction would be in place (e.g. *frog — flesh ; cat — flesh, hair*), or, again, where the supraordinated concept is even wrong (e.g. *frog — is an insect*). If reactions of this kind occur only once or are very exceptional the diagnosis of slight imbecility would be rather speculative, but if they occur frequently its probability is great.

So far as the sentence reactions are concerned, the discovery of imbecile traits becomes rather more difficult. Taken as a whole, the sentence form gives rise to a suspicion of slight imbecility, or at least of a very low grade of culture. Marked leaning to the meaning of the stimulus-word is a differential factor from the reactions of certain hysterics who also employ the sentence form ; but these use it with a school-like restriction often deliberate, and with great circumlocution as to that meaning of the stimulus-word which is of most importance to the patient.

As we have seen in every case, the tendency to definition is of the greatest importance in the reaction of the feeble-minded. The more striking this tendency in the reactions, the more probable, on the whole, is the imbecility of the patient. Special attention should be paid to tautologies, to awkward turns of the reaction, to examples which denote a very peculiar temperament (e.g. *friendly — the man is friendly; glaring — that is a glaring colour ; sweet — the new cider is sweet; ill — I have been ill; child — the father has children ; emperor — is a person*, etc.).

5. Time Measurements

As previously mentioned, 764 time measurements were taken in five subjects ; the measurement was recorded on a one-fifth second stop-watch, set when the stimulus-word was spoken and stopped at the utterance of the reaction. The time was measured in patients 6, 5, 8, 11, 13. The stimulus-words were divided into concrete, abstract, adjective, and verb. The mean numbers, which I give individually for each of these groups, are the probable mean in seconds.[1]

	No. 6	No. 5	No. 8	No. 11	No. 13	Average of uneducated normals[2]	Average of the subjects
Concretes . .	4	4	4·8	3	1·4	1·8	3·4
Abstracts . .	4·4	4	5	3·4	2	2·3	3·7
Adjectives . .	3·2	4	5	3·4	2	1·9	3·5
Verbs . .	3·8	4	4	3·4	1·4	2·2	3·3
Probable mean of all times . .	3·8	4	5	3·4	1·6	2	3

Patient No. 6 is not so feeble-minded as she seems to be from her position in this series. She was only treated as among the most difficult cases because she has a certain similarity with these cases by reason of her emotional stupidity. By her intelli-

[1] The method of reckoning is the same as given by Aschaffenburg.

[2] I am indebted for these figures to Dr. Jung ; they are taken from 2200 time measurements. The average figures are the arithmetical mean of the individual subjects.

gence she belonged to about No. 9. Viewing the table with this correction, we notice that with the increasing degree of intelligence there is a shortening of the probable mean. No. 8 is the only one who affords any considerable exception to this. No. 8 is the idiot with the hysterical characteristics who in daily intercourse shows also much retardation and inhibition.

The average figures of our patients, which I have placed alongside those of the uneducated normals, show prolongation of the association times among imbeciles, although No. 13 is below the probable mean of the uneducated normals. As will be seen from the table, the longest times occur, on the average, with the abstract stimulus-words ; this is also the case among the uneducated normals. The shortest times, however, do not occur, as among normals, with concretes but with verbs ; the cause of this is not at once obvious.

The marked prolongation of the association times among imbeciles is chiefly due to the difficulty of intellectual effort. But that this is not the whole ground is shown by No. 6, in connexion with whom I possess two series of experiments. The first of the series was taken at the beginning of his detention in the asylum, after continuous and exhaustive examination ; the second about a week later. The probable mean of the first series is 8·6 seconds, that of the second 3·8.[1]

These figures show that, besides intellectual difficulty, emotional factors have also a considerable influence upon the reaction-time. A first set of experiments upon an imbecile therefore possesses only very relative value so far as reaction-time is concerned (and also quality).

6. RECAPITULATION

One of the most striking peculiarities of the imbecile reaction as contrasted with the normal consists in the fact that the feeble-minded seldom react with one word ; generally they employ several words or make whole sentences. In the introduction I quoted the view of Jung and Riklin, who say that the uneducated conceive the stimulus-word as a question, i.e. as standing in some fictitious connexion with a sentence. That is the explanation of the greater care bestowed upon the reaction by the uneducated, as shown by their reproducing on the average more inner associations than the educated. The imbeciles, who in every respect are linked to the lowest grade of the uneducated, show fundamentally the same phenomena. They apprehend the

[1] The stimulus-words of the first series were in part repeated at the second experiment, but this could have had but very slight effect on the great difference in the figures.

stimulus-word quite unmistakably as a question. That is the explanation of their preference for the sentence form in the reactions. As we have seen, school reminiscences play no small part ; as Cordes [1] pertinently remarks, it often seems as if the teacher's behest " to answer in a whole sentence " was still taking effect. The tendency to " answer " with a whole sentence is strongly marked in my patients ; when they were requested to give the reaction in one word and shown by example how to do so, the experiment was soon ruined by the limited apprehension, the verbal poverty, and the consequent formal method of expression.

The frequent sentence-formations render the classification of imbecile associations considerably more difficult. The Kräpelin-Aschaffenburg classification is only helpful in exceptional cases ; in the majority of cases this logical-verbal classification is out of the question ; its application to sentences is a forced one. For these cases we must use the points of view which follow from the analysis of my material.

We have found that the *tendency to definition* is the chief sign of the feeble-minded reaction. The feeble-minded tries by reason of his sluggish temperament to explain the stimulus-word, or at least to express something which is a characteristic of it. The association experiment thus loses something of the character it has acquired from experiments with the educated. The reaction does not follow directly ; it no longer arises automatically from the unconscious, but it is something sought for, it is a construction that follows a definite scheme. The reproduction of the first (verbal) thought that occurs, as demanded by the original experiment, thus completely fails ; this is replaced by the conscious evoking of a series of associations in a definite direction. We thus find an " adjustment " which is exclusively directed to the meaning of the stimulus-word, the exact opposite of the adjustment which Jung and Riklin have demonstrated in highly cultured persons, whose reactions were chiefly determined by the uttered word. Between these two extremes lie all the remaining possibilities of reaction in the educated and the uneducated. The tendency to definition can, as we have seen, obtain expression in many forms. The primary form is :

(A) *Tautological Elucidation*

This is a very simple form of explanation and is expressed rather in the form of the spoken word than in the words themselves, in so far as it is concerned with the most rudimentary form of

---

[1] Wundt's *Phil. Studien*, Bd. XVII.

the mere repetition of the stimulus-word (i.e. finally with the article and translation into dialect : *cat — the little cat*). The *when* form is not much higher : *quarrel — when you quarrel, angry — when you're angry*. Tautologies, to which any more or less indifferent predicate is added, belong here : *mountain — the high mountain ; hair — the beautiful hair*. Rising above these primitive forms there is a whole series of tautological elucidations, which approximate more or less to an analysis and thus cannot be sharply separated from this form of explanation.

(B) *Analysis*

The meaning of the stimulus-word is formally defined by a sentence, as general as possible, with numerous factors conditioning it : *prison — consists of cells where useless people are locked up ; year — twelve months*.

(C) *Supraordination*

The stimulus-word is supraordinated to some universal concept, always with a tendency to explanation. The following possibilities occur :

(1) The supraordination is an appropriate one, i.e. the stimulus-word is marked with sufficient sharpness by the supraordinated general concept (*cat — domestic animal ; table — furniture ; bread — food*).

(2) The supraordination is inappropriate ; the general concept is too wide and too indefinite to characterize sufficiently the stimulus-word (*head — part ; tree — thing ; father — a man ; son — human being*).

(3) The supraordination is too wide a general concept but it is limited by some particular by-concept—generally some designation of time or purpose (*cherry — a garden thing ; star — part of the sky ; wood — thing for burning*).

(D) *Definition of Time, Place, Means, Purpose, Origin, etc.*

The stimulus-word is denoted by the addition of one of these designations (*book — for reading ; stove — for heating*).

(E) *Statement of the principal Quality or Activity*

The meaning of the stimulus-word is explained or defined by giving the chief action or quality of the object in question (*bird — flies ; wood — burns*).

(F) *Statement of the Subject of the Activity or Quality*

The stimulus-word is an adjective or verb. The reaction is a
noun, whose chief activity or quality is given by the stimulus-
word (*swim — fish swim ; blue — the sky*).

(G) *Example*

The example, which is given to explain the stimulus-word,
can be universal (e.g. *war — when two countries quarrel with one
another*) or particular, i.e. of a subjective nature, e.g. :

Ill	I have already been ill
Sorrow	when you have much work and can't do it
Wreath	there is one at a gymnasium festival
Wages	that is when you work in a factory
Father	he once threw me downstairs

So far as my experience goes, these groups include pretty
well most of the possibilities that occur. The overwhelming
majority of imbecile reactions (the sluggish variety) betray the
tendency to definition. As we have seen, however, in the slighter
forms of imbecility, sentences occur which have no pronounced
character, but are merely school-sentences which state something about the stimulus-word. These reactions, of course,
remain outside our schedule.

CHAPTER IV

ANALYSIS OF THE ASSOCIATIONS OF AN EPILEPTIC

By DR. C. G. JUNG

EPILEPSY is one of the few mental diseases whose symptomology is thoroughly known, and its limits defined, by a wealth of cases and of systematic studies. Psychiatry has proved that together with the epileptic fits mental degeneration is extremely common; of the latter it may be asserted that it is specific and therefore of diagnostic value. We will merely mention the chief features of epileptic degeneracy as given in any good textbook:

(1) INTELLECTUAL : Feeble-mindedness, retardation of mental reactions, loquaciousness, limitation and poverty of the imagination, with a corresponding poverty and stereotypy of speech, frequently abnormalities of fantasy.

(2) EMOTIONAL : Irritability, waywardness, marked egocentricity, exaggeration of all intellectual feelings, especially of religiosity.

These qualities form the so-called epileptic character, which, once set up, must be regarded as a permanent structure. Temporary augmentations of one or other quality, which spring from an intercurrent fit, are probably present. Even without knowledge of the epileptic attacks the diagnosis can be made with sufficient certainty by the presence of the epileptic character, although cases of this kind seldom arise. When the attacks are rare it frequently happens that the epileptic character is only slightly developed. From a practical point of view it becomes therefore of some value to find an exact expression of epileptic degeneration.

Attempts have been repeatedly made of late to investigate the epileptic aberrations by experimental methods. Colucci [1] and Breukink [2] have experimented with the ergograph ; Sommer [3]

[1] Colucci, "L'Allenamento ergografico nei Normali e negli Epilettici," *Riforma medica*, Anno XVIII, No. 36, 1902.

[2] Breukink, "Ueber Ermüdungskurven bei Gesunden und bei einigen Neurosen und Psychosen," *Journal für Psych. u. Neur.*, Bd. IV, 1904.

[3] Sommer, *Lehrbuch der psychopath. Untersuchungsmethoden.*

and more especially his pupil Fuhrmann,[1] directed their attention to association in epileptics. We regard these latter investigations as peculiarly adapted for a more exact formulation of epileptic degeneration.

Fuhrmann gives an account of the investigation of the associations in two epileptics. The first case was that of a patient who had suffered since the age of ten. The author demonstrated in this case that the predicates were strongly marked and that the egocentric factor played an unusually large part. The reactions in this case could not all be regarded as " associations " ; there were also word-reactions whose content and form were in no inner connexion with the stimulus-word. Fuhrmann calls these reactions " unconscious." These reactions were found (according to his tables) at the beginning of the experiment. Series 1 began with the following reactions :

1. Light	belief	5. Red	parents
2. Dark	health	6. Yellow	father
3. White	arm	7. Green	chair
4. Black	blue	8. Blue	arm

Furhmann did not attempt any interpretation. Kräpelin [2] has accepted this observation in the new edition of his textbook, vol. ii, p. 626, where he makes the following remarks :

" It seems as if these images, which were liberated, but not produced, by the experiment, proceeded from permanent general tendencies of ideas. Their content was mostly related to the state of the disease, or, anyway, to the personal relationships of the patient. We must take it that the frequency of such associations, determined by inner conditions, not by outer excitation, are more peculiarly favoured by the sluggishness of the epileptic. It is this which, unlike the healthy person, prevents his finding quick and easy links to the stimulus-word."

In 1903 I showed in my work " Ueber Simulation von Geistesstörung" (loc. cit., p. 181) the disproportionate occurrence of similar meaningless associations in an imbecile during a state of emotional stupidity. Wehrlin [3] has proved this exhaustively with documentary evidence in his investigations on imbeciles and idiots. In our experience such meaningless reactions always occur when the subject is in a condition of emotional stupidity ; this may, of course, occur in every possible condition of mental aberration. There is, thus, nothing specific of epilepsy in these " unconscious " reactions.

[1] Fuhrmann, *Analyse des Vorstellungsmaterials bei epileptischem Schwachsinn* (Diss : Giessen, 1902).

[2] Kräpelin, *Lehrbuch*, VII. Auflage, 1904.
    See chapter iii.

To return to Fuhrmann's work : after about a month the experiment was repeated with the same stimulus-words in the first case.

The second case was that of a patient who had been ill since his seventeenth year. Four repetitions of the reactions were made here within eight months, demonstrating a considerable limitation of the " field of association," a marked monotony of the reactions. Upon the basis of the associations of two female idiots Fuhrmann holds it as a " delimitating " difference between epilepsy and idiocy that the latter knows no supraordinated concepts. But Wehrlin has shown that the idiot does recognize supraordinated concepts although they are extremely primitive. The distinction must therefore really be something much more subtle than Fuhrmann seems to suppose.

Riklin [1] in his valuable article on " Hebung epileptischer Amnesien durch Hypnose " (Occurrence of Epileptic Amnesia through Hypnosis) refers to some association experiments on epileptics. He enters more into the quality of the reactions and thus reaches various important conclusions.

He demonstrated *adherence to the content of the reaction, clinging to the same grammatical form, marked relation to the ego, personal constellations, frequent emotional accentuation of the content of the reaction, and poverty of the imagination.*

These peculiarities are for the most part nothing but reflections of the epileptic character. Riklin has proved the possibility of reading the signs of epileptic degeneration from a series of association experiments. In criticism of Riklin's observations it must, however, be stated that (1) perseveration of the grammatical form is not necessarily an epileptic symptom—Wehrlin has shown enormous perseveration of the form in imbeciles and idiots (chapter iii) ; (2) perseveration of the content occurs also in normals, as I have shown in my joint work with Riklin (chapter ii). Ego-relationships and personal constellations also occur among normals and feeble-minded, as does likewise the emotional accentuation of the content of the reaction. Poverty of the imagination is obviously not characteristic of epilepsy, but of the feeble-minded as a whole ; as it is also, in a certain sense, for emotional stupidity, where it acquires the peculiar form of " blank association."

In epilepsy, therefore, we have rather to do with a greater or lesser degree of the symptoms which have something of a specific character. My endeavour has been to clarify these conditions and to attempt to separate what is specific in epileptic associations from the different types of normal persons and

[1] Riklin, *Jour. für Psych. u. Neur.*, 1904.

from congenital feeble-mindedness. Work of this kind must obviously rest upon a large material. The Swiss Asylum for Epileptics in Zurich, with its large number of patients, afforded me an exceptionally favourable opportunity. The greater part of the material was collected by the superintendent of the asylum, Dr. Ulrich ; a small part was obtained in the Burghölzli Asylum for the Insane. The total number of persons examined was 158 ; the total number of associations, 18,277. This extensive basis permitted, to a certain degree, an estimate of the various possibilities in the associations of epileptics : Dr. Ulrich and myself therefore undertook a methodical working up of this field, which covers so much that is of great interest. In order to apprehend the essence of the alterations of associations in epileptics as closely as possible, I proposed the following division of the material :

First of all I separated those cases who were not born feeble-minded and who were attacked by epilepsy only after the completion of their development, or at least after puberty.

I was thus able to reject from among the epileptics those extremely numerous cases where congenital feeble-mindedness complicates the picture of the disease. As Wehrlin's work shows, the imbeciles, in so far as they are to any extent distinctly feeble-minded, appear to have a fairly characteristic type of association, marked chiefly by the tendency to " definition " of the stimulus-word. The first investigation of epileptics showed us association types which had, at first sight, great similarity with the imbecile type. The similarity was still greater in the case of epileptics congenitally imbecile or with marked deterioration in early youth. This separation was thus absolutely essential for the recognition of what is specifically epileptic.

For external reasons a further division of the work was made ; in the first instance I analysed the reactions of a typical case as exhaustively as possible, whilst Dr. Ulrich investigated the different possibilities of the epileptic reaction types.[1]

Before beginning the report on the observations I must make a few remarks on the technique of the procedure.

The preparation of the patient for the experiment is an absolutely necessary step. It must be remembered that these persons have, as a rule, no notion of what the experiment demands from them ; they thus become easily confused, and this, when at all pronounced, affects the result most distinctly, as I have repeatedly seen. Therefore we provide some kind of instruction before the experiment. The patient is told that some word will be called out to which he is to answer as quickly as possible—

---

[1] Dr. Ulrich's work is not included in this volume.

without thinking at all about it—with the very first word or the very first idea that occurs to him. Some examples are then given, the experimenter giving a pretty complete selection of the different associations. The subject is thus placed in a position freely to select the mode of reaction proper to him. If he is not prejudiced he will naturally choose the mode which is characteristic for him. We take care that the subject is not cramped by restricting himself to a reaction with a single word. Should this be the case the characteristic mode of reaction is quite effaced and the reaction-time considerably affected. With women it is not infrequently necessary to subdue impending emotion by a rather simple explanation. I usually do this by representing the experiment as a kind of game of thoughts.

A fresh list of stimulus-words was used in these experiments. It was composed of two hundred different words, of which seventy-five were concrete, twenty-five abstract, fifty adjectives, and fifty verbs. The serial order is noun–adjective, noun–verb. The intermixture was as complete as possible, so that related words did not follow one another. No notice was taken of the number of syllables. The stimulus-words were taken from quite different spheres of daily life, practically avoiding all rare words. A series of emotionally toned concepts such as love, kiss, luck, friendly, etc., were purposely interspersed, for a peculiar significance attaches to such words.

I select the following case from our material :

M. Joseph, machine-locksmith, born 1863, a widower, childless. Has been convicted nineteen times. Alleged to have no familial predisposition. Good at school ; served a three years' apprenticeship to a locksmith, good testimonial as to work. No illness of moment in his youth, no signs of epilepsy : was married in 1888. His wife became insane in 1893 and died in an asylum. Since his wife's illness the patient, till then settled and industrious, began a restless life, travelling nearly all over Europe. He soon ran away from any settled work took to drink, travelling without any plan and wandering about in the forests. In this period he was often in the hands of the police, mostly for theft. Patient states that he has amnesia for the greater part of this period. During 1893–94 he was three times in an asylum for severe " mania transitoria." In 1896 patient fractured his skull. In 1896–98 he was again in various asylums with delirium. In 1898 tremors were observed confined to one side, occurring in paroxysms. At this time there was noticed a rather connected delirium with plastic and very stable visions, which were described by the patient with much emotion. At the end of 1904 patient wandered about aimlessly and half starved in the mountains. Then he wound up a drinking bout by stealing a bicycle. After this he again wandered about aimlessly, and was caught by the police. Placed in this asylum for observation, the following report was made :

" Feeble-minded, with epileptic character. There are frequent brief seizures of momentary unconsciousness with aura : Sees dark points, five to six in a row, which are always going up and down ; feels as if his head were pressed in or fastened together by screws ; his chest feels as if drops of water were trickling down; there is a buzzing in the ears; then anxiety and dread gets hold of him as if he had done something wrong, or he feels pains in his back which mount up to his head; he has the feeling as if he must tear everything, or he feels as if a locomotive were suddenly rushing towards him."

He becomes dizzy after this aura, everything turns round and he loses consciousness. These lapses of consciousness were also objectively observed during conversation, and especially whilst card-playing. Very marked intolerance for alcohol.

The associations of this case seem to me in many respects very typical for epilepsy, although all the characteristic symptoms were not present. Each case has its own peculiarities, for even here individual differences between the reaction types play a great part.

1. Coal	pit coal: 7·2 seconds	
2. Moderate	not eat much: 12 seconds.	
3. Song	sing, to sing a song: 6·2 seconds	
4. Suppose	I suppose, what do I suppose? many things: 23·2 seconds	
5. Pain	because I am ill: 4·2 seconds	
6. Dirty	when an apple is dirty, a plant, everything can be dirty: 5·8 seconds.	
7. Moon	that is the moon in the sky, the moon is there: 3·4 seconds	
8. Laugh	people laugh: 4·2 seconds	
9. Coffee	people drink it, people drink it every day: 4 seconds	
10. Wide	that is the width of a distance (with explanatory gesture): 6·2 seconds	
11. Air	that is the air, the air of nature, healthy or unhealthy, good air is good air: 2·2 seconds	
12. Carry	I carry something, a burden or good clothes: 5 seconds	

These first twelve reactions allow us to draw certain conclusions. The most striking thing is that the patient does not react merely by one single word but generally by a whole sentence. A certain significance attaches to this fact. In my experience, based upon an investigation of over thirty thousand normal associations, normal persons prefer, as a rule, the reactions in one word (*N.B.*, after preliminary instruction as described). There are exceptions where educated persons favour the sentence form; Riklin and myself quoted an instance of this in our work on the associations of normals. This particular person belonged to the "complex constellation type," that is, to the reaction type whose associations at the time of the experiment were under the influence of a presentation complex marked by emotion.[1] In cases of that kind we recognize at once the peculiar constellation by the content of the associations. Among normals there is another type who prefers to express his reactions not exactly in the sentence form but in two or more words:

---

[1] See p. 140.

The Predicate Type [1]

Persons of this type form judgments upon and evaluate the object designated by the stimulus-word. This naturally takes the form of a predicate, which sufficiently explains the use of several words. In any case these two types cannot be mistaken for the reactions with which we are now concerned.

The sentence form is, however, so frequent and widespread in the pathological sphere that it becomes difficult to regard it as pathognomonic. An observation worth mentioning—which I cannot, however, support by figures—is that uneducated mental patients seem to have a greater tendency to the sentence form than educated ones. Should this observation be confirmed, it could easily be brought into harmony with the fact that the uneducated attach much greater importance to the stimulus-word than the educated—a fact repeatedly brought out in the previous chapters. Extremely uneducated persons, whose aim is to give the most " appropriate answer " and to explain the stimulus-word as well as possible, require for this purpose many more words than the educated, who frequently just string the words together verbally. This tendency is seen most distinctly in idiots and imbeciles, where sentences are very frequently constructed.[2]

It would be difficult to understand the preference for the sentence form in our case without some such special supposition this preference entitles us to believe, with great probability, that there is some abnormality.

Before investigating the content of the reactions, we must pay some attention to the reaction-times. These are abnormally long. (The average reaction-time of the uneducated is two seconds.) No conclusions can for the moment be drawn from this, for there is no form of disease in which the reaction-times may not be prolonged. Aschaffenburg has found the reaction times somewhat prolonged in maniacal excitement. It is not advisable to investigate the reaction-times in association experiments for themselves, apart from the analysis of the content of the association, for they are absolutely dependent upon the momentary content of consciousness.

Now consider the quality of the associations.

It is at once apparent that the patient gives himself up to the meaning of the stimulus-word, with a pronounced tendency

[1] See p. 142.

[2] In Bleuler's view another fact favours the occurrence of the sentence form in the feeble-minded. The feeble-minded not only grasp with great difficulty a word apart from its context in a sentence, but can hardly think of words apart from the context.

to elucidate and characterize the thing designated by the stimulus-word. Wehrlin has regarded this tendency as peculiarly characteristic of congenital feeble-mindedness. Our case is certainly not one of congenital feeble-mindedness. Perhaps this tendency to explanation arises in every high-grade feeble-minded person ; perhaps it should be assumed that the demented approximates to the congenital imbecile in certain points, even if the causes of the two conditions are quite different. In our case the tendency towards explanation is so distinct that we can readily confirm the forms found in Wehrlin's work on imbeciles.

As " tautological elucidation " consider, for instance :

Suppose	I suppose, etc.
Carry	I carry something, etc.
Air	that is the air, etc.

As explanation by " example " we have :

Moderate	not eat much
Dirty	when an apple is dirty, etc.
Wide	that is the width of a distance (with explanatory gesture)

As " statement of the principal quality or activity " we have :

Laugh	people laugh
Coffee	people drink it

In this respect we can demonstrate obvious agreement with the imbecile tendency to explanation. It can be even said that the patient endeavours not to be misunderstood in this respect. For instance, when there might be some possible doubt as to whether there is a superficial current verbal connexion, as *song — sing, coffee — people drink*, he adds something so as to confirm and complete the explanation :

Song	sing, to sing a song
Coffee	people drink, people drink it every day. (Similarly 4, 11, 12)

These instances show that the patient seems to need to emphasize this tendency to explanation.

Besides this tendency, three of the twelve reactions exhibit the word " I." Reactions of this kind are egocentric. Egocentric reactions occur also in normals, where they are found in persons with the " egocentric attitude." [1] This adjustment can be found in three different forms :

(1) The subject uses a series of personal reminiscences in his reactions.

(2) The subject is under the influence of an emotionally toned presentation complex. He refers nearly every stimulus-word to

[1] See p. 138.

himself (i.e. to the complex) and responds to it as if it were a question touching the complex.

(3) The subject belongs to the predicate type and evaluates the thing denoted by the stimulus-word from the personal stand-point.

In these three types the ego comes occasionally to the front. Besides this, egocentric reactions occur, on the average, more frequently in the educated than in the uneducated, and most frequently when the subject is unembarrassed. We found the average figures of egocentric reactions to be 1·7 per cent. in uneducated men, only 0·5 per cent. in uneducated women. This makes the marked occurrence of egocentricity all the more striking in this case. One might think the chief cause of it to be feeble-mindedness. Imbeciles use personal reminiscences relatively often, for their limited horizon provides no others.

Wehrlin has given some beautiful instances of this. Subsequent figures from our material on imbeciles have shown that the figures for egocentric reactions vary between 0 and 2·4 per cent. Among fifteen imbeciles there were in əll only nine who exhibited egocentric reactions. But it should be stated that in Wehrlin's material there was an imbecile [1] who exhibited no less than 26·5 per cent. egocentric reactions. That is quite an exception, and has its own special basis. This imbecile is differentiated from the others by having no true tendency to explanation, but by forming whenever possible a school-sentence to each stimulus-word, which so frequently begins with " I ".

Fall	I fall down	Advice	I ask my father for advice
Run	I run quickly	Head	I have a head
Sick	I get sick with bad fish	Wages	I have earned the wages

These examples show, as Wehrlin points out, that this imbecile endeavours above everything to form school-sentences, using *I* where other imbeciles would say *we* or *people*. The term " egocentric " should be, therefore, only used with caution for these reactions. This case is, as we have said, an exception, and does not alter the fact that imbeciles do as a rule avoid the reference to self. Egocentric reactions do not force themselves on the imbecile, who prefers, on the contrary, such expressions as *one, a person, people*, etc., in order to get round the " I " form. Hysteria also, with its innumerable references to the ego, prefers the use of the less incriminating *one*.

Our case, with its pronounced tendency to explanation, exhibits the occurrence of egocentric reactions in a way not

---

[1] No. 13 of Wehrlin's cases.

found among imbeciles with the same kind of tendency to explanation. It may be objected that the reaction

<blockquote>To carry   I carry something, etc.</blockquote>

is a school-sentence. This objection cannot, however, be made to reaction 5 :

<blockquote>Pain   because I am ill</blockquote>

If this egocentric factor tells somewhat against imbecility, still more so does the peculiar method of explanation adopted by the patient.

I have already drawn attention to the fact that the patient to a certain extent accentuates his tendency to explanation by repeating his reaction by way of confirmation, or by the addition of an attribute. But he goes still further ; he does not content himself with a simple reaction, but can obviously not go far enough to satisfy this need for the full completion of his explanation.

In reaction 4 :

<blockquote>Suppose   I suppose, what do I suppose ? many things</blockquote>

one sees by the form how he endeavours to add something characteristic. He passes into a really abnormal exuberance in reaction 11 :

<blockquote>Air   that is the air, the air of nature, healthy or unhealthy, good air is good air</blockquote>

The impulse towards completeness becomes a pleonasm in reaction 10 :

<blockquote>Wide   that is the width of a distance</blockquote>

(with explanatory gesture) (cp. also reactions 6, 7, 12). In reactions 11

<blockquote>good air</blockquote>

and 12

<blockquote>good clothes</blockquote>

the predicates seem to express some quite special emphasis. The effort with which he reacts has something altogether inadequate, for this display of concepts exceeds for the most part anything that was really necessary to cover the stimulus-word. This behaviour at once gives the impression of an unnecessary and exaggerated exuberance. It is this factor which is absent in the imbecile, who contents himself with a fairly short reaction—one which appears to him more or less appropriate, but one which is frequently limited to the most primitive hints and to the most unfinished ideas. Our patient, on the contrary, has a strong tendency to heap up as much as possible and to exhaust the reaction, occasionally giving far beyond what is necessary.

The twelve reactions hitherto referred to give us grounds
for the supposition of *intellectual feeble-mindedness*, specifically
tinged by *a marked egocentric factor* and by *exaggerated exuberance*.
Now consider these further reactions of our patient :

13. Plate   dinner-plate—dinner-plate—for dinner

The reaction is repeated for confirmation. But that is not
sufficient, and another designation is added which is simply an
unnecessary piling up. Constructed similarly but much more
specific is reaction

14. Tired   I am tired—aye, tired—the body is tired : 3 seconds
15. Notion   I have a notion—to discover a machine—to draw—to
                 place—to live properly : 13 seconds

This reaction is exaggerated in its completeness ; it contains
two explanations through definite examples, one of which, a
personal constellation (the patient is a machine locksmith), is
thrice determined :

16. Fly   the bird flies : 4·8 seconds
17. Eye   the eye sees : 2·8 seconds
18. Strong   I am powerful, that is strong : 4·6 seconds

Again a blunt reference to the ego with a confirmatory but
unnecessary addition.

19. Seed   that is a pip, a seed-pip

The tendency to confirmation and completion here leads to
the formation of a neologism, *seed-pip* (see below concerning
this reaction).

20. Producing   working industriously is called producing : 3·6 seconds

Working is endowed with an emotionally toned attribute.

21. Sail   a sail is a sailing ship on the water : 6·8 seconds

Note the frequent recurrence of the stimulus-word in the
reactions. So far only three associations have occurred in which
the stimulus-word does not recur in some form in the reaction.

22. Modest   indeed the man is modest who has learned something :
                 9 seconds

Indeed is an expression which represents an emotion, and is
designed to objectivate self in presentations and words (cp.
R. 14).

In all places where vivid emotions, either easily aroused or
very intense, take part, *indeed, yes and no* frequently occur (as
in hysteria and certain organic affections of the brain). The

content of this association suggests a trend of thought which
we are hardly likely to meet in congenital idiots.

23. Floor   floor of a room : 3·8 seconds
24. Whistle   I whistle : 3·2 seconds
25. Purpose   for what purpose ? for what purpose are you doing that ?
                for what purpose ? 5·6 seconds

This reaction is peculiarly remarkable by reason of the extreme
repetition of the stimulus-word.   It will be seen that the patient
conceives the stimulus-word as a question.[1]

26. Hot   it's too warm, too hot : 2 seconds

Perhaps none of the previous reactions portray so well as
this one the patient's tendency to confirm and to strengthen the
reaction.   It is as if he wanted to illuminate the meaning every
time by additional impressiveness.   This energetic emphasis is
beautifully expressed in the ascending *too warm, too hot.*

27. Resin   resin from fir, resin grows on fir-trees, on pine-trees :
                3·8 seconds
28. Awake   I awake my friend, he is asleep : 8·4 seconds

Both reactions are marked by their completeness, especially
the latter, where the patient adds *he is asleep.*

29. Apple   there's different apples : 6·6 seconds

This reaction, exactly in the same form, is found with extraordinary frequency among imbeciles.

30. Bad   one says who is bad ? he's and he's—bad, that's a bad
                man : 6 seconds
31. Case   letter-case : 3 seconds
32. Drink   I drink lemonade : 3 seconds
33. Bed   for sleeping—I have the bed : 3 seconds
34. Worthy   the man is worthy, which the honour is due to him : 9·4
                seconds

This reaction has gone verbally wrong.   Thus the epileptic
feeble-minded seems to have, in common with the congenital
feeble-minded, the defect of handling speech clumsily and arbi-
trarily.   We find among imbeciles a number of faulty constructions and impossible neologisms.   But verbal clumsiness should
not be too easily assigned to the feeble-minded in association
experiments, for the verbal expression may be due to some
passing affective inhibition.   We shall return to this later.

35. Danger   I am in danger, in danger of life : 4·2 seconds
36. Visit   I visit a patient : 4·8 seconds

This reaction must be another reference to the ego.

[1] Chapter ii, p. 131.

37. Locksmith   I'm a locksmith, artisan : 2·8 seconds
38. High   the church steeple is high usually : 4·8 seconds
39. Hatchet   the hatchet is an axe : 3·4 seconds
40. Meddle   don't meddle in other's affairs : 6·2 seconds

This reaction recalls a colloquial phrase ; it is the first of the kind in this case.   Such reactions are, as we know, very frequent among normals.

41. Path   is a footpath, a field path : 3·2 seconds
42. Round   is a ball, otherwise it is not a ball, if it is not round : 3·8 seconds

A reaction very characteristic of this patient's pedantic exaggeration.[1]

43. Blood   has every man, every animal, but good or bad, that's the difference : 3·4 seconds

In these long-winded reactions we find the same estimates as in R. 11.   There it was a question of *healthy or unhealthy air*, here *good or bad blood*.   The constellation in common is obviously the question—important for the patient—of health.   Reactions 5 and 16 also refer to this complex.   Fuhrmann has also emphasized the marked occurrence of the disease complex in the associations of the epileptic.

44. Hire   I hire an apartment : 6 seconds
45. Prudent   Man be prudent : 4·8 seconds
46. Jolly   I'm jolly, I'm gay : 3·6 seconds

---

[1] Reactions of this kind are notably differentiated from certain reactions which may be exceptionally received from talkative imbeciles. Instances of this type are :

Sunday   consists of a day when you do nothing, when you go to church
Mountain   a high mountain, with houses or without houses
Salt   something to salt, bread is salted
Copy-book   consists of paper. A newspaper is made of it
Ring   on the finger, jewellery, chain
Attendant   who attends in hospitals, asylums, homes
Piano   when there is music, upstairs, where the organ is, near there. The young lady played it. (Tells another story about an organist)
Swim   in the lake, in the water, in the Rhine, you require swimming drawers
To cook   necessary for eating, soup, flour, meat, kitchen utensils, kettle
Star   part of the sky, planets, sun, moon, and stars

In these associations the insistence and the confirmation of the epileptic are absent, they do not so nicely strike the emotional factor ; they are more like stories suggesting rather a flight of ideas—the flow of thought goes on and does not stick doggedly to the stimulus-word.

47. Market   annual market, that is a market, there has just been the
                 fair in Basle : 7 seconds
48. Forget   I have forgotten something : 5 seconds
49. Drum   the tummy is a drum : 3·2 seconds
50. Free   I am free—I am free, I am a free citizen, it would be fine
                 if it were so : 4 seconds

In this reaction, besides the insistent emphasis on *free*, one
is struck by the egocentric reference in the form of the valuation
fine.

51. Cart   a cart, a team : 4·4 seconds
52. Eat   I eat, I eat a hash : 2·4 seconds
53. Impudence   if a man—there are men who are impudent, impudent
                 in their talk, impudent manners : 6·8 seconds
54. Quick   quick—the machine runs : 3·8 seconds

A constellation from his daily occupation.

55. Fireside   chimney—a factory chimney : 2·4 seconds
56. Enjoy   I enjoy a talk in the evening, I enjoy the pleasures : 4
                 seconds
57. Clergyman   is a priest, a parson, he must be a good man : 2·2 seconds

To the reaction, quite enough by itself, there is added a
valuation of feeling.   This recalls 15 :

        Notion   to live rightly

Are these, perhaps, hints of the moralizing tendencies of the
epileptic ?

58. Easy   what is not easy is difficult : 5 seconds
59. Neck   this is the neck (points to his neck)—every man has a
                 neck : 2·8 seconds
60. Wish   I wish you good luck for the New Year : 3 seconds
61. Stone   marble stone, there are different stones, stone is a naturality :
                 4·6 seconds

A tendency to the use of learned words is also found in imbeciles (e.g. substance, element, composition, etc.), which they
frequently use in quite a grotesque way.

62. Eminent   the educated man is eminent : 6·2 seconds
63. Hose   India-rubber hose is a hose : 4 seconds
64. Love   I love my neighbours like myself

This reaction seems to me characteristic of the epileptic ;
Biblical form, marked emphasis of feeling and egocentricity.   For
comparison I give the ten reactions to *love* of ten imbeciles selected
at random :

1. Friendly   6. I love my father
2. Angry   7. When you love one another
3. Bridegroom   8. When two persons like each other
4. When you love somebody   9. When you like some one
5. Pleasant   10. When you love some one

With one exception (6) the imbeciles react quite impersonally and ever so much more colourlessly than the epileptic.

65. Tiles   there are grooved tiles in Basle
66. Mild   it is mild weather, it's mild, it's warm : 2·8 seconds

It is hardly necessary to add to these examples. The further associations of this case contain nothing new in principle.

A few general remarks will not be out of place. It is to be noted that the patient accompanied most reactions with a gesture (which has occasionally been noted in the above formula). Whenever possible the gesture expressed something of confirmation and completeness. In 30 per cent. of the reactions the stimulus-word was repeated. As will be shown in chapter v, the repetition of the stimulus-word in normals is not something accidental but has its deeper reasons, as may be said of all disturbances occurring in the experiment. Apart from those rare cases in normals where the stimulus-word, owing to some kind of embarrassment or other, is quickly and softly repeated, this disturbance mostly occurs in those places where an affect perseverates from a previous reaction and inhibits the association in the one following. Among hysterics I have also seen that the stimulus-word which is a " complex excitant " [1] causes a certain repetition of the stimulus-word in a tone of inquiry. These observations show us that, among normals, the places where repetitions of the stimulus-words occur are not indifferent places. But other mechanisms may be in question in epilepsy. In our case the first four stimulus-words were repeated, the fourth (*suppose*) three times. The next to be repeated was the 15th (*notion*).[2] A general embarrassment may be presupposed at first. In *suppose*, the " difficulty " of the word, perhaps, had something to do with it, as also with *notion*. Both had also very prolonged times (23·2 and 13 seconds), which far exceed the reaction-times to the words in close proximity. But perhaps the repetition of the stimulus-word *notion* is not entirely to be explained by the difficulty of the word, but may be conditioned by the perseveration of an emotional tone. The previous reaction runs :

I am tired, aye, tired, the body is tired : 3 seconds

the next reaction-time is 13 seconds.

[1] Certain stimulus-words can encounter a very personal, important, and markedly emotional presentation complex; certain disturbances of the association result, which we term " complex signs." The chief of these are : abnormally long reaction-times, repetition of the stimulus-word, abnormal behaviour at the critical reaction or at the one following.

[2] " Notion " is a very insidious word for some people.

Apart from the context, the word *aye* points to the existence of some strong emotional tone. The next repetition of the stimulus-word is in R. 19 : *seed.* The previous reaction runs :

Am powerful, that is strong : 4·6 seconds (following R.T. 7 seconds)

21. *Sail* is repeated. Previous reaction :

Work industriously *is called* producing : 3·6 seconds (following R.T. 6·8 seconds)

22. *Modest* is repeated. Previous reaction :

A sail is a sailing-ship on the water : 6·8 seconds (following R.T. 9 seconds)

We have two repetitions of the stimulus-word following immediately upon one another, where the reaction-time rises in step-ladder fashion : 3·6–6·8–9 seconds.

The reaction to *sail* is a verbal slip. (In my investigations in reaction-times verbal slips proved to be complex signs.) At the foot of the ladder we have *work industriously*—an emotionally charged, probably egocentric reaction. The third reaction (22) runs :

Indeed *the* man is modest who has learnt something

It is not difficult to recognize a substantial relationship with *work industriously.* The supposition that the emotional tone of *work industriously* perseverates amid the verbally disturbed reaction and constellated reaction (22) is thus not improbable.

47. *Market* is repeated. Previous reaction :

I am joyful, I am jolly : 3·6 seconds (following R.T. 7 seconds)

51. *Cart* is repeated. Previous reaction :

I am free, I am a free citizen, it would be fine if it were really so : 4 seconds
(following R.T. 4·4 seconds)

With the exception of the first four reactions, most of the repetitions of the stimulus-words occur in reactions which immediately follow egocentric associations. The reaction-time is, as a rule, abnormally prolonged in these places ; not to dilate further upon this, I will not give more instances, but I can assure the reader that, with insignificant exceptions, all the other repetitions of the stimulus-words occur where the emotions are strongly aroused.

A certain verbal clumsiness occurred in some reactions. One is tempted to make epileptic feeble-mindedness, like that in imbecility, responsible for these faulty constructions. But we know another source for these verbal errors—the strong emotional complex aroused by the stimulus-word. In my article on the behaviour of the reaction-time in association experiments (chapter v) I shall bring forward a series of examples from which it will be seen that the reaction is influenced, in normals, by an emotional complex. Verbal slips, apparently quite accidental, which the subject scarcely notices himself, prove to be the purposeful, determined mixed product of two concurrent ideas.[1]

Before ascribing the verbally incorrect reactions to feeble-mindedness, it behoves us to investigate whether the mechanism which we have discovered among normals be not here also the cause of the faulty construction of sentences or words. There are three such verbal errors in the associations. I put these three associations together with the previous ones (the faulty construction is in italics).

18.	Strong	I'm powerful, that is, strong : 4·6 seconds
19.	Seed	that is a pip—a *seed-pip* : 7 seconds (the stimulus-word is repeated)
20.	Producing	working industriously is called producing
21.	Sail	*a sail is a sailing-ship* on the water : 6·8 seconds (the stimulus-word is repeated)
33.	Bed	for sleeping, I have the bed : 3 seconds
34.	Worthy	the man is worthy, *which the honour is due to him* : 9·4 seconds (the stimulus-word is repeated)

These three faulty constructions have the following in common :

(1) The stimulus-word of the faulty association is invariably repeated.

(2) Each of the faulty associations has a reaction-time which is not only higher than that of the previous reaction but is delayed far beyond the average of the others.[2]

(3) Two of the faulty associations follow reactions having an emotional tone ; in the third case this is at least probable from its content and by analogy with similar cases.

These observations entitle us to say that we are scarcely justified in ascribing the faulty construction to feeble-mindedness.

From this exposition it follows that no specific epileptic mechanism is to be found either in the frequent repetitions of the stimulus-word or in the faulty construction of sentences. There merely remains for discussion, therefore, the question of whether anything specifically epileptic may be found in the intensity of these otherwise normal processes. Perhaps the reaction-times can help us, as these are a valuable aid for judging emotional processes.

[1] Cp. also Freud's observations in *The Psychopathology of Everyday Life.* (English translation by Dr. A. A. Brill.)

[2] I have found in normals that those reactions which are constellated by a conscious or unconscious complex very often have an abnormally long reaction-time ; the emotional tone can be carried on to the reaction following, when the reaction-time becomes likewise prolonged.

All the mean times, which I quote, are the probable mean.[1]

From the time-measurements made on this subject we obtain as the general probable mean 4·2 seconds (uneducated normals 2 seconds). The general reaction-time is thus more than double that of corresponding normal. But this mean is only "gross," it is composed of different non-comparable measures. As I shall show in the next chapter, reactions complicated by emotion are usually prolonged. Therefore, if there are many such reactions the general mean becomes, other things being equal, strongly affected. If we exclude all those reactions which, according to the criterion we have laid down, are marked by an emotional egocentric content, and also the reactions immediately following, we get as the probable mean for all presumably non-complicated reactions 3·8 seconds, whilst the probable mean for those discarded amounts to 4·8 seconds.

The emotional tone thus makes a difference of 1 second. This behaviour is not so very far removed from that of normals. We have given many instances to show that there is a considerable difference between the time of an emotional association and that of the reactions immediately succeeding. We have, therefore, investigated the times of these two groups apart. The mean of the reactions containing an emotional presentation is 3·6 seconds, a number which is 0·2 seconds lower than the mean of the non-emotionally toned associations ; but the mean of the associations immediately succeeding the foregoing is 5·8 seconds. This extremely high mean, which exceeds the non-complicated reactions by no less than 2 seconds, expresses the important fact that the emotional tone which inhibits association perseverates from the critical reaction and only reaches its full effect in the succeeding reaction. As a rule, therefore, the inhibitory effect of the emotional tone is not shown in the critical reaction itself, but only in the succeeding reaction. It must be, therefore, taken that in this case the emotional tone only sets in properly at the end of the critical reaction, swells very slowly, and then, gradually running down, influences the next reaction. This behaviour is the more remarkable when one takes into account that meanwhile the experimenter has to write down the reaction, to read the time, to call out the next stimulus-word ; the writing down of the reactions, often pretty lengthy, taking up most time. I have tried to investigate this on the associations of normals. I have taken the associations of a case of which I possess an extremely detailed analysis so that I was fully initiated into all the associations constellated by a complex.

---

[1] Cp. Aschaffenburg: Kräpelin's *Psych. Arbeiten*, Bd. I. (As regards the counting I must refer to chapter v on reaction-times.)

The probable mean of all associations not complicated by emotion amounted to 1·2 seconds. The mean of the emotionally toned associations was 1·6 seconds. The mean of the reactions immediately succeeding to those emotionally toned was 1·2 seconds ; it is therefore equal to the mean of the non-complicated reactions. Consequently, if in mentally healthy subjects the " complex-excitant " stimulus-word is followed, on the average, by a reaction-time 0·4 seconds longer than the stimulus-word which immediately follows or which is indifferent ; this means that in normal persons the emotional tone arises much more quickly and is obliterated incomparably more quickly than in an epileptic. Hence the reaction-time of the associations following is on the average not affected at all among healthy persons, whilst, as we have seen, in our epileptic an extraordinary prolongation of the time occurs in the association following the critical one.

This important and interesting peculiarity seems to be of a pathological nature ; how far it is typical of epilepsy will be learnt from the working out of our large material.

The phenomenon seems to have something characteristic for our case, for the existence of such an abnormal emotional process can be presumed also from the quality of the associations. I have repeatedly called attention to the fact that the subject frequently gives subsequent confirmation in an emphatic tone, often with expressions betraying an emotion (e.g. *hot — it's warm, too hot ; tired — I'm tired, aye tired, the body is tired*, etc.). This peculiar form of the reaction also seems to speak in favour of the emotional tone setting in slowly and gradually swelling up, thus liberating more associations with a similar tendency. The emotional tone has very probably a higher intensity among epileptics than among normals, which again must conduce to the prolongation of the tone. But it is difficult to say whether the epileptic emotional tone is not itself abnormally prolonged.[1]

In my analytical investigations on the reaction-times of normals I was able to demonstrate the existence of one or more presentation complexes charged with emotion which constellated a great number of the associations. I have already referred to the fact that a complex exists in our epileptic which constellates

---

[1] This conception would explain the epileptic fixation by the abnormality of the emotional tone. But it is not inconceivable that the epileptic presentation in this respect has something abnormal, that it lasts longer than in normals and thus produces a series of associations which cling to the original presentation. Under these conditions relatively numerous perseverations of the context would be expected. None was present, however, in our case.

a series of associations. It is the complex of disease. The following associations must be referred to this complex :

Pain	because I am ill : 4·2 seconds (succeeding R.T. 5·8 seconds)
Tired	I'm tired, aye tired, the body's tired : 3 seconds ; S.R.T. 13 seconds [1] ; R.S.[2]
Strong	I'm powerful, that is strong : 4·6 seconds ; S.R.T. 7 seconds ; R.S.
Blood	every man has—but good blood or bad blood, that's the difference : 3·4 seconds ; S.R.T. 6 seconds ; R.S.
Joyous	I'm joyous, I'm jolly : 3·6 seconds ; S.R.T. 7 seconds ; R.S.

A constellation somewhat more remote might be :

Air	that is the air—healthy or unhealthy : 2·2 seconds ; S.R.T. 5 seconds
Visit	I visit a patient : 4·8 seconds

The reaction following runs :

Locksmith	I'm a locksmith : 2·8 seconds

The patient is confined to an asylum in consequence of his disease and this has powerfully affected him. He was afraid that he would not get free again, not be able to work and earn money again. Home-sickness troubled him likewise. The following reactions perhaps refer to this side of the complex :

Producing	work industriously means producing : 3·6 seconds. S.R.T. 6·8 seconds ; R.S.
Danger	I'm in danger, in danger of life : 4·2 seconds ; S.R.T. 4·8 seconds.
Free	I'm free—it would be fine if it were so : 4 seconds ; S.R.T. 4·4 seconds ; R.S.
Wish	I wish you good luck for the New Year : 3 seconds ; S.R.T. 4·6 seconds ; R.S.

About this last association it should be said that the tests were carried out just before Christmas, a period when sensitive patients find the confinement doubly difficult to bear.

These few instances should suffice to show that a whole series of associations are constellated by an emotionally toned complex. This behaviour is not in itself anything abnormal, for the associations of normals are constellated by the same kind of complexes.

RECAPITULATION

(1) As in the associations of normals.

a. Patient adapts himself to the importance of the stimulus-word like uneducated persons. Consequently superficial word-associations are absent.

---

[1] S.R.T. = reaction-time of succeeding reaction.

[2] R.S. = repetition of the stimulus-word in succeeding reaction.

b. The associations are in part constellated by a diseas
complex.

(2) As in the associations of imbeciles.

a. The attitude towards the meaning of the stimulus-wor
is so intense that a large number of the associations must b
apprehended as " explanations," in the sense used by Wehrli
in his work (chapter iii).

b. The associations have the sentence form.

c. The reaction-times are considerably prolonged as compare
with normals.

d. The frequent repetition of the stimulus-word.

(3) Peculiarities as compared with normals and imbeciles.

a. The " explanations" have an awkward, circumlocutia
character, particularly expressed by the confirmation and com
pleteness of the reaction (*tendency towards full completion*). Th
stimulus-word is frequently repeated in the reaction.

b. The outer form of the reaction is not stereotyped or limited
with the exception of the egocentric form, which occurs wit
peculiar frequency (31 per cent.).

c. Frequent emotional references which are fairly obviou
(religious, moralizing, etc.).

d. The reaction-times only display their greatest variation
after the critical reaction. The abnormally long times do no
occur in particularly difficult words, but in places which ar
determined by a perseveration of the emotional tone. From thi
it may be concluded that in this patient the emotional tone set
in later and lasts longer than in normals.

In conclusion, I would observe that my analysis is for th
moment of value only for this case, and that I do not venture t
draw any universal deduction. There are many different kind
of epilepsy which perhaps exhibit different psychological charac
teristics. Inasmuch as my case is complicated by fracture o
the skull, it is perhaps exceptional.

CHAPTER V

REACTION-TIME IN ASSOCIATION EXPERIMENTS

By Dr. C. G. JUNG

THE present investigation deals with the behaviour of the time interval which occurs between the calling out of the stimulus-word and the utterance of the reaction-word. I term this interval simply " reaction-time," with the knowledge that it is made up of a composite series which can be deductively and empirically reduced into numerous components. I forbear venturing upon an analysis of that kind, for the results would be just like hypotheses which had to be supported by anatomical data to which they were not entitled. The components of our " reaction-time " are only known to us in part, and in an exhaustive critique would prove extremely complicated, as Claparède's summary shows [1]:

(1) Transference of the sound to the ear of the percipient.
(2) Nerve conduction to the acoustic centre.
(3) Recognition of the word (primary identification).
(4) Understanding of the word (secondary identification).
(5) Evoking of the induced presentation, i.e. the pure association.
(6) Naming of the presentation evoked.
(7) Excitation of the speech-motor apparatus or of the motor centre of the hand, if measured by means of the Morse communicator.
(8) Nerve conduction to the muscle.

A superficial consideration of these eight factors shows that we have only emphasized some of the most important factors. The innumerable possibilities of intracerebral processes have been in no wise exhausted.

So far as we know these components, they are of very short duration, the longest not exceeding 50 σ. (Ziehen). Under normal

[1] Claparède, L'Association des Idées, p. 275. The scheme is based upon Ziehen, Die Ideenassoziation des Kindes, 2. Abhandlg., p. 14.

conditions some of these components, e.g. the time for nerve conduction, excitation of the centre, etc., have a fairly constant duration. In any case, variations here take place within relatively narrow boundaries. Variations in identification time are greater, and greatest of all are the true association time and the time for the verbal formation of the reaction. In the association experiment the last factors have therefore greatest importance.

Whoever has undertaken association experiments knows how wide are the limits of the reaction-times. In our experience times up to six seconds are not at all exceptional even among normal persons. This great difference of the times gives us a needful hint as to the methods of time measurement. So long as we have not sufficient knowledge of the causes of the variations, small differences in the times cannot tell us anything. We do not, therefore, require any complicated experimental conditions to measure times of one-thousandth of a second ; we may quietly ignore slight differences so long as the causes of the greater differences do not escape us. Apart from the fact that complicated methods of measuring the finer intervals disclose nothing more than measurements with the one-fifth second stop-watch, there are weighty considerations against the use of mouth-whistles, trumpet-calls, or dark chambers. If Mayer and Orth [1] regarded it as necessary to shut the eyes during the experiment to avoid all disturbing sense impressions, the apparatus mentioned certainly does nothing to simplify the experiment or prevent disturbing influences. In any case unpractised persons cannot be employed in these experiments if gross disturbances of attention are not to be risked. Finally, in mental patients the more exact time measurements are obviously excluded.

Measurement by the one-fifth second watch seems, therefore, not only quite sufficient but has stood the test in the investigations of several workers. Mayer and Orth [2] have worked with it, as have Thumb and Marbe,[3] Wreschner,[4] Sommer, and others. Claparède's view is that it suffices for all experiments in successive association.[5] Besides simplicity in handling, the stop-watch has the especial advantage of disturbing the experiment least, and this fact was important in the experiments with the uneducated, who are prone to emotion.

[1] Zeitsch. f. Psychol., Bd. XXVI.
[2] Loc. cit.
[3] Experimentelle Untersuchungen über die Grundlagen der sprachlichen Analogiebildung (Leipzig, 1901).
[4] Allgemeine Zeitschrift für Psychiatrie, Bd. LVII.
[5] Loc. cit., p. 261.

With the great differences in time that have to be considered, it is of little consequence that the times measured are all somewhat too large. Any one who has worked with this stop-watch knows that the apparatus is only approximately correct in its working, for the stop arrangement does not always put the hand exactly at the place at which the stop is liberated. To this must be added certain variations in the personal equation which may influence the measurement. Although the uncontrollable disturbances are not minimal, one can, at least in my experience, take it that the measurements are correct to about one-fifth of a second $= 200 \ \sigma$. This slight disadvantage has hitherto done no real harm to our experiments.

The material upon which this investigation is based consists of the time measurements which were published by Riklin and myself [1] on the associations of normal persons. Of the thirty-eight persons whose associations are there reviewed, the reaction-time was measured in twenty-six persons. Approximately one-half were measured by Riklin. The difference of the personal equation in the measurements of the two experimenters is less than one-fifth of a second, as we have proved by control experiments ; it may therefore be left out of account.

The number and composition of the measurements are :

1. In 7 uneducated women there were 1201 time measurements
2. In 7   „   men   „   1007 „   „
3. In 6 educated   women   „   948 „   „
4. In 6   „   men   „   988 „   „

Total 26 persons   4144 time measurements

(A) *The Average Duration of an Association*

In his studies on association Aschaffenburg says [2] : " It is of the greatest importance that the duration of an association of a normal subject can differ by one-half from the average duration of the rest, which lies between 1200 and 1400 σ. It teaches us in the most striking way what little value should be ascribed to the absolute length of time."

Aschaffenburg bases this judgment on the observation that the reaction-time is subjected to great individual variations. In accordance with this fact, we find in the literature of the subject rather wide divergences as to the average length of associations. Féré [3] gives as the mean for men 700 σ, for women

[1] See chapter ii.
[2] Kräpelin's *Psychol. Arbeiten*, Bd. I, p. 272.
[3] *La Pathologie des émotions.*

830 σ.[1] Galton gives the average time as 1·3 second. Trautscholdt's [2] figures vary between 1154 and 896 σ.

These figures will suffice to show how little agreement there
is among investigators. The differences are probably referable
to the following points :

(1) The methods of measuring vary with the apparatus and
other conditions of the experiment.

(2) The amount of practice varies in the subjects.

(3) The methods of reckoning the mean figures are different.

Practically there are only two methods of reckoning the
mean figures :

a. The arithmetical mean.

b. The probable mean (Kräpelin).

In view of the fact that in association experiments excessively
long times frequently occur, the use of the arithmetical mean
does not seem advisable. In this method high values affect the
otherwise low average value in a very disturbing way and may
be quite misleading. This difficulty is overcome by the method
of the probable mean. In this method the figures are arranged
in a series according to their value, and then the nearest mean
figure is taken. This excludes the effect of excessively high
values. In the great majority of cases the probable mean is
lower than the arithmetical. For instance, three of my subjects
exhibit the following values :

Probable mean   : 1·8, 2, 1·6.
Arithmetical mean : 2·8, 3, 3·6.

As this instance shows, differences of this kind can influence
the general mean to a high degree. It is therefore not a matter
of indifference which method of reckoning has been used.
Ziehen's " representative value," which demands a pretty detailed
calculation, should not, for this reason, find much appreciation,
although it renders possible a very accurate review of the individual figures. The *composite value* is dependent upon external
accidents, and is only to be used under certain conditions.

These considerations seem to indicate that the probable mean
is the method most to be recommended for calculating the mean
figures more quickly from great numbers of figures.

(4) The number of subjects is generally too limited and the
selection too one-sided in the previous writers.

I have not endeavoured to find absolute mean figures but
only approximate probable figures which will give us to some
extent the heights to which the values tend in normal subjects of

----

[1] " Psychometric Experiments," *Brain*, 1879, vol. ii, p. 149.

[2] Wundt's *Phil. Studien*, Bd. I.

different social status. Believing that the association experiments used somewhat as they have been for some years in this clinic will play an important part in the future diagnosis of mental diseases, it seems to me of practical importance to discover universal normal mean values, which will afford a certain basis for judging pathological values.

The universal mean value for the duration of an association was found to be :

1·8 second

This was arrived at in the following way : First, the probable mean of each of the twenty-six subjects was calculated, and from the individual values so obtained the arithmetical mean was drawn. The latter method was then chosen because twenty-six persons are, after all, but a small number, and it was therefore unfair to exclude the individual values from the calculation by the use of the probable means.

This mean figure shows a pretty long duration of the association time. It exceeds by quite a good deal the values given in the literature of this subject. The causes of this prolongation are :

(1) The points already above mentioned (measurement by the second-watch, unpractised subjects, who in part come from the lower classes).

(2) The majority of the subjects are Swiss, a circumstance whose importance in acoustic-verbal experiments was discussed in chapter ii.

This summary of principles will clear up the way in which the significance of the values is conditioned. The variability of the mean figures is shown much more simply by grouping the subjects from certain simple points of view and comparing the individual groups with one another.

(B) Sex and Reaction-time

As already mentioned, Féré gave a longer association time for women than for men. We can confirm this by our figures :

Men	1·6 second
Women	2 seconds

which show that the women reacted considerably more slowly in our association experiments. It should be mentioned, however, that the educated women are approximately at the same level of culture as the educated men, but, on the other hand, the uneducated women are somewhat below the level of the culture of the uneducated men. As Ranschburg's [1] and our

---

[1] *Allgemeine Zeitschrift für Psychiatrie*, 1900.

own previous investigations [1] have shown, uneducated persons, and especially women, exceed the educated in inner associations by a considerable percentage, whilst in purely verbal associations they are left far behind.   According to Ziehen's [2] observations on children, their associations are marked by the inner references (relationship of significance) having longer reaction-times, whilst the verbal associations require the shortest time.   These facts, emphasized by Ziehen, are, it is true, contested by Aschaffenburg, [3] who finds " there are no characteristic differences in the reaction-times of forms of association."   The figures given by Aschaffenburg certainly allow no other interpretation, but they may perhaps be explained as the consequence of the one-sided selection of his subjects.   Ziehen's [4] contention that " presentations having greater external relationship, as, e.g., rhymed verbal presentations," are reproduced more quickly is fully in accordance with everyday experience.   This point should therefore be taken into consideration in the explanation of the longer association times of women.   Whether this is the whole explanation we shall learn in our further inquiries.   In any case, before discussing a difference of sex in the reaction-time we must investigate the influence of education.

(C) *Educational Rank and Reaction-time*

	Educated	Uneducated
Men	1·3 second	1·8 (1·6 [5]) second
Women	1·7 ,,	2·2 seconds
Educated in general	1·5 ,,	Uneducated in general : 2 (1·9) seconds

Our earlier investigations invariably showed that the uneducated subjects produce more inner associations than the educated. The ratio of inner association to outer is among the uneducated 43 : 53 per cent., among the educated 36 : 59 per cent.   One is tempted to connect the difference in the reaction-time with this relationship, and to maintain that the smaller number of inner associations among the educated corresponds with the shorter reaction-time, and, inversely, the greater number of inner associations among the uneducated corresponds with the longer reaction-time.   However plausible this assumption (especially in view of

[1] Chapter ii, p. 144.

[2] *Die Ideenassoziation des Kindes.*

[3] *Psych. Arbeiten*, Bd. I.

[4] *Leitfaden der Physiol. Psychologie.*

[5] Among the uneducated male subjects there was a young man with slight hysterical disposition whose mental stability we have perhaps overestimated. His probable mean is no less than 3·4 seconds (i.e. an abnormally high value). If this suspicious case is excluded, the mean of the men is only 1·6 second.

Ziehen's results) might seem, a consideration of the figures for the two sexes shows us that the facts are not so simple. On a closer examination of the educational rank of the subjects, it must be stated absolutely that the difference in culture between the educated and the uneducated is incomparably greater than that between the educated men and women. It therefore remains quite inexplicable why the time difference of 0·4 is the same between the educated men and women as between the educated and the uneducated. Add to this that the reaction-time, 1·7 of the educated women as compared with 1·3 of the educated men, does not correspond at all with the percentage ratio of the inner and outer associations : that of the women is 38 : 61 per cent., whilst that of the men is only 36 : 56 per cent. Analogous to this, the time difference of ·4 (or ·6) between the uneducated men and women in no wise corresponds to the difference of culture between the sexes in the uneducated group. In both cases there remains a time difference to the debit of the women corresponding in no wise with the difference of culture. If we take the time difference of the men of the two groups by themselves and that of the women by themselves the difference in culture suffices for an explanation, and this is very nicely shown also in the ratio of the kinds of association to each other. This supposition is also supported by the observations of Wreschner [1] and Wehrlin,[2] who have dwelt upon the general prolongation of association activity in pathological absence of intelligence and culture (congenital feeble-minded). Wehrlin has shown that together with the prolonged reaction-time there goes an increase of inner associations.

Whilst the uneducated women exhibit slightly more inner associations than the men, the facts are reversed in educated men and women, for the educated women have fewer inner associations than the men ; nevertheless there is a time difference between the sexes which is in part greater than that between educated and uneducated. As we have seen, neither a higher number of inner associations nor the lesser difference of culture can be held responsible for this. There seems a new factor interposed—presumably a sex difference.

We shall consider the justification for this supposition later. Before discussing this theme it becomes necessary to investigate the influences which the individual stimulus-word exercises upon the reaction.

[1] *Allgemeine Zeitschrift für Psychiatrie*, Bd. LVII.
[2] Chapter iii.

(D) *The Influences of the Stimulus-word upon the Reaction-time*

The previous investigations on association times have been chiefly concerned to discover a connexion between the quality of the association (i.e. of the reaction) and its duration. Trautscholdt has already tried to establish certain relationships. He states that the verbal associations require the shortest time. We have already mentioned the observations of Ziehen and Aschaffenburg. We must now see if the two components of the association, stimulus-word and reaction, cannot be examined separately as to their influence upon the duration. Definite results can only be expected from an enormous material. I have already tried with Riklin to estimate the influence which the stimulus-word has upon the quality of the reaction. Certain laws were established :

(1) The grammatical form of the stimulus-word has a great influence upon the form of the reaction ; that is to say, the subject betrays a distinct tendency to give the reaction the grammatical form of the stimulus-word.[1]

The individual figures with this tendency show great variations. My stimulus-words, which consist of 60 per cent. nouns, 18 per cent. adjectives, and 21 per cent. verbs (mixing the different word forms so as to prevent perseveration of the reaction form), gave the following :

The individual figures for grammatical agreement vary between 26 and 95 per cent. The average figure for the educated amounts to 51 per cent., for the uneducated to 59 per cent. The uneducated thus show a rather more distinct tendency to be influenced by the form of the stimulus-word. (This holds good not only of the grammatical forms but also of the number of syllables and of alliteration.)

(2) The tendency to agreement in grammatical form is under the limiting influence of the law of frequency. In language, adjectives and verbs occur about one-half as often as nouns.[2] The noun has thus a higher frequency value, so that the probability of the reproduction of a noun is greater than that of an adjective or verb.

[1] Münsterburg, Kräpelin, and Aschaffenburg have to some extent dealt with this question. Kräpelin finds in reactions to nouns 90 per cent. agreement ; Aschaffenburg, among sixteen subjects, 81 per cent. It should be noted that " on principle " he only used nouns as stimulus-words. But this circumstance encourages to a great degree the favourite perseveration of the same form of reaction, and thus his figures have at most but conditional value. As grammatical forms I understand purely the form as noun, adjective, or verb.

[2] I have made adequate calculations from newspapers and dialogues of the feuilleton kind and have found approximately this ratio.

In our experiments noun stimulus-words were followed on the average by nouns in 73 per cent. (Aschaffenburg 81 per cent.). Since verbs and adjectives have a lesser frequency value, their influence upon the reaction form is correspondingly lower. Experience confirms this supposition : to verb stimulus-words there followed, on the average, 33 per cent. verbs. The number of nouns amounts to, on the average, 49 per cent., and has thus been reduced by the tendency to agreement in grammatical forms. Adjective stimulus-words have a rather stronger influence, being followed by 52 per cent. adjectives. The number of nouns is reduced by adjective stimulus-words to 44 per cent. on the average. We see from these facts that by the use of verb and adjective as stimulus-words the frequency of nouns can be lessened by about one-half on the average.

(3) Our previous investigations [1] have shown that the quality of the association is not inconsiderably influenced by the grammatical form of the stimulus-word. Whilst, for instance, among uneducated women the inner associations were to the outer as 1 : 1·06, the ratio of the associations to adjective stimulus-words was 1 : 0·62 and to verb stimulus-words 1 : 0·43. The number of inner associations to adjective and verb stimulus-words is quite considerably increased. We find the same phenomenon in the educated, only in a much weaker degree. The increase of inner associations seems to rest upon this—that in consequence of the lower frequency value of verbs and adjectives there are much fewer current word connexions with these than with nouns. The associations that follow verbs and adjectives are thus much less prepared and demand a greater stress of attention ; this naturally gives rise to significant relationships rather than to superficial and purely external connexions. We therefore see that more inner associations result with verbs and adjectives than with nouns.

From the observations of Ziehen, who has proved that higher figures occur when there are relationships of meaning, it is to be expected that verbs and adjectives will be, on the average, followed by higher figures than nouns. But as the nouns can themselves consist of presentations with different values, and as this can itself greatly influence the reaction-time, the nouns are classified into concrete and universal concepts, a further reason for this being that uneducated persons are also easily confused by many universal concepts.

The probable mean of all subjects is :

| For concrete concepts 1·67 second | For adjectives 1·70 second |
| „ universal „ 1·95 „ | „ verbs 1·90 „ |

---

[1] Chapter ii.

The figures agree with expectation; reactions to verbs and adjectives show a longer time than those to concrete stimulus-words. Reactions to universal concepts require the longest time, which also agrees with expectation.

Probable Mean of the Reaction-times to Concrete and other Stimulus-words

	Uneducated		Educated	
	Women	Men	Women	Men
Concrete concepts　.　.	2	1·7	1·6	1·4
Universal concepts　.　.	2·8	1·9	1·8	1·3
Adjectives　.　.　.　.	2·2	1·7	1·7	1·2
Verbs　.　.　.　.	2·4	2	1·9	1·3

The table shows that the uneducated have higher reaction-times than the educated.[1] The longest time occurs among uneducated women when the stimulus-words are universal concepts, whilst these stimulus-words require among educated men a shorter time than the concretes. It is curious that, in contrast with all other subjects, the educated men have their longest times with concretes. This fact is important in so far as it shows that the influence of the stimulus-word upon the duration of the association does not consist merely in the factors just discussed. Comparing these figures with the values given by Aschaffenburg for similar subjects, it is seen that our figures taken with the second-watch are approximately the same as those obtained by him when using the whistle and chronoscope.[2]

(E) *The Influence of the Reaction-word upon the Reaction-time*

We have discussed the behaviour of the reaction-time when the stimulus-word is a noun, adjective, or verb. We have now to find out how the reaction-time behaves when the reaction-word is a noun, etc.

---

[1] The individual values upon which this table is based vary between 1 and 4·4 seconds.

[2] A whole series of questions could easily be opened up here. For instance : what is the reaction-time when verb is followed by verb or noun by noun, and how does this compare in the different subjects ? But these would take us too far from the object of this investigation.

The probable means of all subjects are :

With concretes as reaction-words .	.	.	.	1·81 second
„ universals „ „	.	.	.	1·98 „
„ adjectives „ „	.	.	.	1·65 „
„ verbs „ „	.	.	.	1·66 „

If these tables are compared with the previous one of the mean values for the correspondingly classified stimulus-word, it is seen that the universal concepts have in both cases the longest duration (1·95 and 1·98 second). When the reaction-word is a concrete it shows a longer duration than when caused by a concrete stimulus-word (stimulus-word 1·67, reaction-word 1·81 second). This difference must rest upon the fact that many more current word connexions exist to a noun, whilst noun to noun generally means an inner relationship, or at least an association by coexistence (which for the rest behaves among the uneducated as an inner association—see chapter ii). Under the heading "concretes as reaction-words" numerous inner association words have been grouped, which is probably the cause of the prolongation of the reaction-time. We find the contrary in verbs and adjectives as reaction-words. Their mean values are diminished as compared with those of the previous table (1·7, 1·9 : 1·65, 1·66 second) because in these classes, especially among the verbs, many current verbal connexions occur.

The probable mean values of the individual groups of the subjects are as follows :

Probable Mean of Reaction-times for Concrete, etc., Reaction-words [1]

	Uneducated		Educated	
	Women	Men	Women	Men
Concretes	2·2	1·85	1·7	1·5
Universals	2·7	2	2	1·4
Adjectives	2	1·7	1·7	1·2
Verbs	1·9	1·7	1·8	1·3

The relatively low values above mentioned for adjectives and verbs are here present in all four groups. Here again the uneducated women present the highest figures. The relatively

[1] The individual figures upon which this table is based vary between 1 and 4 seconds.

high figures for the concretes are striking. The fact mentioned in the last section, that the educated men have their longest reaction-times with the concretes, is found here also. Perhaps the explanation of this may be sought in the fact that in this group there occur very many significant relationships and these prolong the duration.

(F) *The Influence of the Quality of the Association upon the Reaction-time*

As we have seen, Aschaffenburg's investigations on the influence of the quality of the association upon the reaction-time led to no unequivocal result ; Ziehen's success, already alluded to, is therefore all the more encouraging. I have likewise investigated the influence of the quality of the association upon the time, limiting myself to the three groups of our former classification : inner and outer associations and clang-reactions. The average figures are as follows :

	Uneducated		Educated	
	Women	Men	Women	Men
Inner associations . .	2·8	1·9	2·1	1·6
Outer associations. . .	1·9	1·7	1·8	1·3
Clang-reactions . . .	2·6	2·4	2	1·3

There is a distinct difference between the time duration for inner and outer associations, the outer associations requiring a distinctly lesser time. The matter is different in clang-reactions, where we should, from all we know, have expected the shortest times, since these are the lowest and simplest associations and should arise in the shortest time. Obviously in practice the relations are not so simple as one might expert theoretically. I have frequently found that it is just the most superficial clang-reactions which are often very long. It is my experience that, as a rule, clang-reactions are abnormal reactions due to some kind of distracting disturbance. The following section shows us what is the usual nature of this disturbance.

(G) *The Overlong Reaction-time*

To limit practically the concept " overlong " reaction-time, I shall call that time " overlong " which is above the probable mean of the subject in question. If, e.g., the probable mean amounts to 2·5 seconds, 3 seconds is an "overlong" reaction-time.

Let us first of all recapitulate what is so far known as to the causes which (we are naturally referring to our experiments only) prolong the reaction-time :

(1) Certain grammatical forms of stimulus- and reaction-words.

(2) A significant relation between stimulus- and reaction-word.

(3) The rarity or difficulty of the stimulus-word (universal concepts).

(4) Ziehen [1] has proved the remarkable fact that (as con-trasted with reactions in common currency) individual associations prolong the reaction-time.

(5) Mayer and Orth [2] found in their experimental studies on association that the reaction-time was prolonged when conation interpolated itself between stimulus and reaction. If an emotional content of consciousness occurred at all between stimulus and reaction the reaction-time was considerably increased as compared with the rest of the associations. Painful emotions more especially prolonged the time.[3]

(6) In our previous investigations (chapter ii) we called atten-tion to the fact that abnormally long reaction-times more especially occur when an emotionally accentuated complex was aroused by the stimulus-word. We were thus able not only to confirm the observations of Mayer and Orth, but could also prove in many cases—

(1) The complex is generally the cause of several, or indeed of very many long times, and

(2) What is the nature of the complex.

The fact that the overlong times can denote the presence of emotional complexes seems to us of great importance. That would perhaps give us the means by a short and simple examina-tion to discover things of personal import, especially the com-plexes which characterize the psychology of the individual. Pathology would get much help also, for in this way we should get valuable sign-posts, say among hysterics, for the discovery of the complexes making for disease, of which the hysteric is himself not always aware.

[1] *Die Ideenassoziation des Kindes.*

[2] *Zeitschrift für Psychol.*, Bd. XXVI.

[3] Ziehen was the first to point out that in cases of prolonged reaction-time "a relatively strong emotional accentuation" had often arisen. Op. cit., p. 36,

To elucidate these questions further I have undertaken, with the co-operation of some educated subjects, who possessed good powers of introspection, the detailed analyses of the individual associations.

No. 1 is a married lady who placed herself in the readiest way at my disposal for the experiment and gave me every possible information. I report the experiment in as detailed a way as possible so that the reader may receive as complete a picture as possible.

The probable mean of the experiment amounts to 1 second.

1. Head	-cloth	: 1	second
2. Green	grass	: 0·8	,,
3. Water	-fall	: 1	,,
4. Prick	cut	: 0·8	,,
5. Angel	-heart	: 0·8	,,

These reactions followed without the slightest emotion, smoothly and indifferently. Reaction 5 is striking: subject cannot explain to herself how she comes to *heart*, which was used by her as a composite word. Then there suddenly occurred to her *Angelard*, a name formerly very familiar to her. It is, therefore, an indirect association following the known type of displacement by clang-similarity. The question now arises: What is the reason for this sudden appearance of an indirect association? Our earlier investigations have shown (chapter ii) that, under certain conditions, the indirect associations are increased in states of disturbed attention. It must therefore be accepted that disturbance of attention can produce indirect associations. The subject rejects altogether any disturbance from without, nor can she disclose any internal disturbance. Although the conscious can render no data, it is possible that some unconscious stimulus has disturbed the reaction. The stimulus-word *angel* has no special emphasis for her. As we already know, emphasis from a previous association can resound, and can constellate the reaction unconsciously,[1] especially when there has been something of strong emotional interest in the previous associations. Reaction 4, *cut*, calls up a certain slight shade of anxiety, an image of blood,[2] etc. The subject is pregnant and has now and then feelings of anxious expectancy. Whether the presentation *blood* also determined the reaction *heart* I leave undecided.

The emotional tone of *cut* was, the subject stated, so slight and so secondary that the connexion did not occur to her. It was for this reason that the prolongation of the reaction-time, common at such places, was here absent.

6. Long	short	: 0·8	second
7. Ship	journey	: 0·8	,,
8. Plough	field	: 1	,,
9. Wool	silk	: 1	,,
10. Friendly	amiable	: 1·2	,,
11. Table	chair	: 1·2	,,
12. Carry	lift	: 1·2	,,
13. State	make	: 1·2	,,
14. Haughty	naughty	: 1·2	,,
(*trotzig*)	(*protzig*)		

---

[1] Regarding perseveration, cp. Muller and Pilzecker, *Experim. Beiträge zur Lehre vom Gedächtnis* (Leipzig, 1900).

[2] Cp. later reaction 143, *blood*.

The rhyme is a constellation : the subject remembers having read it in one of my association lists.

15. Dance	jump	: 0·8 second
16. Lake	sea	: 0·8	,,
17. Ill	well	: 1·2	,,
18. Proud	fiery	: 1·2	,,

The last two reactions have some emotional tone, though very weak.

19. To cook	to learn	: 0·8 second
20. Ink	black	: 1	,,
21. Evil	good	: 0·8	,,
22. Needle	cotton	: 1	,,
23. To swim	to learn	: 0·8	,,

Reaction 19 returns here with the same short reaction-time. The subject admits that she has not properly learnt either cookery or swimming.

24. Journey	Berlin	: 1·2 second

Constellation of a journey a few months back ; the date, moreover, is about the same as that of the beginning of pregnancy.

25. Blue	sky	: 0·8 second
26. Bread	eat	: 1·2	,,
27. Threaten	fist	: 1·2	,,
28. Lamp	green	: 1·4	,,

This is the first longish time. The subject scarcely noticed her hesitation and perceived no special emotional tone. But the previous stimulus-word *threaten*, is rather insidious. Recalling the feeling of anxious expectancy already mentioned, we have perhaps a point of departure for the explanation of this delayed time : it is another perseveration. It is not necessary for the emotional tone to arise at the previous reaction. Affective processes always arise somewhat more slowly and proceed somewhat more slowly than purely associative processes. The emotional tone follows a little later, as can be observed in certain hysterics.

The reaction *green* is a constellation derived from her home life (lamp-shades).

29. Rich	poor	: 1 second
30. Tree	green	: 0·8	,,

Reaction 28 returns here with a very short time, a phenomenon which may rest on associative processes which have just emerged from consciousness, have a tendency to recur, or can be very readily reproduced.[1]

Our previous investigations (chapter ii) have also taught us that repetitions of the reaction frequently rest upon a peculiar emotional tone, for the words repeated are associated with an emotionally toned complex. The emotional tone resting upon such words is the mechanism which again pushes it forth at every opportunity.

31. Sing	can	: 2·4 seconds

A very superficial reaction, like *learn* to *cook and swim,* with a remarkably long reaction-time. The subject is very musical, but has always regretted that she could not sing, a deficiency which has occasioned her more pain than, for instance, her inability to swim.

32. Pity	have	: 1 second
33. Yellow	gold	: 1	,,
34. Mountain	ascend	: 1	,,
35. Play	children	: 1	,,
36. Salt	salty	: 1·4	,,

---

[1] Cp. Müller and Pilzecker, loc. cit.

This is the first reaction where this subject found an inhibition; the previous ones had followed quite "smoothly." She states that at first she did not apprehend the meaning of the word *salt* at all and had to imagine it to herself by an effort of will. Despite the long reaction-time and the stress of attention a very superficial reaction followed, one largely determined by clang. She cannot explain this disturbance. We notice the previous reaction, *children*, that obviously belongs to the pregnancy complex; its tone has perseverated and produced the disturbance.

37. New	old	: 1	second	
38. Manners	customs	: 1	,,	
39. Ride	drive	: 1	,,	
40. Wall	-maps	: 1	,,	
41. Stupid	clever	: 1	,,	
42. Copy-book	slate	: 1	,,	
43. Despise	mépriser	: 1·8	,,	

Again a long reaction-time, and moreover, oddly enough, the reaction is in French. The reaction is very superficial and adds nothing new to the presentation content of the stimulus-word.

Despise is accompanied by an unpleasant emotional tone. Immediately after the reaction it came to her that she had had a passing fear that her pregnancy might in different ways decrease her attractiveness in the eyes of her husband. She immediately afterwards thought of a married couple who were at first happy and then separated—the married couple in Zola's novel "Vérité." Hence the French form of the reaction.

It is scarcely necessary to add that these reminiscences were not conscious at the moment of the reaction.

44. Right	time	: 1	second
45. Tooth	false	: 1	,,
46. People	faithful	: 1·4	,,

Again a longish time with a slightly unpleasant tone; thinks it could refer to a song called "Faithful People," but has the feeling of something personally unpleasant.

The previous reaction, which is without any perceptible emotional tone, runs *false*; *faithful* is the opposite. This observation suffices for the subject to find the correct explanation. The reaction *false* excited the pregnancy complex more especially the fear of losing her husband's affection.

47. Smell	scent	: 1	second
48. Book	read	: 1	,,
49. Unjust	just	: 0·8	,,
50. Frog	-leg	: 1·2	,,
51. Separate	avoid	: 0·8	,,
52. Hunger	thirst	: 0·8	,,
53. White	black	: 1	,,
54. Ring	finger	: 1	,,
55. Take care	listen	: 1	,,
56. Fir-tree	woods	: 1	,,
57. Gloomy	jolly	: 1	,,
58. Plum	pear	: 1	,,
59. Meet	certain	: 1	,,
60. Law	follow	: 1·2	,,
61. Dear	husband	: 1·2	,,
62. Glass	glad	: 1	,,

The strong clang-like determination of the last reaction is probably likewise conditioned to some extent by the previous reaction.

63. Dispute	quarrel	: 1·2 second
64. Goat	bleat	: 1·2	„
65. Big	little	: 0·8	„
66. Potato	field	: 1	„
67. Paint	painter	: 1	„
68. Part	piece	: 1	„
69. Old	young	: 1	„
70. Blossom	red	: 0·6	„

She explains this short reaction-time by saying that the first syllable of the stimulus-word *blo-ssom* brought up the presentation *blood*; cp. reactions 4 and 143. Here we have a kind of assimilation of the stimulus-word to the strongly accentuated pregnancy complex.

71. Hit	prick	: 1	second
72. Box	-bed	: 1	„
73. Bright	brighter	: 1·4	„
74. Family	father	: 1·4	„

These four reactions are of interest. It will be remembered that in the association *prick — cut* (R. 4) the pregnancy complex was first encountered. Without the subject's having had the slightest feeling of the significance of the reaction, the association *prick* is consequent on *blood* brought up by the word *blo-ssom*. Reaction 72, which followed, went quite smoothly without any tinge of emotion. But the reaction is curious. The subject has now and then paid a visit to our asylum and was alluding to the deep beds used there, the so-called " box-beds." But the explanation rather surprised her, for the term " box-bed " was not very familiar to her. This rather peculiar association was followed by a clang-association (73) with a relatively long time, a phenomenon which we have already had occasion to regard as suspicious. *Bright* is the name of an individual who had a certain, though somewhat remote, significance for her. In any case there are no strong emotional reminiscences linked with the name. The subjective feeling present was merely that of slight hesitancy. The supposition that the clang-reaction is connected with the previous curious reaction does not, therefore, seem quite baseless. The reaction *bed* is repeated later on, with a distinct feeling of word-making, at the stimulus-word *mild — bed* (R. 199), a meaningless connexion quite inexplicable to her; but assuming a clang-alteration at the suppressed pregnancy complex, the association becomes the very sensible *child — bed*. Accepting this hypothesis, the above series becomes quite clear; it is again the pregnancy complex with *blood, operation, child-bed*. The emotional tone becomes more accentuated and disturbs the following reaction (perhaps *bright* cannot be assimilated to the complex), and finally comes *father*.

75. Washer	washerwoman	: 1	second
76. Cow	stupid	: 0·8	„
77. Odd	-ness	: 1	„
78. Happy	-ly	: 0·6	„
79. Tell	mother	: 1·4	„
80. Angle	bi-right	: 2	seconds

Reaction 78 is very short, which is rather curious in a stimulus-word which might so easily have aroused the complex. So the next reaction requires a much longer time, 1·4 second, and this has hitherto always been a complex symptom. The reaction *mother* explains the long time. Reaction 80 is disturbed, which is not surprising since the complex has been so distinctly encountered. The reaction *right* takes 2 seconds, having been preceded by the uttering of the syllable *bi*. To the subject herself the emotional tone of *mother* is still present. She cannot find any connexion between *angle* and *bi*. She cannot think at all what word she thought of beginning with *bi*. We are thus altogether thrown back on conjecture. In reaction 79 the pregnancy complex again occurs. We have already seen several times that it is chiefly marked by anxious expectancy. We have also seen that the first syllable of the stimulus-word can be assimilated to the complex (*blossom — blood*); the first clang-syllable of *angle = ang*, assimilated as *anxiety* and then *bi = birth*? This suggestion was accepted by her immediately. The construction may appear to many as an interpretation by omens; I should not report it were it not that I have had numerous analogous phenomena both in healthy people and patients.

81. Narrow	-hearted	: 0·6 second
82. Brother	sister	: 0·8	,,
83. Injure (*schaden*)	avoid	: 1·2	,,

This recalls *separate — avoid*. Possibly *schaden* (injure) is repressed as being emotionally unpleasant in view of the complex and has been assimilated as *scheiden* (to separate). Such repressed assimilations are frequent among hysterics. The subject is not able to confirm this explanation.

84. Stork	bring	: 3·4 seconds

The causation of this abnormally long time by the complex is clear.[1]

85. False	cat	: 1 second
86. Anxiety	have	: 1	,,
87. Kiss	me	: 1·2	,,

The marked emphasis on the personal ego in reaction 87 is perhaps also determined by the critical reaction 86.

88. Burning	fire	: 1·2 second
89. Dirty	yellow	: 1	,,
90. Door	shut	: 0·8	,,
91. Choose	choice	: 1·2	,,
92. Hay	grass	: 1	,,
93. Quiet	peaceful	: 0·8	,,
94. Scorn	ridicule	: 1	,,
95. Sleep	wake	: 1	,,
96. Month	May	: 1	,,
97. Shade	blue	: 1·2	,,
98. Dog	cat	: 1	,,
99. Talk	speak	: 1	,,
100. Coal	dust	: 1	,,
101. Moderate	drink	: 1	,,
102. Lid	eye	: 1	,,
103. Suppose	believe	: 1·2	,,
104. Smart	heart	: 0·8	,,

She states that this rhyme, which has a relatively short time, was dragged in by her.

105. Lazy	idle	: 1 second
106. Moon	calf	: 1	,,
107. Laugh	cry	: 1	,,

---

[1] The popular explanation given to children in Switzerland (as in Germany) is that new babies are brought by storks.—TRANSLATOR.

108. Coffee	drink	: 1 second
109. Broad	narrow	: 1 ,,
110. Air	thick	: 1 ,,
111. Carry	lift	: 1 ,,
112. Plate	round	: 0·8 ,,

Reaction 110 is rather curious ; it looks as if the constellation *broad — narrow* had acted particularly strongly. Is it possibly still acting at reaction 112 ?

The succeeding reactions were entirely objective ; neither the subject nor the observer found anything noticeable about them. We can therefore omit them.

143. Blood	red	: 0·6 second
144. Award	award	: 1·2 ,,
	-avoid	: 2 seconds
145. Foresight	forbear	: 1 second

Reaction 143 followed with great promptness. It is the same reaction that occurred at *blossom* (70). It is followed by a longer time and the repetition of the stimulus-word—the only case in the whole experiment. Reaction 145 is likewise very superficial, not even making sense but simply linked by a motor-clang association.

The succeeding reactions I omit as unimportant.

| 162. Rank | noble | : 1·2 second |
| 163. Slide | sly | : 0·8 ,, |

The subject states that the emotional tone of *rank* was still there at the moment of the subsequent reaction. The lady was formerly in better financial circumstances and occasionally feels the change.

| 172. Turn | round | : 1·4 second |

The cause of the longer reaction-time is here obscure, unless *round* has the emotional tone suspected above. She can give no explanation.

| 175. Confidence | me | : 1·4 second |

Here again we have the fear bound up with the complex of the husband's estrangement.

190. Bring	something	: 1·2 second
191. Hotel	Stork	
	(hotel)	: 1 ,,

What *something* means is seen by the reaction that followed.

| 195. Mirror | glitter | : 1·4 second |
| 198. Punish | prison | : 1·4 ,, |

The two long reaction-times cannot be satisfactorily explained. The subject states that at 195 at first the presentation of *glaze* rose up, but it became changed to *glitter*. It is difficult to say why *glaze* was repressed.

At 198 she could only say that she felt a slight hesitancy. Even though we cannot discover anything plausible, we may be sure from previous experience that some kind of emotionally toned complex is at the back of it. As a later instance will show, it need not be anything current but can be a reminiscence of something apparently long done with.

| 199. Mild | bed | : 1 second |

Cp. what was said about this reaction at reaction 72. Particularly interesting in this case was the complete absence of any suspicion in the subject herself as to the significance of this reaction.

Others are:

164. Love	faithful	: 1	second
167. Change	false	: 1	„
181. Duty	faithful	: 0·8	„
187. Serpent	false	: 0·8	„

In reaction 45, *false — tooth* 1 second, *faithful* 1·4 seconds. These words, for which she has obviously a predilection, seem to occur with gradually abbreviated reaction-time.[1] It is also interesting that words of this kind referring to the complex seem to have a tendency to become stereotyped in places where they do not quite make sense; it is not the case here, it is true, but we have demonstrated it in one case in an earlier investigation.

The analysis of the reactions of this subject has shown that the times exceeding 1·2 seconds, with the exception of the few reactions referred to, may be traced in two ways to the influence of an emotionally toned complex.

(1) The association has too long a reaction-time when the complex is aroused.

(2) The association directly following the one arousing the complex has a prolonged reaction-time in consequence of the maintenance of the emotional tone.

Besides the associations with prolonged reaction-time, numerous others contained complex constellations. On the whole, reactions with strong emotional tone and distinct reference to the complex have longer reaction-times. Her awareness of the significance of an association was only constant in the following respect : a very strong and differentiated emotional tone or a very marked style of the reaction alone awakened the consciousness of the complex. In the above reactions this was only once the case : in *stork — bring*. In all the other reactions the emotional tone or peculiar style of the reaction merely formed the indications for the subsequent recognition of the complex. At the moment itself there was only present to consciousness that portion more or less represented in the reaction. Here is evidence of how slight is the importance of the conscious for the activity of association.

Our whole thinking and doing, which seem to us so overwhelmingly conscious, are in reality composed of these small fragments which are determined to the minutest degree by the innumerable factors lying quite outside the conscious. To our conscious self the association process appears to be our own work, subordinate to our valuations, our free will, and our attention ; but in reality, as our experiment shows beautifully, the conscious self is merely the marionette dancing upon the stage to a hidden automatic impulse.[2]

---

[1] In cases of this kind a more exact measurement of the time would be desirable.

[2] Those, therefore, who maintain the mind = consciousness really take a part for the whole.

The analytic consideration of this experimental series shows the effect of a complex upon the association activity. Although, we are wont to say, the association is subject to a free valuation and the subject can say what he will, he really does not say what he will, but must disclose that which he believes is most secret. The reactions are not in any way free associations, but merely symptomatic acts (Freud) [1] conditioned by a psychical factor which behaves as an independent entity. The emotionally toned complex, momentarily separated from consciousness, is an activity constantly in successful rivalry with the intentions of the ego complex. Despite the distracting and repressing adaptation of the ego complex, this complex brings forth subjective reactions and associations of whose significance the ego complex has no suspicion. In our subject we find a series of intimate secrets given away by the associations ; not merely those of the moment, but all the presentation complexes of most import to the individual, all those which make up the content of her personality in joy and in sorrow. We find her strongest actual complex to be bound up with thoughts about her pregnancy, her rather anxious expectancy, and love for her husband with jealous fears. This is a complex of an erotic kind which has just become acute ; that is why it is so much to the front. No less than 18 per cent. of the associations can certainly be referred to it.[2] In addition there are a few other complexes of considerably less intensity : loss of her former position, a few deficiencies which she regards as unpleasant (*singing, swimming, cooking*), and finally an erotic complex which occurred many years back in her youth and which only shows itself in one association. (Out of regard for the subject of the experiment I must, unfortunately, omit a report on this.) The probable mean of this person amounts to 1 second, 30·5 per cent. of the times exceed this mean. 20·5 per cent. of the times have 1·2 second ; of these 32 per cent. can be definitely referred to the influence of complexes. Six per cent. of the times are 1·4 second, 75 per cent. of these being certainly determined by the complex. Three per cent. exceed 1·4 second, all of which are certainly due to the effect of a complex.

Subject No. 2 is a cultured gentleman of middle age. The reaction type is like that of No. 1, objective and superficial. I shall therefore confine myself to the critical reactions. He is a physician and often takes part in our experiments, which he follows with interest.

The probable mean of the series is 1·2 second.

---

[1] Cp. Freud, *The Psychopathology of Everyday Life.*

[2] Whilst only 4 per cent. can with certainty be referred to other complexes.

1. Head	part	: 1·21 second
2. Green	blue	: 1 ,,
3. Water	to clean	: 2·6 seconds

The stimulus-word immediately aroused an unpleasant emotional tone recalling something sexual, with an accompanying feeling of inhibition. Directly after the reaction he clearly recognized that water had been apprehended in the sense of urine.

4. Prick	hit	: 1 second
5. Angel	pure	: 1 ,,
6. Long	big	: 1·2 ,,
7. Ship	big	: 1 ,,

Here there is a distinct perseveration. At *big* in reaction 6 there first occurred a distinctly sexual feeling, then followed the second reaction, and immediately afterwards there was clear knowledge of its cause. It is a reminiscence. He had heard from us that certain female patients frequently associate sexual suggestions to *long*.

8. Plough	plough up	: 1 second
9. Wool	sheep	: 1·2 ,,
10. Friendly	bude bud	: 1·2 ,,
11. Table	gable	: 0·8 ,,

Reaction 10 is clearly disturbed. A slip of the tongue occurred which the subject at once corrects to *bud*. A mildly unpleasant feeling of uneasiness is experienced which continues during the next reaction. Hence the aimless rhyme. *Friendly — bud* is curious; he cannot explain it. The slip of the tongue seems to him as if it should really have been *bad*. But this reaction would be equally unintelligible to him. (For the probable explanation see below, reaction 86.)

15. Stalk	long	: 1·2 second
16. Dance	lance	: 1·8 ,,
17. Lake	big	: 1·2 ,,

In reaction 15 the sexual tone of *long* recurs and almost simultaneously the reminiscence already referred to. Reaction 16 is a clang-association with an abnormally long time. The sexual tone of reaction 15 kept up, mixed with vexation, and led again up to the former association, *long — big*.

18. Ill	poor	: 1·2 second
19. Pride	dried	: 1·6 ,,

Poor is accompanied by a slightly unpleasant tone of feeling, but there is no definite presentation. *Pride* is still more unpleasant, with a feeling of distraction and inhibition. The meaningless rhyme and the long time are doubly determined. He has an unpleasant money affair which has worried him for some time. He was frequently reproached, more especially formerly, with pride. This reproach affords a painful contrast with the money affair. The clear presentation of this connexion did not, of course, occur until after the reaction.

20. Cook	good	: 1 second
22. Ink	come	: 1·4 ,,

The association runs *come in the ink* and has a mixed unpleasant tinge referred by him to the money affair, but there immediately arises the reminiscence of an erotic complex, with strongly unpleasant tone, dating back several years.

24. Swim	good	: 1·2 second
25. Travel	jolly	: 1·6 ,,

Numerous indistinct reminiscences of travel of a predominantly pleasant tone.

26. Blue   lake   : 1·2 second
27. Bread   daily   : 2   seconds

Bread arouses a slightly unpleasant feeling; something like that at *poor* obtrudes itself with a feeling of inhibition. Afterwards a clear bearing upon the money affair.

28. Threaten   bad   : 1·2 second

Very unpleasant tone, subsequent recollection of the erotic complex which is bound up with feelings of guilt.

29. Lamp   shade   : 1·2 second
30. Rich   poor   : 1·4   ,,

Poor has again a painful tinge and again arouses subsequently the reminiscence of the money affair.

31. Root   shoot   : 1·2 second
32. Sing   jump   : 1·8   ,,

Root again arouses the sexual tone like *long* and for the same reason, then annoyance; the rhyme and long reaction-time are referable to this.

33. Pity   the poor : 1·42 second
34. Goal   much   : 1·2   ,,

The poor again arouses the money complex, this time with distinct and adequate emotional tone. Goal is assimilated as gold, although the stimulus-word is correctly apprehended. The money complex overcomes the ego complex with its telltale *much*.

36. Play   ball   : 1·2 second
37. Salt   fault   : 1·4   ,,

The association *play — ball,* which is in itself quite innocent, at once took on an erotic emotional tone, the word *ball* changing its meaning to *evening dance.* The erotic complex again made its appearance; hence the rhyme with the long reaction-time in the following association. I need scarcely add that at the moment of the reaction the chain of thought here exposed did not exist in consciousness, but was only represented by passing feelings. The presentations belonging to these feelings arise as a rule only afterwards, when the attention is especially directed to the emotional tone.

38. New   old   : 1·2 second

The *o* in old was spoken with a curious drawling, as if $oo = (p)oor$ were coming; but *old* came out. The money complex has lately reached a more acute stage.

39. Habit   bad habit : 1·8 second

Feeling of hesitation; in *bad habit* there is a slight shade of a feeling of guilt. The erotic complex again.

40. Ride   drive   : 1·4 second
41. Wall   place   : 1·8   ,,
42. Stupid   clumsy   : 2   seconds

No. 41 is quite inexplicable to the subject; a feeling as if it should be *no place in the sun.* In reaction 42 a very painful tone leads at once to the money complex, with the distinct knowledge that *drive* is determined by the complex, although the feeling tone peculiar to the complex did not distinctly arise till reaction 42. The reaction *place* thus belongs much more to the money complex than to *wall.* Reaction 42 has also something of the erotic complex attached to it.

43. Copy-book   book   : 1·4 second
44. Disesteem   esteem   : 1·4   „
45. Paint   money   : 1·4   „

Esteem seems to have hit the money complex very hard, for *paint* was assimilated as *pay*—hence *money*. The money complex here again overcame the ego complex.

46. Right   wrong   : 1·2 second
47. People   poor   : 1·8   „

Again the money complex with a long time.

60. Meet   defence   : 1·2 second
61. Law   lord   : 4·8 seconds

At reaction 61 an inexplicable feeling of inhibition, which for a long time would not permit any reaction to take place, then a very disturbed meaningless reaction accompanied by something like disgust. Afterwards a whole series of painful reminiscences about actions which did not correspond with the *laws of morality*, among these the erotic complex.

The following reaction:

62. Dear   good   : 2 seconds

is also entirely under the influence of these memories, of all his past iniquities.

69. Part   part of the
                   body   : 1·8 second

We have again the sexual constellation of reactions 6 and 15.

76. Wash   filth   : 1·6 second

Slight feeling of guilt and repentance; afterwards erotic complex. As regards the blunt expression cp. reaction 90.

78. Strange   new hand : 2 seconds

At first a feeling as if *poor* should come, then a reaction which is determined by reaction 38—*new — old*. Naturally the reaction occurs without the slightest consciousness of this constellation. *Strange* again struck the money complex.

79. Luck   ill luck : 1·4 second

Constellated by the previous reaction.

80. Tell   mother   : 1·2 second
81. Propriety   improper : 3·6 seconds
82. Narrow   narrow-
                   hearted   : 1·8 second

Reaction 80 occurred without any special emotional tone; but at *propriety* an immediate inhibition, with unpleasant feeling, which distinctly persisted during the next reaction; afterwards immediate recollection of various scenes of childhood which are distinctly constellated by *mother*. Instances are impressed upon him when his mother was really angry, and said that the boy behaved improperly and would always do so. One scene is very distinct, when as a hobbledehoy he behaved improperly and was rude to a lady. This reminiscence at once led back to the erotic complex, where a somewhat similar reproach must be made to himself. This is certainly the complex which is concealed behind this long reaction-time, and various *cover memories* (Freud).

86. False   bad   : 1·4 second

Here the reaction *bad* returns for the third time. (In the experimental series it recurred six times and *good* five times.) *Bad* carries the feeling of guilt with it proper to the erotic complex. It will be seen that this word, together with *good,* has a similar tendency to arise, as has *poor* for the money complex. (*Poor* occurs four times as a manifest reaction, and three times as a repressed one.) *Bad* occurred for the first time in reaction 10, but was obviously repressed there, since in his present emotional life there are strong inhibitions against the emotional complex.

89. Brand   poultice   : 1·8 second

The stimulus-word was correctly apprehended, but was at once changed into *bran,* to which *poultice* was associated with a rather long time. Thus *brand* was assimilated. The previous association contained no constellation for this assimilation. *Brand* has, however, an unpleasant tone and is forthwith associated with the idea of acute alcoholism, and therewith a reminiscence of that state on one occasion, which is accompanied by very painful feelings. This time the ego complex got the lead of the old, but still watchful reminiscence, and assimilated the stimulus-word in a most appropriate sense. The painful memory was thus disguised or concealed from himself. This mechanism (censure in Freud's sense) [1] plays a very prominent part in hysteria. It is not a case of a function of the conscious which must find expression, but of an automatic regulation thereof, which may or may not come into consciousness.

90. Dirty   filthy   : 1·4 second

The blunt style of this reaction is determined by moral repugnance, which is bound up with the erotic complex.

91. Door   to show   : 1·4 second

This reaction with its uninviting, repellant manner is determined by the same feeling.

92. Choose   mayor   : 2·2 seconds

Here a new complex is met. It is the hope of advancement, of a *mair* (more) from different points of view. It is at the same time the hope of a leading position, not of a subordinate one. The determination of *mayor* is therefore not merely a pure clang, but it is something conceivable—in a symbolic form, however. The correct reaction would be *superintendent.* But this word is associated with the secret wish, and therefore the inhibition which represses the whole desire extends to this word. Instead of the correct reaction we obtain a presentation associated with it which is externally determined by the word *mair* (more), this being again characteristic of the mood of the moment.

This process is very similar to the hysterical talking at random in the Ganser complex, [2] or perhaps even more with the associating at random of dementia præcox, where metaphors of this kind are especially employed. Similar phenomena are found relatively frequently in everyday life; I mean in melody and word automatisms. A lady gave me the following delightful instance: she told me that for some days the word *dagon* was constantly on her lips, although she had no idea whence it came. I asked her for any recent affect towards events or suppressed wishes. After some delay and hesitation she told me that she had very much wanted a "morning-gown" but her husband had not seen his way to it. *Dagon = day-gon = day-gown = morning-gown* shows the partial relationship of sense and clang. The determination of the form *dagon* arose from the fact that about the same time she was reading about Dagon.[3] Similar combinations can be demonstrated in great number if the trouble is taken to

---

[1] Freud, *Interpretation of Dreams.*

[2] Riklin, "Zur Psychologie hysterischer Dämmerzustände und des Ganserschen Symptoms," *Psych.-neur. Wochenschr.,* 1904, No. 22.

[3] For a similar word automatism see chapter ii, p. 153.

go into the tunes one is humming oneself or that are being hummed by others. A colleague who on his round caught a glimpse of a nurse who was said to be pregnant presently caught himself softly humming, " Es waren zwei Königskinder, die hatten einander so lieb," etc. (" Fondly two royal children loved "). At the same time he was consciously occupied with a quite other matter. Another colleague betrayed to me through his automatic humming the ending of an unhappy love complex.

These instances give us some insight in what direction trains of thought move when conscious attention is absent. Every association occurring in consciousness arouses to a certain extent an echo of similarities and analogies which runs through all stages, from similarity of meaning through similarity of form to merest similarity of clang. The most beautiful instances of this are furnished by dreams.

> 95. Ridicule   derision   : 1·4 second
> 96. Dead   dog   : 1·6 „

This association surprised the subject. He does not understand how he came to this unusual association. The somewhat prolonged time leads one to suspect an emotional tone which he first acknowledges as vague and then as painful. At the catchword " painful " a distinct recollection returns ; it is now more than twenty years ago. He was obliged to shoot a favourite dog and the loss was " painful " to him for a long time.

> 102. Moderate   immoderate : 1·6 second

The somewhat longer time in this superficial reaction is explained by its relation to 89 (brand).

> 104. Suppose   believe   : 2 seconds

Suppose is an insidious word and there are very few persons who do not find themselves caught by it. The erotic complex was encountered here.

> 105. Pain   derision   : 1·2 second
> 108. Laugh   prate   : 2·8 seconds

The p of prate was drawled out. At first, just for an instant, pain distinctly came up ; hence the long time. But pain was involuntarily at once suppressed. The emotional tone has something amounting almost to nausea ; he agrees that he has an almost morbid sensitiveness to ridicule. Reaction 95, ridicule — derision, 105, pain — derision, 108, laugh — pain (prate), are now seen to be intimately connected. The determination of prate is on one side an alliteration, on the other a significant relationship, " prating about people."

> 120. Create   work   : 2 seconds

The professional complex is the cause of the prolongation of the reaction.

> 127. Hart   deer   : 2 seconds

The first feeling was as if the association was hard — poor, and the word poor was almost uttered. Another assimilation to the money complex.
The next reaction :

> 128. Waken   awaken   : 1·6 second

is on this account very superficial, with a relatively long time.

> 130. Wicked   bad   : 0·8 second
> 131. Portfolio   hold   : 0·8 „

Portfolio had the sense of pocket-case, where he used to hold his money. The reaction hold is quite meaningless and at first surprised the subject, who then recalled the meaning he had given to *portfolio*. Another reference to the money complex.

148. Forget	-fulness	: 2	seconds
149. Drum	beat	: 1·2	second
150. Free	-dom	: 1·2	,,
151. Wagon	-burg	: 3	seconds

Reaction 148 has a very unpleasant tone; nothing special was noticed at 149 and 150; there is a marked and inexplicable inhibition at 151.

Forget arouses an event of many years back—a breach with an unfaithful friend. Reaction 149 is " The Trusty Comrade " :

> " The drums beat up to action
> And he was by my side," etc.

Reaction 150 refers to the breach. Reaction 151, *wagon*, seems to have been only assimilated with great difficulty ; its completion, *burg*, is curious. It becomes clear when the subject explains that it was at Augsburg that his friend's falseness was first recognized. All these data were unconscious at the moment of the reaction. The complex was represented at reaction 148 only by an unpleasant feeling, which could not at first be more closely defined. The connexion between the reactions in this series was only recognized subsequently.

153. Impudence	accursed	: 2	seconds
154. Rapid	-ity	: 0·6 second	

Reaction 153 belongs to the mood of the above reactions (the analysis was only taken up after the completion of the experiment). It is anger at the impudence of his false friend. The strong emotional tone seems to have extended even to reaction 154.

167. Change	of time	: 1·8 second

The stimulus-word again hit the money complex, hence the long time.

184. Deaf	neat	: 2·6 seconds

He assimilated *deaf* as *deft*, although he understood the stimulus-word. (He knows the list well and has even used it himself a few times in experiments.) The reaction-time is very long. *Deaf* causes a slight anxiety complex. He has several times had catarrh of his Eustachian tube, leaving the hearing in one ear slightly deficient. He has an exaggerated fear of becoming entirely deaf. *Deaf* has too unpleasant a tone and is therefore quickly suppressed.

190. Bring	money	: 1·2 second
191. Wording	fetch	: 2·2 seconds

The last reaction is meaningless, but it is explained by the money complex aroused by *bring*.

195. Mirror	mind	: 1·8 second	
196. Full	filth	: 1·4	,,
197. Reason	good	: 1·6	,,
198. Punish	for evil	: 2·2 seconds	
200. Beautiful	good	: 1·6 second	

Reaction 195 is somewhat inhibited for an unknown reason. Perhaps the *mirror of the mind* had something of the ethical tone of the subsequent reactions. In *full* this is, of course, self-evident: *the mind is full of* . . . The strong expression expresses the disgust already demonstrated (reaction 90). The following *good* is loosely connected with the stimulus-word and is repeated at the earliest opportunity (200). It likewise refers to the erotic complex.

Reaction 198 is obviously constellated by the complex.

In contrast with the previous subject, there is here a whole series of emotionally toned complexes which have little or no connexion with each other. Whilst in the female subject No. 1 the sexual complex (pregnancy) with its offshoots (anxiety, jealousy) dominates the scene, in the male subject No. 2 the sexual complexes play a less important part. Out of personal consideration for the latter I cannot review the whole of the reactions. But it is easy to demonstrate :

(1) Sexual complexes.

An erotic complex belonging to the past and now closed, which expresses itself almost exclusively in ethical emotional constellations (disgust, repentance).

An erotic complex of the moment which is expressed merely by erotic emotional constellations (not reviewed).

There are at least three sexually toned presentations independent of each other.

(2) Money complex.

(3) Ambition, with at least four secondary memory complexes.

(4) Personal sensitiveness with at least three secondary memory complexes.

(5) Friendship.

(6) Two emotional-tinged reminiscences independent of one another (*dead dog, deafness*).

We thus have something like ten complexes which are, so to say, independent of one another. Subject No. 2 is a few years older than No. 1 ; in the latter 18 per cent. of the associations refer to the sexual complex, whilst only 4 per cent. occur with other emotionally toned constellations. In No. 2, on the other hand, 53 per cent. of the associations can be referred to the influence of a complex. This greater number of complex constellations does not merely mean that the analysis was driven further, or that No. 2 gave us better information than No. 1, but it can be objectively recognized that the emotion of No. 2 (at least at the time of the experiment) was greater. This is recognized by the frequent disturbed reactions, and by the curious assimilations and repressions.[1]

Of the 53 per cent. complex constellations 10 per cent. only are really sexual, i.e. refer to an erotic complex of the moment ; 11·5 per cent. refer to the money complex, 2·5 per cent. to ambition, 4·5 per cent. to personal sensitiveness, 3 per cent. to the breach of friendship, 9 per cent. to an erotic complex now closed and constellated by feelings of disgust and repentance ; 12·5 per cent. relate to about six small more or less separated complexes with emotional tones. The really sexual

[1] Cp. also "complex signs " in chapter ii.

complex falls into the background as compared with many of the other constellations (10 : 43).

This case shows us even better than the first how much of the individual element is contained in the associations. The experiment furnishes us with information of great importance about his mental content ; to a certain extent it gives us a cross-section of the present psychological personality.

No. 3 is a younger man of education. I limit myself entirely to the critical associations, and review the case chiefly to point out that we find here, in principle, the same thing as was found in the two previous cases. The probable mean of the subject is 1·6 second.

1. Head	neck	: 1·2 second	
2. Green	mouse	: 0·8	,,
3. Water	green	: 1	,,

This series strikes one by the peculiar reaction *mouse*, and the perseveration of *green*. *Neck* is a reminiscence of the day before the experiment ; he had seen a cinematograph scene of the death of Marie Antoinette.

He is not certain whence came *mouse* ; he has rather the feeling that it was a slip of the tongue—supposes it was *house*.

4. Prick	fight	: 1·2 second
5. Angel	house	: 1·6 ,,

Here the conjectured reaction to No. 2—*house*—returns with a long reaction-time and the recollection comes up also. His grandfather was often in the habit of singing "Through all the lands an angel goes," etc ; but with equal frequency he used to sing "My house in the green field stands." Linked with these songs are a series of emotionally toned images, which are only partly pleasant. The perseveration *green* and the slip of the tongue—*mouse* for *house*—now become clear.

13. State	church	: 1·8 second

The reaction took place with hesitancy, for *church* stands for the great complex of a strong religiosity.

16. Dance	not	: 1·8 second

The reaction really is *I cannot dance*, with which is connected a very disagreeable feeling, for he has experienced a rebuff in love which a friend, who can dance well, has been spared.

18. Ill	not	: 1·6 second

This stimulus-word he again ascribes to himself ; in spite of the unfortunate result of the affair, he was yet not entirely without hope.

22. Wicked	friendly	: 1·8 second
23. Needle	need	: 1·2 ,,

Wicked arouses the feeling of jealous animosity which he manifests towards a certain rival. The clang-association following is conditioned by perseveration of the emotional tone.

30. Rich	fairly	: 2·8 seconds
31. Tree	gnarled	: 1·6 second

Reaction 30 belongs to the lost fiancée, hence the long reaction-time. The subsequent reaction is also somewhat long and has a rather affected and remote character; the tone seemed somewhat ironical, and this holds true also in the following reactions :

| 32. Sing | amiable | : 1·4 second |
| 33. Pity | absolutely none | : 1·8 „ |

By which is meant that he really deserves no pity, for every one is master of his destiny.

44. Despise	fellows	: 5 seconds
47. People	religion	: 1·6 second
48. Smell	disgusting	: 1 „
50. Unjust	abominable	: 1·8 „

In reaction 44 by *fellows* are meant the Jews. The lady in question is a Jewess. *People* again arouses the presentation " Jews," but it is repressed. *Religion* takes its place because to the religiously disposed subject the religion of his sweetheart caused scruples. The subsequent predicates, strongly tinged with emotion, really refer to the complex and not to the stimulus-words that aroused them (as with No. 2, where the coarse form of the reaction likewise betrayed the affect).

| 54. White | snow | : 1·8 second |

A feeling of " finished " or " death " ; refers to the love complex.

| 61. Law | absolute | : 1·4 second |

This is again the reaction 33 and expresses the same feeling : so the law says it, it must be so.

| 62. Dear | beautiful | : 1·2 second |
| 66. Big | fine | : 1·2 „ |

Both reactions have an ironical tone and refer to the complex.

| 74. Wild | animal | : 1·8 second |

Wild (which in dialect = *wicked*) the subject attributes to himself on account of the complex.

| 75. Family | house | : 1 second |

The word *house* seems to be the representation of the complex of all family recollections (also *to cook — house*). It occurs here with a relatively short time.

| 79. Fortune | play | : 1·8 second |

distinctly refers to the love complex.

| 80. Relate | talk | : 1·6 second |

The reaction was given in English. We have already learned to view French reactions with suspicion ; the reaction in English also refers to the complex. He at first wanted to relate the story of his disappointment to a brother who was living in America, but afterwards altered his intention. The English form is determined by this.

| 83. Brother | sister (in English) | : 2 seconds |

Another reaction in English with a long reaction-time. *Brother* probably aroused again unconsciously the presentation of the former reaction. *Sister* comes because the sister of the subject was then about to go to a French boarding-school, just as the brother had shortly before gone to America. This analogy was condensed in the *sister*.

88. Kiss   absolutely   : 1·6 second

Absolutely is a word standing for the love complex.

91. Door   mouse   : 1·6 second

The slip of the tongue to reaction 2 occurs again, probably to mask the complex *house*.

92. Choose   Kaposi

The word *caprice* was really the word that emerged for a moment, but was immediately inhibited and changed into *Kaposi*. The choice of the lady in question was a *caprice*. *Kaposi* is only a clang-similarity and constellated by a conversation which took place the day before, when *Kaposi* was mentioned.

105. Pain   kiss   : 1   second
106. Lazy   sow   : 1·4   ,,

The coarse expression of the last reaction rests upon the feeling of anger which perseverates from reaction 105.

115. Resolute   kiss   : 1·8 second

Resolute was assimilated as " absolute," the representative of the complex, and the reaction was in accordance with this meaning.

125. Purpose   absolutely
                 none   : 1·2 second
126. Hit   yes   : 2·2 seconds
134. Worthy   purblind   : 1   second
135. Danger   liking   : 1·4   ,,
136. High   no, low   : 2·8 seconds
140. Mix   blood   : 2   ,,
143. Blood   mix   : 1·4 second

These constellations are all more or less constellated by the love complex; the constellating factor was, of course, not a clear image at all but merely a kind of indefinable mood.

144. To let   family   : 1·6 second

For a moment *house* came up, but it was repressed and replaced by the rather curious *family*. This is association 75 suddenly taken up again to mask the word *house*, which stands for the complex.

145. Retribute   resolute   : 2 seconds

Again *absolute* at first forced its way up, but was inhibited and masked by *resolute*, by a clang-association in which perhaps reaction 115 had some effect also.

160. Wish   absolutely
                 none   : 1·8 second

I will not accumulate further instances; they do not show anything new in principle but merely confirm what has been already demonstrated in the previous subjects.

The love complex was well to the front in this case; 52 per cent. of the associations certainly refer to it. The family complex can be demonstrated in 11 per cent. of the associations. Then there occurs, here and there, a complex of ambitious endeavour, provable in 7 per cent. Numerous single emotional reminiscences can be shown in 27 per cent. of the associations. The general probable mean of this case is 1·6 second : 31 per cent.

R

of the reaction-times exceed this mean; 17 per cent. amount to 1·8 second; of these 85 per cent. are constellated by the complex, whilst in 15 per cent. this influence is doubtful or not proven. 4·5 per cent. of the associations take 2 seconds; 89 per cent. of these can be referred certainly to the complex, whilst in 11 per cent. the influence is uncertain. Nine per cent. of the associations take over two seconds; they are all referable to the complex influence.

There is no object in multiplying instances, for it would be only a constant repetition. So far as my experience goes the complex phenomena are the same in all subjects. Naturally the nature of the complex varies with sex and education.[1]

The perseveration of the emotional tone deserves attention. Perseveration plays, as we know, a peculiarly large share in the pathology of the association process. Perhaps the investigations on normals have helped to elucidate the essential problem of morbid perseveration. In these experiments, the perseveration of the emotional tone occurred so often that it can be expressed to some extent statistically. For instance, No. 2 shows thirty-two reaction-times over 1·6 second, of which sixteen are likewise followed by prolonged reaction-times. The reaction-time following is prolonged on ten occasions, the two next reactions thrice, and once the third, fourth, and fifth reactions following. As this summary shows, a *quasi* step-ladder increase of the reaction-times is not infrequently observed. In certain cases of hysteria and dementia præcox I have seen the same increase, but much more distinctly, of the step-ladder pattern, and this usually in places where a complex was suspected.

To recapitulate :

(1) These figures demonstrate that almost without exception very long reaction-times are caused by the interpolation of a strong emotional tone.

---

[1] The concept *repression*, which I have so frequently used in my analyses requires a brief exposition. With Freud the concept (as, moreover, the word suggests) has the character of an active doing, frequently indeed that of a function of the conscious. In hysteria there is certainly the impression that *repression* = willed forgetting. But when it comes to normal persons a more passive transference to the background is found; to say the least the repression here is something unconscious to which the idea of willed, or rather of *desired*, can only be indirectly attributed. If I still speak of "repressing" or "concealing," this use of the word may be regarded, if preferred, as a metaphor from the psychology of the conscious. Materially it is all the same, for objectively it is perfectly indifferent whether a mental process is conscious or unconscious. (Cp. Bleuler, "Versuch einer naturwissenschaftliche Betrachtung der psychologischen Grundbegriffe," *Allgemeine Zeitschrift für Psychiatrie*, Bd. L.)

(2) Strong emotional tones belong, as a rule, to extensive and personally important presentation complexes.

(3) The reaction can belong to a complex of this kind and bear the emotional tone of the complex without the complex necessarily being present in consciousness. The constellation (Ziehen) of an association is mostly unconscious (or " not conscious ") ; the constellating complex then plays the part of a quasi-independent entity, of a " second personality."

(4) The emotional tone can also, unconsciously, influence the succeeding reactions, when diverse phenomena may be observed :

a. The reaction under the influence of the perseverating emotional tone has too long a reaction-time.

b. The reaction is an association which still belongs to the sphere of the presentation of the previous complex.

c. The reaction is abnormal : it can

(α) be disturbed by a slip of the tongue or repetition of the stimulus-word ;

(β) be abnormally superficial (clang-reaction).

(5) The emotional tones in question are mostly of a disagreeable nature.

(6) The signs of an unconscious constellating complex are : long reaction-time, peculiar reaction, fault, perseveration, stereotyped repetition of a reaction-word (" representative of a complex "), translation into a foreign tongue, energetic expression, quotation, slip, assimilation of the stimulus-word (or misunderstanding of the stimulus-word).

(7) Erotic complexes seem to play a peculiarly important part.[1]

(H) *On the Quantitative Behaviour of the Delayed Reaction-times in a Large Number of Subjects*

a. STIMULUS-WORD AND DELAYED REACTION-TIME.—It would be of interest to learn whether the laws deduced from the above analysis could be employed on a larger number of subjects about whom we possess but meagre information. Practical experience teaches us that there are very few people who can follow their own psychological processes to the minutest details. Subjective analysis has therefore very narrow limits. But it ought to be

---

[1] The analysis of the associations of an uneducated person would require to be differently formulated, and in a more complicated way. As Riklin and I have shown, the uneducated attaches chief importance to the meaning of the stimulus-word ; therefore he has a longer reaction-time, making it difficult to judge out how far this is conditioned by the emotions or by the difficulties of the adaptation.

possible, guided by the results obtained, to penetrate objectively into the complexes concealed in the associations, and at least to demonstrate the probability that the laws obtained by subjective analysis are universally true. On the same lines I have therefore investigated the kinds of stimulus-words that, as a rule, produce delayed reactions. The material was eleven persons, of whom nine were uneducated and two educated.

(1) Five subjects always reacted with long times to the following stimulus-words :

Needle	False	Hope
{ Hair [1]		Strange
{ Salt	Fern	Resin
{ (Tooth) three persons [2]	{ Disgust	{ (Disguise) seven persons [2]
{ Window	{ Increase	{ Inn
Pyramid	Remember	Hit
Ripe	Threaten	Weave

It is not surprising that stimulus-words like *fern, increase, resin, pyramid*, require a delayed reaction-time, for they are rather rare words to which the uneducated have not at their disposal an off-hand connexion. But this cannot be maintained of the words *needle, hair, hit*, etc. ; these are extremely common in colloquial speech. The reason for the delayed reaction-times for these words must be sought for on the basis of the above analyses. On the whole, these are words which usually evoke emotionally toned combinations, like *hope, false, hit, threaten, remember, ripe*, etc, for they have in themselves a certain emotional value. For women *hair* must have a certain emotional value. The words *salt, window, increase, inn*, have, it is true, no emotional value which at once springs to the mind, but in the original they follow on stimulus-words that do excite emotion ; thus, as repeatedly demonstrated, they still come within the sphere of the perseverating emotional tone. *Hair* and *tooth* can, especially among women, cause long times, whilst *disgust* and *despise* universally excite emotion. *Needle* does not follow any stimulus-word exciting emotion, but here another factor comes into play. This word is in German *nadel*, and as pronounced, the nearest and only clang-association for those who speak the Swiss dialect is *nabel* (navel). Thus *nadel* (needle) for these persons almost invariably arouses the word *nabel* (navel). As we have seen, it is not at all necessary that this fact should come into consciousness, but it can nevertheless occasion an inhibition

---

[1] The stimulus-words bracketed together followed each other directly in the original.

[2] The word in parentheses was given because as a complex excitant it is more suspect than *window* or *inn*.

in the association. That this is no idle speculation is seen from the occurrence of the same phenomenon in other words where a similar tendency exists.[1]

(2) Six out of eleven subjects always reacted with a long time to the following :

Dream	Injure	Swing
Paper	Indulge	Omen
Book	Shocking	Smell
Frog	Soft	Forge
Attendant	((Guess) eight persons	Caress
Right	(Of age	Family

Words like *swing* and *omen* can be regarded as difficult words in which the rarity may overcome the emotional value. From the ubiquity of *paper* it is difficult to say what is in general the factor that arouses emotion. *Attendant* acts under the constellation that the uneducated persons were all male and female attendants in our asylum. The factor in *soft* was due to the German clang-similarity with another word, *leise = soft*, apprehended as *läuse = lice*. It is curious that to the word *frog* there was so frequent a prolonged time. Those in whom it occurred were, with a few exceptions, women. The male subject who reacted with a long time was able to give us an explanation ; *frog* had encountered the emotional complex arising from the recent birth of a son. Possibly for the woman's unconscious, *frog* has an emotional similarity with the small, naked, crawling infant ; thus encountering a sexual complex which is surely present in every woman, even if entirely unconscious.

The emotional value of the remaining stimulus-words is clear and requires no further discussion.

(3) Seven of the eleven reacted to the following stimulus-words with prolonged time :

(Freedom	Sick
Unjust	Despise
World	Take care
Faithfulness	Kiss
Consciousness	

The only " difficult " word is *consciousness*. It is not difficult to understand that the stimulus-words *freedom, unjust, take care,* cause a prolonged time-reaction among the asylum attendants. *World* seems to be within the sphere of influence of two stimulus-words that excite emotion.

[1] It is also seen in stimulus-words that have more than one meaning, especially when one meaning has a vulgar or obscene usage.—TRANSLATOR.

(4) Eight to ten of the eleven persons reacted with prolonged time to the following :

Heart	Suppose
Violence	{(Kiss) seven persons
Wonder	{(Naturally) nine persons

With *suppose* it was less the somewhat rare occurrence of the word than its effect upon the emotions. *Wonder* seems frequently to have aroused religious complexes attended by inhibitions. *Naturally* is erotically constellated by *kiss* immediately preceding it, and therefore a very "insidious" word for both sexes. *Violence* obtained the maximum of the delayed times. The fact that all the subjects are very closely connected with the asylum perhaps played an important part here.

We see from this critical analysis that the difficulty or rarity of a stimulus-word has no inconsiderable effect upon the duration of the reaction-time, but that in the overwhelming majority of cases the stimulus-words with delayed reactions are marked by a high emotional value.

I have tried to estimate the quantitative values of these four series in the following table :

Of the two hundred stimulus-words, forty-eight excited in five or more persons a delayed reaction-time.

In five subjects there were delayed times with seventeen words ; 76 per cent. took place with presentations of emotional value.

In six subjects there were delayed times with seventeen words ; 76 per cent. took place with presentations of emotional value.

In seven subjects there were delayed times with nine words ; 89 per cent. took place with presentations of emotional value.

In eight to ten subjects there were delayed times with five words ; 90 per cent. took place with presentations of emotional value.

Thus, on the average, 83 per cent. of the stimulus-words with a prolonged time had an emotional value, whilst only 17 per cent. of the prolongations were due to difficulty of the words. Of the stimulus-words arousing emotion at least 28 per cent. had an emotional value, chiefly erotic.

b. OCCURRENCE OF DELAYED REACTION TIME AMONG INDIVIDUALS.—We can conclude that abnormally long reaction-times are mainly due to emotional processes. Daily experience tells us that it is just in the world of the emotions that the greatest individual differences exist. It is, therefore, worth while to investigate the behaviour of the abnormally long times in the different subjects. In this investigation I have used the material supplied by twenty-six persons (uneducated—seven women, seven men ; educated—six women, six men), with a total of four thousand individual measurements.

As already mentioned, all reactions which exceeded the individual probable mean were regarded as delayed. In that way a series of reactions was encountered which showed neither long duration nor distinct influence of complex. But, on the other hand, if the upper individual limit for normal times is raised, one is thrown on to the arithmetical mean, in which the delayed times are included. But this limit is far too high for individuals and the method brings out no characteristic figures. I therefore resolved to choose the individual probable mean as the upper limit: first, because the abnormally long times are not considered therein (the probable mean is, as a rule, lower than the arithmetical); and secondly, because about one-third of those times (see analysis of No. 1) which exceed the probable mean by merely 0·2 seconds is constellated by emotional complexes, whilst the very long times are all due to complexes. In this way we deal pretty well with all the times delayed by emotion. As many of the examples show, there exists a certain ratio between the intensity of the emotion and the length of the reaction-time. From very long reaction-times one may deduce, *cum grano salis*, very intense emotion. On calculating the average by the arithmetical mean the delayed times become too abundant. In the following table I present the figures of the probable and the arithmetical mean for the four groups as well as the percentage figures of the delayed times, in addition to the difference between probable and arithmetical mean.

		Prob. mean	Arith. mean	Difference	Delayed times in per cent.
UNEDUCATED	Women	2·2	2·9	0·7	49·2
	Men	1·8	2·4	0·6	40·9
EDUCATED	Women	1·7	2·2	0·5	42·4
	Men	1·3	1·7	0·4	41·8

All the columns of this table express in different ways pretty much the same thing ; the uneducated women have the highest probable mean and the greatest number of delayed reaction-times. The differences between probable and arithmetical mean are instructive : the group of educated men have a lesser difference than the other three groups. This fact says that the long reaction-times of this group are, on the average, shorter than that of the other groups ; that the emotional inhibition (for that is the chief import, and not differences of culture) in all the other subjects, even if they do not always occur absolutely more frequently, are more fundamental and excessive than those of the Educated Men. In this I see the expression of the fact that the experimenter, who in every respect stands at the level of the group of Educated Men, is for the remaining groups a person of the opposite sex or a person placed over them. This seems to me to be a sufficient reason for the universally stronger occurrence of emotional inhibitions in the remaining groups.

With the demonstration of the emotional influences upon the duration of reaction-time I have opened up a territory which is so complicated and subject to such great individual variations that for the present there would be no advantage in communicating the individual figures which form the bases of the above tables.

General Recapitulation

(*A*) The average reaction-time of the measurements taken with the second stop-watch among the educated and uneducated is 1·8 second.

(*B*) The times for the male subjects (1·6 second) are, on the average, shorter than those of the female subjects (2·9 seconds).

(*C*) Likewise the times of the educated (1·5 second) are, on the average, shorter than those of the uneducated (2 seconds).

(*D*) The quality of the stimulus-word exercises a definite influence upon the reaction-times. The shortest average times are responses to concretes (1·67 second), the longest to universal concepts and verbs (1·95 and 1·9 second). The educated men form an exception to this rule, for in their case the concretes are, on the average, followed by the longest reaction-times.

(*E*) The quality of the reaction-word also seems to have a distinct influence upon the duration of the reaction-time. The longest times occur with universal concepts (1·98 second). The shortest times occur with adjectives and verbs (1·65 and 1·66 second). The concretes (1·81 second) are in the middle. The educated men here again form an exception, for their longest time is again with concretes.

(*F*) The nature of the association has a distinct influence upon the reaction-time. Inner associations demand a longer reaction-time than outer ones. Clang-reactions show, generally, relatively long times because they are abnormal and their occurrence is due to certain disturbances from inner distraction.

(*G*) The reaction-times which exceed the probable mean are, in large part, caused by the occurrence of intense emotion which belongs to the presentation complexes significant to the individual. The reason for the prolongation is generally not conscious at the moment. The delayed reactions can therefore serve as a means for the discovery of affect-toned (often unconscious) presentation complexes (of importance in hysteria).

(*H*) Certain stimulus-words are commonly followed by a delayed reaction. About 83 per cent. of these stimulus-words are chiefly characterized by their emotional value, whilst only about 17 per cent. have delayed times on account of the difficulty or rarity of the word.

The emotional tone often calms down slowly, extending to the subsequent reaction, which thus becomes disturbed (perseveration).

CHAPTER VI

CONSCIOUSNESS AND ASSOCIATION

By PROFESSOR E. BLEULER

MENTION is often made in this volume of unconscious or sub-conscious mental functions, or of unconscious processes that influence mental functions.

Curiously enough, these things, which one meets with at every step in psychological investigation, are in Germany generally ignored, misunderstood, or attacked upon doctrinaire grounds. In France it would be unnecessary to make any special reference to the existence of unconscious mental phenomena ; both the Janets, for instance, imply this constantly in their experimental work, and Grasset has even formed a special theory (anatomical) for it.

In Germany the concept of the unconscious has become so twisted by Ed. v. Hartmann, among others, that it has become quite useless for scientific psychology. Others base their ideas on a theoretical standpoint, which to some extent is defensible enough : mental is conscious, the essence of the mental lies in its consciousness ; it is then, nonsense to speak of unconscious mental processes.[1]

But these professors forget, strange as it may sound, that observation is unable to draw any border-line between conscious and unconscious. Exactly the same functional formations and mechanisms which we find in the conscious are demonstrable outside it, and these are just as capable of determining our psyche as the analogous conscious processes. In this sense there are, then, unconscious sensations, perceptions, deductions, feelings, fears and hopes, simply and solely distinguishable from similarly named conscious phenomena by the absence of the conscious quality. Their separation is, therefore, entirely artificial, and can never be justified by observation ; whoever denies the existence of these functions renders the explanation of conscious processes impossible, for unconscious mechanisms are ever

---

[1] Ziehen, *Leitfaden der phys. Psychologie.* This limited view is to me as if some one were to describe the life of the amphibia as observed on land, whilst ignoring their life in water.

modifying or even determining the course of conscious processes.

It seems to me that Wundt's psychology is at present the chief hindrance to any impartial investigation of the facts. I do not wish to be misunderstood: Wundt has done more, very much more, for scientific psychology than any other psychologist, but his attitude towards the questions with which we are immediately concerned is not justified by the facts, although from many expressions one might conclude that he is aware of these facts and even subscribes to our theory.

Wundt says in his *Physiologische Psychologie* (5th edition, vol. iii, p. 521): " On the mental side an association of immediate events is that condition by which consciousness invariably appears in experience." This sentence is, of course, quite correct, but if nothing more is said many readers may forget, as perhaps the writer did himself, that it cannot become reversed. As we hope to show, there are numerous associations of presentations, following the same laws, where consciousness is absent. The ordered association of presentations is therefore only a condition of consciousness in the sense that without this probably no consciousness can exist ; but not in the sense that whenever the association is present then there is consciousness. On p. 320 consciousness is said to be the condition of every experience. That may be in harmony with the theory of apperception, but it is a somewhat bold statement. A spider clearly gathers experience, a bee gathers manifold experiences. But is it so certain that these creatures have consciousness ? One may believe this or accept it, but not prove it.

In the *Psychologie* (1st edition, p. 238) consciousness itself is said to be the association of psychical images. But it is difficult to say what is to be made out of this idea. In other places the concept of consciousness is approximated to that of apperception, the latter being presented as a kind of personification at the back of the rest of the psyche. According to Wundt this feeling is the subjective reaction " of consciousness " or of " apperception " to an impression ; our consciousness criticizes the word and its course (*Physiologische Psychologie*, 3rd edition, vol. ii, p. 3).

With such lack of clearness it is not surprising that Wundt confuses things with one another which have nothing to do with one another, as, e.g., a latent memory-picture and unconscious psychical function. Is the " latent memory-picture " (the memory-trace) constantly reproduced in a feeble way, or is it only revivified at times by a new stimulus ? This question passes on to the related one whether the acquired presentations have a permanent existence (somewhat in Herbart's sense), or whether they arise afresh every time by some kind of functional act when they emerge into " consciousness " or become otherwise active.

This sets out from the view that there can be memory-traces (physical and psychical) which only become active at times. A memory-trace, a predisposition, would then be generally of no importance at all, something like the predisposition of a stationary pendulum to swing, or of a canal in which for the time being there was no water running. The trace would only take on function when the memory-picture played any kind of part in a new mental process. Whether it then became conscious or not does not come into the question; although most people, implicitly or explicitly, generally consider *conscious* memory-pictures only.

Despite the similarity of names, unconscious actions, reflections, and presentations in our sense differ from these *toto cœlo*. We are here dealing with actual functions which are not conscious to the individual. Wundt amalgamates both latent memory-pictures and unconscious mental happenings, and even mixes up with these the question of inborn presentations.

In his *Physiologische Psychologie* (vol. iii, p. 748) the conception of a mental occurrence, resulting from the analogy of conscious motives, but which is at the same time not conscious, coincides completely with the concept of the life-forces of vitalism.

Such obscure concepts are useless in the practical psychology of the asylum, or in the investigation of normals. They have, moreover, the great disadvantage that they stand in the way of impartial observation and must be first of all pushed aside by those who wish to arrive at any kind of useful view.

There is no better testimony to the value of a psychological theory than its applicability in psychopathology. The philosophic psychology of the study must seem to be pure phantasy in the eyes of every physician because its theories are valueless in practical life. Psychiatry (one could almost say each individual psychiatrist) has to create for itself a psychology for home use.

However fruitful other sides of Wundt's "physiological" psychology have been in pathology, his theories have failed completely where we tried to unravel all that is denoted by "conscious, unconscious," "dissociated personality," etc. His theories have not even helped their originator to appreciate the significance of such relatively simple phenomena as occur in hypnotism.

It becomes our task to show briefly that there are unconscious mental phenomena, and to point out the diverse means by which these find expression.

Experience tells us, however, that this will not be enough. Even scientists, as a rule, only assimilate new ideas which harmonize with their previous content of presentations.

I shall, therefore, in conclusion, indicate briefly a theory of these unconscious phenomena which has enabled me for twenty-six years to "explain" all these observations. The whole psychology of the unconscious, all the phenomena of hypnotism, of dissociation of the personality, of hysterical conscious conditions, are brought into harmony with the rest of our knowledge, while the theory helps to remove the odium of the weird and inconceivable which so many people still attach to these phenomena.

Much of this I shall only suggest here. A psychology of the unconscious with any pretension to completeness would fill volumes.

THE FACTS

Most people agree that there is no conscious quality in the actions of the works of a watch or of physical events in general. But the expression "unconscious" is not properly used in this connexion, but only of processes in our brains where consciousness is absent, although in all other respects equivalent to or obviously like conscious processes.

We deduce these processes from their effects, or are able to learn about them in individual instances from their memory-pictures becoming subsequently conscious.

I am walking in the street occupied with some problem, make way for other people, go the right way; of all the sense-impressions not one-hundredth part becomes conscious to me, yet they guide my steps.

That these are not simple reflex processes may be deduced from the following facts, among others :

Embarking on and maintaining the direction in walking, making way, and so on is originally a mental act which has only become unconscious (" automatic ") in many cases, and that quite gradually, without one being able to state exactly at what moment or during what action consciousness completely disappeared. The activity which has become automatic cannot be something different in principle from the action originally conscious ; at any moment it can become again more or less conscious.

Our whole pathology shows that in man, at least, such activities are governed by the cerebral cortex and become disordered in agreement with the corresponding conscious functions.

The purpose and choice of the road set out upon is generally consciously determined by the mind beforehand. A reflex process cannot thus be voluntarily managed ; a reflex is distinguished from psychical functions by being non- " plastic." Now and again the unconscious psyche (the " unconscious ") commits the same kind of mistakes as the conscious psyche ; for instance, instead of taking the preselected but unusual path, another is taken to which one is more accustomed, or a side street which one intended to take is passed by if the buildings have undergone any alteration.

In such cases purposeful, unconscious changes are made in the original plan ; if a street for any cause is impassable I can choose another without reference to my consciousness. Such unconscious choice of action has analogies with conscious mental activity, but not with reflex activities.

Later on everything that my senses have perceived can emerge as memory-pictures identical with the memory-traces consciously grasped. It is relatively frequent for a spoken sentence, a word read in passing, the stroke of a clock, and the like to pass into consciousness after an interval, sometimes only after several minutes. Thus after a considerable time some passing incident, some dream or hypnotic suggestion, a memory-picture received unconsciously, may emerge into consciousness.

Here we have to do with the analogies to sensation and perception in the region of the unconscious. Again, it is unconscious sensation when, my attention being strongly fixed, a boot-nail sticks into my foot; I get up, feel worried. I notice this fact without recognizing the cause of my change of mood until for some reason or other my attention is turned towards the slight pain. All unconscious sensations and perceptions can suddenly pass into consciousness.

Among the passers-by, for whom I make room without taking notice of them, is a friend or a negro; there is some very strong smell; danger of some kind threatens me; I see fruit for sale when I am thirsty; some clumsy person pushes me aside—in all such cases consciousness is suddenly added to the unconscious process without our being able to notice any other change.

I am awaiting my fiancée and see her coming through the garden shrubbery; I am amazed at not feeling the usual pleasurable excitement. A minute later she comes out of the shrubbery—and it is not my fiancée at all; I have mistaken her for another girl, who wears dresses of the same colour. The same thing happens to me again : recalling the previous occurrence, I meant to be cautious, and nevertheless arrived at the same (false) conclusion, that the girl approaching must be my fiancée. A third time, in a mist, I get joyfully excited at the approach of a person whom I consciously did not recognize as my fiancée. The unconscious was right there also.

When reading I am accustomed to adopt various postures, which are more comfortable than elegant. Should some one knock at the door before whom I do not feel quite at my ease I sit up automatically. I have an old housekeeper from whom I do not hide my inelegant postures. Now it has happened to me to feel quite sure that the step and the knock belonged to another person—to my younger servant; and yet I could hardly make up my mind to sit up. Once, indeed, just before the expected servant entered I had time to reflect a little; I decided, in a way quite foreign to my usual thoughts and feelings, that I must accustom the girl also to see me on the sofa with my legs on the table. In all these cases, as in all similar incidents, my unconscious was right—it was the old housekeeper who was at the door.

These are cases of unconscious recognition in contrast with the conscious malcognition; add to this that the unconscious phenomena dominated the conscious feeling, the motor reaction, and even reflection.

When I was working in the physiological laboratory I frequently had to carry a lot of rabbits in a net an hour's walk. Naturally my hand got tired and I often had to change hands. I wanted to study the phenomenon of fatigue, and find out how long under conscious strain I could stop from changing hands. I did not once succeed in determining the moment of fatigue ; when I turned my attention to the rabbits, either I was not as yet tired or I had already changed hands. The sensations of fatigue had already, without appearing in consciousness, informed my brain and set an activity in motion which cannot possibly be apprehended as a mere reflex.

Just as every unconscious sense-image or its memory-picture may, from any kind of accident, become conscious, so conscious doings may become unconscious. You have only to think of the well-known instances of piano-playing, reading aloud whilst thinking of something else, or of any similarly complicated functions which have become automatic through practice ; at any moment they may become, in part or wholly, conscious and again unconscious.

But there are also unconscious analogies to reflections, to logical thinking. Carpenter in his *Mental Physiology* cites a number of instances which have become known to all since then, which prove that long series of reflections can be made in the unconscious, the result only appearing in consciousness.

Unconscious poetical productions have been made as well as discoveries ; long-sought-after mathematical problems have suddenly emerged into consciousness ready solved. Lord Mansfield certainly spoke from a ripe experience when he advised a young and newly appointed judge, " Never give reasons for your decisions : your judgments will very probably be right, but your reasons will almost certainly be wrong." [1]

By inferences which scarcely ever become conscious to us perceptions are formed from sensations. The size of an object we infer from the size of the retinal picture ; the convergence of the eyes and other sensations, again, enable us by unconscious inference to determine the distance. In the analysis of peripheral illusions of sense it is quite common to speak of such unconscious inferences (Helmholtz).

From " impressions " which we cannot analyse we often make far-reaching conclusions which we know only from the results. People who have no knowledge of graphology diagnose a rascal from the handwriting without knowing why ; a young and inexperienced girl gives an acute and poignant character of a new friend after a brief acquaintance ; a physician makes a

[1] Carpenter, *Mental Physiology*, p. 482.

correct diagnosis in difficult cases, the grounds of which he cannot properly give. A little girl from the outset distrusted a swindler who had introduced himself into a respectable family as one in great need, and who was liked by every one else.

Compare also the explanation of the cases published in the literature of so-called clairvoyance.

In unconscious reflections unconscious motives very frequently play their share. One cannot adequately explain on conscious grounds many of one's own decisions ; he who often conscientiously analyses himself will often find the decisive factor in a motive which was quite unconscious at the time of deliberation and decision. Try and find out the reasons for the doings of those dearest to you ; you get at nothing without the acceptance of unconscious motives. (For beautiful examples as to how opinions arise, see Forel, *Die Zukunft*, 1902–1903, p. 1.[1])

In this respect self-observation is very interesting when a quick action or response is demanded. The conscious self is quite unable in such cases to exercise exact reflection. The " feelings " are often derided. This word comprises, as a rule, two quite distinct things : real affects (fear, anger, etc.), then ill-considered intellectual motives and reflections. The latter must be thought out more thoroughly somewhere—" in the unconscious "—otherwise our actions would only be correct by accident ; they would become in every way equivalent to the doings of those weak-minded persons who never get beyond

---

[1] Those who know something about the alcohol question or wish to know something about it should study the arguments of the moderate drinkers for wonderful examples of the ignorance of motives. Teetotalism is opposed, e.g., by pointing out that people drank as much or even more in former days— in direct contradiction to the fact that the development of breweries and distilleries belongs to the last century, almost to the last decades. (In Switzerland the brewery was practically non-existent fifty years ago.) It is said that moderation strengthens the character—although millionfold observation has shown that alcohol weakens the character on the psychical side. In every other field care is taken to protect youth against corruption ; who, for example, would send his daughter into bad company so as to strengthen her character ? It is said in all seriousness that God has made wine so that man may drink of it. But we have long lost the habit of swallowing everything which God permits to grow. Moreover, God has at most let the grapes grow ; without man's additional effort there would be no wine. Such halting statements, such as otherwise one is only accustomed to get from imbeciles, one can hear on the drink question by the hundreds from the most intelligent people. They are easily shown to be false by the simplest person who here thinks objectively. The true motives can easily be discovered from any moderate drinker whom you know at all well. Most persons cannot be among wolves without joining in the howling, they cannot bear being regarded as peculiar. Others cannot give up their habits, their usual pleasures ; others feel embarrassed before their wives or neighbours or some relative who is a brewer or innkeeper, and so on.

uch obscure concepts. But it is quite the contrary; the individual is often astonished, on working out the matter, how orrectly his " feelings " have guided him.

Just as unconscious motives condition conscious activity, he reverse is also true. At every moment we decide on actions which are afterwards carried out quite unconsciously, so whilst without previous practice the adjustment of any kind can be nal or persistent. In my school days and up to my fifteenth ear I had warts on my left hand with which I was always dgeting; I used to get blood out of them for writing and suchke things. I was then told that warts were kept up by bestowing ttention upon them, whereupon I resolved to ignore mine. Six months later my warts were accidentally brought back to my mind; they had disappeared; in the interval I had not thought nce about them nor of my decision. From my youth upwards used, when I was alone, to spin a fairy-tale of adventures many ears ahead. I then read in a grammar-book the sentence, ' It is a disease of the soul to think the impossible." My fairyale became suspect and from that time disappeared from my involuntary fantasies without any effort of will, without any onscious prohibition. Some ten years ago I had some new shirts made; the buttonholes of the cuffs were in unwonted places, o that in putting on my coat I always used to pull out the studs.

finally succeeded in putting on the coat without dragging out the studs; it was not till a year later that I had the old difficulty gain. It was on a walk when under difficult conditions I wanted o put on the coat and the studs slipped out; up till then the adjustment made on a single occasion had sufficed.

In all these cases we are dealing with the conscious influencing of processes usually counted as mental, which, in any case, belong not to the reflex, but to the plastic functions. The transformed motive worked on permanently, although it became quite unconscious for a long time after the new adjustment.

There are similar adjustments towards centripetal processes. One is looking for a certain plant on a walk; after a while ne ceases to think about it, but as soon as the plant comes into view the attention is at once directed to it with an inhibition of ll other processes present at the moment in consciousness. You re running through the pages of a book to find a name, get interested in the book; are not thinking, perhaps, for the next our why you took up the book, but as soon as you come across the name, it is noted and brought into connexion with the original urpose. In such cases the adaptation is directed to what we all, in the conscious, the attention. There is an " unconscious adjustment of attention."

But there is also a continuous unconscious attention, as when in the street traffic I push by or step aside, feeling for the most convenient way, or when I unconsciously search the hedges for some flower.

The equivalency of unconscious presentations is best shown in the course of series of associations which jump from presentation to presentation, quite unconcerned as to whether the individual associations are conscious or not.

Many instances are found in this book ; I mention only three types. Stimulus-word : *mild* ; the reaction *bed* slurs over the words *child — child-bed* conditioned by a constellation which remained unconscious. To *high* a subject was about to answer *deep* ; she corrected it before she had quite uttered the word and said *low*. She did not know why ; analysis shows that *deep* read backwards is the name of a former adorer—a fact about the word of which she was previously not aware. To *despise* there came the reaction *mépriser*, the only reaction in French. The word is given by the stimulus, but the French form is conditioned in the unconscious by the reading of a French novel, which had reminded the subject that she might be herself despised under certain conditions.

Hypnosis gives us the means of experimenting with unconscious processes. Sense-images can be made completely unconscious by suggestion of anæsthesia, of negative hallucination, and they can be nevertheless employed to direct movements, whilst after any desired interval their existence can be established as memory-pictures. In conditions of experimental hyperæsthesia sense-images can be turned to other unconscious uses and even to better uses than the conscious ones.

In mirror-reading by letters reflected from ordinary writing paper, in the recognition, by the sense of smell, of movements taking place in any object, all the factors are scarcely conscious (The literature of hypnotism contains numerous other examples of unsuspected finer qualities of sensations which would be quite impossible to " supraconsciousness.")

If during hypnosis I give a command for a visit to be paid one hour after waking, the subject performs the action, in most cases, in his normal consciousness ; but the real motive of his visit remains quite unconscious, he believes he has other grounds for it. If I require the post-hypnotic visit to be made sixteen days later, the days are counted unconsciously, or the mental mechanism is so attuned that the action is carried out on the appointed day. If I say, " When I have clapped hands twenty seven times you will go to sleep again," sleep takes place even if the subject on awaking has quite forgotten the command, and take several days over the twenty-seven hand-clappings. The clapping must have been counted unconsciously. If I say, " If a mouse rustles in the wall you will feel an itching in the nose," the unconscious attention is attuned to the rustling of a mouse.

Many inferences made by hypnotized persons are unconscious ; the best known is the clever guessing of the hypnotist's aims, which has so frequently simulated thought transference. The subjects do not always know that they have made a deduction, and scarcely ever know out of what elements they have formed it. If we use the experiments, stupidly forbidden, of thought-reading, of the planchette (unconscious writing), and of table-rapping, we find among hypnotized and unhypnotized, among healthy and unhealthy persons, remarkable unconscious activities. Memory-pictures quite inaccessible to consciousness emerge with wonderful distinctness and are combined in logical ways as well as in fantasies. A girl writes (from left to right) an Arabic dedication which she must have seen at some time without understanding it ; she displays knowledge which she certainly never consciously possessed.

In trance, with automatic writing, she composes stories, the incidents in which she must have stored in her childhood, but which have not left a trace in her consciousness (cryptomnesia).[1]

Automatic writing, in particular, deserves more attention from psychologists than it has received. In so-called mediums it is a very common function. In Mulhouse there is a Nature Doctor, without professional qualifications, who successfully trains most of his patients in this automatic activity and gets them to write the diagnosis.

Automatic speaking is found in dementia præcox. The patient hears himself talking (mostly cursing) as if he were a third quite disinterested spectator. In the visionaries of Cevennes, about whom we possess fairly accurate reports, this phenomenon was so developed that they delivered whole sermons without their consciousness taking the slightest part. The study of all forms of " possession " furnishes other examples of this.

In thought-reading, the guide makes unconscious movements of the extremities and muscles which the thought-reader interprets, in many cases quite unconsciously, as I have been able to convince myself from many instances. Here again unconscious sensation and interpretation extend far beyond anything we can accomplish consciously. By a mere touch, direction can be much more accurately determined than might be expected, and the guess is often so extraordinary that at present we can offer no explanation. For instance, whole words or concepts are trans-

[1] Flournoy, *Des Indes à la Planète Mars.*

ferred in this way. Jung placed his hand on the back of the medium and thought of Cæsar, whereupon the medium automatically wrote "Brutus." According to Jung's unpublished experiments numbers can be correctly given if the medium only joins in the first movements of the answering table, and then interrupts all contact with the table and the medium.

These unconscious thoughts have often a tendency to express themselves in quite uncommon ways, e.g. they prefer a symbol which is foreign to the consciousness. If an innocent young girl much taken up with some strapping youth just introduced to her, makes the table say, "I am hungry and thirsty for human flesh," we easily recognize a disguise. Freud in his work on dreams, which has not met with the recognition it merits, has shown that somewhat similar ideas exist in dreams, and Jung and Riklin have found similar ideas to be the conscious or unconscious core of the bizarreries of dementia præcox.

I came across another instance of this to-day in the sphere of dreams. A girl about whose dreams I inquired on medical grounds, who would be very unhappy if I explained to her the meaning of her dream, told me the following : She was with her former teacher in the garden. He showed her an outline of the map of Switzerland. She showed him the Bernina range. He then wanted her to point out to him something else, the Popocatepetl. She wished to look for the mountain, when he bade her show him the Pacific Ocean ; she had only to go up a step when she would see it. She did so and remarked that it was a beautiful kind of "Pacific Ocean" ; it was most stormy, the foam spurted up to the sky and up to her herself, the sky was quite dark (this repeated with emphasis). Those unpractised in dream interpretation may take as key the clang to Popocatepetl with this key the rest, up to and including the black sky, easily made out (with the exception of the Bernina range).

We notice again in "unconscious cerebration" a tendency to witticisms foreign to our waking state.[1] One of our assistant physicians named Woerlin was selected for a better post and had to leave at once, which put us into great difficulty. In reporting the case to the authorities I left out the "r" in the name (Woe – lin) ; consciously I had never thought of such a pun. Observation has convinced us that Freud is right in claiming that most of these slips have a deeper meaning.

Unconscious feelings often express themselves in snatches of tunes which seem to spring up from nowhere, and their significance is undiscoverable to the subject himself without analysis

[1] Fundamentally these are not so much witticisms as unexpected associations of ideas which give the impression of wit.

Quotations serve the same end ; in association experiments they very frequently conceal emotional complexes (see chapter v).

Automatic writing and the related expressions of unconscious activity (designation of letters with the planchette, tables, movements, etc.) often conceal a " mood " of the unconscious which so far remains unexplained—words, syllables, and even sentences are misplaced in various ways or even written backwards. An acquaintance experimenting with the planchette (which, it should be noted, succeeds with most people) received words which were quite incomprehensible. To the question, " What language might this be ? " his own unconscious replied to him by the planchette, but with the letters now correctly in place, " Idiot, turn it round." This gave him the key. Jung [1] quotes a case from Myers where the automatic writing furnished complete anagrams.

Such complications are not only foreign to conscious thinking, but they require work of a kind that very few persons could carry out consciously in their heads. In this connexion we must again recall the hypersensitiveness of unconscious sense-perceptions and the hyperintelligence of many unconscious deductions.

And, nevertheless, in all these experimental expressions of the unconscious there is scarcely ever produced any really original piece of work, whatever similarity such play of ideas may have with the creations of genius. Some day we shall certainly succeed in interpreting all these things in the manner of Freud's explanation of dreams, and of the instance given above of hunger and thirst for human flesh.

The same tendency to witticisms and tomfoolery is found, as is well known, among the mediums of the spiritualists and among hysterics, whose symptoms arise to a great extent in the unconscious.

Unconscious feelings are somewhat more difficult to understand. We find their effects in association and we see their influence most markedly in changes of consciousness, in the dissociation of the different personalities, and similar phenomena (see below).

The way in which they first arise in the unconscious, by an unconscious elaboration of the content of experience, and can then be transferred to conscious personality, the following example will show. I once received some unpleasant news when I was very busy. The full extent of the matter had not become quite clear to me whilst listening to the messenger. For an hour or more I gave various instructions and orders. During this time the news had quite vanished from my mind. I had forgotten

[1] Jung, *Collected Papers on Analytical Psychology*, chap. i, p. 54.

it and was quite as usual. I then went to the wards, when it seemed to me suddenly as if I felt a heavy weight on my chest, as if I had had some accident. It was only after long reflection that I discovered the cause to be the unpleasant news which was unconsciously at work; it had linked itself to further associations, and had succeeded in obtaining notice by the conscious self through a movement of the feelings.

Every novelist knows that, besides the feelings, the instincts play a large part in the unconscious. Two examples from real life will suffice. A young man went to a ball fully determined to get engaged to a girl who was, on rational grounds, a good match for him. He there got engaged it is true, but to another lady, who did not correspond so well to his conscious wishes, but, as the sequel showed, was the right woman for him (communicated by Jung). A rather elderly bachelor discovered that he was in love with a girl who did not come up to his former conscious ideal of a " housewife." He first noticed this when stopping at an hotel; he found himself always asking for letters, even when he knew that none could possibly have arrived. Here again the unconscious instinct had chosen, as against all the fine theories of the conscious.

In the region of psychopathology we also find the unconscious in constant activity.

Hallucinatory paranoiacs complain daily about voices which seem strange to them, but which must undoubtedly have arisen from the unconscious working of the mind. The Maid of Orleans had hallucinations in which the Mother of God told her exactly what to do; these proved the right things to do until the Maid's mission was accomplished; they must have arisen from a highly intelligent unconscious mechanism. (The writer has studied the documentary evidence and is convinced that no other explanation is possible.)

Here likewise belong the common teleological hallucinations. For instance, a hebephreniac wanted to throw himself out of the window; on coming to the window he saw that it was filled up by a flood of light and he felt at the same time that he was knocking against an irresistible obstacle (hallucination of sight and of perception of resistance). In hysteria there are a number of other teleological symptoms which have hitherto been insufficiently observed. For some time past a young lady has always had an attack of aphonia when she goes into a shop to buy something. Previously she had never been able to resist the importunities of the salesman, but had often taken things home which she did not want, and which, moreover, far exceeded her means. The aphonia was a defence of the unconscious which, as a rule, sufficed, but it was a means really unworthy of the lady's highly developed intelligence.

One of my college friends suffers from paranoid dementia præcox which set in late and is of very slow course. He tries to prove to me that the injunctions, voices, etc., have not arisen in his brain. He therefore keeps a very exact account of all events which refer to these things. On one occasion he thought of the word *retour*. Then he heard a voice calling out, " *Retour-chaise.*" He assured me, quite truly, with the greatest conviction, that neither immediately nor long before had he thought of this word; it must have come from another person. He hears on many occasions things of which he would never think: surely he would not insult or threaten himself? He had been accustomed for a long time to observe himself with hypochondriacal exactitude, and his intelligence is still so good that on this occasion he allowed they were not " outside " influences, but hallucinations.

This is one case among hundreds. Independently of the conscious personality, wishes and fears regulate ideas to their liking and combine them in a compact complex, whose expressions emerge as " hallucinations " ; these appear to be so consequential and deliberate that they simulate a third person. This third person sometimes criticizes the subject, his thoughts and actions (" voice of conscience "). But it is merely a piece of the split-off personality ; it represents aspirations of this personality which would otherwise be suppressed.

We thus find in the unconscious all those activities which we usually ascribe to the conscious mind, sensation, perception, logical thinking, imagination, attention, aspiration, action.

But that is not the end. We have yet to add the chapter of multiple personality, although in these cases both complexes possess a conscious quality. But we shall see that dissociation of personality is fundamentally nothing else than the splitting off of the unconscious ; unconscious complexes can transform themselves into these secondary personalities by taking over so large a part of the original personality that they represent an entirely new personality.

In the dream of the normal individual personality is already changed. The dream shows traits and memories foreign to one when awake. Such dream-personalities are rarely complete ; they sway hither and thither and have but an ephemeral duration. A permanent grouping of experiences in two or more personalities we see in cases of doubled or multiple " consciousness." The most famous of these is Azam's Felida, who is well known to every psychologist. A young girl suddenly forgot most of her former circumstances, and from being a serious person became witty, jolly, almost boisterous ; after a time her normal state returned, and then both states interchanged at irregular intervals throughout life. In her normal state she had no recollection of her experiences in the second state ; in the latter, however, she remembered in later years the events of her normal state.

Thus several distinct personalities (up to a dozen have been observed) can interchange in the same individual.

In these cases memory behaves in various ways. As a rule the abnormal and its experiences are quite unknown to the normal consciousness, whilst the abnormal state can often make use of the memories of the normal—but not invariably ; sometimes the subjects live like two personalities, completely separated in time and content.

Jung [1] has carefully described the case of a girl at puberty who in trance exhibited an idealized personality, together with two groups of persons of another sort. In the former he suspected that he saw the later character of the girl breaking through, whilst the two others personified traits of character which were to be cast off. The patient's subsequent development has shown that he was right.

Such personalities can, however, exist permanently side by side, and not merely in succession ; it seems probably true that in every one groups of psychical elements lead a more or less independent life.

Max Dessoir has brought together in his *Doppel-Ich* [2] ("Double Self") a number of points in favour of the view that by the side of the conscious ego there is also present a "subconscious." This work, otherwise of great merit, suffers from the mistake of speaking always of one subconscious only. In truth, a practically endless number of different unconscious groupings is possible, and these all occur, although only the one or other complex, as a rule, besides the "supraconscious," seems to reach expression.

Naturally the different complexes representing different types of personalities have much in common. The ordinary acquired capacities such as gait, eating, speech, etc., are generally the same. More than this, the universal concepts, etc., acquired by experience are generally the same in the different complexes. They do not, therefore, lead an absolutely separate life, and activities of the subconscious often interact on the "supra-

---

[1] Jung, *Collected Papers on Analytical Psychology*, chap. i, " On the Psychology and Pathology of so-called Occult Phenomena."

[2] Leipzig, 1890.

conscious " and conversely in just the same way that we have indicated when speaking of unconscious activity alone.

In many cases the different personalities are only distinguishable by the absence or presence of a few memory complexes. Riklin has related a pretty instance of this (*Psych.-neurol. Wochenschrift*, 1904–1905, No. 22). A prisoner under observation got into a state of hysterical delirium at certain questions ; at one moment he was the father of a family and a driver (as in fact he was), then he became an unmarried servant who did not know his name ; both personalities were for the rest very much alike in this, that neither knew anything about the crime.

The selection and grouping of elementary constituents of the memory in the different personalities always arise under the powerful influence of affects, just as in delirium and dreams.

In the instance just quoted one could, by arousing the complex during examination, produce at will the greater part of the patient's past, and by arousing emotional reminiscences about his family reproduce his whole position in life as the father and the mainstay of the family.

THE THEORY

The foregoing observations show us indisputably that all conscious psychical functions can occur also in the unconscious, without any change in their character on that account. Sensation, perception, deduction, desire, action, can all take place in us without becoming conscious. In this sense we are obliged to speak of "unconscious sensation, thinking and doing," if we do not wish to make new words for these concepts. The conscious quality, the becoming aware of a psychical process, is therefore something of quite secondary importance in the consideration of our psyche, although the centripetal side of our psyche is only of importance to our ego in so far as it is conscious. (We only suffer from conscious pains, we only rejoice at conscious pleasures.[1])

We must now ascertain under what conditions psychical processes are conscious.

I believe they become so by association with our ego, that is, with the presentations, sensations, desires, which at any given

---

[1] What is to be understood by the word *conscious* is, unfortunately, by no means a uniform concept. There is no definition of this concept and there can scarcely be one. I hope, nevertheless, that I shall be understood here : by this word *conscious* no one must think of conscious reflection, orientation and other equally different things, but of the essential characteristic which distinguishes us from an automaton who might behave like a man, of the common components that are fundamental to the concepts sensation, perception, doing, willing, feeling.

moment compose our personality.[1] Hence it follows that all those processes which are at the moment not in associative connexion with the ego complex are unconscious.

The difference between conscious and unconscious is often presented as essentially a dynamic one. Strong sense-impressions will certainly, *ceteris paribus*, receive attention sooner than weak ones. Probably strong psychical processes correspond to these. I say " probably," because we have no test of the strength of our psychical processes. But if we start with the presumption of such a test the dynamic theory becomes at once impossible. But, assuming that strong stimuli correspond to strong sensations, we see that the strength of a sensation is of very slight importance as regards attaining consciousness ; it is by no means the most striking feature. Amid the loud roar of the railway-train we notice only the interesting conversation, even if it is much softer than the noise around. I had been exactly one year in Rheinau when I first consciously heard the clock strike eleven, and yet the church tower, which contains a very clear-sounding bell, is next to the superintendent's house. I used to wake at any hour of the night at the slightest sigh of a sick member of the family, when the fire-alarm cannon which was quite near my open bedroom window never awakened me. The brightest flashes of lightning are often unobserved, whilst scarcely perceptible changes in the lighting or the tint, for instance in picking out unhealthy plants, may strike us at once. During an attack an officer was shot in the right arm ; but he did not notice this until he wanted to use his sabre. It is a commonplace fact that strong stimuli of one sense-organ do not prevent the weak stimuli of other sense-organs from becoming conscious, unless the question of pain enters, which then, properly, dominates everything. I do not hear a soft sound in bright light any worse than in the dark.

It is not possible to exhaust this theme here, but it can be strongly maintained that in all the differences which we know, " adjustment " alone plays any substantial part. What this is, upon what it rests, we do not yet know, although many scientists write about " attention," which about corresponds to this kind of adjustment, as if it were something known.

What at present can be stated with certainty about adjustment, or attention, is simply that it facilitates certain definite associations and inhibits others. If we may be allowed to employ again the illustration of the railroad used in chapter i, adjustment is a definite points-station, or, to use the popular comparison

[1] The question whence our conscious ego complex derives its consciousness we shall not here discuss. It is quite irrevelant to our purpose.

of an electric storehouse, a definite place of contacts, which only allows connexions to and from definite directions.

Let us test our hypothesis by a few examples.

I go along the street making way for people without being conscious of the fact. At the time I am occupied with some question which entirely absorbs my conscious thinking. This complex of ideas inhibits, according to known laws, other psychical activities which do not pertain to it, including, therefore, this making way. This inhibition is certainly not to be understood as meaning that the making way will not occur at all or only with more difficulty when I am entirely lost in thought than at other times ; on the contrary, such automatic movements generally are made better unconsciously than consciously. The inhibition does not, therefore, in this case concern the function itself but only the connexion with the ego complex—or, in other words, with the becoming conscious. The automatic process of maintaining your direction is, as we have shown, an act solely distinguished from other psychical functions by the absence of the quality of consciousness. The function has in so far made itself independent that, once begun, it can carry on with or without connexion with the ego complex. None the less, the whole content of memory is at the individual's disposal : the dangers from bicycles, motors, electric cars, and, as recent investigations have shown, their rate of travelling and their direction, are better appreciated by this independent complex of ideas than by conscious deliberation. Probably Stern's remark (*Psychologie der Aussage*) applies here : that time is better appreciated when the attention is otherwise occupied, e.g. in reading, than when the interval of time to be estimated is not filled up.

If we observe ourselves whilst learning to ride a bicycle, the whole process of our detachment from the complex of propulsion is very distinctly conscious. At first we set out with conscious effort, sometimes aided by deliberation ; we must now turn the left handle-bar to the left and bend the body to the same side. By and by everything goes smoothly and we begin to look at other things on the road ; finally we learn to think of things quite unconnected with riding—at first timidly, superficially, and at short intervals, then more boldly and connectedly. The thought complex inhibits the development (not the function) of the motor complex more and more ; this complex becomes more hazy to consciousness as the links with the ego decrease, for the ego is now engaged elsewhere and is hence shut off on this side. At the same time the motor complex becomes more "habitual." Through habit there is not merely an easier and safer disposal of nervous activity but also a binding of the psycho-chyme (*sit venia verbo*) to the absolutely essential paths.   This we see in the infant's every habit as well as in ourselves.   An increasing tendency must exist within the motor complex to limit or to inhibit associations with other complexes.   Finally, this tendency of both sides to close leads to both activities, thinking and riding, working independently of each other ; we can then ride for hours together without thinking of the machine or of the road.

The complex which has here become unconscious behaves as a dissociated piece of the mind, gathering experiences and making use of them.   Some years ago I had frequently to traverse a much broken up road.   The getting out of the way disturbed me exceedingly.   Even if the street was only slightly crowded I was obliged to walk much more slowly than I was accustomed to.   It was only after some time and after much resolution that I found courage to jostle along somewhat faster.   The consequence was that I kept to the tramway lines, the dangers of which my conscious self did not know at all, whilst something within me had carefully calculated how quickly and quietly I could get along the lines without danger.   Such instances could be freely multi-plied by the dozen.   I will just call attention to the fact that only the unconscious of an asylum officer is perfectly at home with the different locks of his asylum.   If for some particular reason he has to open a lock consciously he gets worried, because he does not know how far he should insert the key, upon which side to turn it, how much force is required ; all things which his lock complex knows and carries out accurately.

Unconscious perceptions exist by the myriad, but they would not afford us anything new.   Special mention need only be made of those which later arrive at consciousness or of those which influence our conscious feeling or doing.

If I am busy with some mental work I do not, as a rule, hear the clock strike.   If a few minutes later I am recalled to the time by some association or other, the memory-picture of the clock's striking is frequently revived—sometimes so accurately that I am able to count the beats up to five.   The mind has unconsciously perceived the clock striking, without association with the momentary ego complex ; this association is only restored later by the revived memory-picture.   The clock striking has simply become conscious because the thought which had occupied me has now been disposed of.   The inhibition which it was exercising upon all other mental processes thus ceases.   It should be noted that the memory-picture of the unconscious perception can subsequently become conscious without any onscious association causing a scearh for the memory-picture ; he amnestic after-image of the clock striking can now unite ssociatively with the personality and is thus consciously erceived.

If I have a nail in my shoe which I have not noticed but which s obviously spoiling my temper the same mechanism comes nto play. Every civilized person has become practised in not aying attention to such small inflictions whilst otherwise engaged. Iental occupation also prevents the conscious perception of ain—the associative union of this pain with the self is busied ʋith other matters. But the pain is none the less present in he mind ; it influences the behaviour, the temper, the affect, s if it were conscious. For the total separation of emotional mpulses from the conscious part of our mind is much more ifficult than that of the purely intellectual processes ; teleologi- ally expressed, it is the purpose of the affects to govern the ʋhole mind.

In the earlier cited cases where my unconscious correctly ecognized the servant or her knocking, whilst my conscious hinking was in error, the explanation is likewise easy. Sitting ιp is automatic as soon as I can decide, from the kind of knocking, ʋerhaps also from the unconsciously perceived steps and the like, hat the person approaching is some one with whom I am not quite ,t home. Lying still, when the opposite decision is arrived at, is ikewise automatic, if this expression may be allowed for the non- arrying out of an action. In ordinary cases I feel that the eaction to the knocking of a stranger consists in a movement of he corresponding muscles, or at least in a tension of these muscles ; ʋeyond this no correct knowledge of anything else passes through ɩonsciousness, which recognizes at most the knocking and the ιitting up. Whether in the unconscious there has really been ι recognition of the person, or whether the reaction here is merely *Sit up or lie quiet,* I am unable quite to settle. From the daily ιccurrence of much more complicated processes in the unconscious t does not seem very likely that the only suggestion from the ʋerception is a knocking, leading one to sit up or lie quiet, and ιot a knocking of a definite person. But it is certain that an ιnconscious part of my mind correctly recognized the kind of ɩnocking requiring me to sit up, whilst the conscious mind ʋas at fault.

My unconscious reaction through my feelings to a (false) perception of my fiancée cannot be the result of rapid deduction. We can exclude the view that a sense-impression, e.g. the look ɔf a bit of dress, had aroused the reaction of feeling without the assistance of the (unconscious) concept of the fiancée herself.

The reaction corresponded so exactly to the perception of a person, and not to that of a fetishism—towards which I am, moreover, much less sensitive than most people. The change of mind on seeing my fiancée approaching was so specific that it is not easy to separate it from the concept of the fiancée under normal conditions.

If we have once proved the absence of associative links between the slighter complexes and the ego, the occurrence of more complicated chains of thought and reflections in the unconscious can occasion no surprise. They do not show anything new in principle. When carrying my rabbits to the laboratory I did not notice that I got fatigued, although the fatigue occasioned the unconscious changing of hands : complicated unconscious associations have here nothing surprising. A part of the mind works out a task, under the guidance of some instinct, without union with the ego ; then some mental product, such as the solution of a problem or a poem, emerges suddenly into consciousness as a finished result, or it may be written without full participation of the ego, semi or entirely automatically.

We stand in need of a critique of those cases where but part of an apparently unitary process is unconscious.

Indirect associations come in here. The concept *child-bed*, which served as a bridge between *mild* and *bed*, was associatively linked on one side with the conscious stimulus-word, and on the other with the reaction-word about to be conscious : why did it not become conscious also ? [1]

First of all, it must be said that for anything to become conscious a certain time, a certain direction of the presentation, is necessary. The concept which served as a bridge had a very short life, as the time-measurement of the whole association showed ; no wonder, then, that it was unnoticed. Add to this that it only possessed two links with the conscious processes (with the stimulus-word and the reaction-word) and no direct one with the ego complex. The latter was obviously the essential. Only the presentations directly connected with the ego become conscious, not the indirect ones ; if otherwise, when I consciously turn down a certain street all the requisite movements of the muscles would have to become conscious also.

Such a bridge concept can be both " quite obscure " and transiently conscious, so that one is afterwards not quite clear

---

[1] Wundt, indeed, regards it as remaining " obscurely conscious." But in agreement with our conception, he accepts a whole scale of degrees of consciousness ; may not this extend to 0 or almost to 0, so that for practical purposes our inner perception touches 0 ? Moreover, Wundt's conception of indirect association is a little different from what it is in these papers.

whether it should be ascribed to conscious or unconscious presen
tations.   For a time it was just on the border-line or it contained
only one link, or at most few links, with the ego.   In observing
oneself it will be seen that on arriving at consciousness the time
element and the number of links play a great part.   A decline of
both these factors lowers also the degree of consciousness, which
finally sinks to 0.   We thus understand that the conscious must
be regarded as relative, that there are no clear boundaries
between the conscious and the unconscious.

Like the bridge concept of indirect associations, the unconscious motive of a decision or of a reflection has a kind of link
with the conscious self, otherwise it could not work towards a
decision.   Here the brevity of the time plays no part, whilst the
boundary of the association connexions becomes more obvious.
For the elucidation of these latter we must remember that in
reality whole functional complexes are never fully conscious
to us.   When I write I have no suspicion of the innervation of
the muscles, not even of the formation of the letters, and frequently
I am so occupied with the content of the writing that probably
for relatively long intervals of time I do not know that I am
writing.   When bicycling, even after many years' practice,
certain individual manœuvres which I make in passing others
become conscious, but not in all their components.   In short,
we can prove a thousand times over that individual components
of complexes which are proceeding unconsciously can become
immediately conscious—that is, can become associated to the
conscious thought complex.

A peculiarity of the psyche must here be considered which
obviously possesses great importance, but, unfortunately, has not
been sufficiently studied.   Wundt rightly lays stress upon this :
that the psychical complexes do not merely represent the sum
of their parts.   Every complex has, as a whole, definite qualities
which belong only to the whole.   An apparently simple concept
like that of " water " is composed of a number of sense-presentations ; we operate with it as if it were a unit.   Under other
circumstances it is decomposed or partially or wholly blended
with other concepts to a new unity.   If I speak of " water " in
chemistry a number of associations are excluded which under
different circumstances apparently belong to the concept " water."
Nobody then thinks of its importance in navigation, in the landscape, in nourishment, etc.   In other words, in ordinary life we
never operate with one concept, " water," but with a number of
concepts, wider in one direction, narrower in another : " water
in the chemical sense," " water in connexion with the land " ;
the associations to be linked on to this are not formed, in normal

persons, from the partial concept " water " but from the concept " water with a definite connotation." [1]

Every concept, in the usual sense of psychological abstraction, has also a very different value according to the momentary connexions with which, for the time being, it forms a whole. This whole, as a unity, has also its special connexions ; just as the associations which are linked to the concept " rose " are quite other than those of its individual components (form, colour, smell, growth on stalk, etc.). All the complexes, from the simplest presentations of a sensation to the most complicated and elaborate presentation of a scientific theory, behave thus, and the ego complex behaves in like manner. A presentation can be as readily associated to the whole ego complex as to one of its components. But in the former case it is conscious, if our view is correct ; while if it is united with some individual partial presentation it remains unconscious.

When I go into town I often make it consciously clear to myself whether I am going to walk, or bicycle, or take the tram. But not always ; occasionally, I am only thinking of my business there. Then somehow, on the way, I find that the street is really too muddy for bicycling when I am bicycling, or, inversely, that I should have done better to have cycled than to have walked. In the cases which arrive at consciousness when I have made a mistake, that complex of mine which is occupied with the means of transit is associated only with the thought of going to town, but not with my whole ego, to which the settling of the proper way should belong. In those cases where I consciously decide how I shall go to town, the preparations for departure, different according as I walk or cycle, are separated by an (unconscious) adjustment from the concept of the mode selected ; it is unconnected with the aims and thoughts of the ego, it remains unconscious.

In the case of a logical idea controlled by an unconscious motive the activity will usually encounter some affect (wish, fear, instinct) which is more or less conscious, but was liberated by the unconscious motive. From other experiences we are well acquainted with the power the affects possess of inhibiting opposing associations, of expediting others, and controlling logical thought even when all the motives are conscious.

It is unpleasant to the drinker to be disturbed in his habits. He therefore adduces silly reasons to justify drinking, gives them an importance which they do not possess, and suppresses any critical thoughts he may have.

[1] In dementia præcox we find that these complexes lose their unitary value ; the chain of ideas thus becomes ill-regulated—the dement who speaks about " water " often mixes up its different significances.

For centuries great thinkers believed in the sophisms about the proofs for the existence of God ; Kant, who demonstrated their complete futility, shrank before the consequences. So without noticing the weakness of his logic, he reintroduced by another route into his philosophy the idea of the Lord, the freedom of the will, and the other pretty things which he had first rejected.

When we thus learn to recognize the power of the affects, their influence upon the dissociation of personality is more readily understood. These manifestations are not really so very peculiar ; in the healthy mind they have far-reaching prototypes, of which they are only pathological exaggerations. If you test a child's knowledge by questions in a pedagogic manner, he is a very different being from what he is when you are able to test his knowledge accidentally in a tactful conversation. He is shy and inhibited, or he displays the whole school psyche in the deplorable manner and accentuation of the child repeating its lesson ; great effort is often required to make a natural being again out of the child.[1]

We have here a complete analogy to the hysterical delirium of the carter previously described.

What a difference there is between the associations, ideas, aspirations, and character of a young man who has just said " good-bye " to his parents when setting forth into the world, and these mental processes in the same youth when a few days later he is at some jolly party. He is another person just as is the hysteric in delirium, though the change is a slighter one. A whole mass of presentations and motives which were then in the forefront are now inaccessible ; his good resolutions have been blown to the winds, to reappear next day when he is down in the dumps.[2]

In the joyous mood in this case, in depression in another case, a wish or a fear selects those associations which can be immediately formed. The criminal under medical observation

---

[1] It is extremely probable that most of the published cases of extraordinary ignorance among recruits have only been misinterpreted on account of an " emotional stupidity " (Jung) readily to be understood.

[2] One difference between the child and the frivolous youth on the one side, and the hysteric on the other, is that in the latter there is a sharper division of the two states on account of the action of the affects being heightened by disease. The transition from one state to another is a gradual one in normals—in hysteria often takes place suddenly. But the content is also different : the hysteric as a rule only carries over a small part of his personality into the delirium, just as much as corresponds to the affect ; in healthy persons the greater part of the ego is common to the two states. Amnesias are hence rare in healthy persons, the rule in hysterics.

thinks, more or less consciously, that if he could only pretend to be mad he would get off better. Without any effort on his part—it would be quite impossible for him to interfere voluntarily to the same degree with his psychical mechanisms—his associative inhibitions and paths become set, following his desire, in accordance with his notion of madness. He says and does everything upside down : he gets the Ganser syndrome.

A woman received, just after childbirth, a letter from her husband, full of reproaches and threatening to leave her. If only the letter had not come ! A few moments later and it hasn't come, she knows nothing more about it, and everything has vanished from her mind that was connected with the letter and the bad news ; what does not fit in is altered—the woman has an attack of hysterical delirium. A young woman who had once gone through an attack of dementia præcox falls in love with a young man who one day makes her clearly understand that she is nothing to him. Her wishes now take control of her associations ; she sees only the possibilities of their fulfilment, and soon has hallucinations in this direction ; during the next few months she is convinced that she is married to him and that she is pregnant. An imbecile feels injured by his brothers and generally badly treated by them. He would like to get into a furious temper and do something to the wretches. And then he gets into a rage. His blind impulse of destruction is directed against everything in his reach, without regard even to himself or to the things that belong to him. And when the anniversary of the day returns on which he was injured he recalls it all, and a repetition of the attack is the consequence. A great number of outbursts among imbeciles are due to such a mechanism

In these cases the mechanisms which have led up to the disease symptom are alone unknown. The dissociated complex of ideas is united with the ego like other real events ; the normal experiences have sunk into the subconscious, that is, their associative links with the ego complex are quite inhibited. In hysterics, portions of the normal personality can at any time be rejoined different ways, but it is not so in hebephreniacs, whose chain of thought we are quite unable to direct.

Sometimes a double personality of this kind is formed entirely in the unconscious. Some wish, some fear, groups the corresponding presentations, as in the instances cited of hysterical delirium, but no direct union with the ego is formed ; in addition to the permanent presentations the complex makes use of indifferent elements of a general nature, such as speech, writing muscular co-ordinations, etc. These personalities, which can be perhaps, formed in great numbers, can be manifested through automatic writing and similar procedures without ever arriving at consciousness. In Flournoy's *Hélène* there was a person of this kind who signed herself Marie Antoinette, in whom Hélène's desire for a great position thus became embodied.

Such partial personalities can sometimes become more complete by assimilating some of the most important elements of the ego ; they then arrive at consciousness. They have thus passed from hysterical delirium, from trance conditions, into the " second person " in Azam's sense. There is, therefore, no difference in principle between unconscious complexes and these several personalities endowed with consciousness. When an unconscious complex associates to itself an increasing number of the elements of the ordinary ego, without linking itself with the ego as a whole, it becomes finally a second personality.

The influence of unconscious emotional presentations on experimental associations, as proved in this work, finds ready explanation on our theory. We know that an effect has the tendency to influence the entire psyche. If I have experienced anything sad, I am not only sad when I think of it, the sadness is also shown in all my actions which are not in associative connexion with the cause of it, even in the more automatic actions such as carriage, gait, writing, etc.

Should a stimulus-word arouse an emotional presentation in the unconscious, the affect corresponding to it must exercise its influence upon the associative activity. According to well-known laws every affect has a tendency to inhibit all psychical processes which are foreign to it ; the affect thus disturbs the experimental associative activity, makes it longer or superficial. That the affect itself does not usually reach the conscious is understandable ; it is too weak, lasts only a brief time, is inhibited by the attention paid to the experiment and by the unpleasant feeling of being disturbed (which on its part may likewise inhibit secondarily the associative activity).

The phenomena of hypnosis are too complicated for us to review here. It must suffice to remind the reader who has followed us so far that, bearing our exposition in mind, they can be all explained quite easily as inhibitions and mental paths ; inhibitions which only permit definite complexes of ideas to arrive at function, and which also separate complexes at will, e.g. a pain from the conscious ego, whilst the ready-formed mental paths act in just the reverse way. But nothing new enters the mind ; individual functions in daily use are simply aroused in a one-sided way and exaggerated as regards the relationships of ordinary life. I hope soon to find time to show that suggestion only uses the known mechanisms which hourly set our affects in motion so that I may corroborate the view which has often been expressed, but which is, strangely enough, still often contested— that suggestibility is but a normal and necessary quality of the mind.

In accordance with these views, the phenomena of dreams receive an explanation which suffices to make them lose the odium of obscurity and mystery.

In dreams we see that the rudder which controls the direction of thought whilst awake is absent entirely or in great part.

The associations thus penetrate in directions which they avoid in the waking state. One of the first consequences of this is that the ego becomes composed of other partial presentations and partial complexes ; hence the personality becomes different. That is why we " forget " dreams so easily. There are but few associations formed by the events of the dream which proceed from that other ego, the waking ego ; few associations which the dream could link (consciously) as revivified memory-pictures to the ego. If one awakes slowly, the dream complex has time to join some links with the ego during the act of returning to the normal self, and recollections become easier than on sudden awaking. We see the same thing in the transition from the self, changed by conditions of illness (twilight states, periodic attacks, intoxications) to the normal state. In sudden changes amnesia occurs, *ceteris paribus*, more easily and to a higher degree than in gradual transition.

The altered self must have other desires, a changed aim for the direction of thought, and this increases still more the abnormality of the associations. As a rule, we can say that in dreams a correct idea of purpose, according to the self when awake, is absent, or is at least weak and vacillating. The associations are directed by other motives than in the waking state, when one or two dominant impulses guide conscious reflection in the required direction, using as far as possible the laws of thought. In the dream, logic goes to the wall and the dominant places are taken here, as in children, by the feelings accidentally present and by the affects of the moment. In Freud's sense, the dream associations are governed chiefly by the emotional life.

We have still a few remarks to offer on the relationship which transition into the conscious bears to memory and will, although this is not the place to go into the matter thoroughly.

The revival of memory-traces has been hitherto attributed to the associative paths. Those traces, whose function form the concept of the " rose," are in close union with those which represented the concept of "thorns." The psychochyme goes from one to the other and thus makes the association real. A we have seen, this process also takes place in the unconscious. The fact that a memory-picture passes again into function thus does not in itself condition the memory-picture's becoming conscious. The aroused memory-picture only becomes conscious when it passes at the same time into associative union with the ego.

The study of conscious psychical phenomena has long since shown that, together with the concepts and other memory-pictures, their associative connexions become fixed at the same time. Psychical elements thus stimulate common associations if at their first occurrence they were associatively united. That is why things we have experienced in the unconscious can only exceptionally be brought to conscious memory. The objects against which I have unconsciously jostled in the streets I can only in rare cases remember again. But these traces remain united with their contemporary unconscious functions, otherwise habit would be impossible to the unconscious. The great number of pictures of movements which make bicycling possible for me have become unconscious ; unconsciously they again become active and control my actions on the bicycle without my having a suspicion of them ; the conscious mental thoughts and the body's balancing go on separately although side by side. In order to bring the co-ordination of movement into consciousness I must direct my attention to them just as if they were something outside me. They then become united associatively to the conscious ego, and can remain so if I do not prefer to render them automatic again.

Should the self change naturally, many of the memory-pictures which are not firmly fixed by practice become inaccessible. What has been experienced in a dream, in a twilight state, in intoxication, is united to an abnormal self. Hence a mass of associative links with these occurrences are absent from the normal self ; consequently one does not remember at all, or but vaguely, the twilight state, whilst during a recurrence of the same condition there may be a very clear recollection of it.

It is perhaps in place here to note that *conscious* and *willed* are by no means synonymous concepts in all cases. In the morning I wish to get up, dress myself, wash myself. Consciously, I only introduce the automatism, whilst my consciousness seems quite separated from these proceedings ; the action has become automatic and goes on without connexion with my ego, which meantime is occupied with other things. The dressing is desired but is not conscious.

Obsessions are not desired, but they are certainly conscious, because they remain in union with the self. In another way many actions are conscious which are not desired, e.g. the automatic actions of the insane, of catatoniacs. In these cases the purely motor act is carried on without any connexion with the conscious ego. The patients see themselves, hear themselves doing something, and thus come to consciousness of an action as if they were perceiving the action of a third person.

The mechanism of attention is too little known to us in the conscious for us to be able to " explain " it in the unconscious. But it is easy for us to imagine that those same dispositions which form conscious attention can exist also without associative connexion with the self. I resolve to pay attention to a certain plant and then think no more about it. If I come across the plant its identity at once occurs to me. I must take it that not only was the latent disposition prepared to form further associations at the sight of the plant, say to gather it, but to establish union with the ego at the same time. That the latter process is no necessary partial manifestation of the adjustment is proved by the daily occurrence of adjustments which do not become conscious to us. Whilst still at home I propose to go to such and such a place. On the way thither I no longer think about it but at every crossing I take the correct turning. This is not an unconscious adjustment of the attention but an unconscious attention, or, to follow the convenient usage of many psychologists in personifying the "unconscious," an attention of the unconscious. The mental complex which unconsciously governs my direction notices all the crossings and chooses the correct ones without uniting itself with the otherwise occupied self.

Association is a process dominating our entire psyche and one we already find in reflexes [1] which are not psychical. Our conception introduces no new element into psychology. That processes can run their course outside the ego complex as well as within, the instances quoted in the first part of this chapter will prove ; that they are not associated with the remaining content of our thought is obvious ; it is equally obvious that everything which proceeds in " our conscious " is associated with the presentations which for the moment form our personality, our ego. What is new in our conception is this : that the presence or absence of consciousness depends upon whether connexion with the ego is present or absent ; this factor can be always made out.

I am not in a position to give a strict proof of the correctness of this hypothesis. It seems to me highly probable because it

[1] This and other points pertaining hereto I have examined more thoroughly in the *Allgemeine Zeitschrift für Psychiatrie*, Bd. L (" Versuch einer naturwissenschaftlichen Betrachtung der psychologischen Grundbegriffe ").

fully explains all the facts which I have noticed during twenty-six years' observation both in healthy and in sick people ; nor is anything postulated which is not already known. Its simplicity is a further recommendation. Whether it is right or not, it seems to me, anyway, to fulfil a weighty task. It links the unconscious psychical phenomenon to the rest of our knowledge and removes it from the realm of the mysterious. I hope, therefore, that it will serve to destroy the current prejudices against an objective investigation of the facts in this sphere, and will thus pave the way for further fruitful studies.

Many have already said something similar, but so far as I know either they have not worked out the idea, or, like Wundt, they have turned aside from the consequences. Of the former I will only mention Janet, Exner, Löb, who set out from very different points of view. It must indeed astonish every observer that the consciousness which we observe in ourselves is so closely united with those functions which we term association and connected recollection (associative memory ; Löb).

It is more difficult to understand the position of those who absolutely deny the "unconscious." So far as I know, the consequential carrying out of their supposition is never made by them, and they are unable to reconcile themselves with many facts. Just two recent instances. Raimann [1] says, clearly and definitely, "there is no unconscious knowledge." Ten pages further we find, "Experience forces us to assume that hysterics do not distinguish between conscious and unconscious." Hellpach,[2] in his denial of the unconscious, first of all brings to his aid a *petitio principii* : "But the unconscious which lies between *b* and *a* seems to have changed the first presentation within these, and can, naturally, not be the object of psychology, for the psyche has only to do with the conscious " (p. 222). And on pp. 403–406 he begins a really beautiful deduction which is to show that the mechanisms which can condition false connexions do not require any unconscious for their explanation. At one moment it is said that the hysteric is naturally not conscious of the associations which have developed in him. But this unconscious is only a subjective essence, for objectively all these phenomena are causally connected quite as well as they are in the normal way. The last sentence is the coping-stone of the whole edifice and suddenly introduces the concept of causality, which has as much to do with the deduction as a straw hat with the arch of a bridge. This quite apart from

---

[1] *Die hysterichen Geisstesstörungen* ("Hysterical Mental Disorders "), p. 232.

[2] *Grundlinien der Psychologie der Hysterie* (" Foundations of the Psychology of Hysteria"), pp. 222, 403–406.

the fact that there is so far no objective consciousness, and thus in what preceded the unconscious psychical mechanism was already granted. On p. 35 again the obscurities of Wundt's concept take revenge on their adept.

That the unconscious mental functions do not fit into most of the theories is certainly not their fault. They are facts to which theories must accommodate themselves, however often the reverse process be tried. The difficulties attending the recognition of the unconscious are truly significant of the power of preconceived opinions and academic speculation.

If we mean not only to prove the existence of the unconscious but to apprehend it in its connexion with other mental happenings, with the reserve which science everywhere enjoins on us, we must accommodate ourselves to the idea that there are a number of functions of the brain of which only a portion becomes conscious. And this becoming conscious is sometimes only a secondary matter and occurs, according to our hypothesis, by association with the ego. The independence of the mind from the function of the brain is about as demonstrable as the dependence of water considered in its aggregate state on warmth and pressure [1]; so far as I know, the heinousness of pressure has not been a reason for denying this dependence. We are therefore not in bad company if we ignore the "psychophysical parallel," which helps us to no understanding but only conceals the renunciation of any understanding by a positive expression; nor are we in bad company when we do not allow preconceived opinion to brush aside the facts of daily observation.

SUMMARY

There are effective and numerous processes in us which comport themselves in all respects like conscious processes with the one exception that consciousness is absent.

Psychology cannot ignore them because the processes influence the conscious mind just as well as conscious sensations, thoughts, and wishes.

The study of these unconscious (mental) functions are quite indispensable in psychopathology for they often control its symptoms.

We can best represent such processes to ourselves by imagining that physical processes in the brain, which form the foundation of all psychical happenings, only become conscious when they become functionally linked—associated—with the ego complex.

[1] We as little possess an "explanation," like that of the effect of the (hypothetical) phenomena of ether upon the (hypothetical) molecules of water, as we possess any presentation of the transference of the movement of one body to another—or the effect of the physical upon the psychical.

CHAPTER VII

PSYCHO-ANALYSIS AND ASSOCIATION EXPERIMENTS

By Dr. C. G. JUNG

It is not easy to give in a few words the basis of Freud's theory of hysteria and his psycho-analytic method. The nomenclature and Freud's conceptions are still in flux—fortunately, I would add. For despite the extraordinary progress which our knowledge of hysteria has made in the last few years, thanks to Freud's works, neither Freud nor we who follow him have reached finality. No one must be astounded, therefore, if Freud in his most recent work on hysteria [1] has again, to a large extent, abandoned the nomenclature of his *Studies in Hysteria*, and has substituted a series of other and more fitting expressions. Freud's terms should not be always regarded as strictly limited scientific concepts, but rather as occasional expressions of a language rich in new forms. Those who write about Freud should avoid logomachy but should keep in mind the essence of the thing.

Freud traces every hysteria back to a series of psychical traumata, which finally reach their apex in a sexual trauma of prepuberty. Naturally, the so-called psychogenic character of hysteria was known before Freud. (For a precise demarcation of the psychogenic we are particularly indebted to Möbius.) It was known that hysteria arises from presentations which are distinguished by their strength of emotion. But Freud was the first to show us the path traversed by the psychological process. He found that the hysterical symptom is essentially a symbol for presentations (sexual in the ultimate analysis) which are not present in the conscious, but are repressed from the conscious by strong inhibitions. Repression arises from the critical presentations being so charged with pain (unpleasure) as to be insupportable to the conscious self.

Inseparably bound up with this conception is the psycho-

[1] " Bruchstück einer Hysterieanalyse," *Monatsschrift für Psychiatrie u. Neurologie*, 1905. Republished in *Sammlung kleiner Schriften zur Neurosenlehre*, zweite Folge.

analytic method. It provides us with the knowledge of the repressed material of presentation that has become unconscious. If we ask patients directly as to the cause of their illness we always receive incorrect, or at least imperfect, information. If we did receive correct information as in other (physical) illnesses, we should have known long ago about the psychogenic nature of hysteria. But it is just the point of hysteria that it represses the real cause, the psychic trauma, forgets it and replaces it by superficial " cover causes." That is why hysterics ceaselessly tell us that their illness arose from a cold, from over-work, from real organic disorders. And many physicians thus allow themselves again and again to be deceived. Others go to the opposite extreme and maintain that all hysterics lie. But that is because they completely misconceive the psychological conditionings of hysteria, which really consist in this, that presentations insupportable to the conscious ego are repressed and cannot be therefore reproduced. Freud's psycho-analytic methods circumvent the inhibitions which the conscious ego sets up towards the repressed presentations. The essence of the method consists in the patient simply relating everything, without selection, that comes into his mind (Freud called this " free association "). The method is completely presented in Freud's work, *The Interpretation of Dreams* (1900).[1] Although it is theoretically a priori certain that law will control all the thoughts that occur to a person, it is readily understandable that a person without great experience would go astray in this labyrinth of ideas, and would finally get hopelessly stuck. It is, and will remain, one of the chief reasons against the general application of Freud's method that delicate psychological intuition in the doctor is as much a requisite as technique for a psycho-analysis ; the physician must possess individual characteristics which cannot be presupposed to exist in every doctor or psychologist. Then for psycho-analysis one's thoughts must have a particular bent, having in view the understanding of symbols. But this adjustment is only to be gained with industrious practice. It is a tendency of the mind, inborn in a poet, but carefully avoided in scientific thought, the constellation here being towards sharply-cut images. Thinking in symbols requires a new adjustment from us just as if we had to begin to think in flight ideas. It would seem that these are some of the reasons why Freud's methods have only been understood by few, and practised by even fewer ; there are, indeed, but a few workers who value Freud's work theoretically or practically.

Despite the many valuable experiences which Freud has

[1] English translation by Dr. A. A. Brill, 1912.

expounded for us, psycho-analysis is a very difficult art, for every beginner rapidly loses courage and orientation in face of the innumerable obstacles. Safe foundations are wanting from whence to start ; when you have to begin with a patient at haphazard, so to say, you are often at a loss where to begin the attack.

Association experiments have helped us to get over these first and chief difficulties. I have shown in the chapter on time-measurements (chapter v) that the emotionally charged presentation complexes give rise to characteristic disturbances in the experiment ; their presence and probable nature can be recognized from the disturbances themselves. This fact forms the foundation of *The Psychological Diagnosis of Facts* founded by Wertheimer and Klein,[1] Hans Gross,[2] and Alfred Gross.[3] It seems fairly possible by this method to diagnose by the associations the complex of a crime. Every one has naturally one or more complexes which make themselves manifest in some way in the associations. The background of our consciousness (or the unconscious) consists of complexes of this kind. The whole material of memory is grouped around them. They form higher psychical unities analogous to the ego complex (Bleuler,[4] chapter vi). They constellate the whole of our thinking and doing, hence the associations also. We sometimes join a second experiment to that of the association one, *reproduction*.[5] The experiment consists in making the subject repeat his reactions to the stimulus-words in the first experiment. Where memory fails we have generally to do with a constellation due to a complex. Reproduction, therefore, assists in the closer circumscribing of the complex disturbances.

All psychogenic neuroses contain a complex which is differentiated from normal complexes by being endowed with extremely strong emotional tones, possessing such constellating power that it brings the whole individual under its influence. The complex is hence the *causa morbi* (given, of course, the predis-

---

[1] Wertheimer, *Experimentelle Untersuchungen zur Tatbestandsdiagnostik* (Dissert : Würzburg, 1905.)

Wertheimer and Klein, "Psychologische Tatbestandsdiagnostik," *Archiv. für Kriminalanthropologie*, Bd. XV.

[2] Hans Gross, "Zur psychologischen Tatbestandsdiagnostik," *Archiv. für Kriminalanthropologie*, 1905.

[3] Alfred Gross, "Die Associationsmethode im Strafprocess," *Zeitschrift für die gesamte Strafrechtswissenschaft*, Bd. XXVI. Grabowsky, "Psychologische Tatbestandsdiagnostik," 1905.

[4] Bleuler, "Versuch einer naturwissenschaftlichen Betrachtung der psychologischen Grundbegriffe," *Allgemeine Zeitschrift für Psychiatrie*.

[5] Jung, "Experimentelle Beobachtungen über das Erinnerungsvermögen," *Centralb. für Nervenheilk. u. Psych.*, Bd. XXVIII.

position). The associations often enable us to recognize the nature of the complex, thus obtaining valuable clues for causal therapy. A by-product, not to be under-estimated, is the scientific knowledge which we thus gain of the origin and inner construction of the psychogenic neuroses. Freud has assuredly long since given us the substance of this knowledge, but he has anticipated by a long way the understanding of his time. It will not, therefore, be superfluous if I offer some new approach on the experimental plane to the Freudian store of knowledge. In previous chapters Freud's principles have several times been drawn on in explanation. Here I would present the connexion between psycho-analysis and association experiments by some practical examples. I choose an ordinary case of obsessional neurosis which I treated in June 1905.

Miss E. came to me for hypnotic treatment for sleeplessness of four months' duration. Besides the sleeplessness she complained of inner unrest and excitement, irritability towards her family, impatience and quarrelsomeness. She is thirty-seven, a teacher, cultured and intelligent; has always been nervous; has a younger sister feeble-minded; her father was an alcoholic. Condition: well nourished; physically nothing of moment was found. Her agitated and convulsive movements are remarkable. Whilst talking she seldom looks at the doctor, as a rule not addressing him but speaking out at the window. From time to time she turns away still more, is often obliged to laugh involuntarily, frequently shrugs her shoulders as if shaking off something disagreeable, protruding the lower part of her abdomen in a peculiar manner.

The anamnesis which she gives is very incomplete and indefinite. She had formerly been a governess abroad, but had not then been ill. The illness only occurred in recent years and has gradually developed to its present pitch. She says she has been unsuccessfully treated by many doctors. She would now like to try hypnosis, but immediately adds that she is firmly convinced that hypnotism will not succeed. Her disease is incurable and she is sure she will go mad. She has, indeed, often thought that she cannot be normal now and that she is already insane. It here occurred to me that the patient was obviously talking round something that she would not or could not say. On being urged she finally explained, with many gestures of resistance and constant blushing, that she could not sleep because whenever she disposed herself to sleeping the idea came to her that she would not, of course, be able to sleep, that she would never sleep again until she were dead; she would then wake right up and be unable to sleep again the whole night. Whenever she felt worn out and desired to sleep a terrible fear would rouse her up again—she would never sleep again until she were dead or mad. She had to wrench this explanation out of herself in such a way, and with such gestures of aversion, as almost to arouse the impression that she was telling something sexually improper which caused her to be ashamed. Again there were the movements of the abdomen. She frequently laughed as if abashed, which made a peculiar impression of inadequacy. This peculiar state caused me to ask if there were other ideas present which troubled her during the sleeplessness: "No, I can't remember anything—things just pass through me—oh, it's thousands of things that keep running through my head." She was unable to recall anything, made gestures of aversion and said suddenly: She has really such stupid thoughts; these force themselves upon her and she cannot possibly shake herself free from them. She is sorry she cannot communicate these ideas to me for she is afraid I would then get these obsessions. She had once told a doctor and a clergyman about her thoughts and now she is always thinking that she had infected those people and that they also had obsessional ideas. She was sure she had already infected me. I reassured her; I had already heard many ideas of that kind and they had not injured me in the least. Upon this she admitted with the same gestures that, besides the ideas mentioned with which she had infected the doctor and the clergyman, she was chiefly bothered by the thought that a neighbour, a woman, who had recently died, had on her account died unhappy and had had to suffer all the torments of hell. She had only had that idea since her death; previously, she had had for many years the idea that a boy whom she had formerly educated had subsequently died from the punishments she had occasionally imposed upon him. Her anxiety was so great that she had been obliged to write twice to the family for news about his health. She had done it each time in a way that would not arouse suspicion. The good news which she received each time had momentarily quieted her, but a few days later the anxiety was as great as ever. That idea had now ceased, but she had now to reproach herself with the unhappy death of her neighbour. Reason told her that these ideas were nonsense (she said this in a very uncertain voice) or was it perhaps the truth ? (she quickly added). Thus she did not entirely correct herself, but was obviously completely mastered by the obsessional ideas.

The anamnesis did not succeed in discovering any sexual abnormalities, that is to say, anything which could in any way refer to sexual matters was denied as a matter of course.

Any attempt at hypnotism was useless because she could not fix her attention in any way. Not to spoil this method at the beginning by useless attempts, I decided first to obtain some certainty about the psychical material which was at the root of the illness. I therefore arranged an association experiment with her.

I. The Association Experiment

The whole experiment is reproduced here.

Stimulus-word	Reaction	Reaction-time	Reproduction
1. *Head* [1]	*thoughts*	: 2·2 seconds	hair
2. Green	grass	: 1·8 „	† [2]
3. *Water*	*drinker — drink*	: 2·4 „	glass
4. Prick	needle	: 3·6 „	†
5. Angel ‡[3]	heaven	: 2·6 .,	†
6. Long ‡	short	: 4 „	†
7. Ship	sea	: 1·4 „	†

I note that I am not in a position to give an exhaustive analysis of the associations. The subject met all questions by assuring me that nothing special occurred to her mind at the so-called critical places. In this way it was impossible to discover the determinants of the individual reactions by subjective analysis.

[1] Associations which were absent or incorrect in reproduction are in italics.

[2] † denotes correct reproduction.

[3] ‡ denotes that the patient quickly repeated the stimulus-word. This phenomenon is frequently encountered both with and after complex reactions.

But, after all, the objective result of the experiment suffices for a diagnosis, at least in its outlines, apart from the statements of the subject. I should like to give in as much detail as possible how I arrived at my diagnosis.

The probable mean (Kräpelin) of all the reaction-times of the experiment amounts to 2·4 seconds. This mean is far too high for an intelligent and cultured person. The mean figures I obtained in twelve educated persons are 1·5 second. As the effects of emotion are chiefly responsible for the prolongation of the reaction-time,[1] a marked emotivity of the subject may be concluded from this rather high figure. I beg the reader to keep hold of this figure, 2·4 seconds, during the following consideration of the reactions.

Reaction 1, *head — thoughts*, reproduced incorrectly. The complex of the illness may have been at work here. Reaction 3, *water — drinker — drink*, is verbally disturbed. *Drinker* has been improved to *drink*. Her father was a heavy drinker. The subsequent three reaction-times are all prolonged to over 2·4 seconds ; there are besides two repetitions of the stimulus-word. One may therefore accept a perseveration due to emotion after *drinker*.[2] Reaction 5, *angel — heaven*, may have aroused the obsessional idea of the unhappy death of her neighbour.

Stimulus-word	Reaction	Reaction-time	Reproduction
8. Pluck	sow	: 2·2 seconds	†
9. *Wool*	*spin*	: 3·4 ,,	— [3]
10. *Friendly*	*lovable*	: 3·6 ,,	good
11. *Table*	*woman*	: 4·6 ,,	—
12. Ask	answer	: 2·4 ,,	†
13. State	church	: 2·2 ,,	†
14. *Haughty*	*spirited*	: 1·8 ,,	friendly
15. Stalk	flower	: 1·8 ,,	†

What disturbance caused the prolongation at *wool* I cannot say. Experience has shown that with reaction 10, *friendly*, erotic reminiscences readily occur. The striking reaction 11, *table — woman*, which patient cannot explain, seems to refer to an erotic significance of reaction 10. In sensitive persons, as all neurotics are, stimulus-words are always taken personally. One can easily suppose that the patient would like to be the " lovable, good woman." That the word *friendly* has a certain tendency to reproduction in the patient is seen in its recurrence in reaction 14. (Naturally emotional presentations have a stronger tendency to reproduction than indifferent ones.)

[1] See chapter v.

[2] I cannot here enter into the justification for this deduction and must refer the reader to chapter v.

[3] — means not reproduced.

Stimulus-word	Reaction	Reaction-time	Reproduction
16. Dance	jump	: 1·8 seconds	†
17. Sea ‡	water	: 2·4 ,,	†
18. Ill	healthy	: 2 ,,	†
19. Proud	arrogant	: 5 ,,	†
20. Cook	roast	: 2 ,,	†
21. Ink	barrel	: 2 ,,	†
22. *Wicked*	*good*	: 3 ,,	—
23. Needle	prick	: 2·2 ,,	†
24. Swim	water	: 2 ,,	†
25. Journey	railway	: 2·2 ,,	†
26. Blue	red	: 1·8 ,,	†
27. Bread	knife	: 2 ,,	†
28. *Threaten*	*naughty*	: 8 ,,	—

Reaction 16, *dance*, is prone to arouse erotic reminiscences. This supposition is not unjustified here, for the reaction following is disturbed. Reactions 18 and 19, *ill* and *proud*, may have easily had personal references. With *proud* there are distinct complex signs, likewise *wicked* and *threaten* have obviously aroused feelings. The reaction to *threaten* — *naughty* sounds like the association to the presentation of a child. Perhaps the reminiscence of her pupil has been aroused ? *Threaten* is capable of arousing many emotional relationships. People with vivid complexes generally have some anxiety about the future. We often see that they refer *threaten* to the threatened uncertainty of their future. Naturally concrete references frequently underlie this emotion. It should not be forgotten that a word like *threaten* is not quite usual, and by its " difficulty " alone has a somewhat exciting effect, without there being necessarily a definite complex beneath. All the same, it seems more prudent to put it down to the influence of a complex than to " difficulty." (I would remind the reader of Freud's analyses.)

Stimulus-word	Reaction	Reaction-time	Reproduction
29. Lamp	light	: 1·8 seconds	†
30. Rich	poor	: 1·8 ,,	†
31. Tree	green	: 1·2 ,,	†
32. Sing	dance	: 2 ,,	†
33. Pity	poor	: 2 ,,	†
34. *Yellow*	*flower*	: 4·2 ,,	green
35. Mountain ‡	mine	: 2·8 ,,	†
36. *Play*	*children*	: 2·2 ,,	dance
37. Salt	bread	: 2·8 ,,	†
38. New	old	: 1·6 ,,	†

In this series *dance*, which was the stimulus-word of reaction 16, recurs twice, betraying a distinct tendency to reproduction, corresponding to the not inconsiderable emotional tone which obviously clings to it. Frequent repetition can betray a person in this way, as the following case indicates : A gentleman, whom

I asked to take part in an experiment, was convinced that he would disclose no complexes. On his way to me he thought over what words he would answer to my stimulus-words. It at once occurred to him to say *Paris*, a word that seemed to him void of all personal significance. In the experiment he repeated *Paris* several times, explaining that the word was absolutely accidental. Six months later he admitted to me that, at the time of the experiment, he was entirely absorbed by an affair which greatly upset him which was taking place in Paris. But at the time it seemed to him that *Paris* had no significance at all for him. I have no reason to doubt the truthfulness of this person. Reaction 34, *yellow*, certainly had a personal reference, to judge from the surrounding complex disturbances. Patient has a rather yellowish complexion, giving her an elderly appearance. Women are very sensitive to these things, especially when an erotic complex is present.

That *children* (reaction 36) is not reproduced but is replaced by another of erotic nature is worth mentioning.

Stimulus-word	Reaction	Reaction-time	Reproduction
39. *Habit* ‡	*ugly or bad*	: 12·2 seconds	bad manners
40. Ride ‡	drive	: 2·4 ,,	†
41. *Wall*	*room*	: 3 ,,	—
42. Stupid ‡	clever	: 2·8 ,,	—
43. Copy-book ‡	book	: 3 ,,	†
44. *Despise* ‡	*disesteem*	: 15·2 ,,	to disesteem
45. Tooth	abscess	: 1·4 ,,	†

In this series we meet various severe complex disturbances. At reaction 39, *habit*, and reaction 44, *despise*, the patient made gestures of aversion and stamped her foot. An "ugly or bad habit" can easily be understood in a sexual sense : onanism, for instance, is a bad habit. People are despised who have such bad habits. Reaction 42, *stupid*, can be personal or can be a perseverating emotional tone extending over from *habit*. The movements accompanying the expressions are certainly not against a sexual complex. *Habit* might also be *drinking habit*, and thus have aroused the complex of her drunken father.

Stimulus-word	Reaction	Reaction-time	Reproduction
46. *Right* ‡	*I always feel like saying exactly the opposite*	: 7·6 seconds	wrong
47. People ‡	father	: 6 ,,	†
48. Smell	pleasant smell	: 4·8 ,,	†
49. *Book* ‡	*pen*	: 4·4 ,,	copy-book
50. *Unjust* ‡	*opinion*	: 3·6 ,,	just
51. Frog	green	: 2·4 ,,	†
52. Divorce	marriage	: 2·2 ,,	†
53. Hunger	thirst	: 1·4 ,,	†
54. White	black	: 1·8 ,,	†

If, as we presume, the subject takes the stimulus-word personally and has a sexual complex in the direction suggested, it will be readily understood that in reaction 46, *right*, she *always feels like saying the opposite*, for that agrees with her actions ; it is more suitable also in regard to her father's drunkenness. Double or manifold determinations should not be excluded ; according to Freud, they are indeed the rule.

It is noticeable that reaction 47 runs *people — father*. She seems still to be within the region of the emotional tone of *right*. We might conclude that there is some obscure connexion between her self-reproaches and *father*. (This connexion will become clear later.)

What was the nature of the disturbance in *book — pen* is not easy to say. (Book = German *Buch*, and, thus pronounced, means in the Swiss dialect *Bauch* = belly.) An assimilation of this kind could easily occur with a sexual complex. I have often come across it in other persons.

The constant decrease of the reaction-times from *right*, 7·6 seconds, speaks, however, rather in favour of a severe complex disturbance which began at this stimulus-word and gradually decreased in the seven reactions that followed. Reaction 50, *unjust*, seems to be taken personally, which bears out the idea of self-reproach.

Stimulus-word	Reaction	Reaction-time	Reproduction
55. Cattle ‡	cow	: 4·2 seconds	†
56. Take care	disobedient	: 4 ,,	†
57. *Pencil*	*sharpen*	: 3 ,,	pointed
58. Cloudy	weather	: 1·8 ,,	†
59. Plum	tree	: 3·8 ,,	†
60. Touch	certain	: 1·4 ,,	†
61. Law	state	: 2·8 ,,	†
62. *Dear*	*good*	: 4 ,,	child
63. Glass	wa–water	: 1·6 ,,	†
64. *Quarrel*	*dispute*	: 2·2 ,,	discord
65. *Goat*	*milk*	: 2 ,,	to give milk

I cannot explain the disturbance at reaction 55, *cattle*. Reaction 56, *disobedient*, recalls the previous *naughty*, which one should probably refer to the pupil. The disturbance in the succeeding reactions speaks for perseveration of the emotion. Reaction 59, *plum — tree*, judging from the length of the reaction-time, does not seem to have gone quite smoothly. Plum is not an everyday word, but it is not likely that an educated person would require so much time for the reaction. (In Wehrlin's idiots the average times varied from 3 to 3·7 seconds ; in an educated person 3·8 seconds thus seems far too long.) *Plum* (like an egg-shaped plum), Swiss *zwetschge*, is a favourite sexual symbol in Swiss colloquial speech.

Reaction 62, *dear*, can be readily claimed as an erotic complex. In reaction 63, *glass*, the complex of the alcoholic father came again to the surface, with the strong emotion bound up with it. (Hence the disturbance of the two subsequent reactions.)

Stimulus-word	Reaction	Reaction-time	Reproduction
66. Big	small	: 2·6 seconds	†
67. Potato ‡	mealy	: 0·6 „	†
68. Paint	mill	: 2 „	†
69. Part ‡	small	: 11·6 „	†
70. *Old*	*ugly*	: 3 „	young, not beautiful
71. *Flower*	*beautiful*	: 2 „	scent
72. Hit	cane	: 2·8 „	—
73. Chest	table	: 2·8 „	—

Reaction 66, *big*, is usually taken personally. The patient is of very small stature. In an erotic complex there will be, as we have already seen, many references to the body. That must be the explanation of the disturbances in the subsequent reactions. Reaction 69, *part*, has a greatly prolonged reaction-time ; part(s) taken as sexual part(s) is very common. The strong emotional tone of this is characteristic. That among these constellations reaction 70, *old*, is apprehended in the personal erotic sense is not to be wondered at. How strongly marked the question of personal beauty is in the patient is seen from the perseveration *beautiful* (reaction 71). Reaction 72, *hit* — *cane*, may have been especially constellated by the obsession that she was responsible for the death of her former pupil.

Stimulus-word	Reaction	Reaction-time	Reproduction
74. Wild	child	: 2·4 seconds	†
75. Family	big	: 2·4 „	†
76. Wash ‡	clean	: 3 „	†
77. Cow	milk	: 1·8 „	†
78. Strange ‡	home-sick	: 14·8 „	†
79. Luck ‡	ill luck	: 3 „	†
80. Relate	stories	: 1·6 „	†

The slight disturbance at reaction 76, *wash*, is explicable by the previous erotic associations, *child* and *family*. Reaction 78, *strange*, has obviously awakened a personal reference of which we shall get the explanation later.

Stimulus-word	Reaction	Reaction-time	Reproduction
81. Standing	understanding	: 4·6 seconds	†
82. Narrow ‡	small	: 3·2 „	†
83. Brother	sister	: 1 „	†
84. Injure ‡	neighbour	: 4 „	†
85. Stork ‡	church	: 2·4 „	†

Stimulus-word	Reaction	Reaction-time		Reproduction
86. False ‡	faithless	: 3	seconds	†
87. Anxiety	feeling	: 2·4	,,	†
88. Kiss	mouth	: 2·2	,,	†
89. Burning	fire	: 1·8	,,	†
90. Dirty	clammy	: 2·2	,,	†
91. Door	crease	: 1·6	,,	†

The clang-association *standing — understanding* [1] is very striking ; we recall the disturbance evoked by *habit*. We there suspected the *bad habit* of onanism. This complex may have been aroused here also. The popular belief is that onanism destroys the understanding (mind). Remember also the subject's complaint that she feared she would go mad. Reaction 82, *narrow — small*, is under the influence of the previous reaction : *small* probably belongs by analogy with its former occurrence to the bodily complex ; *narrow* can be referred, under the constellation of the previous association, to the introitus vaginæ and thus be linked with the *small*, which hints at her stature ; the suspicious "part(s)" are *small*. (This supposition will be confirmed.) Reaction 84, *injure*, is probably taken personally. *Neighbour* agrees well with this. She caused immeasurable injury to her neighbour by being the cause of her unhappy death. But *injure* can be also taken personally under the sexual constellation ; one causes oneself physical and mental injuries by onanism (as above). The neighbour is thus only a cover person cp. Freud's similar demonstrations). Her neighbour is an easy means of concealing herself. Subsequent disturbances indicate that an emotional tone set in here.

In reaction 86, *false — faithless*, a definite erotic reminiscence may easily have emerged in an elderly single woman.

Stimulus-word	Reaction	Reaction-time		Reproduction
92. Choose ‡	teacher	: 4·4	seconds	†
93. Hay	straw	: 1·8	,,	†
94. *Still* ‡	*stool*	: 13	,,	child
95. Scorn	derision	: 1·4	,,	†
96. Sleep ‡	wake	: 3·4	,,	†
97. Month	year	: 1·6	,,	†
98. Tinted	bright	: 2·4	,,	†
99. Dog	cat	: 1·2	,,	†
100. Talk	silence	: 1·4	,,	†

Reaction 92, *choose*, women are prone to link on to thoughts f marriage. The subject's father was a teacher, she is a teacher. is a likely supposition that she thinks of marriage with a

---

[1] This should be understood as *standing in society*: the German is *Anstand* tation, demeanour, etc.), *Verstand* (understanding).—TRANSLATOR.

teacher. Again the father-complex comes up for consideration (see later about this.) Reaction 94, *still — stool*, is a striking clang-association. The explanation is given by the eroticism *child*. A child can be *still*, but the dead are also *still* (obsessional idea— she caused the death of her pupil through ill-treatment). But erotic relationships can be also present; for *stillen* means in German to *suckle, nurse, hush* an infant. One can "still" a child, " still " the sexual impulses.

Reaction 96, *sleep*, has many sexual references. Patient is unable to sleep. Sleeplessness in younger people is frequently the expression of want of sexual satisfaction (Freud).

Those without experience in the sphere of pathological association-psychology will probably shake their heads at the above suppositions; perhaps they will not only see herein hypothesis, but also fantasies. Very likely the same criticism will be made here as at Freud's *Dream Interpretation*.

We will first recapitulate the result of the association and reproduction experiment. As already mentioned, the patient gave no explanations; I am thus thrown entirely upon the objective data of the experiment, and on my experience.

The probable mean of the reaction-times amounts to 2· seconds; 44 per cent. of the reaction-times exceed 2·4 seconds Among these are figures up to 15·2 seconds, from which we may deduce a considerable emotion, or, in other words, a considerable want of command over the psychical material.

We have pointed to the existence of various complexes during the analysis. The erotic complex seems to play a chief part. It will not be superfluous if I again summarize the individual complex reactions so as to obtain a better perspective.

The following refer to an erotic complex [1] :

Stimulus-word	Reaction		Reaction-time	Reproduction
10. *Friendly*	*lovable*	:	3·6 seconds	good
11. *Table*	*woman*	:	4·6 ,,	—
12.		:	2·4 ,,	
13.		:	2·2 ,,	
14.		:	1·8 ,,	
16. Dance	jump	:	1·8 ,,	†
17. Sea ‡	water	:	2·4 ,,	†
34. *Yellow*	*flower*	:	4·2 ,,	green
35. Mountain ‡	mine	:	2·8 ,,	†
36.		:	2·2 ,,	
39. *Habit*	*ugly or bad*	:	12·2 ,,	bad manners
40. Ride ‡	drive	:	2·4 ,,	†

[1] To emphasize the complex disturbances I add the phenomena of perseveration, especially the gradually decreasing times of the succeeding reactions.

Stimulus-word	Reaction	Reaction-time	Reproduction
41. *Wall*	room	: 3 seconds	—
44. *Despise* ‡	disesteem	: 15·2 ,,	to disesteem
45.		: 1·4 ,,	
59. Plum	tree	: 3·8 ,,	†
62. Dear	good	: 4 ,,	child
66. Big	small	: 2·6 ,,	†
67. Potato ‡	mealy	: 6 ,,	†
68.		: 2 ,,	
69. Part	small	: 11·6 ,,	†
70. *Old*	ugly	: 3 ,,	young, not beautiful
71. *Flower*	beautiful	: 2 ,,	scent
72. *Hit*	cane	: 2·8 ,,	—
73.		: 2·4 ,,	
74. Wild	child	: 2·4 ,,	†
75. Family	big	: 2·4 ,,	†
76. Wash ‡	clean	: 3 ,,	†
81. Standing	understanding	: 4·6 ,,	†
82. Narrow ‡	small	: 3·2 ,,	†
83.		: 1 ,,	
86. False ‡	faithless	: 3 ,,	†
87.		: 2·4 ,,	†
88.		: 2·2	
89.		: 1·8 ,,	
92. Choose ‡	teacher	: 4·4 ,,	†
93.		: 1·8 ,,	
94. *Still* ‡	stool	: 13 ,,	child
95.		: 1·4 ,,	
96. Sleep ‡	wake	: 3·4 ,,	†
97.		: 1·6 ,,	

These reactions, all showing characteristic disturbances which are *ex hypothesi* of a sexual nature, can be linked together into the following story :

The subject feels that she is *old, ugly* ; she finds her *yellowish* complexion very disagreeable and her physique, upon which she bestows anxious attention, displeases her as being too *small*. She has a great longing for *marriage*, she would be a *loving wife* to her husband and would like to have *children*. Beneath these erotic yet quite innocent symptoms there seems to be a sexual complex which the patient has every reason to suppress more strongly. There are hints from which it may be inferred that she bestows unusual attention upon her genitalia ; in a respectable and educated single lady that can only signify *onanism*, of course, in the wider sense of perverse sexual self-satisfaction.

Onanism is one of the most frequent sources of *self-reproach* [1] and self-criticism. We find suggestions of this

---

[1] The reproaches need not, of course, be limited entirely to the sexual complex but are rapidly generalized.

complex, or rather this side of the sexual complex, in the associations :

Stimulus-word	Reaction	Reaction-time	Reproduction
14. *Arrogant*	*courageous*	: 1·8 seconds	friendly
19. *Proud*	spirited, stupid	: 5 ,,	†
22. Wicked	good	: 3 .,	—
23.		: 2·2 ,,	
42. Stupid ‡	clever	: 2·8 ,,	—
43. Copy-book	book	: 3 ,,	†
46. *Right* ‡	I always feel like saying exactly the opposite	: 7·6 ,,	wrong
47. People ‡	father	: 6 ,,	†
48. Smell	pleasant smell	: 4·8 ,,	†
49. *Book* ‡	pen	: 4·4 ,,	copy-book
50. *Unjust* ‡	opinion	: 3·6 ,,	just
51.		: 2·4 ,,	
52.		: 2·2 ,,	
53.		: 1·4 ,,	

Referable to the complex of the alcoholic father are :

3. *Water*	*drinker — drink*	: 2·4 seconds	*glass*
4.		: 3·6 ,,	
63. Glass	wa-water	: 1·6 ,,	†
64. *Dispute*	*quarrel*	: 2·4 ,,	*discord*
65. *Goat*	*milk*	: 2 ,,	*to give milk*

It is obvious from this summary that the sexual complex is very prominent. Although, as has been said, no direct confirmation of this interpretation could be obtained from the subject, I regard the complex diagnosis as certain upon the basis of the considerations I have advanced.

I therefore said to her : " I am certain that your obsessional ideas are merely excuses and screens ; in reality you are tormented by sexual ideas." The subject contested this explanation with affect and sincere conviction. If I had not been persuaded by the association experiment of the existence of a strongly marked sexual complex my conviction would probably have wavered. I made an appeal to her intelligence and her love of truth : she assured me that if she knew of anything of the kind in herself she would say it, for she knew it would be stupid to conceal such thoughts from the doctor. She had thought of marriage " like every one else, but not more." I then ended the interview, and made an appointment for two days later.

II. THE PSYCHO-ANALYSIS

In psycho-analysis the mental condition of the patient is important, but still more important is the mental condition of the doctor. This must assuredly be the reason why Freud's psycho-analysis is treated by science with silence. The analyst who goes into a case without assured conviction is soon lost in the pits and snares which the hysterical complex constructs at every turn. He must know beforehand that everything in the hysteric resists the bringing forth of the complex. When convenient, not only do interest and sympathy for the doctor disappear, but the subject loses the power of thought, the possibility of recollection, and finally even speech. But it is exactly these peculiar measures of defence that serve to betray the complex.

Just as in the association experiment hesitation, prolongation of time, absence of reproduction occur when the complex is aroused, in analysis likewise difficulties occur where the complex is being approached. To circumvent these difficulties Freud insists upon " free association." It is a very simple method which has only to be used a few times to be understood to a certain degree. In this case I undertook the psycho-analysis, following exactly Freud's method. I made the subject sit in a comfortable chair and seated myself behind her so as not to confuse her. I asked her to tell me quietly everything that came into her mind, to be quite indifferent as to what it was. The subject laughed : " One can't tell every bit of nonsense that occurs to one." I stood to my demand. A couple of times she tried to say something, but broke off each time with the excuse that it was silly, that I should be obliged to laugh and would think that she was a stupid or ungrateful person. I confined myself again to urging her to speak out, and finally she brought out these sentences : " I think that I never shall be well—now you'll laugh—but I'm convinced that I shall never be well. You can't hypnotize me, for I'm convinced that nobody can hypnotize me. You'll not be able to cure me any more than any other doctor. It will only be worse for me, for I shall reproach myself for having taken up your time unnecessarily with my rubbish." This idea was not quite unjustifiable, for the patient only threw the sentences out after long pauses, so that we had required almost half an hour to produce this meagre result. She went on : " I am now thinking of the people at home, how they are working and require me whilst I am here for nothing but my own silly thoughts —of course, you'll be infected by them—now I am thinking that I cannot sleep, that last night, despite your order, I took a gramme of veronal—of course I shall never be able to sleep again, how will you cure me then ?—what am I to say to you ? (There was here noticeable a certain restlessness.) I can't tell you all the silly thoughts that come into my head. (Restlessness increases, shrugs her shoulders, stamps up and down, shakes herself as if in great depression.) Now this is rubbish—I don't know anything more—nothing else occurs to me—let me go home now, nothing else comes to me." (Very restless—turns about on the chair, gestures of disgust, shaking the upper part of her body to and fro and her elbows moving as if thrusting aside ; at last she jumps up to leave.) Nothing else comes to her. With gentle force I persuade her to sit down again and point out to her that she has really come to get better, so she must carry out my prescription. After much discussion as to the purpose and meaning of my method she finally agrees to remain and continue. But the same depression and gestures of disgust soon recommence ; she twists about on the chair, from time to time sitting upright with a forced movement as if after a great victory she had come to a determination, and finally says despondingly : " Something silly comes to me—you will certainly laugh—but you must not tell it to anybody else—no, I really can't tell you, never—it is something very simple—it has nothing to do with my illness—I am robbing you of your time—it is nothing important— am I really obliged to tell it you ? It is not easy to say it— here goes : Well, once I was in France—it won't come, not if I sit for a month in this chair—(then with sudden determination) well, once I was a governess in France—no, I really can't tell it— there was a servant there—no, there was a gardener there—my God, what will you think of me !—this is martyrdom—I have never thought of anything like this."

Amid such interjections of distress there came out in the end, with innumerable stoppages and interruptions in which she swore that this would be her last consultation, that to-morrow she would go away, the following story :

There was among the servants a gardener who once said to her he would like to sleep with her. Whilst saying this he tried to kiss her, but she pushed him away. At night on going to bed she listened at the door and imagined what it would be like if he were to come and sleep with her ; she got fearfully excited lest he might come. In bed her thoughts again turned to what it would be like if he were to come, and then she drove these ideas away. But she could not get rid of thinking what it would be like, although she again and again shuddered at the idea that she could be thinking of anything of the sort. In this turmoil of thought she could not get to sleep until the morning.

This first sitting had lasted no less than an hour and a half. The result was a sexual history. Especially interesting was the fact of the disclosure being accompanied by the same mimetic manifestations which I had noticed at the first consultation. These tic-like phenomena were thus in very close and easily explicable connexion with the repressed sexual incidents. I made an appointment for the day after next, which she at once agreed to, seeming much relieved, and saying no more about going away.

At the time of her appointment I was engaged with some urgent work, and therefore requested her to come in the evening. But she sent me a message that it was impossible for her to wait, it was absolutely essential for her to talk to me. I supposed that something special had happened and went to her. I found her greatly excited ; she had not slept at all, not a minute ; she had been obliged to take sleeping medicines. I asked her if she had been again worried about her obsessions : "No, something much worse ; my head is now full of that nonsense about which I spoke to you last time. Now I can only think of these stories and of nothing else ; all night I have been tossing and turning about and cannot banish the thoughts for a minute. I must have a talk with you at once; it gives me no peace." She stated that on the last occasion she had felt much relieved and calmer and had gone home in good spirits, hoping that she would now be able to sleep ; but then she recalled an affair which she ought really to have mentioned last time, but which she thought wasn't worth while. She was now firmly resolved "not to act so stupidly" as last time but to speak out freely whatever came up into her mind. In this way the confessions would soon be ended. I began the analysis again, hoping that it would now go smoothly, without the endless preliminaries of the last time. But I was hopelessly mistaken. The patient went through almost exactly the same interjections as in the first sitting. After an hour and a half of real spiritual torment I had brought out the following history :

In the same house where my patient was a governess there was a servant-girl [1] who had a lover ; the girl had also had sexual intercourse with the gardener. The patient had frequent talks with her about sexual matters, especially about the sexual intercourse of the master and mistress. She and the servant had from time to time even examined the bedding of their master and mistress for spots of semen and other signs of coitus. After these conversations the patient used every time to reproach herself bitterly with her immorality, and passed sleepless nights in which she would be tossed about by painful reproaches and voluptuous fantasies.

When the story was brought to an end after wearisome struggles, the patient said "that was the last, there was nothing more in her mind." If only she could sleep; repeating these events was no help at all.

[1] Cp. the mention of this servant at the first sitting.

Two days later she came for the third sitting and stated : After the last interview she felt fairly calmed, but hardly had she got into bed when another event at once occurred to her which had tormented her ever since, together with the self-reproach of not having told me everything the last time. She was now certain that to-day she would tell me about it quickly, without the constant resistance of the previous occasions. But the third sitting was exactly the same : continuous interjections, excuses, etc. Most remarkable was a tendency to present the affair as a matter of course, as if there were nothing in it. It concerned a second servant-girl in the same house. The master had a page-boy who pursued the girl, but did not succeed in seducing her. Finally, one evening when there was a party going on he managed to seduce the girl in the garden. But the couple were taken unawares by the mistress at the critical moment. The lad is said to have exclaimed, " What a pity ! I was just ready." The governess had been told this story by the servant-girl first mentioned. At first she pretended that the story had no interest at all for her, as if it were disagreeable, but she was lying, for in reality she had the greatest interest in it ; she had tried a couple of times to bring the girl back to the story so as to learn all the details. That night she could scarcely sleep on account of her curiosity and was ceaselessly asking herself " what the couple were doing in the garden, in what position were they when the mistress discovered them, for what was he ready if his mistress had not arrived ? " Although she knew the answers to these questions quite well, she could not rest without putting the questions to herself over and over again. Then she was constantly considering what she would have done in such a position. The excitement lasted several days.

In telling the story her attitude was, as mentioned, that it was a matter of course. For instance, under great resistance she told how the boy had pursued the servant. From the resistances one supposed that something unpleasant was to come ; but then she went on in a tone of indifference : " True, the page-lad was in love with the girl ; there's nothing wonderful in that ; that frequently happens, doesn't it ? Ah ! now something else comes—oh well, that's nothing." During the recital she tried again and again to minimize the importance of the event to herself by throwing in general rhetorical questions of this kind.

From that time on the former obsessional ideas were absent during the whole time of the analysis (three weeks), but the sexual ideas took their place ; as soon as one story was finished another took its place, worrying the patient with a real obsession.

She found no peace again until it had been told. She expressed herself as much astonished at the change ; the stories would come up like clockwork, just as if they had been " experienced yesterday." Things came back to her of which she had lost all remembrance, but which she now recognized again (Freud's hypermnesia). These excuses must naturally be accepted with the same reserve as were the common " I don't know." The subject may easily have nourished and jealously cherished all the sexual ideas up to the present moment without on that account being able to recall them when she has to speak of them objectively. Her mimetic expressions during the talks are often in themselves sufficient to let me know what is coming, whilst she assures me a dozen times that she really can remember nothing more. Her ordinary self and her sexual self are really two distinct complexes, two different consciousnesses, which neither desire nor dare to know anything of each other. There is here but a suggestion of the dissociation of personality (as, moreover, in every vivid complex whose peculiarity is a striving after autonomy). But it is only a step to the classical cases of dissociation of personality, which are naturally all conditioned by Freud's mechanisms.[1]

A certain termination had been reached in these three sittings, so far as concerned the obsession that she was responsible for the death of her former pupil and the self-reproaches connected with her sexual stories. The patient felt this obviously, for she stated herself that many years had passed since these affairs, and the idea that she was responsible for her pupil's death had not troubled her for a long time. Probably to circumvent the unbearable sexual ideas she had transferred the reproaches from this sphere and fastened them on to her educational methods, in the well-known way. If one has constantly to reproach oneself about one set of ideas compensation is sought elsewhere as if a similar defect were present there. This is especially noticeable in onanists (hypercriticism, obsessions of cleanliness and tidiness). It does not seem to be mere accident that those incidents were first related which lay at the root of a past obsessional idea. As in her actual consciousness no obsessional ideas were present which could directly support these incidents, no special inhibitions were present. These incidents were therefore relatively indifferent material.

I do not want to describe the succeeding sittings in detail; they all followed the type described. No exhortation, no allusion to the ridiculous nature of her stereotyped resistances, could

---

[1] Cp. Jung, *Collected Papers*, " The Psychology and Pathology of Occult Phenomena " (Baillière, Tindall and Cox ; 1916).

induce the subject to a quicker and less embarrassed narrative. Each fresh sitting was a fresh torture, and in nearly every one the subject assured me that it was the last. Usually the night following new material came up which afforded her no rest.

To the governess reminiscences there were appended a series of indecent stories which had served as the themes of talks with her neighbour for whose unhappy death the patient reproached herself. The dubious past of her neighbour was whispered on every hand. The subject, who is a highly respectable person and comes of an honourable family, has in her sense a dubious past also ; she indeed reproached herself about it. It was therefore not psychologically wonderful that she had been immediately attracted by her interesting neighbour. The *chronique scandaleuse* was discussed there, and the patient was obliged to narrate a whole series of highly obscene stories and jokes which I need not repeat here. To this she had again linked a number of self-reproaches. When the neighbour rapidly succumbed to an illness the subject transferred the reproaches, really due to her own sexual curiosity, on to the death of her neighbour, who must have died unblessed since the patient's visits had induced her to sinful talk. The nature of the reminiscences and of the chain of thought seem to be in favour of the view that these obsessional ideas were simply a new edition of her earlier ideas about her pupil's death. She had brought the religious obsessional ideas first to the clergyman and then to the doctor. To both she linked the presentation that she had infected them with her obsessions, to a certain extent in the same way as she had infected her neighbour, and originally her pupil. At the root of all this there is the general idea that she is a terrible creature who infects every one with her own corruption.

In the following sittings the patient chiefly disclosed a number of incidents which she had talked over in earlier years with a friend. This friend had a position in the office of a large business. There she heard all kinds of piquant things from gentlemen, which she brought post-haste from time to time to the patient. One day her friend said she would like to have relations with a man to see what it was like. This idea excited the patient powerfully ; she was obliged to keep saying to herself she would like to do the same. That was reason enough for renewed reproaches. From this narrative onwards the sexual incidents become more distinctly fastened on to her own person, although at nearly every sitting obscene jokes and the like had to be reproduced. Of the stories referring to her own person there were first of all reminiscences of earlier love affairs and expectations. The reproduction of these events, innocent enough on the whole, went pretty smoothly. Only one story had a more marked emotional tone. She had been in love with a young foreigner and believed he wished to marry her. But afterwards he left without a good-bye and she heard no more of him. She waited a long time, always hoping that he would write again to her. Reaction 78, *foreign — home-sick*, 14·8 seconds, refers to this affair. As already mentioned, the subject could not at the time explain the meaning of this reaction. Whilst the old love affairs were related without too great difficulties, there recurred at the end of this phase considerable resistances. The subject wished absolutely to leave ; she had nothing more to tell. I suggested to her that I had heard nothing about her earlier youth. She thought that would soon be got over, for she had not much to say about her youth. Hardly had she spoken this sentence when she was obliged to repeat a couple of times her tic-like gestures of disgust—an infallible sign that some important material was to be expected. Amid inconceivable stoppages and painful twistings she told me, by fits and starts, about a book that at the age of ten she had found at home called *The Way to a Happy Marriage*. She assured me that she had no longer any idea of what was in the book. But as I remained inexorable, memory after a time returned, and it was seen that the patient remembered all the details, frequently indeed the very words. She described the first coitus and its complications ; this academic description seemed to me peculiar and unusual. I suspected that at the back of this general description much must lay concealed. There was not long to wait before the patient related how at the age of fourteen she had found in the pocket of her elder brother a small book in which a letter was pressed. The letter was addressed by a young woman to a bosom friend and treated the secrets of the wedding night in a very obscene and lascivious way. As this showed, I was obviously on the right path. The next thing that came to the patient referred to erotic dreams which she had had in earlier days. The dreams were distinct pollution dreams and represented coitus without disguise. She then confessed to having sometimes tried to retain the dream-picture and to masturbate. Bound up with the onanism was a constant thinking about her own genitalia ; she was concerned as to whether she was " properly formed," if her introitus was not somewhat too narrow, and she felt compelled to investigate this problem with her finger. She was frequently obliged to look at her naked body in the looking-glass, and so on. She felt compelled to make a whole series of imaginary pictures about coitus—how she would behave at the first coitus, etc. Finally she acknowledged feeling violent sexual libido (which she had at first vehemently denied), admitting that she would very much like to marry, and had sexual images about most of the men with whom she had associated. She could not resist putting herself in the leading part in all the sexual events which she had piled up. For instance, she told about a young, naïvely frank acquaintance who in an excursion in an overfilled railway carriage had sat her teacher on her lap. The girl said afterwards, laughingly, that the teacher never failed to play his part, he had even taken a ruler with him in his trousers pocket. The patient was always thinking how pleasant it would be for her also if a teacher sat upon her knees, and she would know then what the ruler in the trousers pocket signified. (The earlier reaction, *choose — teacher*, must have been constellated by this incident.)

Amid great resistance she related how at the age of fourteen she had once lain upon a younger sister " as if she were a man." In one of the last sittings she succeeded in recalling an event which agrees in every way with the importance attributed by Freud to early psychical trauma. At the age of seven or eight she had on several occasions overheard the coitus of her parents. Once she heard her mother preventing it and refusing to give in to her father at all. After that it was a long time before she could look at her parents. Her mother became pregnant and gave birth to the patient's younger sister. She hated her sister from the first moment and was only able much later to overcome a deep antipathy to the child. It is not at all improbable that the subject had imagined herself as the second person in this affair, and she has indeed taken over the rôle of mother. The strong emotional tone which occurred in all the associations to " father " is readily comprehensible from this intimate link.

The psychological trauma of a perception of this kind is naturally preserved in the child's mind as an extremely emotional complex which constellates thinking and doing for years. This was classically the case in this patient. Her sexual function was thus given a very definite direction.[1] The analysis of her repressed presentations shows this; it is chiefly concerned with the grubbing out and picturing of coitus situations. It is remarkable that despite her extraordinarily vivid fantasy, she had never got deeply entangled with men and had rejected all attempts at seduction. On the other hand, she has been attracted by women of dubious character and equivocal conversation with an almost magical compulsion, an unexpected

---

[1] With this may be compared the fact that many sexual perverts (fetishists) have acquired their abnormality through an accidental sexual event. Cp. v. Krafft-Ebing, *Psychopathia Sexualis*.

tendency in a woman of her education and intelligence.   The two last sittings were peculiarly instructive in this respect. She reproduced a cunning accumulation of the most disgusting indecencies which she had occasionally heard in the streets. What was common to all these indecencies, the repetition of which we may be spared, was the different abnormalities of coitus (too wide or too narrow an introitus, coitus of a young man with a big, fat woman, etc.).   The amount and the deep vulgarity of these jokes seemed to me almost incomprehensible in so cultured and respectable a lady.   The phenomenon is, however, explained by the early perverse direction of the sexual function, which was chiefly concerned with the hunting out of sexual filth, that is, the symbolical repetition of the overheard coitus.   This complex has therefore affected the whole of her previous life and determined a mass of sexual doings and associations in its particular form.   That is, for instance, why the patient carried out a kind of coitus action with her little sister, why her listening at the door to find out whether the gardener is coming is still so impressed upon her, why she engaged in the disgusting business of snuffling in the bed of her master and mistress, why she sought the company of sexually despicable people.   Her defensive gestures and the peculiar projection of her abdomen show the effect of the complex at work everywhere. It is also very noticeable that at every sitting she appeared in another dress.

Such a use of the sexual function is bound to be unbearable to an otherwise finely planned character ; a repugnance to and repression of the tendency, as absurd as it is detestable, must arise.   It is impossible that an educated and finely sensitive woman could bring these obscenities into union with the rest of her mental content.   These things can therefore only exist in repression.   But they do exist, they carry on a separate existence, they form a state within a state, they constitute a personality within a personality ; or, otherwise expressed, two consciouses are present which are kept apart by violent emotional inhibitions. One mind can and does know nothing of the other mind.   That is the explanation of the remarkable disturbances in reproduction which work against analysis.   The ethically higher mind does not deal with the associations of the other mind ; that is why it seems to her that she has forgotten these ideas, as if she had never known about such things.   I am inclined to agree with her conviction that she really knew nothing more, that it was not a lie when she assured me with the greatest obstinacy that she had nothing more to say.

But although a complex be repressed ever so much from normal consciousness it must still influence and constellate the content of normal consciousness—for the deepest dissociation of the conscious does not extend to the unitary basis of personality. Repression must therefore leave behind a certain residue in the functions of the conscious; normal consciousness must in some way direct the state of feeling which a repressed complex leaves behind. What is simpler than for any one of the ideas compatible with normal consciousness to be projected and accepted as the explanation of the constant self-reproaches and discontented mood ? To find a motive for the pangs of conscience attributable to her sins at the time she was a governess, the patient projects her reproaches on to her methods of education. These must have been bad is the view taken by her conscious self, for she would not otherwise have a constant feeling of reproach when she recalls memories of that time. As we have already seen, the origin of this obsession becomes the model of the obsession about her guilt for the unhappy death of her neighbour. The accumulation of obsessional ideas around the doctor and clergyman were well grounded, for, as the subject confessed to me, these persons were not sexually indifferent to her. Inasmuch as they affect her sexually they are quasi-accessories in her depravity; hence they must also be reproaching themselves.

After this analysis we can understand the part her father played in her erotic complex, a part that was not clear in the associations. The analysis confirms, in the fullest way, the suppositions aroused by the associations. The associations served me as a safe signpost in the maze of moving fantasies which sought to put the analysis at each step on a wrong road.

The analysis was undertaken during three weeks every second day and lasted each time from an hour and a half to two hours. Although at the end of the three weeks there were neither proper sleep nor real quiet, I dismissed the patient from further treatment and did not hear from her till the end of November. In the last days of November 1905 she came to see me unexpectedly and announced that she was cured. After breaking off the analysis she said she was in the most violent, agitated mood, and remained thus for some four weeks. At night she was either tormented by her sexual images or by the re-emergence of her obsessional ideas. The obsessions about her neighbour were particularly frequent and gave her no rest until she had again visited the daughter of the deceased, to be told for the xth time about the death scene. When the daughter again assured her that her mother had died quietly, the subject became suddenly convinced that the woman had died at peace. Then at one blow all her obsessions disappeared.   Sleep returned and was only on rare occasions troubled by sexual images.

To what is this fortunate end of the treatment to be attributed ?

Obviously the daughter's version, which the patient had repeatedly heard without result, was only the occasion of the removal of the obsessions.   A real turn for the better took place at the beginning of the treatment, when the sexual images replaced the obsessional ideas.   The confession of her sinful thoughts must have enormously lightened the patient.   But it seems improbable that it was to this speaking out or to the " abreaction " alone that the cure was attributable.   To keep down such fancies permanently great energy is required.   People with obsessions are weak, they are incapable of holding in their images with a tight rein.   Treatment therefore always works best with them. The best treatment is to compel them, with a certain ruthlessness, to reproduce and display all the presentations incompatible with their consciousness.   The energy is thus not only put to a severe test, but the conscious gets accustomed to the existence of images formerly repressed.   The mental separate existences become crushed, since they are dragged by an effort of will from repression into daylight.   In the process they lose considerably in nimbus, and hence in danger ; the subjects receive at the same time the feeling of being masters of their images. I therefore lay stress upon the strengthening of the will, and not upon the mere " abreaction," as Freud did formerly.

It seems from some recent works that Freud's theory of obsessional phenomena is still systematically ignored.   It is hence a great satisfaction to me to be able to recall attention to Freud's theories—even at the risk of falling into the sphere of this systematic amnesia.

Summary

(1) The complex appearing in the associations of a psychogenic neurosis exhibits the *causa morbi* (excluding the predisposition).

(2) Associations can be a valuable aid for the discovery of the pathogenic complex as well as serving for the shortening and lightening of Freud's psycho-analysis.

(3) Associations give us experimentally an insight into the psychological structure of the neurotic symptoms : Hysteria and obsession phenomena arise from one complex.   The physical and psychical symptoms are but the symbolical pictures of the psychogenic complex.

CHAPTER VIII

CASES ILLUSTRATING THE PHENOMENA OF ASSOCIATION IN HYSTERIA

By Dr. FRANZ RIKLIN

THE following investigations deal with association experiments in eight cases of hysteria.

FIRST CASE

CATTERINA H. showed signs of hysteria whilst still at school. She studied at a Russian high school and took an active part in the tumults of the last few years. She had a friendship, probably platonic on her side, with a student. The patient has a peculiar sexuality which gives evidence of her hysteria. She is able so to repress all sexual experiences, and that knowledge which every one necessarily acquires in the course of growth, that she was over twenty without having any correct ideas on the subject, although she was a student. She even took part in a discussion on prostitution without really knowing what prostitution was ; and she praised an acquaintance who afterwards admitted that he had once taken up with a prostitute. She believed it was a question of a girl despised by society, and considered he had acted meritoriously. Later, when a catastrophe had opened her eyes, she could only think shamefacedly of that " silly " conversation. It was, moreover, obvious how little she recognized her sexuality even later.

Her friend R. loved her, but not merely platonically. He wrote to her from abroad, confessed his love, and wished to marry her. Annoyed by these " bourgeois and conventional outbursts," she wrote him an indignant letter, whereupon he committed suicide. Going one day in high spirits to some compatriots, she saw the news in a Russian paper. She wanted to make herself believe that it must be somebody else with the same name, and did not change her light-hearted mood. Nevertheless the news drove her to the house of a friend who would be likely to know more about it. After a prolonged search she saw her friend in the distance, and when with one word she was told everything the patient collapsed and had her first hysterical attack. (She is said to have once had a slight twilight condition as a school-child, also from some psychical cause.) It was not possible to obtain any more exact account of the fit. Soon afterwards she went to another university. The attacks repeated themselves, especially on certain anniversaries (day of the week, month, year of R.'s death) and on other occasions connected with this event. (I cannot here discuss in more detail the analysis of the attacks and twilight states. Her condition was made worse by another circumstance. The patient was informed by a woman acquaintance, a midwifery student, about male sexuality and the sexual act, upon which the knowledge on the subject hitherto repressed, entered completely into consciousness. She felt herself

322

unhappy; mankind, hitherto idealized, became a beast; the idea that R. loved her sensually (perhaps also repentance that her ignorance was responsible for his death) troubled her terribly. In slight twilight states she would often say, "I must go to his grave and ask him if he knew it." She hated mankind on account of its sexual function, hated also her doctor, whom she imagined was also like the rest; she could only esteem him when she saw him in attendance upon his patients and was then able to exclude the sexual image. About two years after R.'s death the patient entered the asylum, after having been treated at different places.

I must mention some of the individual phenomena of the numerous minor twilight states and symptomatic actions (Freud [1]), because they illuminate the fundamental phenomena of hysterical associations and of hysteria in general—the pathological dissociation and the disposal of repressed complexes in the acts and thoughts of the hysteric; elements which we also find among normals.

The patient often wanted to learn the violin and inquired earnestly about a teacher, especially on days when she was in a minor twilight state. Her sweetheart had played the violin. She cannot look at closed or half-open eyes because she then thinks that a dead person is there. She does not see the flowers on the table because she would then have to see the doctor who is in the room; she dares not look at him because she thinks blood is flowing from his temples. Apparently as an innocent joke, she placed some crushed rose-leaves on a little pimple on her forehead (gunshot wound). She liked to sing music-hall songs where the name R. occurs (false, inadequate affect). She is frightened at any meeting (first attack). She represents her illness as if she had two souls, a big and a small one; the small one has been poisoned and has been exchanged with the big one; when the small one acts upon the big one she is ill. This is a very pretty image of a repressed complex which became noticeable in the reactions.

The five hundred associations employed were made in four tests; the first and last were carried out with German test-words and with time-measurements, in the second and third experiments Russian words were used without any time-measurements. The first three experiments took place in the early part of her stay in the asylum, on the first, fifth, and eighth day, the last one was made ten weeks later.

Her two complexes—the relationship to R. and her sexuality, both intimately connected—run like a thread through all the reactions—those carried out the first two days as well as those carried out later, i.e. at a time when we had a fairly complete analysis of the case.

Working out the two hundred associations of the first experiment, we find that 15 per cent. refer to the R. complex, about 7 per cent. to the complex "sexual knowledge," and about 12 per cent. to a third, a political complex (Russia, socialism, revolution). This also stands in the closest connexion with the others, as we shall learn in detail; on the whole, therefore, 35 per cent. of definite complex reactions.

The number of egocentric reactions exceeds that found among

[1] Freud, *The Psychopathology of Everyday Life.*

normals ; in our patient it is 8–9 per cent. (In normal educated women it is, on the average, 2·1 per cent.)

EXAMPLES OF EGOCENTRIC REACTION

Needle	cruel	Frog	brr
Needle	fright	Water	fearful
Lake	fear	Dance	stupid
Mountain	cruel	Cat	pfui
Dream	fearful	Bird	darling
School	fearful	Now	bad
School	hateful	Bad	me
Hair	unpleasant	Time	weary
Attendant	good		

Most of these highly subjective reactions are explained by particular events.

EXAMPLES OF COMPLEX REACTIONS

R. = Repressed complex; S. = Sexuality; P. = Political complex; D.T. = Delayed reaction-time.

I. *Test :* Table	books	: 7·2 seconds R.
II. „ Table	letter	R.
III. „ Table	dissection-table	: 1·4 „

Patient thought of the table in R.'s room on which lay his revolver ; then of a letter of farewell. Dissection-table signifies the reminiscence of a psychological experiment on a frog, which made a very unpleasant impression upon the patient. All reminiscences of blood are closely connected with R.'s *bloody death* and play a rôle similar to the symptomatic action—as the " representative " of the repressed complex.

I. *Test :* Bread   nourishment : 5 seconds, S.
II. „   Bread   daily

The latter is an abbreviated quotation (" Give us this day our daily bread "), and therefore suspect of being a complex indicator. In the patient's view eating belongs to what is animal in man, like sex (cp. Freud). This idea is also expressed by the fact that she invariably eats *very little*, and will *not eat in company*

I. *Test :* Hit   cruel   : 3·4 seconds, R.
II. „   Hit   whip, knout, R.

She first saw R. bleeding at a Russian demonstration ; he had been gashed by Cossacks.

I. *Test :* Dark red   " I can think of nothing," R.

A so-called fault, a complex indicator ; nothing comes up to the patient. Dark red is associated with blood, as is seen from many of her expressions ; it is a colour which occupies her a good deal.

I. *Test :* Sweet   fruit, melon : 2·2 seconds, R.
II.   „   Sweet   mankind, R.

In the second experiment patient immediately adds a quotation ; I cannot enter into its accuracy : " Bitter is also the sweet fruit of the sweetest woman ; the warrior may not have it, and so he would have the woman." Surely a symbolism of the conception of her relationship to R.

In the third test she reacts *raspberry — bitter*, 4·6 seconds, founded upon the same ideas.

IV. *Test :* Idle   " Show me the fruit which rots ere it is broken " : 0·8 sec.

It is a quotation (therefore probably a complex indicator) which the patient refers to herself. In this test she explained, when she was less repressed (i.e. less hysterical) after the long treatment, that she referred this association to herself : " When you understand nothing (of sexual matters) you are not spoilt ; now you will be spoilt in time." According to her view she is the early rotting fruit.

I. *Test :* Divorce   woman   : 6 seconds
II.   „   Divorce   dead . . . for ever ; 4 seconds, R.

The first reaction, *woman*, is clearly a cover reaction for the idea which emerges clearly in the second experiment.

I. *Test :* Game   children : 2·2 seconds
II.   „   Game   woman, a woman is a toy (quotation)
IV.   „   Game   I am too old to enjoy games, too young to be without
                      desires : 1·6 second (quotation)

The references to the sexual complex seem to me obvious. Here are two quotations, and at the suspect first reaction a prolonged reaction-time.

I. *Test :* Babble   author : 3·6 seconds
II.   „   Babble   go on talking, gossip
III.   „   Babble   impossible ; I will not narrate it : 2·2 seconds
IV.   „   Speak   I would rather not : 3·6 seconds ; " and they speak
                      like our deeds," S.

All the reactions refer, even on the patient's own declaration, to her " secret "—i.e. to the sexual complex ; at the first, apparently unequivocal, reaction there is suspiciously delayed reaction-time, at the last an apparently mutilated quotation ; in the third reaction a sentence which the patient uses in stereotyped fashion in her twilight states, when she speaks of her " secret," the sexual complex.

I. *Test :* Love   father—occurs to me : 2 seconds

The patient laughs loudly hereat, and cannot make out how she arrived at this answer (mimetic reaction !).

III. *Test :* Love   in order to forget again

The next moment the patient knew nothing about this reaction, she did not even understand what it could mean. She had said it quite unconsciously ! The connexion is obvious to us.[1]

I. *Test :* Love   I do not know what to say

No reaction. A fault. Patient contorts her face (mimetic reaction).

IV. *Test :* Love   child : 1 second

Patient uttered this reaction imitating the voice and tone of a patient in the asylum, who constantly used the expression (a kind of quotation therefore).

I. *Test :* Tears   uneasy : 2·6 seconds
III. „ Tears   death ; tears are shed at death

The two reactions complete one another, the first by its delayed reaction, the second by its transparency. Reference to death, which occupied her more than anything.

IV. *Test :* Month   when budded every shrub and tree in the wondrous month of May, love into my heart did steal to make me like them fay

This quotation, again a complex reaction, glosses harmlessly over the memory of R.'s death, *who shot himself in May.*

I. *Test :* Right   (Shrugs her shoulders, no reaction) " The word doesn't come " ; at last after 11 seconds, " universal "

Patient frequently reacted with " universal vote," but that is only a cover reaction, apparently belonging to the political complex. In reality this hysterical inhibition was caused by the sexual complex, the idea being that nothing was right, that mankind ought not to have sexual feelings. The patient later gave this explanation herself in a series of cases, especially in the later tests ; this holds good of the following reaction :

IV. *Test :* Law   (Fault—with a gesture of warding off—mimetic reaction)

Patient thinks of the natural laws of sexuality.

II. *Test :* Right   none, it doesn't exist
I. „ False   women : 5 seconds
II. „ False   man, S. (in the sense of man is falsely organized)
II. „ False   corruption of man, S. (in sexual sense)
III. „ Correct   not everything, S.
I. „ Unjust   Russia : 2·8 seconds

Apparently a political complex ; in reality the idea was again present that man was created wrongly ; the sexual complex is

---

[1] Cp. Jung, " Experimentelle Beobachtungen über das Erinnerungsvermögen," *Centralbl. f. Nervenheilk. u. Psychiatrie,* September 1905, for a review of methods of reproduction.

here masked by the political one. (Unjust, wrong, unrighteous are terms more allied in the Russian than in the German language.)

  I. *Test :* Revenge   friend, a particular one : 7·6 seconds (R.'s brother)
  II. „   Despise   N. (name of the brother)

" That doesn't tell you anything." She laughed and, whilst laughing, took the portrait of N. from the table ; we have here an inadequate feeling reaction in consequence of repression. The inadequacy is very clear when it is known that revenge, hatred, and scorn of the brother of the dead man, and her fear of him, play an important part in her twilight states. Thus we get the following reaction :

  II. *Test :* Threaten   no, he will not do it to me . . .

This is a stereotyped sentence in the attacks : " No, no, he will not kill me," i.e. N. But suddenly she cannot recall her reaction ; she must have been absent-minded. We have here a kind of twilight state, which is dissociated by " amnesia " from consciousness.

This fear of N.'s revenge, which possessed the patient after R.'s death, is quite unfounded. In reality her relationship to him was quite good. She thinks she must worship him as a kind of martyr, as he must have suffered immensely from the same cause.

  I. *Test :* Pure   the Germans : 6 seconds, D.R.
  II. „   Pure   life, my ideal ; it is no longer so : 2 seconds, S.

The Germans are obviously a cover reaction. The effect of the sexual complex is obvious. Here belong the following reactions :

  IV. *Test :* Dirty   thoughts : 2 seconds
  I. „   Murderer   minister : 3 „

(Laughed aloud.) " I wanted to say Kaiser." Political complex, R. occurring again (inadequate emotional reaction).

  II. *Test :* Murderer   myself ; it is only an accident that this word came
                 out. (Inadequate, apparently indifferent)
  IV. „   Intention   no, without : 14 seconds

" I had no intention to kill him," is one of her constant sayings in the twilight states.

  I. *Test :* Suppose   (fault ; patient sighs !)
  IV. „   Suppose   never, nobody would ever have supposed it : 1 sec., S.
  I. „   Soft   quiet : 2·4 seconds
  II. „   Soft   in the churchyard
  IV. „   Quiet   grave : 1 second

(Weeping.) " I was at the cemetery with him."
Here we have, as frequently in the repetition of the same reaction-word, an increase of the cover reaction from Test I

to a distinct expansion of the association pertaining to it in
Test IV.

I. *Test :* To wipe   goloshes : 7·2 seconds (cover reaction)

Patient laughed, making a grimace, R. (inadequate emotional
reaction, mimetic reaction) ; *to wipe* signifies for the patient to
wipe the blood away from his face. She remembers a childhood's
game with a refrain "To wipe, wipe, wipe !" sings it over and
over again, laughing at the same time [1] (complex song with
inadequate emotional tone).

I. *Test :* Natural   (fault)

Nothing comes up to the patient ; she turns aside. The natural
law of sexuality is again meant.

I. *Test :* Remember   carry on a revolution : 3 seconds
III. „   Remember   R. That tells you nothing, that is a dead person ;
                    I could have answered anything else

The first reaction seems to belong to the political complex.
The second reaction, with its apparently superficial, indifferent
tone (inadequate affect) explains itself.

This collection of examples of complex constellations, which
could be easily increased, demonstrates its extremely frequent and
intense occurrence in hysteria. By means of comparison with
other reaction-times in the same patient, apparently indifferent
reactions with a delayed reaction-time are discovered to be
complex constellations. The so-called faults, the mimetic reactions, quotations, etc., prove to be nearly always complex
representatives.

We have even seen phenomena occur, in response to definite
stimulus-words, behaving as cheats of consciousness ; we see,
moreover, how a complex (the political one) in reality stands
for and conceals the sexual complex. We see that *forgetting*,
both in Freud's investigations and in Ganser's symptom complex,
is a function of repression. *It is not the kind of mechanism but the
frequency and intensity of the complex indicators which distinguish
hysteria from the normal.*

SECOND CASE

ANNA L., 20 years, a seamstress. The patient is a poor, simple girl. Her
stepfather treats her badly, although she works diligently and contributes towards
the household ; her mother is good ; there is thus a mental conflict. She would
like to marry in order to avoid this conflict and to assuage her desire for peace,
quietness at home, and love. Her first sweetheart was faithless, for he never
wrote again after going abroad. She has another now, but is worried as to
whether her wish is to be fulfilled. Together with some other hysterical symptoms
she is suffering from enuresis nocturna.

---

[1] Cp. *Melody Automatisms*, chapter v.

Two hundred associations were carried out. I give some of the results, omitting, for the sake of concentration, a small number of indifferent reactions. Patient had, especially during the first half of the test, a frequent embarrassed laugh. The predominance of subjective values will be noticed.

Prick	needle	: 1·2 seconds
State	beautiful	: 6·2 „ (latter in the sense of stately)
Angel	beautiful	: 1·6 „
Long	street. Later: at night-time with my sweetheart in the street	
Insolent	hateful	: 3·4 seconds (at home)
Stalk	flower	: 1·6 „
Ship	big	: 2 „ (a trip on a gondola when they got acquainted with one another)
Plough	field	: 1·6 seconds
Wool	sheep	: 1·2 „
Friendly	good	: 2·6 „
Carry	child	: 5·8 „
Dance	jolly	: 3 „
Lake	nice	: 3·8 „ (the gondola trip)
Angry	(fault). After 10 seconds: " Nothing occurs to me." (Laughs.) " Father is angry, very."	

She then tells the experimenter, who was not previously aware of her circumstances : " My stepfather does not like me, he can't bear me ; he doesn't even like my mother to be good to me." (There is meaningless laughter at this memory.)

Needle	prick	: 1·4 seconds	Bread	hard	: 1·8 seconds
Swim	not	: 2·6 „	Threaten	father	: 3 „
Travel	far	: 3 „	Rich	money	: 1·6 „
Blue	sky	: 1 „	Tree	green	: 1·6 „
Sing	nice	: 1 „	Play	children	: 2 „
Mountain	high	: 1·2 „	Salt	bitter	: 1·2 „
New	clothes	: 3 „	Ride	horse	: 2 „
Habits	country	: 4·4 „	Wall	white	: 2·2 „

Stupid (fault). " Nothing occurs to me." Then: " That one should not get the person one likes, and the other one doesn't want it either."

Copy-book	write	: 1·4 seconds
To despise	not nice	: 2·2 „
Tooth	painful	
Right	(fault). " Nothing occurs to me." Then she says, weeping : " It is not right that I was happy with mother and then father is so cross "	
Prudent	(fault). Later : " I am that in choosing "	
Forget	(fault). The unhappy affair with her first sweetheart	
Love	Patient laughs for 5 seconds ; after 19·6 seconds she says : " Those belonging to you—and those you like—these are questions "	
Understand	to understand one another well : 2·8 seconds (laughing)	

THIRD CASE

MATILDE R., hospital nurse, about 25 years. She is full of enthusiasms. Her father, a drunkard, was a riding-master. The patient first worked in a country house and was better treated than a servant-girl. In a gynæcological clinic where she wanted to train as nurse she was seduced, as alleged, through being made drunk. Afterwards she brought an action against the seducer. She wanted to conceal the pregnancy from her people, and by night duty earned a miserable pittance, giving out that all was well with her. She gave birth quite alone, without help, and then took the premature stillborn child (8–9 months) and ran with it to the river, where she placed it in the water. The affair was found out. There was an inquest, but the patient was not arrested, as it was proved that it was not a case of infanticide.

The privation and the court proceedings had strongly affected the girl and brought about a series of hysterical symptoms (shriekings, tremors as if in a rigor). Afterwards she became a hospital nurse and found a refuge and an altruistic aim in life which was of therapeutic value. Besides many other hysterical features and physical symptoms, she is a noctambulist and has remarkable somnambulistic dreams.

The reactions of this patient are distinguished by the preference for the sentence form. But they are quite different from the sentence reaction of imbeciles. Wehrlin has shown (chapter iii) that among imbeciles the tendency to definition in its various forms is the chief characteristic. In hysteria, on the other hand, the occurrence of strong emotional tones seems to be crowded into sentence formation. The sentences often have the character of cover reactions, the form of school answers that apparently tell you nothing.

I. EXAMPLES OF SENTENCE REACTIONS WHICH EXPRESS EMOTION

Tree	the leaves are now falling :	4	seconds
Flowers	are now all shed :	2·4	,,
Bird	are already all away :	3·6	,,
Mountain	I should like to climb one :	3·2	,,
Book	something delicious for me:	1·8	,,
Dance	I like it :	1	,,
Swim	I can't :	1·6	,,
Proud	I am very :	4·2	,,
Flatter	I don't like it :	2	,,
Child	I'm no longer one :	1·4	,,
Friendly	that I'm not :	2	,,
Soldier	oh, how I'd like to be ! :	1·6	,,
Rich	unfortunately, I am not :	2	,,

It will be noticed that the subject soon leaves the objective sentence type and then produces only " I " sentences.

II. Examples of Cover Reactions

Lake   the lake of Zurich is very beautiful : 7·7 seconds

Patient once thought of jumping into the water, when she was in a very unhappy situation among relatives and was suffering from home-sickness ; she went to the lake but had a fit and was brought back to the house.

Water   is a very useful . . . : 2·2 seconds

Sudden stoppage—betraying much. We think of the foregoing and the event at the river previously mentioned. The stoppage can also stand for the word *drink*, which would complete the sentence. The following reactions favour this view :

Thirst   drunkards have . . . : 10·4 seconds

The subject has never touched alcohol since that one excess with its fatal results ; it makes her sick to think of it. This is behind the affect :

Public-house   is something disgusting : 4·4 seconds

Other examples :

Evil   one must avoid : 18·6 seconds

The subject at first wanted to quote the words " Deliver us from evil." It is thus a cover reaction coupled with a most significant delay in the reaction-time. The reaction refers to the fatal occurrences.

Decorum   one must have : 2·2 seconds

Again refers to her complex.

Suffer   yes . . . our patients do, much : 5·6 seconds

Thought, " I must suffer much."

Despise   everybody sometimes : 2·6 seconds

Spoken with feeling ; thought of her seducer who left her in misery.

Remember   one sometimes thinks of something . . . and forgets it again : 7 seconds

Refers again to the events of her life.

Faithfulness is something beautiful : 7·4 seconds

with a deep sigh, mimetic reaction.

Unjust   are many men : 3·8 seconds

with the same reference (prosecution).

False   snakes are : 2·6 seconds

same reference.

Sin   every man sins : 6 seconds

Thinks of the same affair.

Love   I don't know—is a feeling : 15 seconds

(Says afterwards, " That is stupid ; there is no real love.")

III. EXAMPLES OF SENTENCES WHICH EXPRESS WISHES

Mountain   I should like to climb one
Soldier   I wish I were one
Bicycle   I should like to be able to ride it
Carriage   I should like to drive

(Partly reminiscences.)

Ride   a jolly sport : 4·4 seconds

Her father was a riding-master ; she had a situation in a country house where she often used to ride.

Dance   I like it
Charm   when one's very beautiful : 10·2 seconds

then adds, " I should like to be very charming ! "

IV. EXAMPLES OF SENTENCES DEMONSTRATING HER EDUCATIONAL LEVEL

Faust   Goethe wrote that
Arithmetic   I'm pretty fair at it
Potatoes   came from America
Powder   Gutenberg discovered powder—didn't he ?

V. EXAMPLES OF SENTENCES WHICH EXPRESS HER COMPLEX MORE OR LESS DISTINCTLY

White	innocence is	: 2·4 seconds	(quotation)
Prison	preserve me from it	: 1·8 ,,	(Inquest)
Marriage	I shall never marry	: 1·8 ,,	
Appearance	is oft deceptive	: 1·6 ,,	(quotation)
Youth	has no virtue	: 2 ,,	(quotation)
Sorrow	I have had much already	: 2·6 ,,	
Kiss	is a sign of love	: 6·8 ,,	
Natural	everything in nature is natural	: 5·6 ,,	
Bad	many people are	: 3·4 ,,	
Pool	is a town in D.	: 3·4 ,,	

This is explained by there being a prison in Poole. See the stimulus-word *prison* above.

Love   I love my patients : 3·8 seconds
Tears   I have shed many : 1·6   ,,   (quotation)
Terrible   murder   : 10·6 ,,

The experimenter repeated the stimulus-word with affect—we recall her anamnesis.

Hope	if there were no hope	: 2·4 seconds (quotation)
Love	so long as you can love	: 3·2 „
Misery	in London there is the greatest misery	: 3·8 „

The reaction refers to her own misery in the big town of X.

Corner	a life in the corner	: 3·6 seconds (quotation)
Hot	love burns hot	: 5 „
Consciousness	one has not always got it	: 3 „

Says she means our patients ; but it refers to her seduction.

| Snare | to put a snare for some one | : 3·8 seconds |

Certainly belongs to the same complex.

The two following cases also show sentence reactions. The sentences are here chiefly cover reactions for the complex. I have published the histories of these two patients elsewhere in another connexion.[1]

FOURTH CASE

MRS. MARIA C. The point about this history is that the patient was in the women's clinic on account of a thrombosis following labour when she received a letter from her husband that excited her. The latter, a labourer (Italian), had made the unpleasant discovery that his wife had incautiously lent a sum of eight hundred francs which he could not recover. Although they loved each other he considered this an unwarrantable folly, for it made his savings illusory, and he threatened that he would have nothing more to do with her. This threw the woman into a hysterical twilight state with the Ganser syndrome complex, and she was taken to the clinic.

One hundred and fifty associations were carried out on the third day of her sojourn in the asylum, when the patient's mind was fairly clear but still troubled as to whether her husband would forgive her. Twenty further associations were made on the next day after a reassuring visit from her husband.

Most of the reactions are in sentence form and are usually cover reactions. The expression *one* is frequently repeated. Generally this means the patient's husband or herself ; a confirmation of the view which we expressed in the work on the associations of normals, that *one* is a cover word for the principal characters in emotionally toned presentation complexes. This view cannot be extended to the associations of imbeciles, when *one* more often appears in the reactions as a tendency to definition.

More than half of the associations are certainly complex reactions and probably a good part of the rest, about which, however, we have no sufficient evidence.

Mimetic reactions are strikingly frequent, e.g. *friendly — one* is at times 3·2 seconds. Patient laughs and explains, " My husband is friendly." Cover reaction in sentence form with mimetic reaction.

---

[1] " Zur Psychologie hysterischer Dämmerzustände und des Ganserschen Symptoms," *Psychiatr. neurol. Wochenschrift*, 1904.

Carry   one carries many things : 3·2 seconds

(What ? " Water to table." Then " a helpless creature."
(The last child is very weakly.)

Stubborn   one is sometimes : 2·8 seconds

Then " I am like that ; obstinate people are stubborn."

Lake   that is a great mass . . . water : 9 seconds

Note the hesitation. The patient had intended jumping into
the lake when she was stopped by her husband.

Ill   one is : 3·2 seconds

(Laughs.) " I and my baby."

Proud   an unfriendly person : 14·4 seconds

At first thinks, *My relatives — aunt.* Refers to the dissatisfaction
of her relatives on account of her marriage with the Italian.

Angry   I am . . . myself

but adds softly, " but I hope to alter."

Threaten   and if one is disobedient, one is threatened : 4·2 seconds

Under this generalized form of the sentence is to be understood
herself and her husband.

Rich   a man is who has plenty of money : 6 seconds

Patient begins to cry and recalls the story of the eight hundred
francs.

Sing   one does this when glad : 4·4 seconds

Cp. the remark about *one.* The patient means herself and
thinks of the contrast with the happy times when she could be
full of joy.

Pity   a fine man has that : 3·6 seconds

Then, " I do not know who has pity for me " (cries). Does not
mean her man (husband) but her relatives, who were against
her marriage and had a malicious joy in her misfortune.

Mountain   there's many mountains : snow mountains : 16·8 seconds

Cover sentence for the reminiscence of her joyous youth
when she lived in F. mountain. A contrast determined by the
complex between now and then.

New   new, are . . . new buildings, a new building : 7·2 seconds

(Laughs). Her man is a mason.

Habits   man has good . . . and bad habits : 4 seconds

Again thinks of her story. Again *man* and a cover sentence in
the most generalized form.

Stupid   that is the insane man, some one who is not quite right in
             the head (*ego reference*) : 4·6 seconds

Despise   the proud man does so : 2·4 seconds

Explains : " My relatives ; perhaps my man."

Tooth   that is man's (3·8 seconds) help . . . for eating, at least not to control oneself

Patient had the habit of biting something when defending herself in altercation with her husband.

Right   the honourable man is : 4 seconds

A very forced complex reaction.

People   there are many kinds—Italians, Germans, Swiss—oh, many kinds of people : 4·2 seconds

Patient immediately said, " I would like to see how it finishes between Franz and myself.

Book   library book, novels are also books, also *book-keeping* : 3 seconds

(The eight hundred francs.)

Separate   separate that . . . : 4 seconds ; a pause of 4·8 seconds. Then, " That hurts me " (begins to cry)

Hunger   one must often suffer that (2·2 seconds) . . . animals sometimes also

The latter sentence in High German—a phrase to complete the cover reaction because the patient always reacts in dialect ; cp. the complaint in her husband's letter that he has to work for the family whilst his wife is so careless of the money.

White   is snow (2·2 seconds) and white clothes . . . linen

(Laughs, and then suddenly cries.)   " I thought of burial clothes." The laughter at the beginning is to be regarded as an expression of affect inadequate to the occasion.

Cloudy   that is . . . (2 seconds) water often is. (After a further 5 seconds) Sometimes one is, first occurred to me

Dear   my man is that   : 3·2 seconds (spoken very softly)

Quarrel   when two persons quarrel : 3·2   „

Patient laughs, shrugs her shoulders.

Imbeciles can make answers like this,[1] but the explanation here shows it to be a cover reaction. The mimetic play favours this view ; the reaction is probably evoked by the idea of the present relations between the patient and her husband.

The same holds good of the following reaction :

Family   that is when there are a couple together and they have children : 5·2 seconds

Patient thinks of her family.

Stranger   the wanderer is a stranger : 3 seconds

Patient thought of herself. She again reacted in High German instead of the usual dialect. To the stimulus-word *happiness* there was no verbal reaction (fault), but after about 15 seconds she began to cry. At the stimulus-word immediately following,

---

[1] See Wehrlin, chapter iii.

tell, the patient was still unable to control her crying, but after 30 seconds reacted somewhat more quietly with *to tell stories*.

We have here a clear perseveration ; the reactions that follow do not, however, seem to be influenced by it.

Decency	one should have	: 3·2 seconds
Narrow	a small space is narrow	: 4·2 ,,
Stork	that is . . . (3·2 seconds)—my husband (spoken softly)	

To the stimulus-word *kiss* patient reacted after 3·8 seconds, "That is a question I cannot answer." She sobbed violently and meant she did not know whether her husband will kiss her again. "He will not forgive me ; and I have little happiness." We see here the stimulus-word apprehended as a question, as among the normal uneducated, and as usually among imbeciles.

Song	kind-meaning people have songs: 5 seconds

formed after "Where singing is then all is quiet and still ; for wicked people have no songs at will." Patient thought of herself who had lost her joyousness.

Idle	lazy people are idle : 7·6 seconds

(Refers to herself.) "I do nothing." Her husband had written her he alone must keep the family, he could not count upon her.

References to her husband now become increasingly frequent :

Bear	my man must bear heavy sorrows : 14 seconds
Tired	my man is tired in the evening ; he wrote it also in the letter : 3·4 seconds
Intention	my man perhaps means I did it intentionally : 3·6 seconds
Strong	my man is : 2·2 seconds
Modest	my man is : 1·2 ,,
Mix	people often mix : about 50 seconds

Thinks of her husband being an Italian.

Blood	that is in man (2·6) . . . and in animals

"Thought of mine and my husband's blood."

After her husband's visit the next day the complex reactions somewhat diminish.

Light	(laughs) I am light (= light-minded) : 11 seconds
Wish	I wish that I may be soon home : 3·6 ,,
Love	I love my husband : 2 ,,
Gentle	my man is that : 7·4 ,,
Seek	all seek (6·6 seconds) . . . would most like to seek flowers if I could go home with my man
Good	my husband is that : 3 seconds

A number of reactions refer to another presentation complex, which occurred before her marriage, when she participated in jolly club meetings and dances, e.g. :

Dance	that is done in the dance, with music : 2 seconds	
Play	with music, play music	: 7·6 ,,
Jolly	I'm no longer that	: 3·8 ,,
Drum	the gymnasts use that (2·2 seconds) . . . with whom I used to enjoy myself and act before I got married	

FIFTH CASE

MRS. VERENA D. This is a case of hysterical twilight state which set in when shortly after her husband's death her only child ("Roseli") got ill. I have published it together with the previous case.[1]

During the twilight state there was amnesia for the child's illness. When she learnt that her child was going on well she became clearer in her mind, and after seeing her child again, a cure rapidly set in. Ten years before she had had her first slight twilight state, when late in the night after the birth of her first child her husband came home drunk.

This is another case of pathological affect. Here likewise at least 50 per cent. of the reactions are complex reactions. Four hundred and twenty-eight associations were taken in all. This person also reacted with a pronounced sentence form, which, however, in the first test (128 associations), before her child's visit, began only at the fifty-third reaction to the stimulus-word.

Beat	the mother beats : 2·8 seconds (patient had beaten her child)
Console	children console : 3·4 ,, etc.

The sentence type remains till the end of the test. In the second test the first sentence form occurred at the seventh reaction :

Father	the child obeys her father : 3·4 seconds

Then a few reactions in one word came in between ; finally after reaction 21, which ran :

Copy-book	school-children use copy-books : 3 seconds

The reactions are almost all sentences ; many are cover sentences, others extremely subjective, dependent upon the " complex." On the whole, however, these sentences are much more school-like and childish than in the last patient. It also seemed as if the imitation of apparently clumsy school sentences was a " symptomatic action." The reactions with *child* and *pupil* refer to her sick child " Roseli." The first fifty-two reactions, not in sentence form, are of a very superficial type, and all belong to the group of the verbal-motor form (chapter ii). The reaction-time does not, as a rule, exceed the probable mean (chapter v), ·4 seconds.

[1] See foot-note, p. 333.

Sunday	Monday	: 1 sec.	Hair	hairpin	: 2·4 sec.
Father	land	: 1·2 ,,	School	school-house	: 2·2 ,,
Table	cloth	: 1·8 ,,	Window	pane	: 0·8 ,,

A few have a prolonged reaction-time ; some of these are connected with the idea " school " or " pupil."

| Copy-book | copy-books : 17·6 sec. | Asylum | educational asylum | : 3·2 sec. |
| Sing | sing late : 6·4 ,, | Play | evening play : 4·4 ,, |

The last refers to an arrangement made by the school in which her child took part. A delayed reaction-time occurred in *begging—go*, 6·8 seconds ; it clearly arises from an idea which worried the patient very much—the worry and struggle for existence after her husband's death.

Reactions in sentence form :

Console	children console	: 3·4 seconds
Child	children play : 6·4 seconds (thought : " you, my child ")
Friendly	children are friendly	: 3 seconds (my child)
Thank	the child thanks her mother	: 2·6 ,,
Send	the mother sends her child	: 4·6 ,,
Well-behaved	children should be well-behaved	: 3·6 ,,
Youth	a child plays in his youth	: 5·6 ,,
Take care	children take care at school	: 3·2 ,,
Arithmetic	children do arithmetic at school	: 2·4 ,,
Indulge	the mother indulges her child	: 5·2 ,,
Kiss	the mother kisses her child	: 2·6 ,,
Play	the children go to evening play	
Walk	the children go for a walk	: 3·6 ,,

In the first test of 128 reactions we find 13, i.e. 10 per cent., of the sentences with the word *child*. We never find such frequency among normals. Nearly all these reactions have delayed reaction-times.

From the second test (after her child's visit) :

Father	the child obeys her father	: 3·4 seconds	
School	children go to school	: 1·6 ,,	
Play	the children play	: 1·8 ,,	
Stubborn	children are stubborn	: 1·8 ,,	
Child	the child is good	: 3·4 ,,	
Amiable	children should be amiable	: 1·4 ,,	
Thank	children should give thanks	: 2·2 ,,	
Send	the child is sent by mother	: 6 ,,	
Naughty	the children are rather naughty	: 4·8 ,,	(" Roseli," adds the patient)
Threaten	the father threatens the boy	: 2 ,,	(laughs)
Manners	the children should learn manners	: 1·8 ,,	(see above)
Joke	children like to joke	: 3 ,,	
Small	the child is small	: 1·8 ,,	
Love	the mother loves her child	: 2·6 ,,	
Fruit	children like fruit	: 1·4 ,,	
Run	the child learns to run	: 4·4 ,,	

Out of 200 reactions in the second test there are 20 sentences with the word *child*—again 10 per cent. In those places in the first test where the sentences contained *child*, it usually occurred again in the second test ; but the reaction-times in the second test tended to become shorter.

Nowhere is it more clearly seen than here that this kind of complex reaction must be placed among Freud's symptomatic actions.

In the third test five days later we find a similar relationship, almost all the reactions were sentences, and among them 9 per cent. had *child*.

The word *schoolboy* plays a similar part ; it stands for *child* and *Roseli*.

In the first test—

Schoolboy	schoolgirl : 3·2 seconds

Then we find :

Song	school-children sing songs : 4 seconds

In the second test—

Schoolboy	school . . . slate	: 4	seconds
Copy-book	school-children use copy-books	: 3	,,
Book	school-children use books	: 3·8	,,
Pay attention	school-children pay attention	: 2	,, (cp. above :
	children pay attention at school)		
Song	(as in first test) : 2·6 seconds		

In the third test—

Praise	the teacher praises the school-child	: 2·4 seconds
Favour	the schoolboy tries to get the	
	master's favour	: 13·4 ,,
Forget	the schoolboy forgets his lessons	: 4 ,,

With the same chain of thought we have :

Correct	the lesson must be done correctly	: 6·2 seconds

Her husband often helped Roseli with her preparation.)

Sentences to *schoolboy* are not as frequent as those to *child*, but belong to the same group of symptom reactions. I must refer to what was said in chapter ii about repetitions. It is a question of complex action. To the same category belongs a series of sentences in pedagogic form :

Manners	children should have good manners	
Thank	children should give thanks	
Justice	we should always bestow justice	: 17·4 seconds
Self	we should help our neighbours	: 4·4 ,,
Proud	we should not be proud	: 5 ,,
Clean	we should be clean	: 4·4 ,,
Behave	we should be well behaved	: 9·2 ,,
Prudent	we should be prudent	: 4·4 ,,
Modest	we should be modest	: 2 ,,

Her way of falling into the child's kind of associations recalls the phenomena of pathological dreamy states as described by Pick among hysterics.

Symptomatic is the frequent emerging of the word *Rose*, conditioned by the image of her child (*Rosa*, *Ros-eli*).

In the first test the patient reacts

Some people like to gossip (klatschen) : 8·4 seconds

This is a cover reaction and refers to a naughty act which she had to forbid her child.

I. *Test* :	(Klatschen) Gossip	klatsch-rose (corn-poppy)	: 5·2 seconds
II. „	Dark red	a dark red rose	: 2 „
III. „	Smell	the rose smells nice	: 1·4 „
	Yellow	a yellow rose	: 4·8 „

We find a mass of associations which refer to her child, to her husband and his agreeable and especially his disagreeable characteristics (drunkard !), his death, the family life, care about the future. Among these we find the best examples of sentences which are actually *cover reactions*. Perhaps it is proper to distinguish between the common *symptom* reaction and the peculiar cover reaction ; both are complex phenomena. The reactions with *child*, *schoolboy*, and especially the school sentences framed like a child's, are partly only simple symptom reactions (e.g. *yellow — rose*). One gets the impression that instead of a customary reaction (*yellow — green*, *yellow — colour*) there occurs a reaction dictated by the preference of the complex. In the cover reactions, on the other hand, we get the slurring over of a disagreeable fact, of a reminiscence emotionally toned, by an apparently innocent reaction, by some seemingly indifferent sentence universally valid. As I tried to show before, these cover reactions are by-associations of a complex which arise when the stimulus-word directly encounters the complex ; the complex is then under repression, under the dissociation of what is incompatible with consciousness. Varying with the degree of repression, of the dissociation of the complex, it becomes possible to inquire of the subject as to the motive for the origin of the cover reaction and to bring the repressed complex into consciousness.

In the higher grades of repression (hysteria) the significance of the reaction is inexplicable to the subject herself ; the dissociation is then too strong. Hypnosis, or Freud's method of Free Association, then often discovers the explanation. All degrees of normal concealment and hesitation (delayed reaction-time from ejaculation to complete repression, and dissociation of consciousness (amnesia) occur objectively ; it makes no difference whether the mechanism occurs in the conscious or the unconscious

When necessary the explanation is given in the following instances :

I. *Test :* Come   to me (spoken softly) : 12·8 sec. (thought of Roseli)
         Year   yes, I'm coming   : 15·8 ,,   (thought :   I'm
                      going home to my child)

These were two successive reactions in our schedule. With the first there was a mimetic reaction (spoken softly) ; in the second a perseveration of the emotional tone ; in both a marked adaptation of the complex to the stimulus-word.

I. *Test :* Heart   thou my heart : 22·4 seconds
II.   ,,   Bird   the bird   : 5·6   ,,

The reactions were successive. The second reaction, a repetition of the stimulus-word, is, as mentioned in earlier chapters, a phenomenon of perseveration where the attention is riveted to the previous reaction.

II. *Test :* Heart   (fault). After 40 seconds, explanation : " I thought
                    of papa "
I.   ,,   The words are successive
       Rich   there are many rich people : 3 seconds
       Leap   out of my reach

Patient was asked what was the second stimulus-word : answer, *reach.* We here see an assimilation by the apprehension of the second stimulus-word (*reach — rich*) to the awakened complex, which perseverates so that the patient has not taken in the stimulus-word. Economic worry is the complex here (since her husband's death), as expressed in numerous other reactions. We find this phenomenon of the assimilation of the stimulus-word, of which indications are found among normals, very strongly marked in hysteria.

I. *Test :* Sunday   I like Sunday : 2·4 seconds (is expecting her child's
                    visit on Sunday)
II.   ,,   Inn   one gets alcoholic drinks at an inn : 7·4 seconds

(A cover reaction. Hates all inns because her husband used to drink. Much delayed reaction-time.)

I & II. *Test :* Family   family happiness   : 4·8 seconds

Explains : " It was so nice whilst papa was alive."

I. *Test :* Sorrow   cares make sorrow   : 5·6 seconds
II.   ,,   Sorrow   one has some sorrow   : 6   ,,

Explains : " When papa was away."   (Cover reaction.)

I. *Test :* Hunger   the poor are hungry   : 10   seconds
II. ,,   Hunger   poor people are hungry : 7·4   ,,

Explains (superficially) : " They often came to the house and asked for food." The delayed reaction-time refers rather at her own economic troubles.

| I. *Test :* | Bad | the apple is rather bad | : | 12·6 seconds |
| II. „ | Bad | there are bad people | : | 15·4 „ |

Explains : " or bad things like vegetables," etc. " Oh, my husband promised me he would get home earlier " (and did not keep it). (Cover reaction.)

| I. *Test :* | Rich | riches are not everything | : | 15 seconds |
| II. „ | Rich | there are many rich people | : | 3·8 „ |

(Cover reaction, economic troubles.)

| I. *Test :* | Quarrel | nasty people like to quarrel | : | 4·2 seconds |
| II. „ | Quarrel | people quarrel at times | : | 8·2 „ |

Explains : " with her husband on account of his drinking."

I. *Test :*	Beat	the smith hits	: 2·8 seconds
II. „	Beat	naughty children hit one another : 6 seconds ;
		" at first I think one beats the tree "

" Children hit one another." " Roseli is so wild " (omitted). " I once hit Roseli when we had visitors."

I. *Test :*	Three	the tree is high : 4·6 seconds (stimulus-word mis-
		understood)
II. „	Three	(fault ; after 20 seconds still no reaction)

" Three is an odd number." (Why so long before reacting ?) " I had first to make sure that it was odd." Then : " We were three—papa, Roseli, and myself."

| I. *Test :* | Thirst | water | : 7·2 seconds |
| II. „ | Thirst | we are rather thirsty | : 7·4 „ |

Explains : " One drinks when thirsty." Then : " Papa used to be thirsty." (Thinks of her own illness of ten years before.)

We note the successive explanations, which at first are to conceal the explanation and are resistances to the repressed idea ; it is the same resistance with which we meet in Freud's psycho-analysis.

I & II. *Tests :* Separate	death separates us : 8 seconds ; and 8·6 seconds,
	thinks of her husband's death
I & II. „ Ill	I am ill : 5·6 seconds and 4 seconds

" Thought of Roseli, but she's all right." We see here the repression which during and directly after the twilight state had led to a full amnesia emotionally grounded for the illness of her child.

| II. *Test :* Faithful | servants should be faithful : 8 seconds |

Explains : " The wife should be faithful to her husband." Then " I feared when my husband was away so long that he was unfaithful to me." It should be mentioned here that in Test II after her child's visit, the complex *husband* occurs much more frequently.

| Wreath | my husband got many wreaths : 7·4 seconds (at the funeral) |
| Elect | the boroughs elect . . . (18·2 seconds) mayor |

("At election times her husband was always in the public-house.")

| Law | a vote is taken about a law : 8·4 seconds |

Explains : " Her husband had to vote." Then : " He then came home, but he was drunk."

| Right | we must bestow the right : 17·4 seconds |

Explains : " I was often in the wrong at home."

| Annoying | vermin are annoying (explains : " drinking ") |
| Unjust | (20 seconds no reaction ; then at 25·6 seconds, " The unjust must suffer ") |

In her endeavour to form a sentence according to pattern, patient was unable to produce anything. Explains : " I had to suffer much injustice. He believed that I was unkind to him when I warned him against drinking."

| Misery | the poor are in misery : 5·8 seconds (her economic position) |
| Suppose | one rather supposes : 6·6   ,, |

Explains : " When Roseli had a headache I thought she was going to die."

| Much | I go walking a lot : 18·2 seconds (she was in the park yesterday, looked down into the town and had home-sickness) |

To give an impression of the whole, I append a series of reactions from the first test without further remarks. The beginning of the sentence type is nicely seen at the stimulus-word *beat*.

Frog	leg	:	1·4 seconds
Flower	flower-pot	:	1·6 ,,
Cherry	cherry-tree	:	1·6 ,,
Asylum	educational asylum	:	3·2 ,,
Warder	asylum warder	:	3·6 ,,
Piano	piano-stool	:	1·6 ,,
Fern	ferns	:	7·2 ,,
Oven	door	:	1·6 ,,
Walk	go for a walk	:	1·6 ,,
Cook	cookery book	:	1·8 ,,
Water	water-bottle	:	1·4 ,,
Dance	dancing floor	:	2 ,,
Cat	cat's paw	:	12 ,,
Begging	to go	:	6·8 ,,
Dark	darkness	:	1·2 ,,
Heart	you, my heart	:	2·8 ,,
Swim	swimming-bath	:	about 3·8 seconds
White	white bread	:	1·6 seconds
Play	play evening	:	4·4 ,,
13	Number 13	:	2·4 ,,

Emperor	empire	: 2	seconds
Moon	half-moon	: 2·4	,,
Beat	the smith beats	: 2·8	,,
Console	the children console	: 3·8	,,
A fire	the house is on fire	: 2·4	,,
Star	the star is beautiful	: 2·4	,,
Stroke	the cat is stroked	: 4	,,
Wonderful	natural events are wonderful	: 4	,,
Child	children play	: 6·4	,,
Dark red	the mouth—blood is dark red	: 4·6	,,
Ride	the rider rides	: 7·4	,,
Sweet	sugar tastes sweet	: 5·6	,,
Friendly	children are friendly	: 3	,,
Bread	the bread is cut	: 2·2	,,
Bronze	in mines there is bronze	: 3·6	,,
Crown	the Crown Hotel	: 5·4	,,
Thirst	water	: 7·2	,,
Greenish	leaves are greenish	: 2·8	,,
Thank	the child thanks her mother	: 2·6	,,
Raw	potatoes are raw	: 1	,,
Stinks	rotten meat stinks	: 6·2	,,
Bright	the colours are bright	: 3·8	,,
Sends	the mother sends the child	: 4·6	,,
Seven	seven o'clock	: 12·2	,,
Prison	the thief is in prison	: 6·2	,,
Separate	we are separated from the dead	: 8	,,
Ill	I am ill	: 5·6	,,
Song	pupils sing songs	: 4	,,
Potatoes	one eats potatoes	: 2·2	,,
Sacrifice	the ancients made sacrifices	: 5·6	,,
Wedding	people enjoy a wedding	: 7	,,
Now	I am going home	: 4·8	,,
Angry	the dog is rather angry	: 5·4	,,
Soldier	the soldier obeys the rules	: 3	,,
Gossip	many people like to gossip	: 8·4	,,
Come	to me (spoken softly)	: 12·8	,,
Year	Yes, I'm coming	: 15·0	,,
Above	the stars are above	: 4·4	,,
Long	the old woman goes slowly	: 10·4	,, (mother)
Behave	children should be well behaved	: 2·6	,,
Rich	there are many rich people	: 6	,,
Sour	the apple tastes sour	: 2·8	,,
Suffer	one offers the hand	: 6·8	,,
	(*stimulus-word heard as " offer* ")		
Suffer	the sick must suffer	: 5·2	,,
Eye	the eye is beautiful	: 4·4	,,
Doctor	the doctor prescribes medicine	: 4·6	,,
Sunday	I enjoy Sunday	: 2·4	,, (visit)
Youth	the child plays in his youth	: 5·6	,,
Indulge	the mother indulges the child	: 5·2	,,
Inn	alcoholic liquors are drunk in the inn	: 7·4	,,
Stupid	the donkey is stupid	: 13·2	,,
Family	family fortune	: 4·8	,,
Trouble	sorrow produces trouble	: 5·6	,,

Pay attention	the children pay attention at school:	3·2 seconds
Fist	the angry man clenches his fist	: 10·6 ,,
End	everything comes to an end	: 6·4 ,,
Hunger	the poor are hungry	: 10 ,,

SIXTH CASE

BERTHA SCH. This patient, 28 years of age, has suffered for the last three years from hystero-epileptic attacks; her sister has suffered likewise for the last seven years. Before her marriage patient had sexual connexion for about a year with her present husband, a drunkard. When a neighbour in a dispute accused her of this she got a brief aphonia—" The words stuck in her mouth." She had her first attack when the marriage was definitely settled. She would rather not have married the drunkard, but dared not go back. During the attack gestures of repugnance and abhorrence played an important rôle. The marriage was unhappy; the patient separated from her brutal husband and went back with her rather delicate and nervous child to her family. Her husband frequently annoyed her again. Owing to these causes attacks took place from time to time. After hypnotic treatment the woman remained for six months without any attack and was vigorous and able to work. After having been again waylaid by her husband some isolated attacks took place after violent scenes.

In the associations we find at least 35 per cent. that certainly belong to the hysterogenic complex—husband, unhappy marriage and its consequences; poverty, hard work, worry about the child. The patient is one of those persons who react, on the average, pretty quickly, and not in sentence-form; with them the accent is on the more or less abrupt, long prolongations of the reaction-time and on the faults. In the latter the stimulus-word strikes the complex and no verbal reaction follows at all. In this case, as in many cases of hysteria, the patient is quite unable to say why she cannot answer, whilst in hypnosis she gives a correct answer. In many normals no verbal reaction is produced in quite analogous places; we register a fault, and finally we can, in the waking state, get information as to the correct grounds of the fault. There are " faults " of different intensity. In both cases we have a fault, due to the " complex." The mechanism of its occurrence, whether conscious or unconscious, is the same, only the degree of dissociation of the complex is much stronger in the first case; the complex is removed from consciousness.

Examples :

Journey — (fault). Cannot give the reason for the fault. In hypnosis : " Honeymoon journey."

Proud — (fault). Subsequently *bag*. In hypnosis : " Purse-proud," thinking of her brother's wife with whom she is now living.

Strange — (fault). No reason found in waking state. In hypnosis : " After the separation I wanted at first to go to some strangers, not to my brother's wife, but finally I did so." She complains, however, that she has to eat humble-pie there.

Mix — (fault). Cannot state the reason. In hypnosis : " Sexual connexion with her husband." The stimulus-word *mix* is often taken in this sense (cp. the stimulus-words *mix* and *blood* in Case 4—Mrs. M. C.).

Forget — (fault). In hypnosis : " Misery, my husband." Her husband worries her all the time.

(*Gleich*) *similar* — (fault). Laughs ; she cannot explain why nothing occurs to her, that she cannot say anything. In hypnosis with a great deal of resistance she thought of a *part of the body*. (The dialect word *gleich* is a slang word for limb or penis.) Her husband is again persecuting her, wishing to renew sexual life.

Stalk — (fault). In the waking state patient cannot give the meaning of the fault. In hypnosis she states that her husband is a " withered stalk." Is that the final explanation ? We have seen that in many cases *stalk* arouses the presentation of penis and causes a long reaction-time. Our case is to some extent an answer to the question how far complex reactions influence the succeeding indifferent associations (cp. chapter iv).

The series

Disesteem	esteem :	1·6 seconds	Folk	right :	19·6 seconds
Tooth	mouth :	3·6 „	Stink	smell :	1·4 „
Just	unjust :	7·2 „			

shows a gradual increase of the reaction-times up to *folk — right*. The next reaction is short and seems to be independent of the previous ones. It could not be definitely proved whether the first ones are independent of one another.

In

Just	unjust :	7·2 seconds	Folk	right : 19·6 seconds

that is certainly not so ; the first influences the second ; we have a kind of perseveration.

In

Just	unjust : 7·2 seconds

we get the explanation in hypnosis, latterly her husband is again pursuing her ; that is *unjust*.

Folk (*Volk*) right (*recht*)

is a form of perseveration to *unjust* ; perhaps there is a slang association to *Volkrecht*, the title of a newspaper which circulates among the patient's friends and neighbours. Hypnosis shows she was thinking about her husband. We find, moreover, in the associations the following :

Unjust	treatment : 7 seconds	Frog	toad : 9 seconds

Both associations refer to her husband. The first obviously, as was confirmed in hypnosis ; to the second the hypnotized patient said *frog* gave her a feeling of nausea ; immediately adding, " so does my husband." We find a similar after-effect in the reactions

| White | black : 3·6 seconds | Ring | finger : 6·8 seconds |

Her husband's name is Black, hence the delayed time. To *ring*, the immediate association was *wedding-ring*.

A few other typical complex reactions require notice. There is a complex *child*, which means an increase of the attacks. The patient complains that she can no longer sleep or rest ; since her separation she must keep herself and look after her restless child.

Angel	child	: 5	seconds
Quiet	noise	: 2·4	„ (refers to the child)
Sleep	get up	: 3·4	„ „ „
Tired	courage	: 3·2	„ „ „
Modest	child	: 8·8	„
Wake	child	—	
Bed	sleep	: 1·4	„

The reaction *sleep* is frequently repeated. She generally uses such repetitions when there is a complex, in this case about the child.

| Separate | come | : 1·6 seconds | Certain | come : 9·2 seconds |
| Meet | come | : 1 | „ | |

A repetition of the reaction referring to the last invitations and plottings of her husband. To a reaction *wild — hunter*, 12·2 seconds, patient explains that her brother is a hunter. Then : " I thought of myself ; I'm often wild (with rage) ; my husband often came home wild."

SEVENTH CASE

JULIUS SCHW., a clerk, 23 years. Many tests were tried with this patient ; on twenty-third, first, seventh, eleventh, fourteenth ; eleven without time-measurements, on fifteenth with time-measurements ; six hundred and ninety associations altogether. The patient had perpetrated eleven arsons within six weeks in a hysterical twilight state with amnesia and under the influence of drink.

We will limit ourselves to repeating peculiar manifestations of perseverations which were strongly marked in this case.

From the first test—

Light	fire
Star	red (thought of fire)
Strike	a match

This short series shows a peculiar form of perseveration of the content in three successive reactions. In the reaction

| Strike | a match |

it comes out very clearly. That this phenomenon of perseveration began at the stimulus-word *light* explains itself.

In the second test we meet this phenomenon more and more ; stimulus-words set up far-reaching series of presentations, the *stimulus-word being forgotten.*　We find a beginning in the following places :

Head	red
Ink	black
Needle	pointed
Bread	bath　"What was the stimulus-word ? "　" Ink "—a little later
Mountain	book
Hair	beard　(" Stimulus-word ? "　Pat bare)
Salt	water　(" Stimulus-word ? "　Old ; or was it Old salt ?)
Dream	foam
Copy-book	skittle　(" Stimulus-word ? "　Patient, dazed and laughing, says : " Here's copy-book "—laughing more and more obviously in hallucination)

After a while he points with astonishment to the examiner and says, " I thought I saw some one else ; I have—played skittles somewhere in W——, surely ? " The patient suddenly thinks the examiner has given another stimulus-word.　This dream state was certainly set up by the stimulus-word *dream.*　The patient is frequently concerned with a dream of playing skittles in W—— ; what is connected with this could not, unfortunately, be found out.

The ten reactions that followed had nothing noteworthy ; the patient seemed clear-headed.　Then the following series came (the vertical lines denote the length of the perseveration) :

Window	fowl
Frog	dog
Flower ⌐	good.　(Patient gets a staring look, gradually increasing, but still reacts regularly)
Cherry │	sun (long reaction-time)
Asylum │	star
Warder —	flower (long reaction-time)
Piano ⌐	music (beats with the hand upon the table as if lost in thought)
Fern │	Mignon
Stove │	mirror
Walk │	orange
Cook │	lemon (the head sinking more and more upon the table)
Water │	Mozart　(long reaction-time)
Dance │	Philine　　"　　　"
Cat │	Laertes　　"　　　"
Dozen └	—　(no answer.　" What word did I say ? "　" Italian ")
Dark	light　(Patient awakes)
Heart	hand
Bird ⌐	air
Swim └	fly (perseveration)
White	blue, etc.

It then occurs to the patient himself that he is always falling asleep ; he often "dreams" in the same way, calling up melodies.

In the second test similar phenomena occur :

Wonderful	┬ beautiful
Child	blue
Dark red	fire
Sweet	cry
Ride	┴ jump

Shortly after—

Crown	trumpeter
You	room (does not know stimulus-word or reaction immediately afterwards)
Greenish	red
Against	again
Raw	┬ brilliance
Smell	fortune
Bright	Count
Sweet	Duke
Love	veranda
Prison	carpet
Separate	Walberg (Walpurg ?)
Ill	┴— orchestra

We see that states arise set up by certain stimulus-words, when the stimulus-words are not followed by any reaction that make sense, but serve as sparks for a reaction. The reactions that follow correspond to a circle of ideas aroused by the first stimulus-word, remaining active for some time. Careful examination of the patient at such moments shows him to be in temporary twilight states which are produced by the particular stimulus-word. A definite circle of ideas is aroused ; the patient forms it while subject to complete hallucination, ignores the sense-presentations, is untroubled about his surroundings, and lives in a quite other *milieu*. (Passion for fire, skittles, a bit out of *Mignon* at the play.) On the particular day when the above tests were given the patient was much inclined towards twilight states ; but in the other tests much the same thing occurred. The tendency to twilight states was very common, and was so far under control that it was usually determined by some affect— a visit from his parents, moving books, and especially sentimental love scenes in performances given at the asylum, and "lyrical" music.

In the series of perseverations there is some strong emotional situation. Emotions are often the cause of perseveration in association experiments (where it is not a distraction of attention). Attention is concentrated for some time on the critical presentation ; hence the subsequent reactions come up shorn of attention, then the phenomenon of distraction occurs. In well-pronounced cases this expresses itself by no reaction occurring to the stimulus-words, but only to the content of the previous critical reaction. It is in this wise that we are to understand the occurrence of the perseverating series.[1] The situation aroused by the critical stimulus-word is so emotionally powerful that it completely chains the interest, so that the patient quite loses consciousness of his surroundings ; he passes into a twilight state (Pick's dreamy state). These examples are of theoretical interest because they show how the common complex perseverations are only separated by degree from the hysterical twilight state.

EIGHTH CASE

BETTY SL. This patient, 19 years old, was an illegitimate child brought up by a foster-mother. Her own mother later married somebody else. At the age of fourteen Betty returned to her mother, but was soon badly treated. She was driven, after all kinds of dissensions, to take a place as servant in the same town.

After taking the situation she once unexpectedly met her mother, who looked at her with hatred and scorn. The patient staggered home and had her first hysterical attack. The content of the attack corresponded to this origin. The patient had a hallucination—her mother's face with its expression of hate and scorn. The last attacks occurred when the patient got news from home.

The associations were taken in French. There are markedly long reaction-times.[2]

Récalcitrant	aimable	: 8	seconds
Malade	convalescent	: 7·8	,, (refers to herself)
Menacer	caresser	: 6	,,
Mépriser	agréer	: 6	,,

Peculiarly remarkable in this case is the frequent distraction from the surroundings, which we have already met with in a more rudimentary form in the associations of normal persons. It is a complex indicator. The correct reaction is blocked ; as a cover reaction some external perception is taken, some object in the room or something similar. We find the same phenomenon in the associations during states of *emotional paralysis*[3] (examination paralysis), showing manifestations similar to affective complexes. In this state faults, repetition of the stimulus-word, etc., occur also. In the case under consideration there are peculiar relationships between the emotional stupidity which expressed itself at the beginning of the experiment, chiefly in her distraction

[1] Cp. Stransky, *Ueber Sprachverwirrtheit*, 1905.

[2] The associations have been left in the original French.—TRANSLATOR.

[3] Jung, " Ueber Simulation von Geistesstörung," *Journal für Psych. u. Neur.*, Bd. II, 1903.

to her surroundings, and the complex to which the associations with the delayed reaction-times belong.

Tête	rue (looking through the window)			
Vert	lampe (in the room)			
Eau	feu	: 2	seconds	
Piquer	encrier	: 1·2	,,	(in room)
Ange	fenêtre	: 1·4	,,	,, ,,
Long	lunette	: 1·2	,,	(on the table)
Bateau	arbre	: 2·2	,,	(through windows)
Labourer	feuille	: 3	,,	(looking at a tree)
Laine	pierre	: 3·4	,,	(outside)
Aimable	méchant	: 1·8	,,	(gives place to laughter; this is an instance of appropriate emotion, to which attention was called in Case 1)
Table	cuiller	: 3·4	,,	(Is the delayed reaction-time an aftermath of the previous complex reaction ?)
Porter	tableau	: 1·4	,,	(in room)
État	volet	: 2·2	,,	(through window)
Récalcitrant	aimable	: 8	,,	
Danser	boire	: 3·2	,,	
Tige	loup	: 2	,,	(Patient can give no explanation at all of these " meaningless " reactions)
Lac	rivière	: 1·2	,,	
Malade	convalescent	: 7·8	,,	(reference to her condition)
Orgueil	simplicité	: 1·6	,,	
Cuire	bruler	: 4·8	,,	
Encre	plume	: 1·6	,,	
Méchant	sage	: 2·4	,,	
Aiguille	fil	: 2·6	,,	
Nager	noyer	: 2	,,	
Voyage	repos	: 7·2	,,	(Journey from her home in Switzerland, away from her mother)
Menacer	caresser	: 6·9	,,	(complex)
Lampe	chapeau	: 2·2	,,	(chapeau de lampe)
Riche	pauvre	: 0·8	,,	
Arbre	branche	: 4·8	,,	
Chanter	pleurer	: 1·6	,,	etc.

The distraction to the surroundings (the corresponding reactions are in italics) as shown at the beginning is an expression of the slight emotional stupidity present in this reserved, somewhat frightened girl. We see that these reactions, with the exception of the superficial reaction *eau — feu*, are only interrupted when complex reactions occur, and that they quite disappear after the second complex reaction :

Récalcitrant   aimable : 8 seconds

In the fifth case (Verena D.) it was a complex which set up the continuous reaction in sentence form ; here the complex breaks down the reactions due to emotional stupidity. We found a similar phenomenon, the liberation, by a definite word, of an almost unbroken series of complex reactions, in the associations of normal persons (Subject No. 7, Educated Men). Emotional stupidity is also seen in the associations of many imbeciles and epileptics. In some cases of hysteria it persists during nearly the entire experiment. These often present a picture similar to certain pictures obtained from persons in a twilight state. In later experiments carried out with the same person it may quite disappear.

SUMMARY

In the forefront of the hysterical type of reaction we find more or less independent and active presentation complexes with much affect, whose expansion seems to be much more powerful than among normals. The reactions are frequently interrupted by complex disturbances. Together with the usual complex indicators, we occasionally find some with *amnestic manifestations* and *phenomena of consciousness*. The critical stimulus-word is often forgotten and in its place the previous one is named.

The cause of the fault is unknown to the subject ; the " distraction to the surroundings " and the misunderstanding of the stimulus-word are other complex indicators. A further large group of complex indicators is formed by reactions which do not denote the complex by the stimulus-word, but are only associated in the remotest way with the word denoting the complex. This arises in one of two ways : either the complex excited by the stimulus-word is repressed and the reaction is superficially associated with the complex, being so apprehended as not to betray the complex but to call up instead a seemingly indifferent reaction. Take as examples the cover reactions in Cases 4 and 5 (Mrs. M. C. and Verena D.).

Mrs. Verena D. reacts :

> Faithful　　　servants should be faithful

Behind this innocent sentence lies the fear about her husband's infidelity. The *replacement of the complex presentation by a seemingly innocent reaction is a symptom of repression.* I interpreted similarly the " conversion symptoms " of Lina H.[1]

The physical conversion symptom is associated to the complex, but is not noticeable to the observer and to the consciousness of the patient, thus guaranteeing the dissociation between

---

[1] *Analyse der Sympt. und Assoz. eines Falles von Hysterie.*

the complex and the conscious. Or the action of the complex is so powerful that its influence reaches out to a distant series of presentations, determining them likewise. (Cp. a number of the reactions in sentence form in Cases 4 and 5.)

Among the complex indicators, distraction to the surroundings and the non-understanding of the complex excitant stimulus-words play a certain rôle. I have adduced numerous instances. The stimulus-word may be assimilated to the complex. (The stimulus-word is apprehended as best suits the complex or as best conceals it.)

Distraction to surroundings often appears when it is a question of an affect-determined distraction in order to avoid the critical stimulus-word. I once had the following experience : A boy of twelve injured his knee one Sunday from a fall. Numerous stitches were required to close the wound. The anæsthesia was very light, so that the boy still reacted at each stitch, although faintly and with amnesia after the operation. In this light narcosis he carried on a conversation, the whole meaning of which was to distract himself from the operation, to repress all thoughts about it. It partly recalled Ganser's answers, partly wish-fulfilment dreams, which have likewise their roots in repression and distraction from a disagreeable complex. He said sponta-neously and loudly : " To-day's Monday ! Then come along, Tony, we're leaving off and going for a game." Then, as if in scorn of the intense pain of the operation, he told a friend what Christmas presents he had got, and so on. Not infre-quently we find this occurring. Jung[1] quotes the case of a woman who during an operation fell into a twilight state where in hallucination she was walking among flowery fields.

The observations in Ganser's twilight states speak partly in favour of these answers and the formation of wish-fulfilment deliria as semi-complex phenomena of a related nature ; partly, however, the observations speak in favour of an unconscious simulation.

The complex can alter the apprehension, remove the stimulus (or stimulus-word), produce hallucinations favouring the repres-sion or wish fulfilment, so that the contrary of that which is the content of the repressed presentation complex occurs.

So far as my observations permit a conclusion, my view already expressed several times in this work has been confirmed, that *the complex with its activities is the all-important matter in hysterical psychology, and that all the hysterical symptoms can be derived therefrom.*

[1] *Occult Phenomena.*

CHAPTER IX

ASSOCIATION, DREAM, AND HYSTERICAL SYMPTOMS

By Dr. C. G. JUNG

I. The Associations

THE object of this investigation is to support and elucidate the views expressed in chapters vii and viii about the nature of the anomalies of association in hysteria. The following is the case :

A young woman, aged 24, intelligent and of average education, physically healthy. Her mother suffers from osteomalacia, which has entirely crippled her; otherwise there is no demonstrable taint. The patient is the youngest child, the only daughter, and has four elder brothers. She was well until school began; was very sensitive at school, but made good progress. In her second year tremors of the right arm set in, which soon made writing impossible; the tremors became generalized, till finally a hysterical chorea occurred. The patient became the starting-point of a small school epidemic of St. Vitus's dance. The chorea expressed itself in tic-like attacks which sometimes lasted one to two minutes. In these attacks the patient hit out around her and stamped, occasionally giving vent to a shriek. Consciousness was not disturbed during the attacks. The attacks occurred fifteen to twenty times a day. Menstruation began at the age of fifteen. With the occurrence of the first period the choreiform attacks ceased as by magic. (The patient had two years before consulted a specialist, who said that the attacks would leave off with the periods.) But in the same week the patient experienced one day, towards evening, a dull feeling in her head. The feeling gradually took on the character of heat, which became far worse during the periods. The pain increased as the years went on. From about ten o'clock in the morning these hot feelings increased regularly and gradually until they became " insupportable." For the last three years the pain had been so bad that she was completely prostrated by these hot feelings in the head lasting nearly all day long. Innumerable treatments with all kinds of methods had been unavailingly tried. Sometimes the patient could assist a little with the housework in the morning. From ten o'clock onwards she went about doing nothing, continually complaining about her head. She became gradually misanthropic and withdrew altogether from society. During the summer, on hot days, she remained in the cellar. During the winter she would not be in any heated room. She consulted me in the summer of 1905, when she was getting rapidly worse. She felt she was going out of her mind, and had hallucinations of white and black figures. She begged to be admitted to the local asylum. In the autumn of 1905 she was admitted.

Condition.—Well nourished, slender person ; her appearance of suffering seemed to be directed towards obtaining pity ; entire absence of energy in her

354

behaviour, this is indicated by her extremely fine, frail handwriting. Constant complaints about feelings of heat in her head. The tone of the complaint is pronouncedly elegiacal. She describes her feelings in the following way: " The whole head is stopped from the neck up and quite hot; I have at least forty degrees of fever in my head—it is quite tense, choking. My neck is strangled, hot, dry, withered up. The feeling of dry heat and warmth is most terrible at the back of my neck, the top part. It's always worse after eating. My body is quite cold and my hands blue-black; my feet are like ice. My idea is that if I could but once have a great bleeding of my nose I would be much better. I am always imagining that I am *bleeding* from the *nose and mouth*, a basinful; I am always imagining *big clots of fresh blood. I am always dreaming of blood.* I often dream that I am wading in blood, that the room is full of blood, or that *blood is spurting out of my nose, mouth, eyes, and ears.* I likewise often dream of *fire;* everything is then in *flames.*"

On going to sleep she often has the vision of a black man stretching out his black hand towards her and seizing her arm; occasionally she also sees indistinct white figures of women.

Her *periods have stopped* since February 1905; she is very constipated; *meteorism,* noticeably distending the lower part of the abdomen, has been present for several months. She has great *resistance to sitting down ;* generally stands up or walks up and down the room. *Great repugnance to meat ;* avoids everything which makes heat. If she but hears the steam ascending in the heater her bad condition increases. She indulges in *cold ablutions* every day and does gymnastics in her room, attaching great importance to these activities. This is in strange contrast with her repugnance to and fear of any continuous work, which she believes is very injurious to her. She has a *morbid love of order and cleanliness* (she states that formerly she had for a time an obsession to touch things, which showed itself in an impulse, whilst walking about the room, to touch any objects). She has no insight into the mental nature of her pain but is firmly convinced that there is an organic change in her head; but she laughs involuntarily when telling us that one of her doctors took it to be a case of Basedow's disease. Naturally she has no more idea what was the cause of her illness than have the doctors who have hitherto treated her.

There can be no question but that this is a case of hysteria. The extraordinary chronic nature of the case and the absence of any change in the chief symptoms, rather unusual in hysteria, speak in favour of a profound paralysis of energy and complete subjugation of the personality to the disease complex. She has been ill seventeen years. In considering the peculiarity of the symptoms it must be remembered that the " St. Vitus's dance " (choreiform tic) developed by continuity into the present condition. We cannot accept the view that the " St. Vitus's dance " was healed ; on the contrary, everything is in favour of the view that the effect of the first menstrual period was simply to change it suddenly into another form of the fundamental disease. Her completely childlike and asthenic personality show all the signs of the infantile, Meige-Feindel type of tiqueur.

To make the description of the case quite clear I will first describe the association experiments which were carried out with the patient, who was under treatment in the asylum from

October 1, 1905, till December 21, 1905. The experiments were spread over this period. The treatment had a certain measure of success, which was not without an important influence on the experiment. The tests were at times carried out in a room only moderately warm (13°), for the patient could not permanently bear more than 11° of heat.

THE ASSOCIATION TESTS

FIRST SERIES

July 23, 10 a.m., with the Reproduction Test

Stimulus-word	Time [1]	Reaction	Reproduction
1. Head	6	-ache	
2. Green	33	stone	
3. Water	—	—	
4. Prick	9	bee	
5. *Angel*	105	hotel	—
6. Long	65	knife	—
7. *Ship*	35	steamship	—
8. *Plough*	21	field	garden
9. Wool	75	knit	
10. Friendly	11	-ness	
11. Table	30	cloth	
12. Ask	—	—	
13. State	—	—	
14. Stubborn	40	person	
15. Stalk	11	of flower	
16. Dance	10	dancing floor	
17. Lake	29	of Zurich	
18. Ill	—	—	
19. Proud	19	haughty	
20. To cook	13	cookery school	
21. Ink	9	ink-bottle	
22. Wicked	9	wickedness	
23. Needle	10	pincushion	
24. Swim	45	swimming school	
25. *Travel*	60	travelling rug	—
26. Blue	35	Blue-street	
27. Bread	20	breadless	
28. *Threaten*	60	punishment	punish
29. Lamp	11	lamp-shade	
30. Rich	21	riches	
31. Tree	23	fruit-tree	
32. Sing	16	choral society	
33. Pity	35	to regret	
34. Yellow	25	yolk of egg	
35. Mountain	23	Utli mountain	
36. Play	16	chess	
37. Salt	12	salt-cellar	

[1] These figures give the time in one-fifth seconds.

Stimulus-word	Time [1]	Reaction	Reproduction
38. New	15	Newbury	
39. Custom	46	propriety	
40. Ride	18	riding school	
41. *Wall*	12	Spanish wall	—
42. Stupid	45	stupidity	—
43. Exercise-book	15	school exercise-book	
44. Despise	—	—	
45. *Tooth*	15	eye-tooth	—
46. *Correct*	25	to arrange	—
47. People	23	people's paper	
48. *Smell*	50	sink	—
49. Book	15	reading book	
50. *Unjust*	—	—	—
51. Frog	25	tree-frog	
52. Separate	32	divorce	
53. Hunger	19	eat	
54. White	18	snow	
55. Cattle	32	herd of cattle	
56. To take care	30	esteem	
57. Pencil	31	pencil-holder	
58. Cloudy	—	—	
59. Plum	66	plum jam	
60. Meet	—	—	
61. Law	—	—	
62. Love	15	loveless	
63. Glass	8	tumbler	
64. *To quarrel*	23	dispute	—
65. Goat	12	goat's milk	
66. Big	15	generous	
67. Potato	20	potato-meal	
68. Paint	21	oil paintings	
69. Part	26	part-payment	
70. Old	49	Oldtown	
71. Flower	51	nosegay	
72. *Strike*	30	stroke with hammer	
73. Basket	21	clothes-basket	
74. Wild	21	wild duck	
75. Family	26	family party	
76. Wash	—	—	
77. Cow	10	cow's milk	
78. Foreign	30	foreign book	
79. Happiness	53	congratulations	
80. To narrate	15	stories	
81. Deportment	55	lesson in deportment	
82. Narrow	—	—	
83. Brother	—	—	
84. Malice	10	malicious joy (*Schadenfreude*)	
85. Stork	26	stork's nest	
86. False	37	falsity	
87. Dread	20	feeling of dread	
88. Kiss	65	sisterly kiss	

[1] These figures give the time in one-fifth seconds.

Stimulus-word	Time [1]	Reaction	Reproduction
89. Fire	28	huge fire	
90. Dirty	—	—	
91. Doors	21	lock of door	
92. Choice	55	choice of comradeship	
93. Hay	19	hay-wagon	
94. Still	39	peace	
95. *Ridicule*	10	ridiculous price, ridiculously cheap	
96. Sleep	17	sleeplessness	
97. Month	15	monthly meeting	
98. Coloured	—	—	
99. Dog	15	dog-faithful	
100. Speak	67	consultation	

This test was made at the consultation. Let us first of all consider the associations from the statistical point of view. I content myself with the classification into inner and outer associations, clang-associations, faults, and indirect associations (see chapter ii). This summary classification suffices for our purpose. These are :

Inner associations	16 per cent.
Outer „	60 „
Clang-reactions	9 „
Faults	14 „
Indirect associations. . . .	1 „
Reproduction anomalies . . .	14 „

The outer associations are the most numerous, predominating in a most unusual degree. The patient is not without intelligence, but she has not been highly educated. (She only went through the elementary schools, and this with many intermissions.) A glance at the reactions shows that the outer associations consist chiefly of verbal-motor connexions, of *word-combinations*. Side by side we find a good many *word-completions* (clang-re-actions). The number of faults is striking. Compare the figures with these :

Average Figures of Educated Women [2]

Inner associations	35 per cent.
Outer „	58 „
Clang-reactions	3·3 „
Faults	1·4 „

and we see that the figures for this patient show a much more superficial mode of association ; they approach the figures of the distraction test.

[1] These figures give the time in one-fifth seconds.
[2] P. 146.

Average of the distraction test with 100 metronome beats per minute :

Educated Women, excluding the Predicate Type

Inner associations	20·8 per cent.
Outer „	62·8 „
Clang-reactions	13·2 „
Faults	0·4 „

One might believe that there had been distraction of attention during the test. The question then arises to what the distraction must be referred or what factor this disturbing influence had upon the attention. There were no external causes, so that we are led to consider some psychological disturbance. We need not seek very far, for the patient is entirely occupied with one thought which extinguishes every kind of interest in her surroundings ; she is absorbed entirely in the *presentation complex of her illness*. Her whole attention is focussed on the symptoms of her illness, so that only a small remainder is left at the disposition of the association test ; hence the superficial reaction type. Her illness makes so great a claim upon her that she scarcely allows the meaning of the stimulus-word to reach her. As a general rule she contents herself simply with apprehending the outer form of the words ; and her intellectual work is limited to finding some ready-made connexion to the stimulus-word. Hence she only listens with " half an ear " and allows the stimulus-words almost to slip off of themselves. She cannot rouse herself to direct her attention to the experiment ; obviously this is far too unimportant to her compared with her disease complex. Her slight degree of self-control sinks from time to time to zero (fault), not infrequently just where some ready-made verbal connexion is not at hand ; this also occurs frequently when the stimulus-word has aroused emotionally toned connotations, as we shall see later. As soon as she noticed that the reaction was not immediately at hand she abstained entirely from enforcing one. We have here an experimental expression of the clinically remarkable abulia, which, as usual, consists in the surrender of the entire interest to the disease complex, the hysterogenic complex which is at the root of her symptoms ; hence nothing remains over for what is going on around. (A similar case of distraction phenomena is referred to on p. 69, where, however, the cause of the disturbance was a quite recent affect).

The probable mean time of this test was 5·2 seconds, a very high figure. We believe that such prolongations rest upon certain emotional inhibitions.

Just as in the case reported in chapter vii, an analysis of the patient was impossible for she was utterly indifferent, and would not enter into any questions which did not refer to her symptoms. The repression or the inhibition arising from the pathogenic complex was obviously too strong at that time.

After the consultation when this test was made the patient returned home, and, as mentioned, her illness rapidly got worse. Three months later she was admitted to the asylum.

Test II

October 5, 5 p.m.

Stimulus-word	Reaction	Time
1. Head	headache	1·6
2. Green	—	—
3. Water	water-carriage	2·8
4. Prick	thorn-apple	2·7
5. Angel	—	—
6. Long	longing	2·2
7. Ship	—	—
8. Plough	—	—
9. Wool	cotton-wool	2·2
10. Friendly	friendliness	3
11. Table	table companion	2·2
12. Ask	note of interrogation	6·6
13. State	—	—
14. Stubborn	person	3·2
15. Stalk	flower-stalk	6
16. Dance	dancing floor	4
17. Water	water-lily	9
18. Ill	illness	3·4
19. Proud	—	—
20. To cook	—	—
21. Ink	ink-eraser	4·6
22. Wicked	wickedness	—
23. Needle	pincushion	2·4
24. Swim	swimming pool	4
25. Travel	—	—
26. Blue	—	—
27. Bread	—	—
28. Threaten	—	—

At reaction 28 the patient refused to proceed, declaring that she could not hold out any longer. She could not be persuaded to remain any longer in the examination room. It was also impossible to add a reproduction test or any analysis. Nevertheless certain results may be noticed. First of all, there is the strikingly peculiar character of the associations; they are mainly word-combinations and there are numerous faults. Comparing the two tests we find :

Test	I	II
	Per cent.	Per cent.
Inner associations . .	16	—
Outer „ . .	60	46·4
Clang-reactions . . .	9	14·2
Faults	14	39·2
Indirect associations . .	1	—

This is a most unusual record. The patient's behaviour during the examination was characteristic ; she supported her head with both hands and sighed from time to time about the unbearable heat in her head which the heated room caused her (13° ! It did not trouble her in the least that in summer she found a temperature of 13° pleasantly cool whilst the same temperature in winter was unbearable. The part played by the temperature of the air was therefore only due to imagination !) She was obviously quite obsessed by her disease complex during the test. It is not surprising that she had no attention left for the dull experiment. We have again an experiment in distraction, but in a much higher degree than in Test I. The decline in her condition had increased the distraction of attention ; that is, attention is now more than before directed to the disease complex, so that there is less attention to give to the experiment. It clearly cost her enormous trouble to direct her attention to the tests ; she is worn out after twenty-eight reactions and is obliged to relinquish the experiment. The energy at her disposal is reduced to a minimum. The enormous increase in faults is an expression of this fact, they are almost threefold those of the first test. She rejects all stimulus-words which do not lend themselves to ready word-connexions. But all the faults are not absolutely referable to the absence of a ready-made word-connexion (e.g. to *cook*, there are such common combinations as cookery, cooking ; to *State*, state affairs ; to *travel*, travelling bag, etc.). Nor are all the long reaction-times attributable to verbal difficulties (e.g. *water* with 9 seconds, to which there are numerous combinations). We are obliged to think of some affective causes for these disturbances, which may be conditioned by unconscious inhibitions arising from the pathogenic complex which is at the root of the disease complex.

The probable mean time of the test was 5·2 seconds (taking the faults at 20 seconds, although one usually waited up to thirty seconds). The probable mean is, therefore, very high.

Test III

October 9, 5 p.m. With Reproduction Test

Stimulus-word	Reaction	Time	Reproduction
1. Lamp	lamp-glass	1·8	—
2. Rich	riches	1·8	—
3. Tree	tree-trunk	1·4	—
4. *Sing*	*choral society*	5·2	sing-song
5. Pity	—	—	pitiful
6. Yellow	golden yellow	3·2	—
7. Mountain	mountain chain	4·8	—
8. *Play*	sing-song	6·6	play at ball

Stimulus-word	Reaction	Time	Reproduction
9. Salt	salt-cellar	6·8	—
10. New	new moon	3	—
11. *Habits*	—	—	customary
12. Ride	riding school	3	—
13. Wall	wall paintings	4·6	—
14. Stupid	stupidity	4	—
15. Copy-book	school copy-book	2·2	—
16. *To despise*	—	—	despicable
17. Tooth	toothache	2	—
18. Right	—	—	—
19. People	people's holiday	2	—
20. Smell	—	—	—
21. Book	reading book	3·8	—
22. Unjust	—	—	—
23. Frog	tree-frog	2·4	—
24. *Separate*	—	—	conjugal separation
25. Hunger	heat hunger	5	—
26. White	snow-white	2	—
27. Cattle	drove of cattle	4·1	—
28. To take care	caution	2·4	—
29. Pencil	pencil-holder	6·6	—
30. Cloudy	—	—	—
31. Plum	—	—	—
32. Meet	—	—	—

This test shows some changes as compared with the earlier ones. The results expressed in percentages are :

Test	II	III
	Per cent.	Per cent.
Inner associations . .	—	3·1
Outer ,, . .	46·4	59·3
Clang-reactions . . .	14·2	6·2
Faults	39·2	31·2
Anomalies in reproduction .	—	18·7

This is therefore another experiment in distraction. The probable mean time is :

First Test	Second Test	Third Test
5·2	5·2	4·6

There is a certain diminution of the reaction-time, which must be chiefly attributed to the relative decrease of the " faults." It may perhaps be inferred from this result that the patient has pulled herself together a little. This seems also to be expressed by the fact that despite her early abandonment of the experiment, she allowed herself to be persuaded into the reproduction test. This test also went four reactions further than the first one (28, 32). The number of clang-reactions has considerably diminished in favour of the outer and inner associations. This must be also regarded as a certain improvement in attention.

TEST IV

October 17, 5 p.m. With Reproduction Test

Stimulus-word	Reaction	Time
1. Law	lawless	5
2. Love	loveless	3
3. Glass	glass chest	2
4. Quarrel	—	—
5. Goat	goat milk	2·8
6. Big	big city	4·8
7. Potato	potato patch	5·6
8. Pain	painting studio	5·4
9. Part	parties	3
10. Old	Old-town	9·6
11. Flower	calyx	2·4
12. Hit	—	—
13. Basket	clothes-basket	5·6
14. Wild	—	—
15. Family	family party	4
16. Wash	—	—
17. Cow	cow milk	3·2
18. Foreign	foreign book	3·4
19. Luck	lucky wish	2·8
20. Narrate	—	—
21. Deportment	teaching deportment	2·8
22. Narrow	—	—
23. Brother	—	—
24. Malice	malicious joy	3·6
25. Stork (stimulus-word at first misunderstood, then fault)		
26. False	falsity	8·2
27. Anxiety	anxious feeling	3
28. Kiss	sisterly kiss	4
29. Flame	black flames	6·8
30. Dirty	dirty speck	7
31. Door	door-trap	4·8
32. Vote	—	—
33. Hay	—	—
34. Quiet	—	—

This test was carried out at a time when the patient was not feeling so well (one of those variations which are not uncommon in the course of hysteria). This test looks, likewise, as if it were a distraction test. With the exception of a few individual reactions (*kiss — sisterly kiss*) the patient never enters into the meaning of the stimulus-words, but contents herself with apprehending the outer form of the word. There were no disturbances in reproduction. The test went two reactions further than the previous one (32, 34). Expressed in percentages :

Test	II	III	IV
	Per cent.	Per cent.	Per cent.
Inner associations . .	—	3·1	2·9
Outer ,, . .	46·4	59·3	58·8
Clang-reactions . .	14·2	6·2	5·8
Faults	39·2	31·2	32·3
Reproductive anomalies	—	18·7	—

The probable mean time is

Test	II	III	IV
	5·2 seconds	4·6 seconds	5·4 seconds

There is an increase of the reaction-time referable to the temporary unfavourable condition of the patient. The absence of reproductive anomalies may be accidental in such a small series of reactions, but may be also attributed to the fact that the patient did notice the reactions this time so as to make no mistakes in the reproduction.

TEST V

October 9, 5 p.m.   With Reproduction Test

	Stimulus-word	Reaction	Time	Reproduction
1.	Scorn	—	—	
2.	*Sleep*	rest	1·8	tired
3.	*Month*	—	—	time
4.	Coloured	painter	6·8	
5.	Dog	domestic animal	3·4	
6.	Talk	narrate	4·8	
7.	Coal	to iron	4	
8.	Moderate	—	—	
9.	Song	singing	3·6	
10.	Suppose	facts	10	
11.	*Pain*	*ill*	5·2	*illness*
12.	Lazy	work	5·4	
13.	Moon	—	—	
14.	Laugh	jolly	—	
15.	Coffee	breakfast	2·2	
16.	Broad	measure	3·6	
17.	Air	warm	5	
18.	Frighten	dread	7·6	
19.	Plate	cat	7	
20.	*Tired*	*sleep*	4·4	*bed*
21.	*Aim*	*injure*	7·4	?
22.	Fly	—	—	
23.	Eye	—	—	
24.	Strong	powerful	2·6	
25.	Fruit	—	—	
26.	*Create*	*industrious*	3	*work*
27.	Sail	ship	7	
28.	Modest	content	6·4	

Stimulus-word	Reaction	Time	Reproduction
29. Floor (does not understand the stimulus-word at first)	land	10	
30. Whistle	tune	6·4	
31. Purpose	cause	3·4	
32. *Hot*	yes, yes, in there	4	*light*
33. Hand	limb	3	
34. *Wake*	*awake*	3	*get up*
35. Apple	don't know	15·6	
36. Bad	—	—	
37. Mouth	teeth	7·2	
38. Drink	fluid	4·4	
39. *Bed*	*tired*	7·2	*sleep*
40. *Beautiful*	*pretty*	4	?
41. *Danger*	—	—	*terrible*
42. Visit	—	—	
43. *Artisan*	*occupation*	6·4	*make*
44. High	mountain	4·6	
45. Axe	wood	9·4	
46. Notice	take care	2	
47. Way	walk	5	
48. Round	ball	2·4	
49. *Blood*	—	—	*red*
50. To yield	—	—	
51. Caution	take care	—	
52. *Jolly*	*stories*	4·8	*laugh*
53. Market	buy	3·6	
54. *Forget*	*thoughts*	5·4	*stories*
55. Thunder	noise	5	
56. Free	outspoken	6·6	
57. Carriage	drive	3·2	
58. Eat	appetite	5	
59. Impudence	—	—	
60. Quick	go	2·4	
61. Chimney	smoke	2·6	
62. Enjoy	pleasure	3·2	
63. Vicar	preach	2·4	
64. Light	weight	3·6	
65. Neck	slender	7	
66. Wish	present	5·6	
67. Stone	hard	8·8	
68. Superior	rich	1·4	
69. Tube	rubber	2·6	
70. *Love*	*beautiful*	9·4	?
71. Slate	roof	3·4	
72. Mild	temperature	4·8	
73. Avarice	miser	6·4	?
74. Seek	—	—	
75. Cover	—	—	
76. Good	—	—	
77. Leaf	—	—	
78. Complain	illness	6	
79. Railway	travel	4·8	

This test presents a very different association type from the others. It is as if the patient had suddenly found another adaptation.[1]

The percentage relationships are :

Test	II	III	IV	V
	Per cent.	Per cent.	Per cent.	Per cent.
Inner associations . .	—	3·1	2·9	56·9
Outer „ . .	46·4	59·3	58·8	18·9
Clang-reactions . . .	14·2	6·2	5·8	1·2
Faults	39·2	31·2	32·3	21·5
Indirect associations . .	—	—	—	1·2
Anomalies in reproduction .	—	18·7	—	21·5

We see from these figures that the patient has now achieved a normal type. She now enters into the meaning of the reaction-word, linking with it a preponderating number of inner associations.[2] The abnormal components have been pretty well abandoned, so that, e.g., the clang-reactions do not exceed the normal mean. The number of faults remains high, but has also considerably decreased. The patient is now able to hold out much longer, for this test exceeds the others by forty-five reactions. The mean time is 5·4 seconds, as in the previous tests ; it thus remains very long.

This test was made three weeks after the previous one. Meanwhile treatment had much improved the patient's condition. In the earlier tests we pointed out the *absence of entering into the meaning of the stimulus-word,* the *dominance of outer associations,* the enormous *number of faults,* and the rapid fatigue as pathological signs showing her extreme subjection to the disease complex. The improvement of the condition is psychologically shown, particularly by the patient's having acquired an interest in objective processes, although her interest was quickly exhausted ; the treatment had assuaged the tyranny of the complex. Her personality gradually became free from the tyranny of her illness and able to assimilate objective facts ; in other words, she could now adapt herself to her environment. Certain hysterical stigmata were maintained : the enormous number of faults, the long reaction-times, and other signs of a complex—signs of pathological emotivity which, as we know, is the psychological foundation of hysteria.

[1] But in fact this is not the case, for in Test I the patient had shown tendencies to a less superficial association type.

[2] This patient now exhibits a type which we not infrequently see amongst the uneducated : very many inner associations, few outer, and very few clang-reactions.

TEST VI

December 1, 5 p.m.   With Reproduction Test

This test consisted of 100 reactions, concluded at this number not on account of the patient's exhaustion, but because 100 reactions seemed to me sufficient for analysis. I will therefore give a critical review of the test in sections. The probable mean time of this test, I will begin by remarking, was 5·2 seconds— not longer, therefore, than the previous tests. Despite this apparent agreement the time relationships are, on the whole, quite different from the earlier attempts. To bring out these relationships I have split each test up into series of six to ten reactions and calculated the arithmetical mean time of each series.[1]

The results of the six tests would show curves of the following nature :

Test I.—The curve shows a strong fluctuation. At first a level of relatively " short times " is soon reached, which after various fluctuations keeps ascending higher. Towards the end very strong prolongations of time occur, which to some extent are again made up for but never quite reach the first level. The curve gives one the impression that the patient had noticed the long times and had in consequence pulled herself together during a few reactions. Test I was carried out at the first consultation. As already mentioned, her condition afterwards got worse. This aggravation is seen in the curve of

Test II, where the curve begins pretty high and, after a brief recovery, is rapidly followed by a collapse.

In *Test III* the curves begin low : the patient had (as she then said) made the good resolution to take every pains to react quickly. But the energy so painfully aroused is not long maintained ; the times become progressively longer until very high figures are reached. The perception of this weakness probably determined in the patient a slight final effort, which, however, exhausts her last trace of energy.

Test IV.—The curve begins rather higher than last time (as stated, the patient was having a bad turn at the time of the experiment). There occurred here also an uninterrupted rise in the reaction-times.

Tests I–IV had furnished predominantly *outer associations and faults.* We see from the curves that this mode of assimilation is linked with rapidly rising reaction-times.

Test V.—The curve begins very high (perhaps because the patient had been greatly discouraged by the previous tests and had thus resistances towards the experiment). The curve rapidly falls, and after one strong variation is maintained at a moderate level, which, however, slowly ascends. There follows a strong and a final effort maintained for a long time, which ends in a rapid and uninterrupted ascent of the " times." The final effort had entirely exhausted her energy.

Test VI.—In this last test (after two months' treatment) the curve begins at a moderate height and then rapidly sinks to a very low level, which is maintained more or less during the whole experiment without noteworthy fluctuations,

---

[1] The faults have been each reckoned as 20 seconds.

only towards the end showing a tendency to rise. Test V shows, at least in its middle parts, a tendency towards stability, which is fully expressed in Test VI. But Tests V and VI are those which exhibit a normal mode of association. The normal type occurs here with the tendency to stability in the reaction-times. At the same time a very low level is reached and maintained in Test VI. The one hundred stimulus-words which are the basis of Test I were employed also in Tests II and IV and in Test VI. As the curves show, we cannot perceive any shortening of the reaction-times from the repetition of the same stimulus-words. From Tests II to IV we might rather suppose the opposite. According to Kräpelin's investigations we should rather expect a fixation of the reactions to produce a relatively rapid abbreviation of the time. In Test VI there are, however, not only no fixations but quite other reactions (corresponding to the new adaptation whose beginning was seen in Test V).

The prolongation of the reaction-times is seen to be connected with a great loss of energy, i.e. with an entire inability to withdraw attention from the disease complex. It cost the patient great trouble to direct her attention for any length of time upon anything else than her illness, her fatigue corresponding with her endeavour. The curves which exhibit the prolongation of time are therefore *curves of want of energy*. This becomes clear if we turn them round and read them from right to left. Then they look rather like the work curves of a very exhausted neurotic (exhaustion of will !). In curves I, V, and VI we notice the *increase due to practice*, and the reactive rises in curves I, III, and V, which is the final effort. In curves I and VI this progressive fatigue is clearly marked. Thus the association experiment gives us information in certain cases about energy and fatigue.

ANALYSIS OF THE ASSOCIATIONS IN TEST VI

I place the associations of Test VI parallel with those of I–VI for analytical comparison.

Tests	I		II, IV (V)		VI	
		sec.		sec.		sec.
1. Head	-ache	: 1·2	headache	: 1·6	pain — pains in the head	: 1·8
2. Green	corn	: 6·6	—		forest	: 5·2
3. Water	—		water-carriage	: 2·8	deep	: 1·4
4. Prick	bee	: 1·8	thorn-apple	: 2·4	bee	: 2·8
5. *Angel*	hotel	: 2·1 [?][1]	—		—	
6. *Long*	knife	: 9 [?]	longing	: 2·2	street	: 5
7. Ship	steamship	: 7 [?]	—		sea	: 4
8. Plough	field (garden)	: 4·2	—		demand—give	7·4
9. Wool	knit	: 1·5	cotton-wool		(stimulus-word not understood) knit	: 10·2

---

[1] Absence of reproduction is shown by the brackets.

Tests	I		II, IV (V)		VI	
		sec.		sec.		sec.
10. Friendly	-ness	: 2·2	friendliness	: 3	— (men)	
11. Table	(does not un-		table com-		room	: 9
	derstand		panion	: 2·2		
	stimulus-					
	word at first)					
	-cloth	: 6				

Reaction 1, *head*, naturally arouses the disease complex, for the patient has localized her chief symptoms in her head. The times are not long, but we find in Test VI a disturbance through a slip of speech. The two earlier reactions have the superficial character which is not infrequently seen in complex reactions, which the patient would like to slide over lightly.

Reaction 3, *water*, seems to have the well-known signs of perseveration of an emotional tone.

Reaction 5, *angel*, has complex signs. The patient is not religious but is still very childish. In the last few months she had frequent thoughts of death, she had hallucinations in the evenings of a " black skeleton " stretching out his hand to her. That is reason enough for a complex disturbance ; but we must go deeper. The patient has an inner and intimate relationship to her mother. The two women have another link in common through illness. Her mother suffers from osteomalacia and is a complete cripple. Her daughter takes her mother as her pattern not only from a moral point of view, but perhaps also as presaging her own fate. The fear of a fate similar to that of her mother is never very distant. Finally, it must be remembered that young girls and hysterics talk of death when they wish to have love. Disturbances proceed from *angel* to reaction 8. In Test I there even occurred a slight amnesia here.[1]

At reaction 8 in Test VI another stimulus-word was inserted in order to bring out the complex—*demand*; it requires 7·4 seconds for the reaction, and the succeeding stimulus-word, *wool*, is at first not understood and requires 10·2 seconds. To *demand* I obtained some further thoughts. In her own words, ' I thought that you demand too much of me ; it is *too much* when you always want me to be well." It seemed to me that the patient was here rather sliding lightly over something—although thoughts about the doctor who is treating her seem to be accompanied in hysterics by a strong emotional tone (transference to the doctor ; see Freud). I therefore simply said, " The demand." The patient jerked herself slightly together and said : " I don't know what you mean—I can't make out what you are now wanting of me." Then she suddenly broke out into loud laughter, flushed, and said nothing more. The course of this bit of analysis is as follows : At first the patient complains that I am demanding too much from her, then the well-known negative subterfuges appear, and finally a strongly emotional thought with laughter, the cause of which is not difficult to guess. Laughter is of diagnostic importance ; in psycho-analysis it often shows that one has struck a complex. It is clear that it is not any one but the patient herself who is demanding too much. Freud [2] says : " Many of my neurotic patients are during psycho-analysis regularly wont to show by a laugh that one has succeeded in correctly showing to their conscious perception what the unconscious had concealed ; they even laugh when the content of what has been concealed has nothing in it to justify their laughter.

---

[1] Cp. " Experimentelle Beobachtungen über das Erinnerungsvermögen," *Zentralblatt für Nervenheilkunde und Psychiatrie*, 1905.

[2] *Der Witz* (" Wit and its Relation to the Unconscious "), by Professor Sigmund Freud. (London : Fisher Unwin.)

This happens when the physician having recognized the condition has prepared the way for the patient to recognize himself this bit of his unconscious when it looms up."

Reaction 10, *friendly*, seems to be critical in Test II but not in Tests I and VI.

Analysis.—At first strong resistances ("I don't know anything," etc.); then: "I thought of you, doctor. Recently you were not very friendly to me." This reminiscence refers to a definite event when the patient transferred her ill-humour to me and afterwards maintained that it was I who was in a bad temper (transference of affect). This reminiscence seems sufficient to explain the disturbance. I have already pointed out that the patient transferred the "demanding too much" to me; she also endows me with her own ill-humour and complains that I am not friendly to her. Her "demand" is therefore that I should be friendly with her, and as I always am, then that I am not friendly enough, for she still complains of my unfriendliness. She is ever wanting greater friendship from me—which means that I am indifferent to the patient in an erotic sense. Naturally I cannot agree to this demand. Thus the *patient is demanding too much*. This piece of complex she only acquired here, and so the complex disturbances were bound to increase at *friendly*.

Test	I		II-IV		VI	
		sec.		sec.		sec.
12. Ask	—		note of inter-rogation	: 6·6	answer	: 5·8
13. State	—		—		state build-ings	: 11·6
14. Stubborn	stubborn person	: 8	stubborn person	: 3·2	character	: 6
15. Stalk	flower-stalk	: 2·2	flower-stalk	: 6	flower-stalk	: 10·6
16. Dance	dancing floor	: 2	dancing floor	: 4	ball	: 5·4
17. Water	Zurich	: 5·8	water-lily	: 9	deep	: 7·2
18. Ill	—		sickly	: 3·4	hospital	: 6·2
19. Proud	haughty	: 3·8			longing—home-sick	: 7·4
20. Cook	cookery school	: 2·6	—		kitchen	: 3·6
21. Ink	ink-bottle	: 1·8	ink-eraser	: 4·6	write	: 2

Reaction 12: at *ask* there were obvious complex disturbances which affect the subsequent reactions also.

Analysis.—"I thought that you asked me a lot, but I know absolutely nothing—I certainly know nothing more." The patient says this with emphasis and with a nasty ill-tempered expression contrasting strikingly with her usual good-nature and submissiveness. She then broke out into loud laughter, which she tried to suppress by the expression of her ill-humour. "Oh, what a nuisance —that won't do—I never thought of that at all." At the moment of the reaction she had not thought of the peculiar meaning of the word *ask*, so fraught with meaning to any young woman. She believes that this meaning has only just occurred to her; "she really never thinks about anything of the kind." We have here another hint of the presence of an erotic complex.

Reaction 16, *stubborn*, is well adapted for ego relationships. If the reaction is *character* or *trait* or *bad habit*, reference may be suspected to the patient under examination. The ego relationship occurs clearly in *character*. and thus we get stronger disturbances than in the earlier reactions.

Analysis.—" People are often stubborn—I was as a child—once I was awfully stubborn and wouldn't go to school at all—I think I was about twelve then—after that I did not go to school again."

It will be remembered that the patient attributed her inability to go to school to the St. Vitus's dance; now she is regarding this illness as naughtiness, and even says it was from stubbornness that she stopped going to school. But if during the course of another conversation she is asked why she stopped going to school she says that she was then very ill. We can be content with this explanation. But her twelfth year has another significance of much greater import, as we shall see later.

Reaction 16, *dance — dancing floor*, also gets away from the deeper meaning. It is only with the reaction *ball*, which shows a deeper penetration into the meaning of the stimulus-word, that we rouse the complex. *Dancing — saloon* is something that horrifies the circle in which the patient lives, whilst *ball* is quite a legitimate occasion for erotic relationships. The patient was obliged to laugh directly she was asked what came into her mind about *ball*. Erotic thoughts were again to the fore.

To reaction 19 the stimulus-word in Test VI was *longing*.

Analysis.—Patient declared obstinately and with obvious resistance that nothing except *home-sickness* occurred to her at *longing*. I maintained that something would occur to her. There was then suddenly loud laughter, which was at once angrily suppressed. " No, no, this disgusts me; it's a bore." We had the same reaction as at *demand*. There was certainly some strongly repressed erotic desire.

Test	I		II-IV		VI	
		sec.		sec.		sec.
2. Wicked	wickedness	: 7·8	wickedness	: 3·8	disobedient (child)	: 7·6
3. Needle	pincushion	: 2	pincushion	: 2·4	child; work (love)	: 7·8
4. Swim	swimming school	: 9	swimming pool	: 4	bathing-place	: 6·4
5. Travel	travelling rug 12 ?		—		railway	: 4·8
6. Blue	Blue-street	: 7	—		colour	: 1·8
7. Bread	breadless	: 4	—		baker	: 2
8. Threaten	(does not understand the stimulus-word) punishment 12 (punish)				expect—visit	: 3·6

This was the end of Test II

Test III

		sec.		sec.		sec.
9. Lamp	lamp-shade	: 2·2	lamp-shade	: 1·8	light	: 4
0. Rich	riches	: 4·2	riches	: 1·8	money	: 6·8
1. Tree	fruit-tree	: 4·6	tree-stem	: 1·4	garden	: 3·6
2. Sing	choral society	: 3·2	choral society	: 5·2	concert	: 5·2

Reaction 22, *wicked*, is taken personally; *disobedient* seems to express the complex most clearly.

Analysis.—" Recently I was angry with you—formerly I was often wicked and disobedient » school " etc. Association 23, *child — work*, is peculiar and could not be explained by the patient. In reproduction came the more appropriate association *love*. The school complex comes first, which is most deeply bound up with the idea of " work." Remember that the stimulus-words *create* and *artisan* in Test V caused complex disturbances. Moreover, the patient is always insisting that she is not " lazy " ; she would like to find some real work ; she also complained about certain relatives who said she was only suffering from laziness. The stimulus-word *child* is a word which as a rule has a critical effect in erotic complexes among women.

Reaction 25 : at *travel* there are complex indicators.

Analysis.—" I am thinking of a beautiful journey to Italy which I should so much like to make one day "—a long pause, then with great embarrassment " honeymoon journeys are made to Italy."

Reaction 28, Test VI, *expect*.

Analysis.—" I am expecting nothing, absolutely nothing, health and "—again loud laughter, which the patient, annoyed, tries to suppress. The same reaction again as at *demand* and *longing*.

Reaction 30, *rich*.

Analysis.—" I should like to be rich, then I could remain longer here under treatment " ; then a block occurred which stopped all further flow of thought. " Longer under treatment " means " remain longer in the present relationship to the doctor."

Test	I		II-IV		VI	
		sec.		sec.		sec.
33. Pity	regret	: 7	(full of pity)		—	
34. Yellow	yolk of egg	: 4·8	golden yellow:	3·2	canary bird	: 5
35. Mountain	Utli moun-tain	: 4·6	mountain chain	: 4·8	mountain chain	10·8
36. Game	chess	: 3·2	singing (game of ball)	: 6·6	game of ball	: 6·8
37. Salt	salt-cellar	: 2·4	salt-cellar	: 6·8	cook	: 2·2
38. New	Newbury	: 3	new moon	: 3·8	house	: 7
39. Custom	propriety	: 9·2	— (decorum)		expect happy (joy)	: 8·2
40. Ride	riding school	: 33	riding school	: 3	path	: 1·8
41. Wall	Spanish wall	: 2·4 (?)	wall paintings	: 4·6	room	: 5·2
42. Stupid	stupidity	: 9 (?)	stupidity	: 4	un—derstand	: 7·2
43. Exercise-book	school exercise-book	: 3	school exercise-book	: 2·2	exercise-book	: 5·2

Reaction 33, *pity*.

Analysis.—" I can't think what pity has to do with me—oh, perhaps with my illness—people ought to have pity on me."

I have only given a sample of the resistance the patient had at this word in reality the resistance lasted much longer and was expressed also mimetically in her sorrowful face. The tendency to evoke pity has great significance the history of the patient's illness. Through her illness she managed not go to school any more. Later she is the central figure for the pity of the whole family. The patient must have some consciousness of this even if obscurely the strong inhibition is probably referable to this.

Reaction 35, *mountain*.

Analysis.—Refuses to acknowledge anything. She has had nothing do with mountains, the word doesn't concern her at all ; she has never been on a mountain. Certainly she would enjoy a tour in the Alps, but that's been impossible on account of her illness; besides, she could not travel by railway, she could not bear that. The patient speaks here in negations as if a mountain tour had no meaning for her. A few days before this test I had been away on an excursion to the mountains; the patient was afterwards unhappy because I had not taken her—she had never seen the mountains in the neighbourhood, etc. She suppresses this circumstance altogether, for which there was no obvious ground if *travel* had not some complex import. She has all kinds of imaginary relationships to the doctor; a journey with the erotic " symptomatic figure " is a metaphor for "honeymoon journey." This is certainly the reason why this event takes part in the sexual repression.

Reaction 38, *new.*

Analysis.—The patient has been intimate with a lady who has moved into a *new* house for which the patient exhibits an extraordinary liking. She envies the lady her whole household : " I should like to have something of the sort." The interest appears to be symptomatic. The analysis discovers great resistances (" people often move into a new house—we have also got a new room at home," etc.). I now ask pointedly, " When does one move into a new house ? " This apparently most general question causes the patient great confusion ; she blushes and admits, " When they marry." She had assimilated the " *new house* to her erotic complex.

Reaction 39, Test VI, *expect.*

The analysis arouses at once laughter—which says enough. The laughter is here quite appropriate.

Reaction 23, *child*, likewise caused a disturbance. We shall return to this complex at reaction 69.

Reaction 42, *stupid.*

Analysis brings out self-reproaches relating to the time when she left school (aged twelve). She reproaches herself that from want of energy she learnt too little and is therefore *stupid.*

Test	I		II-IV		VI	
		sec.		sec.		sec.
44. Despise	—		— (despicable)		people	: 7·2
45. Tooth	eye-tooth	: 3 (?)	toothache	: 2	mouth	: 3·6
46. Correct	arrange	: 5	—		control	: 6·6
47. People	people's paper	: 4·6	people's holiday	: 2	crowd	: 5
48. Smell	sink	: 10	—		die—cemetery	: 3·4
49. Book	reading book	: 3	reading book	: 3·8	read	: 2·2
50. Unjust	—		—		marriage : church	: 3·2
51. Frog	tree-frog	: 5	tree-frog	: 2·4	green	: 2
52. Separate	divorce	: 6·4	— (divorce)		divorce	: 4
53. Hunger	eat	: 3·8	violent hunger	: 5·6	dog—bark	: 6·8
54. White	snow	: 3·6	snow-white	: 2	snow	: 3·2
55. Cattle	herd of cattle	: 6·4	herd of cattle	: 4·2	herd of cattle	: 9·4

Reaction 44, *despise.*

Patient feels herself always at a disadvantage ; her want of education she regards as something for which people must despise her; people also despised her on account of her illness, which they regarded as laziness. Perhaps there is something else in the illness which makes her peculiarly despicable? We know that sexual self-reproaches are readily made here.

Reaction 46, *correct*, also shows disturbances. The analysis gave nothing but generalities, which are difficult to interpret. Perhaps there is something in her actions which is, or was not, *correct*?

Reaction 53, *dog* (Test VI) has a very long reaction-time—6·8 seconds.

Analysis.—Patient dreamt about two dogs which probably have an erotic meaning (see below).

Test	I		II-IV		VI	
		sec.		sec.		sec.
56. Take care	esteem	: 6	esteem	: 2·4	esteem	: 2·8
57. Pencil	pencil-holder	: 6·2	pencil-holder	: 6·6	black	: 5
58. Cloudy	—		—		weather	: 2
59. Plum	plum jam		—		cat—domestic animal	: 8
60. Meet	—		—		protection	: 3·6

This is the end of Test III

Test IV

		sec.		sec.		sec.
61. Law	—		illegal	: 5	illegal	: 5·4
62. Love	loveless	: 3	loveless	: 3	child	: 2
63. Glass	tumbler	: 1·6	glass-cupboard	: 2	bottle	: 8
64. To quarrel	dispute	: 4·6	—		want of peace	: 7·8
65. Goat	goat's milk	: 2·4	goat's milk	: 2·8	fire : house	: 3·8
66. Big	generous	: 3	big town	: 4·8	sea	: 11
67. Potato	potato-meal	: 4	potato patch	: 5·6	food	: 6·8

Reaction 57, *pencil*.

Analysis.—The patient thinks of the attempts at work when I sat opposite to her, and from time to time during the additions marked her copy-book with a blue pencil. Nothing else occurred to her. These attempts took place shortly before beginning Test VI. It may, however, only have to do with some past memory which must be constellated somewhere. There is perhaps some masturbation complex or some other sexual fantasy. I avoided the sexual theme as far as possible during the whole time of her treatment and only got her to speak about it at the end. If there was some masturbation or other physical sexual complex, this was not aroused during the treatment (i.e. before Test VI) but was more or less dormant, especially if it was not actual at the moment.

Tests I-IV took place at the beginning of the treatment, when the complexes were more strongly stimulated; Test VI only occurred in the third month. This perhaps explains the absence of complex indicators at this point in Test VI. In Test I the after-effects could be seen up to reaction 61.

In reaction 62, *love*, the more obvious *child* has stronger perseveration than the earlier and more superficial reaction *loveless*.

Test	I		II-IV		VI	
		sec.		sec.		sec.
68. Paint	oil paintings	: 4·2	studio	: 5·4	picture	: 2·4
69. Part	part payment	: 5·2	participate	: 3	birth—difficult	: 4
70. Old	old town		old town	: 6·6	greybeard	: 3
71. Flower	nosegay	: 10·2	calyx		garden	: 5·4
72. Strike	stroke with hammer	: 6 (?)	—		sit : tired	: 2·2
73. Basket	clothes-basket	: 4·2	clothes-basket	: 5·6	room	: 7
74. Wild	wild duck	: 4·2	—		lion	: 3·4
75. Family	family party	: 5·2	family party	: 4	big	: 5·2
76. Wash	—				kitchen	: 6
77. Cow	cow milk	: 2	cow milk	: 3·2	man—father	: 8·8
78. Foreign	foreign book	: 6	strange book	: 3·4	guest-room	: 5
79. Happiness	congratulations	: 10·6	congratulations	: 2·8	joy	: 5·2
80. Narrate	stories		—		stories	: 3

Reaction 69, Test VI, *birth — difficult.*

Analysis.—" My mother had difficult childbirths ; she told me her illness came from these." (Recall reaction 23, *child — love* ; reaction 39, *expectat — happy.*) Reaction 69 does not show any outer complex indicators at all striking but it contains a definite designation of the complex. Her mother's fate was a warning example to the daughter, and she may readily fear that she may also suffer from osteomalacia if she were to marry. It is not to be wondered at if her sexual ideas are accompanied by very gloomy emotions and can only be dwelt upon with a certain *reservatio mentalis,* i.e. with repression, for they were not linked with any joyous expectation but, on the contrary, with a strong feeling of unpleasantness. This knowledge came, perhaps, very early in life and had a share in the formation of the illness.

Reaction 76, *wash,* may have been constellated by the obvious disturbance from *family,* or by her obsession of cleanliness (see the dream analysis).

Reaction 77 : that it is somewhat connected with family is seen by *man — father of family :* 8·8 seconds.

Test	I		II-IV		VI	
		sec.		sec.		sec.
81. Deportment	lesson in deportment	: 11	teaching of deportment	: 2·8	habits	: 2·4
82. Narrow	—		—		place	: 3·6
83. Brother	—		—		brothers and sisters	: 7·8
84. Malice	malicious joy	: 2	malicious joy	: 3·6	loss	: 8·2
85. Stork	stork's nest	: 5·2	(does not catch the stimulus-word)		fly	: 7·4
86. False	falsity	: 7·4	falsity	: 8·2	men	: 3·2
87. Dread	feeling of dread	: 4	feeling of dread	: 3	trembling	: 3·8
88. Kiss	sisterly kiss	: 13	sisterly kiss	: 4	sisterly kiss	: 3·8
89. Fire	huge fire	: 5·6	cinders	: 6·5	house	: 8·8
90. Dirty	—		dirty speck		street	: 1·8
91. Door	lock of door	: 4·2	door-latch	: 4·8	door-lock	: 2

Test	I		II-IV		VI	
		sec.		sec.		sec.
92. Choice	choice of comrade	: 11	—		—	
93. Hay	hay waggon	: 3·8	––		barn	: 2·2
94. Still	peace	: 7·8	—		peaceful	: 6·8

End of Test IV

Test V

95. Ridicule	ridiculous price	: 2	—		laugh	: 2·8
96. Sleep	sleeplessness	: 3·4	peace (tired)	: 1·8	night	: 6·8
97. Month	monthly meeting	: 3	— (time)		long	: 6·4
98. Coloured	—		Moor	: 6·8	painter	: 2·6
99. Dog	dog faithful	: 3	domestic animal	: 3·4	river : broad	: 3
100. Speak	consultation	: 13·4	narrate	: 4·8	people	: 6·2

Reaction 81, *deportment,* readily arouses sexual complexes.

Reaction 85, at *stork* there are obvious disturbances which may refer to this stimulus-word (whose erotic significance is well known) or to the previous *malice.*

Reaction 88, *kiss,* is covered by the innocent *sisterly kiss* and clearly shows the naïve impulse at repression (similarly *stork — fly*). But perhaps *sisterly kiss* had a deeper meaning, one could not suspect at the time (cf. the dream analyses).

Reaction 89, *fire,* shows long reaction-times throughout. It is one of the expressions that the patient uses for her headaches. The reaction *house* is constellated by the dreams of fire, where she often saw houses burning.

Reaction 92, *choice,* arouses the far-off reaction *choice of comrade.*

Analysis.—" Many things can be chosen, e.g. a town councillor or anybody else." (Block—then laughter and confusion.) We know very well what a young woman associates with *choice* ; it is indeed an election of membership—for life partnership. This explains the subsequent reactions, for that is the burning question *par excellence.*

Reaction 97, *month,* frequently arouses in women the idea of the periods, and this has a special significance in this case ; hence the complex disturbances.

SUMMARY OF THE ANALYSIS

The association experiment and its analysis have given us some impressions about a number of processes, which are, however, very obscure as a whole. The analysis was carried out under peculiar difficulties, for very few reactions in the three series presented normal relationships.

Complex signs abound, and this is further evidence of how greatly the patient is under the yoke of her complexes ; it might be almost said that it is not she, but her complexes, which carry out the reactions. Great as are the difficulties of analysis from the unwonted extent of the complex signs, the task is even more difficult when it seemed necessary to get further help from the patient as to what was going on within. The patient frequently stops short after a few generalities and her laughter alone betrays the idea that is coming up. There are rarely any suggestions which the patient can confirm. She is so greatly under the influence of her complex that where she should be able to appraise its emotional value she is unable to form any judgment about it and does not know whether it is important or not. We are therefore driven to suppositions, which, however, do allow of certain conclusions. It has been probably noticed that I have only seized upon certain complex constellations, although a good many others were present. These relationships are, however, only of secondary importance, so that for the sake of brevity I leave aside their analysis.

There are a whole series of associations which show complex signs in all the tests, and these may therefore be regarded as constant complex constellations. A fairly thorough interpretation is possible in the majority of these cases. For instance, it cannot be doubted that erotic ideas play a great part ; here and there they can be recognized in relationship to the physician. The disease complex comes next. These two complexes, apparently independent of one another, have side chains which are connected.

Analogous to the patient's illness is that of her mother's, which in its turn touches the daughter's sexual complex (*birth — difficult*, etc.). There are also certain signs of a possible *physical sexual complex*. Finally there is a school complex.

These are the threads which can conduct us through the patient's labyrinth of thoughts. The patient, however, raises barriers ; by her want of self-control, by her impotency towards these complexes, she makes it difficult for us to find the confirmation of our suppositions, and we must discover other help for this.

Nature has a mechanism which works up the complexes into a concentrated essence and brings them into consciousness in an unrecognizable and therefore non-dangerous form : this mechanism is the dream. As I thought I had only discovered general ideas from the association experiment, I collected the patient's dreams. Earlier ones that could be remembered were only the stereotyped dreams of blood and fire, and these were very indistinct. Naturally, one could not rely on obtaining from the past anything but a carefully selected material, from which the strong inhibition would have blotted out everything at all obvious. The patient dreamt very little during the treatment, that is, she remembered very few dreams. The material is therefore less voluminous than might be wished.

THE DREAMS

In the first months of her treatment I frequently asked for dreams. Apparently there were few; now and then the patient said that she had again dreamt of *fire*, or of *blood* : " the whole room was full of fire or blood." Occasionally she dreamt that blood was spurting out of all the orifices of her head, or she dreamt this about another patient whom she saw in a dream in her room. She did not mention any other dreams. These dreams of fire and blood seemed to me to be stereotyped expressions for the dream, like the feelings of heat in her waking life— mainly a symbolical expression of her way of speaking (that she had too much blood in her head, the blood was too hot, it was 40°, she wished she could have a good flow of blood, her whole head was on fire, everything was withered up and burnt out, etc.). In the second place, these stereotyped dreams are, as usual, symbolical expressions of the complex which we have not yet clearly described. To mitigate these dreams, which were often attended with anxious dread, was my therapeutic aim, and to see whether she could forgo these stereotyped dreams, replacing them by something else, was my theoretical aim. I therefore determined to experiment, and said to the patient : " Blood is red, red signifies love ; fire is red and hot ; you know the verse, ' No fire, no coal can burn so hot,' etc. Fire also signifies love."

This explanation made a strong impression on the patient. She could not control her laughter and was extremely embarrassed. My explanation had, therefore, found a re-echo. The simplicity of my dream interpretation was based on the supposition that the dream symbolism of any one with the mentality of the patient would be simple and childish. The explanation was given in the middle of November. The following dreams occurred in the latter half of November :

FIRST DREAM, *Nov.* 27.—" *The room is full of cats, which are making a horrible noise.*" During the dream great dread and anger. Further details were denied ; there remained but this rather general setting. The analysis was conducted in the same way as the associations : avoiding all suggestive remarks, I obtained the first ideas that came up and only urged the patient when she seemed to be labouring under some stronger inhibition. (The decline of energy before a complex thought is just the same as the absence of any reaction at critical places.) In the following analysis the conclusion is placed first, and the material afterwards in small print. Any one only interested in the conclusions can omit the material.

Result of the Analysis.—She lived for eleven years at a place where she was frequently disturbed by the noise of cats. The noise arose from the combats of the animals when pairing. Ideas of pairing are concealed in the dream-picture.

Material.—Cats: "The last few nights cats were in the garden in front of my room. Otherwise I can't think of anything, absolutely nothing." (Note the strong negations, which are preparatory to intense resistance. I insist.) "Nothing at all occurs to me—oh, yes, once we had a fine Angora cat which, unfortunately, was stolen from us." It is odd why such a simple reminiscence is subject to such strong inhibitions; one supposes that this reminiscence has another side of some more personal significance. I beg her to go on with her ideas. (In a tone of annoyance) "There are lots of cats which run about in our garden, yellow, black, white. I can't make out what you want" (becomes very indignant, as if one were forcing her to something repugnant)—"well, nothing more occurs to me." This decided refusal had to be parried; I therefore asked her, "Were you ever disturbed at night by cats?" "No, that was impossible, for where I slept at home we could not hear the cats; as I've said, I was never disturbed by them." (Then in a superficial tone, as if by the way) "Oh, yes, I do remember that when I was about ten or eleven—oh, no, nine years (!) old—we were living at a place where there were always such lots of cats making such a noise at night-time we thought the house would tumble down. Sometimes there were about sixteen cats together that made this horrible noise at night."
I then asked, "How long did you remain in that place?" "Eleven years, from my twelfth to my twenty-third year." The patient was now twenty-four. So for eleven years until last year she was living in a place where she was disturbed by the noise of cats. The inhibition at the reminiscences of the cats is so extremely strong that it leads her to the most obvious contradictions. It is to be noted that the patient's voice, usually so amiable and unassuming, became irritable and aggressive during the analysis. At the same time her face grew more and more mournful, until it was one of extreme suffering; it took on the mask which belonged to her disease complex. I next asked her if she knew the meaning of the nightly noise of the cats; this she indignantly denied; I insisted, but there was only instant refusal. A normally intelligent young woman of twenty-six who has herself kept cats and, moreover, has had plenty of opportunity of learning all about their habits does certainly know the meaning of these meetings. If she is a hysteric her ego complex may not know it, but her sexual complex certainly does.[1] I thereupon explained to the patient that the noise meant *pairing*. Visible excitation followed this explanation; she did not answer, blushed, and looked out of the window. So far as concerned the dream, I said to her the cats were really symbols, she would discover the explanation later. Dreams about cats or dogs always mean something definite. The next few days the patient frequently asked about the meaning of the dream as it interested her.

SECOND DREAM, *Nov.* 30.—"*The whole room is full of mice, which are running about everywhere, making a great noise. The mice look very peculiar; their heads are bigger than ordinary mice, more like rats, but they have great black ears, and they also have remarkably brilliant hot eyes.*"

[1] Cp. Bleuler, chapter vi.

Result of the Analysis.—The mice covered reminiscences about two dogs (a male and a female) which the patient has often seen playing together. She has noticed how dogs jump upon one another. She had also seen a dog standing up on a maid-servant. It is again a question of *pairing*.

Material.—This dream repeats the general situation of the last one, the cats being replaced by mice, which, however, do not appear to be ordinary mice. The " brilliant hot eyes " seem to be part of the fire dream. I make the patient review the text of the dream ; she has nothing to add.

Thoughts about the mice : " It struck me that the mice all ran out of small wooden houses." (This essential modification was obviously dependent upon some inhibition, and therefore could not be reproduced beforehand.) " The little houses looked like dog-kennels." This is a new track, for dogs do not occur in the dream. But in the last dream I called the patient's attention to dogs. The idea of " dog " seemed to be hinted at indirectly (i.e. repressed) in the dream. So I made " dog-kennels " the starting-point of the analysis.

Ideas called up by " dog-kennels " : " There are lots of dog-kennels " (annoyed). " I don't know what you mean ; no one in our neighbourhood had a dog. You can see dog-kennels anywhere—in gardens and in yards ; I can't understand what you can imagine about that—what could be behind that ? For instance, a garden was just at the back of our house where there was a dog-kennel. There were two dogs, two black ones ; I think they were setters— perhaps a male and a female, but the female was soon got rid of ; they used to play together—they used to tear up paper or wood, or they barked." Then came a complete block with extreme ill-humour : she does not want to speak any more about dogs. After much resistance it at last comes out that she often saw how the dog jumped upon the maid-servant when she went into the garden ; she vehemently denies that the male dog ever jumped upon the female. But we know that it is impossible for the patient to say certain things because the inhibitions are too strong. It is extremely probable that she did see it ; that may be concluded not only from the way in which the thing was said, but from the situation as a whole. I said, " But one often sees a dog jumping on the back of another." " Yes, I've often seen that in the street, but the two dogs did not do it." I asked her what this jumping meant ; she said it was a kind of play, she did not know any other meaning. The last was said in a tone of irritation. As of the last dream, so of this we may remark that it is inconceivable that she did not know the meaning ; at all events we are obliged to consider the influence of the sexual complex upon perceptions of the ego complex. In this wise the dream may be reconstructed somewhat as follows : The mice are cover figures which at various places are broken into by the elements of the cat dream. Mouse is a ready association to cat ; the two words can replace one another in dreams (in a condition of diminished attention).[1]

The mice, like the cats, make a noise in a room and are very numerous. The mice have big heads, so they are not really mice but bigger animals. They have great black ears like the black setters. The mice jumped out of dog-kennels. The analysis leads to a very ambiguous situation, the interpretation of which is not difficult ; it is pairing again as in the former dream. That the dog jumps

---

[1] We have proved that in conditions of distraction the indirect associations are increased and that some very ready or current association replaces either the stimulus-word or the reaction ; so that it often seems as if the stimulus-word had been misheard or the reaction misspoken (see chapter ii).

up on a maid-servant seems to be a delicate hint as to the person to whom these thoughts of pairing refer. There was no such hint in the first dream. It is not unreasonable to suppose that the patient's sexual complex was aroused by the first analysis, so that she herself was more markedly dragged into the next dream. Note also that, just as in the earlier blood and fire dreams the whole room was full of blood and fire, so here the whole room was full of cats and mice. The analysis took place on December 1, after the third dream, which I now give. I did not inform the patient about the result of the second dream, so that at her third dream she had received no explanation about the content of dream two.

THIRD DREAM, *Dec.* 1.—" *She goes into town to a shop to buy something. A great black dog comes in which is fearfully hungry and jumps up on her as if she might be giving him something to eat.*"

Result of the Analysis.—In this dream the patient takes the place of the servant in the previous dream, thus expressing the idea that the pairing concerns herself.

Material.—After the analysis of the previous dream the form of the dream is enough to betray its meaning. The patient is now in the servant's position, so that the critical point which remained unexplained in yesterday's dream is cleared up, and exactly in the form which the patient could not understand the day before. Had she understood this symbol it would probably not have been used, like the cats, the significance of which had been brought home to her.

Thoughts about " the dog jumping up." At first, as usual, we get generalities, evasions, and blockages, which, in order to save time, I will not repeat. Finally, the scene between the dog and the servant occurs to her. Naturally this was the first scene that occurred to us in considering the dream ; with the patient it was different. She was seeking for a long time as if for some memory which had been long forgotten and buried. She had first to overcome all the resistances which gathered round this reminiscence. We had not these resistances. Her dream analysis is just like the association experiment, where at critical places exactly the same hindrances occur at a second or repeated repetition, although one would really think that a reaction obtained at such great pains would remain more fixed than an indifferent one.

The same night I carried out the analysis of her chief symptoms (see below). That night she had the following dream :

FOURTH DREAM, *Dec.* 2.—*She is standing in the corridor of her section and sees a great black man coming ; he is leading somebody through the corridor, but she does not see whether the person led is a man or a woman.*

Result of the Analysis.—The black dog becomes a black man, the scene is shifted into the asylum. The black man is the sexual complex which had formed her illness and has led the patient into the asylum. It is to no purpose that she seeks to still her craving for love by falling in love with her doctor, for he is already married.

Material.—In form the dream recalls the dog scene, only the big black dog is now changed into a big black man. The servant from the dog scene (the patient herself) has become indistinct (she does not know whether it is a man or a woman).

The patient does not seem to participate further in the dream ; we must look for her, therefore, in some dream figure, and are probably correct in supposing that she is this vague figure.

Thoughts in regard to the " black man " : " The man is coming from the entrance door as if leading some one to the section. He is dressed like a *vehm-richter* (whom she had once seen on the stage) ; he looks like a ghost, " like the black man whom I once saw as I fell asleep." I asked her if she was afraid then. " No, I was not afraid at that—oh, yes, I wanted to flee into a room through fear. A nurse called out, ' Stop, that's not allowed ; the room is occupied.' " There was obviously an inhibition at " fear." We have now led the " black man " of the dream back to the " black man " of her vision. In the vision the black man was stretching out his hand towards her and wanting to take her, and she experienced great fear. The vision was a stereotyped complex expression like the blood and fire dreams ; it is a stable psychical formation which it is not very easy for analysis to overcome. The analysis does now really impinge upon powerful obstacles which the patient cannot break through. Hence we find the way out in some combination. The black man who approaches wants to seize her, and is analogous to the black hungry dog which jumps upon her. The dog had a strong sexual background, which must apply also to the black man. The vision arose at the crisis of her illness, when the patient had frequent thoughts of death, and feared that she would die from her illness. As was hinted in the analysis of the associations, thoughts of death by no means exclude the sexual background—on the contrary, they can stand for sexuality. As we have seen from the analysis of the associations and the previous dreams, the patient is utterly possessed by a sexual complex. It is therefore highly probable that in this dream also there are thoughts about pairing. But we will leave this aside for the moment and consider the action of the black man more closely. At the height of her illness she feared she would die, and expressed this belief symbolically : the hand of Death is stretched towards her—that is, the illness will carry her off into the grave. The black man in the dream is leading a shadowy figure into the asylum and to that section where the patient really is herself ; the illness, it is true, has not brought the patient to the grave, but it has led her to the asylum.

The black man arises from the sexual dog, and the disease from the sexual complex.

For the understanding of this sentence we must recall all that has been established up till now. In the associations the distinct and intense reality of her sexual complex was brought out ; in the dreams we have hitherto found nothing but metaphors for this sex complex. At first we have the stereotyped dreams of blood and fire, which are naïvely symbolic ; they say, " My blood is hot ; I have strong sex feelings of love." The dreams speak of pairing. Her illness is obviously connected with the monthly periods. The patient recognizes herself that the illness is connected with the first period. Thus everything that we have hitherto been able to establish speaks in favour of the sexual origin of the illness. *What the patient is longing for is obviously the man.* She would like a husband, but has an illness instead, and as long as she is ill she cannot marry. Does she want to be ill ? We know the will to be ill of the hysterics. From some ground or other they take refuge in illness, they wish to be ill. That is a truth which is forced upon the observer in many cases of hysteria. From the asthenic nature of the patient, who for no obvious reason broke down in a simple and non-fatiguing association experiment, I could not help inclining to the view that she was at no pains to react normally or to be healthy. On the contrary, she behaved in such a way as to make one bound to see how ill she was and how slight was her interest to be well. The illness must stand for her as a hindrance to marriage. Her choice is therefore between illness and a husband so far as her relationship to her surroundings is concerned ; a choice, then, between the joy of sexual love and the protected mothering of a sick child, which to a naïvely feminine disposition is not without its advantages. Some days before I had explained to her that she wanted to be ill because she dreaded marriage and health. Her dream is the answer. Scores of times I had said to her, " You are again fleeing into your illness ; you mustn't, that's forbidden." I said this whenever she wished to keep back something that was unpleasant to her, hiding it away behind a headache or feelings of heat. What does the dream say ?

" A nurse called out, ' Stop, that's forbidden.' " The nurse (therefore my representative) called this out when the patient wanted to rush into a room from fear of the black man. (This part of the dream, as was obvious from its telling, is fraught with peculiar obstacles ; it was only reproduced whilst the analysis was going on.) Fear of her sex future and of all its consequences is too great to enable the patient to decide on abandoning her illness. As hitherto, she prefers to be ill—that is to say, in practice, to be nursed and cosseted by her mother.

But this is not the whole of the chain of thoughts in the dream ; she cannot flee into the room, it is occupied. As our analysis shows, we take it that " to flee into the room " is a symbol for flight into the illness, therefore " room " equals " illness." But the patient is occupied by her illness, so that it cannot be occupied by some one else. But we must remember that the " illness " has a double meaning. Her illness is the sex complex—the repressed sex feelings. The prohibition, therefore, runs : It is forbidden to have sex feelings because something has already " taken possession " of sexuality. From want of time I was obliged to break off the analysis here, postponing it to the next day. I had intended her to tell me what room it was in the dream. The next day I at once asked the patient which room it was. She promptly answered, " No. 7." So as not to spoil anything, I asked the patient before beginning the analysis about her dreams of the previous night. She had had dreams again.

FIFTH DREAM, *Dec. 3.*—" *I was outside standing next to Miss L. We both saw that a house was in a blaze. Suddenly a white figure came behind the house ; we were both afraid and exclaimed as with one voice, ' Lord Jesus ! ' *"

Result of the Analysis.—The black man is changed into a white figure, the burning house is the sex complex. Miss L. is a patient who gushes about the writer. Like the patient, she had become ill through an erotic complex. Miss L. is used by the patient to express her having fallen in love with the writer. The patient has now replaced the too affectionate relationship to her mother, so harmful to her will-power, by the erotic relationship to the doctor.

Material.—The form of the dream shows us that by reason of our earlier explanations the black man must now assume another garb ; he is changed into a white figure, who, however, plays the same terrifying rôle as before. The situation is somewhat the same, since the patient is suddenly prevented from doing something which she had begun. It may be presumed that in the burning house we get the ardour of her sex feelings. As a guide to the analysis we make use of the bit of the former dream which was not concluded yesterday—the room No. 7. In this room Miss L. lives, who is of the same age as the patient. This is a new starting-point for the earlier dream, the dream idea running like this :

" I go into Miss L.'s room, I am doing the same as Miss L." A marked feature of Miss L. is that she is in love with the writer, and that it is hopeless, since he is already married. Thus in a double sense the patient finds the room is occupied : (1) Miss L. is already in love with the writer, so that there is nothing left for the patient; (2) the writer is married, so that any tender feelings are out of question. In to-day's dream this idea of yesterday's dream is carried further. Throughout the dream the patient is doing exactly the same as Miss L. She sees the burning house. She has, therefore, red-hot desires or burning love. The patient knows that Miss L. became ill through an unhappy love affair. Here is a further and alluring analogy : that is why they both see the white figure, *alias* the black man, *alias* the illness, suddenly emerging behind the fire, *alias* love, and they are both frightened, for both have become ill through love. Miss L. suffers from sudden attacks of depression, when she behaves quite confusedly and senselessly. The patient was often struck by this, and often maintained with joy that she was not so ill as to behave like that. I had often told her (our patient) that if she had allowed herself to go on much longer she would have become much worse. In her wild jealousy of Miss L. it was easy for her to think that Miss L. had allowed herself to go further and that was why she became so ill. This would be a further reason for " room No. 7." This point was not settled at the time; therefore, we meet it again later on.

The content of this dream throws light upon the former ones in the same kind of way : fear of the black man (the sex future) drove her to flight in her illness, but that is forbidden ; therefore, seeking some fresh outlet, she finds it with Miss L. ; she falls in love with the doctor, who knows what estimate to place upon the illness ; he is a man not sexually dangerous, so the dream finds a lucky compromise. It replaces her mother, who gives her tenderness but causes her illness, by a man who can cure her and is also of sexual significance. But there is a difficulty ; the patient is poor and will not be able to remain much longer here because she has not enough money. Miss L., however, is very rich, and can remain a long while if she wants to. So she takes Miss L.'s place and occupies the " room."

This rendering remained unsolved also, and therefore usable. When I discussed the content of the dream in cautious terms she made a *disappointed and sad face*—the explanation was obviously too crude—and said in a tone of suffering : " Oh, if my mother knew what things are being brought out of me ! "

This reaction was noticeable, for these fine shades of feeling on the daughter's part were hardly noticed by her mother. But the answer portrays the cooling off and turning away of her infantile sexual need for affection from her doctor, and her return for security to her mother's love ; a sure sign that the compromise was untenable, and that the patient could not rid herself of her infantile relationship to her mother.

SIXTH DREAM, *Dec. 6.*—" *My father is here and I am showing him the asylum, and am going through all the sections with him.*"

Result of the Analysis.—This satisfies her wish to be able to remain longer under the treatment of the writer, whom she hopes will cure her.

Material.—The patient states that this is only a fragment of a much longer dream, of which she can remember no more. The dream is not difficult to understand, it represents an unfinished piece of yesterday's dream. In this dream she behaves as if she were more or less at home in the asylum. I had occasionally asked her if her father was not going to visit her, whereupon she would suggest that since she would be only here for a short time it would not be worth while for her father to travel so far. In the dream a situation is accepted which has made the visit worth while. She can therefore remain longer here (which she also wished). The dream also shows the patient in an unexpected position of trust; she has the master-key by which she can open all the sections; from which we must conclude that she enjoys the full, special confidence of the doctors. It is not difficult to guess the meaning of this position of trust in regard to the doctor.

SEVENTH DREAM, *Dec.* 6 (the same night as the last one).— *" I am at home. My mother is at table; you, doctor, are opposite to her and are eating. There is an empty chair between you and mother. I want to sit on this empty chair and eat also. Whereupon my mother has a hot flat-iron which she pushes towards me so that I get hot in the head. I tell mother she ought to put the flat-iron away, it makes me hot so that I can't eat; I wanted to eat with you. You, doctor, then stand up and shriek at me that I need not eat now at all, I can very well eat later."*

Result of the Analysis.—The patient is desiring a sexual affair with the doctor, hoping by this to rid herself of her mother's influence, which induces her illness. But since the doctor is married the wish cannot be fulfilled. Therefore she must remain ill.

Material.—The symbolism of this dream is very obvious; through the indications obtained from Dream IV we can solve it without difficulty. In that dream we saw that she had begun to make a compromise between her infantile relationship to her mother and her sex relationship to a husband, the doctor appearing clearly in the rôle of husband. The animal symbolism was dropped in the latter dreams because it had been explained and had become too obvious. She must, therefore, create other coitus symbols. So the dream begins by the patient being at home. That is the main question which she places before me every day: " How will it be when I get home ? I'm afraid it will all go wrong again at home." At home the danger means, of course, her mother, who as the too tender guardian and pattern of her early childhood had brought the patient to hysteria. The question, therefore, again arises concerning her life at home : " Am I to play again the rôle of the sick child who needs a nurse, or shall I, following the doctor's advice, courageously trust myself to a sex future ? " She is therefore between doctor and mother. The doctor is eating; she would like to join him. But how far can she do the same as the doctor ? There is only one possibility, and that is the one so frequently considered—marriage. She would like to sit on the chair next to me, that is, to sit at my side, which is again nothing but assimilating me in the sense of " husband." Does eating stand for the conjugal function ? We know the Freudian basic principle of *displacement from below upwards.* What takes place in the mouth (in dream, in hysteria, in dementia præcox) is taking place at the genitalia. In the act of eating, something is placed in the mouth.

(An early case of dementia once expressed this idea in her delirium when she asked that the man she wanted as her bridegroom should give her something to eat with a spoon so that she might become pregnant and beget a child.) She would like to enter into sexual relationship with the doctor. Whereupon her mother makes her so hot with the flat-iron so that she cannot sit down at table ; her mother again calls up her illness (feelings of heat in her head) and so prevents her marriage. The fear that she will get worse when she goes home here plays its part. Up till now the doctor had only played a passive part; it was only her mother who was preventing her carrying out her inclination towards the doctor. But now he stands up and repulses her rudely, forbidding her to eat with him, i.e. to have sexual thoughts about him, and consoles her at the same time by telling her she will be able to marry later. This passage refers to a conversation that I had with her a few days before, when I cautiously hinted that later, when she was quite well, the question of marriage would not be so difficult. We see that the patient deals again in the dream with the scene of the occupied room, plus a few variants; to this is added the deep impression which the earlier analysis had made when I pitilessly disturbed her illusions. By this refusal she finds herself thrown back upon her mother; and in the company of her mother she becomes ill because her mother does not wish her to marry (see below). Hardly had I finished this analysis when she said, quite unprompted: " I just recall a dream that I often used to have; I used always to dream about worms, red and white ones—the floor and the whole room was full of them (like the blood, the fire, cats, etc.). It seemed, also often, as if some one was pulling an enormous worm out of my mouth." The dream in this connexion can hardly be anything else than one of those penis dreams as frequent among normals as among the sick (early dements often have particular neologisms for this, such as snakes, stalks of a lily, etc.). The mouth is again the displacement from below upwards.

It is improbable that her mother's objection to marriage was the fundamental hysterogenic event. With the patient's vivid eroticism one would rather expect some sexual trauma. I explained to the patient that I was not yet satisfied; there was some event which she had not yet told me, which must have been of great importance. Perhaps she would disclose it in her dreams. Perhaps the event was connected with her obsession about cleanliness. During the next eight days she could not remember a single dream, although she was aware that she had dreamt. During this time I tried, as always, to get her to take an interest in some occupation, and was planning with her to find some way by which she could earn something. At the end of eight days she remembered a dream.

EIGHTH DREAM.—" *I am at home and am gathering up small gold coins on the floor ; I also find some beautiful stones, which I wash. I then place the money and stones on the kitchen table and show them to my brothers.*"

Result of the Analysis.—The patient is thinking about returning home; she has various good resolutions, and is thinking that she may find in her family, particularly among her brothers, compensation for her impossible relationship to the doctor. But the background of the dream remained unexplained.

Material.—In this dream she realizes that she will be earning money in the future. The " beautiful stones " are a new factor; she washes them (a cleanliness obsession ?) and shows her brothers what she has washed, on the kitchen table (this perhaps is called up by the dining-table ?). The analysis only resulted in generalities; the strongest obstacles prevented any deeper penetration into this dream. What are the brothers doing at the kitchen table ? Do they, perhaps, stand for the doctor at the dining-table of the earlier dream ? I could not solve the question.

ELEVENTH DREAM, *Dec. 12.*—"*I go for a walk in Zurich, but suddenly it is my home. In front of my house I see standing a rural policeman who is speaking to some shadowy-looking man. The policeman has a fearfully sad expression and goes into the house. Then Miss L. suddenly goes along the street, also with a fearfully sad expression. Then we are together in a room and sitting at a dining-table. Suddenly we know there is a fire. Miss L. says, ' I'm going to bed now.' I can't make that out at all, rush into the corridor, but then it appears nothing is the matter ; it was only a false alarm. I now go in again and find myself at home with mother, and my two brothers are also there. A basket with splendid apples is there. One brother says, ' That's something else for me.' "*

Result of the Analysis.—Like Miss L., the patient is disappointed in her expectation about love ; she understands this in Miss L., whose minor defects she mockingly emphasizes. Therefore she goes home, where she enters into a suspiciously intimate relationship with one of her brothers.

Material.—The general situation of the dream resembles that of Dream VII. There is again the appearance of the dining or kitchen table. In the first part of the dream there is a " policeman " with a fearfully sad expression. Immediately, thereupon, Miss L. appears with the same traits. The policeman goes into a house, whereupon the patient is eating together with Miss L. in a room. Obviously Miss L. and the policeman stand for one another.

Why and how is it that Miss L. is changed into a policeman ? I ask her about any striking characteristics of Miss L. She replies that Miss L. has such peculiar ways, she is only half a woman ; besides, she is very thin. In Switzerland we have a long thin sausage which we call a " dried-up policeman " [1] (*dürren Landjäger*). This word is also used as a nickname for thin people. The patient has symbolized the less striking sides of Miss L. The reason for her doing this is seen in the fact that the policeman is speaking to a shadowy man ; when Miss L. is speaking to a man in a dream that man is certain to be the writer. Probably the patient is therefore jealously emphasizing Miss L.'s feelings for the writer and depreciating Miss L. Then she sits down at table with Miss L. ; that is, she enters into some sexual situation with her. We are not to think, however, of anything homosexual, for the sexual significance of " dining-table " has already been exploited for the doctor; thus it would be too obvious. Here it merely means, " I have sexual feelings like Miss L." The alarm of fire which follows has the same meaning.

The patient goes out to see what is happening ; but Miss L. goes to bed, i.e. becomes ill from love. To understand this it must be known that whenever Miss L. gets excited she goes to bed. At the beginning of the dream the patient depreciates her rival, and as soon as the sexual situation (the fire alarm) develops, Miss L. even becomes ill, and hence quite innocuous. So the rival is overcome. But the patient now finds that it is only a false alarm ; that is the disappointment (" the room is occupied," " she cannot join in eating "). The writer has destroyed her illusions, the transference of her need for affection towards a man has not succeeded ; so she must go back to her mother, where at least she will find an

---

[1] Cp. our English term " soldier " for a red herring.

equivalent for her need of love. So the scene changes in the second part of the dream. She is suddenly at home; instead of at the dining-table she is in the kitchen with her mother. Were it only a question of her relationship to her mother, her brothers would be superfluous. But two brothers are here as in Dream VIII, at the kitchen table; instead of the " beautiful stones " there is only a basket with " beautiful apples " ; one brother says, " That's something else for me." The scene of the dining-table in Dream VII, like the one in this dream with Miss L., is scarcely susceptible of other than a sexual meaning ; and immediately following the sexual scene we get a very similarly constructed picture, " dining-table " being replaced by " kitchen." First of all, the beautiful apples look like the " beautiful stones " which lay on the kitchen table, and secondly, they are also something edible (cp. Eve's apple) ; that is, something for the brother, he gets something. We must realize this picture. In the first part of the dream a sexual wish is destroyed ; the second part can hardly refer to her mother only, some sexual element plays a part somewhere. I asked for her thoughts about the " apples." " I thought about the apples which I saw yesterday in a shop where they sell Southern fruits. I was there with your wife." This opens up a track. The analysis now stops and cannot be further followed up. So I go to the brother : " It was my brother who lives in Italy ; he has often invited me to make a journey to Italy and pay him a visit."

Recall here reaction 25, Test VI.

Travel : Patient supposed *a nice journey to Italy — honeymoon journey.* Her brother had no share in that and yet the apples are intended for him. Here I must add a dream which the patient had right at the beginning of her treatment. She dreamt that I came into the room and she said to me : " It's a pity we can't gather the nuts yet, but at home there is a whole basketful." In this dream she offers me the fruit, nuts. Nuts are hard stones, they have to be opened to be eaten. We recall the " beautiful stones," the " splendid apples " which are now intended for her brother. What her erotic hopes at first promised me is now given to her brother after she has turned away from me. Here I think there is obviously something connected with the brother which proceeds from some brother-sister relationship. The importance of the brother to his sister seems suspicious (cp. *kiss — sisterly kiss*), and we cannot forbear the suspicion that here is something we have long sought which might explain much if it could be known.[1] Some adventure of childhood where her brother played some rôle which left a deep impression seems to lie at the root of this—a Freudian trauma. The secret was, however, well guarded and the analysis brought out nothing.

I only communicated the results of the analysis very superficially to the patient so as to avoid giving any hints of a sexual nature. I wished to prevent an explanation of the symbolism leading to greater concealment in the next dream. The inner development of the patient which this dream suggested, i.e. the alienation from the writer, the renunciation of his standpoint and the invalidation of his advice and teaching, manifested itself (apart from any objective set-back) in the important fact that she now again began dreaming of fire and blood, she " heard the fire-horn every night, the alarm was raised."

[1] We may also recall that in the dream of the occupied room it is said, " Stop, that's forbidden." Perhaps this expression became fixed because it aroused a complex, and expressed something of great significance to the patient.

The time for her departure was now fast approaching, and I was hoping for some decisive dream, but she did not remember any more dreams with the exception of the fire dreams, save for a small fragment, which said nothing, on the morning of the day she was to leave. I asked her, as usual, if she had dreamt. She said " Yes," but quickly added : " But I know already what the dream means, I saw it at once. But I couldn't tell it you ; it is something about earlier times which I can, perhaps, only tell mother." All my requests were fruitless ; she maintained it was something of a kind that she could only tell her mother. Finally I said to her, " Then it's a very unpleasant sexual matter." She did not answer, but stared out of the window. More I dared not.

So, unfortunately, our dream analysis and the analysis of the illness as a whole remained incomplete at this point, which seems, however, narrowly circumscribed.

Summary of the Dream Analysis.—Although none of the dreams reached the complete understanding that was wished, and the last broke off at an important point, we have obtained a series of valuable suggestions. We see that the dreams fully confirm the complex of the association tests. The associations exhibited an intense sexual complex, and the dreams, it may be said, treat only of the theme of pairing. We recognize that the complexes which constellate the associations of her waking life constellate likewise her dreams. The dream analysis presents the same obstacles that occurred in the association experiment. By the analysis of the dreams the sex complex was made clear— its displacement to the writer, the disappointment and the falling back of the patient upon her mother, and, again, the resumption of some mysterious childhood relationship to her brother. The next section shows the sex complex in the hysterical symptom as the cause of her illness.

III. THE HYSTERICAL SYMPTOM

It remains to turn the knowledge gleaned in the two previous sections as to the form and content of her sex complex to the symptoms of her illness. We will begin with the " St. Vitus's dance."

According to the anamnesis as given by the patient, this simply began from reasons unknown. She answered all questions as to its origin in the negative, and it seemed as if it were impossible to arrive at the cause because this was unknown to the patient. But we know fully the resistances which are put forth to the reproduction of all complex ideas. Hysterics are only able to carry out mental introspection in so far as indifferent matters are dealt with ; where it is the question of a complex they are powerless. The complex does not belong entirely to the hierarchy of the ego (conscious) ideas ; by reason of its powerful emotional tone it is (like, moreover, every strong affect) more or less autonomous, and drives the association in its direction even when the ego complex strives to think and to act in its own way. For this reason we cannot reproduce " intimate " things with the same certainty and quietness that we can objective things. The impetus to the concealment of " intimate " things can amount to an almost total incapability of reproduction, as we saw in the case given in chapter vii. To obtain information from a hysteric about " intimate " things, about a complex, we must make a flank attack. Freud has built this into a method—it is psycho-analysis. First of all we liberate all the general cover ideas which stand in any kind of associated (often symbolical) relationship to the complex ideas, and then we gradually approach the complex from different sides. At bottom the method is the same as used by a clever examiner towards some shy candidate. The candidate cannot answer specific and direct questions, he is too excited ; so the examiner first gets answers to a series of general and easy questions where the emotional feeling is not so great, and then the desired answer comes of itself. Were I to ask the patient directly as to the cause of her St. Vitus's dance, I should get nothing ; I therefore first obtain her answers to simple indifferent questions, and arrive at the following :

She liked going to school and liked her teachers. She did not like all the lessons, although she does not recollect that there were any which she especially disliked, or that there were any teachers she especially disliked. She did not like the writing lesson, indeed she disliked going to these. It was during a writing lesson (her second school year) that her (right) hand first began to tremble. The trembling grew gradually stronger, so that she was unable to write ; so she had to miss the writing lesson. Then the tremors began in her right leg, so that very shortly she could not go to school at all. Thus the St. Vitus's dance gradually arose. She remembered also that she could not help crying fearfully and was afraid to go into the streets when it rained, so that she often missed school on this account. The attacks were sometimes stronger, sometimes weaker, so that some days she could go to school, sometimes she couldn't. In her twelfth year the illness became so extreme that she had to give up school altogether.

I think that this narrative brings out clearly enough that the patient was an extremely pampered child who used every opportunity to stop away from school ; as if on purpose to cut out the hated writing lesson, the tremors began in the right arm, and finally these served to keep the child away altogether. The patient admits that when she took the trouble she could suppress the tremor. *But it suited her to be ill.* It seemed to me instructive that at the beginning of the analysis she spoke with uncertainty of her feelings about her school recollections. At first it seemed to her that she liked going to school, then we got the feeling expressed that it was not quite so, and then we got the exact contrary, which corresponds to the facts. This inconsequential way of revealing herself points to method in her (cp. the earlier analyses). There is nothing to show that the patient was conscious of this inconsistency ; on the contrary, it seemed that she believed everything she said at the time of saying it. The school complex, the well-known phenomenon in all asthenic children, led to the formation of a hysterical symptom. It is understandable that the success of an automatism affords a suitable *locus minoris resistentiæ* out of which other automatisms can be developed.

The day after this analysis her tone had again changed. She maintained that she could not say she disliked going to school, she quite liked going. School never made any special impression upon her. Other events occupied her much more, e.g. that once a teacher (female) violently quarrelled with her. Here again we get the same uncertainty and inconsequence.

The St. Vitus's dance got worse in her twelfth year. This was the year when (according to the analysis) the recollections of the sexual cat dreams were produced. In the twelfth year the first feelings of puberty become distinct in many girls, and they begin to be interested in sexual matters. But her twelfth year had still another significance for the patient. In reference to the mother complex the following was obtained :

It occurred to her (after a long pause) her mother was so ill, and still so contented and jolly ; if she could only be like that. Her mother always used to say that her osteomalacia came from being married. But she had become ill twenty-eight years ago, and the doctors say the disease is now curable.

These remarks caused me to ask : " Has that any meaning for you ? " " None ; I can't think of any meaning it would have for me—I have never thought about it." I threw out that it was just possible she had the idea that she might inherit such a disease. " She had never feared that ; in spite of that she could have married." I remarked that some kind of fear like that had perhaps arisen at the time of her first period. " That's impossible, for my mother had said to me long before I was twelve years old that I ought not to marry or I might get the same illness."

We may conclude from this remark that in her twelfth year there were conversations of far-reaching sexual significance, which must have made a strong impression upon the patient to judge from the strength of the resistance with which she sought to hide the explanation of this point. At any rate, we find in her twelfth year one of the first components of her sex complex. The first period had two complexes before it, one having a fully developed automatism, the other one associated with sex feelings.

The possibility of the transposition of this decisive event into a hysterical symptom is given, but not the necessity for it, for the non-ability to marry seems insufficient. One requires the existence of some event which would prepare the way for the repression of the sex complex, some sexual event of childhood. This would be the right place for a sexual trauma, at which the dream seems to hint.

With her menstrual period a new phase in her existence begins —the sexual. It is not surprising that the school complex gives place to the sex complex, although only apparently so. As we have seen, it is still present in the associations, forming a wound which is still scarred and kept up by self-reproaches. That her school complex, the St. Vitus's dance, is still potentially present is seen from the following. One day she felt particularly bad. She described the feelings of heat as unendurable ; whilst speaking, her right arm twitched from time to time, then her left arm. I drew her attention to these movements ; then her legs began slowly to tremble and she said, " It is only with great trouble that I pull myself together, that I am not hitting all round me like before ; I've the greatest desire to do it." We see that at a moment when her energy is quite slackened the old automatisms are again ready to break forth (a confirmation of Janet's theory that every *abaissement du niveau mental* is accompanied by a flaring up of the automatism).

Her first period supplied the provocation for the origin of her present difficulties—feelings of heat in the head and neck, feelings as if there was nothing but blood in the head, that her blood was 40°. Her hands, feet, and body are cold. With these feelings there are always the same obsessional ideas : she is compelled to imagine that she is bleeding from the nose, from all the orifices of her head ; she imagines that clots of the blood which came at her first period are in her head, she is always wanting a whole basin of blood·to come away from her head.

This peculiar symptom complex is undoubtedly referable to her period ; it is nothing else than " a displacement from below upwards " (Freud). The mechanism for this displacement is present in the patient ; we have already seen it unmistakably in her dreams. The heat (blood and fire in the dream) is certainly the sexual heat which occurs at the period. The periods have stopped for some months after having been previously very irregular ; distinct meteorism arose and a posture which made the lower half of the abdomen more prominent. For Freud these are imaginary symptoms of pregnancy. Psychological experience speaks to the same effect ; in any erotic expectation complex in a young woman the child plays a definite part in the associations and dreams.[1] It will be recalled that this takes place also in the associations of our patient. Pregnancy has, moreover, for the patient the particular significance of the danger of osteomalacia—a significance that must be repressed. But I cannot adduce any positive evidence from this case in favour of Freud's views.

The following symptomatic actions are probably dependent upon sex feelings :

(1) The constant seeking for cooling.

(2) The cold ablutions.

(3) The repugnance to meat in any form.

(4) The inability to sit down.

(5) The predilection for gymnastic exercises in her room, accompanied by aversion from all other physical exercises.

These symptomatic actions correspond exactly to the popular hygienic ideas for decreasing sexual excitement.

Positive evidence of the repression of sexual feelings is found in her consequent and obstinate circumlocution in all sex questions. As soon as the examination touched anything relating to sex a full stop was reached, and we were generally left with invincible resistances. On theoretical grounds I was able to be convinced by careful questioning that the patient was correctly informed about sex matters ; but she could not tell me whence came her knowledge, and stubbornly denied ever having read anything on the subject or hearing anything from anybody. She simply knew it. Just before the conclusion of the treatment she admitted, after long hesitancies, that once a girl friend had explained things to her when she was twelve years old. This only serves to show again how strong were the barriers which guarded her sex secrets.

I need not go any further into the visions, they have been explained through the analysis of the dreams.

The course of improvement was tedious, with frequent relapses. Her energy visibly improved, so that her ability to work gradually extended to four or five o'clock in the afternoon (previously she was exhausted by ten o'clock in the morning). She was again able to read and do normal work. But the feelings of heat remained, although they seemed less intense ; in the third month of her treatment she began not to speak about them any more to me ; she expressed surprise that latterly she had had such frequent depressions, the cause of which she could not under-

---

[1] E.g., cp. the somnambulic fantasies of the case described in the " Psychology and Pathology of so-called Occult Phenomena " in *Collected Papers on Analytical Psychology*, by C. G. Jung. Authorized translation edited by Dr. Constance C. Long. (London : Baillière, Tindall and Cox.)

stand. (Formerly if anything unpleasant happened she had no depression but increased feelings of heat.) But the patient still spoke about her feelings of heat to my assistant (a lady doctor). After the dream about the dining-table where I had cleared up her relationship towards me, the earlier nomenclature returned with me also ; she heard the fire-alarm in the dreams and several times, especially in the last week of her sojourn here, the black man returned ; he had disappeared after her first analysis. The dream-analysis explains these recrudescences. The patient could not give vent to her inmost secret ; the sexual compromise as regards myself had failed (in me she could obviously find nothing beyond the sexual as to make it worth while to depart from her rôle of invalid). Unable to tear herself away from her secret, she was obliged to remain with the repressed meaning of the feelings of heat ; she was thus driven back to her earlier symptoms, and to the corresponding terminology, thus assuring herself that my explanations were all lies ; for she could not acknowledge that I was right—this would have jeopardized the apparent genuineness of her illness.

About a month after her departure her doctor wrote to me that she was as bad as before, and that she was full of abuse of the asylum and the doctor, with hints that the doctor had only sought opportunities to have immoral conversations with her. Her morbid personality, i.e. her sexual complex, thus entrenched itself behind an aggressive defence ; the complex discredited the doctor's morality as far as possible in order to obtain the normal mental equilibrium.

The automatism of the disease creates in this wise a free path for its unimpeded development, for every complex has the urge to live itself out unrestrained.

SUMMARY

The complex discovered in the associations is the root of the dreams and of the hysterical symptoms.

The disturbances caused by the complex in the association experiment are but the resistances found by Freud in psychoanalysis.

The mechanisms of repression are the same in the association experiment as in dreams and hysterical symptoms.

In hysteria the complex has an abnormal autonomy, and leads to an active separate existence which progressively degrades and destroys the constellating power of the ego complex. A new morbid personality is then gradually created whose tendencies, judgments, and resolutions proceed entirely in the direction of the will to disease.   The remainder of the normal ego is absorbed by the second personality and forced into the rôle of a secondary dominated complex.

A practical treatment of hysteria must endeavour to strengthen the normal rest of the ego, which is best done by introducing a new complex which shall free the ego from the dominance of the morbid complex.

CHAPTER X

ON DISTURBANCES IN REPRODUCTION IN ASSOCIATION EXPERIMENTS

By C. G. JUNG

THE reproduction method which I first described in a short communication in 1905 in the *Centralblatt für Nervenheilkunde und Psychiatrie*, has been recently subjected to frequent criticism (A. Gross,[1] Heilbronner,[2] Isserlin [3]).

Being overwhelmed with other work, I was unfortunately unable till now to supplement my former incomplete communication by means of the statistical results. In 1905 I maintained : If after completing about one hundred word-associations the subject is requested to repeat the answers to each stimulus-word separately and any of the following conditions occur : (1) memory fails at certain places, (2) the former reaction-word is not given at all, (3) it is given incorrectly, (4) there is silence, (5) it is reproduced with great hesitation—the analysis of the associations distorted in any of these ways in reproduction proved that in most cases this failure was constellated by a " complex." As most investigators in this branch seem disinclined to recognize the slightest heuristic value in Freud's psycho-analytic method, I am, unfortunately, debarred from taking the shortest way, which would simply be to give the analyses in support of that statement. In order to exclude that subjective factor in analysis which is so much feared, there remains no course other than to separate out the objective signs of the complex constellations, the " complex indicators," and their relation to the failure in reproduction ; this will be untainted evidence. I discovered the complex indicators empirically in the analysis ; I saw that in the associations which were distinguished by certain indications a complex was, as a rule, constellating with particular strength and had sometimes led to a " disturbing " interference. If these indicators are

[1] A. Gross, " Kriminalpsychologische Tatbestandsforschung," *Jurist.-psychiat. Grenzfragen*, Bd. V, H. 7. (Marhold : Halle, 1907.)

[2] Heilbronner, " Die Grundlagen der psychologischen Tatbestandsdiagnostik," *Zeitschrift für die gesamte Strafrechtswissenschaft*, Bd. XXVII, p 601.

[3] Isserlin, " Ueber Jung's ' Psychologie der Dementia Præcox,' etc.," *Centralblatt für Nervenheilkunde und Psychiatrie*, Bd. XXIX, p. 329.

really characteristic, i.e. if the analytic method has led to a correct result which will stand proof, the indicators must be in close relation to one another. They will recur preferably at certain associations—for instance, at failures in reproduction and at delayed reactions. If that is not the case, and if the complex indicators are distributed without any selection over the whole test, analysis will have led us to a false conclusion. In my former communication I mentioned, further, that :

(1) The failures in reproduction have occasionally an arithmetical mean time which exceeds the general arithmetical mean (one example).

(2) The failures in reproduction are apparently as frequent at the critical as at the post-critical reactions.

(3) Occasionally there is a tendency to disturbances in reproduction, which may be serial or isolated.

(4) The theory of this phenomenon was sought in the general characteristics of the complex. I there emphasized one characteristic—repression (Freud), because this seemed to me peculiarly well fitted to explain the inhibition to correct reproduction. The chief characteristic of the complex is, at all events, its relative autonomy, which may find expression in two directions : by increased emphasis and stability in consciousness, and by repression—that is, resistance to reproduction in the unconscious. Hence the associations which belong to the complex lack the "flexibility" of the remaining and more indifferent psychic material. (This only holds good of the case when the special complex is inhibited and cannot reach reproduction. The complex itself naturally has complete command of its material, it is even hypermnestic.) This reference of the disturbance in reproduction to a more general psychological peculiarity seems to me a helpful explanation. Obviously the hypothesis is not true of all cases, for one must be first sure that all external sources of disturbance (accidental) have been entirely excluded. My hypothesis is only true for the majority of cases, and, speaking generally, for the majority of complex indicators also.

(5) The complexes exhibited in the association experiment have usually a tone of unpleasure, so that the exceptional condition in which the complex stands during the test may be well qualified as " repression."

I must now prove in detail the fundamental principles of this conception ; that is, that the disturbances in reproduction are complex indicators and agree, as a whole, with the other complex indicators. The method adopted for obtaining this proof is not quite simple, for we must remember that the disturbance in reproduction, like all complex indicators, is no necessary accompaniment of the complex; furthermore, like the other complex indicators, it is not exclusively linked to the critical places but can arise also in the subsequent reactions. The commonest complex indicator is the reaction-time.

DISTURBANCE IN REPRODUCTION AND REACTION-TIME

The readiest method of comparison would be simply to compare the arithmetical mean time of the failures in reproduction with the arithmetical mean of all times or all the rest of the times. But this method would be only adequate if the disturbances in reproduction agreed with the "too long" times. But that is not the case at all; the relationships are much more complicated.

The following very different cases occur:

(1) Critical reaction with $<$ too long time. / disturbance in reproduction.

(2) Critical reaction with too long time.
   Post-critical reaction with disturbance in reproduction.

(3) Critical reaction with disturbance in reproduction.
   Post-critical reaction with too long time.

(4) Post-critical reaction with $<$ too long time. / disturbance in reaction.

(5) Disturbance in reaction at a critical and post-critical reaction (two-limbed series of disturbances).

(6) Disturbance in reproduction at a critical reaction and at three or more subsequent reactions (three- or four-limbed series of disturbances).

The method has to take account of these complicated relationships. In chapter v I made use of the probable mean for the definition of the "too long" reaction-time, with due regard to the fact that the arithmetical mean, as a rule, is disproportionately high in consequence of the influence of the exceedingly long times; these cannot be compensated by exceedingly short times, for the reaction-time is only infinitely variable at the top. The probable mean, therefore, gives, on the whole, a far better picture of the average rapidity of the reaction. Whatever exceeds this average should be regarded, as a rule, as not quite normal. But the probable mean should be only used for large series of figures; it becomes too inexact otherwise, for it is considerably affected by slight accidents. In small series of numbers we must use the arithmetical mean. I start, therefore, from the probable mean of the whole test, and first of all count how many reaction-times with absence of reproduction exceed, how many agree with, and how many are below the probable mean. If my previous suppositions are correct we should expect to find that the majority of disturbances in reproduction exceed the probable mean. Those disturbances in reproduction which exceed or are below the probable mean may be perseverations and may directly follow a too long time ; in these cases the reaction - time immediately preceding cannot be examined. Properly speaking, the reaction - time immediately following should be investigated, because the prolongation of time might only follow afterwards. But that would take us very far. I have hitherto not attempted this examination because it seemed to me that such cases are not very frequent. We will first see how far we get with the above two methods. Be it noted that in these methods my subjectivity is entirely excluded. This makes any re-examination perfectly safe.

The material selected as the basis of my investigation consists of twenty-eight cases which were all picked out considerably earlier and for a purpose quite other than the examination of this particular question. Rather less than a third were selected by myself ; the other two-thirds were selected by various assistants, some of them many years previously. Among the persons tested there were only three mentally healthy, the others were nervous and mental patients of different kinds and of the most diverse reaction type. The material is thus as varied as could be desired, presenting the fewest possible chances of any uniformity in the results. I summarize the results in the following table :

			Association reproductions with absence of reproduction.				
			Above the probable mean.	At	Under	I.[1]	II.[1]
G.	Hebephrenia .	100 associations	22	5	8	10·6	12·5
		Probable mean (P.M.) = 8·5					
		Arithmetical mean (A.M.) = 9					
		35 per cent. failures in reproduction (F.R.)					
A.	Moral insanity	100 ass., P.M. 12·30	—	6	9	14·1	10·2
		A.M. 15·2					
		45 per cent. F.R.					
R. ♀	Hebephrenia	100 ass., P.M. 13·5	11	—	4	—	11·7
		A.M. 20·6					
		15 per cent. F.R.					

[1] The figures in these two columns give the arithmetical mean of the reaction-times of the associations immediately preceding the reproductions that failed : (I, the associations in reproduction absent at the probable mean ; II, for those that were absent below the probable mean.

			Association reproductions with absence of reproduction.				
			Above the probable mean.	At	Under	I.	II.
P.	Paranoia	100 ass., P.M. 11 A.M. 12·9 22 per cent. F.R.	13	2	7	13	13·?
H.	Catatonia	100 ass., P.M. 22 A.M. 30·3 53 per cent. F.R.	33	1	19	25	31
G. ♀	Hysteria and imbecility	50 ass., P.M. 14 A.M. 17 16 per cent. F.R.	6	—	2	—	16
W. ♀	Dementia præcox	100 ass., P.M. 10·5 A.M. 11·3 53 per cent. F.R.	29	—	24	—	10·?
G.	Organic feeble-mindedness	100 ass., P.M. 47 A.M. 57 67 per cent. F.R.	34	2	31	165	67·?
Z. ♀	Dementia præcox	100 ass., P.M. 10 A.M. 14·4 51 per cent. F.R.	32	6	13	14	16·?
H. ♀	Dementia præcox	100 ass., P.M. 10 A.M. 11·5 41 per cent. F.R.	22	5	14	9	10·3
V.	Imbecility	100 ass., P.M. 11 A.M. 11·1 28 per cent. F.R.	16	5	7	10·2	16·1
E	Moral insanity	100 ass., P.M. 15 A.M. 18·1 30 per cent. F.R.	21	5	4	17·8	18
K ♀	Dementia præcox	100 ass., P.M. 17 A.M. 21·8 38 per cent. F.R.	23	—	15	—	24·4
K. ♀	Dementia præcox	100 ass., P.M. 5 A.M. 7·1 25 per cent. F.R.	18	4	3	4·7	9·6
A.	Paranoia	100 ass., P.M. 13·5 A.M. 13·9 14 per cent. F.R.	7	—	7	—	10·4
B.	Psychopathia	113 ass., P.M. 18 A.M. 19·5 27·4 per cent. F.R.	16	2	13	19	17·6
S.	Catatonia	100 ass., P.M. 11 A.M. 14·3 32 per cent. F.R.	24	3	5	11·6	16·6
H.	Imbecility	104 ass., P.M. 18 A.M. 30·4 27·8 per cent. F.R.	14	4	11	56·7	24·?

			Association reproductions with absence of reproduction.				
			Above the probable mean.	At the probable mean.	Under the probable mean.	I.	II.
S.	Psychopathia .	100 ass., P.M. 12	26	4	7	19	16·4
		A.M. 17·4					
		37 per cent. F.R.					
R.	Dementia præcox .	50 ass., P.M. 32	14	2	2	12·5	33·5
		A.M. 38·3					
		36 per cent. F.R.					
R. ♀	Cerebral syphilis	100 ass., P.M. 14	23	3	20	12·6	15·3
		A.M. 17·3					
		46 per cent. F.R.					
S.	Imbecility .	100 ass., P.M. 26	13	—	8	—	55·8
		A.M. 37·5					
		21 per cent. F.R.					
J. ♀	Normal . .	100 ass., P.M. 7	8	—	—	—	—
		A.M. 7·9					
		8 per cent. F.R.					
H.	Alcoholism and imbecility .	100 ass., P.M. 10·5	28	—	9	—	13·3
		A.M. 13·5					
		37 per cent. F.R.					
P.	Normal . .	100 ass., P.M. 7	20	6	7	7·7	8·6
		A.M. 7·9					
		33 per cent. F.R.					
A.	Normal . .	100 ass., P.M. 7	11	—	4	—	8·1
		A.M. 7·8					
		15 per cent. F.R.					
S.	Moral insanity	100 ass., P.M. 12	27	2	11	9	13·3
		A.M. 13·9					
		40 per cent. F.R.					
W.	Neurasthenia .	100 ass., P.M. 15	21	1	9	9	16·8
		A.M. 17·2					
		31 per cent. F.R.					

We may conclude from these figures that, on the average, 62·2 per cent. of the absent reproductions lie, as regards the reaction-times, above the probable mean, 7·5 per cent. coincide with it, and 30·2 per cent. are below it. This agrees with expectation. On the average, 33 per cent. of the associations were not reproduced. The mean time of the two last columns must be considered with the critique mentioned above. They contain cases of very different import. As we have said, we have only taken note of the reaction-time which immediately preceded the disturbance in reproduction, and that, moreover, only in those cases where the disturbed reproduction itself was below the general mean time. But it is quite possible that the disturbance in reproduction is itself no perseveration, but takes place at the critical reaction with a short reaction-time, and that the long reaction-time only follows subsequently. This occurrence would make the result much worse.   So we must here work with minimal figures.   Still the time of the disturbed reproductions here under review exceeds, on the average, the common probable mean by 7·8 and the common arithmetical mean by 4·1.   The values which form the basis of this calculation vary extraordinarily.   The series of figures of the last column are more uniform and yield richer material, but are subject to the same consideration as the figures of the last column but one.   We find here also that, on the average, the reaction-time which precedes this disturbance in reproduction exceeds by 4·2 the probable mean, and by 0·4 the arithmetical mean.   We must remember that the arithmetical mean tends to be displaced upwards, out of all proportion, as our figures sufficiently demonstrate.   In my opinion these figures also speak in favour of, not against, expectation.   If it be remembered how infinitely complicated psychical processes are and how difficult to control, especially in the region of association, we cannot help being astonished at the relative regularity of the results, which are not to be impugned by an incomplete scheme.

DISTURBANCES IN SERIES AND REACTION-TIME

In my material 63·9 per cent. of all failures in reproduction are arranged in series.   This fact shows that there is every reason to relate the failure to the complex, for the complex with its perseveration is in the association experiment a factor *par excellence* for the formation of series, just as it is in ordinary psychological life (which according to the opinion of some ought not to be brought into connexion with psychology at all).   If this deduction from analogy is correct the serial disturbances should exhibit the same complex indicators as the series of complexes—that is, before all, delayed time.   Not to accumulate tables unnecessarily, I omit the tables of the individual series.   The percentage numbers already furnished show that the material is large enough for statistical averages.   The number of disturbances in reproduction which serve as the foundation of these statistics amounts to rather over six hundred.   We calculate the arithmetical mean of all failures in reproduction associations which follow directly on one another, and we compare the mean figure with the individual probable mean and arithmetical mean of the subject in question.

2-limbed series of disturbances are, on the average,   7·7 above the P.M.

2-	,,	,,	,,	,,	,,	3·6	,,	A.M.
3-	,,	,,	,,	,,	,,	9·6	,,	P.M.
3-	,,	,,	,,	,,	,,	6·3	,,	A.M.
4-	,,	.	.	,,	,,	11·6	.,	P.M.

4-limbed series of disturbances are, on the average, 6·4 above the A.M.
5- „ & over „   „   „   „   6·7   „   P.M.
5- „ „ „   „   „   „   2·4   „   A.M.

There is a rise of the time values up to the series of four.
Series of five and over are again lower. This result does not
agree badly with the analytical considerations. We not infrequently find a strong complex perseverating over three or more
terms with a final step-ladderlike decrease of the reaction-times.
The stronger the complex that is aroused the stronger become,
cum grano salis, the disturbances proceeding from it. In longer
series, however (which are also much rarer), other kinds of
experimental disturbances often enter into play.

We can summarize the foregoing by saying : The main
disturbance in reproduction occurs at a too long reaction-time ;
if it does not coincide with this the previous reaction-time is
wont to be too long in the majority of cases. (The question
as to the subsequent reaction-time we leave unsolved, as it is of
slighter importance.)

Another method, perhaps even more instructive, can be used
to demonstrate the higher time values of the series of disturbances.
Taking the twenty-four cases with well-developed series, I
arrange them in two classes, one upon another, in the following
way : First I take those series which begin with a reaction-time
longer than the association immediately preceding, e.g. :

Association correctly reproduced	1st disturbance	2nd disturbance	3rd disturbance	4th disturbance	Association correctly reproduced at the end of the series
9	10	8	6	6	7
10	82	15	—	—	11
6	92	15	8	—	8
12	35	16	16	—	14
		and	so on		

In this way I arranged 119 series of this class, one upon
another, added together the individual columns, and divided
by the number of the terms of the sum.

The second class relates to those series where the disturbance first set in with a reaction-time that is shorter than the
association correctly reproduced that immediately preceded.
For comparison I take the reaction-time of the two previous
associations (it is a matter of indifference whether this is correctly
or incorrectly reproduced). I have excluded from the calculation

all those complicated by "faults," although such series would have supported my results much more strongly.

This class can be thus summarized :

Previous association	Correct reproduction with increased time	1st disturbance	2nd disturbance	3rd disturbance	Correct reproductions at end of series
14	17	8	21	—	10
12	15	13	55	12	13
8	40	12	20	—	9
		and	so on		

There were fifty-six series in this category. A few series where the correct reproduction and the first disturbance in the series had the same reaction-time I have divided equally among the two classes. The results are as follows (given in the arithmetical mean and in one-fifth seconds).

CLASS I

Correct reproduction	1st disturbance	2nd disturbance	3rd disturbance	4th disturbance	5th disturbance	Correct reproduction at end of series
14·8	37·2	22·8	23·9	33	27	17·9

CLASS II

Previous association	Correct reproduction with long R.T.	1st disturbance	2nd disturbance	3rd disturbance[1]	Correct reproduction at end of series
18·3	22·5	13·3	22·7	30	17·6

The average arithmetical mean time of the twenty-four cases made use of here amounts to 19·8. We thus see that with one exception all the times considerably exceed this mean. The exception is in those disturbances in reproduction (Class II) which immediately follow on a longer time.

[1] I omit the fourth and subsequent disturbances, because they are based upon too small a series of figures (under 20)   But they are all considerably above the general arithmetical mean—for this reason alone, that the number and the series of disturbances in reproduction frequently increase with the length of the reaction-time.

DISTURBANCES IN REPRODUCTION AND PROBABLE MEAN TIME

If, as seems proved by this investigation, the disturbance in reproduction occurs chiefly in connexion with the too long times, we may venture to suppose that the number of disturbances increases with the longer individual mean times. That seems, at least, to be the fact in my (limited) material.

With a P.M. time of 5-10 there are, on the average, Dist. Reprod. 29·7

„	„	10·5–15	„	„	„	31·8
„	„	15·5–20	„	„	„	31·8
„	„	20·5 and over „	„	„		44·2

But for the elucidation of this question a far larger material is required.

DISTURBANCES IN REPRODUCTION AND COMPLEX INDICATORS WITH THE EXCLUSION OF THE TOO LONG REACTION-TIMES

Besides the too long reaction-times I have found as complex indicators : a reaction with two or more words where the subject usually reacts with one word, repetition of the stimulus-word, misunderstanding of the stimulus-word, faults, slips of speech, translation into a foreign language, reaction with an otherwise unusual foreign word, interpolation of " Yes " or some other exclamation before or after the reaction, unusual content of the reaction, perseveration in essence and in form. Estimation of the unusual nature of the content and judgment as to perseveration is open to subjective influences. I have, therefore, omitted these two criteria in the investigation. I only except obvious perseveration of a reaction-word when it appears identically the same in the reaction following. I have selected out of the material the nineteen cases characterized by their generally reacting with one word. I count off how many of the complex indicators are present in the whole test and how many of these correspond to the association which failed in reproduction.

The following table presents the results of this investigation in individual figures :

	Correctly reproduced associations.	Absence of reproduced associations.
	Complex signs	Complex signs
1	0·08	0·16
2	0·11	0·31
3	0·03	0·27
4	0·03	0·11
5 . . . . · .	0·15	0·20

	Correctly reproduced associations.	Absence of reproduced associations.
	Complex signs	Complex signs
6	0·11	0·28
7	0·37	0·40
8	0·08	0·26
9	0·06	0·16
10	0·12	0·42
11	0·27	0·39
12	0·03	0·18
13	0·06	0·15
14	0·01	0·02
15	0·06	0·33
16	0·23	0·29
17	0·04	0·15
18	0·31	0·54
19	0·18	0·29

If it be remembered that all complex reactions do not necessarily lead to absence of reproduction, and that the absent reproductions only occur in one-third of all the associations, the result shown by the above table is sufficiently striking. We see that, without exception, in every case more complex indicators occur at the associations with absence of reproduction; so that as a rule they are signalled out beforehand. Those associations with absent reproduction exhibit, on the average, rather more than twice as many complex indicators as those which are correctly reproduced.

Summary

There is in my very diverse material an undoubted connexion between absence of reproduction and too long reaction-time; the main disturbances in reproduction occur when the reaction-time has been too long, and sometimes partly also subsequent to too long reaction-times. Moreover, the association which afterwards fails to be reproduced has, on the average, double as many complex indicators as those correctly reproduced. We have excluded complex indicators which depend upon a subjective estimation of the content of the reaction and the corresponding perseveration. We learn from this that the complex indicators have a tendency to group themselves round certain definite associations; without analysis we cannot, of course, perceive what is the origin of the relationship between these very diverse complex indicators.

CHAPTER XI

STATISTICAL INVESTIGATIONS ON WORD-ASSO-CIATIONS AND ON FAMILIAL AGREEMENT IN REACTION TYPE AMONG UNEDUCATED PERSONS

By Dr. EMMA FURST

At the instigation of Professor Bleuler and Dr. Jung I undertook a statistical investigation of the associations that chiefly occur among normal persons, and as to modifications in these associations due to age, education, and family.

For practical reasons the work divides itself into two parts; the first part deals with the results obtained among the uneducated.

I. Arrangement of the Experiment

Associations were obtained in twenty-four families comprising one hundred subjects, forty-two males and fifty-eight females, aged between nine and eighty-one years.

Those taking part in these tests were :

4 families each consisting of				2	subjects
6 ,,	,,	,,	,,	3	,,
3 ,,	,,	,,	,,	4	,,
4 ,,	,,	,,	,,	5	,,
3 ,,	,,	,,	,,	6	,,
2 ,,	,,	,,	,,	7	,,
1 family		,,	,,	10	,,

So far as language is concerned the material is very much the same, only the last family of ten being of Austrian nationality ; all the other subjects are Eastern Swiss with dialect as their usual speech. But so far as regards intelligence and education the material is very unequal. The subjects were of all degrees of intelligence and class, from the quite unintelligent class up to highly intelligent and educated persons. Twenty-nine of the subjects had only an elementary, and thirty-five a secondary schooling ; fourteen had gone through an intermediate school, and eight had an education corresponding to this ; fourteen of the subjects had had a university career.

Out of the twenty-four families all the subjects in thirteen of these families had about the same degree of education; in eleven families it was pretty equal as to some members, very diverse as to others. In eleven families all the members lived together. The experiment was carried out among normals. Nevertheless among these persons there were some of a very low degree of intellect, with imbecile traits; a few others, especially women, showed slight hysterical symptoms, whilst among the older subjects were some with the physiological changes of age. But all were capable of living in society.

Care was taken not to carry out the tests in conditions of fatigue, after a heavy meal, or late in the evening. In two cases where the tests could only be carried out late at night quite abnormal results were obtained. One subject always saw the stimulus-word as if written before her, but could find no associations. With another the experiment was made at ten o'clock at night after a heavy day's work and moderate indulgence in alcohol. For external reasons no second test could be made. Naturally these two results are not included in the statistical averages. A man of eighty-one had also to be excluded because he proved to be suffering from dementia senilis, with hallucinations of persecution and gave 61 per cent. clang-reactions. These three cases were all men; so that the number of men was reduced to thirty-nine, and the total number of subjects to ninety-seven.

Before beginning the tests an explanation was given by means of a few examples of the various possibilities of association, and the subject was enjoined to react with the first word that occurred. With ninety persons two hundred, with ten persons four hundred associations were made. As a rule two hundred associations were carried out at a session. In two cases with high definition figures and very long reaction-times the test had to be carried out in two sessions both on the same day. The tests were carried out with each individual quite alone, that is, not in the presence of any other member of the family. The stimulus-word was called out in literary German. Jung's list of words was used, the peculiarities of which have been described in chapter ii. The total number of associations carried out and used amounts to twenty-two thousand in round numbers. With eighty-one persons I carried out the tests personally; another nineteen were investigated by four colleagues (men or women); they were their nearest relatives. Unfortunately, time measurements were not made; the experiments began in 1903, when the importance of time in the reaction was not so well known. That my investigations are but little, sometimes not at all, concerned with the effects of the complexes, although these are of chief importance as regards the constellation, be attributed to this circumstance.

II. Classification

I have classified the material according to the Kräpelin-Aschaffenburg [1] method as improved by Jung.

The same criticism has been made against Jung's classification as was formerly made against the Kräpelin-Aschaffenburg classification. Despite Jung's express warning, some critics, e.g. Watt, made the mistake of thinking that Jung claimed to have found, by his classification, the intrapsychical association. There is no suggestion of this anywhere, as any attentive reader of the second chapter in this book can convince himself. Jung's classification is entirely logical-verbal and in no wise prejudges the intrapsychical association. Nevertheless, taking the result as a whole, some conclusions can be drawn as to the general intrapsychical process ; thus in chapter ii a conclusion was made as to attention. The outer classification cannot of itself settle anything about the inner conditions of the association ; it does not, indeed, deal with the question. That belongs to the psychoanalytic method as demonstrated in chapters vii and ix.

That a classification based upon logical points of view does not afford merely accidental and arbitrary results is best seen by the changes of the reactions in disturbed attention, changes which follow certain laws and can be expressed in figures. Naturally the classification does not bring out everything ; still it brings out a great deal which makes the investigation valuable. In spite of the many difficulties of this classification, I decided on it because no better one is known to me ; for its principles I refer the reader to chapter ii.

III. Results of the Tests

As the following investigations show, the subjects showed a preference for certain association forms. This is particularly true of the predicative relationship, substantive-adjective, and inversely (predicate type). According to the frequency of the different kinds of associations in a subject, five types of association may be distinguished, among which there are transition types. In fifty subjects we found two or more kinds of associations about equally represented, e.g. co-ordinations and motor reactions, or co-ordinations and predicates, or predicates and motor reactions. These I grouped as *mixed types*. In the rest of the subjects one definite kind of association predominated over the others, amounting, approximately, to more than 40 per cent. of all the associations.

[1] Aschaffenburg, " Experimentelle Studien über Assoziationen " (Kräpelin's *Psychologische Arbeiten*). *Investigations on the Associations of Normal Persons*, chapter ii. Certain changes were made in Jung's list, as will be seen.

In nearly every subject I came across more or less well-marked complex phenomena. A detailed investigation of these was not possible in all cases on account of the amount of the material, the absence of time measurements and the absence of analyses. In the following descriptions of individual families a particular description of the individual subject is often necessary. I have begun with those families standing lowest in the scale as regards intelligence and education, in order to show the change in association type with increasing education. This procedure is justified by the fact that education is one of the factors which most seriously influences the nature of the reactions. All the figures in the tables are given in percentages.

In several families a striking agreement was found between the members of the family as regards the nature of the associations. To express this agreement or this difference, as the case might be, by a simple figure, Dr. Jung devised the following calculation :

The individual figures of any two members of a family who are to be compared are placed together, the differences are written out, these differences are added together, and the sum is divided by the number of classes in the classification.

Example

Kind of association	Husband	Wife	Difference
1. Co-ordination	6·5	0·5	6
2. Sub- and supra-ordination . . .	7	—	7
3. Contrast association	—	—	—
4. Predicates as to value	8·5	95	86·5
5. Other predicates	21	3·5	17·5
6. Relationship of subject and object . .	15·5	0·5	15
7. Designation of time, place, means, etc. .	11	—	11
8. Definition	11	—	11
9. Coexistence	1·5	—	1·5
10. Identity	0·5	0·5	—
11. Verbal-motor connexion	12	—	12
12. Word-formation	6	—	6
13. Word-completion	—	—	—
14. Clang-association	—	—	—
15. Remainder group (faults, meaningless, indirect associations)	—	—	—
Total		=	173·5

$$\text{Average difference, D} = \frac{173 \cdot 5}{15} = 11 \cdot 5$$

$$D = 11 \cdot 5$$

D gives, not perhaps in the most ideal way, the typical measure of the difference ; in practice it is a very useful figure, considerably abbreviating the exhibition of the differences and avoiding much repetition. As the above table shows, the calculation of this difference was not based upon Jung's detailed classification ; first, on account of greater simplicity, and secondly, because a nicer classification increases the number of unavoidable vagaries. Therefore all divisions which seemed uncertain or were infrequent were grouped in one class. All coadjuncts with the same supraconcept, similarity, inner and outer relationship, by example, and causal dependence were included in the class of co-ordination ; similarly, the verbal-motor connexions and quotations were put together. The inclusion of indirect associations, faults, and meaningless reactions in one class is justified by the fact that these are, as a rule, all to be regarded as disturbances ; their individual estimation is unimportant in this inquiry. The distribution of the associations among these fifteen groups is, on the whole, very simple if one keeps to certain logical norms, and it should lead to approximately satisfactory conclusions. The following results seem to justify this view :

DESCRIPTION OF THE INDIVIDUAL TEST FAMILIES

FAMILY I

Daughter, 16 years, polisher ; mother, 45 years, laundress ; father, 47 years, tailor. All three test persons are very unintelligent and very badly educated.

Test persons	Value predicates	Other predicates	Other inner associations	Outer associations	Clang-reactions	Sentence reactions	Type
Father, 47 years.	8·5	21	51	19·5	—	9	mixed
Mother, 45 „ .	95	3·5	1	0·5	—	63	predicate
Daughter, 16 „ .	98	0·5	—	1·5	—	95	predicate

Stimulus-word	Father	Mother	Daughter
1. Green	colour	joy	is nice
2. Water	bluish	good	is useful
3. Prick	with a knife	disagreeable	is not good
4. Angel	appearance	good, always good	nice
5. Long	measure	correct	it's long
6. Table	furniture	is nice	is useful

Stimulus-word	Father	Mother	Daughter
7. Haughty	question of the heart	unpleasant	is not nice
8. Proud	vulgar	bad sign	is also not nice
9. Wicked	not good	disgusting	is wicked
10. Friendly	good feeling	is pleasant	is nice
11. Bear	a burden	is good, is pleasant	is nice
12. State	the people's laws	is proper	useful
13. Stalk	liquorice root	must be so	is nice
14. Ink	black	good, useful	also useful
15. Rich	private income	good in all cases	is also nice
16. Mountain	high	O, beautiful	nice
17. Salt	marriage	very good	useful
18. Habits	of the people	very good, good habits	nice
19. Stupid	silly	it's stupid	it's stupid
20. Tooth	in the mouth	is good, is useful	is nice

The daughter is an extreme predicate type. Throughout the whole experiment she makes use almost exclusively of the same reactions—*good, nice, useful*, and their negatives.

In many places the form of the reaction is quite unsuitable and without meaning, as, e.g. *bear — is nice ; part — is nice ; month — is nice ; broad — is nice.* Very characteristic of her limitations are the identities she makes which vividly recall imbecility. She even notices herself her frequent repetitions, and tries to find another association ; finds none, and simply repeats the stimulus-word in sentence form : *long — is long.* Probably a slight emotional stupor had a share in this, although at the time of the tests she did not seem embarrassed.

Still the general impression is that of embarrassment ; we may recall the difficulties of adjustment that Wehrlin's imbeciles had (chapter iii) ; there seems to be something of the sort here. Comparing the examples we have given, a high degree of resemblance between daughter and mother will be noticed.

The mother shows the same disposition towards the finer peculiarities of the reactions as her daughter, but she has a freer choice of predicates, which is further expressed by the existence of a few objective predicates ; still, she also has a very limited vocabulary.[1] Thus we find *good, is good, very good, always good, is not good,* 54 times ; *beautiful, is beautiful,* 17 times ; *useful,* 10 times ; *necessary,* 7 times ; *must be,* 5 times ; *also right,* twice.

In contrast with the daughter, in whom we find, it is true, judgments as to value, but without strongly pronounced subjective

---

[1] This remark is, of course, only made as regards her mental condition during the experiment.

valuations, her mother does show rather more distinct traces of her own personality.

Examples

Stimulus-word	Daughter	Mother
Yellow	not nice	no, delicate colour
New	nice	much better than old
Book	useful	I like a good one
Frog	not nice	I don't like
Plum	good	I like
Coffee	useful	I love my coffee

This rather freer way of reaction suggests a lesser degree of embarrassment. Many awkward reactions (*is nice, pleasant, unpleasant*, etc.) point to her very low intellectual level.

The father belongs to the mixed type, deviating in behaviour both from his wife and his daughter. We get, nevertheless, 29·5 per cent. of predicates, which show, however, but slight agreement in kind with those of the other two persons.

His intellectual and educational level is well expressed in the following figures :

Designation of place, time, etc.   .   11 per cent.
Definition   11   ,,

As is well known, imbeciles prefer the use of these forms. There are, besides, many awkward and affected reactions.

Examples

Fear	pressure over the heart
Kiss	delivery of love
Family	consists of parents and children
Cow	does chew the cud
Sofa	pleasant piece of furniture
Understanding	lies in the brain

This kind of reaction is very similar to that found by Wehrlin (chapter iii) in slight degrees of imbecility. In this case, as in his, the adjustment is towards the meaning of the stimulus-words, with a tendency to explain the meaning of the stimulus-word and to give the reaction in sentence form. But there are essential differences ; we have a greater wealth of ideas, better powers of abstraction, greater verbal facility—all shown by the quite appropriate predicates, which are external and rather objective, and by verbal reminiscences, quotations, and word-formations, which are almost entirely absent in imbeciles.

Examples

Soldier	servant of the State
Love	affection
Eye	of the law
Book	of life
Laugh	in one's sleeve
Prudence	is the mother of wisdom
Folk	crowd of people
Moon	a heavenly body

This family shows various types. The two females belong to one type with a difference between them in the subjective and egocentric apprehension of the stimulus-word. The husband belongs to an objective type. So far as age is concerned the relationship of inner to outer associations discloses no laws ; in mother and daughter the classification is almost the same ; the father, as the oldest test person of the family, has fewest inner associations. Common to all three is a verbal want of facility corresponding to their low level of intellect and education. This is noticed in the frequent sentence form, the many repetitions and the clumsy reactions, partly in dialect, partly new formations.

Average difference of the reaction type [1] :

$$\left.\begin{array}{l}\text{Father}\\\text{Mother}\end{array}\right\} 11{\cdot}5 \qquad \left.\begin{array}{l}\text{Mother}\\\text{Daughter}\end{array}\right\} 0{\cdot}5 \qquad \left.\begin{array}{l}\text{Father}\\\text{Daughter}\end{array}\right\} 12{\cdot}1$$

Agreement between father and mother is extremely slight (be it remembered that by the method of calculation used the greatest difference could only be 13·3) ; it is still less between father and daughter. On the other hand, there is an extraordinary agreement between mother and daughter, the daughter proceeding still further in the direction of the maternal reaction type, withdrawing still more from the father. It is difficult to say on what the difference, on the one hand, between father and mother, and the agreement, on the other hand, between mother and daughter are founded. One is inclined to think first of all that the female sex of the experimenter has an effect upon the adjustment of the subject. We need only think here, of course, of a phenomenon of adjustment, for the type of reaction is not necessarily constant, as Jung and Riklin have already proved. It is conceivable that the subject would have had a different attitude towards another experimenter. Again, the fact that the experimenter (a woman) is of higher intellectual and social grade than the subject may influence the result. Experience shows that such factors are of great importance in the reaction type. We must, above all, realize that we are here only dealing with relative

[1] The figures are from calculations made by Dr. Jung.

values which are in no wise chiefly connected with the intellectual qualities of the subject, but mainly with the emotions. Jung and Riklin have shown that, influenced by relaxation of attention, the reaction type can undergo considerable changes in the same experiment. But attention is after all but a fragment of affectivity [1] (Bleuler). We must consider the possibility that the experimenter, by reason of her sex, her intellectual and social class, touched specific complexes in the subjects which condition the peculiar phenomena of the adaptation. Finally, the striking differences between husband and wife would also find its explanation in factors concerned with the test persons themselves ; such an explanation would require information about the " spiritual bond " between the couple, and about their complexes, obviously a very delicate and complicated investigation. That perhaps some repelling complex was here in question seems suggested by the fact that in other married couples there is a striking agreement in type between husband and wife. That many other complicated mental factors do enter into consideration is, of course, perfectly obvious ; but these are beyond our present knowledge. The explanation of the agreement between mother and daughter we are disposed to find in their common life and *milieu*, as well as in the mental dependence of the child upon her mother. But it is questionable whether the matter is quite so simple for there are cases where this assumption does not hold. It would rather seem as if greater importance must be attributed to the individual complexes and their more or less accidental agreements.

FAMILY II

The associations were carried out in two sisters and three brothers aged 31–43 years, and for comparison in the wife of the youngest brother. All belong to the artisan class and are uneducated ; their intelligence varied from weak to moderate.

Test persons	Value predicates	Other predicates	Other inner associations	Outer associations	Clang-reactions	Sentence form	Type
1. Brother, 34 years	20	47·5	25·5	6·5	—	11	predicate
2. His wife, 32 ,,	29	40	20	7·5	—	8	,,
3. Brother, 41 ,,	17	35·5	28·5	19·5	0·5	22	,,
4. ,, 39 ,,	12	12·5	35·5	39·5	0·5	—	mixed
5. Sister, 43 ,,	7	16·5	26	45	1	13	superficial
6. ,, 31 ,,	12·5	3	33·5	49	0·5	2	,,

[1] *Affektivität, Suggestibilität u. Paranoia* (Halle : Marhold, 1906.)

Stimulus-word	No. 1	No. 2	No. 3	No. 4	No. 5	No. 6
Head	big	hard	hair	brain	hair	neck
Green	grass	grass	carpet	blue	field	red
Water	cold	thin	to wash	wine	cold	cloud
Prick	needle	pain	needle	to lighten	holly	sensitive
Long	short	short	meter measure	short	—	short
Ship	big	round	sail	anchor	sea-ship	water
Plough	nice	nice	lie	field	hero	field
Bear	heavy	heavy	children	lie	ill	lift
State	big	big	hat	Swiss	taxes	republic
Haughty	wild	not	when angry	soft-hearted	Anna	soft-hearted
To dance	difficult	jolly	schottische	jollity	—	jump
Lake	big	big	Vevey	sea	Zurich lake	river
Ill	heavy	heavy	nose-bleeding	healthy	Mrs. X.	healthy
Proud	wild	not nice	calling	unpleasant	M.	high-spirited
Wicked	peaceful	not nice	often	good	Anne	good
Swim	difficult	jolly	water-bird	sing	not I	water
Travel	nice	nice	often	pleasant	I should like to, to Italy	nice
Blue	green	colour	nice	green	lake	red
Threaten	danger	not nice	often	obedient	—	punish

Subjects Nos. 1 and 2. Both very unintelligent and uneducated ; artisans.—The similarity between these two, husband and wife, is very striking both in the chief and in the sub-classes. In both the predicates are high (67·5 and 69 per cent.); there are very few motor reactions, co-ordinations, and coexistences. The agreement extends to the more subtle peculiarities of individual reactions. Both react to the same stimulus-word thirty times with the same reaction. The associations are very simple and obvious and refer, especially in the wife, to their immediate surroundings. The predicates mainly give colour, form, and size, or some very general estimate of the stimulus content such as *good, nice*, without subjective estimate ; they are frequently repeated. The wife more especially reacts to verbs by general concepts, as *mankind, child*.

The agreement is seen not only in the general quantitative relationships, but also in both persons having a strong tendency to repeat certain words. The husband reacts with the word *big* 23 times, his wife 15 times (in the other members only, on the average, 0·7 times). *Beautiful* is repeated by the husband 11 times, by the wife 25 times (by the other members, on the average, thrice). The word *difficult* is repeated 9 times by the husband, 4 times by his wife ; it does not occur at all among the others.

In both subjects there are distinct complex constellations, which are rather more numerous in the wife. To stimulus-words suggesting a certain agility, the man who is physically weak and clumsy reacts several times by *difficult* (*dance, swim, take care, meet, sing*). A few other reactions are constellations from the family and household life of the subjects, worried by economic troubles.

The wife's complexes are mainly economic worries, a great number of children, and quarrels with her husband's relatives. She feels herself despised and unjustly treated. The complex reactions are sometimes expressed very openly, sometimes by motor and meaningless reactions and particularly by general concepts. The latter are found exclusively in response to stimulus-words with an emotional tone (as *unjust, despise, stranger*, etc.) to which *mankind* is always the reaction. But we cannot hold the complexes altogether responsible for the frequency of these general concepts in the uneducated as contrasted with the educated. The verbal want of facility among the uneducated is partly responsible. Whilst educated persons are usually able to find a motor reaction when there is a momentary blockade to the activity of association evoked by some emotionally toned stimulus-word, no such motor reaction occurs to the uneducated and unintelligent, who then employ some general concept which means nothing.

The want of education in these two subjects is again shown : by reactions that are inappropriate or make no sense ; by taking the stimulus-words in their dialect sense and by reactions in clumsy or dialect forms ; by the use of numerous designations of place, time, purpose, and means with the preposition ; by the small number of motor reactions. The wife shows this, furthermore, by her numerous, though extremely simple, general concepts and her difficulty in reacting to rarer words, especially abstracts.

A fire	difficult (thick smoke)
Colour	wild
Deaf	bull (*taub* (deaf) in dialect = mad)
Hatchet	cutting
Dog	free (dialect = good-natured)
View	of the dog

Subject No. 3. Elder brother of No. 1, of medium intelligence and slight education ; holds a responsible position as warder in a house of correction.—Quantitatively there is great resemblance to No. 1. But there is a very essential difference ; in his reactions

No. 3 shows himself influenced to a large extent by indifferent recollections and by emotionally toned events of the past and present. The associations thus receive an extremely individual turn ; i.e. were we to reckon up with how many other ideas this subject makes the like reaction to the same reaction-word we should obtain a great number of associations which were entirely individual. Thus this subject was the only one out of one hundred subjects who reacted *proud — occupation.* We shall be certainly right in assuming that by this reaction he expresses joy at his present position, which means an advance for him which he made great efforts to obtain. A few other emotionally toned chains of thought may be gathered from the associations. In the following associations he touches upon the relationship to his superiors.

Modest	question of occupation
Trust	with a certain treatment
People	civil servant
Choose	authority
Honour	yes
Haughty	when angry
Seek	large orders

The strongest emotional tone is found in his feeling of responsibility for the criminals, in his fear of their attempts at escape, and especially in his apprehension of the danger of his being attacked. The latter very intensive affect constellated a whole series of associations :

Wild	interned
To take care	of the interned
Danger	every day
Meet	unfavourable
Fear	little
Blood	human blood
Door	open
Caution	master
Locksmith	proper guard
Pipe	weapon

Besides these there are a number of more or less emotionally toned reactions, part of them arising from his former occupation of tailor, part from narrower or wider surroundings.

Bring	on requisition	Public-house	little
Paper	examine	Write	much
Wagon	three pieces	Travel	often
Forget	what, already	Angry	often
Free	a little	Pity	may be
Soldier	none	Luck	seldom
Smell	air of cells	Family	three in family

Pencil	pocket-shaped	Lake	Vevey
Copy-book	examine	Full	anger
Punish	often	Threaten	often
Railway-station	best when near	Brother	two

His want of education is documented by some awkward, coarse expressions, with formation of new words or word combinations, e.g. *purpose — family-purpose*, by dialect expressions and by the wrong use of words, e.g. :

Eat	with good taste (in the sense of enjoyment)
Neck	formerly tainted (had a goitre)
Fireplace	necessity for a Russian

He belongs to the complex-constellation type described by Jung and Riklin, in whom a stimulus idea arouses a whole memory complex. We recognize in this case that the feeling of responsibility and fear of his own life, perhaps also the thought that he is not quite adequate to his position, determine the subjective constellation of the associations.

The divergence from these two subjects, 4 and 6, is clearly seen in the eldest brother and the youngest sister, who both belong to the mixed type and agree with each other in many respects ; for instance, in the classes supraconcept, similarity, contrast, coexistence, and motor reactions, as also in their common tendency towards reaction with the same grammatical form (the sister 54·5 per cent. and the brother 66·5 per cent., corresponding with the greater number of co-ordinations). Whilst both subjects had to the same stimulus-word the same reaction in twenty-eight cases and a very similar reaction in thirty-eight cases, the brother has the following reactions in common with the rest of his family :

With subject No. 1	.	.	.	11 reactions
,, ,, ,, 2	.	.	.	7 ,,
,, ,, ,, 3	.	.	.	1 reaction
,, ,, ,, 5	.	.	.	3 reactions

The number of predicates is considerably less in both these subjects, the number of coexistences and motor reactions much greater than in subjects 1 and 3. Still there are considerable differences between subjects 4 and 6. The brother, who is the most uneducated and rather imbecile, gives a very objective and but slightly individual impression quite unaffected by personal memories, and this despite the many value predicates. Beyond the predicates *big, beautiful, good, friendly, pleasant,* and *unpleasant,* the associations are mainly coexistences, slang phrases, and contrasts. There is very little that is individual.

Subject No. 6. Unmarried sister, 32 years old ; no better educated but rather more intelligent.—Her reactions are rather

more superficial than her brother's ; she has far fewer co-ordinations and objective predicates but more verbal reminiscences.
In contrast with her brother, she shows more complex indicators,
which are sometimes quite open and expressed by very frank
subjective judgments, whilst sometimes they are concealed in
faults and ve y long reaction-times at emotionally toned stimulus-
words :

Beloved	grand	Suppose	one can
Make	I like	Kiss	nice
False	hateful	Quarrel	hateful
Decency	one must have	Love	nice
Beat	hateful	Dirty	hateful
Stupid	—	Wild	hateful
Right	—	Choose	—
Pain	suffer	View	to have
Modest	be	Fear	to have
Visit	we can	Understand	understood
Worthy	be	Separate	hurts
Caution	to have	Hunger	hurts[1]
Forget	we can		

The reactions are likewise very simple, with many familiar
phrases ; there were no affected or meaningless reactions.

*Subject No. 5. Elder sister, unmarried, 43 years old ; of medium
intelligence, secondary education ; fairly read, vivacious and
energetic, with many interests.*—The relationship of inner to outer
associations is the same as her sister's, with whom she has most
similarity—especially seen in the complex phenomena as faults
and delayed reaction-times. But the association type is much
more superficial. Despite the large number of predicates there
are very few value predicates. On the other hand, there were
30 per cent. word-formations, some very simple, taken from
her immediate surroundings, her housekeeping and occupation ;
others were more unusual, showing fair reading. The rest of
the associations are also simple and appropriate. There were no
meaningless, affected, cumbersome reactions. There were 4·5
per cent. of faults. It is not impossible that this is connected
with the motor type. Faults are chiefly found in persons with a
lively complex. But a strong complex demands much psychical
energy, leaving less power of concentration at the disposal of
indifferent matters ; this results in decrease of attention and a
superficial type. She is chiefly differentiated from her sister by
a greater number of individual associations. The faults are all
found at emotionally toned stimulus-words : *friendly, dance,
manners, threaten, despise, take care, worthy, impudence.*

---

[1] Perseveration from the previous reaction.

As will be seen from the tables, the ratio of inner to outer associations shows no relationship to age reducible to rule. There is no great similarity in type between the brothers and sisters ; they were separated in early youth and only lived together for a time. Although the ratio of the figures is relatively similar, the qualitative relationships are most diverse, dependent principally upon difference in the complex constellation.

In one subject the complex constellation is chiefly expressed by a freer occurrence of individual associations exhibiting the chief complex without disguise ; in another subject it was chiefly shown by its effects in causing disturbances in attention and inhibitions to associations ; this naturally conditions a great difference in the reactions. According to Dr. Jung's calculations on my material $D = 5\cdot9$ for all uneducated men who are not related, for women it is 6. The relationship of the husband and wife, $1\cdot8$, is considerably below these figures ; that of the husband and his eldest brother is $2\cdot7$; the intermediate brother and younger sister is $2\cdot8$; all the other differences exceed $5\cdot9$, sometimes even 6. The familial similarity is thus very limited. But, in contrast with the previous family, there is very considerable agreement between husband and wife.

FAMILIES III AND IV

Six subjects. The associations were taken in three brothers aged 74, 71, and 63 years ; a sister aged 67 and her children, a son of 31 years, and a daughter aged 27. The intelligence in all was but medium ; all were uneducated, peasants or artisans.

Test persons		Value predicates	Other predicates	Definitions	Other inner associations	Outer associations	Clang-reactions	Remainder group	Predicate
I	1. Brother, 74 years	40	21·5	11	17	10·5	—	—	predicate
	2. ,, 71 ,,	10	14·5	34·5	30	11	—	—	predicate definition
	3. ,, 63 ,,	31	27	1·5	27·5	13	—	—	predicate
II	4. Sister, 67 ,,	24·5	14·5	—	36·5	24	—	0·5	predicate co-ordination
	5. Her son, 31 ,,	6·5	22	—	32	39	—	0·5	mixed predicate
	6. Her daughter, 27 ,,	18	30·5	—	33	17·5	—	1·5	predicate

We must divide this family into two groups : Group I with subjects Nos. 1–3 ; Group 2 with subjects Nos. 4–6.

Group I have all considerably more inner associations and

are strongly differentiated from Group II in the finer relationships also. They are very similar among themselves ; all three have relatively few outer associations. The eldest and the youngest of the brothers are pronounced predicate types with many value predicates ; the intermediate brother is a mixed type in whom definitions predominate ; the eldest has also 11 per cent. definitions. All three react extremely slowly, with great attention and reflection ; this is especially true of subjects 1 and 2, who usually suppressed or did not speak out the first unconscious association in order to give a " better answer " (e.g. *head — green — who is unskilled*).

Subject No. 1. Eldest brother, 74 years old, uneducated.— Together with 11 per cent. of definitions, there are 40 per cent. value and 17 per cent. objective predicates ; some of them such as occur in many uneducated or elderly persons.

The intense striving to produce something " good, clever," leads to a series of affected, studied, awkward reactions, to dialect forms and neologisms.

Examples of Ordinary Value Predicates

State	good	Way	wearisome
Rich	pleasant	Salt	indispensable
Quarrel	unpleasant	Air	blows away (i.e. violent wind)
Hay	nice smell	Wood	agreeable
Bread	tastes good	Hit	objectionable
Sail	indispensable	Deaf	objectionable
Dog	pleasant	Good	encouraging
Unjust	insulting	Fear	fatiguing
Law	orderly	Seek	deceiving
Beloved	uniting	Tired	uneasy
Brother	amiable	Family	widespread
Long	sadly	Great	remarkable
Ill	pitiable	Ring	holding together
Haughty	disapproving	Proud	fatiguing
Flower	nice smell		

Although many of these reactions belong to the predicate type, it can be seen that there is an easy transition to the definition type ; the predicate, which is largely charged with emotion, gradually assumes an explanatory character. The subject endeavours to make some intellectual addition to his personal estimation of the object designated by the stimulus-word ; this quite corresponds to the tendency to react as " cleverly " as possible. The following associations show a further stage of this tendency ; they consist essentially of combinations of value predicates with subordinations, some of which are appropriate, some of which are too general ; these lead again to true explanatory reactions such as are found among imbeciles :

Blue	beautiful colour	Month	part of the year
Stork	clever animal	Resin	preparatory substance
Coffee	valuable drink	Neck	part of the body
Ask	valuable answer	Sleeper	part of the railway
Laugh	comfortable frame of mind	Looking-glass	reflection
Market	old custom	Moon	heavenly body
Chimney	heavy work (building)	Bed	household furniture
Hatchet	dangerous object	Stone	material
Goat	useful animal	Railway-station	halt for travellers
Potato	pleasant food	Sofa	pause for a rest
Clergyman	indispensable teacher	Write	business matters
Coal	useful substance	Bone	substance
Kiss	recognition of friendship	To make	industry
Locksmith	fatiguing work	Angel	life
Plate	necessary object	Portfolio	writing stuff
Pipe	dangerous substance	Play	for pleasure

In the stress upon the meaning of the word, the far-fetched association, and especially in the tendency to explanation these reactions resemble those found among imbeciles. The tendency to explanation is particularly expressed by the universal concepts, which are either too narrow or too broad and by the true explanations. The difference consists in the large number of predicates, which are to a large extent subjective, in the far bigger vocabulary, in the appropriate concepts, and in the rarer use of the sentence form.

The reactions of this subject, who is by no means an imbecile and is not a senile dement, are theoretically very remarkable ; the question therefore arises : Why does this subject react as if he were an imbecile ?

We have seen that not only does he belong to a family where predicates predominate, but he himself shows an unmistakable tendency to predicates. As Jung and Riklin have shown, in the predicate type the stimulus idea is very plastic, and thus arouses associations that are very rich in their content. The plasticity of the stimulus presentation depends in the first place upon the adjustment, i.e. upon the question whether the reaction carries with it great strain of attention or not. This increased attention can arise from different emotional considerations. In the first place, the unusual and exciting situation which recalls a school examination plays a part. People mostly conceive the experiment as an examination of intelligence, and so endeavour to react as " cleverly " as possible, so as not to appear " stupid." This feeling is, furthermore, aroused by the fact that many uneducated persons feel themselves mentally inferior to the educated even if they do not always openly admit it. Many people are, indeed, very sensitive in this respect. We may, then, really speak of an " intelligence complex." The like holds true of imbeciles (who, moreover, do not all exhibit the typical definition), who frequently have an insight into their own intellectual defects and have therefore a certain ambition not to appear so " stupid."

Our subject is an old man who obviously fears that he will be regarded as stupid and therefore takes the experiment very seriously. Hence the amount of thought and reflection given to the reactions. This emotional constellation is, moreover, easily read in the associations (e.g. *knowledge — to wish*). This case throws a certain light on the imbecile way of reacting and illuminates something fundamental in the predicate type. We see that between the definition and the predicate type there is a transition ; in the predicate type it is not a question of an entirely new attitude but only of something that has been changed in form. The extreme predicate types really at bottom also make " explanations " ; their predication reaction, *pleasant, beautiful, to be recommended*, always means *that is something pleasant, beautiful*, etc. These are emotional explanations without any intellectual addition.

Subject No. 2 reacted very slowly ; the experiment lasted four hours. Despite a quantitative difference, No. 2 has qualitatively a fair resemblance with No. 1. The attitude is likewise explanatory, the intellectual factor overcoming the more moderate emotional predicates. We therefore find here an increased number of definitions and co-ordinations, whilst the value predicates decrease considerably. The following examples show the similarity of the attitude with that of No. 1.

Air	necessary for life	Pay	a duty
Give	good deed	Swim	great advantage
Bring	kindness	Tooth	advantage for the stomach
Proud	improper	Hit	necessity
Needle	of good steel	Head	of man
Mug	beautiful gift	Basket	for clothes
Ride	better than running	Mock	improper behaviour
Ring	is not square	Speak	fortunate gift
Big	certain States	Laugh	jolly mood
Part	of a piece of land	Hot	means of warming
Table	in the room	Market	place for sale
Sleep	for strengthening	Wagon	transport
Month	a part of the year	Chimney	smoke conductor
Moon	part of the world	Portfolio	paper-holder
Plate	kitchen utensil	Forget	neglect
Pain	interrupts sleep	Eat	necessary for stomach
Fruit	healthy food		

Subject No. 3. Here the tendency to definition and explanation recedes somewhat and is chiefly replaced by predicates ; among these are many value predicates and co-ordinate relationships in which the tendency to explanation can be indistinctly recognized. As compared with the two previous subjects these reactions leave a much more natural and less forced impression ; they are not so affected and far-fetched ; the individual reactions also show a freer treatment of the stimulus-word and much less limitation to the meaning of the stimulus-word.

Month	to record	Air	necessary
Purpose	carry out	Wicked	dangerous
Floor	good, guaranteed	Ask	adverse
Bear	powerful	Flower	costly
Haughty	nervous	Ring	fits
Husband	intoxication	Ink	brilliant
Fear	unavoidable	Salt	necessary
Hot	pleasant	Hatchet	dangerous
Plough	uneven	To cook	troublesome
Lake	melancholy	Narrate	difficult
Play	quarrel	Law	acceptable
Strong	overspirited	Pride	imperious
Needle	useful	Soldier	necessary exercise
Tooth	serviceable	Family	comfortable
Stupid	insufficient	Hunger	devouring
Useful	pleasant	White	soilable
Song	unschooled	Intention	accident
Work	difficulties—in writing	Pipe	transport
Coffee	shortly	Duty	responsible
Broad	spread out	Give	charitable

Subject No. 4 is the married sister of these persons. As the tables show, she does not differ greatly from her brothers' type ; she is relatively most like her youngest brother but shows rather more tendency to value predicates. These consist in numerous repetitions of *beautiful, useful, painful*, etc. There is also a certain tendency to explanation, which is, however, only hinted at in the rather numerous supraordinations and frequently partakes rather of the nature of value predicates.

Examples

Moderate	virtue	Clergyman	learned man
Coffee	plant	Deaf	illness
Modest	virtue	Sing	virtue
Floor	wood	Folk	mankind
Apple	fruit		

There is a distinct tendency to give the " material " of the object called up by the stimulus-word, e.g. :

Wall	iron	Ship	wood
Cover	iron	Copy-book	paper
Needle	steel	Portfolio	leather
Floor	wood		

A like tendency is often very pronounced in imbeciles.

Subject No. 5 (the son of No. 4) deviates somewhat from his mother, for the number of value predicates is considerably less, whilst the outer associations increase. He approaches his mother's type, for description of the material of the object plays a part and predicates are rather numerous ; but, in contra-distinction to his mother, the predicates are less emotional relationships than some external or objective quality. That his attitude towards the meaning of the stimulus-word is less intensive is seen also by the increased coexistences and frequent colloquial phrases. He is an artisan and relatively intelligent ; hence his somewhat greater adaptability to the new position. The following comparative list shows how much more objective and unrestrained his reactions are.

Stimulus-word	No. 1	No. 2	No. 3	No. 4	No. 5
Goat	useful animal	small milch animal	useful	useful	milk
Potato	pleasant food	food	indispensable	food	earth
Old	troublesome	buildings	different	weak	young
Hit	reprehensible	necessity	powerful	painful	hammer
Family	widespread	parents and children	agreeable	beautiful	members
Narrow	unpleasant	difficult to breathe	objectionable	painful	broad
False	unpleasant	unfaithful	quarrelsome	vice	understood
Quiet	pleasant in old age	lonely	lonely	wild	the lake is quiet
Speak	with caution	happy gift	naughty	lovable	tongue
Rich	pleasant	who has much knowledge	tempting	beautiful	money
Mountain	extensive view	view-point	great strength to climb	high	stone
Stupid	not clever	weak-minded	insufficient	pity	clever
Unjust	injurious	innocent	shame	punishable	affair

Subject No. 6 approximates more closely to her mother's type both quantitatively as well as in the finer relationships of the reactions. The tendency frequently to repeat certain predicates is even more pronounced. Such words as *big, beautiful, high, naughty*, are repeated. The following list shows this similarity between mother and daughter.

Stimulus-word	Mother	Daughter
Prick	to pain	painful
Angel	lovable	lovely
Wool	warm	dyed
Dance	beautiful	jollity

Stimulus-word	Mother	Daughter
To cook	good	art
Ink	black	black
Wicked	silly	naughty
Swim	drown	dangerous
Travel	beautiful	pleasure
Mountain	high	high
Play	joy	jollity
Habits	virtuous	beautiful
Ride	art	pleasure

In 11·5 per cent. of like stimulus-words mother and daughter react with the same word. This is a very high concordance in association. The difference between mother and daughter is only 2·5, whilst between mother and son it is 4·2 ; between son and daughter it is a little higher, 4·4. The mother is differentiated from her brothers by, on the average, 4·4.

FAMILY V

Husband, wife, son, and sister of the husband who, however, was not living with the family. Their intelligence is medium ; they are all uneducated—an artisan family.

Subjects		Value predicates	Other predicates	Co-ordinates	Relationship of subject and object	Other associations	Clangs	Type
Father,	42 years .	14	39·5	14·5	12·5	19·5	—	predicate
Mother,	42 ,, .	18	22·5	15	13·5	30	1	predicate (superficial)
Son,	12 ,, .	7·5	17·5	19	17	29	—	mixed
Sister of father, 41 ,, .		14	22·5	9·5	23	31	—	predicate (superficial)

Subject No. 1 has a large number of predicates (in this family the predicates increase with age), which, however, disclose the emotional factor far less than, e.g., certain subjects in the last family. Subject No. 2 shows more emotionally toned reactions and value predicates than the others. As the table shows, the relationships of the reactions are very uniform in this family, although there are great differences of age, and the single sister does not live with the family. The average difference of all the members of the family among themselves amounts to 3·1 ; subjects No. 3 and 4, nephew and aunt, approach nearest to one another (D = 2·1).

Examples

Stimulus-word	Father	Mother	Son	Sister of Father
Prick	pain	poisonous	hurts	needle
Angel	pure	heaven	beautiful	innocent
Bear	heavy	child	heavy	child
State	kingdom	greater	great	America
Ill	difficult	old	difficult	mother
To cook	good	good	good	kitchen
Ink	black	black	black	teacher
To threaten	ambush	bad luck	insult	storm
Rich	proud	men	poor	health
Separate	distance	hurts	parents	sad
Quarrel	like to	not nice	naughty	men
Old	grandmother	people	young	grey-headed
Memory	dance lesson	good	duty	nice
Dog	angry	nicer	St. Bernard dog	faithful
Choose	people	people	President	walk
Kiss	girl	love	mother	mother
Laugh	joyous	jolly	about nonsense	gay
Air	cold	good	good	clear
Intention	wicked	good	closed windows	useless

This family has no other peculiarities worth mentioning.

FAMILY VI

Husband, wife, three daughters, and two sons (twins). Uneducated but relatively intelligent people. The husband is a merchant in a small way.

Subject	Value predicates	Other predicates	Other inner associations	Relationship of object and subject	Outer associations	Clangs	Type
Father, 60 years . .	17	28·5	17	14·5	23	—	predicate
Mother, 53 ,, . .	40	28	11·5	11	9·5	—	,,
Daughter, 30 ,, . .	23	20	27·5	12	17·5	—	,,
,, 20 ,, . .	14	32	16·5	18·5	19	—	,,
,, 13 ,, . .	11·5	38·5	18·5	23·5	8	—	,,
Son I, 17 ,, . .	12·5	29	24	15·5	18	—	,,
,, II, 17 ,, . .	8	23	17·5	19	32·5	—	mixed

The female members of this family show an increase in their value predicates with increasing age ; with the exception of the mother, however, these value predicates are not strongly marked, although in most cases a pronounced predicate type is present. The more objective type, the opposite of the predicate type, is stronger in the males and in the youngest daughter than in the mother and the two elder daughters. The relationship of the twin brothers should be the most interesting because the conditions are here favourable, one would expect, for a high measure of agreement. But their average difference amounts to 3·7, which is not an especially low figure, and the figures given above suggest a divergent behaviour. Son No. 1 approximates most closely to his sister, who is nearest to his age ; the difference is here only 1·9—the agreement is thus very great. Son No. 2 approximates more nearly to his father's type, the difference being 2·3 (son No. 2 differs from his father by 2·8).

The following examples illustrate these relationships :

Stimulus-word	Son No. 1	Daughter No. 2	Son No. 2	Father
Head	part of body	part of man	man	round
Green	grass	grass	forest	frog
Water	clear	wet	lake	sugar-water
Angel	in heaven	gracious	heaven	heaven
Ship	warship	on the lake	sea	big
Plough	peasant	peasant	field	field
Wool	soft	soft	sheep	sheep
To bear	a soldier the gun	commission-aire	burden	hat
Haughty	naughty child	pupil	child	child
Proud	high-spirited	vice	horse	fool
To cook	the cook	the cook	mother	coffee
Ink	for writing	fluid	write	copying-ink
Needle	pointed	fine	sew	dull
Journey	pleasure	beautiful	business	honeymoon
Bread	food	food	eat	black
To threaten	enemy	enemy	war	teacher
Tree	green	tall	forest	cherry
Ride	cavalry	on horseback	horse	horse
Wall	part of a room	part of a room	room	carpet
Tooth	should be white	hard	mouth	contagion
Book	means of learning	square	read	Bible
Hunger	unpleasant	the best cook	bread	hurts
Pencil	writing material	long	write	ink
Big	house	buildings	land	tree
Luck	gracious	beautiful	in games	advantageous
Manners	necessary	necessary	man	beautiful
Kiss	the beloved	the loved one	love	bride
Door	for opening	for opening	wide	imperfect
Hay	dry	brittle	barn	tastes good
Month	period of year	part of the year	February	year
Surprise	mistake	event	something	stolen
Moon	heavenly body	part of the world	night	full

This comparative table shows pretty clearly the similarity between son No. 1 and the second daughter. They have not only several associations verbally alike but there is a striking harmony in the tendency of their reactions. Their predicate attitude is also shown in the reactions which are not counted among the predicates ; there is attention to the meaning of the stimulus-word, whilst son No. 2 and his father show a somewhat more objective and superficial adjustment. These examples seem to show that the difference in reaction type does not correspond with any merely intellectual difference but rather with peculiarity of affect. This probably consists in the two first subjects (son No. 1 and the second daughter) having a particular emotional relationship towards the experimenter, which accidentally (?) is the same in both ; it is absent in the other two.

Whilst the eldest daughter has but few more value predicates than other predicates, her mother has a preponderance of value predicates. In this family she exhibits the highest number of predicates ; the youngest daughter comes next to her, but her predicates are chiefly objective.

Stimulus-word	Mother	Daughter
Dance	pleasure	in ball-room
Swim	healthy	child
Journey	pleasure	the traveller
Bread	healthy	we eat
To sing	beautiful	loud
Habits	good	old habits
Ride	healthy	rider
Tooth	intolerable	white
Book	useful	rectangular
Plum	good	blue
Potato	useful	round
Cow	useful	gives milk
Hay	smells nice	light

We see that the daughter, with her definite tendency to predicates, expresses these chiefly as positive attributes ; her mother seems to put much more personal feeling into her reactions. The father with his moderate predicate type is, on the whole, much nearer the type of the children than the mother. Jung's calculations make the average difference between father and children = 2·8, between mother and children = 4·2. The relationship between father and sons = 2·5, between father and daughters = 3. The relationship of the mother shows corresponding but higher figures : between mother and daughters = 3·9, between mother and sons = 4·7. These figures prove the fact, confirmed by the nature of the associations, that in this family the sons approximate to the father's type and the daughters to the mother's. This would have been even greater in the case of the eldest daughter if a particular cause of disturbance had not arisen in the second hundred test words. In the second hundred there was an increase of the motor reactions, especially of the word completions and definitions, to the prejudice of the predicates and co-ordinations. The cause was as follows : The experiment took place on a day when she was expecting to meet her betrothed at a party in the evening. She was able to keep her attention directed to the experiment during the first hundred, showing no distraction. Her attention wandered in the second hundred and she reacted very slowly. Being repeatedly requested to take notice of what she was doing, she reacted for a little while with supraordinations and definitions, again slacking off into verbal reactions.

FAMILY VII

Very unintelligent and quite uneducated artisan family.

Subject	Value predicates	Other predicates	Relationship of subject to object	Definitions	Other inner associations	Other outer associations	Types
Father, 46 years	3·5	1	2·5	60	26·5	6·5	definition
Mother, 44 ,,	5·5	30·5	18·5	8	24	13	mixed predicate
Daughter, 14 years	7	32·5	22·5	3·5	24	6	,, ,,
Son, 9 ,,	2	15	6·5	55·5	15·5	5·5	definition

The peculiarity of this family which at once strikes the eye is the sharp division into two different types—the father and son having a definition type, the mother and daughter a mixed type leaning towards the predicate. The associations of father and son, the ratio of whose figures shows such close agreement, have a very different appearance on the surface, and deserve therefore special review.

The son's associations :

Water	clear and cold	Potato	grows in the field
Lake	deep and much water	Plate	what's flat
Resin	what's sticky	Smooth	feather
Stories	to tell	Narrow	clothes
Understand	arithmetic	Stone	hard
Apple	what one eats	Steeple	what's high
Book	what one reads	Cart	where sacks are loaded
Visit	to friends	Station	where trains go

Coffee	people can drink	Goat	what has horns
Tree	what bears fruit	Public-house	where you drink beer
Hay	what the cow eats	Lamp	to make it light
Angel	is not seen	Friendly	to greet relatives
Buy	cow	Rich	when you get lots of
Needle	which pricks		money
Clergyman	who preaches	Mountain	where you must climb
Punish	if you gossip		up
Satchel	where you put your exercise-books	Quarrel	when one person says another thing than
Bed	when you sleep		the other
Stork	what has a great beak	Impudence	to take something right
Cupboard	where you put clothes		away from somebody
Pipe	where water goes through	Quick	when you run
		Sleep	when the eyes are closed
Sheet	what you write upon	Strong	when you can lift something heavy
House	where people live in		
Sofa	what you sit upon	Modest	when you don't say much
Soldier	who is in military service	Locksmith	who works with iron
Air	what floats about the earth	Free	after being shut in

The form of the association with its numerous sentences, 70 per cent. beginning with *what the*, etc., conditions a reaction type which is deceptively similar, on a cursory examination, to the method of associations Wehrlin found in high-grade feeble-minded.

A more thorough examination shows that the similarity is only superficial and that the associations go far beyond that kind.

In comparison with the associations of imbeciles and idiots we have :

Points in Common

(1) In the majority of the associations the meaning of the stimulus-word is apprehended as if it were a question.

(2) The reaction is not automatic but is thought out with great attention and straining ; it has a tendency to explanation. The subject became emotional and reacted very slowly. (The experiment lasted three hours.)

(3) The reaction is in many words or whole sentences (70 per cent. with *where you, when you*).

(4) The formation of school sentences.

(5) The circumlocutions.

(6) The large number of associations of purpose and example.

(7) Many definitions (55 per cent.) and many tautologies.

(8) Many associations of activities.

Points not in Common

(1) The relatively large number (35 per cent.) of normal non-explanatory reactions in a single word, or with selected, appropriate, changing, objective, outer and value predicates, which show very few repetitions.

These reactions alone show that this subject stands above imbeciles in regard to wealth of words and understanding ; for imbeciles when they use predicates do so monotonously, using very few words, perhaps *black* and *white*, throughout the whole experiment and using them most inappropriately.

(2) The ordinary coexistences and associations of activities.

(3) The almost complete absence of far-reaching and specialized general concepts (such as *tree — portion of ; cherry — thing in the garden*), of superordinations, simple tautologies where the stimulus-word is explained by a synonym, diminutive, attribute, or by the opposite with the negative, such as : *mountain — a high mountain ; flower — a mayflower ; flower — a little flower ; light — is not dark.*

(4) The greater developed power of abstraction. The examples and true definitions are more general and abstract, and generally explain the meaning of the stimulus-word neatly and sufficiently by bringing out the essential. We do not find here instances as we do in Wehrlin's idiots, where the subject explains the stimulus-word by some quite secondary, external and visible attribute, nor do we find the specially concrete examples of the idiot such as *prison — that's got a little window ; father — he once threw me downstairs ; hair — what gets cut ; mountain — there's a tree upon which cherries grow.*

Although the father's associations are very near the son's qualitatively, externally they differ considerably ; but the same tendency is present, as the following instances from the father's list show :

Head	part of body	Stalk	part of plant
Wool	factory	Resin	sap of tree
Snake	reptile	Soldier	liable to service
Ink	liquid	State	corporation
Ship	means of transport	Table	furniture of room
Decency	human nature	Wall	part of house
Coal	stuff for burning	New	thing just made
Ill	natural thing	Goat	domestic animal
Hay	part of plant	Sail	part of ship's body
Coloured	colour combination	Plum	stone fruit
Talk	human need	Axe	tool
Despise	human vice	Tree	plant class
Clergyman	personality	Threaten	human wickedness
Book	reading matter	Copy-book	mass of paper

Angel	unseen being	Write	work
Bread	daily food	Mountain	a massive
Quick	rapid movement	Swim	bodily exercise
Folk	community	Month	calculation of time
Law	is caution	Hunger	bodily feeling
Quiet	human nature		

The subject is an extreme definition type. 85·5 per cent. of the associations have a defining quality, 60 per cent. of these being direct definitions. The subject showed strong emotion during the tests and endeavoured earnestly to give correct answers. The reaction-times were very long ; the experiment lasted two and a half hours. After repeated reminders to give the first reaction he could not be turned away from his association type.

In contrast with the son, the similarity of the associations with those of imbeciles are here rather in content than in form, whilst many of the associations sound like those of an affected hebephreniac. Here again we find the apprehension of the stimulus-word in the sense of a question and the tendency to explain or to define it. But the associations differ from those of the imbecile in many respects ; the superordinations are generally more appropriate and sufficiently characteristic of the content of the stimulus-word. Only occasionally do we come across general concepts used too specifically, and subordinations used too broadly, giving a very imperfect characteristic of the stimulus-word.

In contradistinction to the imbecile, the true definitions are more general and more abstract and really explain the stimulus-word. Associations such as *family — corporation ; fire — mass of heat ; song — combination of tunes ; sail — part of ship's body* make a curious impression, scarcely explicable by want of intelligence. Such reactions, which one must regard as affected or extravagant, speak in favour of a lively impulse to react in " as educated " a way as possible. In this wise he seeks to compensate for a vivid feeling of inferiority (cp. Jung's *Psychology of Dementia Præcox*, p. 74). I have seen the same thing among intelligent people, e.g. in a student who was also a pronounced definition type but naturally expressed himself in a more educated way. The young man was somewhat embarrassed and obviously endeavoured not to display his intellectual nakedness before me. He could not have found any better way of demonstrating his embarrassment.

The comparison of father and son shows much similarity in their tendency of reaction, although the reactions appear outwardly very different ; this is again evidence that emotional factor play the chief part in the difference of reaction type.

The associations of mother and daughter also show an extreme adaptation to the meaning of the stimulus-word, but there was less embarrassment ; there was no special emphasis on the intellectual factor so distinctly found in father and son.   There is great agreement both in type and in individual reactions, as the following examples show :

Stimulus-word	Mother	Daughter
Angel	innocent	innocent
Haughty	bad boy	bad boy
Stalk	leek's stalk	stalks for soup
Dance	couple	gentleman and lady
Lake	much water	great
Threaten	father	father
Lamp	burns bright	gives light
Rich	king	king
New	dress	dress
Tooth	biting	pains
Take care	industrious pupil	pupil
Pencil	long	black
Law	God's command	Moses
Love	child	father and mother
Glass	light	breakable
Great	God	father
Potato	bulb	bulb
Hit	father	bad boy
Family	several persons	of five persons
Strange	traveller (male)	traveller (female)
Brother	loves me	love
Kiss	mother	mother
Fire	great pain	painful
Door	wide	big
Hay	dry	dry
Mock	shame	stupidity
Month	many days	thirty-one days
Air	cool	moist
Coal	sooty	black
Fruit	sweet	sweet
Make	father	parents
Jolly	happy child	little children

These examples, which show a far-reaching similarity between mother and daughter, are still more striking on comparing the reactions of father and son.   According to Jung's calculations the difference between father and mother is 9·4, between mother and daughter 2, between father and son 4, between mother and son 7.   The son therefore is more like his father than is his mother by 2·4.

FAMILY VIII

An artisan family with the usual schooling and of medium intelligence; it includes a sister of the mother who lives with the family.

Subjects	Value predicates	Other predicates	Relationship of subject and object	Other inner associations	Outer associations	Clangs	Type
Father, 37 years	20	37·5	12	10·5	20	—	predicate
Mother, 35 ,,	19	28·5	7·5	12·5	32·5	—	,,
Mother's sister, 29 ,,	12·5	35	17	13·5	18	3	,,
Daughter, 15 ,,	21·5	38	13	16·5	11	—	,,
,, 12 ,,	22	44	14·5	7·5	12	—	,,

The whole family present a definite predicate type. Like Families VI and VII with their twelve- and thirteen-year-old daughters, the twelve- and fifteen-year-old daughters have a more pronounced predicate type than the mother. The greatest agreement is found between father and the two daughters (D = 1·2 and 1·65), then between the two daughters (D = 1·8).

Stimulus-word	Father	1st daughter	2nd daughter
Family	large	large	large
Time	perishes	short	long
Ground	deep	deep	firm
Sleeve	long	long	wide
Thousand	number	big number	big number
Smart	beautiful	new	big
Slate-pencil	short	pointed	black
Raspberry	sweet	good	sweet
Hedge	thorny	thick	long
Vinegar	sharp	sharp	bitter
To crack	glasses	egg	egg

These examples will serve as illustrations of their common predicative adaptation. The mother's associations do not differ considerably from these. Her difference from the father is 2·6 Her type is rather more superficial than her husband's (12·5 more outer associations). Otherwise we find in her, as in her husband, a preponderance of indirect predicates as compared with value predicates (she belongs to the " reserved " predicate type). It is chiefly in consequence of her more superficial type that she differs by 3·6 from her daughters, who, as mentioned present an intense predicate type.

The mother's sister, living with the family, likewise shows a similar predicate type, which approximates rather to the type of the daughters (her nieces) than to that of her sister (difference from her nieces 3, from her sister 4·4).   The cause of this difference is partly to be found in the fact that she, like her nieces, produces considerably more inner associations than their mother.   We shall investigate this relationship more closely in the following family.

FAMILY IX

Artisan family.   Husband and wife of medium intelligence, unedu- cated.   The wife is the third sister of the wife in foregoing family ; has been married several years and lives in another milieu.

Subjects	Value predicates	Other predicates	Relationship of subject and object	Contrasts	Inner associations	Outer associations	Clangs	Type
Husband, 33 years .	1	3·5	2·5	23·5	20·5	47	1·5	Co-ordination
Wife, 34 ,, .	1·5	0·5	0·5	21·5	36	38·5	0·5	,,

This family exhibits a type diametrically opposed to the last one.   Only traces of predicates are present, whilst we find a surprising number of inner associations, especially of contrasts.

Whilst there were practically no contrasts in the last family (0·4 per subject), here they average 22·5.   There is an unusual agreement between husband and wife in their associations (D = 1·4), which seems the more remarkable for there is an appearance of the wife having possibly had another type formerly. We may perhaps venture to suppose, from the facts hitherto observed, that members of the same family approximate in type to one another, especially if they are of the same sex.   It is likely, therefore, that the wife did belong rather more to the type of her two sisters ; it was only subsequently, after her joint life with her husband, that she took on his type (i.e. acquired the same affective factors which produce the type).

By the following comparative results of this family and the two sisters of Family VIII the reader can judge of the differences in attitude, uninfluenced by any differences of views as to classification.

Stimulus- word	1st sister, mother in Family VIII	2nd sister, Family VIII	3rd sister, wife in Family IX	Her husband, Family IX
Ink	black	black	water	Indian ink
Bread	fresh	white	sweet	potatoes
Lamp	light	light	flower-vase	umbrella

Stimulus-word	1st sister, mother in Family VIII	2nd sister, Family VIII	3rd sister, wife in Family IX	Her husband, Family IX
Tree	leafless	tall	shrub	root
Copy-book	dirty	thick	book	book
Book	thick	learned	album	copy-book
Pencil	black	short	penholder	ink
Sing	nice	entertaining	jump	laugh
Tooth	white	false	tongue	-ache
Flower	scent	red	bushes	grass
Water	cool	clear	milk	cold water
Dance	joy	waltz	jump	drink
Haughty	naughty child	little children	friendly	soft-hearted
Song	nice	hymn	music	zither
Potato	good	frozen	bean	carrots
Threaten	wicked	stupid	complain	to adjust
Manners	nice	in company	and customs	no manners
Family	big	widespread	congregation	sex
People	big	warlike	town	country
Foreign	wander	foreigner	home	liveable
False	bad	snake	friendly	like a cat
Fruit	good	dear	wine	vegetables
Public-house	great	frequented	shop	restaurant
Kiss	child	fiancé	cuddle	love
Blood	red	red	water	frog's blood
Love	love God	parents	praise	hate

These examples will suffice to show the similarity between the first two sisters and the dissimilarity of the third. Jung's calculations show that the first and second sisters differ from the third by 8–8·8, whilst their difference from each other is only 4·4. Our classification may have its own defects and vagaries but such cases teach us that, at least, they suffice to express statistically such differences. Thus we have an instrument which enables us to reap the firstfruits in these still uncultivated fields.

SUMMARY OF THE RESULTS

The material here reviewed consists of nine families with thirty-seven subjects aged from nine to seventy-four years. With the exception of one person who is rather more highly educated, all the subjects are quite uncultured. Only ten had attended the secondary schools for two years; the remaining twenty-six had only an elementary schooling; the persons all lived in an uncultured *milieu*. We were able to examine the relationship of inner to outer associations in regard to parents and children in six cases. In five families we experimented with both parents, in one family with the mother only. Let us first of all consider the relationship of mother and child and compare it with the results of Jung and Riklin.[1]

In three families all the children had more inner associations than the mother. The children were between nine and fifteen. In two families the youngest child (a thirteen- and a twenty-seven-year-old daughter respectively) had more inner, all the others more outer, associations than the mother. We can express these results in a formula : all children under sixteen have *more inner associations than the mother and (with one exception) all children over sixteen have more outer associations than the mother.*

The relationship of children to father is somewhat different. Eight children had more inner, and three more outer, associations than the father. No rule can be laid down as regards the age of the child. Hence Jung and Riklin's statement is only confirmed conditionally. A further result is that *the husbands tend to have more outer associations than their wives and, in general, the sons more than the daughters.* From this we may conclude that in my investigations the attention of the female subjects was less inhibited towards the experiment.

A comparison of brothers and sisters shows that in youth the sisters have a greater tendency towards inner associations, in the intermediate and later years the brothers have the greater tendency.

We are unable, so far as these tests are concerned, to draw any definite conclusions as to the effect of age ; we have considered the sisters and brothers, all the male and all the female subjects, and all the subjects in general, and we find enormous individual differences ; the conclusion of Ranschburg and Balint seem therefore to require revision. The examination of this question in married couples gave no results. In seven families the husband had more inner associations (the wives were aged between thirty-two and forty-four, the husbands aged between thirty-four and forty-six). In three cases the wives (aged between thirty-four and forty-six) had more inner associations than their husbands (aged from thirty-three to sixty). On the other hand, the more intelligent and better educated or better read individual of a married couple seems to have more outer associations.

The predicate type preponderates among these uneducated persons. The following table shows in individual figures

---

[1] Jung and Riklin, chapter ii, pp. 50–57, point out that there is not only a familial type relationship between mother and daughters, but apparently a regularly quantitative behaviour of the individual associations. This behaviour is such that as we proceed from the mother towards the youngest daughter the type become increasingly more superficial. They bring forward two cases of this, although with certain reservations.

and percentages the frequency of the individual types of associations :

Predicate type,	21 subjects	= 54 %	Men :	8
			Women :	13
Mixed type,	11 ,,	= 29 %	Men :	6
			Women :	5
Definition type,	2 ,,	= 5 %	(father and son)	
Co-ordination type,	2 ,,	= 5 %	(husband and wife)	
Superficial type,	2 ,,	= 5 %	(women)	

Besides the twenty-one persons of the predicate type having more than 40 per cent. predicates, there were six persons in the mixed type with a great number of predicates ; in them the number of predicates exceeded the numbers of all the other chief groups, such as co-ordination, coexistences, and motor-speech reactions. If we add these six of the mixed type with their predicative tendency to the predicate type we have twenty-seven persons of the predicate type = 72 per cent. of all the subjects.

The frequency of the predicate type is rather greater in women (seventeen women to ten men), which corresponds with the findings of Jung and Riklin.

The remaining types are so poorly represented in this material that nothing definite or characteristic can be said about them, with the exception of the *definition type,* which was seen exclusively in males, both in its pure form and in a mixed form (three cases). Jung and Riklin have put forward the hypothesis that the predicate type corresponds to a psychological peculiarity, which is even preserved during artificial distraction (chapter ii, p. 160). They hold that the mechanism of the predicate type consists in the primary appearance of vivid pictures which by reason of their powerful emotional tone give rise to a corresponding subjectively coloured, predicative, verbal reaction. From my tests I can but confirm their view of a marked emotional factor. But it is difficult to say upon what psychological factor this predicate attitude rests. An accidental individual complex can hardly be the cause ; the type is too common and likewise too familial for that. The most probable supposition seems to me to be that this arises out of a general emotional attitude towards the experimenter. The frequency of the predicate type makes it worth while to study its occurrence more accurately ; let us first of all consider its quantitative behaviour in males and females.

The ratio of value predicates to other predicates is, in males

1 : 1·55 ; in females, 1 : 0·84. That means that among men the positive predicate predominates as against the subjectively toned value predicates ; in women it is the reverse.

How does the predicate type behave as regards different age periods ?

We will first investigate the ages between ten and forty and then between forty-one and eighty ; we get these results :

In men :

Years 10–40, value predicates : objective predicates = 1 : 2·17
„   41–80, „   „   „   „   = 1 : 1·27

In women :

Years 10–40, value predicates : objective predicates = 1 : 1·14
„   41–80, „   „   „   „   = 1 : 0·38

In both groups there is seen a greater tendency to value predicates in age than in youth ; greater in women than in men. In women the preponderance of value predicates begins at forty-one years, in men only at sixty-one years (from sixty-one to eighty years the ratio among men is 1 : 0·68 ; from forty-one to sixty years it is 1 : 2·14).

Should these figures be confirmed we should be able to say that in these experiments the disposition peculiar to the predicate type, i.e. an increase of the subjective tendency, undergoes a considerable increase in women about the fortieth year, but in men much later, about the sixtieth year. If we venture to regard this tendency as an inflow of more personal emotions, it must be accepted that about this period of life there are important changes in the affective disposition.

We can give the main classes in the following percentages so far as regards the general figures of the individual groups :

	Male subjects	Female subjects
	Per cent.	Per cent.
Inner associations . . .	76·9 (40·5)	78·9 (46·6)
Outer „	21 (55·6)	19·7 (49·4)
Clang-reactions	0·1 (0·6)	0·2 (0·7)
Remainder group	0·1 (2·4)	0·7 (2·3)

The figures in parentheses are the corresponding ones from the work of Jung and Riklin (chapter ii). In contrast to theirs, my figures show a considerable preponderance of inner associations. This difference cannot be due to classification, for Dr. Jung confirmed my conclusions and compared my material with his earlier one. Besides, the important differences in those reactions where abnormalities are easily recognized (clang-reactions and remainder group) show that it is not a question of classification. The difference must be in the material. Jung and Riklin took as their uneducated subjects the male and female attendants of the asylum, whilst my material was gathered from persons less intellectual and of a lower social grade. Another circumstance is probably not without importance : in Jung and Riklin's experiments the persons were in the service of the experimenters ; this influences the affectivity. The increase of inner associations as the intelligence and social scale decreases, as shown by the figures, is the expression of a well-known fact, which has been fully explained in earlier chapters. The finding of Jung and Riklin corresponds to the rather more superficial type of reaction in men as compared with women. The details of the individual classes are shown in the following table.

Kind of association	Males	Females
Co-ordination	10·1	9
Sub- and supra-ordination	6·4	5
Contrast	2·6	1·7
Value predicates	12·9	24·6
Objective and outer predicates . . .	23·2	24
Subject and object relationship . . .	9·7	12·1
Definition of place, time, means, purpose, etc..	1·8	1·5
Definition	10·2	1
Coexistence	9·2	6·2
Identity	1·7	1·6
Verbal-motor connexion	7·1	7·7
Neologisms	3	4·2
Word-completion	—	0·2
Clang-association	0·1	—
Remainder group (fault, meaningless, indirect).	0·1	0·7

Among the inner associations the greatest difference is in the number of value predicates. Jung and Riklin pointed out a preference among women, especially among the uneducated, for the predicate type. The difference ought to come out markedly here, because I have separated the individual predicates as far as practicable, whilst they were all reckoned together by Jung and Riklin. The difference lies, we find, chiefly in the value predicates. Another prominent difference is the *preference of the definition* type by men. The above figures show that the female subjects have a subjective " personal " attitude, whilst the men have generally an objective intellectual attitude. Whilst in Jung and Riklin's figures the remainder group, which chiefly contains the results of disturbance, shows higher figures, on the average, among men, here the women have the higher figure. Whether this is related to the sex of the experimenter or is a merely accidental difference is hard to say.

The familial agreements in the tendency of the reaction, which I found to be qualitative and pointed out in the individual cases, have been worked out by Jung statistically. Based upon 268 comparisons of unrelated men and women in my material, requiring 8000 single comparisons, the mean difference of non-related men is 5·9 and of non-related women is 6. These mean figures are valuable because they give a measure for the estimation of the intrafamilial differences, clearly shown in the following figures.

The mean difference of related men is 4·1, that of women 3·8. These figures are considerably lower than the difference of non-related persons, and we may conclude that relations have, on the whole, a tendency to agree in their reaction type. The mean deviation [1] of the series of figures lying at the base of the first figures amounts to 1·2, that of the latter is 1·5. The difference among the men rests, therefore, upon a series of fairly uniform composition, whilst the mean difference among the women is composed of an unequal series. Verbally expressed : Some related women differ very strongly, whilst others agree in their reaction type much more than do related men.

Mean difference between fathers and children   : 4·2 (2·4)

    ,,   ,,   ,,   mothers and children : 3·5 (1·0)

(The figure in brackets is the mean deviation of the mean.)

Mothers and children present a relatively strong and uniform agreement, whilst fathers and children, on the whole, agree less, although there are some exceptions where there is close agreement, as the high figure for mean deviation shows.

Mean difference between fathers and sons   : 3·1 (0·6)

    ,,   ,,   ,,   mothers and daughters : 3   (1·0)

    ,,   ,,   ,,   fathers and daughters : 4·9 (3·5)

    ,,   ,,   ,,   mothers and sons   : 4·7 (1·2)

[1] The mean deviation is calculated in this way: first calculate how much each figure of the whole series differs from the arithmetical mean of the series, add the difference figures, and divide the sum by their amount. The quotient gives the mean deviation of the mean.

The agreement between fathers and sons is almost uniformly even, likewise that between mothers and daughters. The crossed relationships show the same thing by their relatively high differential values :

Mean difference of brothers among themselves   : 4·7 (14)
   ,,   ,,   ,, sisters   ,,   ,,   : 5·1 (2·4)

Brothers show a relatively slight agreement, that of the sisters is still less ; but the figure for the mean deviation of the mean shows that there are exceptions. This is at once seen when one excludes the married sisters from the comparison :

Mean difference of unmarried brothers among themselves : 4·8 (1·0)
   ,,   ,,   ,,   ,,   sisters   ,,   ,,   : 3·4 (1·7)

Whilst the difference among brothers does not alter essentially, the difference among sisters sinks considerably. This signifies that the married sisters differ considerably among themselves but not the single ones. It would seem that marriage disturbs the agreement in reaction type (in so far as the husband may belong to another type ?).

Mean difference of brothers and sisters : 4·4 (1·5)

In this relationship a relatively uniform, slight agreement seems to prevail.

Mean difference of husband and wife : 4·7 (3·2)

Here we note a fairly slight average agreement, which, however, varies very greatly, i.e. there are cases of higher agreement, and others of the greatest divergence. This was already brought out in the presentation of the individual families.

The best and most uniform agreement is found among parents and their children of the same sex. The children differ more among themselves than from their parents ; they differ more from the father than from the mother ; the daughters approximate more to their mothers than do sons to their fathers. Unmarried daughters agree in their reactions among themselves more than do unmarried sons, just as related women in general agree more among themselves than do related men. Marriage seems only exceptionally to lead to a greater agreement of the pair.

Tabular Summary of some Cases of Familial Agreement and Difference

Kind of association	Husband	His wife	Father	Mother	Daughter	Father	1st daughter	2nd daughter	Father	Son	Mother	Daughter
Co-ordination	16·5	33·5	6·5	0·5	—	7	7	4	3	8·5	17·5	13·5
Sub- and supra-ordination	4	2·5	7	—	—	3·5	9	2·5	23·5	3	5·5	7
Contrast	23·5	21·5	—	—	—	—	—	—	—	—	0·5	0·5
Value predicates	1	1·5	8·5	95	98	20	21·5	22	3·5	2	5·5	7
Objective and outer predicates	3·5	0·5	21	3·5	0·5	37·5	38	44	1	15	30·5	32·5
Subject and object relationship	2·5	0·5	15·5	0·5	—	12	13	14·5	2·5	6·5	18·5	22·5
Definition of place, time, etc.	0·5	—	11	—	—	—	—	0·5	—	4	0·5	3
Definition	—	—	11	—	—	—	0·5	0·5	60	55·5	8	3·5
Co-existence	20·5	20	1·5	—	—	6·5	5	1·5	0·5	2	1	4·5
Identity	2	2	0·5	0·5	1·5	1·5	1	—	4·5	0·5	4	—
Verbal-motor connexion	16	14·5	12	—	—	9·5	4·5	7·5	1	2	6·5	4
Neologisms	8·5	2	6	—	—	2·5	0·5	3	0·5	1	1·5	2
Word-completion	0·5	—	—	—	—	—	—	—	—	—	—	—
Clang-association	1	0·5	—	—	—	—	—	—	—	—	—	—
Remainder group	—	1	—	—	—	—	—	—	—	—	0·5	—

The whole material is too limited for these figures to be regarded as authoritative and final ; they should be merely considered as indications.

Finally, let me express my best thanks to Professor Bleuler for his stimulus in this work, and especially to Dr. Jung for his kind co-operation and valuable advice when carrying t out.

CHAPTER XII

ON THE PSYCHOGALVANIC PHENOMENON IN ASSOCIATION EXPERIMENTS

By Dr. L. BINSWANGER

PART I

INTRODUCTION : HISTORICAL SURVEY : TECHNIQUE OF THE EXPERIMENTS

At the instance of Dr. Jung I have carried out association experiments as modified at the Zurich psychiatric clinic on twenty-three healthy persons, who during the entire experiment were subjected to a very feeble electric current.

The source was in most cases one Bunsen cell of not more than 15 volts tension ; the electrodes were made of thin brass plates which were placed on the hands. In the current there was inserted a sensitive Deprez-d'Arsonvals mirror-galvanometer (constants : $5100 = 10^{.10}$ amperes : 0.08 mm. in diameter), which registered the fluctuations of the current during the experiment ; there was also a shunt which reduced the oscillations of the current upon the galvanometer and quickly brought the excursions of the mirror to rest again.[1] A celluloid scale divided into millimetres and centimetres, with a lamp upon it, was placed one metre from the galvanometer, the lamp throwing a perpendicular beam of light upon the galvanometer mirror. The variations of the mirror and the variations in the strength of the current are measured by the excursions of the beam of light upon the scale.[2]

When associations are carried out with this arrangement it is noticed that in almost any reaction under normal conditions the beam of light undergoes a greater or lesser excursion on the scale ; at first this is in the direction of the conducting current (in our tests always from left to right) ; it then halts a moment, thereupon returning again to the proximity of its first position. This excursion of the beam of light, which corresponds to a change in the strength of the current in our circuit, is called the galvanic

[1] S. Veraguth, "Das psychogalvanische Reflexphänomen," I. Bericht Monatsschrift für Psych. und Neurol., Bd. XXI, Heft 5, p. 387. We always placed the stopper contact at 1/1.

[2] Cp. Jung, "On Psychophysical Relations of the Association Experiment," Journal of Abnormal Psychology, vol. i, p. 247. The entire arrangement of the tests is given there in detail with a figure of the apparatus.

deviation. As psychical processes in the subject influence the changes in the strength of the current, we designate the whole phenomenon, after Veraguth, as the psychogalvanic phenomenon.

Attempts to connect galvanic changes with psychical processes are not new. The history of these attempts shows two widely separated movements which originally were quite distinct. In these movements (Tarchanoff,[1] Sticker [2]) the reactions of the subject towards a current were not investigated, but the currents which occur on the superficies of the skin of the subject during psychical processes were directly measured. For this purpose unpolarized electrodes were used, by means of which the current is led through the galvanometer. I agree with Tarchanoff, despite Sticker's objection, that this is essentially a measurement of the secretory current of the skin (sweat glandular system). The experiments of Sommer and Fürstenau [3] form a transition from the first method to the second, to which latter we adhere. They used zinc and charcoal plates as electrodes but without using any galvanic cell as the source of the current. I speak of this method as a transition because it is still partly a question of " secretory currents " [4] ; to this, however, a second factor is added, which probably plays the chief part : changes in the resistance of the subject to electrical conduction. This method can be combined with the second method by using a galvanic cell as well as electrodes of zinc and charcoal.[5]

Féré [6] was the first to make investigations of the effect of psychical processes upon the changes in resistance to electrical conduction ; he applied sensory stimuli to his subjects.

From a certain point of view one might include here the investigations begun in 1878 by Romain Vigouroux [7] on hysterics

[1] Tarchanoff, " Ueber die galvanischen Erscheinungen in der Haut des Menschen bei Reizungen der Sinnesorgane und bei verschiedenen Formen der psychischen Tätigkeit," Pflüger's Archiv., 1890, Bd. XLVI.

[2] Sticker, " Ueber Versuche einer objectiven Darstellung von Sensibilitäts-störungen," Wiener klin. Rundschau, 1897, Nos. 30 and 31.

[3] Sommer und Fürstenau, " Die elektrische Vorgänge an der menschlichen Haut," Klinik für psychische und nervöse Krankheiten, Bd. I, Heft 3, 1906.

[4] It should not, however, be forgotten that we are dealing here with currents which owe their origin to the potential difference between skin and electrodes, whilst the true secretory currents arise entirely in the living body.

[5] The latter must then, of course, be placed in the direction of the circulating current.

[6] Féré, " Note sur des modifications de la résistance électrique sous l'influence des excitations sensorielles et des émotions," Comptes rendus hébdomadaires des Séances et Mémoires de la Société de Biologie, 1888, p. 217 ff. Féré remarks that the resistance diminishes " sous l'influence d'émotions sthéniques " and increases under " l'absence d'excitations," p. 218.

[7] R. Vigouroux, " Sur la résistance électrique considérée comme signe clinique," Le Progrès medical, 1888, Semestre I, pp. 45 and 86.

and Graves's disease and those made by his nephew, A. Vigouroux,[1] on melancholics. These works show us clearly the effect of psychic factors upon the electrical resistance of the human body. In 1904 the engineer E. K. Müller made experiments in Zurich upon " the changes in physical resistance to the galvanic current "; Veraguth [2] learnt the phenomena from these experiments, to which Jung [3] then drew attention.

I cannot enter here into the physical and physiological sides of the phenomenon. So far it seems to me that even with the tests in a conducting current the sweat-glandular system plays a great part. That does not mean that we only deal with sweat perceptible to our senses, but rather that it is a question " of the secretory process brought about by stimulation of the nerves." I am here in agreement with the views expressed by Biedermann [4] in his *Electrical Physiology* (" On the Electro-motor Effects of Epithelial and Sweat Cells "). That the secretion of sweat is intimately bound up with psychical processes is current knowledge, experimentally proved by Adamkiewicz [5] in 1878. Nevertheless, despite numerous experiments we are still in the region of hypothesis, and do not even know if we really measure the same physiological processes under different arrangements of the experiments.

All these investigators noticed the influence of psychical action upon the galvanic processes. Tarchanoff,[6] who seems to have been the first to confirm the connexion of sweating with psychical activity, concludes : " Nearly every kind of nerve action, although there may be a time limit, from the simplest impressions and sensations to the highest mental activity and spontaneous motor expression, is accompanied by increased activity of the sweat glands." He regards this increased activity of the sweat glands as the cause of the variation in the electric current, shown by the galvanometer. Sticker[7] writes : " I have repeatedly convinced myself that the origin of the galvanic skin phenomenon is under the influence of exciting mental impressions, and that the will has no effect upon it ; this reflex could be used with great advantage for the discovery of words and pictures

[1] A. Vigouroux, *Étude sur la résistance électrique chez les mélancoliques.* Thèse de Paris, 1890.

[2] Veraguth, loc. cit., p. 387.

[3] Jung, loc. cit.

[4] Biedermann, *Elektrophysiologie* (Jena, 1895). See also Hermann, *Lehrbuch der Physiologie,* 12th edition, p. 145 ff.

[5] Adamkiewicz, *Die Sekretion des Schweisses : Eine bilateralsymmetrische Nervenfunktion.* (Berlin : Hirschwald, 1878.)

[6] Tarchanoff, loc. cit., p. 53.

[7] Sticker, loc. cit., p. 518.

that influence the emotions. In a word—which will be listened to by many without any reaction—whoever takes the meaning of something to heart will react with a strong galvanic skin phenomenon. Whoever is from any cause emotionally roused on looking at a picture will react with a definite increase of the current ; whilst whoever is unmoved by the picture, or in whom it arouses no memory, will have no skin excitation." Sticker calls attention to the forensic importance of the phenomenon.

Sommer, on the other hand, writes : " We have not observed with any certainty that psychical processes have any influence, such as Tarchanoff has noticed, upon the current, apart from the reaction phenomena after tickling." When some psychical influence does occur, as after fright, it is conditioned, according to Sommer and Fürstenau, by the muscular contractions that arise and the contact changes thus caused in the electrodes. We shall see later that such muscular contractions do now and then play a part in the psychogalvanic experiment, but they do not explain the whole phenomenon.

A. Vigouroux, referring to Féré on this point, says : " Ce dernier observe que la résistance électrique de ces sujets (he is dealing with hysterics) est diminué par le fait d'excitations sensorielles diverses, visuelles (verres colorés), auditives (diapason à poids), gustatives, olfactives, etc." ; and adds : " On pourrait également rapprocher de ces faits la diminution de la résistance chez les malades atteints de la maladie de Basedow : une émotivité extrême est, en effet, la caractéristique de l'état mental de ces malades." [1]

Müller [2] writes : " Toute influence psychique, propre ou étrangère, a pour effet immédiat, les cas échéants, une énorme différence dans les résultats de mesurage (diminution de la résistance jusqu'à $\frac{1}{3}-\frac{1}{5}$)."

Veraguth insists as clearly as possible upon the effect of psychical factors, especially of the emotions, in sensory and psychical stimuli causing changes in the current.[3] But when he says (p. 420), " It is not the emotional tone alone which conditions the strength of the galvanic reaction ; in higher psychical stimuli further factors to be considered are their actuality," I must submit that the division of these two factors does not seem necessary. The only concept we can frame about *actuality* is surely its increased emotional tone in regard to non-present things.

---

[1] A. Vigouroux, loc. cit., 46 ; Féré, loc. cit., p. 218.

[2] *Conférence expérimentale de M. le directeur E. K. Müller à Zurich à la Société suisse des Sciences naturelles (Section médicale).* I am indebted for this quotation to Dr. Veraguth.

[3] Veraguth, loc. cit., p. 420 ff.

It is noticed that stronger deviations occur when a stimulus-word arouses a presentation which is " actual " for the subject, i.e. one which occupied him just before or during the test ; it is stronger than when a complex is touched which years ago played some part. But " actuality " is not an addition to the emotional tone, the actuality is the emotional tone ; it is only another expression for " increased emotional tone."

I have myself avoided the word " actual " because we can always replace it by the less dubious expression " emotionally toned." In many cases, moreover, it is difficult to say whether a complex is really actual for the subject in Veraguth's sense. The analysis in many cases discloses undoubted relationships of an " old " complex to the present ; in the same way an apparently " actual " complex, which momentarily seems very much to occupy the subject, may derive its essential affect from events of long ago. Both will come to light quite clearly in Test I. For this reason also I have avoided the designation " actual."

This survey of the views of other authors shows us that they nearly all have observed deviations at emotionally toned psychical processes only. Tarchanoff alone claims to have found galvanometric changes in " every kind of nerve action." At all events, in our experiments with the conducted current we could only perceive that the psychogalvanic phenomenon occurred in affective processes. With associations indifferent to the subject, which aroused no emotion, there was no deviation, any more than when reading something indifferent (an observation that Veraguth had already made) or on adding up easy figures, which entail no effort. In the same way purely intellectual sensations produce no deviation when their emotional tone is lowered (e.g. by repetition) ; this we shall call attention to in the section on physical movements and deep inspiration. Naturally the expressions " not emotionally toned," " purely intellectual," must be taken *cum grano salis*. They are entirely relative to the order of the research as a whole, and particularly to the sensitiveness of the galvanometer used. Reactions which evoke no response in one galvanometer, which are for us therefore " not emotionally toned," may evoke response in a more sensitive instrument. Hence it is very important to consider the sensitiveness of the galvanometer. With an extremely sensitive instrument we could receive responses during an indifferent reading, addition, etc., for we are never in a state completely devoid of emotion—free from innervations altogether.

To Veraguth are due our thanks for having been the first to take associations with the galvanometer : he noticed that the association curve moved in an ascending line, in contradistinction to the "rest curve" (which is obtained when the subject sits quietly, taking as little part as possible) ; that in the same person different words evoke extremely different changes in the curves, that those stimulus-words which touch an "actual emotional complex" produce stronger fluctuations than indifferent words. He also observed that the excursions are stronger when the subject reacts by words than when he does not, and that the first (indifferent) stimulus-words usually evoke stronger fluctuations than the later indifferent ones. Tarchanoff had previously determined the influence of expectation upon the galvanic phenomenon ; Veraguth noticed its occurrence in association experiments (fluctuation from expectation).[1]

Besides these psychological effects upon the galvanic phenomenon there are a great number of physiological and physical effects which we cannot here consider. In so far as they influence the experiment they will be discussed later. We shall just mention the enormous effect of cold and warmth and the degree of moisture of the epidermis upon the conducting powers of the skin.[2] If despite these effects we still regard the psychogalvanic phenomenon as an invaluable instrument in the analysis of the emotions, it is because we were able to convince ourselves in the course of months of investigations that the psychological factors can generally be separated pretty easily from the others ; when the former are at all pronounced we may disregard the physical and physiological influences. Of course these psychological factors, in order to be noted by the galvanometer, must of themselves produce physiological and physical changes, which will be of an extremely fine kind. In the striking promptness and exactitude found in the connexion between the galvanic phenomenon and the psychical processes there can be no question of gross physical (or chemical) processes interpolated between the two. Above all, it is no question of processes which, once aroused, pursue their path independently of psychical events ; rather are we constrained to admit processes whose course is continually controlled, furthered, or stayed by the central organ.

The experiments demand no further detailed description. Of the thirty subjects, tests in twenty-three were undertaken with the conducted circuit and brass or nickel electrodes, in two with the conducted circuit and "water contact," in five with the Sommer-Fürstenau arrangement (zinc and charcoal

[1] Cp. Veraguth, "Der psychophysische galvanische Reflex," *Bericht über den II. Kongress für experimentelle Psychologie*, pp. 219–224. (Barth: Leipzig, 1907.)

[2] Hermann, loc. cit., pp. 303, 305, especially E. du Bois-Reymond, *Untersuchungen über tierische Elektrizität*, Bd. II, chapter viii, section 4. (Berlin, 1849.)

electrodes or galvanic cell).   We shall return to this in reviewing the single groups.

Reading off and Registering the Galvanometer Deviations: Determining and Marking the Reaction-time

The subject is instructed, as usual, how to react and is requested to avoid all movement as far as possible ; this is not asking too much, for the sitting only lasts thirty to forty minutes, and the patient can rest quite comfortably.   The test is then begun.   Before calling out the stimulus-word a glance is given at the scale and the place noted where the beam of light (its right margin) persists.   The stimulus-word is called out, and as a rule a galvanometer deviation follows at once.   The deviation is taken to be the greatest excursion which the beam of light makes in a positive direction on the scale.   As soon as the positive fluctuation returns again, i.e. becomes negative, the beginning and end of the excursion are written down.[1]   The reaction-word is then noted, and then, last of all, the reaction-time ; the latter is fixed by the one-fifth second watch, whilst the two former data must be kept in the memory.   The reaction-time is determined by pressing on the button of the watch held in the left hand at the moment the stimulus- and reaction-words are pronounced.   At first it is easy to forget this because the experimenter's attention is taken up with observing the beam of light. But it soon becomes automatic.   At the reproduction test it is best to calculate the difference in the figures noted for the deviation and to write it down.   For each reaction there is the following schedule :

Stimulus-word	Deviation	Reaction-word	Time in $\frac{1}{5}$ sec.	Deviation absolute in mm.	Reproduction[2]
Head	12·5–14	nice	9	15	$\pm$

At the conclusion of the test the *reproduction* test is at once carried out.   When the subject does not remember the reaction-word or states it incorrectly, or when he has to reflect about it a long time, it is nearly always a question of disturbance from some emotionally toned presentation complex.   We then speak of

[1] It not infrequently occurs that whilst writing it down the negative deviation again changes into a positive one ; this arises from perseveration or from fresh emotional tone, and would in any case be noticed in the subsequent reactions since these would begin with a higher figure.   If the subsequent positive fluctuation is again followed by a negative one, it is best to correct the lower figure that has been written down by adding the second positive movement to the first.

[2] Here we only give the absolute value of the deviation.   Its height on the scale can be read off on the accompanying curves, at least for the big analyses.   In the reproduction test the — sign will be given or the incorrect reaction.   No sign means that the reproductions are correct.

disturbances of reproduction.[1] It may be here said that the complex which causes the disturbance in reproduction need not necessarily be contained in the particular reaction, it may have been incited in one of the previous reactions. It must not be, therefore, assumed that in the reaction where there is disturbance in reproduction there is a complex. To which reaction the disturbance in reproduction is due must be cleared up by other means.

The analysis is then added after the reproduction test. These can be combined. The figures of the movements and the reaction-times are exhibited graphically by the " bar " method, as seen in the illustration. The original curves are shown on 2 mm. paper, 1 mm. of the paper corresponding to 1 mm. of the scale, and each one-fifth second is expressed by 1 mm. In the repro-duction of the curves in this work the relationships have all been reduced by one-half. In the presentation of the galvano-meter deviations it was found necessary, instead of placing the absolute values on an abscissa side by side, to express also their position to one another ; this was done by placing the deviations on the paper directly after their course on the scale. It is only in this way that we get a curve of any real use. The reaction-times are shown by the " bars " placed next one another on the abscissa. The deviation and the time pertaining to it are placed exactly on top of each other. Faults in this method are easily recognized. But it had the great advantage of showing the individual deviations directly and clearly, and that is the chief thing.

Jung [2] devised a very beautiful method for registering the movements but it was less useful for our purpose ; he devised a movable slide which follows the beam of light on the side. A pulley transfers the movements of the slide to a kymograph. This method is indispensable for finer investigations, but it had the disadvantage for us that it requires two experimenters, and that it does not give a good general view (100 associations may take up a roll of paper of almost 2 metres).

The Tempo of the Test : Latent Time : Oscillations due to Expectation

The *tempo* in which the words are called out deserves a few remarks. The pauses should not be too long between the indi-vidual reactions, so as to avoid the interpolation of too many

[1] Jung, " Experimentelle Beobachtungen über das Erinnerungsvermögen," *Centralblatt für Nervenheilkunde und Psychiatrie*, Bd. XXVIII; also chapter 10.

[2] " On Psychophysical Relations of the Association Experiment," *Journal of Abnormal Psychology*, vol. i, No. 6.

fresh ideas which are not directly conditioned by the reactions, but sufficient time must be allowed for the positive oscillation which sometimes follows the negative one to come to rest; this takes longer with strong than with weak deviations. I took a middle course by only slightly varying the pauses, waiting rather longer when the movements were strong but not for the negative oscillation to cease entirely, if it did not last too long. In time one learns fairly well to estimate how far a deviation will follow from the *tempo*. If the stimulus-word is pronounced whilst there is still a negative oscillation this will continue for a time until it changes into a new positive one. The time spent between the occurrence of the psychical process and its galvanic expression is the *latent time*.[1]

A further reason for not waiting too long between the single reactions is the occurrence of oscillations due to *expectation*. If there is no stimulus-word for a longish time there suddenly occurs, quite regularly with some subjects, an oscillation when the subject believes the next stimulus-word is about to be given. These expectation oscillations can be beautifully exhibited on the kymograph, and they show that these occur as a rule just before pronouncing the new stimulus-word. Several such expectation-waves can be obtained one after another if one waits long enough. Raising one's eyes from the association formula and looking at the scale often suffices to obtain an expectation oscillation. For the experimenter to look at the scale generally means calling out a new stimulus-word, and the subject then becomes disposed to concentrate his attention on the coming stimulus-word. In other words, he is in a state of " strained expectancy "—a concentration of the attention upon what is to come (Lehmann).[2] It is better, therefore, for the subject not to observe the experimenter. By an approximately uniform *tempo* the expectation oscillations are for the most part excluded. When they do occur they can generally be separated from the fluctuations due to the stimulus-word itself, for there is a slight pause between the two ; the expectation oscillation often falls a little so that an interval may be noticed between the two on the kymograph curve. It is then that we must separate this expectation oscillation from that due to the stimulus which follows, for it has nothing to do with the stimulus-word in question. It only gives us

[1] The latent time can be always observed whether the mirror is at rest or in movement. According to our observations it varies between 1·5 and 5 seconds if the electrodes are placed on the hands.

[2] We shall often have occasion to consider the influence of attention upon the psychogalvanic phenomenon. I refer the reader to the section upon attention in Bleuler's book, *Affektivität, Suggestibilität, Paranoia* (Halle, 1906), p. 31, where Bleuler is very insistent that attention is nothing but a " special case of affect."

information about the degree of attention which the subject is giving to the experiment.

CONCERNING THE EFFECT OF BODILY MOVEMENTS AND DEEP INSPIRATION ON THE PSYCHOGALVANIC PHENOMENON

We shall here only consider such movements as change the contact between the subject's hands and the electrodes ; chiefly, then, movements of the hands and arms, but of the legs also if these are of such a nature as to affect the subject's position as a whole. Such fluctuations in the current caused by contact alterations to the electrodes are readily recognized, for they are much more brusque than those psychically determined, and display no temporal or psychological connexion with the particular reactions. It is often a question of negative oscillations. If a disturbing oscillation of this kind arises one must wait before going on until it has spent itself. For later orientation I marked at the appropriate place in the list of words, " Moved." With strong disturbances the experiment is interrupted. Not to exaggerate the contact changes, it may be added that within narrow limits their effect is very slight as compared with that due to psychological causes. On pressing voluntarily a little harder on the electrodes so that a distinct movement of the hand is just noticed, one occasionally obtains slighter galvanometer movements than with emotional reactions when the hand is quite at rest. To produce such strong galvanometer deviations as many persons make at strong complexes one would have to press with a good deal of force upon the electrodes. Besides these voluntary movements, which occur when the subject finds his position uncomfortable and wants to change it, involuntary movements may also have a share. Many subjects themselves admit that they had felt that they had pressed now and then more strongly upon the electrodes at complex than at indifferent reactions. We must not regard this kind of " movements " as faults, for they take place quite regularly at any increased stimulus of affectivity [1] and increase the fluctuation set up by other processes of innervation. We here quite agree with Sommer [2] when he says that involuntary movements affect in a remarkable degree the strength of the circuit. But since we know that in the use of water contact, when the hands and electrodes do not touch, the psychogalvanic phenomenon likewise occurs, we cannot regard the

[1] We use the term affectivity in Bleuler's sense. He understands thereby not only affects in the ordinary sense, but also slight feelings or tones of pleasure and unpleasure at every possible kind of experience.

[2] Sommer and Fürstenau, loc. cit., p. 202. Cp. E. du Bois-Reymond, loc. cit., Bd. II, p. 321 ff.

changes in contact of the electrodes as the essential conditio
for the occurrence of the phenomenon.[1] Besides increase
pressure on the electrodes the movements of the muscles ma
also increase the galvanometer movements by exciting th
activity of the sweat glands (cp. du Bois-Reymond's experimen
and its interpretation by Hermann [2]).

We are not always justified in regarding what occurs at dee
inspirations (laughter and coughing) as *faults*. We must distinguisl
between those which are entirely accidental, caused by fatigue, anc
those which we must regard as "complex indicators," standing i
close relationship to the affectivity, like the involuntary increasec
pressure on the electrodes. This occurred very noticeably in
young lady who, whenever she could not find the reaction
word (and Jung has shown that this is almost invariably due t
emotion), heaved a deep sigh. The complex reactions in questior
are strongly shown on the galvanometer curve. Very dee
inspirations can so affect the strength of the current that a
the whole thorax rises, contact with the electrodes become
loosened. There is then a brusque negative oscillation. Tha
seldom occurs. Much more frequently the deep inspiration
sighing, works by and through the emotional tone only whicl
produces it. The emotional tone connected with the sigh car
act more powerfully upon the physical expression of that feeling
than the sigh by itself would have evoked. But if the sigh is
rather accidental, due, say, to fatigue, it can itself produce a
strong emotional tone by reason of its associative connexion witl
ideas of grief, anxiety, worry, etc. That a sigh does not affect
the strength of the current apart from its accompanying emotiona
tone follows from the experiments of Jung and Peterson,[3] whc
often caused their subjects to make deep inspirations in quick
succession. The first inspirations produced strong deviations, the
succeeding ones were smaller and smaller, the last of all again
became large as the business began to be disagreeable and wearisome to the subject. Vasometer changes evoked by inspirations
are therefore no criterion for the occurrence of oscillations. The
deep inspiration behaves exactly like a psychological stimulus. In
one of Jung and Peterson's cases the excessively large deviations
in deep inspiration were caused by the reawakening of the subject's
fear that he was consumptive.

The systematic repetition of one and the same stimulus shows
very neatly that it is not the perception of the stimulus itself,
but the emotional tone connected with it which affects the psycho-

---

[1] Water contact was first used in these tests by the engineer E. K. Müller.
[2] Hermann, *Lehrbuch der Physiol.*, 12th edition, p. 146.
[3] Jung and Peterson, *Brain*, July 1907, p. 153.

galvanic phenomenon. If the emotional tone of a sensation, e.g. pricking with a needle, can be reduced by frequent repetition, there is no oscillation of the current. What is true of sensations is also true of presentations, as shown in the work of Veraguth, and in the experiments made by Jung and Peterson and by the present writer.

The Material

Our subjects were educated and uneducated men and women : doctors, students, male and female asylum nurses, and three male patients, two of whom were found to be mentally sound and discharged ; the third did not show any disturbing deviation from the normal in those experiments. One female subject was an obvious hysteric. There were in all 23 subjects with 2160 reactions. The smallest number of reactions in one subject was 20, the largest 200 ; as a rule between 50 and 100 associations were carried out. With some subjects second experiments were carried out on different days.

PART II

Report on some Experiments and their Results

I will begin with an experiment on a subject remarkable for penetrating and reliable self-observation.

Experiment I

A married doctor well acquainted with the association experiment.

The probable mean (P.M.) of the reaction-time (R.T.) in these tests was 9/5 or 1·8 second, that of the galvanometer deviation was 8 mm. Times or deviations (so-called " too large values ") above the average are to be regarded, therefore, as disturbances due to emotionally toned complex (see chapter v). The average values or reaction-times which I obtained cannot be directly compared with Jung's, for my personal equation is greater and the conditions of the order of my research are also different from his. The lowest probable mean that I obtained, and that was only in one normal experiment, was 8/5 = 1·6 second ; so that 1·8 second is a low average value.

Curve 1 shows the experiment graphically :

Stimulus-word	Reaction-word	Reaction-time in one-fifth sec.	Galvan. deviation in mm.
1. Head	hand	7	16
2. Blue	sea	9	6

These times disclose no particular emotional tone. A deviation of 16 in Test I demands an explanation. Veraguth had already pointed out that the first deviations in an experiment are usually greater than the subsequent ones. Besides complicated physical causes, it depends also on the fact that most persons are somewhat embarrassed and excited at the beginning and their attention is stretched. So that, quite apart from its content, the first word will discover a complex connected with ideas of the experiment itself, such as : " What will my reactions be like—long or short ? Shall I be able to find a reaction-word at all ? Will any of my secret thoughts and wishes come out ? What will the experimenter think about them ? " These are all ideas which strongly excite the ego complex, and are hence emotionally toned in a striking degree.[1] The relationship of the subject to the experimenter has a particular influence which produces its effect throughout the whole experiment. Jung has brought this out very clearly (see chapter v) and Veraguth likewise (loc. cit., p. 35). In this case, where the subject is relatively unembarrassed as regards the experimenter and has often had the tests carried out on himself, the second deviation already falls below the mean.

		R.T.	G.D.
3. Wall	star	9	14

Whilst the time is average, the deviation as compared with the previous one exhibits a considerable difference. *Wall — star* is an unusual association requiring explanation. Asked what had here occurred to him, he explains that he really wished to say *stone*.[2] I got his free associations to *stone* and we obtained the following series : *stone — stone-blue* (blue sky) ; *star — sister-in-law* (who when engaged often reacted with the word *star*) ; *brother-in-law — wife*—a Mr. St. No. 1 and another Mr. St. No. 2. He now recollected that the word *wall* sounded for a moment like *will*, and the connexion became clear to him. He has been waiting for some time for a work from Mr. St. No. 1 which he very much wants. He had often said to himself, " *Will* the work ever appear and has Mr. St. finished it ? " He had exactly the opposite feeling about the second Mr. St., about whose power of working he was astonished. (Both names have a close clang-relationship to the above series of associations.)

The reaction could be therefore expressed somewhat as follows : " When will Mr. St.'s work appear ? If only Mr. St. No. 1 were as energetic as Mr. St. No. 2 ! " The determination of the reaction *wall — star* is thus disclosed ; we see the way in which, through the complex of Mr. St.'s work and its emotional tone the word *wall* gets the clang of *will*. But from *wall* to *star* there are chains of thought which pass alongside the former, although more " superficially." [3] The *over-determination* which Freud has shown to take place in dreams is also true of association tests. The subject states that at *wall* he had thought of the walls of the asylum, and had thereat the feeling of something severing, inhibiting, insurmountable. In seeking an explanation of these determinants for *star*, the (English) word *stone* given in the above scenes occurred to me, and I noticed that the previous reaction-word was *sea*, which with *star* was the title of a well-known book in which England played a great share. The subject affirmed that

---

[1] Naturally such thoughts need not be clearly conscious although the affect be present. Cp. Jung, " Affects have as a rule an intellectual content, which need not always be conscious." (*The Psychology of Dementia Præcox*, by Dr. C. G. Jung. Translated by Peterson and Brill. New York : The Journal of Nervous and Mental Diseases Publishing Coy., 1909, p. 34.)

[2] The word *stone* was said by the subject in English.—TRANSLATOR.

[3] Freud's *Interpretation of Dreams*.

he had read *Star of the Sea*, 1906, with great interest, and it at once occurred to him that on the title-page of the book there was a blue flag with a *white star*. He further explains that he had described a great star in a poem just as it was illustrated in the *Star of the Sea*, 1906. In reality there is no star on the title-page of the book, as he thought. It was, as the subject himself recognized, a paramnesia by assimilation. A third reference to England is the association *brother-in-law*, who had frequent opportunities of travelling to England and was not so fixed to one place as the subject himself. He was also recently trying to arrange with a colleague for a journey to England which was of some importance to him, but his work at the asylum stood in the way, hindered him. (The subject is, be it remarked by the way, passionately fond of travelling.) *Wall* thus seems to signify a hindrance to this journey through his work in the asylum. Finally it occurred to him that his colleague had advised him to combine with the voyage to England one to America, and not to take the Norddeutscher Lloyd but to travel by the White *Star* Line. We shall find a third determinant for this reaction in reaction 59, where I purposely interpolated the word *star* as a stimulus-word during the test so as to obtain further evidence about the curious reaction 3. Although this analysis is incomplete, it does show the wide ramifications and chains of ideas leading up to two strong complexes; it is enough to show us why the deviation was so extensive here. We also learn at the same time that the complexes need not be conscious, at the moment of the reaction, to obtain such large deviations. The subject had only a "vague feeling of hindrance." The intellectual content of the "feeling" was quite concealed from him.

		R.T.	G.D.
4. Prick	knife	6	6

The subject had carried out several association tests with the same stimulus-word; this reaction, which is one frequently heard, is for him merely verbal, without emotional tone.

5. Devil	angel	7	9

He knew that the stimulus-word *angel* followed *prick*, and was therefore surprised when *devil* was pronounced. (We changed the stimulus-words of our usual list at several places because he knew the list.)

6. Lame	ill	7	7

Lame is again my stimulus-word; subject is surprised.

7. Boat	row	9	8

The day before he had passed by a Mr. Boat without seeing him and so had not saluted him, which made him feel uncomfortable. No distinct influence upon the two values could be recognized.

8. Plough	field	7	1

As in reaction 4, this has become through usage a purely verbal-motor reaction. The low deviation clearly shows the difference in the emotional tone between this indifferent reaction and the above reactions.

9. Will	strive	7	12

The subject has a strongly pronounced striving for knowledge, work, and recognition. The long deviation accords with this strong complex.

10. Friendly	hateful	7	5

Wanted to say *to hate*. Constellated by a dream of the previous night which referred to an old complex not recently revised and which will be dealt with later. So far there had been a rapid rise of the whole curve,[1] as is usually observed in normal tests. The more rapid or slower rise of the curve at the beginning has become for me a valuable criterion of the (psychical) sensibility. The more finely organized the subject, the more labile his affectivity, and the greater the consequent excitation through the experiment, the more rapidly does the curve rise. Physiological and physical influences also have a share in this, but the psychological peculiarities of the subject still seem to me the most important. There is no doubt as to the effect of psychical factors at the beginnings of the curves in Tests II (c), III, and IV.

		R.T.	G.D.
11. Fish	water	9	7

Fish was put in by me ; it therefore seemed " strange " to the subject.

12. Ask	answer	7	4
13. State	law	7	3
14. Haughty	hateful	6	5

In reactions 12 and 13 the same holds good as for 4 and 8. Reaction 14 is constellated by the same dream as reaction 10. Note that the complex shows no signs in reactions 10 and 14 except the rather indirect content of the reaction.

15. Thorn	flesh	7	10

It at once occurs to him that *thorn* signifies a sexual symbol and has replaced the similar *stalk*. During the reaction he is thinking that Paul says of himself he has a thorn in the flesh.

16. To dance	joyous	12	12

Time and deviation obviously increased. The subject is annoyed at having to go to a ball next day ; thereat a mass of strongly toned reminiscences.

17. Sea	lake	6	5

Lower values for time and deviation, but the curve nevertheless rises. Possibly reactions 15 and 16 are here at work, but there is an emotional tone at reaction 17, for he formerly had great longings for the sea which were again aroused by the promised journey to England. The emotional tone is not expressed in the deviation itself but by a positive fluctuation which is not followed by any negative, as usual, but by a second strong positive fluctuation. The emotional tone does not diminish but is strengthened after saying the reaction-word (see curve).

The flat course of the curve from reactions 10–17 is explained by the low emotional tone of most of these reactions. It is only after reaction 15 that stronger fluctuations arise, and at reaction 17 cause a rise in the level.

18. Ill	poor	6	6
19. Proud	eminent	9	15

He is often reproached by his family with being too proud ! He has, in general, a strongly developed conscience.

20. England	France	9	14

(See reaction 3.)

---

[1] By " curve " I designate the whole graphic course of the experiment, whilst the expression " complex wave " is only used for the individual undulations interposed in the total curve, and which are again composed of individual deviations.

		R.T.	G.D.	Reproduction
21. Ink	drink	7	10	

He meant to say *drinker*. On his last journey to England he had charge of
a female patient, a " drinker." The reaction belongs to the strong complex of
the journey planned to England.

22. All	ton	7	14	

Alton is the name of the estate where his wife's parents live and where his
wife grew up. The size of the deviations and the rise of the curve show that
complexes were met with in reactions 19–22.

23. Nidel	bath	7	10	

Was surprised at the dialect word *nidel*. Nidelbad is a sanatorium near
Zurich.   The deviation = 10 is partly related to surprise at the stimulus-word—
it was inserted instead of *needle*.   He subsequently recalled " Cleopatra's Needle "
in London and the Needles at Southampton.   England is here again.

24. Swim	water	7	7	
25. Leave	take	11	12	have

Three complex signs in this reaction : prolonged time, increased deviation,
and disturbance in reproduction. *Leave* is a strong complex for, as mentioned,
he is very fond of travelling, but as physician to a State asylum only receives
short leave. The journey to England is again involved.

26. Rude	gruff	11	8	

The reaction-time 11 is due to the perseveration of the reaction 25 (see later
about the influence of perseveration on time and deviation).

27. Red (rot)	blue	9	10	

Apparently a purely verbal reaction. But the deviation points to a complex.
He thinks of the pathologist Rot, who did a post-mortem on his father, and of
the proverb " To-day red, to-morrow dead."   He can think of nothing further.
For the analysis see reaction 63.

28. Threaten	hit	9	11	lengthy reflection

The complex aroused in reactions 10 and 14 occurs to him on account of
which he was for a time " threatened." Whilst there were no complex signs
there, here we get two.

29. Asylum	have	11	8	

Believed he had answered too soon, before the stimulus-word was quite
spoken.
   The reaction-time 11 shows that he deceived himself. He at first thought
it was *manners*. *Manners* is connected with the complex in reaction 28, and
was heard in the sense of the complex.[1]   Asylum at the same time was repressed.[2]

---

[1] These cases are spoken of as assimilation of the stimulus-word to the
complex. See Riklin, chapter viii.
[2] For repression consult Freud's works, and Jung, chapter v.

Analysis 3 showed us that in *asylum* there is a tone of unpleasure.

		R.T.	G.D.	Reproduction
30. Rich	poor	8	20	

Twenty is the biggest deviation so far. Money complex plays a large part in this subject and is closely connected with his love of travelling, his salary at the asylum, and his future way of living.

31. Place	time	7	13

Place is apprehended in its philosophic sense. He asked himself whether I had inserted the word to arouse his "philosophic complex." Was, then, the emotional tone, which the galvanometer showed, not to be brought into connexion with a complex already present and only conditioned through the person of the experimenter ? Not at all, for the transference of the emotional tone to the experimenter points to a definite source of affect, which has, however, another origin. The period when he was much engaged with philosophy is emotionally toned to an extreme degree for him.

32. Ring	swing	7	6
33. Pain	heavy	14	14

The rhyme in reaction 32 accords with the weak deviation. It is a purely verbal mechanism which in a subject so practised in language as himself demands the minimum of attention. But we may note that the clang-association, with its slight deviation, follows directly after a reaction with distinct emotional tone.

Reaction 33 was heard as *rain*, a good example of repression and of the assimilation of the stimulus-word to the sense of a complex. That *pain* should be repressed is not astonishing ; he would like to enjoy life but has a slight disposition to hypochondriacal ideas (as we shall see later).

34. Money	have	9	24

The deviation exceeded No. 30, *rich — poor*, by 4 mm. We see how strongly developed is the money complex with all that pertains to it.

35. Mountain	climb	9	12

He regrets that in consequence of his asylum work he has little time for mountaineering.

36. Play	cards	11	5	(reflects)

Here he thought of his wife and children.

37. Speck	neck	9	6
38. Repent	spent	11	7

The time is prolonged but not the deviation. But the rise of the curve afterwards denotes a rising emotional tone. Reaction 38 is connected with the complex (not gone into) which he had in mind in reaction 10, without its becoming objective there (analysis showed that he wanted to say *to hate* and substituted the more harmless *hateful*). In reaction 14, *haughty — hateful*, the complex was not yet recognizable, but it came out in reactions 28, *threaten — hit* and 29, *asylum — have*. The complex is objectively evident in reactions 38 and 39. It would seem that the complex became more and more autonomous, coming more to the surface with the addition of the stimuli. The "autonomy" of the complex is seen also in the curve, which in the section 34–38 presents for the first time

the picture of a distinct complex curve (long deviation with a subsequent **fall**
of the curve and smaller deviations).

		R.T.	G.D.	Reproduction
39. Custom	manners	9	10	(reflects)
40. Ride	drive	7	11	

Regrets he has now no time for riding.

41. Sand	sea	9	10

Thinks of the journey to England and of a friend's dream where the word
santonin played a part.   It was this friend who suggested the journey to England.

42. Stupid	donkey (Dubel)	9	18

The reaction was the dialect word *dubel* (a fool—donkey).   He explains that
this reaction was emotionally toned; he was thinking of a particular person.

43. Sap	rap	7	6	
44. Despise	esteem	9	6	
45. Tame	wild	11	5	(reflects)

At first he understood *tooth* (instead of *tame*), the word used in the ordinary
schedule.

46. Important	unimportant	7	1	
47. People	ruler	9	10	(reflects)

Here Napoleon occurred to him, and a dream analysis where Napoleon came in.
But the emotional tone is derived from the " will to power " which is strongly
marked in him.   The experiment was here interrupted by a message, and his hands
were removed from the electrodes; after a few minutes the experiment was continued.   We now observed a very rapid rise of the curve, which in four reactions
reached the same height which it took sixteen reactions to reach in the first part.
In general the second part of the curve shows a much more "nervous," labile
character than the first.   On close investigation the same kind of change is
seen between the end of the first part of the curve and its beginning and middle ;
a more distinct effect of the complexes on the curve is noticeable.

48. Drown	swim	17	14

As this is the first reaction in the second part of the curve, the great deviation
must not be regarded as a complex sign without investigation ; but the long
reaction-time, 17 seconds, points to one.   The subject apprehended the reaction-
word as *Aprilchen* (this has rather more clang-association to the German than
to the English reaction-word), and at once thought of a journey to England
which was to take place next April—another good instance of assimilation to
the complex.

49. Belly	lie	8	18

Apprehended sexually and in the sense of " crawling on one's belly " to some
one ; something very antagonistic to the subject, especially in scientific matters.

50. Wrong	right	9	3
51. Kröte	spöte	16	40 !

He thought of the well-known verse with these rhymes to the name of Goethe.
Goethe sets up through a particular constellation, which cannot be here gone
into, a strong emotional tone.
  The subject admits that from this time on he experienced distinct **excitation**.
We shall deal with this section of the curve 51–58 again.

		R.T.	G.D.	Reproduction
52. Divorce	force	9	5	
53. Hunger	thirst	6	6	
54. Knowledge	thirst	9	8	

As thirst for knowledge.

55. Child	have	10	5	

He thinks that his youngest child is slightly unwell. But there seems to be some stronger complex behind this apparently "innocent" reaction. The reaction-word *have* suggests this, for this word only occurs in definite complex places: see *manners — have; money — have;* and later, *fame — have; salary — have.* Jung calls such stereotyped reaction-words complex representatives (chapter v). The complex is quite unconscious here. Besides the stereotyped reaction-word the complex is betrayed by prolongation of the reaction-time—one-fifth of a second above the mean; we shall meet the complex again in reaction 59.

56. Hat	put on	11	6	
57. Pencil	write	11	5	

Remembers that *pencil* is occasionally apprehended as a sexual symbol.

58. Carrot	sugar	7	2	(reflects)

Again a sexual symbol.

59. Star	house	12	20	(reflects)

This reaction enabled us to penetrate into the deepest layers of the reaction, *wall — star.* The subject has the feeling that it was the same thing here as in reaction 3; he really wanted to say *wall.* The wish which accompanied the reaction was, "May a lucky star shine over our house." That refers to the future of his family in general but also to its past (see the poem mentioned in reaction 3 where he described his lucky star). To *star* the subject next thought of *Star of Bethlehem*; and, recalling the associations *sister-in-law* (now pregnant) and *wife* from the series of associations in reaction 3, reaction 35, *child — have,* and also reaction 75, *family — have,* we easily recognize the wish concealed behind all these reactions. But the association *Star of Bethlehem* ("Unto us a son is born") first gives us the correct clue. He has now two daughters. The wish for a son is easily understandable. We can summarize the analysis of reactions 3 and 59 (although it is far from exhausted, as the expert will quickly see):

1st layer: When will Mr. St. No. 1's work appear? If only he were as energetic as Mr. St. No. 2. What was the wall (= hindrance) here was not mentioned.

2nd layer: When *shall* I travel to England? Shall I go on to America with the White Star Line? If only the asylum were not such a wall (brick wall = hindrance).

3rd layer: When shall I have a son? May a lucky star grant him to me. The wall (= hindrance) is fate in general, which has hitherto opposed his desire.

60. Cellar	excellent	9	1	

A very superficial reaction. The very slight deviation is explained by the previous reaction. The deviation of reaction 60 is at the short, descending limb of a complex wave which here consists of two reactions only. We shall see later why the deviations found at the down-stroke of a complex wave are particularly short, and the corresponding reactions particularly superficial.

		R.T.	G.D.
61. Light	beat	13	10

Patient heard the stimulus-word as *fight* and at once thought of an opponent; it is the same complex as in reaction 42.

62. Love	dear	6	7

Note the subsequent rise of the curve; *love* has in itself a strong emotional valuation.

63. Grass	herb	12	7

The reaction-time is prolonged; the deviation indifferent. Biblical sayings are at the base of the reaction : " For all flesh is grass." Again : " Let the earth bring forth grass, the herb yielding seed, and the fruit-tree yielding fruit after his kind, whose seed is in itself, upon the earth."

The second saying was not verbally remembered by the subject during the analysis but its content was present ; moreover, during the reaction he saw the picture illustrating it in the Carolsfeld Bible ; especially vivid was the rain which is so closely connected with the passage. We have already, during the test, come across one saying expressing a similar idea : " To-day red, to-morrow dead." It was at reaction 27, *red — blue* (R.T. 9, G.D. 10), when he at the same time thought of the pathologist Rot, who performed an autopsy on his father. Here again *father* at once occurred to him. The association of *father* was aroused in both reactions by ideas of death, which the sayings " To-day red," etc., and " All flesh " contain. The *father* can be here but a cover figure concealing some other person. We shall not go far astray in suspecting it is the subject himself ; for Freud's remark about dreams—that the chief actor is always the dreamer himself—is equally true here. After much reflection he remembered his father used to say that the L.'s (his surname) never lived long, and it was at the age of thirty that he had expressed these hypochondriacal thoughts most frequently. We know now that, although he does not want to admit it, similar thoughts are passing in his own mind. He is now thirty-one years old. The saying " Let the earth," etc., is a turning away from himself to his successor (son) ; in the two reactions 27 and 63 we thus find the instincts of self-preservation and of the preservation of the species (which are in other ways well marked in him). The saying also leads to our understanding reaction 59 (" May a lucky star "). Very remarkable is the Biblical colouring in which all these complexes are arrayed. The subject was very religious in childhood. Thus past, present, and future combine in the short analysis. One might expect that to the words *red* and *grass* we should get *dead* and *flesh* ; whilst the reactions are *blue* and *herb*— most innocent reactions. This brings out very clearly the censure in Freud's [1] sense. These two sayings containing thoughts of death touch him painfully ; he thus seeks to elude them and succeeds. To put it in Jung's language : the " ego complex " has overcome the very unpleasantly toned death complex and has " assimilated the stimulus-word in a sense appropriate to the ego complex," thus concealing the painful thoughts, or hiding them from himself.

And, as so frequently happens, in the repression of one complex another suppressed complex, that of propagation, found a means to make itself evident. We shall return later to the relationship between deviation and time in this reaction.

---

[1] Freud, *Interpretation of Dreams and Psychology of Everyday Life.*

	R.T.	G.D.
64. To yield yield up	11	3

The disproportion between R.T. and G.D. is explained by perseveration from the previous reaction.

65. Goat buck	7	14

He thought of a gentleman whom a colleague had called a goat the day before. At the same time the thought arose: "The experimenter will draw analogous conclusions about me." The curve now rose rapidly. One gets the impression that the complexes force themselves more to the front, withdrawing from the force of the ego complex. The ego complex has lost its inhibitory action, and so the remaining complexes gain in autonomy. Thus, instead of the fairly regular first half of the curve we find extreme fluctuations in the second half where the individual complexes gain expression.

66. Big little	6	8
67. Potato new	5	5
68. Tired I am	7	5

Reaction 68 is the beginning of the well-known child's prayer. The reaction is constellated by the subject's momentary condition. The fatigue helps in the complex becoming autonomous.

After this reaction the curve shows a tendency to fall, and one might expect that there would be peace again. But a critical stimulus-word followed in which the subject feels that he now has exposed his complexes. He acknowledges in analysis that after reaction 69 he became more excited and had the feeling "Now everything will come out." The curve shows the excitation at reaction 65. The test is more subtle than conscious perception. The feeling of fear that now everything will come out must attain a certain threshold value in order to reach consciousness.

69. Sex determination	9	25

Thinks of Schenk's method of determining sex before birth. We know that he has two daughters and would like a son. Besides, the word *sex* is itself very "complex-rousing" (see the connexion with reaction 65, when the excitation not yet conscious had begun).

70. Young old	7	16

The subject admits that the death complex reverberated here.

71. Fame have	7	15

We have mentioned *have* as a complex representative. We are here dealing with the complex of ambition, thirst for knowledge, "will to power," which we have frequently met. The section of the curve 65–71 can be regarded as an up stroke of a complex curve.[1] On closer examination it can be split into two halves belonging to two complexes which are not entirely separated from one another. The first complex (65–68) was aroused by the reaction *goat — buck*, and was fading when the new complex (*sex — determination*) arose causing a further rise of the curve (together with the subsequent reactions). It is only in reaction 73 that the down stroke of this composite complex curve

---

[1] Hitherto we have only spoken of complex curves when a down stroke with slight deviations followed a long deviation. But in place of one long deviation we can get several deviations, which are then usually found upon the up stroke.

begins; the reactions 74–76, which have but little emotional tone, belong to this down stroke.

		R.T.	G.D.	Reproduction
72. Bear	heavy	11	12	

Thinks of reaction 33; also of pregnancy and his wife (son).

73. Box	bed	11	12	

Perseveration of thoughts about his wife, for *box — bed* is an association due to her former pregnancy.

Notice how the complexes increase and that they are not new ones. They now extend because the inhibition on the part of the ego complex is absent.

74. Coarse	se-sex	8	0	

The hesitation at the reaction-word points to the commencing "emptiness of association" caused by the complexes. No deviation at all; the reaction only detained the descent of the curve for a moment.

75. Family	have	6	4	

Have alone betrays the complex.

76. Wash	pure	8	3	

To the last three associations a minimum of attention was given. The complexes aroused at reactions 69–73 are still at work. In a subject less fluent in speech we might here expect clang or verbal-motor reactions. But for this subject a mere trace of attention is sufficient to find a word that makes sense.

77. Ambition	to be	7	15	

The complex again breaks through without bothering about the verbal form of the stimulus-word. The reaction is very superficial, verbal-motor, which probably accounts for absence of any prolongation of time.

78. Foreign	far	12	7	wide

Foreign is taken in the geographical sense; the incorrect reproduction *wide* points to the love of travelling.

79. Back	rack	7	9	

A verbal reaction, hence the short time; constellated by a reminiscence of a patient.

80. To count	count out	9	8	
81. State	état	12	23	

Three complex indicators: translation of the stimulus-word and the prolongation of both time and deviation. The reaction refers both to the sexual and to the social spheres. Its emotional tone must be very strong for the curve scarcely descends between reactions 81 and 82.

82. Narrow	broad	7	8	

The curve now begins to fall. If we are to regard reactions 81 and 82 as the beginning of a complex wave, reactions 83–87 are its descending limb.

83. Brother	sister	7	3	
84. Harmful	useful	7	2	

The superficial verbal apprehension of these two reactions accords with the lower figures for time and deviation.

		R.T.	G.D.
85. Birth	accoucheur	8	13

Thought of his sister-in-law and his wife. We recognize the old complexes but they no longer exercise the same effect upon the curve for they canno restrain its descent. It is probable they have been somewhat " abreacted by now through their frequent expression in so many reactions.

86. Falsify	deceive	11	10

relates to the " opponent " whom we have already encountered.

87. Regret	lively	8	8

Seems a superficial verbal reaction. Still the curve ascends ; he regrets havin insufficient time for the execution of his scientific and travel plans.

88. Kiss	beloved	9	10

Probably a reminiscence from the subjects with whom he has himself cor ducted experiments ; this is a common reaction on their part.

89. Toy	play	9	25

Was confused by the stimulus-word ; thinks of children's toys, but the lon reaction can scarcely be accounted for by this confusion alone. *Toy* leads t toying, *play* to his children and his wife.

90. Foul	useful	14	14

Death complex. But there is an additional complex referring to himself whos existence seems to him at times quite useless.

91. Doors	open	7	6
92. Choice	trouble	9	18

The question of the future here rose up.

93. Repentance	fast	11	20

See reaction 87.

94. Suckle	suck	11	7
95. Mockery	scorn	3	6
96. Sleep	at night	11	17
97. Salary	have	7	17
98. Vienna	Paris	7	23

Reactions 94–97 require no further explanation now. Reaction 98 : he i contemplating a journey to Vienna as soon as the vacation begins ; he ca hardly wait.

99. Round	earth	7	6
100. Soon	yes	13	33

Is again thinking of the vacation and the Vienna journey. Has a genera feeling " something is soon going to happen." The strong deviation points t the subject's great need of new " sensations."

The analysis shows that we are dealing with a sensitive emotivated subject. This is proved by the great number o complexes (eleven different complexes, which constellate mor than one reaction, and many lesser ones) and the frequenc with which they give rise to strong physical innervations. Th strong emotional nature comes to light also in the increase of the complex waves in the second half of the curve, where we notice a "penetration" of the complexes, i.e. a retrogression of the inhibiting influence of the ego complex.[1]

The reaction-times seem to contradict the results of the psychogalvanic phenomenon. The former are nearly always short, and would often have failed us as complex indicators, whilst the galvanometer behaved with much greater certainty. The comparison of the probable and arithmetical mean more especially eludes us, since the former does not take very long times into account whilst the latter does ; and since there is a certain ratio between length of reaction-time and the intensity of the feelings, Jung thought that he found in the difference of the two means a starting-point whence one could draw certain conclusions as to the intensity of the feelings. In this case the probable mean is 9 seconds and the arithmetical mean, usually greater than the other, is here 8·8 seconds, which is another proof that there are no very long times. But it would be a fundamental error to conclude that there was no intense emotion. We see that in experimental psychology there are, owing to idiosyncrasies, many individual exceptions to conclusions that are correct for most cases. The idiosyncrasies in this case are those to which we have frequently alluded ; the subject is very fluent in speech both by disposition and from usage, and can thus dispose of emotional inhibitions with great facility. The verbal mechanism has attained great autonomy. The numerous rhymes are evidence of this ; they amount to 7 per cent. of the reactions, whilst among educated men Jung found only 0·6 per cent. The verbal-motor reactions are about 30 per cent., a figure which according to my experience is very high, whilst Jung gives them as 34·2 per cent. for educated men. This seems to me extremely high and rests upon a too narrow selection of his " Educated Men."

The galvanometer deviations show a distinct difference between probable and arithmetical mean : P.M. of the deviations, 8 mm. ; A.M. of the deviations, 10 mm.—a difference of 2 mm. (= 25 per cent. of the P.M.), which shows that there were a considerable number of very marked deviations. As a general rule we may infer that, like the very long times, these denote intense emotion.

[1] In phlegmatic subjects the whole curve runs a regular course as this one did at the beginning, without distinct complex waves. The curve then presents almost a line without breaks. In hysterically disposed persons the curve is very different ; it is quite bizarre, interrupted by sudden ascents and as rapid descents. The course of the galvanometer curve has become for me a reliable criterion of the affectivity of the subject.

Much is learned also from the comparison of the mean of those deviations which followed " too long times " [1] with the mean of the galvanometric deviations of the whole test. The deviations occurring with times above the P.M. were therefore written out and their P.M. determined. Since we regard the prolonged times as well as the increased deviation as of intense emotional tone, we must take it that there is a certain agreement between the two. In our case it is seen that though the " too long " times exceed the P.M. by very little, the " too long " deviations do correspond to them :

P.M. of all the deviations : 8.

P.M. of deviations where there are too long times : 10.

The difference in many cases is the same as that between P.M. and A.M. of all the deviations together.

The " clang " associations demand notice ; in our experiment they were in the form of rhymes. Jung and Riklin consider that clangs appear when there is a decline of attention. In their view " clang " associations are the most primitive phenomena of similarity, being but little above simple repetition. Distraction acts in the first place as a bar to inner (" higher ") associations and favours the appearance of the outer associations—these being more mechanical and therefore predominantly clang-associations (chapter ii, p. 42). In order to understand the behaviour of the psychogalvanic phenomenon in clang-reactions we must distinguish carefully whether the distraction which favours the occurrence of clang-reactions is conditioned by one or more previous complex reactions, or is conditioned entirely by the stimulus-word itself, i.e. by a new complex. In the former case the deviation is usually below the norm, in the second case generally above it. The examples in this test help to elucidate this question. We shall later on return to this. We will first set out the instances where distraction was consequent upon a previous complex (remember that the P.M. of the deviations amounts to 9).

			R.T.	G.D.	
1. Previous complex	30. Rich	poor	8	30	
	31. Place	time	7	13	
Clang-reaction	32. Ring	swing	7	6	
2. Previous complex	42. Stupid	donkey (dubel)	9	18	
Clang-reaction	43. Sap	rap	7	6	
3. Previous complex	34. Money	have	9	24	
	35. Mountain	climb	9	12	
	36. Play	cards	11	5	(reflects)
Clang-reaction	37. Speck	neck	9	6	
	38. Repent	spent	11	7	

[1] " Too long " times or deviations always signify those above the P.M. in question.

In the analysis we have already referred to the interesting section of the curve 34–38 and termed it a *complex wave*. The name seemed to me justifiable for these sections of the curve, because it clearly shows how a complex is expressed on the galvanometer curve. (In subjects with fewer complexes the behaviour is much more obvious than here where there are such numerous complexes affecting one another—both in the psyche and in the curve.)

The complex causes first of all, at the reaction where it is aroused, a long deviation, which exceeds by more or less the mean of the deviations of the whole test. But this does not exhaust its effect upon the curve. For we are able to notice in the curve not only the excitation of the complex but its rever-beration, its longer or shorter mastery of the psyche. To the great positive deviation there is a corresponding negative one, and the succeeding deviation begins at the same height as that of the complex reaction. Should the emotional tone conditioned by the complex persist, only a slight negative follows the positive deviation, or if the emotional tone is very strong there is a further ascent of the curve. If the subsequent reactions are also strongly toned by emotion, i.e. if new complexes are added, we may find a long ascending wave as we found in the section 65–71. But after a shorter or longer interval we always find a down-stroke, unless an excitation is added which is in some way conditioned by the test. The wave begins to fall if the subject is no longer susceptible to new stimuli, because he is completely mastered by the complex or complexes.

The attention is completely distracted from the external world by the complex to which it becomes wholly attached. That is why complex reactions so frequently give superficial, verbal-motor or clang associations.[1] Distraction acts similarly as a check upon physical innervations, as we shall have occasion to see. The curve consequently falls and the deviations following immediately become smaller (unless a new complex again rivets attention). This is the origin of the down stroke of the complex wave. We can therefore say : The longer the down stroke of a complex wave, and the shorter the deviations belonging thereto, the stronger is the complex and the longer it perseverates. So that besides the deviation in the complex reaction we have another essential sign wherewith to estimate the strength of the complex in the down stroke of the complex wave. The behaviour of the complex wave in different individuals gives us a criterion of the type of their affectivity. We can notice in a labile character that the wave is like a bonfire that is soon extinct, or in a tenacious

[1] Jung, *The Psychology of Dementia Præcox*, p. 50.

resistant character that it preserves for a long time what has once aroused it. We can only just indicate these relationships here, and refer the reader to Curve II c.

Let us return to our examples (R. 34–38). Since the subject reacts very superficially, we must not lay much weight upon the verbal-motor reactions. But the two clang-associations *speck — neck, repent — spent*, point to the strong distraction which is evidenced by the descending limb of the complex curve. Reaction 38, *repent — spent*, requires attention for itself. It forms the end of the down stroke and the beginning of the ascending limb of a complex wave. This is expressed by the clang-association and the short deviation, both indicating the distraction of attention by the previous complex. The prolonged time, 11 seconds, and its part as the beginning of a new complex curve, shows it to be a new " entrenchment of attention " (Freud), a new complex, the repentance complex already mentioned.[1] In this reaction we had to do with a clang-association of that second kind which owes its origin to the appearance of a new complex and determines a deviation above the mean. The deviation is here also above the mean if we reckon the rise of the curve that follows as belonging to it, a rise that corresponded to a subsequent positive deviation. As we know, a subsequent positive deviation of this kind generally corresponds to a new emotional tone occurring after the reaction-word has been called out ; here this is conditioned by the repentance complex. For this complex developed its effect upon the physical innervation only after the clang-association had been produced. But that it exercised its effect upon the reaction before it entered consciousness we recognize by the prolonged reaction-time. It is for this reason that I would make it, together with the effect of the previous complex, responsible for the clang-association. Freud has discovered in his *Interpretation of Dreams* the mechanism by which a complex leads to the occurrence of clang-associations and of superficial associations in general. In this book, to which we owe an overwhelming fund of new points of view for psychology and psychopathology, he says [2] : " Whenever a psychical element is connected with another by some superficial association there is a real and deeper link between the two which is subject to the resistance of the censure. If the censure makes this normal way of linkage inaccessible, the superficial replace the deeper associations in the presentation. It is as if some barricade, e.g. an inundation in the mountains, had made the

---

[1] For personal reasons this complex was not analysed more thoroughly.

[2] Freud in this book does not make use of the term " complex " but the idea is implied in his conclusions.

large and best roads impassable; transport then becomes restricted to the inconvenient and steep bridle-paths, which are otherwise only used by the hunter" (*Interpretation of Dreams*, p. 310).

The obstacle to transport is the complex which interposed between stimulus- and reaction-word; the censure is shown by the repressing action of the ego complex upon this complex. The inconvenient, steep bridle-paths are in our case the clang-associations of which Jung and Riklin speak (chapter ii, p. 42). What Freud says of the dream is only true in the association experiment of the clang-associations of the second kind. In those of the first kind which owe their origin to distraction from a previous complex, a "more real and deeper" link cannot be proved in analysis. This is also seen by the striking character of the psychogalvanic phenomenon, for this generally shows a diminution in the first kind and an increase in the second kind.

The reaction *repent — spent* led up to the clang-association of the second kind. The deeper connexion between the two associations is obvious. We have had further instances in our experiment of clang-associations with increased deviation.

First Example

		R.T.	G.D.
51. Kröte	spöte	16	40
(52. Divorce	force	9	5)

Despite the clang-association both time and deviation are enormously increased in reaction 51. The deeper connexion between these associations, namely, that both occur in a poem of Goethe's, was the cause of the pronounced effect. But Goethe is an extremely powerful complex for this subject, into which, as already mentioned, we are, unfortunately, unable to enter further.

It is also noteworthy that Goethe was not associated, an association which lay at the root of the whole reaction and which would also have rhymed to *kröte*; instead we get the less "indiscreet" word *spöte*, which the censure can more easily allow to pass. What the censure was particularly careful about was the great embarrassment of the subject at revealing this complex to the experimenter. The complex became at once conscious.

(The reaction 52 that follows, *divorce — force*, with its slight deviation, is clearly a clang-association of the first kind which arose through the strong influence of the previous reaction and had no complex of its own.[1])

Second Example

		R.T.	G.D.
92. Choice	pain	9	18

---

[1] See p. 474.

An indifferent reaction preceded this; clearly it contains the complex in itself. The deep connexion between the two associations is clear (" who has the choice has also the pain "). It refers to the strong complex of the " question of a future." Here the complex was conscious also.

Reactions with " Too Long " Reaction-time and " Too Short " a Deviation

In the one hundred associations we were struck by eleven where the time exceeded the probable mean whilst the deviation was less than the probable mean (P.M. of reaction-time, 9; P.M. of deviation, 8). The reactions in question are 26; 36; 38; 45; 55, 56, 57; 63, 64; 78 and 94.

In looking at the curve we notice that four of these deviations, 26, 36, 78, and 94, follow directly a too long deviation, whilst 38 and 45, the groups 55–57 and 63–64, are separated from " too long " deviations by two, or at most three short deviations. It would seem that here, as with clang-associations of the first kind, distraction has a share through a complex which had acted upon the previous strong deviation. Let us now denote the after-effect of a complex by the term perseveration. Jung has proved so abundantly that the perseveration can prolong the times of those reactions within its sphere of influence that it is unnecessary for us to set forth the proofs of this.[1]

That the perseveration can also diminish the deviation we have just seen (see the down stroke of the complex wave). We shall later return to a detailed instance of this kind (II c); we here want to clear up the disproportion between deviation and time when it arises in the sphere of perseveration.[2]

Whilst in the measurement of the psychogalvanic phenomenon we have to do with a quite involuntary, automatic innervation process, in which the subject does not actually participate, but is merely a spectator, the measurement of the reaction-time is a process which demands the active co-operation of his personality. In order to find an appropriate reaction-word he must now turn part of his attention directed towards the previous complex to the reaction itself. To overcome the resistance that proceeds

[1] Jung, chapter v.

[2] Jung and Riklin understand by perseveration " the continuance of the previous idea so far as it becomes manifest in the nature of the reaction following." The designation is purely " formal " and has nothing to do with " perseveration in organic cerebral processes." Jung and Riklin only consider the effect upon the reaction that follows and " leave aside the effect of a reaction that has been itself influenced "; there they speak of " constellation." I do not draw this distinction, but believe I am justified by the behaviour of the galvanometer curve in speaking of " perseveration " in both cases.

from the complex takes up time, so that the reaction-time is longer than in a reaction where the whole attention is at disposal. But the innervation process (the deviation) measured by the galvanometer gives us information about this residue of attention which is to be turned to the new stimulus-word. The portion of the attention linked to the complex acts, as shown above, upon the whole curve upon which the deviations arise. This is the origin of the down stroke of the complex waves. It can be pertinently expressed in this way : In the galvanometer curve we exhibit complex and new reaction, separated, the former by the course of the curve, the latter by the deviation. In the reaction-time, on the contrary (of course, only in perseveration) we perceive a sign of the intensity of the conflict between the two. The greater this conflict is, the longer is the reaction-time. But this law is only true of the deviation in which we see only one of the parties in the struggle, not the struggle itself. According to whether the complex or the subsequent reaction remains victorious (in the struggle for the possession of the attention) so will the deviation be above or below the mean. The reaction-time thus tells us how " warm " the struggle was, but the deviation tells us which was victorious. Since we measure by these two estimates entirely different things (in cases of perseveration), we must not demand any ratio between them. At the most we can say that when the perseveration is very strong and the new reaction in itself very strongly toned by emotion, the reaction-time tends to be long, the deviation tends to be short.

The following example, a section of which was dealt with in the clang-associations, may clear up this discussion.

In the curve section 51–58 we notice a complex wave which begins with the long deviation at 51, followed by a series of seven short deviations. But we never obtain here, remarkably enough, any down stroke of a complex curve. That obviously depends upon the fact that we are still at the beginning of the second section of the curve. The tendency of the wave to descend, which follows a long deviation, is opposed by the tendency to rise which we encounter at the beginning of almost every normal curve. This wave contains three of the eleven reactions (55, 56, 57).

		R.T.	G.D.
51. Kröte	spöte	16	40

contains the very powerful Goethe complex.

52. Divorce	force	9	5
53. Hunger	thirst	6	6
54. Knowledge	thirst	8	9
55. Child	have	10	5

		R.T.	G.D.
56. Hat	put on	11	6
57. Pencil	write	11	5
58. Carrot	sugar	7	2

The perseveration proceeding from reaction 51 is expressed in the associations, which are very superficial even for this patient : one rhyme, five verbal-motor associations, one coexistence. Moreover, in reaction 54 the reaction-word of 53 is reproduced, which again distinctly points to perseveration. The effects of the perseverating emotional tone upon the reaction-time and deviation above described give us an easy explanation of the striking differences of the two values in reactions 55, 56, and 57. Reaction 55 contains the *son* complex and the *propagation* complex in general, reaction 56 contains the latter. Reaction 57 is erotically constellated by reminiscences of association tests he has himself carried out, and at the same time by the sense of the relation to the ego. The rhyme and the slight deviation show that only slight attention was given to reaction 52, which is the first after the critical reaction. The time shows that in consequence of this there was no great " conflict."

Reaction 53 : The dissociation of association which this reaction demanded must have been even easier than in 52, for the reaction-time is very low.

Reaction 54 : A strong " conflict," for *knowledge* is emotionally toned and demands a greater " entrenchment of attention " (R.T. = 9). The deviation (= 8) shows that in fact the reaction did try to enchain the attention. We next get the three emotional-toned reactions 55–57. A violent " conflict " is renewed (R.T. = 10 and 11). The perseverating emotional tone, which is probably strengthened by reaction 54, retains, in contradistinction to reaction 54, the greatest part of the entrenched attention and has but little left for the new reaction (deviations 5, 6, 5). At reaction 58 the reaction-time, as well as the deviation, show that there was no distinct dissociation of attention, but the reaction became very superficial, purely verbal-motor.

I hope I have shown that, in reactions which occur at a perseverating emotional tone, there cannot be expected the slightest ratio between reaction-time and deviation—that we might, indeed, easily get an inversed ratio between the two. When we find such an inversed ratio we must consider the possibility of a perseveration.

It would not take us any further were we to apply these deductions to the other instances (R. 63–64 ; 26 ; 36 ; 78 and 98). I will here only refer to another factor which may also produce

٭ disproportion between the two values ; I refer to indistinct ٭pprehension of the stimulus-word.

		R.T.	G.D.	Reproduction
45. Tame	wild	11	5	(reflects)

The subject at first understood *tooth*. This indistinct appre-ٮension is more easily understood because the original list con-ained the word *tooth*, which I changed into *tame*.

In such cases the time is prolonged by " the feeling of uncer-ainty " as to whether the word has been correctly heard or not ; ın intellectual feeling in Nahlowsky's sense.   Bleuler [1] has shown hat such "intellectual feelings, which are memory processes, ᵣre utterly different from affectivity."   We see here how impor-ant this sharp distinction is.   According to Bleuler it is only ' affectivity in the strictest sense " that has definite effects upon ᵥody and mind.   Since we only register affective processes by he psychogalvanic reflex when the reaction - time registers ᵥoth memory or intellectual processes as well, the disproportion ᵴ explicable in such cases.   But there need by no means always ᵥe this disproportion in reactions where the word has been indis-ᵼnctly understood.   First, the indistinct apprehension may be a ᵭmplex sign when the deviation is increased by the complex ; ᵴcondly, a real affect in the strictest sense may be added to the ᵼntellectual feeling "—for instance, when the subject is endeavour-ᵻg to react quickly and feels himself inhibited by his indistinct ᵨpprehension so that he is not sure to what he is to react.   Then ᵭnnoyance, confusion, or some similar affect steps in.   This is ᵥoticed in subjects who stand in any kind of affective relationship ᵵ the experimenter, e.g. in attendants, who are often unable to ᵥrget that the experimenter is their chief, and sometimes in ᵫmale nurses, where there is in addition the sex difference. ᵥith close acquaintances—especially if they happen to be ᵥomen—this relationship to the experimenter can act both as ᵵ time and deviation upon apparently most innocent reactions.

Summary of Experiment I

Both halves of the association curves show a rapid rise at ᵵe beginning ; but the second half rises much more rapidly than ᵵe first, due chiefly to the increased excitation of the subject. ᵵe second half is marked by numerous and very pronounced ᵮmplex waves, which point to the complexes becoming autono-ᵥous and to the growing excitation.   The typical complex wave ᵥnsists of a very long deviation, followed by a down stroke ᵼth deviations that are "too short."   The down stroke of the

[1] Bleuler, loc. cit., p. 10 ff.

complex curve and the too short deviations are explained by the distraction of the attention, which is still fettered to the complex reaction (perseveration). In this experiment, where the complexes were so numerous, there were few favourable opportunities for pure complex waves.

" Too long " deviations correspond in most cases to complex reactions, short deviations to non-emotionally toned reactions. Exceptions are seen when a perseveration makes itself felt.

Perseveration acts partly by decreasing the corresponding deviation, partly by prolonging the corresponding time. The explanation is this : the reaction - time gives us information about the intensity of the conflict between perseveration and the new reaction, whilst the deviation informs us about the result of this conflict—that is, about the entrenched attention which the new reaction contains. Having regard to the difference expressed by these two values as regards perseveration we conclude there cannot be any direct ratio between time and deviation ; on the contrary, when perseveration is strong we should rather expect an indirect ratio. That the complexes in our test are indicated with greater certainty by the deviation than by the reaction-times is found in the verbal fluency of this particular patient.

The clang-associations in our experiment exhibit prolonged deviations when caused by a complex, abbreviated deviation when caused by a perseveration.

EXPERIMENT II

The subject is about forty years old, an intelligent mechanic, who rose from being a simple journeyman in a machine manufactory to a position of respectability and wealth. An ineradicable tendency to fraud by the use of his own half-perfected discoveries soon brought him to prison. In the summer of 1906 he was sent to us from prison, where he was undergoing his third term of punishment, as doubt was entertained about his sanity. After three months observation we were obliged to send him back to the prison as " mentally sound in a legal sense." There was nothing abnormal to be found in him save a very strong emotivity, a disposition to quarrel, and a certain want of clarity in his thoughts. As I had to form an opinion about the man, and therefore spent much time with him, I obtained in the three months a good insight into his mind. After association tests had been repeatedly made with him I made the first galvanometer test on July 21, 1906. (The analysis of the three following tests remained very incomplete because at the time when I did them I was insufficiently at home in psycho-analysis. If, nevertheless, I cite these tests here it is because the Curve II c in and for itself, and compared with Curve II a and II b, seems to be to be particularly interesting.)

Test (a) (July 21, 1906).—The subject was greatly interested in the experiment, especially from the technical side, and he had prepared himself for it by various curves which he had drawn for me.

The P.M. of the reaction-times is 11, the A.M. 13·1. The P.M. of the galvan meter deviations is 30, the A.M. 37.   The P.M. of the deviations which coincide with too long time is 35.[1]

From the distinct difference between the P.M. and the A.M. of the times we infer that we are dealing with an emotional personality.

The arrangement of the experiment in all three tests differed from the previous one because two galvanic cells were employed instead of one.   The deviations cannot be compared off-hand with the former because, through the use of a stronger current, the deviations were made stronger.   For this reason the difference between the deviations obtained in the third test with this subject, and the results from Tests I and II become the more evident.[2]

		R.T.	G.D.
1. Head	round	10	15
2. Green	tree	16	16

No explanation could be given for the prolongation of the time.

3. Water	thin	9	10
4. Prick	heart	11	25

He has a pricking pain in the region of the heart and fears he may have heart disease.   There have been several cases of death from heart disease in his family. The complex increases the deviation but it is still under the P.M.

5. Angel	fantasy	16	17

A rather curious association.   In a test carried out three weeks earlier, without the galvanometer, he had used the same reaction-word at this place with obvious complex disturbances.   The reaction-time was then 20.   The time is here increased but not the deviation.   Inasmuch as the subject has already reacted to the same stimulus-words, the conditions are peculiarly complicated.   We as yet know too little about the effect of repetitions of the same stimulus-words on the psychogalvanic phenomenon to be able to give an explanation of the disproportion between reaction-time and deflection.   The reaction is partly rooted in the subject's position towards religion (angels are only imaginary figures), but partly also in his everyday life (it would be imaginary to think one could find " an angel in life ").   He is divorced from his wife and often speaks of her in abusive terms.   He granted the truth of the first statement but could neither affirm nor deny the second.   But it is pretty certainly near the truth to any one who knows the psychology of this subject.

6. Long	fir-tree	25	40

In the first experiment, three weeks earlier, the reaction-time was 37 with the same reaction-word.   Between the associations *angel — fantasy* on the one side and *long — fir-tree* on the other a pathway had been made by the first test, and they have now shorter reaction-times.   But the strength of the complex is still very strong, as is seen by the very long time and the long deviation.

---

[1] At those places where the times are not indicated the deviations have also not been used for calculating the mean, otherwise the comparison between the two means would not be accurate.

[2] I emphasize again the statement that even with the case of the same strength of current the deviations vary in their average size according to the individual tested.   This is somewhat dependent upon physical and physiological conditions (thickness of epidermis, temperature of the skin and of the whole surroundings, more or less pressure upon the electrodes), but predominantly it depends upon the psychological character of the subject.   It is this which stamps the whole curve.

In *long — fir-tree* he had thought of the expression *rolling-pin* used in his occupation, and this was repressed in favour of the word *fir-tree* that got dragged in. The complex which in our experience usually occurs here among patients is the length of the detention. This complex was particularly strong in this subject.

		R.T.	G.D.
7. Ship	sailing ship	7	10
8. Plough	field	7	12
9. Wool	cotton-wool	8	3

Three indifferent associations taken from his first experiment.

10. Friendly	friendly face	16	27

Explains he prefers that people should be friendly to him ; refers to doctors, especially to the experimenter. It matters a good deal to the subject whether the experimenter is friendly to him or not.

11. Table	square	9	14
12. Ask	ask ? words	28	45

That the repetition of the stimulus-word is due to a complex is clear from the very prolonged reaction-time. The complex is the experimenter himself. In the first experiment he associated to *ask — we did !* Since he is the subject of a medico-judicial inquiry we understand the great importance that he attaches to the course of the experiment.

13. State	Federal State	15	35

In his view he cannot help his misfortune, it is the fault of society, of the State.

14. Proud	mankind	8	25

Slipped in and somewhat " abreacted " through the first experiment. *Mankind* almost always represents a complex. Who is here meant (himself ? his wife ?) remains unexplained.

15. Stalk	hempstalks	—	23
16. Dance	little couple	15	35

He was a good dancer and great gourmand.

17. Lake	Lake Zurich	22	25

" Sunday excursions on the lake are very pleasant memories," he said in analysis (contrast with his present life).

18. Disease	heart disease	15	58

The complex of reaction 4 is here fully revealed. This is another instance of how a complex at first appears indistinctly, and by repeated " echoings " shows the complex signs distinctly.

19. Proud	old maid	8	30

Dragged in from the former experiment. The reaction-word may be conditioned by the separation from his wife.

20. Cook	electric cooking	16	50

" He had recently read about it." Cooking reminds him of his wife and his former housekeeping (very extravagant for his means). In the first test he associated to *cooking : housekeeping, household, kitchen.*

		R.T.	G.D.
21. Ink	black	10	45

Not explained.

| 22. Wicked | mankind | 16 | 35 |

He thinks he has been wickedly treated by several people, especially by the
Public Prosecutor, as whose victim he regards himself. But it remained unexplained whether this was concealed beneath the innocent *mankind*.

| 23. Needle | pointed | 10 | 75 |

Wanted to say *needle prick*—unexplained.

| 24. Swim | lake | 11 | 17 |
| 25. Travel | round the world | 15 | 70 |

This stimulus-word frequently acts very strongly upon prisoners, as contrasting
with their confinement and as expressing a flight of ideas. A reaction in more
than one word points, moreover, to the influence of a complex.

| 26. Blue | sky-blue | 8 | 45 |

He here noticed that the experimenter looked for a moment out of the window,
and asked himself, " Is he looking at the weather ? " It is significant how
closely he watches the experimenter (see also R. 54). The curve rises still higher
after reaction 26, a sign of the presence of some excitation.

| 27. Bread | daily | 10 | 95 |

He here thought of " Our Father," etc., and that next day he was to go to
the asylum church. He has no religious beliefs. He only went to church as a
distraction.

The strong deviation remained for a long time unexplained until I learnt
that he only went to church because he saw a female patient there with whom
he had fallen in love at a dance in the asylum. At the time he could hardly
wait for the day of divine service. But this does not sufficiently explain the
strong deviation.

| 28. Threaten | laws | 15 | 80 |

The complex is clear.

| 29. Lamp | table-lamp | 11 | 55 |

" He would like to have the nice lamps he had at home." Unexplained.

| 30. Rich | poor | — | 85 |

He had himself gone from poverty to wealth and from wealth back to poverty.
He had learnt both to know the luxury of a Parisian *salon* and the misery
of the prison-house. Day and night he is thinking of regaining his freedom and
of acquiring wealth by his inventions.

The curve rapidly rises from the end of the first half, after
reaction 13. A glance shows that the deviations are, in general,
considerably greater in the second half of the curve. The arithmetical mean of the reaction-time of the second half of the
experiment (13) is greater than that of the first half (11·7). We
may conclude from the rapid rise of the curve, the increase in the
deviations, and in the arithmetical mean of the times in the
second half of the test that the subject has been somewhat

stimulated by the experiment. We also saw that the individual reactions gave opportunity enough to stimulate a very emotional subject. The fact that the experimenter is likewise the medical judge of the patient, this creating in the latter a marked condition of dependence, also contributes somewhat to increasing the excitation. The latter fact must be added to the general experimental excitation, which experience shows influences the action of complexes.

Test (b) (July 24, 1906).—P.M. of reaction-times, 11 ; P.M. of deflections, 23 ; A.M. of reaction-times, 11·5 ; A.M. of deflections, 30 ; P.M. of the deviations which coincide with the " too long " times, 30.

The " emotive inhibitions " are seen more distinctly in this test in the relationship of the deviations than in those of the reaction-times ; the difference between the P.M. and A.M. of the latter is slight (0·5 as against 2 in Test (a)), whilst the difference of the former (7) is almost as great as in Test (a). That the deviations are, on the average, shorter (P.M. 23 against 30, and A.M. 30 against 38) was due chiefly to a physical cause. The experiment was twice interrupted by making the subject wash his hands in cold water. I tried to prevent the beam of light from overstepping the scale, as this had nearly happened in Test (a), and I also wanted to study the effect of washing hands, for I then ascribed great influence to the amount of perspiration produced.[1]

It is easy to see how slight is the influence of this strong physical interference upon the character of the curve. It cuts the curve into three parts, but each of these parts shows the picture that we have already seen in Test (a)—an almost uninterrupted rapid rise showing no distinct complex waves. The curve of Test (c), where we caused a *psychological* interruption, is quite different, as we shall see.

The same list of words was continued ; we keep to the same numbers for the reactions.

		R.T.	G.D.	Reproduction
31. Tree	green	9	10	
32. Sing	tenor	9	25	

He sang in a small asylum choir which I was conducting. One sees that in some way his " ego complex " must have become more stirred so as to receive a strong deviation. In excitable persons it is a regular rule for a strong deviation to follow any reaction that touches the " ego complex." These reactions need not be strongly emotionally toned ; quite indifferent reminiscences of the long past will produce it. Beyond a certain degree of emotionalness the subject has a definite affect to the experimenter, as was the case here. We see that in everyday life the more we like a person the more emotionally toned becomes every kind of relationship. It is the same with other affects.

33. Pity	mankind	12	18	
34. Yellow	golden yellow	10	13	
35. Mountain	high mountain	9	12	high mountains
36. Play	child's play	13	20	

The subject here thought, " It would be child's play to make a new apparatus " (for galvanometric measurements). His grandiose complex is here distinctly

---

[1] Washing the hands in cold water increases the resistance to conduction of the skin. Moreover, the drying of the previously moist hands diminishes the contact at the electrodes. The curve, therefore, begins each time lower than it was before.

seen. He had, in fact, made me a sketch of a contrivance for transferring the galvanometer fluctuations directly on to the kymograph. On paper this looked, like all his drawings, very neat and serviceable, but there were fundamental difficulties in its execution.

		R.T.	G.D.	Reproduction
37. Salt	race	14	22	

Unexplained.

38. New	clothes	12	25	—

He thinks much of his appearance. He would like to produce the impression of a person of distinction.

39. Customs	country customs	10	15	
40. Ride	horse-ride	10	38	

He had served in the artillery. That the memory is emotionally toned is seen by the reactions 48, *smell — horse-dung*, and 72, *beat — beat horses*. He then had charge of a " kicker " in the stable, and the smell of the manure disturbed his sleep when he was on stable duty. The distinct recollection, in the association test, of his military service, although it was twenty-one years ago, was due to the fact that he did not become an officer. After going through the officers' school he did no more service because he went abroad, where, nevertheless, he gave himself out as a Swiss officer. We had brought that home to him here and it annoyed him.

41. Wall	vertical	11	43	
42. Stupid	hoggishly stupid	—	110	

" It is hoggishly stupid the kind of talk sometimes in the section." A very strong expression indicating strong feeling. As he laughed during the reaction the deviation became peculiarly strong (see R. 55).

43. Copy-book	exercise-book	—	40	

He has a great number of exercise-books in which he made notes of everything he read. The books were clasified into divisions : Philosophy, Art, Crafts, etc. He is very proud of all this.

44. Despise	despise men	12	90	

" Men have a tendency to despise one another." He has often had to suffer from having been in prison. Once he was expelled from a church society when his past became known. When he speaks about this he is seized by strong affect.

45. Tooth	ache	8	53	

At the reaction it came over him that he " got no tooth-powder here " ; again the complex of his present position, which receives its increase of affect from a number of sources. The short time is explained by the speech-motor form of the reaction. In such verbal reactions the speech mechanism, as previously remarked, reacts almost automatically without becoming influenced by the " emotive inhibition."

46. Correct	logical	25	50	

(Did not understand.)

47. People	Swiss people	11	10	
48. Smell	horse-dung	17	22	
49. Book	good book	10	20	
50. Unjust	punishment	12	35	

One cannot say exactly to what extent he himself believes in his innocence : certainly to a very large extent. He overwhelmed the judges and the governor of the prison, the Public Prosecutor and the Chief Superintendent of the Asylum, with endless communications in which he tried to prove his innocence.

		R.T.	G.D.
51. Frog	tree-frog	7	25

Since a strong complex was aroused at reaction 50 we must regard perseveration as acting here. Reaction 51 was a purely verbal reaction without any particular emotion. There can be, therefore, no strong conflict for the possession of attention here. Hence time is very short. In this case we should expect the same of the deviation, but it is here rather above the probable mean. The reaction did, therefore, contain a perceptible measure of attention; in other words, there occurred a distinct splitting of the attention. This happened so easily in this case (R.T. = 7) because the subject endeavoured in Tests (a) and (b) to concentrate himself as far as possible upon the experiment itself, which interested him, in order to be ready for each new stimulus-word. The rapid rise of the curve (a) and (b) accords well with this great straining of his attention to the experiment, and the complete absence of pronounced complex waves (for these are conditioned by the attention being chained to the complex and its distraction from the experiment). In this test we can demonstrate a general experimental excitation.

52. To divorce	marriage, divorce	—	25

The divorce occurred under very unpleasant circumstances.

53. Hunger	heat hunger	7	30

Unexplained.

54. White	snow-white	11	30

The experimenter's collar was meant by this. The experimenter belongs, in a large measure, to the test complex. We saw in reaction 26 how the subject watched the experimenter. Here is a second proof. When reactions occur which refer to the appearance of the experimenter we can be sure that there is an inner bond between the subject and the experimenter. That is why such reactions are much more frequently found in persons of the other sex.

55. Ox	cattle	11	60

He recalled the manager of a factory where he was an apprentice, who often used this word to his workpeople. Reactions which are insults or the like are usually accompanied by a strong deviation. This is because whilst pronouncing the word the feeling usually comes up that the experimenter might regard it as referring to him; for in ordinary life such words are usually addressed to some one else, more rarely to oneself. Nevertheless the latter case does now and then play a part in the experiment. Thus with Subject No. 1 at the reaction *stupid — fool* " he thought that I might think he meant himself." Such delicate shades give us sign-posts for estimating the subject's character. In No. 1, together with the degree of self-consciousness there is a suggestion of " tendency to self-depreciation "; the two very often go together.[1]

---

[1] As a rule strong deviations also occur, as with insults, when the subject is made to hold his tongue out. As most people only do this in their childhood, it is inseparably connected with a strong emotional tone. If we put out the tongue in the presence of some one else and not for a doctor, that affect (anger, contradiction, mockery) is again aroused. But as there is nobody present except the experimenter, we quite unconsciously transfer that affect to the experimenter. It takes much to make it quite clear that this is only an experiment. The unconscious is stronger than our conscious reflections; it is only after frequent repeti-

		R.T.	G.D.	Reproduction
56. To take care	look out	13	50	

He thought of electric circuits. *Look out* is a warning which is in itself emotionally toned.

57. Pencil	sharpen	—	40	

The patient is a distinguished technical draughtsman, a fact upon which he plumes himself not a little.

Interruption by washing hands.

58. Cloudy	weather	11	10	
59. Plum	sweet	10	7	

The deviations are very small in consequence of the hand-washing. But the succeeding reaction showed that a strong centrifugal excitation is but slightly influenced by such physical conditions.

60. Meet	shoot	—	30	

Recalls the shooting competitions in which he used to take part in his good days. Besides that, he has occupied himself very much with artillery problems and claims to have invented a shrapnel bomb.

61. Law	people's law	—	23	
62. Love	have	10	35	

Completes it in analysis with " my children." He is much attached to his children. It is a thorn in his flesh that they live with his wife.

63. Glass	brittle	—	23	
64. Quarrel	parties	14	40	the parties quarrel

He was in constant warfare with his wife and her parents. Whenever he speaks about it he explodes with visible excitement (see also R. 75).

Test (c). *July* 25, 1906.—For easier survey I place the average figures of Tests (a) and (b) by the side of (c).

	I. P.M. of R.T.	II. A.M. of R.T.	Difference	III. P.M. of Dev.	A.M. of Dev.	Difference	P.M. of deviations which follow "too short" times
Test (a) .	11	13	2	30	38	8	35
Test (b) .	11	11·5	0·5	23	30	7	30
Test (c) .	14	14·9	0·9	5	9	4	3

Disturbances in reproduction : (a) 0 ; (b) 4 ; (c) 8.

This comparative table shows us (1) that the P.M. of the reaction-times in Test (c) amounts to 14, as against 11 in the other two tests ; (2) that against this the P.M. of the deviations is only 5—much lower than in Tests (a) and (b) ; (3) that in Test (c) the P.M. of those deviations which occur at too long times is shorter ; (3) that the P.M. of all the deviations together = 5, so that the average " too long " times are simultaneous with " too short " deviations ; (4) that the disturbances of

tions, when it has become purely automatic, that the process loses its affective components and therewith its effect upon the psychogalvanic phenomenon. (Cp. the remarks on repetition tests with deep inspiration.)

reproduction have considerably increased. The remarkable disproportion between reaction-times and the deviations in this test itself, and as against Tests (*a*) and (*b*), must be regarded (after what was found in Experiment I) as due to a strong perseveration. The increased errors in reproduction point also to the distraction of attention.

If we look at the curves we realize at once that Curve *c* has a very different character from Curves *a* and *b*. There is no steep ascent to a summit with big deviations, but, on the contrary, a steep descent with remarkably small deviations. The beginning of the curve recalls the down stroke of a complex wave, again the perseveration of a complex. The riddle is solved when we learn that a strong complex was aroused shortly before the beginning of the experiment. When his hands were just laid on the electrodes, but the galvanometer was not yet interpolated, I purposely declared to him that we had come to the opinion that he was just an ordinary swindler, that his discoveries were valueless because they could not be carried out. This declaration affected him greatly, for he saw the sudden destruction of his hope of winning us on his side, and thus his prospects here were as bad as previously in prison. We have learnt in Tests (*a*) and (*b*) his strong emotionalness ; we understand how he would be bound to react to this communication. Had he not possessed a considerable degree of good nature he might well have refused all further experiments. But he kept his hands quietly upon the electrodes and turned to the experiment, which after the intercalation of the galvanometer I began.

		R.T.	G.D.	Reproduction
65. Goat	animal	14	0	—

The time of the P.M. is maintained but the absence of deviation and of reproduction points to the aroused complex.

| 66. Big | men | — | —1 | (long reflection) |

The word *men* (a word of embarrassment for him) shows the "blankness of association" conditioned by the complex. The reaction could not prevent the fall of the wave for one moment, much less bring about any positive deviation. Only the subsequent rise of the wave shows some slight action. The — sign in front of the deviation shows that despite the reaction the curve sank 1 mm. This is not here a negative deviation conditioned by the reaction, but simply an absence of any effect of the new reaction upon the descending complex wave. This behaviour is only seen when there is strong perseveration, i.e. a complete blockade of the subject against new impressions in consequence of a previous complex action. In the calculation such negative values are reckoned as 0. In the curves the negative deviations are marked by a *.

| 67. Potato | field | 10 | 0 |

The superficial reaction and 0 for the deviation point to the perseveration.

		R.T.	G.D.	Reproduction
68. Paint	faint ? fate	—	3	

The disturbance of attention is shown by the non-understanding of the stimulus-word.

69. Portion	inheritance	13	2	
70. Old	men	—	— 2	(reflects)
71. Flower	red flowers	14	4	red

Constellated by the flowers which one of his fellow-patients had placed in front of the windows.

72. Hit	hit horses	16	2

See R. 40.

73. Box	clothes-box	—	5
74. Pick	good picture	10	8

Understood picture. In a short time there were two misunderstandings of the reaction-word, which never occurred in Tests (a) and (b).

This reaction was the first to claim any large measure of attention. The subject thought of Napoleon I, his hero, of whom he possessed several portraits.

75. Family	nice family	18	15

Means his wife's family. There was a strong complex. The sarcastic expression *nice family* points to a strong emotional content. Nevertheless perseveration acts very powerfully, for in comparison with the deviations (a) and (b) this is still very low.

76. Wash	face	14	— 2	(face-washing)
77. Cow	milch-cow	12	— 2	
78. Foreign	workman	25	2	(reflects)

Explains that he was here thinking of a strike near Zurich in which many of his friends participated, and to which the military were called out. The Public Prosecutor, as whose victim he regarded himself, commanded the regiment in question. He afterwards said that this was the cause of the military handling the strikers so badly ; grounds enough to produce a vivid emotional tone at the memory of the strike.

79. Fortune	domestic fortune 15		0

Said he was longing for this. See reactions 19 and 20.

80. Narrate	stories	13	2
81. Manners	asylum-manners	—	15

A curious composite word. He said he was thinking of the bad manners of the patients in his section. Despite perseveration, a perceptible deviation. We saw that nearly all the reactions which recall his life in the asylum are accompanied by strong deviations.

82. Narrow	pass	35	2	room

He said that he here thought his sentence would be due to narrow-mindedness if it were such as my remarks seemed to indicate. We notice that the conversation has undoubtedly an after-effect during the test. It is remarkable how low the deviation is (see R. 66).

83. Brother	younger	15	3

Thinks of his brother who died young.

		R.T.	G.D.	Reproduction
84. Damage	damage by hail	15	5	

Unexplained.

| 85. Stork | children | 25 | 28 | |

It came to him that his little daughter liked to tell "stories about storks." We noticed in reaction 62 that the reminiscences of his children are strongly emotionally toned. Reaction 88 points to the same.

From here to reaction 89 there is an "island" where the curve takes on the character of (a) and (b). As strong complexes were aroused it is understandable that the influence of that perseverating affect is momentarily interrupted.[1]

| 86. False | mankind | 10 | 12 | |

It would not be going far astray to suppose that the experimeter himself is intended by this reaction.

| 87. Dread | never | 25 | 60 | |

The reaction-word arises from the subject's personal disposition. From the foregoing there must be many emotional-toned associations linked to *dread*.

| 88. Kiss | children | 15 | 30 | |

Although he is fairly amorously disposed, I do not think that children is here only a "cover association." He was always a loving, anxious father towards his children. Nevertheless amorous ideas may play a part.

| 89. Fire | -like | 10 | 30 | |

Unexplained.

90. Dirty	street	7	− 2	
91. Doors	great	10	7	
92. Vote	people	13	3	
93. Hay	parched	15	3	
94. Quiet	room	10	5	
95. Sarcasm	men	20	17	

He is extremely susceptible to sarcasm, as he is to disesteem (see R. 44, where men is also associated).

| 96. Sleep | go | 15 | 3 | room |
| 97. Month | ten | 10 | 16 | |

Says he has now done ten months of his punishment. The short reaction-time betrays how intense is his occupation with the question of finishing his time. Otherwise the reaction *ten* could not so promptly follow *month*. The deviation corresponds to the strength of the complex, which even conquers the perseveration (see the subsequent rise of the curve).

| 98. Coloured | nature | 15 | 18 | |

After the foregoing reaction has broken the ban of the perseveration it can more easily succeed with a marked deviation. He was not able to give any explanation in answer to simple questioning.

| 99. Dog | yard dog | 10 | 5 | |
| 100. Speak | little | 7 | 5 | |

---

[1] This "island" shows clearly that it is no physical cause that is responsible for the peculiar course of Curve c. We see that as soon as the psychological constellation approximates to the Tests (a) and (b) the character of the curve becomes the same.

SUMMARY OF EXPERIMENT II (a), (b), AND (c)

Curves *a* and *b* rise very rapidly ; the deviations are very strong. There are no obvious complex waves. He gives great attention to both tests.

Curve *c* exhibits the up stroke of a complex curve ; the deviations are very slight, they are entirely absent at places. The complex was aroused before beginning the experiment, hence the absence of the long deviation that precedes the up stroke.

Test (c) shows clearly the effect of inner distraction from an affect upon the psychological phenomenon and confirms what was said about perseveration in Test I.

In other words :

A strong affect, independent of the experiment, conditions the decline of the association curve and the diminution or absence of the deviations. It is only in those places where stimulus-words interrupted the action of the affect and a new condition of affect was created that the deviations become greater again and the curve rises (curve section 85–89). The affect perseverates so strongly during the test that the P.M. of the reaction-times is increased from 11 (Tests (a) and (b)) to 14, and the P.M. of the deviations is lowered from 30 (Test (a)), 23 (Test (b)), to 5. With " too long " times we get " too short " deviations, whilst in Tests (a) and (b) the prolonged times are, on the average, accompanied by longer deviations.

EXPERIMENT III

The subject is a young married doctor who has carried out association tests with others very often but has never had one carried out on himself. This in itself shows a certain disinclination towards the psychological investigation of himself. He is also reserved in ordinary conversation. This reserve is a defence measure against his extreme sensibility, but it is not so much inherited as acquired from various events which have acted upon him as boy and youth, and which even to-day are still to some extent active. Since the affect bound up with it cannot be yet " abreacted," the complex in question produces much dissociation. It has taken him very far. The consequences of these disinclinations, partly conscious, partly unconscious, directed against those events are making themselves felt in the whole of his being. The bright, careless boy early became a very serious man who has developed, as compensation, a most unusual zeal for duty, and anxiety about his work.

The arrangement of the experiment was the same as in Test I (one cell, brass electrodes).

The average values are as follows :

P.M. of R.T.	A.M. of R.T.	P.M. of deviation	A.M. of deviation	P.M. of deviations with "too long" times	Disturbances in reproduction
8	8·7	0	4	0	33·3 per cent.

The P.M. of the reaction-times is very short, and the difference from A.M. slight. This shows us that he reacted very nimbly. These two values tell us nothing about emotional inhibitions. The value 0 for the P.M. of the deviations is striking. In no " normal test " with any kind of arrangement of the test have I found 0 as P.M. We must look to some complication. The A.M. of the deviations (4) tells us that there must have been deviations. From the P.M. of these deviations which arise at " too long " times (0) we learn that the prolongation of the reaction-time is accompanied by no average prolongation of the deviations. 33·3 per cent. of disturbances in reproduction is a high figure for an educated man. We must conclude that either very strong complexes were aroused in the experiment or that from some other ground there was present a disturbance of attention. The behaviour of the reaction-time and the deviations favour the latter.

If we look at the curve we shall be struck by the similarity to Curve II c. The curve falls instead of rising as in the normal association curve. But whilst in Curve II c the steepest ascent and the slightest deviations are found at the beginning, in Curve III we have at first moderate deviations, and it is only later that the curve falls and the deviations are absent. We may, therefore, conclude that the disturbance of attention only made itself felt little by little.

The behaviour of the average values and of the curve is explained by the subject's psychological constellation. He afterwards told me that he began the experiment with a certain distrust as to the worth of the galvanometric method of investigation. He thought that the deviations were caused by a certain auto-suggestion, and wanted to find out whether deflections would occur if one did not wish them. Secondly, he felt sure that he, the subject, could control the association experiment and that he would be able to conceal his complexes. He therefore purposely reacted as quickly as possible and took care that no prolongation of time should occur. He succeeded herein to a considerable extent. But the complexes only came out the more clearly in the reaction-words.

He would have been very pleased, as he afterwards admitted, if the deviations as complex signs had left me in the lurch ; this was to a certain extent out of envy that I had time to give myself up to the galvanometric investigations, whilst he himself, overwhelmed with practical work, had no leisure for scientific activities. (The experiment will show how strong was the complex of this hindrance to scientific work.) Then the test took place after dinner, when he was somewhat sleepy. We have, therefore, two motives for a conscious and active barrier to attention, and the fatigue is a further reason towards making concentration of attention difficult.

But by far the most important condition for the successful barring of his attention seems to me the unconscious complexes of which we have spoken ; he afterwards said he could not and did not wish to inform me about one of his main complexes. The inhibition arising from that complex seems to me to have been chiefly responsible for the absence of the deviations. It is as if in this case the stimulus-words were, in consequence of this barrier, generally not apprehended in their full significance, and hence could not evoke any development of affect. The short reaction-times speak also for this view. The reason why I ascribe little value to his conscious barrier is due to the fact that in a second test, upon which he had concentrated his good-will, the curve showed exactly the same course. On this second occasion he was also slightly tired. But fatigue does not of itself suffice to lower the curve, as was shown by a test on a female nurse, taken the day after night duty. That the barrier did not succeed at the beginning is plain from the first part of the curve. According to his own account the test did at first somewhat excite him (easily to be understood). But from about reaction 26 he felt " his complexes were now set aside," and he felt safe after that.

The curve sinks distinctly after reaction 26, although we notice before this a tendency to fall. Whilst in Experiment I the rise sets in before the subject had the feeling of excitation, here the ease of mind was shown by the curve, before the subject himself perceived it. Whilst in Test I the ego complex lost more and more its mastery over the other complexes, here the ego complex grew ever stronger. If we calculate the average values of the section of the curve 1–26 we recognize how much more strongly the attention is claimed, as contrasted with the succeeding section of the test.

P.M. of R.T.	A.M. of R.T.	P.M. of deviations	A.M. of deviations	P.M. of deviations with "too long" time	Disturbances in repro-duction
7	8·1	5	8	11	23 per cent.

That the P.M. of the reaction-times is shorter than in the test as a whole shows that the subject's intention to react as quickly as possible succeeded better at first than later. That there was much more affect at the beginning of the experiment is shown by —(1) the great differences between P.M. and A.M. of the times ; (2) the increased values for the deviations (note the P.M. of the deflections which are simultaneous with too long times) ; (3) the decrease of disturbances in reproduction.

		R.T.	G.D.	Reproduction
1. Head	beautiful	9	16	

Believed I thought that he was thinking about his wife. Naturally this is an immediate association to his wife, at least unconsciously; the thoughts are only subsequently clad in this form. It vividly recalls to me a case of dementia præcox where the patient explained in katamnesis that whenever he was in the presence of ladies he always thought that the lady would think he was in love with her.

2. Green	fields	7	10	
3. Water	blue	6	15	

Unexplained.

4. Prick	deep	7	12	

Here thinks that this reaction is apt to arouse sexual associations in other subjects.

5. Angel	angel ? high	14	18	

At first misunderstood *angle*. The cause of the misunderstanding is the perseveration (cp. reaction 4, *deep*, reaction 5, *high*, and the analysis). Why *angel* was understood is unexplained. The reaction *high* he analysed himself, "He did not want to prick the angel deep." The repetition of the stimulus-word, the reaction-time, and the deviation are objective evidence of the complex, not the least being the reaction-word itself. The symbolism is obvious.

6. Long	deep	8	11	big

He knows that the stimulus-word *long* often arouses sexual complexes. He therefore reacts with what, as we shall see, is his "complex representative"—*deep*. The wrongly reproduced *big* is only a replacement for *long*. That a personal sexual complex was here aroused and that the disturbance was not merely conditioned by his experiences with other subjects seems fairly plain. Reactions 4, 5, and 6 are closely connected.

7. Ship	sail	8	8	big

The incorrect reproduction and the deviation (the P.M. of the first twenty-five reactions is 5) again point to a complex. *Big* is suspicious; the matter only got cleared up when in the test carried out four weeks later he reacted *ship — mast*. He then also had an incorrect reproduction—*water*. I have often received elucidation, in later tests, of apparently innocent reactions of earlier tests which showed distinct complex signs. If we remember that months later an extraordinary percentage of reactions will be exactly the same as in the first test, we shall understand how firmly, as a rule, the associations are held. It does not therefore seem overbold to draw conclusions from a test made four months later, even though I assume that the complex in the meantime has not changed.[1]

8. Plough	field	6	1	

This reaction has an emotional tone for only a few people; we can see how dependent the psychogalvanic reflex is upon the emotional tone of ideas.

9. Wool	cotton-wool	7	13	

The reaction reminded him that some of his subjects had understood the word as *well*, and that in a sexual sense.

---

[1] Cp. "The Experiments in Reproduction," by Peterson and Jung, *Brain*, 1907, p. 187.

		R.T.	G.D.	Reproduction
10. Friendly	beloved	8	13	

He said that *beloved* was always, in the experiment, a word that stood for his wife.

11. Table	chair	6	5	
12. Ask	answer	6	5	

He moved his hands between reactions 12 and 13. But I cannot therefore say the strong fall of the curve was the result of the movement ; the strong deviation, however, may have been. For as a rule one finds a rise of the curve after movements, probably because the hands then generally press more strongly upon the electrodes. It was the contrary here ; his hands were removed from the electrodes. This might be due to a decrease of interest, and, inversely, a stronger pressure of his hands might be ascribed to the occurrence of a stronger complex which evoked motor innervations.

13. State	land	9	2	people

The stimulus-word was misunderstood. He possesses a strong social complex ; has a pronounced social vein but regrets that he has too little time and knowledge to busy himself with politics or economics. *State*, moreover, reminds him of state service and the personal want of liberty it occasions.

14. Haughty	friendly	7	3	
15. Stalk	high	11	17	long

(See R. 6.)

16. Dance	much	11	10	

Thinks of his wife.

17. Lake	blue	6	0	
18. Ill	healthy	9	4	
19. Proud	polite	11	2	

The reaction is constellated by an incident when he was reproached with being too proud.

20. Cook	much	9	0	
21. Housekeeping	wife	7	4	

The thought about his wife's housekeeping is strongly emotionally toned. The reaction influences the next one.

22. Wicked	good	6	12	

Explains he referred to his wife and the housekeeping. The strong deviation is not to be interpreted by the emotional tone of reaction 21 first making itself felt at reaction 22 ; it was only at reaction 22 that the complex aroused distinct feeling.

23. Needle	scissors	7	0	
24. Swim	deep	6	1	

The association omitted is *water*; hence the complex representative *deep*. Cp. reaction 3, when the deviation was so strong at the association *water*. The complex did not become distinct there either.

25. Furlough	long	14	16	

Furlough is for this subject, as for No. 1, a strong complex with a wealth of emotionally toned associations.

		R.T.	G.D.	Reproduction
26. Blue	green	7	3	water

The disturbance in reproduction is obviously conditioned by perseveration. As reaction 3 was *water — blue* too much stress must not be laid upon this.

| 27. Dead | life | 9 | 0 | — |

From here on the first series of absent deviations began.

| 28. Threaten | much | 8 | 0 | — |

It was after about reaction 26 (as we said) that he had the feeling "the sexual complex was now out" and he felt at peace. Note that at this place we get three disturbances in reproduction following one another. It is the expression of an inner distraction at this place.

29. Lamp	wick	6	0	
30. Rich	poor	6	0	
31. Earn	money	7	0	rich

To earn money plays a share in the subject's psyche, although there is no deviation. One had the impression that he was thinking, "Now it's all the same to me; I need not get excited; the worst is over." Only the disturbances in reproduction point to a complex.

| 32. To care | much | 9 | 0 | beautiful |
| 33. Pity | good | 11 | 0 | |

He remarked during the analysis: "I ought to have an occupation complex here, seeing that I'm a doctor."

34. Yellow	blue	9	0	
35. Mountain	valley	8	0	
36. Play	children	8	0	
37. Eager	much	16	0	work
38. New	old	6	3	

At reaction 37 his occupation complex was aroused and he felt distinct excitation (he feels himself hindered in his scientific activity by his profession of doctor). The strikingly long reaction-time accords with this. But there is no deviation. This only occurs at the next reaction—one quite indifferent and with a very short time.

It is not unusual to observe such delayed effects upon the galvanometer; a real delay in the action of affect upon the galvanometer can only be accepted with caution (cp. reactions 21 and 22). One does not know whether the affect was not clearly perceived at the particular reaction. or whether it was not a new complex that produced the apparently delayed deviation. Self-observation left the subject this time in the lurch.

| 39. Customs | old | 9 | 0 | manners |

Old perseveration from reaction 38; a hint that there is a certain emotional tone at *old*—which seems to me very probable for reasons which cannot be gone into (reference to the subject's most important complexes). In the reproduction, when the perseveration is removed the very usual reaction-word *manner* was given—a good example of one of the conditions leading to disturbances in reproduction.

| 40. Ride | well | 9 | 9 | |

During his military service he would like to have learnt to ride well, but an illness prevented his riding. He admits that this worried him afterwards.

We see that everything that hinders him in his ambition provokes vivid emotional expressions.

		R.T.	G.D.	Reproduction
41. Wall	room	11	0	
42. Stupid	clever	7	0	
43. Copy-book	book	8	0	
44. Despise		14	0	deep

The reaction reminds him of one of the events of his youth which have so permanently affected him.

45. Tooth	mouth	14	0

Thinks of his dentist's account and a " tooth extraction " dream of his wife. Both are emotionally toned.

46. Right	false	7	0
47. People	State	9	9

The social complex of reaction 13 again. One of the components of it is that the State makes such demands upon him that he has little time to devote to his wife. Therefore the wife and social complexes are often mixed. This is seen by comparing this with Test II.

	1st Test	Reproduction	2nd Test	Reproduction
47. People	State	+	love	state
50. Unjust	just	+	state	love
92. Vote	love	yes	town council	+

		R.T.	G.D.	Reproduction
48. Smell	bad odour	7	1	
49. Book	exercise-book	8	0	
50. Unjust	just	7	20	—

See R. 47.

51. Child	mother	12	0

At this reaction he thinks of his wife. The reaction ought not, in his view, to be very emotionally toned, for he " split off " the complex it contained.

I omit for the sake of brevity some reactions which proved nothing.

61. Law	State	7	0

Despite the complex, no further disturbance.

62. Love	faithful	9	11
63. glass		29	6	drink

Glass reminds him of *drink* (afterwards reproduced) and of the teetotal movement, of which he is a fervid partisan. The strong emotional tone rests upon the fact that this propaganda takes away very much of his time from scientific work.

64. Fight	to like	11	1	quarrel
65. Worm	soup	7	3	

constellated by a term used among his colleagues. The section of the curve 62–68 presents a distinct complex wave. The fall of the curve is again interrupted by the different complexes in reactions 62–65 and he is shaken out of his calm.

			R.T.	G.D.	Reproduction
Down stroke	66. Big	little	6	0	
of the com-	67. Potato	earth-apple	6	0	
plex wave	68. Paint	picture	7	0	much

At reaction 68 he thought of his wife, which at once produced a disturbance in reproduction.

69. Parts	sex	9	5	
70. Old	young	6	0	
71. Flower	through the	11	0	—
	flowers			

Constellated by a comical use of the word *flower*.

72. Pit	deep	7	0	
73. Box	high	8	0	wall

Pit reminds him of *prick*, hence the reaction-word *deep*, and this perseverates, as in reaction 4, in the subsequent reaction (cp. reaction 5, *high = not deep*).
The perseveration is probably the cause of the disturbance in reproduction.

74. Wild	very	9	0	

Refers to a patient.

75. Family	child	7	0	

As in reaction 51, we note that the content of this reaction plays no great part with him.

80. Narrate	report	10	0	much

That he is thinking about his wife is betrayed by the incorrect reproduction (see reactions 16, 68, 88, 101, etc.). " He ought to tell his wife a lot about his work."

81. Manners	customs	7	2	

Here movement of his hands and rise of the curve. The movement seems to have been due to a complex that cannot be gone into.

82. Narrow	broad	7	1	
83. Brother	sister	6	0	
84. Injure	unfaithful	7	0	
85. Stork	child	7	0	

See reactions 51 and 75.

86. False	good	8	0	faithful

In the second experiment *women* was the association here

87. Fear	yes	11	0	
88. Kiss	much	12	2	

Cp. reaction 80.

89. Fire	fire-brigade	9	0	
90. Dirty	clean	8	0	
91. Door	gate	8	0	—

He was aware of the symbolism, as he was in reaction 82.

92. Vote	love	12	0	yes

See reaction 47.

		R.T.	G.D.	Reproduction
93. Marriage	faithful	11	0	

From about now on he closed his eyes, whilst before he had been drowsily looking about him.

94. Still	soft	7	0	good
95. Mockery	yes	9	0	

Social constellation—recalls an event of his youth.

96. Sleep	together	9	104	

The enormous deviations occurred because the complex was brought out quite unconcealed. He had reacted " as if asleep " ; the reaction was driven out before he knew it and could stop it. He could not help laughing to himself, and his hands trembled so that the deviation became stronger. The most important thing about this reaction is that the curve now remains at the summit—i.e. the excitation is maintained. This proves clearly that the curve is by no means bound to sink (say from physical causes) after every long deviation, but that its behaviour is conditioned by the momentary psychological constellation of the subject. In this case there was a sudden transition from the somnolent to the waking state. The stimulus is so strong that it not only aroused him but evoked an excitation with numerous innervations. So no fall of the complex wave occurred (if the experiment had not been soon after broken off we should, of course, have had a fall).

97. Month	year	12	1	
98. Coloured	green	9	0	blue
99. Dog	hog	9	6	

Unexplained.

100. To talk	much	8	0	entertain
101. Night	much	17	27	—

This complex sensitiveness is well seen here.[1]

102. Sew	grass	9	8	field

Misunderstood stimulus-word. Unexplained.

103. Wine	glass	12	8	

See reaction 63.

104. Beautiful	good	8	0	
105. Watch	-works	8	5	

Unexplained.

The strong deviations that appeared in reactions 99–105 show the action of reaction 96 upon the subject's consciousness. The barrier and the drowsiness were overcome, a state of increased irritability arose.

SUMMARY OF EXPERIMENT III

The experiment shows the influence of the distraction of attention, partly purposely determined, partly determined by the subject's psychological constellation.

He was in a state of " active opposition " to the analysis.

[1] By complex sensitiveness Jung understands " the readiness to react to similar but much weaker stimuli with approximately the same force " after a complex idea has once been aroused. (*Psychology of Dementia Præcox*, p. 40.)

This active opposition causes the "association curve" to fall. A certain time (to R. 26) elapses before this opposition succeeds in making itself felt. Up till then the curve sinks but little. This opposition is responsible for the frequent absence of the deviation, an absence which begins after reaction 26.

In contradistinction to Test II c, the reaction-times are very short; the P.M. of the reaction-times for the whole test is 8, for those of reactions 1–26 it is only 7. This shortness of the reaction-times again shows the influence of activity, of an endeavour to react as quickly as possible so as to avoid tell-tale reaction-times. Active opposition works, therefore, contrary to passive distraction of attention (by a perseverating complex) by shortening the deviations as well as the reaction-times.

The reason for this difference as against Test II c can easily be recognized, in that the whole attention was directed towards one end—to react quickly. The "emotive inhibition" comes into conflict with another much stronger intention working in the opposite direction.

This endeavour to react as quickly as possible, to abolish as far as possible the psychological results of the experiment, causes the stimulus-words in many cases to be apprehended quite superficially; the complexes are not touched, so that no development of the affect arises. The deviations are consequently omitted.

EXPERIMENT IV

After I had recognized the effect of distraction of the attention upon the galvanometer curve in two different ways, viz. by the perseveration of a complex (Test II c) and by active opposition (Test III), I tried to attain by a third experimental method the distraction of attention. I used Jung and Riklin's method of outer distraction (see chapter ii). In order to observe at the same time the behaviour of the psychogalvanic curve, I placed the electrodes on the (naked) soles of the feet so that the subject had his feet resting on the electrodes instead of on the ground. I had previously convinced myself by repeated experiments that this method gave the same results as when the electrodes were placed on the hands. The deviations are even stronger because the area of contact is larger and the contact is closer. In the "normal experiment" the curve rises more quickly than when the electrodes are placed on the hands.

In order to bring out clearly the difference between the normal association curve and the "distraction curve" I will describe a distraction test on the subject of Test I. As he was a highly educated man the *tempo* of the metronome beats had to be as rapid as possible in order to reach any dissociation of attention at all. The metronome was placed at 94, i.e. 94 straight beats, each exactly 1 cm. long (the lengths being assigned by horizontal lines), were executed per minute. The stimulus-words only began to be called out when everything was in order. A comparison of Curve 4 with Curve 1 shows the extreme difference. Curve 1 rises rapidly at the beginning, as it did after the interruption (after R. 47). Curve 4 falls rapidly at the beginning, as it does after the interruption (R. 26). It recalls both the small size and the complete absence, at times, of the deviations at the beginnings of Curve 2 c and Curve 3; it shows in large what we found as the down stroke of a complex wave in the "normal" experiment. The curve begins very high (between 37 and 38 mm.), partly because the soles of the feet form a better circuit for the electric current. But there is also a psychological factor. For if under the same condition the experiment is at one time made with "distraction" and then for a time without "distraction," it is found that those parts of the curve where there was "distraction" begin higher than the other. The psychological factor is conditioned by a certain degree of excitement which is of different strength in different individuals, consequent upon the complicated demands which the distraction experiment imposes. Now compare the average values of the normal Test I and of the distraction Test IV, and remember that in Test IV the deviations are, as a rule, greater and the rise of the curve is more rapid with the use of the soles of the feet. When we find that despite this the deviations are less than in hand contact, we get an estimate of the great influence of the psychical process of distraction upon the psychogalvanic phenomenon.

P.M. of R.T.	A.M. of R.T.	Difference	P.M. of deviations	A.M. of deviations	Difference	Disturbances of reproduction
Test I . 9	8·8	− 0·2	8	10	+ 2	10 %
Test II . 7	8·4	+ 1·4	0	2·5	+ 2·5	21 %

Both the P.M. and the A.M. of the reaction-times is less than in the normal test. This is another distinct difference as against inner distraction from the perseveration of a complex (II c). There the reaction-time was increased, on the average, against the normal test of the same person. We there regarded the prolongation of the time as due to an increased dissociation of attention, which was claimed by the complex, thus leaving only a residue for the reactions themselves. Remember that the quality of the associations was not remarkably superficial because the subject, despite the complex, endeavoured to react according to the sense of the words. In this test (IV) the abbreviation of time is due simply to the dissociation of attention being much more complete, for the patient's reactions are almost entirely verbal. By reason of his great verbal fluency he was able to give his whole attention to making the strokes and allowed the verbal mechanism to work almost automatically. The more autonomically the verbal mechanism worked the shorter became the reaction-times. The conditions are very similar to those in the last test (III). In that case the attention was almost wholly occupied by the endeavour to act quickly, here by making the strokes. The difference between the P.M. and the A.M. of the reaction-time in the test shows that there must have also occurred a series of "too long" times; that emotive disturbances must have crept into the purely verbal course of the reactions. The P.M. of the tests is 0, as in Test III; but the A.M. of these shows that deviations must have occurred. The frequent absence of deviation is explained on the same grounds as in Test III. The distraction of attention is proved also by the fact that disturbances in reproduction are almost twice as frequent in this test as in the normal test. In communicating the associations in this test I chiefly desire to show the extremely superficial type of the associations.

		R.T.	G.D.	Reproduction
1. Head	face	7	16	
2. Green	grass	7	2	
3. Water	water	6	11	
4. Prick	pain	7	14	knife
5. Angel	angle	7	6	
6. Long	gong	6	2	

The four first reaction-words contain the vowel a, and reactions 5 and 6 are entirely clang-associations.

| 7. Ship | ship | 6 | 8 | (reflects) |

The repetition of the stimulus-words at reactions 3 and 7 shows most distinctly how strongly the attention has been distracted.

| 8. Plough | f-fly | 14 | 25 | |

The long time was caused by the stuttering in pronouncing the reaction-word; the long deviation was certainly caused by the disturbance which occurred whenever he began marking a new line; this occasioned a movement of the whole of the upper part of the body and of the legs also. This disturbance is seen in reactions 8 and 16 and at regular intervals after reactions 34, 49, and 62.

On the first two occasions, when the subject was not quite accustomed to the experiment and was still a little excited, the disturbance was expressed by a stronger deviation than later, when it is only shown by a slight rise of the curve.

| 9. Wool | m-knit | 11 | 4 | |

He wanted to say *mull*. Notice the endeavour to react with clangs.

| 10. Friendly | hateful | 7 | 2 | |
| 11. Table | able | 6 | 0 | |

This is the first time there is no deviation. As in the normal experiment, the deviations are at first bigger than afterwards.

		R.T.	G.D.	Reproduction
12. Ask	answer	7	0	task ?
13. State	courage	11	4	Switzerland

At first thought of a "deed" where courage was required. *Courage* is an indirect association.

14. Haughty	friendly	16	0	violent

See reaction 32.

15. Stalk	baulk	6	4
16. Dance	to idle	9	24

The intermediate term was *waltz*.

17. Lake	sea	6	7
18. Ill	weak	6	0
19. Proud	loud	6	0
20. Locks	sock—rocks	9	2

He explained that the stimulus-word had at first evoked the visual picture of a sea grotto, and this again the word *rock*, which gave *rocks*. *Sock* was arrived at by amalgamation of the clang pictures *sea* and *rocks*. It seems more probable that *locks* just evoked the clang-picture *rocks*. Let us remember that in earlier reactions we had the reaction *lake — sea* with a strong deviation. We know from Test I that *sea* is very emotionally toned for this subject. We can understand why it is so suppressed.

21. Ink	to sink	6	0

He wanted to say *fish*. Cp. this reaction in Test I.

22. Wicked	sc—false	14	4

He intended to say *scoff*, which is a dialect expression (*höhn sein*) for *angry*.

23. Needle	pin-prick	11	0

Wanted to say *navel*.

24. Swim	fish	7	0
25. Journey	make	9	0
26. Blue	lake	9	0

Wanted to say *mew ;* a perseveration of the *m* in *make*.

The test had to be interrupted here because the strip of paper was finished. The curve at once rose again to 33·6 ; the electric resistance improved in the pause. With the beginning of distraction the curve at once fell ; the electric resistance rapidly increased.

27. Bread	h'm red	12	9

Wanted to say *cut*.

28. Threaten	hit	7	4
29. Lamp	shine	7	6
30. Rich	poor	6	0
31. Tree	stem	6	0
32. To sing	{ sting [1] { ding	7	9

---

[1] Again two reaction-words. That two words, even if they are often truncated words, are so frequently associated shows that the attention is withheld from the associations, that none has sufficient stress of attention to triumph over the rival associations.

We notice that certain sounds are much to the fore in this experiment. I knew that shortly before the experiment the patient had been informed that a former female patient, whose name begins with this sound, had slandered him. At the end of the experiment I made him rest in order to notice the curves at rest He went to sleep and had a dream in which this lady played the chief part. I thus discovered that his thoughts about her were unconsciously perseverating during the experiment. I am strongly inclined, and the subject agreed with me, to see in the prominence of these sounds a "symptomatic action."[1]

It is also possible that the complex signs in the reactions 14, 22, 28, and 64 refer to this unpleasant complex.

		R.T.	G.D.	Reproduction
33. Pity	the poor	6	0	poor

This reaction, like *friendly — hateful, ask — answer*, are stereotyped replies he gets in his experiments with others and therefore trips off his tongue like rhymes and clangs.

34. Yellow	poor	9	0

Poor, perseveration from reaction 33. See reaction 8.

35. Mountain	climb	7	0
36. Play	children	8	0
37. Salt	paint	9	0

Wanted to say *pot*.

38. New	old	6	12

We must not pay too much attention to the occurrence of too long deviations (unaccompanied by other complex signs) in this test, where movements play a disturbing part.

39. Customs	bad customs	8	1
40. Ride	horse	6	5
41. Wall	stall [2]	7	2

As in Test I, an English word (*wall*) occurred to him (reaction 3 in Test I). Test IV took place seven weeks after Test I. Then *star* was reacted. The word *stall* occurred in the analysis (*Star of Bethlehem*). Despite the distraction the complex can still be recognized.

42. Silly	billy	7	7
43. Copy-book	knife	9	0
44. Despise	esteem	7	0
45. Tooth	time	7	0
46. Right	wrong	7	4
47. People	full	6	0
48. Smell	cattle	9	0
49. Book	Huch	12	0

Thinks of Ricarda Huch.

50. Unjust	just	7	0
51. Frog	h'm—brooch	14	—

---

[1] Freud, *Psychopathology of Everyday Life.*

[2] *Stall* is also the German word and has the same meaning—it is not a rhyme in the original but a clang (*Wand — Stall*).—TRANSLATOR.

Brooch (a clang in the original *Frosch — Brosche*) may be constellated by his intention to give his wife a present.

		R.T.	G.D.	Reproduction
52. Divorce	avoid	7	0	
53. Hunger	thirst	6	0	
54. White	black	6	0	
55. Cattle	herd	6	0	
56. To take over	h'm, to observe	12	0	
57. Pencil	point	6	0	
58. Cloudy	h'm, water	9	0	
59. Plum	sweet	7	0	
60. Meet	greet	7	0	
61. Law	book	9	0	
62. Loving	dear	7	0	
63. Glass	clear	6	0	
64. Strife	str-uggle	12	0	strig striggle

See reaction 32.

65. Goat	h'm, animal	11	0	
66. Big	heavy	9	0	
67. Carrot	capital	9	0	

A very superficial clang-association; *capital* is of momentary importance, for he had just bought some bonds.

68. Panel	picture	7	0	
69. Part	have	7	0	inheritance

See reaction 67.   He has a share (part) in a manufactory.

70. Old	to be	7	0	
71. Bloom	lumen	11	0	

Becoming old and *lumen* both play a rôle.

72. Beat	watch	9	0	(reflects)

Constellated from the metronome beats.

73. Chest	cash	7	0	
74. Wild	mild	7	0	wild
75. Family	have	6	0	
76. Wash	water	6	0	
77. Cow (*Kuh*)	high (*hoch*)	9	0	

Understood as *book*.   Reaction 49 was *book — huch*.

At the end of the test the beam of light went again to 42, i.e. he passed in a few seconds the distance from 13·6–42.   I therefore made the subject rest quite quietly; whereupon he fell asleep and had the dream.   During this time (5 m.) the beam of light went down from 45 to 25, and after he awoke it again rose.   The sleep wave, therefore, behaved like a distraction wave.

Summary of Experiment IV

The test shows the action of "outer distraction" upon the galvanometer curve. The action is here like that of active opposition in Test III : fall of the curve, decrease or absence of the deviations, strikingly small reaction-times. In Test IV the P.M. of the reaction-times is 7, against 9 in the normal experiment on the same subject. Tests III and IV are the opposite of Test II (c) in respect to their short reaction-times. The difference in the behaviour of the reaction-times is to be explained by the fact that in the former tests the attention was actively directed to a definite process, whilst in Test II (c) it was passively fettered by the complex previously aroused. The dissociation of attention is therefore much more complete in Tests III and IV ; the reactions occur without arousing many associations—in Test III through active opposition, in Test IV by the purely verbal-motor attitude. In Test II (c), on the other hand, the subject endeavoured to direct his attention away from the complex towards the single reactions ; hence conflict and prolongation of times.

At the conclusion of the experiment the beam of light ascended very quickly (not shown), whilst usually it falls at the end of the normal test.

Whilst he was asleep (5 min.) the beam of light fell on the scale (about 17 mm.). The sleep-wave thus behaved in this case like waves in distraction, or as if the subject were at rest.

Conclusions derived from Experiments II–IV

In the selection of these three cases from my total cases I had three different aims in mind.

First, I wanted to show what real service the psychogalvanic phenomenon in association tests can render us in psychological investigation, for it enlarges our knowledge by an objective complex sign and gives us more direct information about the affective reactions than other complex signs.

Secondly, I wished to draw the attention of those unacquainted with the association tests to the results, however small they be, of their general experimental-psychological nature—of those, especially, who regard the phenomenon as "an arbitrary means of expression" in experimental psychology.

Thirdly, I selected these tests because one could study in them the physical expression of one and the same psychological process, the distraction of attention. The investigations into the influence of attention in the experiment, when compared

with other investigations, give us some indications as to the
essential meaning of the psychogalvanic phenomenon.

We must remember, in the first place, that in the tests as
carried out we have to do, chiefly or exclusively, with changes
of the electrical resistance of the skin—this, in its turn, causing
fluctuations in the intensity of the current ; the galvanometer
marks these fluctuations. We must accept this, at least until
more exact electro-physiological investigations have been made
on the subject.

The earlier French scientists to whom we have referred accept,
without more ado, these changes of electrical resistance in their
tests. We know nothing at all about changes of electro-motor
power in the experiments.   Therefore we are compelled to regard
the rise of the galvanometer curve (i.e. the increase in the strength
of the current) as expressing the decrease of the electrical resistance
of the skin, and the fall of this curve as expressing an increase of
its resistance.

Féré proved that there was a decrease of electric resistance
on the application of sensory stimuli.   E. Müller, Veraguth, Jung,
and myself have made the same observations.   With the exception
of Féré (who only used sensory stimuli), these workers find that
this resistance decreases also with the higher psychical stimuli.
(Veraguth only speaks of a decrease or increase of the strength
of the current measured directly by the galvanometer, without
saying what conditions it.)   On the other hand, the resistance
increases when at rest and, as we have seen, in sleep.   The
resistance also increases in quiet mental work, e.g. in adding up,
or in uninteresting reading (Veraguth).   We will place these
observations alongside those found in our experiments.

I. *Decrease of the Electrical Resistance to Conduction :*
(a) In sensory stimuli ;
(b) In higher mental stimuli ;
(c) In the course of an association test accompanied by
    attention, which is nothing more than a combination of
    (a) and (b).

II. *Increase of the Electric Resistance to Conduction :*
(a) At rest ;
(b) In sleep ;
(c) In quiet (not exciting) mental work ;
(d) When the attention is fettered by a complex (down stroke
    of the complex wave, Test II (c)).
(e) When the attention is distracted by voluntary opposition
    to the experiment (Test III).
(f) By outer distraction (Test IV).

As we have seen, it is sensory and psychical stimuli that produce the emotional tone which causes the psychogalvanic phenomenon. It is upon this that the usefulness of the phenomenon in association tests is based. The tests have shown us sufficiently the close connexion between the strength of the deviation and the emotional tone which the individual reactions arouse. The psychogalvanic phenomenon owes its origin to purely affective processes, i.e. those which we know are the only ones which act upon the functions of the body.[1] But this action consists of changes in innervation. What the kinds of innervation (secretory ?) in our experiment are we cannot say as yet with certainty ; we only know their specific effect, which is the lowering of the electric resistance of the skin. The deduction, therefore, is that whenever the resistance of the skin to conduction decreases we have an increase, and whenever the resistance increases we have a decrease of innervation.

How is this deduction borne out by the results of Test II ?

It is readily understood that the innervation should decrease at rest, when asleep, and with quiet mental work. For here we get no affective processes. But the explanation is more difficult in cases (d), (e) and (f), for here affective processes have a great share, and we have more or less strong affects. In (e) and (f) the attention is directed towards a certain aim—again an affective process. If, then, we get here a decrease of innervation it can be only the result of inhibition.

Consider, first, case (d).

This is the case Test II (c) with down stroke of the complex wave. May we here speak of an inhibition of innervation ? Certainly. For it is not a question of the galvanometric registration of just that movement when an affect is aroused (this movement is shown by the deviations which occur at the complex reactions) ; what we find is the subsequent manifestations of the affect in the falling of the complex wave and in Test II (c). It is an old and well-known fact that an affect does not only act as a barrier to the associations to which it belongs but is inhibitory to all others. Thus the stimulus-words following the complex reactions or the affect aroused become inhibited in their action upon the flow of ideas and upon the physical functions. This is the explanation of distraction upon a complex and its effect upon the galvanometer curve.

In cases (e) and (f) the distraction follows from the attention being diverted to a particular end. Why does not this tension of the attention, which must be an affective process, produce any innervation ? But this, again, is a wrong way of putting

[1] Bleuler, loc. cit., p. 14.

the problem, for here again we are concerned with the effects of an already existent concentration of the attention. At the moment when the attention is turned towards a definite point a deviation is obtained, as I have often been able to observe. But in Test II (c) such moments occurred before the experiment.

The effect of distraction of attention turned towards a definite process and away from the experiment is just the same as that of an existing affect. Bleuler says of attention : " It is a side of affectivity which does nothing but what we already know about it, for it paves the way for some associations and obstructs others. To these paths (and obstacles), naturally, not only do the intracentral and the centripetal connexions belong, but also a number of centrifugal connexions." Lehmann comes to the same conclusion : " Attention is a pathway to some single point whereby the energy streaming in at the particular point acts at the same time as an inhibition to other simultaneous processes in the central organ." [1]

To sum up :

Whenever the attention is distracted, either through an affect, or through voluntary opposition or through outer distraction, the stimulus-words provoke weakened physical expressions or none at all.

This result is closely related to the findings of Lehmann and of Zoneff and Meumann,[2] who likewise proved that there was a diminution or cessation of physical expression when the stimulus was applied in states of distracted attention. The observations or distraction of attention also lead us to the galvanometric investigations on the insane.

A. Vigouroux [3] found in melancholics an increased electric resistance to conduction which we can thus interpret : the melancholic is in a permanent state of distracted attention. His complexes occupy him permanently, like the affect which, purposely introduced, occupied Subject 2 temporarily.

There is in both cases a hindrance to centrifugal innervation and thus an increased resistance to conduction.

Jung and Ricksher [4] found in catatoniacs and organic dements an increased resistance to conduction and an absence of deviation to stimuli of various kinds. This must be due chiefly to primary disorders of perception rather than to inhibition from

[1] Lehmann, *Elemente der Psychodynamik: übersetzt von Bendixen*, 1905, p. 362.

[2] Zoneff and Meumann, "Ueber die Begleiterscheinungen psychischer Vorgänge in Atem und Puls," Wundt's *Phil. Studien*, 1901, Bd. XVIII, p. 1.

[3] A. Vigouroux, loc. cit.

[4] *Journal of Abnormal Psychology*, vol. ii, 1907–1908, p. 189.

" inner distraction." The observation made by R. Vigouroux [1] that in hysterics the electric resistance is increased on the hemianæsthetic side as compared with the sound side seems to me now understandable. If we regard the hysterical hemianæsthesia as occurring when this side is functionally split off from consciousness, then we see that the innervation flowing towards that side will be slighter. And we have hitherto always found that this decrease of innervation is accompanied by increased resistance.

In conclusion, I would like to point out the difference the " at rest " wave shows according to whether the current used is of lesser or greater strength. In the latter case we always find that the resistance of the skin decreases with the length of the current. Veraguth proved this contradiction in the rest curve with slight currents. The resistance then increases the longer the circuit lasts. The explanation of this contradiction must be that by the use of a considerable strength of current (I cannot give the limits) one is not dealing with a rest wave but always with a stimulus wave, i.e. that we here get physiological and finally psychological effects. We need but recall the stimulus action of the electrodes upon the skin with a strong galvanic current. [2] Moreover, purely physical conditions may have a share in this. A permanent complex (permanent affect, permanent concentration of attention upon something other than the experimental stimuli) hinders the psychical working up of the stimulus, which remains poor in association and feeling. The absence of new innervations, and therefore the disappearance of the deviations, is the result of the absence of new affects. The gradual sinking of the curve is explained by the gradual wearing off of the affect, whilst the intellectual attitude of inhibition created by the affect is maintained for a longer period.

PART III

Extension of the Points of View obtained in Part II to the Material as a Whole

Reaction-time and Galvanic Deviation

We shall review in this section the mutual behaviour of these two complex indicators in their connexion with one another, and shall refer to further conditions which lead to a disproportion of these two values. From the experiments we have learnt that, as a rule, a " too long " reaction-time corresponds with a " too long "

[1] R. Vigouroux, loc. cit.
[2] Cp. Erb, *Handbuch der Elektrotherapie*, 1882, p. 116.

deviation.   It has also been shown that, as a rule,[1] with a prolongation of the reaction-time there goes an affective process ; we shall
not be in error if, with Jung, we make this affective process
responsible for the prolongation of the time.   But we have given
sufficient instances of exceptions to the ratio between reaction-
time   and   deviation,   which   are   largely   due   to   the   influence
of a perseverating emotional tone.   We have seen that in
cases where an emotional tone was handed on from an earlier
reaction there was no question of any direct ratio between
these two factors in the following or next following reaction ;
that, on the contrary, when the perseverating complex is very
strong the ratio is inverse—the time is prolonged and the deviation
shortened.   I have sufficiently explained the reason for this.

We saw a second cause for this prolongation of the reaction-
time without a simultaneous increase of the deviation in the
occurrence of an " intellectual feeling " in Nahlowsky's sense ;
this is of no practical importance but is of theoretical interest.
It was due to a " feeling of uncertainty " when the stimulus-word
was not clearly understood.   It was shown that these cases are
extremely rare because the conditions for the occurrence of
purely " intellectual feelings " only arise exceptionally in the
association test.   To the example *tame — wild*, when *tooth* was
understood, I will add another that seems to me beyond
criticism :

Subject No. 16, *Physician :*		R.T.	G.D.
R. 14. Craft	boat	21	7
		(9)	(19) [2]

He hesitated whether I had said *craft* or *crafty* ; finally he
decided for the former.   It is easy to see that when two words
which clang emerge, neither of which has any particular emotional
tone for the patient, a certain time is spent till the subject decides
on one.   We might speak of a " selection-time " which is added
to the reaction-time in the strict sense.   This hesitation did not
here produce any affect, for the deviation is still below the probable
mean.   The indistinct apprehension of the stimulus-word is often
followed by its repetition or by a *what ?*   In such cases the
reaction-time is particularly long, because I only let go the watch-
spring of the hand when the real reaction-word is pronounced.
The size of the deviation in such cases depends upon whether an
intellectual feeling or an affective process is connected with the

---

[1] We shall find there are exceptions, to which we shall refer later.

[2] The figures in parentheses give the probable means of the two values for
the whole test.   The values only have a meaning when compared with these
probable means.

repetition of the stimulus-word. The latter is commonly the
case, but I have some distinct examples of the former.

Subject No. 13, Female Attendant :	R.T.	G.D.		
82. Bend	end ? beginning	12	1	
		(9)	(2)	

Subject No. 12, Female Student :

4. Prick	what ? pain	18	3
		(11)	(5)
6. Long	what ? many	26	3
15. Stalk	what ? flowers	27	5

The following case of disproportion between reaction-time and
deviation seems due to the difficulty of the word.

Subject No. 11, Uneducated Man :

Salt	mineral	18	2
		(9)	(2)

Delayed reaction-times are often seen at the word *salt*. At
present I can only find the cause in a certain difficulty in finding
appropriate associations (*pepper* and *bitter* are the commonest).
The subject had, like many uneducated persons, taken the
stimulus-word as a question—*What is salt ?* The correct answer
gave him intellectual difficulties without his getting " excited "
about it. The following delayed time seems partly due to special
intellectual effort. The reaction occurred in Test II (c) :

82. Narrow	pass	35	2
		(14)	(5)

We saw that the reaction took place under the influence of a
perseverating emotional tone ; but the excessive prolongation
of the time seems to require explanation. He wanted to say
narrow-hearted, which is extremely emotionally toned for him.
In order to suppress *narrow-hearted* and to find the harmless
narrow — pass required severe intellectual effort, made still more
difficult by the perseveration.

It was remarkable that despite this repression and affect the
deviation was so slight. I cannot avoid the impression that we
had here an inhibition of innervation by the intellectual effort
which made such demands upon the subject's attention.

Whilst we can show that, besides perseveration, intellectual
difficulties may lead to a prolongation of the time without prolongation of the deviation, those cases where the deviation, but
not the time, is prolonged are found chiefly when there are verbal
reasons. These are generally cases of complexes which pass
unnoticed in the reaction-time because the subject was able to

slip in a verbal association. We have seen that emotive inhibitions are manifested with difficulty in such associations. This may be due to the strong pathway between the associations which then rapidly follow each other, although other associations also become aroused. Very often, however, the reason is that the verbal association that slipped in was already formed before the complex became generally aroused and could make its whole inhibitory action felt. I have often observed this in myself. The deviation, which follows much more slowly, has time to come under the influence of the complex.

Other examples :

Subject No. 22, Male Attendant :		R.T.	G.D.
61. Law	opposed	8	24
		(10)	(14)
69. Part	have	8	20
75. Family	relations	8	25
82. Narrow	-hearted	8	17
83. Brother	love	8	17
84. Injure	joy	7	46
89. Fire	cause	6	25

Subject No. 12, Female Student :			
62. Love	have	11	9
		(11)	(5)

Subject No. 19, Doctor :			
79. Book	have	8	16
		(9)	(5)
88. Kiss	like	8	12

(He had heard this reaction in a great many subjects.)

Subject No. 2 :			
45. Tooth	-ache	8	53
		(14)	(5)

Subject No. 18, Attendant :			
68. Paint	painter	9	7
		(14)	(2)

CLANG-ASSOCIATIONS AND GALVANOMETER DEFLECTIONS

Action of " Unconscious " Complexes upon the Galvanic Deflection

Before leaving the individual analyses and proceeding to the purely statistical working out of our material I must again refer to the clang-associations, which will give an opportunity to study the action of " unconscious " [1] complexes upon the psychogalvanic phenomenon.

In the analysis of Test I we were able to prove that the clang-reactions which arose from distraction of attention due to a previous complex showed a " too small " deviation, whilst those which themselves awoke a complex had a " too long " one.

We also saw in the examples *kröte — spöte* (R. 51) and reactions 92 and 38 that beyond the " contact " connexion by the clang-association there was a deeper link between stimulus- and reaction-word. In all three reactions the clang-association was determined by a complex which the stimulus-word aroused ; in reaction 38, *repent — spent*, perseveration also took part, so that the deviation itself did not exceed the probable mean. The complex participating in the disturbance was indicated on the galvanometer by the subsequent rise of the curve. When a perseverating emotional tone had caused both the deviation and the clang-association no deeper connexion could be demonstrated (R. 32, *ring — swing ;* R. 37, *speck — neck ;* and R. 52, *divorce — force*). What we had been able to prove in Test I was also found in the clang-associations of the other tests. The grouping together of cases like *divorce — avoid* is very informative ; of fourteen subjects to whom the word *divorce* was called out five reacted with *avoid*.[2]

We will first give two cases where there was also perseveration, and then three where complexes were at work.

		R.T.	G.D.
Subject No. 1 :			
52. Avoid	divorce	9	8
		(9)	(8)
Subject No. 23, Doctor :			
52. Avoid	divorce	11	6
		(11)	(7)

In both these cases there was the perseveration of an emotional tone. In Subject No. 1 this came at the preceding reaction, which, as we saw, aroused a very strong complex. In Subject No. 23 perseveration is also observed. It is due to

50. Unjust	just	11	13
		(11)	(7)

---

[1] We shall see that these are not " unconscious " complexes in Freud's sense but only suppressed complexes ; that is, they were once in consciousness and can reappear there at any time (Freud's foreconscious). Freud understands by unconscious complexes in the strict sense complexes which have never become conscious to the person and which can only be brought into the conscious by psycho-analysis.

[2] In English *divorce — avoid* is a clang-association ; in the German it is a rhyme—*scheiden — meiden.*—TRANSLATOR.

Upon which follow:

		R.T.	G.D.
51. Frog	water	12	5
52. Divorce	avoid	11	6

The complex in reaction 50, perseverating in reactions 51 and 52, is objectively shown by the long deviation. The reaction-time is, as so often, only prolonged in the next reaction, 51. Subjectively the complex was fully confirmed, for the subject acknowledged that he had had to fight a great deal against injustice and possessed a strong *justice* complex. In the three other cases where there was a complex, the deviations were very prolonged, whilst the time was only prolonged in one case.

Subject No. 12, Female Student :

52. Divorce	avoid	19	12
		(11)	(5)

Both words show the complex. She explained at once that the reaction made her think of a much-loved girl friend who had lately married and left Zürich. This friend, or rather her marriage, plays a great rôle in the experiment.

Subject No. 4, Educated Woman :

52. Divorce	avoid	11	15
		(11)	(5)

One of the rare cases where the clang-association caused by a complex has, for no obvious reason, no time-prolongation. But the deviation, which is thrice the probable mean, is enough. The emotional tone is here on *avoid*.

Subject No. 19, the Writer :

52. Divorce	avoid	8	8
		(9)	(5)

The short reaction-time is explained by the reaction having slipped in from tests carried out on others. Still the complex comes out and is recognizable by the galvanometer. The emotional tone was on *avoid*.

I group these reactions together:

			R.T.	G.D.	
Subject No. 1.	Divorce	avoid	9	5	clang-association due to perseveration
			(9)	8	
22.	,,	,,	11	6	
			(12)	(7)	
12.	,,	,,	19	12	clang-association due to complex.
			(11)	(5)	
4.	,,	,,	11	15	
			(11)	(5)	
19.	,,	,,	8	8	
			(9)	(5)	

Twice I found the rhyme *to prick — brick*, but on both occasions neither complex nor perseveration could be discovered. But the stimulus-word *to prick* is the fourth one in our list, i.e. it comes quite early, when there is still some excitation about the experiment and the attitude towards the meaning of the stimulus-word is still laboured. It might be said that the distraction of attention is here due to the perseveration of a complex, the complex which refers to ideas about the test itself.

The following is another instance of the effect of perseveration upon clang associations.

The probable means are 17 and 10.

Subject No. 15, Female Student :		R.T.	G.D.
11. Young	old	24	28
		(17)	(10)
12. Ask	answer	23	29
13. State	Russia	12	7
14. Stubborn	-minded	14	10
15. Stalk	talk	13	5

Two strong complexes were aroused at reaction 11 which were and are still important to her. Reaction 12 brought up thoughts of her approaching examination for the doctorate—quite enough to provoke an affect. Reaction 13 shows nothing special. Reaction 14 is verbal-motor. The superficiality of this association points clearly to the distraction of attention shown again in the clang-association 15. It is in consequence of this that the deviation reduced the probable mean by a half.

In the clang-associations mentioned so far with " too long " a deviation, the complex became known to the subject during the reaction (see *divorce — avoid*). But I have a number of striking clang-associations showing distinct lengthening of the deviation where the subject was quite unable to assert that the reaction in question was connected with any emotional event, with any complex at all

As, apart from No. 1, I did not obtain many clang-associations in my tests, I have only a few examples to quote, but each one seems to me worth study. They again show what great importance the unconscious has in association activity. The importance of the unconscious in association activity is most clearly seen in Freud's works : *Interpretation of Dreams ; Psychopathology of Everyday Life ; Wit*, etc.[1]

We shall here venture on a proof of the influence of an unconscious or, as we prefer to say, of a repressed complex upon the development of affect, i.e. upon the physical innervations. Here

[1] See also Bleuler, chapter vi, Jung and Riklin, chapter ii, and Jung, chapter iv. In his *Psychology of Dementia Præcox* Jung says, after having spoken of the influence of the complex upon association : " It is of theoretical importance that the complex need not be conscious. By repression it can cause an inhibition of attention in the conscious ; in other words, it can suspend for a time the intellectual activity of consciousness (delayed reaction-time !), or suspend it totally (fault) or diminish its worth (clang-associations)." See also " The Theory of Association," by Münsterberg, *Beiträge zur experimentellen Psychologie*, Heft 4, p. 1 (Freiburg i. B., 1892), and Scripture's penetrating work " Ueber den assoziativen Verlauf der Vorstellungen " (Wundt's *Phil. Studien*, Bd. VII, p. 50). As to the justification for speaking about unconscious psychical processes and as to the part they play in mental life see Lippe, *Leitfaden der Psychologie* (Leipzig, 1903), p. 37 ; Ebbinghaus, *Grundzüge der Psychologie*, Bd. I (Leipzig, 1905), p. 54 ff. ; Höffding, *Psychologie in Umrissen auf Grundlage der Erfahrung*, p. 99 ff.

again Freud has laid down the theoretical principles. In *The Interpretation of Dreams* he says : " This (i.e. the development of the affect) is regarded as a motor activity or as one of secretion ; the key to its innervation is placed in the unconscious."

Before dealing more closely with our examples I should like to add some remarks about the method. It deviates in many respects from that hitherto customary in experimental psychology. In his *Principles of Physiological Psychology*, Wundt, when discussing the analysis of the emotions, says : " It must, moreover, be noticed in all cases that the vasomotor, like the respiratory symptoms, are in themselves only signs of alterations of innervation in the respiratory, cardiac, and circulatory nerve centres. They convey nothing of themselves either about the causes of these symptoms, which are grounded in the mechanism of the nerve centres or about the remoter physiological connexion of the innervations in question. The chief psychological value of these symptoms is rather that they are phenomena which are demonstrated objectively in so far as they regularly accompany emotional ideas ; and by their differences we are enabled to obtain indications of the corresponding psychical differences. But it should never be forgotten that these are only indications and never proofs. If subjective observation does not discover the presence of a definite emotion no amount of objective phenomena can establish it. Experience teaches us, nevertheless, that traces of feelings can escape subjective observation if there is not some special motive for the attention being directed to them."

What is here said of the vasomotor and respiratory symptoms must also refer to the galvanometric phenomena, about whose physiological foundation we have no absolutely certain knowledge. If we were to follow Wundt it would be an error to attempt to discover the relationship of unconscious complexes, which introspection cannot detect, to physical symptoms. But it must have occurred to readers that we have not posited, as the final authority for the connexion of galvanometric with psychical differences, any subjectively demonstrated emotion. In the association test, where the various emotions interchange so rapidly with one another, either increasing or hindering one another, subjective statements as to the nature or form of these feelings are quite unreliable. It is only gross differences of feeling, qualitative and quantitative, that are differentiated by introspection. Wundt agrees that traces of feeling can escape introspection. I believe that the galvanometer, although the shunt does considerably deaden the oscillations of the current, is a far finer reagent for quantitative differences of emotion. As subjective control we found, as we have sufficiently demonstrated, that a reaction which was accompanied by a too long deviation belonged to an emotionally toned complex. In the majority of cases the subject feels the constellation, is often quick to recognize it, although sometimes only after reflection. But when the subjective proof of this connexion is unobtainable we have another means of discovering it. It is the method of psycho-analysis which psychology owes to Freud. It is to be used whenever the information given by a subject about a reaction is unsatisfactory (see, e.g., the reaction 3, *wall — star*, in No. 1), and especially when repression influences the association so that its working is unknown to the subject. Taking the view that unconscious psychic processes can provoke physical changes of innervation, Lehmann's remark will not lead us astray : an outer stimulus must enter consciousness in order to produce organic reactions.[1] He makes Consciousness = Psyche. Naturally, from this point of view he is bound to conclude that if a definite external stimulus creates no definite state of consciousness the organic reactions must be also absent.[2] The contradiction between our view and Lehmann's statement is that Lehmann obviously recognizes only one mental process for the origin of organic reactions, whilst we also recognize unconscious mental processes.[3]

The first example is from a doctor (No. 16), who was kind enough to give me all the information possible. He himself succeeded in discovering the complex repressed during and for a few hours after the experiment.

		R.T.	G.D.
Worry	source	9	15
		(9)	(9)

The reaction-time is the same; the probable mean of the deviation is, however, much increased. He felt at once impelled to seek some deeper connexion between *worry* and *source* (a clang-reaction in German, *quälen — Quelle*). It occurred to him in analysis that he was recently in the town of B. with a female patient who was to be operated upon there. As this particular patient often comes into his associations at other places without giving rise to any increase of deviation, no significance could be attached to this idea. But, as will be seen, the

---

[1] Lehmann, *Die körperlichen Ausserungen psychischer Zustände*, translated by Bendixen, vol. i, p. 158. (Leipzig, 1899.)

[2] See vol. ii, p. 313 ff.

[3] In a certain sense the stimulus, here the stimulus-word, did reach the conscious in the cases now to be related. The subjects reacted to it with one word, afterwards remembering the stimulus-word, and so on. What did not reach consciousness was the relationship of the stimulus to a definite group of ideas. And even here we must put a further limit. A reference to some complex or other is often more or less conscious to the subjects as a " feeling of constraint," some uncertainty, " the reaction might refer to a complex," etc. But what is not conscious to them at all is the complex itself.

town of B. does point to the complex. At any rate, he did not know how he came to this association, and introspection failed to notice any distinct feeling during the reaction. There was no time for a thorough psycho-analysis. I was therefore greatly pleased when my colleague gave me the solution next day in writing. During the course of the evening it came back to him that *source* = *fons amoris* (*sempiterni fons amoris*) was formerly one of his " complex symbols." It was a question of a strong " bachelor complex " which, when he lived in the town of B., was the *source* of much *worry*. The words " sempiterni fons amoris " had become for both the symbol of friendship and service, being used as a formula in greeting. The matter becomes quite clear when we recall the whole strophe of Scheffel's student's song, of which this was the first line :

> Sempiterni fons amoris,
> Consolatrix tristium,
> Pia mater Salvatoris
> Ave virgo virginum.

That *fons amoris* has also a concrete meaning need be merely indicated. It is interesting that for years he had not thought of this episode in his life and that it was only again noticed in his dreams after he had married (about six months before the test). By his marriage the complex had at first increased the associations in the unconscious, thus allowing it to overcome the " censure," first in his dreams and then in the waking consciousness.

The next two examples are from myself.

		R.T.	G.D.
28. Threaten	drone	14	19
		(9)	(5)

The reaction-time and the deviation are markedly prolonged. I was not aware of any complex during the reaction, nor had I any particular feeling after I had uttered the reaction-word. I felt some surprise about it—it seemed to me so remote and I hardly felt that I myself had pronounced it. Nor could I link, at first, any further associations to it, and gave up trying to find any meaning to this reaction. It was only two months later, after returning from a fortnight's journey and looking over my associations again, that its meaning became clear (without my then seeking it) ; it occurred just as my eyes fell on the reaction *the drone*, that's me ! My colleagues had often twitted me with my infrequent appearance in the wards and my not relieving them of some of the work. For bit by bit I had limited myself entirely to the scientific work. A little of their banter had taken effect. Beyond the complete inner certainty that I felt as to the correctness of this interpretation there is in its favour that I only found it after a journey during which I had received many new impressions ; my psychological constellation had become different and so the inner resistances had become displaced. Furthermore, during the journey my real interest in the part I played in the asylum had receded (cp. Freud, *Psychopathology of Every-day Life*). On the first day of my return the complex had acquired an additional affect when I compared the strenuous work of my colleagues with my own life during the journey.

My complex had perceived the opportunity for the application of the stimulus-word to myself by a process of assimilation in the same way as in the other cases of misreading, misunderstanding, etc., which Freud has described in so masterly a way.

To *threaten* is an unpleasurably toned word and at the same time one rather difficult to respond to. There was thus sufficient cause for inhibitory factors.

The complex may have used this moment of hesitation. One of my subjects reacted by *to dry* to this reaction. In that case the time, but not the deviation, was increased ; no reason for the occurrence of the word *to dry* could be found (there must certainly have been one) ; but, on the other hand, *threaten* was energetically parried, for the patient was a female nurse threatened with a crisis in a love-affair which for many reasons caused much excitement.

It was likewise after that journey that I solved the following clang-association :

		R.T.	G.D.	Reproduction
73. Bös (angry)	öl (oil)	9	13	(reflects)
		(9)	(15)	

The series of associations was :

71. To cook	kitchen	7	3	
72. Ink	fish	9	3	write
73. Bös	öl	9	13	(reflects)
74. Needle	ear	9	4	prick
75. To swim	prick	9	10	

The many disturbances in reproduction, the meaningless clang-associations *bös* (angry) — *öl* (oil), the perseveration of the association *prick — to swim*, indicate a great disturbance of attention. This was partly conditioned by a certain degree of momentary fatigue at the time, but chiefly by several complexes. During this section of the experiment I was at the same time the observer who went through the associations almost automatically. It was at the reaction *to swim — prick*, which seemed to me absurd, that I had a distinct feeling of unpleasure. The deviation is here increased. The clang-association *bös — öl* is the centre of interest [1]; this followed as automatically as the others (the reaction-times nowhere exceed the mean). My interest in it only arose later, when my attention had been turned to the action of repressed complexes upon physical innervations. Despite many attempts I could get nothing out of it at first. It was only after my return, when I again took up the forgotten associations, that I distinctly felt that to find the solution I must *translate* something. But the resistance was still so great that the right thing did not occur to me. I was still hitting away in the dark and translating *oil, oleum, œil, oil* (an attempt to get away from the ö) ; then I placed *bös* and *öl* together and wrote in French orthography *beuseul, seul, beul* and similar words, most of them absurd. We shall presently see that the proceeding was correct, but that I went astray in the choice of what to translate. It is remarkable that in my attempts I did hit upon the word *Vesoul*, a station between Basle and Paris. But as there were other resistances to overcome, I was unable to make anything out of Paris. I gave it up, opining that there really was no solution here. Five days later I was drawn back to this association. A thought occurred to me which enabled me to penetrate into the unconscious and break up the chief resistance. At *bös*, which I had entirely neglected, putting all the weight on *öl*, which I had not tried to translate, the proper name, *Böss*, came up to me (it had taken me two months). At once an event which had taken place a year and a half before came up to me very clearly—how I had bought a trunk at Mr. Böss's, a leather merchant in X., and how at the last moment he had painted my monogram with a *black fluid* (see reaction *ink — fish* ; reproduction, *write*) in Latin characters on the brown trunk. At the same time I became aware that I had always connected a *yellow* colour with the sound ö. (The day after the purchase I went to Paris ;

---

[1] In uttering the word *öl* I had no image of it in consciousness but merely the clang-picture.

this only came up to me later). But it became already clear that *öl* meant simply *el* (L), which was by clang assimilated to *bös*. The complex was not cleared up. Trying to call up the monogram L.B. on the trunk, I had a feeling that the word *trunk* had to be translated. I did this step consciously, asking myself what was the French for trunk—*malle*. The solution became instantly clear to me and was also shown involuntarily by a sigh. The *m* in *malle* led to a monogram M. L. B. that I had often seen in Latin letters (like my own L. B.) on a trunk. It is the monogram of that lady who had in the first place suggested my buying the trunk, and who in the second place had intended travelling to Paris with me—an intention which, however, was not carried out. I had been very put out by this. Only in this roundabout way did it become clear who was meant by *angry* (*bös*). (It must be added that this complex is only the portion of a much bigger one which is still present.) *Bös* (angry) thus led to *angry — trunk — L. B. — malle*, and thus to *M. L. B.* There is also a more direct way from *bös* to *M. L. B.* by the translation into *mal*. But here the Latin seems to take part, as indicated by my first association to *öl — oleum. Mala* would be the exact Latin equivalent for *bös* (angry) in this case ; the French *mal* is only a hint. *Mal* also allowed me to understand when I wrote down the analysis why to the following stimulus-word *needle — ear* was reacted. In the reproduction I thought I had said *prick*. It seems highly probable that *malheur* had determined *ear* (*öhr*) both by its clang and its meaning ; it was also now clear why at the beginning I felt compelled to connect the words *bös* and *öl* and write them in French. It was just as if some one had said to me, " Translate into French, combine them, and write down a German clang in French letters—that will give you the answer." We see that the unconscious prescribes the way that psycho-analysis must follow. We know now that a translation had to be made : *bös* into *mal*, written in French ; *öhr* (*heur*) : *mal* and *heur* combined into *malheur*. The word *malheur* was the summit of the analysis.

At *bös* the clang-picture *ör* had become aroused together with the clang-picture *öl* (for from *bös* to *mal* and from *mal* to *malheur* is but a short step). This must, however, have been the stronger for it provoked the corresponding innervation of the speech musculature, whilst *ör* remained unsaid and unconscious. It was only when the word *needle* followed that the clang-picture *ör*, which lay ready waiting, received a stronger impulse and repressed the reaction-word *prick*, which was for me a more labile one. This again appears in the following reaction. Only the chief stages of the analysis can be given here, whilst the psychical impulses of the whole mechanism can only be hinted at. But I hope that I have shown through my trial and error how the psychical course of such an introspection proceeds. The inner feeling of certainty which accompanies such a task can naturally not be communicated to others. Those who attempt analysis on themselves will be the first to adopt our methods.

It is not to be wondered at that a repressed complex which, despite repression, causes physical reactions expresses itself preferentially in clang-associations. It would seem that the common occurrence of clang-associations and physical reactions are an indication of the strength of a repressed complex, or rather of the resistance which a repressed complex has to overcome in order to become conscious. This resistance was striking in all three cases, especially in my own. The occurrence of clang-associations is only a sign that the complex is held back by the " censure " and, just as in dreams, dare only manifest itself in innocent shape. It is a fair conclusion that a repressed complex evokes physical reactions, or in other words affects, when there is strong resistance to its becoming conscious.

I have one other example in which I can prove by the galvanometer the working of a repressed complex. It manifested itself in an educated lady and was as follows:

Subject No. 19 :			R.T.	G.D.	Reproduction
20. Eat	eat ? dinner		18	18	long reflection
			(16)	(16)	

Four complex signs: repetition of the stimulus-word, disturbance in reproduction, prolonged reaction-time, and prolonged deviation. She is surprised at the stimulus-word: that in itself points to a complex. Obviously the word itself cannot cause surprise, but the surprise is a hint that something strange, i.e. unconscious, is going on within her. She had great resistance for a long time, maintaining that nothing occurred to her. Finally, a smile heralded the solution: she does not like eating with her relations before strangers and does not like visitors at her table, because people would then see that she does not like one of her relations (an aunt). The reason of this antipathy was not communicated, nor did I press for it. It is very probable that this antipathy to the aunt exhibits the complex concealed here.

A very pretty example of the influence of a repressed complex on the psychogalvanic complex is given by Jung and Peterson (*Brain*, 1907).

It occurred in a male nurse who was very emotional. The same series of stimulus-words was used three times in succession—a method which brings out the working of a repressed complex particularly well. The greatest deviation occurred with the association *the sun — burns*. Other strong deviations were at the associations *floor — parquet ; pay — write ; warm — the stove*. In the last three reactions there were constant disturbances; all the reproductions were altered. With one exception, all the deflections exceeded the arithmetical mean of each of the series. Of the nine reactions four were above, and two coincided with, the probable mean. The patient said he had no particular thoughts in connexion with these reactions and was not himself aware of anything. But when asked what personal significance *floor* had for him, he suddenly answered, with surprise and embarrassment, that recently a stove had become defective and burned the floor to such an extent that not only the stove but the greater part of the floor had to be renewed. He had to pay for this himself, which meant great expense. Besides, there had been great danger from fire. Thus all the disturbances above recorded were completely explained, including the strong emotional tone of *sun — burns*. The strong resistance on the part of the conscious shows that the patient had not become aware of the complex in the three tests, despite the numerous stimulus-words and its recent occurrence.

PART IV

STATISTICS OF THE NORMAL TESTS

In this last part of the work I shall show from the statistics of the whole material what are the laws between reaction-time and deviation, and between complex signs and deviation. We shall find that the relationships are constant between the factors mentioned and the deviations, and disregard the differences in the methods of the tests, sex, and the educational status of the test persons. We shall review these relationships in the four groups of the educated and uneducated men and women separately, so as to show that they are present in all groups. I must warn the student against comparing the deviation values of one group with those of another, and against drawing conclusions as to the influence of emotionalness, education, or sex. To do this we must be certain that the same experimental methods have been used, and even then regard must be had to the condition of the skin in men and women, in hand or brain workers. It is only the values of the reaction-time that can be properly compared with one another. I shall not, therefore, take notice of the absolute values of the mean of the deviation in the individual groups, and shall limit myself to describing the differences between the probable and arithmetical means. Since these differences are entirely due to psychological processes (for the physical conditions remain exactly the same during the experiment, as a rule, or if there is any change, it is directed equally to those two values) we can compare these group differences.

We have four groups :

1. *Educated Women*

Five tests on five different persons ; 304 associations. In all the tests a current was led through the person tested, brass electrodes were used four times and nickel electrodes once. The number of galvanic cells was once three, twice two, thrice one.

2. *Educated Men*

Twelve tests on eight different persons ; 830 associations. Sommer's method was used once (zinc and charcoal electrodes without any current) ; eleven times we used brass electrodes and a galvanic cell (thrice two, eight times one). We have not included Test II (*c*) in the statistics.

3. *Uneducated Women*

Five tests on four different persons ; 491 associations. Sommer's method was used once, brass electrodes with one galvanic cell twice, twice water-contact and two galvanic cells. In the two experiments with water-contact two nickel electrodes were placed each in a glass vessel and the subject required to dip the second and third finger of each hand in one of the vessels without touching the electrodes. The test does not differ essentially from the others, only the deviation is lower on account of the slight surface contact (two fingers). The probable mean of the deviations was 2 in both tests carried out on the same subject; the arithmetical mean of one test was 1·5, of the second test 2·6 (when the experimenter knew the subject's complexes).

4. *Uneducated Men*

Seven tests on six different persons; 535 associations. Sommer's method was used three times; three times brass electrodes, once nickel electrodes with conducted current (twice two cells, once one cell).

In all, twenty-nine tests on twenty-three persons with 2160 associations. A comparison of the mean of the reaction-time of the different groups follows. (The figures are here given in seconds, not in one-fifth seconds).

TABLE I

	P.M.	A.M.	Difference	Too long times in percentage
Uneducated men . . .	2·94	3·51	0·57	39·8
Educated women . . .	2·9	3·3	0·4	32·2
Uneducated women . . .	2·5	2·7	0·2	33·4
Educated men	2	2·2	0·2	32·2

Compared with Jung's results (chapter v) my results here seem to be, on the average, higher. These depend, as already stated, upon the personal factor, and also to some extent on the very complicated test methods in my experiments. Uneducated women (all nurses) occupy the first place in Jung's work, the third in mine; the other series agree. This is due to the fact that two of the uneducated women (both Swabians!), who took up two-thirds of the associations, were both remarkably fluent in speech. The A.M. of their time is scarcely greater than the P.M. In one of them the association type is remarkably superficial. Only one Swiss brought up in the country showed the type of uneducated women dealt with in former experiments. I am disposed to attribute the great differences of the two means in my uneducated men as much to want of fluency in speech as to lively emotivity. But the great difference in the educated women is a clear sign of emotionalness, as can be proved from the following comparison (see Table II).

Let me first point out that in all groups we find a prolongation of the A.M. of the deviations as against their P.M. In the reaction-time intellectual and verbal conditions share, but this is not the case in the deviations, so that the difference of the two means enables us to draw conclusions as to emotivity. For when the A.M. is very great as compared with the P.M. the deviations must have been very large, and these are caused by affects. The

TABLE II

	Difference between P.M. and A.M. of deflection	Difference between P.M. of time and A.M. of time	Too long deviations in percentage
	mm.	second [1]	
Educated women . . .	7·6	0·4	45·9
Educated men	2·8	0·2	43·8
Uneducated men . . .	2·5	0·57	49·9
Uneducated women . . .	1·1	0·2	40·0

figure for the difference among educated women is surprising. We see clearly that in this group there was great emotionalness, so that we are justified in referring the great difference between P.M. and A.M. of the reaction-time simply to emotional causes. From the contradictory values between the differences of time and deviation means among uneducated men I feel justified in concluding that the great difference in time is not solely conditioned here by their emotivity, but through their unreadiness in speech and their inferior degree of intelligence. For if the time differences were due entirely to emotional conditions the differences in deviation caused by the emotionalness should be correspondingly greater than in the other groups. The low difference in deviation among the uneducated women corresponds with the low difference in time. This led me to deduce a low emotionalness for this group. As a matter of fact, the two subjects mentioned were not greatly excited by the experiment. But as two tests were made with water-contact, which conditions a low amount for deviation and therefore a low difference for both means, I shall draw no conclusions from these values. From a comparison of the values of the educated men one could deduce great verbal fluency (low difference in time) together with highly developed emotionalness, which agrees with the behaviour of these persons as otherwise known to me.

The most important factor for a comparison of the reaction-time and deviations is the measure which tells us how much greater is the P.M. of those deviations which coincide with " too long " times than the P.M. of the deviations of the whole experiment. To obtain this result these deviations are written out and their P.M. calculated. If the P.M. of these deviations is greater than that of the whole deviation it means : in this test " too long " times correspond with " too long " deviations. The following table shows us that this is the case in all four groups. I will not repeat the values for the deviations which coincide

[1] I add the differences of the mean time for the sake of clearness.

with the "too long" times, but take the differences of these with the P.M. of the whole experiment. For comparison I again include the differences of times and deviations.

TABLE III

	Differences between the deflections occurring at too long times and all the deflections of a test	Difference between P.M. of deviations and A.M. of deflections	Differences between P.M. of R. time and A.M. of R. time in seconds
Educated women　.　.　.	+ 5·3	7·6	0·4
Uneducated women　.　.　.	+ 2·8	1·1	0·2
Educated men　.　.　.　.	+ 2·8	2·8	0·2
Uneducated men　.　.　.	+ 1·0	2·5	0·57

Again the educated women exhibit the highest average value, i.e. among educated women the deviations which coincide with "too long" times are most distinctly prolonged. This is a further proof that the prolonged times are of emotional origin in this class. Among uneducated women the difference is strikingly greater than the difference between the P.M. of the deviations and the A.M. of the reaction-times. We can express these relationships by saying : Among uneducated women there are few long deviations and few very long times, but when the latter do occur there is a definitely prolonged deviation (viz. 6·8 against P.M. of deviations for the whole = 4). As the uneducated women in our test are fluent talkers and hence only show a low difference between P.M. and A.M. of reaction - times, their "too long" times are clearly due to emotion (as shown by the great increase of the deviations which coincide with too long times). Among educated men, who, as we have seen, are equally fluent in speech, the prolongation of time is again of emotional origin. The fact that the difference between the A.M. of the deviations and their P.M. is the same as the difference here reviewed indicates that the prolongation of the deviations, coinciding with "too long" times, is less pronounced than among uneducated women. The low difference (+ 1) of the uneducated men confirms the view that the times are only to a small extent prolonged by emotional inhibitions (since the corresponding deviations are so slightly increased) ; for the most part it is a question of speech or intellectual difficulties which, as non-affective processes, are unaccompanied by any prolongation of the deviation.

We see that the comparison of the three differences allows us to draw more accurate conclusions about the emotionalness during the test than the difference between the arithmetical and probable mean times alone.

Besides the relationship between reaction-time and deviation, that between the deviation and the total complex signs was also calculated. Though a definite ratio seemed probable between the length of the reaction-time and the deviation, no constant ratio could be at first discovered between deviation and complex signs. At Jung's suggestion I therefore wrote out all the "too long" deviations which were the only complex indicator; next, those which occurred together with one complex indicator, quite irrespective of its kind; and finally, all those which occurred together with two or more complex indicators. We regarded as complex indicators too long reaction-times, all kinds of reproduction disturbances, repetition and misunderstanding of the stimulus-word, stereotyped repetition of the same reaction-word (complex representative), translation into a foreign language, slips of speech, "peculiar reactions," and clang-associations which were afterwards shown to be conditioned by a complex. There were no "faults" in my tests. It will be seen that sometimes complex indicators need not be conditioned by the particular reaction with whose deviation they are compared, e.g. reproduction disturbances due to perseveration. If, nevertheless, the size of the deviation increases with the number of complex indicators, it shows that these exceptions (which are wont to occur with too small a deviation) need not enter into the final result.

I will again place in juxtaposition the individual groups and give (1) the A.M. of the whole test for each group; (2) that of the deviations which are the only single complex indicator; (3) the deviations which occur with one other complex indicator; (4) the A.M. of those deviations which are connected with two or more complex indicators:

TABLE IV

	A.M. of total deviations	A.M. of deviations forming the only complex indicator	Deviation + one complex indicator A.M.	Deviation + two or more complex indicators A.M.
	(1)	(2)	(3)	(4)
Educated women . . .	13·7	18·2	24·9	29·2
Educated men	13·1	18·3	19·9	21·8
Uneducated women . . .	6·8	7·8	8·8	10·3
Educated men	10	15·5	15·9	17·7

We notice that in all the groups the average length of the

deviation increases with the number of complex indicators. This coincidence is a meaningless and incomprehensible fact without the theory of complexes (and without psycho-analysis). The complex theory shows us the necessary inner connexion of this phenomenon. As far as the individual groups are concerned, I would only point out that again the educated women show the most distinct increase of the single values. In column (4) the value is more than double that of column (1); this is not attained in any other group.

The following table shows in percentages, and in regard to the total number of associations, how often the deviation formed (1) the only complex indicator, (2) how often it occurred with one complex indicator, and (3) how often with two or more complex indicators.

TABLE V

	Deviation the only complex indicator	Deviation + one complex indicator	Deviation + two or more complex indicators
Educated women . . .	13·3	17·5	13·2
Educated men	19·1	15·7	7·5
Uneducated women . . .	15·5	14·3	10·2
Uneducated men . . .	17·1	18·2	10·2

The table speaks for itself. It is too soon to draw any particular conclusions from it. The fact that the educated women show such remarkably large values where emotional factors are concerned may have a common cause apart from any accidental causes. The emotionalness is directed in this group chiefly towards the experimenter; it is only to a small extent conscious or conditioned by external circumstances. It is here a question of " transference to the physician " (Freud),[1] the factor so important in psycho-analysis; in this case it is transference to the experimenter.

SUMMARY

Part I

(1) There are three methods of investigating psychical processes by the galvanometer :

(*a*) The application of unpolarizable electrodes to unsymmetrical parts of the skin (Tarchanoff, Sticker).

(*b*) Use of small metal electrodes having a considerable difference of tension (zinc and charcoal : Sommer and Fürstenau).

[1] Freud, *Bruchstück einer Hysterieanalyse.*

(c) Use of electrodes of the same material and conduction of an electric current through the person tested (R. Vigouroux, Féré, A. Vigouroux, E. H. Müller, Veraguth).

(2) There is still uncertainty about the physiological and physical principles of the psycho-galvanic phenomenon. It would seem that in all three methods the sweat-glands play a prominent part, either (1) by producing the so-called secretory current or (2) by alterations in the resistance to conduction of the skin as against the conducted current. Method (b) seems to be the more complicated as regards a physiological and physical explanation.

(3) Although there are changes in the sweat-glands in all methods of experimenting, we do not yet know whether these changes are absolutely necessary for the occurrence of the psychogalvanic phenomenon, and we do not know whether we are really measuring the same physiological changes in the three methods.

(4) We can only express ourselves in general terms about the final physical changes. In any case, "in view of the extreme promptitude and accuracy which can be observed in the connexion between the galvanic phenomenon and the psychical processes, it cannot be merely a question of gross physical (or chemical) processes which are interpolated between the two. Above all, it can be no question of processes which, once stimulated, pursue their path independently of psychical events ; we are rather constrained to regard these processes as being continuously controlled, furthered, or inhibited by the central organ."

(5) Contact changes of the electrodes cannot be an essential condition for the occurrence of the psychogalvanic phenomenon (in methods (b) and (c)) for it occurs likewise when using water-contact. But involuntary pressure on the electrodes can influence to a remarkable extent the size of the deviation.

(6) Deep inspirations (sighing) act in general just as a psychological stimulus, i.e. on the emotional tone, and not directly by the vasomotor changes which they produce.

(7) In the experimental methods (b) and (c) we have seen that in psychical processes only affective processes (in Bleuler's sense) act upon the psycho-galvanic phenomenon. In pure intellectual work (e.g. adding up figures, the reading of indifferent matter) and in the occurrence of sensations unaccompanied by any distinct emotional tone no deviations occur.

Part II

(8) Too long deviations (i.e. those above the probable mean of the total test) correspond in most cases with complex reactions ; short deviations, with non-emotionally toned reactions. The too long deviation is therefore a new and valuable complex indicator.

(9) We must differentiate between the association curve (Veraguth), which contains the basis of the total deviations of an experiment, and the complex wave, which refers only to that section of the association curve where secondary waves occur.

(10) The typical complex wave consists of a very long deviation followed by a fall of the curve with short deviations. There are frequent deviations from this norm. In the down stroke of the complex wave we find the opposite condition to the whole course of the normal association curve, which always exhibits a tendency to rise.

(11) A picture similar to the down stroke of the complex wave is obtained—

(*a*) By a strong affect which is independent of the experiment (Curve II *c*) ;

(*b*) By active distraction of the attention from the experiment (Curve III) ;

(*c*) By outer distraction (Curve IV).

(12) The observations contained in 10 and 11 may be thus expressed : A constant complex (permanent affect, permanent concentration of the attention upon something other than the experimental stimulus) inhibits the psychical preparation of the stimulus. It remains poor in associations and emotions. The absence of new affects gives rise to an absence of new innervations, and thus also to the disappearance of the deviations. The explanation of the gradual fall of the curve is that the acute affect gradually fades, whilst the mental attitude of inhibition created by the affect is maintained for a long time.

(13) Assuming that we are right in regarding the fall of the galvanometer curve as due to an increase of the electrical resistance, and the rise of the curve to a decrease thereof, we may say : Whenever an increase in innervation occurs (from the application of sensory and psychical stimuli in the normal state, from increased emotivity, or from sudden tension of the attention) the resistance to conduction decreases ; wherever there is inhibition to, or decrease of, innervations, the resistance increases (therefore in the cases given in 10 and 11, also in times of rest, in sleep, and in pure intellectual work).

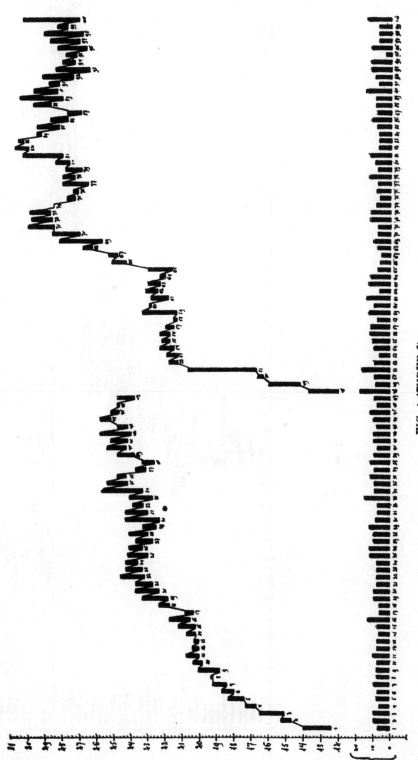

FIG. 1 (CURVE I)

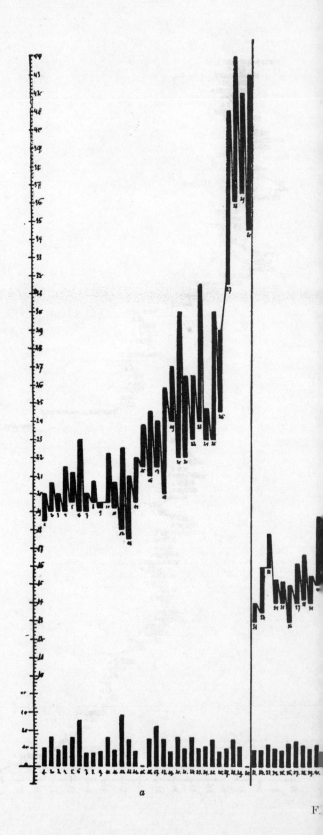

F.

c

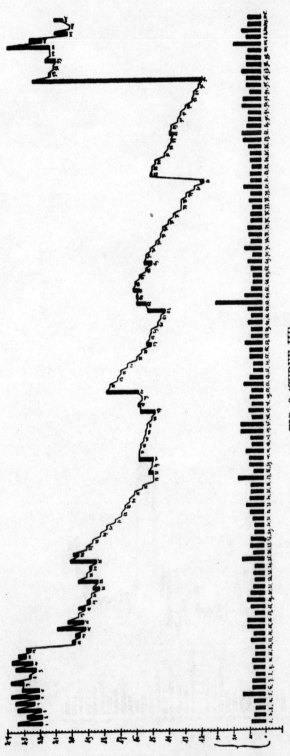

EXPERIMENT III

FIG. 3 (CURVE III)

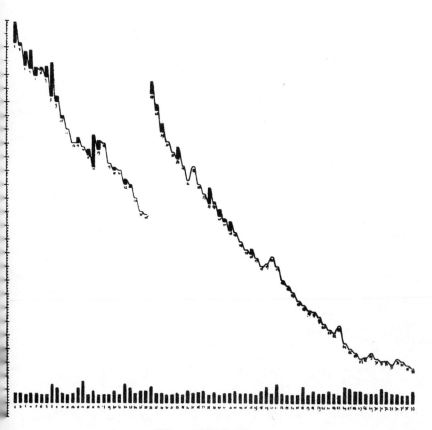

FIG. 4 (CURVE IV)

Part III

(14) Prolongation of the reaction-time without simultaneous prolongation of the deviation can occur :

(a) from intellectual difficulties, such as imperfect grasp of the stimulus-word, its repetition, a rare word given as the stimulus-word ;

(b) from the influence of perseveration—a much more frequent cause.

When a complex perseverates, the times within the sphere of influence of the perseveration can be distinctly prolonged, the deviations distinctly shortened. An explanation of this is found in the difference in a perseveration of what we measure by these two values. The reaction-time gives us the measure of the conflict between the perseverating emotional tone and the new reaction, whilst the deviation gives us the result of the conflict— in other words, the quantity of attention which the new reaction receives. When the perseverating emotional tone is very strong the reaction-time becomes very long, but the deviation will be very short, since the reaction receives but little attention and therefore has only a slight emotional tone.

(15) Prolongation of the deviation without simultaneous prolongation of the reaction-time can arise from purely verbal reasons. The complex, betrayed by the prolonged deviation, may not prolong the reaction-time if the subject has at hand a verbal association he can slip in ; the emotional inhibitions arising from the complex can with difficulty be recognized in such verbally fluent associations.

(16) Clang-associations exhibit generally a too long deviation when they are provoked by a complex contained in the reaction itself ; they exhibit a too short deviation when provoked by the perseveration of a previous complex. In the former case one can usually discover more accurate and deeper connexion between the clang-associations ; in the latter case, usually not. A deviation which is too long, occurring with a clang-reaction, indicates, therefore, some deeper connexion which often lies in the unconscious, and must find its explanation by psycho-analysis.

(17) It seems that complexes repressed from the conscious are able to influence the psycho-galvanic phenomenon.

Part IV

(18) The difference between the probable mean and the arithmetical mean of the deviations is a surer criterion for the emotion of a subject than the difference between the two means

of the reaction-times ; for in the latter intellectual and verbal factors may participate, whilst the deviations are conditioned by affective processes only.

(19) In all four groups of the persons tested (educated and uneducated men and women) the mean of those deviations which coincide with " too long " times is greater than the mean of the total deviations. In all four groups there is an average correspondence between " too long " times and " too long " deviations.

(20) In all four groups the size of the deviations increases with the number of complex indicators. The theory of the complex, which ascribes the occurrence of a complex indicator to the presence of an emotionally toned group of ideas, alone enables us to understand this observation.

EXPLANATION OF FIGURES 1–4

The marks placed next to one another on the horizontal line represent the reaction-times. The (small) figures found at the foot of the ordinate serve as the measure of the length of the reaction-time and refer to one-fifth seconds.

The marks placed on the rising or falling line represent the galvanometer deviations.

The (big) numbers of the ordinates permit their place to be read off upon the scale in centimetres and millimetres.

The reaction-time and deviation of one and the same reaction are placed over one another.

CHAPTER XIII

ON THE PHYSICAL ACCOMPANIMENTS OF
ASSOCIATION PROCESSES

By Dr. H. NUNBERG [1]

AT the suggestion of Dr. Jung I have carried out association tests on a number of persons, investigating at the same time some of the psychophysiological changes that occur during the experiments.

Definite changes in the physical sphere accompany the emotions. Bleuler,[2] e.g., says of affectivity, " Certain affects extend our muscles, others relax them or they produce some other distribution of the muscular tension." When a sudden change takes place in any one—say he gets pale or flushes, sighs, fidgets,—we presume that some definite affective process is going on in him. According to Bleuler (p. 15) the affect is a generalized reaction ; according to Breuer and Freud this reaction exhibits a "whole series of voluntary and involuntary reflexes through which, as experience teaches us, the affects become discharged." [3] A reaction of this kind can apparently occur spontaneously, or it may be provoked by a conversation or by some word ; it can take place consciously if the emerging images are associatively connected with the ego complex,[4] or remain unconscious if they do not enter into this connexion. Since a " complex " represents the " total number of ideas which relate to some definite emotionally toned event " (chapter ii), and the emotional tone is nothing but " an affective condition which is accompanied by physical innervation," [5] such reactions must especially arise after complexes.

Two methods require consideration in investigating the physical

[1] 1909.

[2] *Affektivität, Suggestibilität, Paranoia*, pp. 7 and 15.

[3] *Studien über Hysterie*, p. 5. (Leipzig and Vienna, 1895 ; new edition 1908.)

[4] Jung understands by the ego complex " the ideational mass of the ego which we believe to be accompanied by the potent and ever-living feeling tone of our own body." (*The Psychology of Dementia Præcox*, 1909, translated by Peterson and Brill.)

[5] Jung, *The Psychology of Dementia Præcox*, p. 38.

accompaniments of complexes : the one is the subjective method, the other the objective or method through expression.[1]

Now, the persons tested are not always able to talk about their deepest emotions or to remember emotionally toned events. We are thus dependent upon the method through expression, " which comprises all physical symptoms through which the feelings are outwardly displayed, as well as the movements brought about by the feelings." [2] This objective method can be joined to the association test as elaborated by Jung.

When complexes are present certain disturbances occur in the association experiment—" complex indicators." They are external manifestations of the complex, and conditioned by the emotional tone accompanying it. In our tests we differentiate in this way the indifferent from the complex associations, placing the reactions which show objective disturbances in a special group. We next differentiate between unconscious and conscious complex associations. Our investigations were directed towards finding out whether in the association experiment there are external changes peculiar to each group.

For this purpose we used Sommer's apparatus for the three dimensional determination of tremors, Marey's pneumograph, and the galvanometer.

PART I

Tests with Sommer's Apparatus for Recording Movements in Three Dimensions

Freud says [3] : " All our activities proceed from psychic stimuli (inner or outer) and terminate in innervations." Martius writes [4] that " when a person at rest is submitted to psychological experiments, involuntary movements are not the exception but the rule. They do not only occur with strong and sudden stimuli, or with feelings of fear and expectancy ; they are also connected with every observation, with every effort of attention." Preyer [5] showed that the hand can write down automatically figures which have been vividly present as ideas. These movements are to some extent made accessible to experimental observation by

---

[1] Wundt, *Physiologische Psychologie*, Bd. II, 5th edition, 1903.

[2] Wundt, op. cit. p. 267.

[3] *Interpretation of Dreams*, p. 426.

[4] *Beiträge zur Psychologie und Philosophie*, Bd. I, Heft 4 (Leipzig, 1905); *Ueber die Lehre von der Beeinflussung des Pulses und Atmung durch psychische Reize*, p. 431.

[5] *Die Erklärung des Gedankenlesens.* (Leipzig, 1886.)

Sommer's [1] apparatus.   Sommer writes [2] : " If physiognomy is
(on the other hand) regarded as a factor in the general theory of
expression we try, in place of the old-fashioned physiognomy,
to apprehend the movements of expression just where they are
most readily accessible to presentation and measurement.   The
human hand seems most clearly to express these movements for,
like the face, it expresses mental states through these movements ;
for experimental purposes the hand has the advantage over the
face of relatively greater simplicity."   A detailed description of
the apparatus will be found in Sommer's book, together with an
illustration. [3]

The principle of the apparatus is the decomposition, by means
of a system of levers and apparatus for equilibrization, of the
movements of the hands into the three dimensions of space
and their transference to a kymograph.   Three curves are described on the kymograph, of which the upper corresponds to to-
and-fro or push movements, the middle to lateral, and the lower
to vertical or pressure movements.   The subject's hand is fixed
to the apparatus as described by Sommer.   The index and middle
fingers are fastened to a plate attached to the equilibrization
apparatus, and the arm is supported in an elbow-socket.

The first test showed at once that the apparatus had some
undesirable secondary effects.   First, the pressure and push
movements were very inconstant ; they bent upwards or down-
wards, backwards and forwards, very considerably.   The subject
had to be constantly on the watch to maintain the hand in the
same position.   This caused very great muscular tension, and
so a large part of the finer involuntary movements were lost.
(One subject, indeed, got cramp by endeavouring throughout the
experiment to keep the hand in one position.)   Moreover, the
position of the hand was very largely dependent on the voluntary effort of the subject.   The lateral curve was the most
constant, and so in this work we deal only with observations
about changes of lateral movements.

The association test was carried out in the usual way.   The
moment of the stimulus and reaction were marked by means of
a Morse-key on the kymograph.   The distance of both strokes
was measured at the completion of the test in seconds.   A respiratory curve was also traced on the kymograph because, according
to Martius, [4] the arm movements are influenced by the movements
of the chest.   The respiratory waves and the individual fluctua-

---

[1] Sommer, *Lehrbuch der psychopathologischen Untersuchungsmethoden.* (Berlin
and Vienna, 1899.)

[2] *Ibid.,* p. 95.   [3] *Ibid.,* p. 97.

[4] *Beiträge zur Psychologie und Philosophie,* loc. cit.

tions of the lateral curve were measured by means of a nonius. Before beginning the experiment all the starting parts of the single curves must be brought into a vertical line with a plummet, for any slight displacement of the curves would affect the results considerably.

Curves at rest were first taken, the subject being placed in a position where he was subjected to no stimulus. The fluctuations in the lateral curves were then found to run parallel with the respiratory waves, each respiratory curve corresponding to one fluctuation of the lateral curve, except at several places where a sudden quivering movement was observed. At rest the movements of the arm coincide to a certain extent with the fluctuations of the thorax. Our results agree with those of Martius,[1] who found the same relationship in his investigations with the plethysmograph.

The question now arises whether this relationship holds good in association experiments.

We must mention, however, that we had great technical difficulties in working up the curves, for many of the fluctuations in the lateral curve were so small that they could only be measured with great difficulty. The figures so obtained only approximately express the actual values, and this indirectly influences the results. The results given by Sommer's apparatus, therefore, must be received with caution.

Twenty-five associations were taken on six subjects and the size of the respiratory waves compared with the waves of the lateral curve. The tests were (excepting with two persons) carried out twice, at intervals of two to three days. This plan was adopted in all the tests referred to in this work. One could thus see if the phenomenon was constant in the same person, and whether the experimental excitation was lessened or altogether absent at the second test. Jung and Peterson [2] point out that in consequence of the unusual situation (the submission to experiment) the excitation was so great that the stimulus-words could not be apperceived in their full meaning ; this gave rise to incomplete assimilation and to imperfect preparation for the stimulus-word. Thus the whole experiment was disturbed, whilst in the second experiment, when the subject was more accustomed to the conditions, the changes were much more typical. A decline of the experimental excitation could be proved at the second test, unless, of course, there accidentally arose some cause of disturbance independent of the experiment.

Before reviewing the tests we must briefly explain the figures given. The amplitudes of the single respiratory waves and

[1] Loc. cit.	[2] *Brain*, vol. xxx, 1907, p. 199.

fluctuations of the transverse curves were measured directly after
each stimulus of the series, separated into complex and indifferent
associations,[1] added together, and their arithmetical mean calculated.   The figures in the tables are the arithmetical mean of the
amplitudes in millimetres, the Latin numerals indicating the
serial number of the amplitudes after an association.   These
numbers are represented graphically in the figures.   Each number,
which expresses the size of the amplitude of the representation
as well as the transverse waves, was entered in single (millimetre)
squares of a millimetre paper, the columns thus formed showing
the size of the amplitudes.   But since some of our numbers are
not absolute, but only comparative, values, only as many of the
numbers were entered in the millimetre squares as would make
the comparison of the different amplitudes visible.

The most general numbers taken from the six subjects tested
will be first given ; these refer to the respiratory and lateral
curves which were obtained by adding together the indifferent
and the complicated.

	I	II	III	IV	V	VI	VII
Respiratory waves . .	8·7	8·6	8·8	8·8	8·9	8·7	8·6
Lateral oscillations . .	0·6	0·8	0·8	0·8	0·9	0·8	0·8

As the table shows, the two series run parallel, except for the
first and last waves ; a deeper inspiration follows stronger
movement of the arm.   To a certain extent the strength of
the arm movements depends upon the depth of respiration.

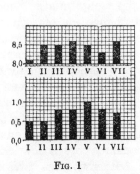

Fig. 1

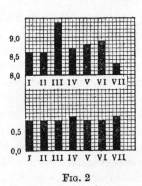

Fig. 2

There are naturally individual deviations from the averages,
but among the individual numbers are some which conform to
this rule in a very high degree :

	I	II	III	IV	V	VI	VII
Respiratory curve . .	13·2	14·1	13·4	13·6	13·9	15·3	12·1
Lateral oscillations . .	0·8	1·1	0·6	0·6	1·0	0·3	0·5

[1] The absence or presence of " complex indicators " distinguishes indifferent
from complex reactions.

Here all the waves agree except the sixth, whose amplitude is very small in contrast with a very large amplitude of respiration.

How do the motor experiments of expression behave with indifferent and complicated associations respectively ?

The following are the changes in the curves with indifferent stimuli :

	I	II	III	IV	V	VI	VII	
Respiratory waves	8·1	8·5	8·5	8·6	8·5	8·3	8·6	} Fig. 1
Lateral oscillations	0·5	0·5	0·8	0·8	1·0	0·8	0·7	

The parallelism is here very slight (Fig. 1), although the figures show at the levels of both curves a certain similarity. After complex stimuli we get the following curves :

	I	II	III	IV	V	VI	VII	
Respiratory waves	8·6	8·6	9·4	8·7	8·8	8·9	8·3	} Fig. 2
Lateral oscillations	0·8	0·8	0·8	0·9	0·8	0·8	0·9	

Although a certain similarity can be noticed after indifferent stimuli, in some places there is, except for the two first waves, which are without significance, not merely no agreement but a marked dissimilarity.

The arm movements and respiration correspond most closely in conditions of rest, least of all with complexes. The deviations shown by the indifferent curve are also probably referable to the fact that the association experiment is a psychical activity. The indifferent stimulus-words may be regarded as small and transitory stimuli which effect changes in the mental state ; " mental processes of the simplest kind exhibit phenomena of activity." [1] These phenomena are naturally expressed by altered innervation. There is, besides, another factor of perhaps greater importance ; among the indifferent reactions there are probably many complexes. The stimulus-words followed in our tests after relatively long pauses, for we had to wait to note the changes in the curves. The subject could consequently recover himself during the pause and compose himself for the new stimulus-word. The influence of perseveration is thus lost, so that probably a few critical reactions are to be found among the indifferent ones. We have seen that after complexes the agreement between the respiratory and lateral curve is removed, so it is possible that some few complexes influenced the indifferent curves.

We are justified in concluding, therefore, that the movements of the hand behave differently with complexes from what they do with indifferent stimuli ; that is to say, with complexes the

[1] Martius, loc cit., p. 512.

arm movements are less dependent upon oscillations of the chest than when at a state of rest.

A few single curves will be now given.

(1) With indifferent stimuli :

		I	II	III	IV	V	VI	VII
Respiratory curves .	.	3·0	3·5	3·5	3·2	3·5	3·4	3·7
Lateral oscillations .	.	0·9	1·6	2·6	2·7	2·7	2·4	2·9

(2) With complex associations :

		I	II	III	IV	V	VI	VII
Respiratory curves .	.	4·5	4·5	4·5	4·7	3·3	4·0	3·4
Lateral oscillations .	.	1·5	0·8	1·6	1·6	0·8	1·1	2·4

The parallelism is present with indifferent stimuli, almost entirely absent with complexes.

We have seen that there is in general a difference between indifferent associations and complexes as regards the kind of movement by which they are expressed. Let us next see if this difference extends to the intensity of these movements.

We shall here compare the oscillations of the lateral curves with indifferent stimuli and with complex associations.

Again we proceed from the most general figures ; they represent the arithmetical mean of the amplitudes obtained by adding all the curves together.

The A.M. of the amplitudes of the lateral curves is :

(1) Indifferent stimuli, 0·5 mm. per association.
(2) Complex   ,,   0·7 mm. ,,   ,,

This ratio was found in five subjects. In three persons with whom the tests were being carried out it occurred in both tests.

Only one subject shows an exception :

(1) Indifferent stimuli, 2·2 mm. per association.
(2) Complex   ,,   1·6 mm. ,,   ,,

Unfortunately, this contradictory behaviour could not be more closely examined owing to lack of material. Whether this was an affect type or only an exception conditioned by the experimental method remains uncertain. It is, however, remarkable that this phenomenon occurred in both experiments with this subject.

Of the six subjects, five showed stronger movements of the hands with the complex associations, whilst one showed weaker movements.

The best single curve of the first group shows the same behaviour (i.e. stronger innervations).

		I	II	III	IV	V	VI	VII
(1) Indifferent stimuli	.	0·5	0·3	0·4	0·6	0·4	0·3	0·3
Complex stimuli.	.	1·3	1·8	1·4	1·1	1·5	0·6	1·4

With complexes, therefore, the involuntary movements of the arm are other than with indifferent stimuli. This points to a condition of altered innervation.

Binswanger has shown in the last chapter that involuntary movements often occur in the association experiment, provoking large galvanic deviations because they are for the most part accompanied by strong emotional tones. Even in a state of rest we noticed an oscillation, and during the association test we also found such isolated oscillations on the curves. These oscillations occurred quite involuntarily, and were apparently quite irregular in their course.

The question arises as to whether the same law may be discovered here likewise.

For this purpose, these isolated oscillations were counted off after each association and the average of these numbers calculated. An endeavour was made to measure the intensity of the thrust, but no general laws could be made out.

The average of these isolated oscillations among six subjects was :

(1) Indifferent stimuli, 1·9 oscillations to an association.
(2) Complex   ,,   2·2   ,,   ,,   ,,

Among three other subjects :

(1) Indifferent stimuli, 2·2 oscillations to an association.
(2) Complex   ,,   1·1   ,,   ,,   ,,

It is noticeable in the case of every subject that when only two tests were made the same phenomenon occurred in both, except in one of the first six subjects tested. In this person there were fewer oscillations after complexes in the first test, but in the second test there were more than after indifferent stimuli.

An example will best illustrate these relationships :

(1) Test I—
With indifferent stimuli, 1 oscillation ; with complexes, 2 oscillations.

(2) Test II—
With indifferent stimuli, 1·7 oscillations ; with complexes, 2·8 oscillations.

There are two types that react differently with complexes. The one shows increased excitability under affect; the other is inhibited by affect. Bleuler says of these types [1] :

[1] Loc cit., p. 25.

"Many people who correspond fairly well to the classical 'sanguinary' temperament react quickly and intensively to emotional impressions, but the affect soon wears off. When the storm is over they are as before. It is as if the acute reaction, the shouting, abusing, hitting out, had 'abreacted' the affect. But if, on the other hand, temperament leads people to suppress the affect, this probably conduces, under conditions not yet ascertained, to displacements and conversions in Freud's sense of pathological reaction. Subsequent abreacting may, under certain conditions, cure the symptoms of the disease which has consisted in a 'converted' affect."

Summarizing our results, we see in the association experiment a series of changes of the psychomotor innervation which deviates from the state of rest :

(1) The relationship between arm movements and the thoracic oscillations is increased with complexes.

(2) The movements of the hand are stronger (with one exception) with complex than with indifferent stimuli.

(3) The frequency of the individual involuntary oscillations is sometimes less with complexes, sometimes greater. This peculiar behaviour leads us to think of the existence of two types.

PART II

RESPIRATION

Affects scarcely ever occur without changes in respiration.[1] Respiration is partly under control of the voluntary nervous system, though under ordinary conditions it proceeds involuntarily. Wundt[2] says of the physical accompaniments of the feelings that they only have value as objective signs of emotional processes when subjective observation confirms the presence of the emotion. But in the next sentence he says : "Experience nevertheless tells us that traces of emotion may escape subjective observation." The association experiment enables us to diagnose emotionally toned complexes, and this means the diagnosis of the emotion that accompanies it.

Let us consider the behaviour of respiration in the association experiment.

It may be premised that the actual pronouncing of the reaction-

[1] Wundt, *Physiolog. Psychologie*, Bd. II, p. 271, 5th edition, 1903.
[2] Loc. cit., p. 271.

word influences respiration very slightly,[1] probably because of the close connexion between respiration and speech.[2] The tension of the laryngeal muscles and the vocal cords is different in expiration and respiration. These changes are not passive but arise from active innervation.[3]

Before proceeding to our own tests we will first deal with the results of previous workers :

Mosso [4] obtained no conclusive results in regard to changes in respiration from stimulation of the sense organs.

Delabarre [5] found that during attention respiration increased in depth and frequency, but decreased during intellectual effort.

Lehmann [6] says that concentration of the attention causes irregular breathing. Strongly unpleasant sensations are accompanied by stopping of the breathing, succeeded by a few short and irregular respirations. Pleasant stimuli cause an increased depth of breathing.

Mentz states [7] that with acoustic stimuli there is generally a simultaneous prolongation of respiration, which, however, decreases if the stimulus is maintained. In involuntary attention there is generally a prolongation of the respiration, in voluntary attention the respiration is much diminished. With affects he found there generally occurred a prolongation of respiration. With increasing strength of the affect there is increasing height or depth of the respiration. He also found changes in the form of respiration with different affects.

Zoneff and Meumann [8] are of opinion that with " sensual " attention the respiration is almost entirely inhibited, with " intellectual " attention it is only partially so or not at all. Directly after the stimulus the breathing increases in depth. With increase of respiration it becomes more superficial. In involuntary concentration of the attention inhibition of respiration occurs. Changes in breathing are, moreover, dependent upon the attention's capacity of adaptation. In pleasurable states there is

[1] Minnemann, *Beiträge zur Psychologie und Philosophie*, Bd. I, Heft 4; *Atmung u. Puls bei aktuellen Affekten.*

[2] Jung and Peterson, *Brain*, vol. xxx, 1907.

[3] Tigerstedt, *Lehrbuch der Physiologie des Menschen.* (Leipzig, 1905.)

[4] *Diagnostik des Pulses in bezug auf die lokalen Veränderungen desselben.* (Leipzig, 1879.) *Ueber den Kreislauf des Blutes im menschlichen Gehirn.* (Leipzig, 1881.)

[5] *Revue Philosophique*, vol. xxxiii, 1892.

[6] *Die körperlichen Aeusserungen psychischer Zustände*, translated by F. Bendixen, Pt. I. (Leipzig, 1899.)

[7] Wundt, "Ueber die Wirkung akusticher Sinnesreize auf Puls und Atmung," *Phil. Studien*, Bd. XI, 1895.

[8] Wundt, "Ueber Begleiterscheinungen psychischer Vorgänge bei Atem und Puls," *Phil. Studien*, Bd. XVIII, 1902.

acceleration and superficiality of the respiration ; in painful states it is slower and deeper. All emotional reactions provoke more changes in the thoracic than in abdominal breathing.

Gent [1] says that in transitory conditions of tension the respiratory curve is scarcely changed ; the same is true of permanent emotional tension. During mental work the curve is somewhat flatter and more extended, but reaches its former height or exceeds it after completion of the work. In emotional excitement the respiration is more superficial, accelerated, and irregular. Gent also investigated various affects, using the reproduction method. He found that under a stimulating affect the respiration becomes irregular, distinctly deeper, and accelerated as compared with the normal curve. With pleasant affects the respiration is more frequent, often more superficial, and the size of the respiration changes considerably. In unpleasant affects which cause excitement and depression respiration becomes irregular, generally flatter and slower.

Martius [2] writes that in mental activity respiration is accelerated as compared with respiration in a state of rest, whilst the fluctuations decreased in height. Neither pleasure nor pain shows anything characteristic in the symptoms which might enable these to be differentiated from one another. There is a type of affect which is marked by a greater slowing down of the pulse and respiration as compared with rest.

Minnemann [3] says : In strong excitement respiration is accelerated and deepened. It becomes irregular under strong affects. It is most regular in the condition of rest of the norm. But a normal curve is only a relative term. There are great differences in the behaviour of different subjects towards affective stimuli. Speaking influences respiration but little.

Now as to our own experiments. The method was the same as that used by Jung with Peterson and Ricksher.[4]

A Marey pneumograph was fastened round the thorax, and the respiratory movements were recorded on a smoothly running kymograph. The amplitudes were measured and calculated as already described.

The tests were carried out on fourteen subjects, twice with each person, and about twenty-five associations were done each time. If we consider the respiratory curve with indifferent

[1] Wundt, "Volumpulskurven bei Gefühlen und Affekten," *Phil. Studien,* Bd. XVIII, 1902.

[2] Loc. cit.   [3] Loc. cit.

[4] Jung and Peterson, loc. cit. ; Jung and Ricksher, " Further Investigations on the Galvanic Phenomenon and Respiration in Normal and Insane Individuals," *Journal of Abnormal Psychology,* vol. ii, No. 5.

associations, the arithmetical mean of the amplitudes of all the respiratory waves in both tests amounted to :

I	II	III	IV	V	VI	VII
11·4	11·7	12·1	12·2	12·4	12·2	12·3[1] (cp. Fig. 3)

The first respiration after the stimulus-word is very small in comparison with all the others. The amplitudes that follow increase up to the sixth, when the amplitude becomes suddenly smaller and increases again after the next deep breath. Respiration increases in depth after the stimulus.[2] The irregularity in the curve after the fifth respiration is probably referable to the fact that some complex associations were included among the indifferent ones. Other factors may also have a share.

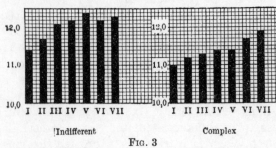

Fig. 3

What is the respiration like with complex associations ? The A.M. of the amplitudes in both series of tests is :

	I	II	III	IV	V	VI	VII	
Complex .	11	11·2	11·3	11·4	11·4	11·7	11·9	} see
Indifferent .	11·4	11·7	12·1	12·2	12·4	12·2	12·3	} Fig. 3

A comparison of the two curves shows that the respiratory curve is almost the same ; the amplitude is smallest directly after the stimulus-word, subsequently the respiration increases in depth. But alongside this there is one remarkable difference : the respiratory curve is distinctly lowered with complex as compared with indifferent associations. The average of the seven amplitudes after indifferent stimuli is 12 mm., and after complexes it is 11·4 mm. In consequence of the more superficial and strained respiration with complexes, the average volume of the inspiratory and expiratory air is less.

Almost all authorities agree that with mental activity breathing

---

[1] That the figures do not agree with those on p. 537 is due to our having had more subjects, none of whom were the same persons. Since the size of respiration fluctuates considerably in individuals, the average with different subjects is very different.

[2] Zoneff and Meumann, loc. cit.

becomes more superficial. Zoneff and Meumann [1] regard this as due to the action of attention, Gent [2] to the action of tension. But attention is accompanied by conditions of tension. According to Bleuler [3] attention is nothing but one aspect of affectivity. In our association experiment we have to deal with complexes, i.e. with ideas which are held together by their affect. (See chapter ii.)

Going somewhat further, we shall now inquire whether the behaviour of the respiratory curve with the complex associations remains the same in both series of tests as against the curve of the indifferent associations. The arithmetical mean of the amplitude with (a) indifferent stimuli :

	I	II	III	IV	V	VI	VII
1st test . .	12·2	12·2	12·8	13·1	13·1	12·7	12·8
2nd test . .	10·7	11·3	11·4	11·3	11·7	11·7	11·9

(b) complex stimuli :

	I	II	III	IV	V	VI	VII
1st test . .	11·4	11·8	12·1	12·0	11·8	12·2	12·4
2nd test . .	10·7	10·6	10·6	10·8	11·0	11·3	11·5

The course of the respiratory curve is similar in the second test to the first, as is the behaviour of the respiratory curve with indifferent and complex associations. In the second test the respiration is not as deep as in the first test with either indifferent or complex associations.

Our subjects were not used to the experiment, and as a rule they did not like it very much, consequently there was more excitement at the first test than at the second. Gent [4] came to the conclusion that with exciting stimuli the respiration was distinctly deeper compared with the normal. Minnemann [5] found the same and says that under constant strong excitation the respiration is deeper. With constant excitation the respiration becomes stronger and the complexes cause a flattening of respiration ; this latter quality of the complex does not seem to be suspended under excitement. We shall discuss an exception to this rule later.

The rule is, accordingly, that with complexes respiration becomes more superficial. As mentioned above, there are exceptions ; five subjects showed at the first test a deepened respiration at complexes. The A.M. of the amplitudes in these cases was :

	I	II	III	IV	V	VI	VII
(a) Indifferent stimuli	10·5	10·7	11·4	11·5	11·5	11·4	11·4
(b) Complexes . .	11·0	12·2	12·2	11·7	11·9	11·9	12·2

[1] Loc. cit. [2] Loc. cit. [3] Loc. cit.
[4] Loc. cit. [5] Loc. cit.

These five subjects showed strong complex constellations, for on the average there were nineteen complexes to ten indifferent associations. In the second test they had thirteen complexes to twelve indifferent associations. In the remaining subjects there were fourteen complexes to ten indifferent associations in the first test, whilst in the second test there were thirteen to eleven. These strong complex constellations in the first five subjects point to great excitation (see p. 555).

The transition from " conscious " to " unconscious " is really fluid,[1] and it must be admitted that many complexes, for the most part actual complexes, can under certain conditions assume such strength and clearness that they can be easily denoted as conscious. For the purpose of marking off the conscious from the unconscious complexes we proceeded as follows : At the end of the experiment the subject was asked if anything definite had come into his mind at the complex association, or if it recalled any event important to him. Those reactions, which showed complex indications and to which an affirmative answer was given, we counted among the conscious complexes. All the others, including those where the statement was not quite certain, were reckoned to the unconscious complexes. There is no doubt as to the conscious complexes, the subject was clearly aware of them ; whilst among the unconscious complexes there may be some which were more or less conscious, as well as perseverations.

The respiratory curve is characteristic for both conscious and unconscious complex associations. The A.M. of the amplitudes for unconscious complexes is :

	I	II	III	IV	V	VI	VII	
	10·5	11·2	11·4	11·4	11·2	11·7	11·7	Fig. 4
(Indifferent . .	11·4	11·7	12·1	12·2	12·4	12·2	12·3	Fig. 3)

This curve (Fig. 4) is somewhat similar to that of the joint common complex curve. This is explained by the fact that the unconscious complexes can influence the curve more strongly than the conscious complexes, for there were 239 unconscious to 111 conscious complexes. It, moreover, resembles the indifferent curve. But there is one considerable difference—the size of the respiration. Almost all the amplitudes are smaller than in Fig. 3, and, moreover, the curve is more irregular than the previous curves. The first respiration is much compressed ; the tension of respiration is more intensive in its after-effect at the end of the respiratory period, i.e. the depth of respiration increases relatively towards the end of respiration. The difference between

---

[1] Freud, *The Interpretation of Dreams.*

the first and last respirations in the size of the amplitude amounts
to 1·2 with unconscious complexes, whilst with indifferent associations it is only 0·9 mm.   The after-effect is, therefore, stronger
with unconscious complexes.   The arithmetical mean of all seven

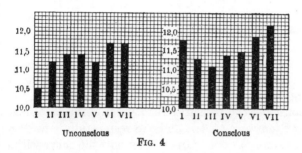

Unconscious   Conscious

FIG. 4

amplitudes amounts to 12 with indifferent associations, and to
11·3 with unconscious complexes.

When these tests are considered separately the unconscious
complexes find expression in the same way in the respiration.
The A.M. of the amplitudes is :

	I	II	III	IV	V	VI	VII
1st test	10·8	11·8	12·0	11·7	11·1	12·3	12·1
2nd test	10·2	10·7	10·8	11·2	11·3	11·2	11·3

So far as curves and size of respiration go these are like Fig. 4.
But the second test series shows smaller amplitudes than the
first.   This must be connected with the greater experimental
excitation of the first test.   The curve also, especially in Test I,
is very irregular.   Two factors may here take part : first, the
strong experimental excitation in Test I ; secondly, the inclusion
of some conscious complexes among the unconscious complexes.
This supposition is supported by the fact that in the second
test the curve is more regular, and the two respiratory curves
with conscious complex association are almost parallel (see
below).

One subject who had only three conscious complexes, although
there were several doubtful ones which were accordingly ascribed
to the unconscious, shows the same respiratory course with unconscious complexes.   In this subject the A.M. of the amplitude
with unconscious complexes is :

	I	II	III	IV	V	VI	VII
	9·7	15·0	15·3	15·7	14·2	15·2	15·8
(Indifferents	11·8	14·6	16·9	16·4	17·5	16·7	18·4)

These tests show that unconscious complexes inhibit respiration.

We now come to the conscious complexes. The A.M. of the amplitudes for both tests is :

	I	II	III	IV	V	VI	VII	
	11·8	11·3	11·1	11·4	11·5	11·9	12·2	Fig. 4
(1. Indifferents .	11·4	11·7	12·1	12·2	12·4	12·2	12·3	Fig. 3)
(2. Unconscious com-complexes .	10·5	11·2	11·4	11·4	11·2	11·7	11·7	Fig. 4)

The first respiration is very deep, then there is inhibition, which becomes even stronger at the third respiration than that at the unconscious complex at the same place ; this occasions a greater release of tension ; at the end the respiration is as deep as with indifferent associations.   In the first half the curve with conscious complexes is quite different from that of the unconscious complex, for in the former the inhibition is preceded by deep breathing, whilst in the latter inhibition follows directly upon the stimulus-word.   We have seen that under strong excitement respiration is deepened.   According to Zoneff and Meumann [1] pain strengthens the activity of respiration.   When a conscious complex is met, excitation follows accompanied by pain ; this can be occasionally confirmed by subjective observation.   The emotional tone of such complexes is very strong ; the emerging mass of ideas engross the attention and this finds expression in the form of subsequent inhibition, while the condition provoked by the attention forms " the psychological background for the emotional toned complex."[2] The curve of respiration is therefore different with conscious complexes from what it is with unconscious complexes, and we can say with Freud [3] "that excitations whose ideas are incapable of reaching consciousness act upon one another differently, proceed differently, and are led to other modes of expression than those we call ' normal,' when we are aware of the content of ideas."

With unconscious complexes the respiratory curve is inhibited as compared with indifferent associations, as it is also with conscious complexes, for the average of the seven amplitudes amounts to 11·7 in the latter (indifferents 12, unconscious complexes 11·3). The fact that this inhibition is less than with unconscious complexes depends, perhaps, upon the excitation occurring at the beginning with the conscious complexes, the after-effect of which does not permit the inhibition to develop completely.   With affects which are composed of isolated kinds of emotion, these

---

[1] Loc. cit.
[2] Jung, loc. cit.
[3] *Bruchstück einer Hysterieanalyse*, p. 102.

emotions influence each other, cross each other, and may even cancel the action of each other.[1]

Do these phenomena occur with conscious complexes in both tests ?

The A.M. of the amplitudes is :

	I	II	III	IV	V	VI	VII	
Test I . . .	12·5	11·9	11·7	12·0	12·0	12·4	12·8	Fig. 5
Test II . . .	11·2	10·7	10·5	10·9	11·0	11·5	11·7	

These curves show not only the same characteristics as the curve in Fig. 4, but are almost the same. The reason for this must be that here we have only selected associations, i.e.

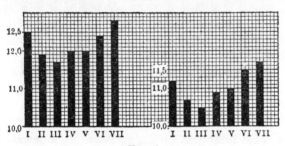

FIG. 5

only purely conscious ones. The second curve is flatter than the first, but that is nothing new.

We gave five tests on p. 543 having deeper respiration with complex associations, which we left over for later discussion. These respiration curves will be decomposed into their components, i.e. into conscious and unconscious complexes.

The A.M. of the amplitudes is :

	I	II	III	IV	V	VI	VII	
(a) Unconscious complexes . .	9·9	11·8	11·6	11·0	11·6	11·5	11·6	
(b) Conscious complexes . .	12·4	12·7	12·5	12·3	11·6	12·4	13·0	Fig. 6
(c) Indifferents .	10·5	10·7	11·4	11·5	11·5	11·4	11·4	

The curve agrees but little with the former curves save with that found in indifferent associations. The curve with conscious complexes has the greatest amplitudes ; with unconscious complexes it oscillates towards the limit of the respiratory curve of indifferent associations. The respiratory curve of unconscious complexes is less like that of the indifferents than the conscious complex ; as compared with the latter it is but slightly deepened. The A.M. of all the amplitudes is 11·2 indif-

----

[1] Wundt, *Physiolog. Psychologie*, Bde. II and III.

ferents, 11·3 unconscious complexes, and 12·3 conscious complexes. The respiratory volume is therefore greatest in the latter. The difference in the indifferent reactions and unconscious complexes is a minimum. So far as the course of the curve is concerned, the curve of conscious complexes approximates most nearly to the average type, i.e. it shows at the beginning a deepened

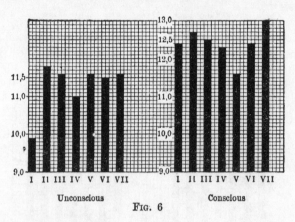

Unconscious   Conscious

Fig. 6

respiration with inhibition occurring later. The respiration with unconscious complexes deviates most of all from the average ; it is the most irregular. Perhaps this curve is caused by a few conscious complexes which are included among the unconscious on account of the subject's faulty introspection. We have already mentioned that these curves occurred with the first test when the subject was excited, and we must add that these experiments had frequently to be interrupted. It would seem that when an affect exists external to the experiment, only the conscious complexes obtain expression in the form of increased respiration, whilst with unconscious complexes this deviates but slightly from that of indifferent associations.

Summary

(1) With complexes the respiration is inhibited as compared with the respiration with indifferent associations.

(2) Unconscious and conscious complexes differ from one another in their type of respiration ; unconscious complexes show strong inhibition of respiration, whilst with conscious complexes there is excitation in addition to the inhibition.

(3) In an affect not directly related to the experiment the conscious complexes seem only to be able to gain expression through increase in the respiration.

(4) Respiration becomes deeper under strong experimental excitation.

(5) There are two types of complex respiration. The one shows itself by laboured breathing. The inspiration is more difficult, there is a kind of dyspnœa, and a feeling of oppression which is probably a partial manifestation of the feeling of anxious dread. The causes of this oppression are not known. Such respiration almost corresponds to the respiration type of unconscious complex associations. In the other type the respiration is irregular, alternately deep and superficial, quasi-sighing. The sighs either occur spontaneously or when a complex is aroused during conversation. When asked the reason for the sighing one is often told that an emotional-toned event has been stirred up. This second kind of breathing corresponds to our respiratory type with conscious complexes. Further investigation must be made to decide the question whether these two types can be separated in practice.

PART III

RESPIRATION AND THE PSYCHOGALVANIC PHENOMENON

We have seen that respiration is influenced in typical ways by conscious and unconscious complexes. As Veraguth's work,[1] and Binswanger's (chapter xii) have shown, the psychogalvanic reflex has a relationship of its own to these conditions.

The experiment was so arranged that changes in the galvanometer and in respiration were simultaneously recorded on a revolving drum. The method was one which was used and described by Jung and his collaborators, to whose works the reader should refer.[2]

Twenty tests were carried out on ten persons. Binswanger has shown in the last chapter the meaning of the psychogalvanic phenomena. A change in innervation is expressed by a decrease of the electrical resistance, as shown by fluctuations of the current. The deviations are stronger with complexes than with indifferent associations. The length of the deviations increases with the number of complex indicators. Unconscious complexes are also shown by the galvanometer. In distraction of the attention the stimulus provokes slight or no deviations, and the resistance of the body increases.

Veraguth [3] has demonstrated the same results. The psycho-

[1] *Das psychogalvanische Reflexphänomen.* (Karger: Berlin, 1909.)

[2] *Journal of Abnormal Psychology*, vol. i, No. 6, and vol. ii, No. 5; *Brain*, vol. xxx, 1907; also Binswanger, chapter xii.

[3] Op. cit.

galvanic reflect consists in a fluctuation in intensity of the electric current. The current decreases when at rest, increases under stimulus. With acoustic stimuli fluctuations only arise when the stimulus excites the attention of the subject. With the strength of the emotional tone the size of the deviation increases. Veraguth maintains, against Binswanger, that besides the strength of the emotional tone actuality plays a part ; but this is only an apparent contradiction, for actuality is included in the concept of emotional tone.

In certain circumstances all objective complex signs may be absent and the complex is only betrayed by the large galvanic deviation. We have found this often in our tests. Morton Prince and Peterson [1] showed in a person with treble dissociation that the ideas split off from consciousness gave galvanic deviations.

If the galvanometer is an indicator of affective processes, all physical manifestations of affectivity should run parallel with the fluctuations of the galvanometer, at least to a certain extent. Veraguth [2] made such tests in a person with injury of the skull, but obtained no definite results. Jung and Peterson [3] took pneumographic and galvanometer curves and came to the following conclusions.

Fluctuations in respiration often coincide in time with galvanometric fluctuations, but often they do not. It may happen that the galvanometer curve shows distinct fluctuations whilst the respiratory curve is quite steady, and conversely (in a case of dementia præcox). Disturbances in respiration come to rest less quickly than the galvanometer. They are influenced by conscious affects, if these are strong ; they are dependent upon the will, while the psychogalvanic phenomena is not ; and they are also dependent upon other intellectual processes.

In a subsequent investigation Jung and Ricksher [4] found that the size of the respiration varies ; that during the rise of the galvanometer curve the respirations become smaller, whilst they become larger during its fall. There is no relationship between diminution of the amplitude and the height of the galvanic curve ; here all kinds of individual variations occur. In dementia præcox no changes may occur in the galvanometer curve, whilst they can be found in the respiratory curve. No rules could be determined as to the rapidity of respiration.

The working out and measurement of our curves was done in

[1] " Experimentelle Untersuchungen über psychogalvanische Reaktionen von mitbewussten (unterbewussten) Vorstellungen in einem Falle von vielfacher Persönlichkeit," *Journal für Psychologie und Neurologie*, Bd. XIII, 1908.

[2] Loc. cit.   [3] Loc. cit.

[4] *Journal of Abnormal Psychology*, vol. ii.

the following way : A straight line was drawn from the apex of
the galvanic curve through the synchronic moment of the respiratory curve, and then the respiratory amplitudes were measured
forwards and backwards and written down as follows :

Before the galvanic apex :	After the galvanic apex :
First respiration wave	First respiration wave
Second „ „	Second „ „
Third „ „	Third „ „

etc.

The apex corresponds to the strongest galvanic deviation,
i.e. to the space between the highest point of the galvanic wave
and its base.

I should like to mention here that there are really two kinds
of courses for the galvanic deviation. The one shows a rapid
rise and fall with great deviations, so that the curve presents
more or less of an acute angled apex. The other, with the same
base, rises more slowly, the deviation is maintained rather longer
at the maximum height, and then again falls slowly ; the apex
is flat and the curve looks like a flattened cone. To measure
such an apex it must be bisected, but this rather alters the relation
of the respiratory amplitudes to the acute-angled apices. This
behaviour, however, only slightly influenced the results.

In working out psychological material, where we have but
few objective points to which to cling, and more especially in an
experimental method which puts very little obstacle to the
freedom of the psychological process, it is impossible to eliminate
all sources of error. It is, e.g., easily possible that a complex
assimilates to a stimulus-word to which it is related without
further disturbance, but that nevertheless there is a considerable
galvanic deviation. In this case the association would be counted
among the so-called indifferents simply from want of objective
signs. This occurs somewhat often. Again, since the distinction
between " conscious " and " unconscious " is really very gradual,
certain complexes of strong emotional tone may be unconscious
in one person with bad introspection which would be long since
conscious in another person with a good insight into himself.
In this way it may easily happen that occasionally complexes,
whose quantum of excitation really depends upon consciousness,
do still remain in the class of the unconscious. The class of
conscious complexes, as may be readily understood, is the
purest and least disturbed. Still, all the irregularities to which
attention has been drawn form the exception and not the rule.

The next question is whether the maximal deviations correspond with the alteration in respiration. The A.M.'s of the

respiratory amplitudes of both series of tests amount to, with indifferent associations :

	Before		Apex of G.D.		After		
III	II	I		I	II	III	IV
11·8	13·0	13·0	6·08	13·0	13·4	13·2	13·1 Fig. 7

The apex corresponds to the height of the deviation, its size is given in the figures under apex of galvanometer

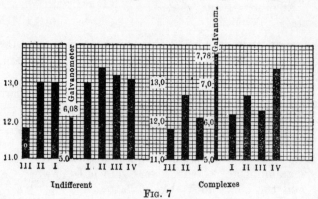

Fig. 7

deviations. The figures before and after the apex, given serially in Latin numerals, signify the size of the respiratory amplitudes.

There is nothing of special interest about this curve except that the respiration seems to be somewhat checked near the apex ; after the apex it increases in depth.

Complex associations :

	Before		Apex of G.D.		After		
III	II	I		I	II	III	IV
11·8	12·7	12·1	7·78	12·2	12·7	12·3	13·4 Fig. 7

The smallest respiratory curves coincide with the height of the galvanic deviation. After the apex the amplitudes are larger than before the apex. The same phenomenon occurs with indifferent associations. Our results agree with those of Jung and Ricksher[1] ; with the up stroke of the galvanometer curve respiration is smaller ; with the down stroke it is greater.

This behaviour occurred in both tests.

(a) Indifferent associations :

		Before			Apex of G.D.		After		
	III	II	I			I	II	III	IV
1st test	.	12·7	13·6	13·7	6·21	13·8	14·5	14·0	13·9
2nd test	.	11·0	12·5	12·3	5·95	12·2	12·3	12·4	12·3

Loc. cit.

(b) Complex associations :

	Before			Apex of G.D.	After			
	III	II	I		I	II	III	IV
1st test	12·7	13·0	12·5	7·38	12·4	12·9	12·8	14·5
2nd test	11·0	12·4	11·8	8·15	12·0	12·5	11·9	12·4

Except with the indifferent associations of the first test the smallest respiratory amplitudes coincide with the apex of the galvanometer deviation. In all the curves respiration is deeper after the apex than before. With indifferent and complex associations respiration is deeper in the first test than in the second. The galvanometer deviations are likewise greater in the first than in the second series of the indifferent associations. The difference of the deviation with indifferent and complex associations amounts to 1·17 in the first, 2·20 in the second tests. The greater deviations with indifferent associations, and the weaker differentiation of these in the first test when respiration is also deeper as compared with Test II, suggest a certain experimental excitation (see p. 534). The contention previously advanced, that under permanent excitation respiration becomes deeper, is supported by these figures.

Now as to the behaviour of conscious and unconscious complexes. The A.M. of the respiratory amplitudes of the two tests with unconscious complexes is :

	Before			Apex of G.D.	After			
	III	II	I		I	II	III	IV
	11·8	12·6	12·1	7·57	12·3	12·6	12·1	12·7	Fig. 8

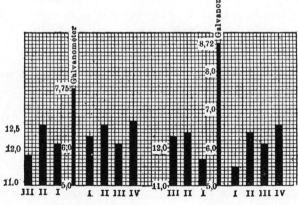

Unconscious   Conscious

Fig. 8

The A.M. of the respiratory amplitudes with conscious complexes is :

Before			Apex of G.D.	After			
III	II	I		I	II	III	IV
12·3	12·4	11·7	8·72	11·5	12·4	12·1	12·6 Fig. 8

The largest deviations coincide with the smallest respiratory amplitudes. This relationship is seen most distinctly by comparing the above figures and tables. The greater the deviations the smaller the amplitudes of respiration grouped in the immediate proximity of the apex. The greatest galvanic deviation and the strongest inhibition of respiration arise at the height of the development of affect. These great changes in innervation occur with conscious complexes. (In the previous section, in conscious complexes the third inspiration was the most superficial; this corresponds here to the first one before the apex. But this will be shown to be no contradiction.)

The same behaviour is observed when the two series of tests are considered apart.

The A.M. of the amplitude of respiration is :

(a) Unconscious complex associations :

	Before			Apex of G.D.	After			
	III	II	I		I	II	III	IV
1st test .	12·7	12·5	12·2	7·95	12·1	12·6	12·4	13·0
2nd test .	11·0	12·7	12·0	7·20	12·5	12·6	11·8	12·5

(b) Conscious complexes :

	Before			Apex of G.D.	After			
	III	II	I		I	II	III	IV
1st test .	12·3	13·0	12·3	8·29	12·1	12·8	12·9	14·3
2nd test .	12·3	11·9	11·1	9·50	10·9	12·1	11·3	10·9

If we place together the galvanic deviations, apart from respiration :

With indifferent associations the G. deviation is 6·08
   ,,   unconscious complexes ,,   G.   ,,   ,, 7·57
   ,,   conscious   ,,   ,,   G.   ,,   ,, 8·72

Conscious complexes therefore form the largest deviations. There is a difference in the strength of the deflections between conscious and unconscious complexes of 0·86, and between unconscious complexes and the indifferents of 1·78.

The ratios are exactly similar in the tests taken separately.

Test I : Indifferent associations, G. deviation, 6·21
           Unconscious complexes, G.   ,,   7·95
           Conscious complexes,   G.   ,,   8·29

Test II : Indifferent associations, G.   ,,   5·95
           Unconscious complexes, G.   ,,   7·20
           Conscious complexes,   G.   ,,   9·50

In the second test the deviations are more differentiated in consequence of the diminution of experimental excitation. The individual figures of the separate tests behave exactly the same as the average figures, with one exception.

On the average, complex associations are accompanied by greater galvanic deviations than are indifferent associations. The conscious especially are more intensive than the unconscious complexes. This fact says that, *ceteris paribus*, the maximum of changes in innervation coincides with consciousness. The action of consciousness seems, as a rule, to belong to complexes of the strongest psychophysical influence. I express this view with diffidence because there are exceptions to this rule, as we shall see below.

We have now learnt that conscious complexes show greater galvanic deviation than unconscious ones. We have already mentioned that in our experiments the effect of perseveration was often unable to find expression. But perseveration can be so strong that after a reaction, apparently innocent, disturbances suddenly occur in the next reaction, such as false reproduction, prolonged reaction, times becoming gradually shorter, etc. Such associations, which only look like complexes because of the perseverating emotional tone, generally appear to be accompanied by smaller galvanic deviations. Sometimes the emotional tone of a complex is so strong that, despite the long pauses in our experiment, perseverations are seen in the reactions following. For this reason it has happened that associations have been sometimes included in the class of the unconscious complex association which were not really complexes, and this naturally has altered the total results. To obviate to some extent this source of error we proceeded as follows : with every subject we first took the total number of conscious complexes and selected from them the largest galvanic deviations (50 per cent. of the total), and then calculated the mean ; the same was done with the unconscious complexes.

This procedure was based upon the following reasoning : if we count among the unconscious complexes all the associations with complex signs when a complex is not conscious, we should certainly have among these no inconsiderable number of pure perseverations. In such cases, according to all previous experience, the galvanic deviation seldom reaches the size of the greatest deviation with true complexes. Thus with perseverations the deviations tend to be relatively low. This method of the greatest galvanic deviations eliminates the perseverations as far as possible.

We had ten subjects for the experiments with the galvanometer. We will first give the average figures of both tests according to the above method of calculation.

A.M. of the greatest galvanometer deviations with

Conscious complexes	Unconscious complexes
11·0	9·0

The average figures of the two tests separately are :

	Conscious complexes	Unconscious complexes
Test I .	10·5	8·7
Test II .	11·5	9·4

On the average, therefore, the greatest (selected) deviations in both tests are stronger with conscious than with unconscious complexes. They are, as we have seen elsewhere, stronger and more differentiated in the second test than in the first.

These are the universal relationships. But if we proceed to the individual figures of the subjects separately the relationships become rather different. There are exceptions, so that individual deviations as well as their total average are in some test cases greater with unconscious than with conscious complexes.

Subject No. 1: Doctor, 28 years old.—In the first test the deviations are, on the average, greater with unconscious complexes than with conscious ones :

Conscious complexes	Unconscious complexes
9·0	9·3

Twenty associations were taken, eleven of which were complexes and four of these eleven were conscious. The A.M. of their reaction-times amounts to 1·8 second, the P.M. 1·7 second. No disturbances of reproduction ; no faults. The complexes are recognized chiefly by too long reaction-times. The subject was acquainted with the association experiment. The second test showed nothing special as regards the galvanometer deviations.

Subject No. 2: Medical Student, 24 years old, rather emotional.—At the first test the average of the galvanic deviations was :

Conscious complexes	Unconscious complexes
9·4	9·8

Altogether thirty associations, among these twenty-two complexes, of which seven were conscious, five reproduction disturbances, one fault. A.M. = 2 seconds ; P.M. = 1·8 second. The subject was acquainted with the association experiment. The second test went quite smoothly and showed nothing special.

Subject No. 3: Student of Chemistry, 20 years old.—In the first test there were eighteen associations, including eight complexes, of which three were conscious; four disturbances in reproduction, no faults. A.M. = 1·6 second; P.M. = 1·4 second. The average size of the galvanometer deviations is smaller with unconscious complexes than with conscious (unconscious 3·9; conscious 4·3), the biggest deviation with the former being, however, just as big as with the latter. The association to this deviation was:

Stimulus-word	Reaction	R.T.	Reproduction G.	Deviations
Water	lake	2 seconds	(fault)	4·3

At the end of the test the subject was unable to suggest anything definite about this reaction. Subsequently he remembered a dangerous incident which had happened to him on a glacier. In the second test with twenty-three associations, there were fifteen complexes (three unconscious) and four disturbances in reproduction; the deviations were, on the average, greater with unconscious than with conscious complexes. The greatest deviation with the latter was 4·2; with the former, 6·4. The individual associations did not explain much about this behaviour. The A.M. and P.M. of the reaction-times is the same as in the first test.

Subject No. 5: Student of Philosophy, 25 years old.—First test shows nothing remarkable as to the deviations. In the second test the average of the galvanometer deviations is 14·5 with conscious complexes and 14·5 with unconscious complexes. Twenty-eight associations, among these being fifteen complexes, five of which were conscious. No disturbances in reproduction. Pronounced predicate type indicating a rather stronger emotional expression (Jung). Very emotional. A.M. = 2 seconds; P.M. = 1·9 seconds. The greatest galvanometer deviation:

			R.T.
Conscious complexes	15·3	(journey — long)	2·7
Unconscious ,,	16	(window — in the garden)	3·0

Subject No. 7: Medical Student, 23 years old.—First test: twenty-seven associations, eighteen of which were complexes, two of these unconscious; nine disturbances in reproduction. The average of the galvanometer deviation with unconscious complexes was 3·9; with conscious, 4·3. The greatest galvanometer deviation:

			R.T.	Reproduction
Conscious complexes	4·3	(frog — jump)	1·9	
Unconscious ,,	4·4	(to aim — good)	1·8	(incorrect)

Second test: twenty-nine associations, eighteen of these complexes, of which two were conscious; nine disturbed reproductions. Average of galvanometer deviations with conscious complexes = 9·5; unconscious = 8·9. Greatest galvanic deviation:

			R.T.	Reproduction
Conscious complexes	9·5	(box — sand)	1·8	
Unconscious ,,	10·6	(love — boy)	1·6	(incorrect)

The reactions in both tests are predominantly predicates.

Subject No. 8: Student of Philosophy, 25 years old.—Nothing special with first test. In the second test twenty-six associations, of which seventeen were complexes and five of these conscious; three disturbances in reproduction; overwhelming number of reactions are predicates. A.M. = 1·7 second; P M. =

1·6 second. Average of galvanic deviations with conscious complexes = 20·2 ; with unconscious = 14·4. The greatest galvanometer deviation :

				R.T.
Conscious complexes	21·8	(marriage	— once)	2·8
Unconscious „	26	(paint	— faint)	2·1

The association immediately preceding this unconscious one was a conscious association :

		G.D.	R.T.
Beet	big	20·6	2·0

We may, perhaps, have a perseveration here.

Subject No. 9 : Lady, Ph.D., 35 years old.—First test : twenty-six associations, fifteen of which were complexes, four being conscious ; one disturbance in reproduction. Average of the galvanic deviations with conscious complexes is 10·9, with unconscious = 10·2.

The greatest galvanometer deviation :

				R.T.	Reproduction
With conscious complexes	11·4	(tired	— jolly)	2·1	(incorrect)
With unconscious „	11·5	(to whistle	— whistle)	1·9	

It is possible that this was a perseveration, for the associations immediately preceding this association were :

		R.T.	G.D.	Ref.		
22. Modest	small	2·0	9·3	Uncertain	said to be conscious	
23. Floor	door	1·9	11·1	+	„	unconscious
24. To whistle	whistle	1·9	11·5	+	„	unconscious

In almost all the subjects there was a deviation which was greater with unconscious complexes than with conscious. Without a thorough psycho-analysis we cannot go more deeply into the individual associations. It must, however, be said that in many cases the deviations with conscious complexes can be very great in comparison with the unconscious ones, e.g. :

Subject No. 6 : Medical Student, 23 years old, extremely emotional.—A.M. = 2·1 seconds ; P.M. = 1·8 second. Twenty-three associations, of which ten were complexes, five being conscious ; four disturbances in reproduction. The average of the galvanic deviation with conscious complexes = 32 ; with unconscious = 17·1. The greatest galvanic deviation was :

				R.T.	Reproduction
Conscious complexes	42·0	(month	— spring)	4·7	(incorrect)
Unconscious „	19·9	(bride	— old maid)	2·5	

This short list suffices to prove that our rule holds good that conscious complexes express themselves more strongly than unconscious ones, but that occasionally this rule has an exception —the unconscious complex producing a stronger deviation than the conscious. Whether this inversion of the law is to be apprehended in the sense of Freud's pathological reaction can be only determined by further experiments.

I would draw attention to the example given in Subject No. 3, where an association capable of existing in the conscious, but not conscious during the experiment, gave a deviation quite as large as the size of the deviation which corresponded to a conscious association.

It will be noted that the criterion of consciousness is based upon a subjective statement which may be often incorrect. But, as psycho-analysis teaches us, this is not of primary importance, for between conscious concealment and unconscious repression is but a step; the difference is not one of kind, but only of degree.

SUMMARY

Part I.   Experiment with Sommer's Apparatus

Sommer's apparatus is, for various reasons, not an instrument adapted for the recording of the finer movements of expression. But by it we were able to prove that the movements of the arm or of the hand are stronger with complexes than with indifferent associations.

The respiratory movement of the thorax communicated to the arm in a state of rest and with indifferent associations seems to be so inhibited with complex associations that it is no longer communicated to the arm.

All the other movements of the curves are of external origin and have nothing to do with movement of expression, with the exception of certain involuntary tremors, which seem to conform to a rule which is not yet precisely determined.

Part II.   Respiration

As contrasted with respiration during indifferent associations the size of respiration shows distinct diminution with complexes. This inhibition is found chiefly with unconscious complexes; with conscious complexes a type of respiration occurs which is alternately compressed and deepened through excitation.

Part III.   Respiration and Psychogalvanic Phenomena

The comparison of the psychogalvanic with the respiratory curves shows (in agreement with the results obtained by Jung and Ricksher) a diminution of the amplitude of respiration with the up stroke, and an increase with the down stroke, of the galvanic curve. The highest point of the galvanic curve coincides with the minimum of the amplitude of respiration. Conscious complex associations result as a rule in a greater galvanic deviation than do unconscious complex associations.

BIBLIOGRAPHY

APTEKMANN, ESTHER. "Experimentelle Beiträge zur Psychologie des psychogalvanischen Phänomens," *Jahrb. f. psychoanalyt. u. psychopatholog. Forschung.*, III (1913), 591–620.

ASCHAFFENBURG, GUSTAV. "Experimentelle Studien über Assoziationen," Kräpelin—*Psycholog. Arbeiten*, I (1896), 209–299; II (1899), 1–83; IV (1904), 235–373.

ATHERTON, M. VALERIS, and WASHBURN, M.F. "Mediate Associations studied by the Method of Inhibiting Associations: An Instance of the Effect of 'Aufgabe,'" *Amer. J. Psychol.*, XXIII (1912), 101–109.

BAWDEN, H. "A Study of Lapses," *Psychol. Rev. Mon. Supp.*, III, 4 (1900), 122.

BECHTEREW. (a) "Ueber zeitliche Verhältnisse der psychischen Prozesse bei in Hypnose befindlichen Personen," *Neurol. Zentralbl.* (1893).

(b) "Ueber die Geschwindigkeitsveränderungen der psychischen Prozesse zu verschiedenen Tageszeiten," *Neurol. Zentralbl.* (1893).

BINET, ALFRED. "Le Diagnostique judiciaire par le méthode des Associations," *Année psychol.*, XVI (1910), 372–383.

BIRNBAUM, KARL. "Ueber den Einfluss von Gefühlsfaktoren auf die Assoziationen," *Monatsschr. f. Psychiat. u. Neurol.*, XXXII (1912), 95–123, 194–220.

BOLTE. "Assoziationsversuche als diagnostisches Hilfsmittel," *Allg. Zeitschr. f. Psychiat.*, LXIV (1907), 619–630.

BURR, EMILY T., and GEISSLER, L. R. "An Introspective Analysis of the Association-Reaction Consciousness," *Amer. J. Psychol.*, XXIV (1913), 564–569.

CLAPARÈDE, ED. *L'Association des Idées* (Paris: 1903), 426.

—— "La psychologie judiciaire," *Année psychol.*, XII (1905), 295–302.

CLAPARÈDE, ED., et ISRAÏLOVITCH. "Influence du Tabac sur l'Association des Idées," *Compt. rend. Soc. biol.* (1902).

CORDES, G. "Experimentelle Untersuchungen über Assoziationen," *Philos. Stud.*, XVII (1901), 30–77.

EASTMAN, F. C., and ROSANOFF. "Association in Feeble-minded and Delinquent Children," *Am. J. of Insanity* (July 1912).

EBERSCHWELLER. *Untersuchungen über die sprachliche Komponente der Assoziation* (Zurich, 1908).

FÉRÉ, CHARLES. *The Pathology of the Emotions* (London: University Press, 1899), 525.

FRANZ, S. J., and WHITE, W. A. "The Use of Association Test in Determining Mental Contents," *U. S. Gov. Hos. for the Insane*, Bull. I (1909), 55–71.

FREUD, SIGMUND. *The Psychopathology of Everyday Life* (Fisher Unwin, 1914).

—— *The Interpretation of Dreams* (Allen and Unwin, 1913).

GALLUS, KURT. " Ueber Assoziationsprüfung," *Zeitschr. f. psychother. u. mediz. Psychol.*, II (1910), 106–127.

GALTON, FRANCIS. "Psychometric Experiments," *Brain,* II (1879), 149–162.
—— *Inquiries into Human Faculty and its Development* (London : Macmillan and Co., 1883), 182–203.

GEISSLER, L. K. "A Preliminary Introspective ˉtudy of the Association-Reaction Consciousness," *Am. J. Psychol.,* XXI (1910), 597–602.
—— " Analysis of Consciousness under Negative Instruction," *Am. J. Psychol.,* XXIII (1912), 183–213.

GIESE, FRITZ. "Das Ich als Komplex in der Psychologie," *Arch. f. d. ges. Psychol.,* XXXII (1914), 120–165.

GRABOWSKY, ADOLF. " Die Anwendung der psychologische Tatbestands-diagnostik in der Strafrechtspraxis," *Monatsschr. f. Kriminalpsychol. u. Strafrechtsref.,* III, 163.
—— " Zur Frage der psychologische Tatbestandsdiagnostik," *Zeitschr. f. d. ges. Strafrechtswiss.,* XVI.

GROSS, A. " Zur psychologischen Tatbestandsdiagnostik als kriminalistisches Hilfsmittel," *Beitr. zur Psychol. der Aussage,* II (1904–1906), 436–439.
—— " Zur psychologische Tatbestandsdiagnostik," *Monatsschr. f. Kriminal-psychol. u. Strafrechtsref.,* II (1905), 182–184.
—— " Die Assoziationsmethode in Strafprozess," *Zeitschr. f. d. ges. Straf-rechtswiss.,* XXVI (1905), 19–40.
—— " Kriminalpsychologische Tatbestandsforschung," *Jurist.-psychiat. Grenz-fragen,* VII (1907).
——· " Zur Frage des Wahrnehmungsproblems," *Ref. in Beitr. zur Psychol. der Aussage,* II (1904–1906), 258–264.

GROSS, H. " Zur psychologische Tatbestandsdiagnostik," *Arch. f. Kriminal-anthrop. u. Kriminalistik,* XIX (1905), 49–59.

HAGGERTY, M. E., and KEMPF, E. J. " Suppression and Substitution as a Factor in Sex Differences," *Am. S. Psychol.,* XXIV (1913), 414–425.

HEILBRONNER, KARL. " Die Grundlagen der psychologischen Tatbestands-diagnostik," *Zeitschr. f. d. ges. Strafrechtswiss.,* XXVII, 601.

HENKE, F. G., and EDDY, M. W. " Mental Diagnosis by the Association-Reaction Method," *Psychol. Rev.,* XVI (1909), 399–409.

HUBER, EDWIN. " Assoziationsversuche an Soldaten," *Zeitschr. f. Psychol. u. Physiol. d. Sinnersorgans,* LIX (1911), 241–272.

ISSERLIN. " Die diagnostische Bedeutung der Assoziationsversuche," *Mün-chener Med. Wochenschr.,* No. 27 (1907).

JONES, ERNEST. " The Practical Value of the Word-Association Method in the Treatment of the Psycho-Neuroses," *Rev. of Neurol. and Psychiat.,* VIII (1910), 641–672.
—— *Papers on Psychoanalysis* (London : Baillière, 1913), 206–240.

JUNG, CARL G. " Ueber Simulation von Geistesstörung," *J. f. Psychol. u. Neurol.,* II (1903), 181–201.
—— " Zur psychologischen Tatbestandsdiagnostik," *Centralbl. f. Nervenheilk. u. Psychiat.,* XXVIII (n.s. XVI), (1905), 813–815.
—— " Die psychologische Diagnose des Tatbestandes," *Jurist.-psychiat. Grenzfr.,* IV (1906).
—— " On Psychophysical Relations of the Association Experiment," *Abnorm. Psychol.,* I (1906–1907), 247–255.
—— " The Association Method," *Am. J. Psychol.,* XXI (1910), 219–269.

KAKISE, HIKOZO. "A Preliminary Experimental Study of the Conscious Concomitants of Understanding," *Am. J. Psychol.*, XXII (1911), 14–46.

KENT, GRACE HELEN, and ROSANOFF. "A Study of Association in Insanity," *Am. J. of Insanity*, LXVII (1910), 317–377.

KOHS, SAMUEL C. "The Association Method in its Relation to the Complex and Complex Indicators," *Am. J. of Psychol.*, XXV (1914), 544–594.

KRÄPELIN, E. *Ueber die Beeinflussung einfacher psychischer Vorgänge* (Jena: Fischer, 1892), 258.

—— "Der psychologische Versuch in der Psychiatrie," Kräpelin—*Psycholog. Arbeiten*, I (1896), 1–91.

KRAMER, F. "Literaturbericht," *Beitr. zur Psychol. der Aussage*, II (1904–1906), 580–586.

KRAMER, F., und STERN, W. "Selbstverrat durch Assoziation," *Beitr. zur. Psychol. der Aussage*, II (1904–1906), 457–488.

KRAUS, O. "Psychologische Tatbestandsdiagnostik," *Monatsschr. f. Kriminalpsychol. u. Strafrechtsref.*, II (1905), 58–61.

KUTZINSKI, ARNOLD. "Ueber die Beeinflussung des Vorstellungsablaufes durch Geschichtskomplexe bei Geisteskranken," *Monatsschr. f. Psychiat. u. Neurol.*, XXXIII (1913), 78–109, 159–178, 254–279.

LADAME. "L'Association des Idées et son Utilisation comme Méthode d'examiner dans les Maladies mentales," *L'Eucéphale*, No. 8 (1908).

LANG, JOSEF B. "Ueber Assoziationsversuche bei Schizophrenen und den Mitgliedern ihrer Familien," *Jahrb. f. Psychoan. u. psychopat. Forsch.*, III (1913).

—— "Zur Bestimmung des psychoanalytischen Widerstandes," *Psychologische Abhandlungen* (edited by Dr. C. G. Jung), No. 1 (1914), 1–35.

—— "Eine Hypothese zur psychologischen Bedeutung der Verfolgungsidee," *idem.*, 35–52.

LANGFIELD, HERBERT SIDNEY. "Suppression with Negative Instruction," *Psychol. Bull.*, VII (1910), 200–208.

—— "Suppression with Negative Instruction," *Psychol. Rev.*, XVIII (1911), 411–424.

LEACH, HAZEL M., and WASHBURN, M. F. "Some Tests by the Association-Reaction Method of Mental Diagnosis," *Am. J. Psychol.*, XXI (1910), 162–167.

LEDERER, MAX. "Psychologische Tatbestandsdiagnostik," *Zschr. f. d. ges. Strafrechtswiss.*, XXVI (1906), 488–506.

LEVY-SUHL, MAX. "Ueber experimentelle Beeinflussung des Vorstellungsverlaufs bei Geisteskranken," *Zschr. f. Psychol. u. Physiol. d. Sinnesorgans*, XLII (1906), 128–161; XLV (1907), 321–340; LIX (1911), 1–90; also Leipzig: Barth (1911), 142.

—— "Ueber Einstellungsvorgänge in normalen und anormalen Seelenzuständen," *Zschr. f. psychother. u. mediz. Psychol.*, II (1910), 141–164.

LEY, AUG., et MENZERATH, PAUL. *L'Etude expérimentale de l'Assoc. des Idées dans les Maladies mentales* (Gand: Van der Häghen, 1911), 199.

LIPMANN, OTTO. "Sammelberichte: Neuere Arbeiten zur Psychologie der Aussage" (Wertheimer und Klein—"Psychologische Tatbestandsdiagnostik"), *Journal f. Psychologie u. Neurologie*, III (1904), 249.

—— "Literaturbericht," *Zschr. f. Psychol. u. Physiol. d. Sinnesorgane*, XLIII (1906), 157–158; XLVI (1907–1908), 306–307.

—— *Grundriss der Psychologie für Juristen* (Leipzig: Barth, 1908), 70–78 (2nd ed. 1914).

LIPMANN, OTTO. "Analyses bibliographiques: Psychologie judiciaire" (Otto Lipmann et M. Wertheimer: "Tatbestandsdiagnostische Kombinationsversuche), *Année Psychol.*, XIV (1908), 493–494.

—— "Die Spuren interessebetonter Erlebnisse und ihre Symptome" (Theorie, Methoden und Ergebrisse der "Tatbestandsdiagnostik"), *Beihefte, Zeitsch. f. angew. Psychol.*, I (1911), 1–96.

LIPMANN, OTTO, und WERTHEIMER, MAX. "Tatbestandsdiagnostische Kombinationsversuche," *Zschr. f. angew. Psychol.*, I (1907–1908), 119–128.

LÖFFLER. "Zur psychologische Tatbestandsdiagnostik," *Monatssch. f. Kriminalpsychol. u. Strafrechtsref.*, III, 449.

MARKUS, O. "Ueber Assoziationen bei Dementia Praecox," *Archiv. f. Psychiatrie*, XLVIII, I.

MAYER, A., und ORTH, J. "Zur qualitativen Untersuchung der Assoziation," *Zschr. f. Psychol.*, XXVI (1901), 1–13.

MENZERATH, PAUL. "Die sogenannten Komplexmerkmale beim Assoziationsexperiment" (Discussion by Sommer, Weygandt, Stern, Wertheimer, Dittrich), *Bericht 5. Kongress f. experim. Psychol.* (Leipzig: Barth, 1912), 170–175.

MEYER, A. "Normal and Abnormal Associations," *Psychol. Bull.*, II (1905), 242–259.

—— "The Problems of Mental Reaction Types, Mental Causes and Diseases," *Psychol. Bull.* (Aug. 1908).

MOLL, ALBERT. "Die Behandlung sexueller Perversionen mit besonderer Berücksichtigung der Assoziationstherapie," *Zeitschr. f. Psychother. u. mediz. Psychol.*, III (1911), 1–29.

MOORE, JARED S. "The Articulation of the Concepts of Normal and Abnormal Psychology," *Am. J. Psychol.*, XXV (1914), 283–287.

MORAVCSIK, E. "Experimente über das psychogalvanische Reflexphänomen," *J. f. Psychol. u. Neurol.*, XVIII (1911), 186–199.

MORAVCSIK, ERNST EMIL. "Diagnostische Assoziationsuntersuchungen," *Allg. Zschr. f. Psychiat.*, LXVIII (1911), 626–673.

MÜLLER, VICTOR J. "Zur Kenntnis der Leitungsbahnen des psychogalvanischen Reflexphänomens," *Monatsschr. f. Psychiat. u. Neurol.*, XXXIII (1913), 235–253.

MÜLLER und PILZECKER. *Experimentelle Beiträge zur Lehre vom Gedächtnis* (Leipzig, 1900).

MÜNSTERBERG. (a) "Die Assoziation sukzessiver Vorstellungen," *Zeitschr. f. Psychol.* (1890).

(b) *Beiträge zur experimentellen Psychologie* (1889–1893).

OTIS, MARGARET. "A Study of Association in Defectives," *Journal of Educational Psychology*, VI, 5 (1915), 271–288.

PELLETIER, M. *Les Lois morbides des Associations des Idées* (Paris: Rousset, 1904), 151.

PETERSON, FREDERICK. "The Galvanometer as a Measurer of Emotions," *Brit. Med. Journ.* (Sept. 1907).

PETERSON, FREDERICK, und JUNG, CARL G. "Psycho-physical Investigations with the Galvanometer and Pneumograph in Normal and Insane Individuals," *Brain*, XXX (1907), 153–218.

PETERSON, FREDERICK, and SCRIPTURE. "Psycho-physical Investigations with the Galvanometer," *Journ. of Nervous and Mental Diseases* (July 1907).

PFENNINGER, W. "Untersuchungen über die Konstanz und den Wechsel der psychologischen Konstellation bei Normalen und Frühdementen (Schizophrenen)," *Jahrb. f. psychoanalyt. u. psychopatholog. Forschung.*, III (1912), 481–524.

POTOTZKY, C. "Die Verwertbarkeit des Assoziationsversuchs für die Beurteilung der traumatischen Neurosen," *Monatsschr. f. Psychiat. u. Neurol.*, XXV (1909), 521–529.

RANSCHBURG, PAUL, und BALINT, EMERICH. "Ueber quantitative und qualitative Veränderungen geistiger Vorgänge im hohen Greisenalter," *Allg. Zschr. f. Psychiat.*, LVII (1900), 689–718.

READ, CHARLES F. "Application of the Word-Association Method to an Acute Psychosis," *Am. J. of Insanity*, LXVIII (1911–1912), 671–681.

RIKLIN, FR. (*a*) "Zur Psychologie hysterischer Dämmerzustände und des ganserschen Symptoms," *Psychol.-neurol. Wochenschr.* (1904).

(*b*) "Analytische Untersuchungen der Symptome und Assoziationen eines Falles von Hysterie," *Psychiat.-neurol. Wochenschr.* (1905), 449.

RING. "The Association Test and Psycho-Analysis," *Boston Med. and Surg. Jour.* (Jan. 7, 1909).

RITTERSHAUS, ERNST. "Ueber Tatbestandsdiagnostik," Vereinsbericht (Vorläufige Mitteilung), *Centralbl. f. Nervenheilk. u. Psychiat.*, XXXI (1908), 877–878.

—— "Die Komplexforschung," *J. f. Psychol. u. Neurol.*, XV (1909–1910), 61–83, 184–220; XVI (1910), 1–43.

—— "Zur psychologischen Differentialdiagnose der einzelnen Epilepsieformen," *Arch. f. Psychiat. u. Nervenkrankh*, XLVI (1910), 1–93, 464–545.

—— "Die Spuren interessebetonter Erlebrisse" und die "Komplexforschung," *Zeitschr. f. d. ges. Neurol. u. Psychiat.*, VIII (1911–1912), 273–283.

ROSANOFF, ISABEL R., and ROSANOFF, A. J. "A Study of Association in Children," *Psychol. Bulletin* (Jan. 1913).

RUSK, ROBERT R. "Experiments on Mental Association in School Children," *Brit. J. Psychol.*, III (1909–1910), 349–385.

SCHNITZLER, JOHANN GUSTAV. "Experimentelle Beiträge zur Tatbestandsdiagnostik," *Zeitschr. f. angew. Psychol.*, II (1908–1909), 51–91.

SCHOLL. "Versuche über die Einführung von Komplexen in die Assoziationen von Gesunden und Geisteskranken," Sommer: *Klinik für psychische u. nervose Krankh.*, III (1908), 197.

SCRIPTURE, E. W. "Experiments on Subconscious Ideas." *J. Amer. Med. Assoc.*, L. (1908), 521–523.

—— Reaction-Time in Nervous and Mental Diseases, *J. Ment. Sci.* (October 1916).

SIDIS, BORIS, and KALMUS, H. T. "The Study of Galvanometric Deflections due to Psycho-physiological Processes," *Psychol. Rev.*, XV (1908), 391–396; XVI (1909), 1–35.

SOMMER, R. *Lehrbuch der psychopathologischen Untersuchungsmethoden* (Berlin, Wien: Urban und Schwartzenberg, 1899), 326–388.

STEIN, PHILIPP, "Tatbestandsdiagnostische Versuche bei Untersuchungsgefangenen," *Zeitschr. f. Psychol. u. Physiol. d. Sinnesorgane*, LII (1909), 161–237.

STERN, WILLIAM. "Mitteilungen," *Beitr. z. Psychol. der Aussage*, II (1904–1906), 275–277, 440–441.

SUTHERLAND, ARTHUR H., *Critique of Word-Association Reactions: An Experimental Study*, Dissertation, Univ. of Chicago (1913), 46.

SWOBODA, HERMANN. *Die Perioden des menschlichen Organismus* (Leipzig: Deuticke, 1904), 135.

THUMB und MARBE. *Exper. Untersuchungen über die psychologischen Grundlagen der sprachlichen Analogiebildung* (Leipzig, 1901).

TOWN. "Associations in Practical Work for the Insane," *The Psychol. Clinic.* (1906).

TRAUTSCHOLDT, MARTIN. "Experimentelle Untersuchungen über die Assoziationen der Vorstellungen," Wundt's *Philos. Stud.*, I (1883), 213–250.

UMPFENBACH. "Literaturbericht," *Zschr. f. Psychol. u. Physiol. d. Sinnesorgane*, XXXIX (1905), 222–3, XL (1906), 69; XLIV (1907), 142–143; XLV (1907), 298–299.

VERAGUTH, OTTO. "Das psychogalvanische Reflexphänomen," *Monatsschr. f. Psychiat. u. Neurol.*, XXI (1907), 387; also Berlin: Karger (1909), 187.

WALITZKI. "Contrib. à l'Etude des Mensurations psychometr. d. aliénés," *Rev. phil.*, XXVIII.

WEBER, ERNST. *Der Einfluss psychischer Vorgänge auf den Körper* (Berlin: Springer, 1910), 426.

WELLS, FREDERICK LYMAN. "Some Properties of the Free Association Time," *Psychol. Rev.*, XVIII (1911), 1–23.

—— "A Preliminary Note on the Categories of Association Reactions," *Psychol. Rev.*, XVIII (1911), 229–233.

—— "Practice Effects in Free Association," *Am. J. Psychol.*, XXII (1911), 1–13.

—— "The Question of Association Types," *Psychol. Rev.*, XIX (1912), 253-270.

WELLS, FREDERIC LYMAN, and CADY, FREDERIC B. "A Critique of the Psycho-Galvanic Reflex, with Some Experiments" (Abstract of the Paper read at a Meeting of the New England Society of Psychiatry), *Amer. J. of Insanity*, LXV (1908–1909), 164–166.

WELLS, FREDERIC LYMAN, and FORBES, ALEXANDER. "On Certain Electrical Processes in the Human Body and their Relation to Emotional Reactions," *Arch. of Psychol.*, II, No. 16 (1908–1911, Mar. 1911), 39.

WERTHEIMER, MAX. "Experimentelle Untersuchungen zur Tatbestandsdiagnostik," *Arch. f. d. ges. Psychol.*, VI (1906), 59–131.

—— "Literaturbericht: Zur Tatbestandsdiagnostik," *Arch. f. d. ges. Psychol.*, VII (1906), 139–140.

—— "Tatbestandsdiagnostische Reproduktionsversuche," *Arch. f. Kriminalanthropol. u. Kriminalistik* (1906), 293.

WERTHEIMER, MAX, und KLEIN, JULIUS. "Psychologische Tatbestandsdiagnostik," *Arch. f. Kriminalanthropol. u. Kriminalistik*, XV (1904), 72–113.

WEYGANDT, WILHELM. "Zur psychologischen Tatsbestandsdiagnostik," *Monatsschr. f. Kriminalpsychol. u. Strafrechtsref.*, II (1905), 435-438.

WRESCHNER, ARTHUR. "Eine experimentelle Studie über die Assoziation in einem Falle von Idiotie," *Allg. Zeitschr. f. Psychiat.*, LVII (1900), 241–339.

—— "Die Reproduktion und Assoziation von Vorstellungen," *Zeitschr. f. Psychol. u. Physiol. d. Sinnesorgane*, Ergängungsband 3, Teil I (1907), 328; Teil II (1909), 599.

WUNDT, WILHELM. *Grundzüge der physiologischen Psychologie* (Leipzig: Engelmann, 1911), III, 436–456, 519–543.

YERKES, ROBERT M., and BERRY, CHARLES S. "The Association Reaction Method of Mental Diagnosis (Tatbestandsdiagnostik)," *Am. J. Psychol.*, XX (1909), 22–37.

ZIEHEN, TH. *Die Ideenassoziation des Kindes.*
—— *Sammlung von Abhandlungen aus dem Gebiete der pädagogischen Psychologie und Physiologie,* Bd. I, Heft. 6, 1898, 1–66 ; Bd. III, Heft 4, 1900, 1–59.
—— *Leitfaden der physiologischen Psychologie* (Jena : G. Fischer, 1906), 176–204.

INDEX

ABULIA, case of, 359
Acoustic motor language, 11, 175
  verbal experiments, 16, 231
" Active opposition," 497, 498
Adamkiewicz, 448
" Adjustment," part played by, 282
Affect, pathological, 333
Affects, influence of, 288, 289
Amnesia, rare in healthy persons, 289
  occurrence in sudden changes, 292
  case of Mrs. Verena D., 337
  case of Julius Schw., 347
  case investigated fully by Jung, 369
Amnestic manifestations, 352
Amplitudes, respiratory, 542–560
Anamnesis, case of Miss E., 300
  incomplete, of patient, 389
Aphonia, its relation to the unconscious, 278
Aschaffenberg's experiments in association, 13, 14, 28, 29, 30, 34, 39, 41,
  48, 49, 61, 124, 229, 232, 234, 235,
  236, 238
Association, Bleuler's theory of, 294
  conscious complex, 532
  unconscious complex, 532
  disturbances in, 407–445
  importance of investigations into,
  1–7
  experiments on educated women,
  40–64
    on educated men, 65–91
    on uneducated women, 91–114
    on uneducated men, 115–122
    on epileptic men, 206–226
    group statistics in, 122–167
    in hysteria, 354–395
    on imbeciles and idiots, 172–
    205
    and the psychogalvanic phe-
    nomenon, 446–530
    important results of, 6
    with Sommer's apparatus,
    532–555

Association, in case of hysteria, 356–
  377
  not intrapsychical, 409
  paraphasic indirect, 30
  psychology, pathological, 308
  verbal, 35
Associations, classification of, 13–38
  influence of attention on, 167
    culture on, 167
    individual peculiarity of subject
    on, 167
    respiration in complex, 542–546
Attention, Bleuler's view, 415, 507
  distraction of, 359, 497–498, 504–
  507, 514, 540
  " intellectual," 540
  its importance in the association
  process, 8–9
  Lehmann's view, 507, 540
  nature of, 122–125, 282–296
  " sensual," 540
Autohypnosis, 49
Automatic speaking, 275
  writing, 275, 277, 291
Automatisms, word, 251

BALINT, 25, 53, 125, 439
Binswanger, 446
  *On the Psychogalvanic Phenomenon
  in Association Experiments,* 446–
  530
Bleuler, 379, 415, 507, 527
  *Upon the Significance of Associa-
  tion Experiments,* 1–7
  Consciousness and Association, 266–
  296
Bleuler's definition of attention, 507,
  543
  " phenomena of adjustment," 67
  use of the term " affectivity," 455,
  477, 506, 531
Bois-Reymond's experiment, 455, 456
Bonhöffer, 152
Bourdon, 16, 35

569